Michael Foot is as distinguished a writer/journalist as he is a politician. For many years he reviewed books for the *Evening Standard*, and he was for long associated with the left-wing weekly *Tribune*, notably as its editor from 1948–52 and 1955–60, and as its Managing Director from 1945–74. He has enjoyed a long and colourful parliamentary career, entered government as Minister for Employment in 1974, and in 1976 was elected Deputy Prime Minister and Deputy Leader of the Labour Party. Under the Labour Government of 1974–79 he became Lord President of the Council and Leader of the House of Commons. He has been MP for Ebbw Vale, Aneurin Bevan's old constituency, since November 1960.

Michael Foot

Aneurin Bevan

Volume 1

PALADIN
GRANADA PUBLISHING
London Toronto Sydney New York

Published by Granada Publishing Limited
in Paladin Books 1975
Reprinted 1979

ISBN 0 586 08194 1

First published in Great Britain by
MacGibbon & Kee Ltd 1962
Copyright © Tribune Publications 1962

Granada Publishing Limited
Frogmore, St Albans, Herts AL2 2NF
and
3 Upper James Street, London W1R 4BP
866 United Nations Plaza, New York, NY 10017, USA
117 York Street, Sydney, NSW 2000, Australia
100 Skyway Avenue, Rexdale, Ontario, M9W 3A6, Canada
PO Box 84165, Greenside, 2034 Johannesburg, South Africa
CML Centre, Queen & Wyndham, Auckland 1, New Zealand

Made and printed in Great Britain by
Richard Clay (The Chaucer Press) Ltd
Bungay, Suffolk
Set in Linotype Ehrhardt

Granada ®
Granada Publishing ®

To the people of
Tredegar, Ebbw Vale, Rhymney and Abertysswg
and to Jill

List of Illustrations

Contents

Preface to the First Edition

In this book – and in the volume which follows – I seek to describe the political values which Aneurin Bevan sustained throughout his life and the major political battles in which he engaged. That, I am sure, is what he would most have wished anyone writing about him to do.

I cannot claim to have portrayed the richness of his personality. Such an achievement is beyond my powers. In any case, no printed words can repair the loss of the voice, the gestures, the mind and vitality of the man. But I hope I have been able to provide something more than a mere external recital of events.

Jennie Lee has given me invaluable assistance and guidance. But she has imposed no limitations on what I wished to write and the responsibility for any errors or misjudgements is mine, not hers.

I also owe an immense, if lesser debt to several others. Members of Aneurin Bevan's family, his closest friend, Archie Lush, and many who knew him in Tredegar, Ebbw Vale and later in his life have provided me with essential information. This should be evident in the text. Tom Driberg, M.P., kindly agreed to read the proofs and corrected many errors. But all these helpers must also be absolved from any responsibility for the final product.

A special word of gratitude is due to Donald Bruce, Aneurin Bevan's Parliamentary Private Secretary between 1945 and 1950. He had made a large compilation of notes and documents with the purpose of writing Aneurin Bevan's life himself. He most generously placed all this at my disposal and has thereby saved me much hard labour and supplied material which might otherwise have been lost.

Finally, I must thank Elizabeth Thomas who has not only given secretarial assistance but who greatly eased the work involved.

The most necessary published sources on which I have drawn are Aneurin Bevan's parliamentary and public speeches, his own book, *In Place of Fear*, Jennie Lee's *Tomorrow is a New Day* and the files of *Tribune*. The other main books quoted or used are indicated in the footnotes.

All the quotations at the head of chapters, with two or three exceptions, are taken from authors who were among Aneurin Bevan's favourites.

July 1962   MICHAEL FOOT

Preface to this Edition

The chief additions to this edition, as compared with the early editions published in 1962, derive from various criticisms made by some of those who knew Aneurin Bevan, in Tredegar and London, long before he became a Member of Parliament, they are indicated in the footnotes. But special mention must also be made of the two most valuable letters from Bevan to John Strachey which were first published in Hugh Thomas's biography of John Strachey (Eyre Methuen 1973).

I also wish to add to the list of those to whom I am indebted the name of one who falls into a different category from most of the others. Howard Samuel was the publisher of the first volume of this book, but died before the publication could take place. He gave me great encouragement in the work required, and had previously given us great assistance on *Tribune*. All the help he gave us was due to his devotion to Aneurin Bevan. Indeed, he and his wife Jane had been close friends of Nye ever since they had first met in his house during the war. They treasured the friendship and so did he.

January 1974   MICHAEL FOOT

1 The Boy 1897–1911

It is hard for any one to be an honest politician who is not born and bred a Dissenter . . . No patriotism, no public spirit, not reared in that inclement sky and harsh soil, in 'the *hortus siccus* of dissent', will generally last: it will either bend in the storm or droop in the sunshine.
                                             – WILLIAM HAZLITT[1]

ANEURIN BEVAN was born at number 32 Charles Street, Tredegar, in the Welsh County of Monmouthshire, on 15 November 1897, of good dissenting stock. His father was a Baptist, his mother a Methodist and the two had first met as members of the choral society attached to the chapels. Tredegar was a working-class town, almost exclusively a miners' town; ninety per cent of the population drew their livelihood from the pits. Yet, despite this binding common interest, there were many shades and gradations of opinion and living standards within the mining community. For some the chapel provided not only a solace from the afflictions of industrial society but the sword and the armour they must use for all worthy striving in the future. 'Drink' was the enemy which appeared to exploit and to ravage more mercilessly than any coalowners. In one sense the chapel-goers led a life apart from the violence and hopeless poverty which Tredegar also knew, and in this God-fearing section of the town the Bevan household in Charles Street held a secure, respected place. The family background was that of Welsh nonconformity in its heyday, with its self-reliance, pride, resource, music and the nurture, through its own logic and past struggles, of the richest soil for the cultivation of new heresies.

Aneurin's father, David, was a native of Tredegar, although his forebears came from Carmarthenshire; he was a miner, the

1. From Hazlitt's essay 'On Court Influence' in his *Political Essays*.

son of a miner, and a Welshman to the fingertips. Most of his working life he suffered from 'a bad chest' which qualified on his death certificate for the title of 'bronchial asthma' but was never scheduled for what it certainly was – the dreaded miner's disease of pneumoconiosis. He was delicately handsome, frail, wayward, a dreamer without a scrap of ambition but with much gaiety and a strong vein of humorous sarcasm. Some even called him a weakling, but the charge could be conceivable only by colliers' standards. Most days he had left the house to catch the colliers' train by five-thirty and was rarely home again much before nightfall, yet he still managed to lead a full life in the home and the community. A fine craftsman at anything he touched, he built on a new room when the family moved to number 7 Charles Street, tended the garden, kept chickens, mended the children's shoes and performed all the other domestic duties directed by his wife. He installed a gas stove – the first in Charles Street – a bathroom, an inside toilet, hot water, a water tub and an organ around which the family assembled to sing hymns and Welsh folk songs every Sunday night. Every Sunday morning and evening he walked to the Carmel Baptist Church in Dukestown and walked back with the deacons and the other mighty arguers, six or seven abreast across the road, debating the sermon and invoking his deep knowledge of the Bible.

At least this was his ritual in the days of Aneurin's childhood. Later his chapel-going enthusiasm faded and perhaps his religious faith too. 'The unholy trinity' of the bishop, the brewer and the squire – not that Tredegar had seen much of the handiwork of the first or the third of these ogres for some decades – had to make way for other opponents. David Bevan became treasurer of his miners' lodge. He was always 'a Federation man', not 'a Company man' – that is, a supporter of the nascent South Wales Miners' Federation and its local branches in their clashes with the quasi-feudal overlord of Tredegar's land, industry and institutions, the Tredegar Iron and Coal Company. In his early manhood he was a Liberal, and voted for Sir William Harcourt in the West Monmouthshire constituency, transferring his allegiance in 1906 to Tom Richards, the miners' nominee.

Once a 'Lib-Lab', like so many of his generation and upbringing, he must have become a Socialist while Aneurin was still at school. Robert Blatchford's *Clarion* was delivered at the house every week. The mixture in its pages of glowing humanity, sentiment, humour, fierce debate and a splendid dream for the future suited David Bevan's taste precisely. As for the struggle to make the dream come true, he was too tired for that, and who will blame him? And besides, there at his elbow was a paradise to be entered at will – the world of music and books. He bequeathed to all his children a love of music. He taught them all to sing, some including Aneurin with no great success, and occasionally pressed sixpence into their hands when they achieved the degree of perfection he desired. He quailed, despite all their mother's promptings, at the thought of teaching them Welsh. He himself belonged to Cymmrodorion, the Welsh cultural organization, and won prizes at the inter-chapel eisteddfodau, one for a love poem which his wife could not read. Yet no communal joys could fully satisfy his spirit. He was a bookworm, begrudging all the other pursuits which dragged him back from his faraway realms of poetry and romance. Gradually and delightedly he discovered that he had one son who would accompany him there. No doubt all children reared in miners' homes at the beginning of the century had hard lives. But a ray of light and tenderness is cast across the youth of Aneurin by the gentle character of such a father.

His mother was the organizer and disciplinarian, stern but just, guarding her brood against all comers, but determined that nothing she could give or inflict would be withheld if it could help them to 'get on' in the world; an English realist among these Welsh romantics. That she was English may at first seem unlikely since she was born in Tredegar, her family came from Radnorshire and her maiden name of Prothero is often considered Welsh. Moreover, her famous son, in later years, could easily be provoked to rail against 'the bovine, phlegmatic Anglo-Saxons', as if not one single drop of alien blood ran in his veins. Yet there seems to be no doubt on the point. Phoebe Prothero's father, John, came from the little town of Hay on the Radnorshire–Hereford border. Whatever Welsh strains or habits she may have acquired, her ancestors were English.[2] Her great-grandfather had been a sheriff's bugler in Hereford and the portrait of him was carried from home to home when they moved as an emblem to prove the slightly greater eminence in the social scale from which the Prothero family had descended. John Prothero was the village blacksmith who moved to Tredegar to get a job in his trade at the Bedwellty pits. His daughter was strong and stubborn, regal in her bearing and the master of the household. She was more even than the matriarchal figure of so many working-class homes of that day. From the accounts of her sons and daughters it is clear that she had exceptional will and capacity.

She cooked, cleaned, ironed and kept house generally with tireless efficiency. No one beneath her roof ever went hungry even in the harshest times. She was up before five in the morning to get her husband's breakfast and later the children's. Then at nine o'clock her own work began, for she was a tailoress or seamstress, as clever with the needle as with the pots and pans. In the early days she ran the trade as a commercial proposition with six apprentices learning dressmaking in her front room and making her own patterns and designs. Later, when the family grew larger, she had to curtail this work and confine her efforts to the task of keeping her own children, on Sunday especially, among the best groomed in the neighbourhood. Clearly she must have made throughout a considerable addition to the household income. In any case, she was always the Chancellor of the family Exchequer, counting every penny. Time and money could be saved, she found, if she bought in bulk; a twenty-pound tub of

2. When the first edition of this book appeared, considerable protest was made against the scandalous revelation that Aneurin Bevan was partly English. One correspondent wrote: 'The Hay-Hereford area was largely Welsh-speaking down to the end of the nineteenth century, and Prothero is a good Welsh name. A sheriff's bugler in Hereford could well have been a Welsh-speaking Welshman.' And another: 'You insist that his mother, hailing from Hay was Saxon – Why? There must have been many Welsh people living just over the Welsh–English border. It is also on record that, a hundred years ago, the Town Clerk of Hereford had to be able to speak Welsh!' These strictures cannot just be pushed aside, but I must still set against them the strongly held belief of the other members of the Bevan family, notably his sister Arianwen.

butter, a side of bacon, or a massive ham. In one room she kept a huge chest of drawers stocked with clothes, new and old. The purchases were made with an eye for bargains when she went on her shopping expeditions to Newport, Cardiff or Bristol. No one but she knew what fashionable treasures the chest held or when they might be produced. When the new room was built at number 7, she was the architect, her husband the skilled labourer. On one occasion, half a century later Aneurin recalled that 'My Methodist parents used to say: have the courage, my son, to say "No". Well, it takes a good deal of courage, but we shall have to say "No" more and more, because only by saying "No" more and more to many things can you say "Yes" to the most valuable things.'[3] The slip about the common religious denomination of his parents was pardonable. Obviously, it was his Methodist mother who taught him the word and the moral. But David's intellect did win one triumph over his formidable helpmate. After the marriage, she too became a Baptist and attended the English Baptist Chapel in Church Street. Usually, however, he was compelled to submit. Once, returning from a meeting of the dramatic society in full regalia, he threw open the door and announced himself: 'Behold, Neptune, King of the Seas.' 'Never mind Neptune,' retorted Mrs Bevan, 'you get upstairs and keep an eye on the children.'

She bore ten children altogether; David John who died at the age of eight; Blodwen; William George; Herbert Luther who died in infancy; Myfanwy; Aneurin; Margaret May; Iorwerth and Idris, twins, but Idris died at birth; and finally, Arianwen who came to be Aneurin's chief worshipper and companion in the family circle. The four-roomed house at number 32 was soon much too small for this growing progeny, and somehow by 1906 Mrs Bevan had scraped and saved enough to buy for about £130, with the help of a mortgage, the seven-room mansion – eight with the home-made addition – at number 7. An uncle came to live there as well, but, says Myfanwy, 'we were never really huddled together, although we had sometimes to sleep three in a bed'. Order could only be produced by careful planning. Every member of the family had his or her duties allocated – one

3. 'Democratic Values' in a Fabian lecture, September 1950.

of Aneurin's was to cut the bread, which he did in thin, delicate slices. All were instructed to be present promptly at mealtimes; all must sit down together formally and all must observe one conversational rule – no gossip about the neighbours. Many friends were eager to join them round the table, for Mrs Bevan spread a liveliness to match her energy and good cooking. 'She was dominating, but not domineering,' says Myfanwy. Sometimes her punctilious taste in dress and habit brought taunts from others in Charles Street. But no one doubted her strength and authority. She had left school at the age of nine and soon 'lost the knack' of reading or writing amid all the endless efforts to fight dirt and slackness and never to owe a shilling. Like other good Christian mothers, she could accept the Bible with one single exception – the story of Martha and Mary. Number 7 Charles Street was one of the homes which only the great Marthas can make.

She was too, in her own way, a feminist, although doubtless she would shudder at the label. Despite all her own proficiency in the home and the instruction she gave both to the boys and girls in the kitchen, she never took the view that the only role for women was to get their men off to work at half past five in the morning and spend their lives at household chores. She knew how much her own skill as a dressmaker had meant to them all. She wanted to see her daughters educated and independent, and once the first tasks of motherhood were over she applied her thrifty prudence to provide for their future. All the children first went up the hill from Charles Street to Sirhowy elementary school. Blodwen was set to learn the millinery business. Mrs Bevan wanted William to try for the secondary school, but maybe he listened more to his father and went to the pits. Myfanwy carried off all the prizes and won a scholarship to the grammar school. And it is at Sirhowy School that Aneurin, two years younger than his cleverest sister, makes his first traceable individual appearance.

He was a sturdy, round-faced boy with large grey-blue eyes and hair almost black. No one detected any spark of genius – least of all Mr William Orchard, headmaster of Sirhowy school. He was a bully and a snob and all the stories of Aneurin's schooldays centre round the physical combats between them. On one occasion Orchard hit him on the chin and Aneurin retaliated by stamping on Orchard's corns. On another occasion Orchard picked on a little boy, asked him why he had not been to school the day before and when he replied that it was his brother's turn to wear the shoes, mocked him and raised a titter from the class. Aneurin picked up an inkwell and threw it at him, but missed. Summoned later to the headmaster's study he made such a show of counter-attacking if a finger was laid upon him that the proposed chastisement was abandoned. Later again he is said to have thrown a snowball with a stone in it at the monstrous red-faced Orchard, ever after lamenting to his friends that he had again missed the target.

Aneurin hated school with an abiding hatred. He could hardly listen patiently to a discussion of formal education. Boys and girls should educate themselves, as he did; any other method he was inclined to regard as new-fangled and distorting. Yet somehow, at Sirhowy, between pot shots at the headmaster and probably with the aid of his intuitive father, he learnt his three Rs – or at least one R. He learnt to read and quickly found it the most precious gift of the gods. He learnt to write an ungainly, sprawling handwriting which he never bothered to improve. As for arithmetic, he was not interested and was even vaguely suspicious. 'Any fool can see that two and two make four,' he would say much later; 'but it takes a real capacity to stretch it to five or, better still, six or seven.' Like his father, he believed in romance and magic; he loved colour and music. What a purposeless drudgery it was to stay in school when he could be sitting at the knee of David Bevan or tramping the hills round Tredegar. He had a body as lithe and strong as a mountain pony's, an eye, an ear and a mind, and he was now beginning to exert all four while a blockheaded headmaster called him lazy and kept him down for a year in a class with younger boys.

He had a tongue too, but there was something wrong with it. He had an appalling stutter which for some years seemed to get worse. Maybe this was the real explanation of the purgatory he suffered at school. Some of his schoolmates would jeer at him and Orchard had a wretched excuse for his impatience. The point becomes stronger still if the stutter was bred at school either by Orchard's bullying or his teaching methods, or a combination of the two. According to some modern psychologists, Aneurin must have been a shifted sinistral, having been born left-handed and forced to write with his right hand. His distaste for the physical act of writing lends strong support to the idea. But no one knows for certain the date when the consequent nervous disorder began. His mother firmly denied that he had had it from the earliest years and offered instead her own comical and less abstruse theory. The brothers William and Aneurin sometimes went to stay with Uncle John who also stuttered. On their return to Charles Street they delighted in reporting Uncle John's conversation with all the appropriate mimicry of his impediment. Gradually, in Aneurin's case, the affectation became compulsive. The explanation is hard to believe. Little doubt is possible, however, about the significance of his inconvenient affliction. He was driven back on his own resources. He was, says Myfanwy, who was closest to him in age, 'a lonely chap'. Any natural bent towards questioning the wisdom of authority was reinforced. Both his mind and his will were influenced by his stutter.

During his last months at school he got a job at Davis's shop in Commercial Street as a butcher's boy.[4] The most valued part of the two and sixpence a week he received for his labours was spent on the *Magnet*, the *Gem*, the penny *Popular* and other boys' magazines. One of his sister Arianwen's first memories is of seeing him ambling along the street with his butcher's basket in one hand while with the other he tried to staunch a bleeding nose and clutch the *Popular* before his eyes. Often he was kept out late at

4. On 18 November 1952 a debate took place in the House of Commons on a bill for fixing the closing hours of shops in which Sir Winston Churchill referred to action he had taken in 1911 as Home Secretary. Bevan said: 'I didn't know until he mentioned it that the right hon. Gentleman, the Prime Minister, was pleading my case when he was making his speech in 1911, because at that time, and for two years previously, I had been a shop assistant working until twelve o'clock on Saturday night and one o'clock on Sunday morning, and I would have been very much more grateful if I had known that he had been so eloquent on my behalf at that time ... I went to work when eleven years old for two and six a week, though I may not have been worth more.'

night on his errands, for Mr Davis had to stay open, particularly on Saturday night, to keep up with his competitors. Eventually Mrs Bevan put her foot down; Aneurin's entry into commerce was abruptly ended. His father, too, made one of his rare and diffident essays in discipline; he banned the *Magnet*, the *Gem* and even the *Popular* from the house; whether in fear that his son might be seduced by these subtle advertisements for the public school system, no one can tell. Not to be thwarted so easily, Aneurin used to hide his magazines in a crevice under Sirhowy bridge. After a week or two he discovered that his copies were being taken while others were being left in exchange by some anonymous student of the same school of literature. The Sirhowy bridge lending library was the first he ever joined. Soon he was availing himself of the richer choice at the Workmen's Institute. The wide empires of Rider Haggard, Nat Gould, Hall Caine and Seton Merriman were opening before him, and David Bevan was assured that he had a boy after his own heart.

Yet there was still no sign, by the tests then applied, of potential intellectual gifts of any special quality. No one, not even his ambitious mother, proposed that he should try for the secondary school. No one believed that he would pass an eleven-plus examination or its less exacting equivalent of that period. The alternative was the pits. So one dark morning he set out with his brother William to catch the miners' train for Ty-tryst colliery. (The name means 'the House of Sadness'.) He was just turning fourteen years old and the date was November 1911.

2 The Miner 1912–21

You can only take what you are strong enough to take and you can only hold what you are strong enough to hold. – A. J. COOK

'I COULD never trace the river to its source,' says one who knew Aneurin Bevan best in the early days, talking of his originality of speech and manner. Many testify that he had already developed his entrancing gifts before he was twenty. One source, therefore, must lie in his early experience as a miner. Somehow between the years 1912 and 1916 or 1917 he grew to manhood and independence of outlook with astonishing speed. No university could have taught him as much as life in the South Wales coalfields through those tempestuous years.

He was proud of being the expert collier which he learnt to become and, like most miners, he treasured the comradeship of the pits which he believed was something closer and finer than any other breed of men could know. But more than most others he recognized the penalties he was forced to pay. 'In other trades,' he wrote, 'there are a thousand diversions to break the monotony of work – the passing traffic, the morning newspaper, above all, the sky, the sunshine, the wind and the rain. The miner has none of these. Every day for eight hours he dies, gives up a slice of his life, literally drops out of life and buries himself. The alarum or the "knocker-up" calls him from his bed at half past four. He makes his way to the pithead. The streets are full of shadows with white faces and black-rimmed sunken eyes. The cold morning echoes with the ring of hobnailed boots. The shadows have such heavy feet.' In another passage he came even nearer to the memories he carried with him from those first years in the pit. 'Here down below are the sudden perils – runaway trams hurtling down the lines; frightened ponies kicking and mauling in the dark, explosions, fire, drowning. And if he escapes? There is a tiredness which comes as the reward of exertion, a physical blessing which makes sleep a matter of relaxed limbs and muscles. And there is a tiredness which leads to stupor, which remains with you on getting up, and which forms a dull, persistent background to your consciousness. This is the tiredness of the miner, particularly of the boy of fourteen or fifteen who falls asleep over his meals and wakes up hours later to find that his evening has gone and there is nothing before him but bed and another day's wrestling with inert matter.'[1] The South Wales minimum rate for a day's wrestling by a boy was fixed at one shilling and fourpence halfpenny just after Aneurin's arrival at Ty-tryst. He brought home about ten shillings a week and gave it all to his mother who thereupon doled out twopence for comics, twopence for chocolate and twopence for a piece of layer cake.

Much more precious for him than these trophies was time; an evening gone was a hideous loss, for his reading became prodigious. With the help of Mr Bowditch, the Librarian at the Tredegar Workmen's Institute Library, he graduated from Rider Haggard to H. G. Wells, from Nat Gould to Jack London. But there was no plan or settled purpose. He seized on everything and would often stay awake reading until the dawn. He wrote poems of his own and declaimed many more. 'A thousand years have I loved thee and wilt thou desert me now?' he shouted to his sister Myfanwy when he wanted some small service done. Arianwen might come downstairs in the morning to find the table strewn with the paper he had scrawled on the night before or the spoons he unconsciously twisted in his hand while his absorption in a book became complete.

In those early years, too, he was still sent to Sunday school. But strange reports percolated back to Charles Street. 'He will keep talking about fish,' complained one teacher – this was her way of explaining Aneurin's attempt to stir a lively debate on his new-found theories of evolution. He was moved from the Baptist school to the Congregational Chapel in Commercial Street. Even

1. Article in the *Daily Express*, 1932.

the less fundamentalist Congregationalists, if they were so, could not contain him. One teacher is said to have threatened to leave if Aneurin stayed as a pupil. The Welsh Sunday schools of those years were occasionally a cover for incipient political debate. One breakaway group from a Sunday school class in Tredegar made contact with the Independent Labour Party in Merthyr and secured their aid in forming a Tredegar branch. At first they could only meet in private houses since the halls were refused them. Aneurin became a regular attender and the most prolific talker, stammer or no stammer. He always remembered how he had carried the platform stool over the mountains for Minnie Pallister, a leading I.L.P. speaker.

Inevitably, one rising interest competed even with his love of reading and made any ructions at the Sunday school look childish. He and his father and his brother and his younger brother were miners and the chief talk round the family table was of coal. Inside number 7 Charles Street, all might be secure and well-managed. Outside, in the pit itself and in the neighbouring valleys, there was violence, anarchy, injustice, cheating and a sense of perpetual struggle. 'Greek mythology,' wrote Bevan many years later, 'had it that each tree was inhabited by a spirit – called, I believe, a dryad – which died when the tree died. The pit is to the mining village what the tree is to the dryad. When the pit dies, the village dies too; when the pit is ill, the village groans. Each is interwoven with the life of the other.' Arguments enough could be had about the health of Ty-tryst and the other collieries round Tredegar – about the efforts of the owners to play off one colliery against another, their drive to circumvent the disadvantages of the recently decreed eight-hour day, their trickery on the men compelled to work 'in abnormal places' and all the intricate technicalities of the industry's wage system which read today like the inflictions of some mediaeval persecution. There was also the persistent fight between 'the Federation men' and 'the Company men'. In Tredegar the South Wales Miners' Federation was strong and growing stronger; but inside its ranks were many who believed that the Tredegar Iron and Coal Company was too powerful to be challenged, that the owners and the miners had an identity of interest, that the lamb must lie down with the lion. This had been the dominant opinion of the old miners' leaders little more than a decade before. It died in convulsions just about the time when Aneurin Bevan was starting work as a miner. In 1910 and 1911 the whole South Wales coalfield had been shaken by the Cambrian Combine strike in the Rhondda which lasted for ten months and ended in pitiful defeat and bitter reproaches that the men had been betrayed by their leaders. In 1912 came the six-week nation-wide strike of more than a million miners for a minimum wage – the most portentous industrial action Britain had known. The Liberal Government of Mr Asquith bowed to the storm, sought to coerce the stubborn coalowners and introduced their Minimum Wage Act. It was a step forward, but not the full stride which the strikers had hoped for; the air was filled with charges of trickery against the Government and, once again, of weakness or worse against the miners' leaders. With the war the terms of the conflict were altered; the rising price of coal enabled the miners to extort better bargains, although little enough compared with the coalowners' leaping profits. When the Government sought to put the whole coalfield under the Munitions of War Act, involving penalties of imprisonment for strikers, South Wales revolted and Lloyd George had to come to Cardiff to apply the ointment of sweet Welsh reason and withdraw the operation of his Act. All these tumultuous events occurred to the accompaniment of shrieking press campaigns against the rapacious, unpatriotic miners. Two deductions could be drawn from the defeats of 1911 and the victories of wartime; only by their own strength could the miners achieve justice and never should they ask for favours or look to Parliaments for salvation. In South Wales particularly a tremendous controversy developed about the proper means of achieving social revolution, and the young Aneurin Bevan drank it in lustily.

In 1912, an Unofficial Reform Committee designed to instil into the leadership of the Federation a more aggressive spirit had been started among the militant miners in South Wales. Much of its inspiration was directly Marxist, but it must be remembered that Karl Marx had not then acquired the prestige and authority which the Soviet Revolution was later to bestow on him and those who claimed to be his true disciples. The doctrine was still far from a dogma, and other prophets were free to enter the field. One was James Connolly, the Irish leader who had founded his Socialist Labour Party on the Clyde in 1905 to propagate his own brand of Marxist syndicalism. 'It is an axiom, enforced by all the experience of the ages,' he wrote, 'that they who rule industrially will rule politically . . . Let us be clear as to the function of Industrial Unionism. That function is to build up an industrial republic inside the shell of the political State, in order that when that industrial republic is fully organized it may crack the shell of the political State and step into its place in the scheme of the universe.'[2] Connolly's ideas or those he had learnt from Daniel de Leon, the American industrial unionist, and the I.W.W. (the Industrial Workers of the World) impregnated *The Miners' Next Step*, the widely circulated programme of the Unofficial Reform Committee. It was an open, scorching attack on parliamentary leaders, the Federation leaders, and the policy of conciliation in industrial struggles. 'An industrial vote,' it said, 'will affect the lives and happiness of workmen far more than a political vote.'[3] One of its authors was Noah Ablett, whom Bevan, Arthur Horner and a whole generation of young miners in South Wales honoured as the most powerful intellectual influence on their youth. Ablett put the case against the roundabout method of acting through Parliament in the simple question: 'Why cross the river to fill the pail?'[4] His theories looked immensely formidable at a time when Labour was much stronger in the coalfields than at Westminster and when the volcanic eruptions of industrial revolt seemed capable of moving the Welsh mountains themselves. Marxism, with or without the syndicalist gloss, had a virility and a topicality which no other creed could supply. 'The relevance of what we were reading to our own industrial and political experience,' wrote Bevan in after years, 'had all the impact of a divine revelation. Everything fell in place.'[4] 'Everything' may be taken to include his own thirst

---

2. Quoted in *The Miners* by R. Page Arnot.
3. Quoted in *The History of the South Wales Miners' Federation* by Ness Edwards.
4. *In Place of Fear* by Aneurin Bevan (Heinemann, 1952).

for a spacious romantic doctrine which Jack London transmuted into a revolutionary philosophy. Did not the coalowners speak the language of the oligarchs in *The Iron Heel*? 'There is the word. It is the King of words – Power. Not God, not Mammon, but Power. Pour it over your tongue till it tingles with it. Power.' To which the revolutionaries reply: 'It shall be done by Power. We of the labour hosts have conned the word till our minds are a-tingle with it. Power. It is a kingly word.' Whether instructed principally by Jack London, Karl Marx, Noah Ablett or the South Wales coalowners, it was a lesson Bevan never forgot or abandoned. Experience was to kill his early faith in syndicalism. But the other moral remained, deeply embedded in all his thinking; *politics was about power*.

It is not possible to fix the dates when these ideas first became rooted in his mind, but undoubtedly all his own experience in the pits fed his rebellious nature. When he wanted he would work like a tiger; all the stories that he was a lazy, inefficient miner were the inventions of his later enemies. Yet he did acquire in his early teens the honourable title of 'that bloody nuisance, Bevan'. He moved from pit to pit, provoking the curses of overmen and the mingled alarm and admiration of his brother William. After a few years at Ty-tryst, following a quarrel, they packed up together and left on the spot. At Bedwellty New Pits they got places in neighbouring stalls and were soon working so hard that they were taking home the highest wage packets. But the peace did not last. Sometimes Aneurin chose to take time off to prove to the authorities with elaborate figures that if he stopped a few hours early he would already have cut enough coal to pay for his own wage and the Company's declared profit. After one row, a deputy-manager met him at the pithead and asked where he was going. 'I am off home,' he replied, 'to put on my best suit and go to see the Mines Inspector at Newport and tell him what is happening here.' In fact, he and William moved on to Whitworth colliery, taking the social revolution with them.

One Christmastime he was securing his stall for the holidays. The order from the under-manager was that only second-hand timber should be used, but Aneurin preferred to use the new timber. Instructed to knock it out, he refused, insisting that any but the new timber would be unsafe and that if the under-manager so desired the argument would be taken to the highest quarters. He won that round, possibly at the price of making the first of his lifelong enemies. The under-manager waited for his opportunity. Some months later Aneurin was sent out of the pit for refusing to unload a dram of rubbish. He carried the dispute to the lodge, eventually proved victimization and had union backing for the demand that the Tredegar Iron and Coal Company must give him another job elsewhere. They decided to send him to Pochin, 'a bad pit' in the miners' eyes and one where the management hoped he would find more difficulty in gaining support from the lodge for his obstreperousness. The manager, a Mr Reynolds, had a special greeting for the young revolutionary. 'So this,' he said, 'is the great Aneurin Bevan. The son of David Bevan, I believe. I used to know him well.' 'In that case,' replied Aneurin, 'you knew a better man than yourself.' One day the same Mr Reynolds found him in a cold downshaft with his over-coat on. 'Fancy a man down a pit dressed like that,' he said. 'Why don't you take that thing off?' 'There's nothing in the Mines Act which says I have to,' was the retort. He became an expert on the Mines Act; soon Pochin was losing its reputation as a tame, reactionary pit, and one old blacksmith there pro-phesied that he would finish up as Prime Minister.

Inevitably, it is the stories of these brushes with authority which his companions of those days remember. During his seven years in the pits he learnt that bullies are usually cowards and much other useful knowledge, including a comprehensive hatred for the whole system of private ownership. Apart from their other crimes, he was disgusted by the waste and inefficiency of the coalowners; every miner knew, he said, that thousands of millions of tons of coal must have been thrown 'in the gob' over the years because the colliery owners would not devise an intelli-gent wage system. And even more immediate and offensive was the manner in which the system conflicted with the men's truest instincts. The common peril encouraged comradeship and re-liance one upon another. But the methods of wage payment subtly set one man's interests against his neighbour's and put a premium on compliance, if not sycophancy, towards the bosses.

Only through the union could a dignified remedy be sought, but the building of a sense of common interest between miners in the same pit and more still between one pit and another was only accomplished painfully over the years by young leaders ready to abandon old habits and take risks. At the lodge meetings Bevan stammered out protests against the alleged lack of initiative shown by the union and had won sharp rebukes from the union leaders. By 1916 he was already prominent in the pit committee and at the end of that year he was made chairman of the lodge – at the age of nineteen, the youngest to be appointed to that office since the union began. He was now able to help put into practice Ablett's strategy. He walked for miles to all the collieries round Tredegar urging some dozen pit lodges to support the amalgamated Tredegar Combine Lodge which eventually became the largest in the whole of South Wales. In 1917 he first went as delegate to a Federation meeting in Cardiff and established closer contact with the other younger spirits in the union who intended to bring in the Ablett revolution when the war was over.

All the while he was reading still more and roaming his favourite mountains on the Monmouthshire–Breconshire border. Bill Hopkins, a fellow collier who lived at the other end, the socially less select end, of Charles Street, was his companion on many of these expeditions. Poetry, he says, was one of Aneurin's early and lasting passions. It had its utilitarian purpose too, for it helped with the stutter; and sometimes they pursued this aim more deliberately by borrowing the *Roget's Thesaurus* from the Library and looking up the synonyms for all the words he found most difficult. This practice which he followed for years helped to cultivate his vast vocabulary and his taste for mixing long Latin words with the best Anglo-Saxon short ones. But he also talked about everything with equal avidity – politics, history, particularly the history of the Welsh Chartists who had marched across those same mountains, the life of the plants they saw by the roadside, the making of the universe. Bill Hopkins recalls one day when they sat on the mountain-top and surveyed the rugged canyons beneath them in which Tredegar and Ebbw Vale are huddled. 'Do you know how it all happened?' asked Aneurin.

Bill Hopkins made some reference to the Book of Genesis whereupon Aneurin launched into a grandiose and meticulous description of the workings of the Ice Age. Often they made their great walks at night, when all was quiet and free and the whole world belonged to them; Bill Hopkins remembers the Tredegar clock striking five in the morning when they made their way home. And once they went on holiday to Blackpool together. Aneurin was taking no chances; he turned up at the station with a bag heavily laden with books. 'I used to have a good time in the pubs,' says Bill Hopkins, 'but Aneurin would not come with me. I would sometimes find him at the Blackpool Speaker's corner preaching Socialism to a bunch of Tories outside the big hotels.' Bill would rarely go to the meetings at Blackpool or anywhere else. 'Why should he?' asked Aneurin. 'He's heard it all before.'

One special speech Bill does remember. The scene was the Hopkins home – a religious one – where, prompted by the family one Sunday night, he stood in front of the fire and announced his text thus: 'O Jerusalem, Jerusalem, thou that killest the prophets and stonest them which are sent unto thee, how often would I have gathered thy children together, even as a hen gathereth her chickens under her wings, and ye would not!' Mrs Hopkins said she had never heard a sermon like it, and we can believe her. Bill Hopkins would never forget the hen and the chickens all his life. He was a wonderful listener, but he was also (and still is) shrewd and fiercely independent. There is no pose or boasting in the way he treasures these memories. Aneurin, he says, was magical and 'clean' in his political aims, eager to escape to the freedom of the countryside, but willing to face the unpopularity which his views at that time often brought upon him.

The war itself helped to develop his Socialism. At first, when still a boy, he was thrilled by the flag-waving and the band-playing; so learned a student of the *Magnet* and the *Boys' Own Paper* could hardly fail to be. During the first months many miners' leaders, including several of the South Wales militants, took their place on the recruiting platforms. For a while the patriotic appeal swept all before it. But many were sceptical, including David Bevan, and his doubts and queries influenced the whole atmosphere at number 7 Charles Street. Mrs Bevan refused to put any of her precious savings in war certificates; she would have no truck with 'blood money'. At the miners' lodge meetings Aneurin heard the reports of the quarrels with the Government over the Munitions of War Act; at the I.L.P. meetings in the town he heard much else – a vast intricate story of how Britain had been led into the conflict by a Government which had refused to tell the House of Commons, much less the people, of its alliances, how capitalism had produced this rivalry among the nations and of how sane men must work for a peace without victors and without vanquished. 'An entirely new world was opened to me and I went to each meeting with a sense of adventure.' By 1916 and 1917 he was firmly ranged on the side of the small minority of miners – larger in South Wales than in most other places, but still small – who were convinced that the class conflict must not be made subordinate to the patriotic pressure – it was 'their bloody war, not ours'.

The Government's Conscription Act introduced a new element into the argument, for many who supported the war opposed the principle of conscription. Throughout 1916 and 1917 the South Wales Miners' Federation, under pressure from the rank-and-file, fought a long sustained action against the application of the measure in the mines. At first the industry was exempted; next 'the comb-out' was to be applied only to those who had entered the industry before 1914; in July 1916 a further agreement was reached between the Miners' Federation and the Government that a fresh recruitment should be made of unmarried miners between the ages of eighteen and twenty-five certified by the Medical Board as being in Class A. Even so, since the union was directly implicated in the control of recruitment, allocations of the numbers of young miners required from each colliery were made and the pit lodges had a big influence in deciding which of their men should join the army. This complicated background[5] needs to be remembered in dealing with the much disputed case of Aneurin Bevan's call-up.

5. Described in *The History of the South Wales Miners' Federation* by Ness Edwards.

A strike had been called by the Tredegar Combine Executive following the refusal of the Company to pay a day's wage to a man who had taken home the body of one of his fellow miners killed in the pit; some six or seven thousand men were out. Frank Hodges, Vernon Hartshorn and other Executive members of the Miners' Federation came up from Cardiff to a crammed meeting at the Olympia cinema in Tredegar to persuade them to go back. At first their pleadings seemed successful until Bevan spoke from the floor and turned the meeting against the platform. Not merely was it agreed that the strike should continue, but a resolution was passed approving the despatch of emissaries to other parts of Wales to seek support for the strikers. Bevan was one of those selected for the task. While he was away his Army call-up papers arrived and were thrown in the fire by his sister Blodwen. He did not worry. He had a tip from the recruiting office that the quota in his colliery was thirty and he was number thirty-one. He would attend to these muddling bureaucrats when his own urgent industrial business had been transacted.

He returned from his speaking tour in West Wales late one night to find his sister, Margaret May, whom he loved dearly, most dangerously ill. Suddenly there was a knock on the door and there stood two policemen. One of them explained that they had come for him because he hadn't answered his call-up papers. He stepped out into the street, told them to be silent and threatened that if they woke up Margaret May he would kill them. Then he invited them into the house, gave them a cup of tea and agreed to go quietly. With one daughter dying and one son arrested, it was a terrible night for the whole family. Aneurin seemed the coolest member of it. 'Everything will be all right, Mam,' he assured his mother. He spent the night at Tredegar police station where his brother William carried him a cooked breakfast next morning. 'This should wake him,' said the policeman; 'we can't.' That morning he was escorted to the court in Ebbw Vale, where he argued that there must have been a mistake about the quota and asked for time to consult the Miners' Federation lawyer. Bill Hopkins paid five pounds for bail and the case was adjourned.

A month later he appeared before the magistrate to conduct his own case. He did not rely solely on the argument about the quota. 'Is it not a fact,' he asked, 'that the War Office would never call up a miner suffering from nystagmus?' The chairman of the Bench agreed. Bevan thereupon produced a medical certificate certifying that he did have nystagmus and the case was closed. Either when the Court was still in session or just after, he elaborated his views: 'I am not and never have been a conscientious objector. I will fight, but I will choose my own enemy and my own battlefield, and I won't have you do it for me.'

His enemies did their best to make the most out of the incident for years afterwards. He was denounced as 'a conchie' or accused of faking a medical certificate to escape military service. But there is no real mystery, once the system of call-up in South Wales is appreciated. He was not a conscientious objector in any religious sense and, with so much lodge work on his hands, had no intention of going to prison as a political objector merely as a gesture. He did have nystagmus (it is an eye disease caused by working in bad light) and had recurrences of it for the rest of his life. Moreover, if he had surrendered to the courts and the police he would have been disregarding the elaborate precautions agreed by his union and making the case worse for others. He never believed in wittingly accommodating his opponents and saw no reason for doing so when his own liberty was at stake. Only one real doubt about the story remains. Some people in Tredegar wondered at the time why he was picked up without the preliminary investigations with the colliery and the pit committee which might have made the whole operation superfluous. A few darkly alleged that the authorities had excellent reasons for getting an awkward young agitator into the army. But no proof exists and Aneurin did not trouble to make any further inquiries. He was free to continue the fight on his own battlefield.

During 1918 and the early months of 1919 he first became a well-known figure in Tredegar. He had always chosen to associate with men older than himself and now the younger men began to look to him as a leader, easily forgetting that he was as young as themselves. Owing to his opposition to the war, he was a marked man among many of the returning soldiers who attempted through the Servicemen's organizations to build up a counter-force against the 'Left' elements which had stayed at home and come to the fore while they were in France. An I.L.P. meeting on the Tredegar Recreation Ground where Aneurin was the chief speaker nearly led to a rough house; the place was invaded by a mob which had sworn to throw him into the near-by pond. He and Bill Hopkins and another friend left the town for a few days and went for a holiday to Llandrindod Wells where they renewed their vows to purge their local Jerusalem which stoned its prophets.

His early fame was not confined to Tredegar. According to the constitution of the South Wales Miners' Federation at that time, the whole coalfield was divided into numerous districts, each with well-nigh autonomous powers. The offices of the Monmouthshire Western Valley District were in Blackwood, ten miles south of Tredegar. Bevan became a regular delegate to the district meetings from his own Combine Lodge Executive and a frequent attender at the lectures given by Sidney Jones, Noah Ablett and other resident or visiting Marxist scholars.[6] Those

6. Noah Ablett's name is the one which often figures most prominently in the records of Socialist intellectual ferment in the South Wales of that time, but some of the correspondence received, following the original publication of this book, convinced me that – certainly without any disrespect for Ablett – Sidney Jones's role has sometimes been underrated. In particular, I received a letter from Mr Richard Jones (no relation) who greatly added to the recognition which Sidney Jones should have been accorded: 'The references to Sidney Jones and to Nye's own "pre-College experience in Blackwood" make me, a native of Blackwood, feel as if he were a stranger there then if not later when he met Lewis Lewis, his brother-in-law, Will Griffiths (N.U.T.), and my friend Harold Finch. Before Aneurin went to the Central Labour College, also during vacations, and particularly for a time after, he visited Blackwood regularly, almost weekly, for the one purpose of spending the evenings with Sidney Jones at his home. During those years Nye and Sid were as thick as thieves. If at any time there was one man Nye admired it was Sidney Jones. Here I come to your remarks regarding Aneurin's "originality of speech and manner" – true Nye was always Nye, but that means he knew a master of the telling phrase when he met one. The art of the stinging reply, the delayed stinging reply, Nye learned from Sidney Jones. He also vastly improved his soap-box oratory by direct imitation of this master soap-box orator and electioneer. Nye's pauses were part due to the impediment, but part to noting Sidney's telling pauses and derisive "uhs". Yes, Sidney was the greatest influence in those formative years. Sidney had a turn of phrase

who first met him there recall how he would grip the table in his contortions to get his words out. But any impression of a callow, stammering youth was quickly effaced. He was not only in re-

---

that was masterly and devastating. (So you will say had Nye.) But I will not bore you with examples.

'Early in life Sidney was brought up in the rigid Baptist code. When about 16 or 17 he showed promise of becoming a leading light in the chapel. Suddenly there was an outcry. This young man was wicked; he talked wickedness; he was wicked in his talk and therefore wicked in his ways. Out with him. And Sidney was kicked out of the Argoed Baptist chapel before he quite realized why. That was several years before he went to the Central Labour College and long before he became a Marxian socialist.

'He worked in the pit; had been working there since he was thirteen years old. His father, William Jones, was one of the nice old chaps one meets in colliery communities. A hard worker, not a particularly keen politician, neither a prominent chapel man; not like my own grandfather Jones who, each Sunday morning and evening, before the sermon was preached, would announce in Welsh that there was bible class on Monday, Band of Hope on Tuesday, and that Morgans would preach again on the following Sunday. But if Sidney's father was a nice quiet retiring man, his mother was a Meredith. The Merediths were good stock hereabouts though the men seem to have recessed now: continuity only in the female line, unfortunately for the name, not the line. Mrs Jones's brother, Sidney's uncle, was employed in the Tredegar Estate archives. He spoke to Sidney after the funeral of William, Sidney's father. He remarked that Sidney's mother, his sister, came of good stock, unlike the Joneses, he hinted. Sidney made a funny noise, but the uncle said he would let Sidney have the family tree. And true to his word a few days later the uncle sent Sidney a postcard showing his mother and consequently he belonged to the Monmouthshire Herberts, which meant their origins went back to Prince Llewellyn and other great Welshmen. Sidney did not show the postcard to everyone; just to his intimates. He would not risk being made fun of being after all a gentleman; for despite his pro-letarian philosophy he was a gentleman. My friend Llewellyn Bowen and I had much fun out of this. Bowen called Sidney a patrician fabian; in reply Sidney said those other things mentioned above.

'Sidney was 7 or 8 years Nye's senior, and he went to the C.L. College earlier. The two were politicians first and what you will afterwards. Nye had immense ambition; Sidney had an easier streak, maybe a lazier one. Yes, the man upon whom Nye Bevan modelled his (political) method of attack was not the Tredegar man but the Blackwood oracle. Sidney was what I call the first local theoretical Marxist – Marxism, that is, cum the philosophy of Dietzgen. I will not bore you here; that is in the dead past; but Nye was a Marxist before he went to the C.L.C., and that he owed to Sidney Jones, not for-getting those you mention at greater length, e.g. Noah Ablett, and others you omit, e.g. the brothers Mainwaring.

'Most of our local Socialists back at the turn of the century and for years afterwards were agnostics. There was one atheist in Blackwood but he was not a Socialist; actually he followed the trade of Christ. Their coming from volt against the coalowners and society. Hardly less was he stirred to stormy outbursts against the bumbledom and complacency of the miners' organization. He wanted the sectional-

---

Christian homes made our fellows aware of such problems as first cause, and as to most of them first cause was God or not God, then there was a choice. Indeed there were three choices: God, not-God or atheism, or some kind of agnosticism. Lewis Lewis, Harry Tucker (Lame Harry), Obadiah Coleman, Hugh Reynolds (Irish Catholic agnostic), were for putting off a decision on such ultimates as First Cause.

'Now, Sidney Jones and, following Sidney, Nye Bevan were never agnostics. I do not quite get this idea from your book that Nye was not an agnostic. He had no time for God or the devil, except the devils that were around him, poverty, grime, slavery (wage) etc. This may not seem to be important but it was so. The trouble with an agnosticism of any kind is that it puts off a decision, e.g. as to God, as to changing the social order, as to any damn thing you can name. Sidney was positive there was no God. "Huh!" His contempt was contained in that expletive or in the shrug of his shoulders.

'Nye Bevan learned from Sidney Jones both the value of being positive on such ultimates and the shrug of the shoulders. Nye went farther than Sidney in calling people names. He was a cheeky chappie, where Sidney was just a nicer fellow and more subtle, that is in facing the enemy, whether big or small. Like Nye, Sidney was always on the fringe of the intellectual roundabout. Always waiting with spragg in hand to upset the applecart. Excuse similes, they do not say much. What I mean is that both were warm (not cold) intellectuals, always ready with a sarcasm or a smile to put to flight any fanciful ideas of what must be done.

'Now this brings me to the crux of what I have to say: Nye, younger than Sidney, was prior to C.L.C. looking for what most of us stumbled upon: he was seeking then a realistic doctrine of revolt; he had the spirit of revolt within him, but it had not then direction. What Sidney Jones supplied may not have been quite what Nye wanted, the message was not always clear: but he had more than hints of the strategy of revolution from Sidney. True a bit of dialectical jargon was added to an old idea of revolution; and as you say, the conditions giving rise to a realistic doctrine of social revolution were not there in the London class room but here in the mining valleys. Will Craik only expected to sharpen our revolutionaries' teeth, which later he did. After all these fellows, particularly those straining at the leash like Nye Bevan, were all for action. I believe that Nye Bevan had his theory of revolution from Sidney Jones. Nothing swallowed whole; not for Nye; but nothing of worth rejected.

'At that time Nye was a philosophical (as distinct from a modern Wilsonian political) pragmatist. He was anti-idealist, anti-agnostic, anti many other philosophical stances; but he believed – and this probably continued throughout his life – he believed the test of any idea or theory was how it worked in practice. Simple, straightforward pragmatism. He and I travelled down in the train and we argued philosophical and other matters, always ending at the point where he affirmed that truth was decided not by a creed or doctrine but how it worked. That was a long time ago.

ized districts swept away so that rank-and-file militancy might meet fewer barriers in reaching the union leaders in Cardiff and London. 'His impudence, his cheek, his brass was colossal,' says Lewis Lewis, one of the leaders of the Blackwood Socialists who marvelled at the spectacle.

Lewis Lewis walked the fields with him, argued and became speedily convinced that the boy was a genius. They read the same books. Aneurin presented Lewis with one of his favourites, Thorsten Veblen's *Theory of the Leisure Class*. Bevan's ideas for action were as fresh as his language. Thus early the meteor blazed. But many of the older men found the intruder insufferable. They were jealous of his gifts and often conspired to humiliate him. 'They sometimes made me ashamed,' says Lewis. Then, perhaps when the unpopularity he had aroused had driven them near breaking-point, he would excite an allegiance even among critics by the towering arrogance with which he treated the employers. Once he went on a deputation to Stephen Davies, manager of the Tredegar Iron and Coal Company. After a violent argument, Davies concluded: 'Look here, Bevan, there isn't room in this Company for you and me.' 'I agree,' replied Bevan, 'and I think you ought to go.' No man was ever prouder of his class. 'Never treat those people as if they are our superiors; that is the first law,' he said to Harold Finch, then miners' agent at Blackwood.[7] Thorsten Veblen, like Jack London, must be accorded a high place among the influences which formed the texture of his mind. Veblen helped to instil a contempt for the manners and customs of capitalist society, adding to the fury evoked by the hardships and indignities inflicted on his own people.

'We had a C.L.C. class in Blackwood with Sidney our tutor. There were links with Abertillery (Heyward), Mountain Ash (Starr), the Rhonddas (Noah Ablett). The Rhondda, again (Will Mainwaring) and so forth. Tredegar stood somehow apart. The tips of the valleys always do: possibly pride in their isolation or being first in the industrial field, which they were. We had Ablett, Mainwaring Will, and Tal; Mark Starr, Will Craik, Tom Mann, John Scurr and dozens of others to address public meetings here but not Nye, not in those earlier days. He was then one of us gropers, though, as Lew Lewis said of him later, clearly a genius.'

7. Later M.P. for Bedwellty.

The tides were in his favour. The armistice, the Russian Revolution, and the high hopes for the peace created a spirit of ferment much more convulsive than anything distantly known before. In 1919 the Tredegar Labour Party was formed and Aneurin was already a prominent spokesman at the Trades Council which controlled it. Liberals and Lib–Labs were now coming over to the Labour Party in shoals, a sure sign of the times. In April he was selected as one of the four official Labour candidates to contest the West Ward in the Tredegar Urban District Council elections. He was beaten, but others had appreciated his talents. He entered for the scholarships offered by the South Wales Miners' Federation to the Central Labour College in London, which the Federation had taken over a few years before as a training establishment for young trade unionists in Marxist economics and Labour history. Harold Finch remembers the eager Aneurin knocking at his door in Blackwood to see whether the results had come through, how when the great news arrived he returned to Tredegar as if he had come into a fortune. The Labour College was then the Mecca of British revolutionaries. Its official prospectus was 'based upon the recognition of the antagonism of interests between Capital and Labour'; its declared purpose was 'to equip workers to propagate and defend the interests of their class'; the final aim was 'the abolition of wage slavery'. Bevan clutched at the opportunity. He would go to London to learn – and to teach.

Oddly, his two years at the Labour College left little mark, apart from a rooted distaste bordering on repulsion for London and all its works. The college was situated in the gloomy backstreets of Earl's Court; he spent many hours on foot exploring the whole city from end to end, and spoke a few times at Marble Arch; but even the London parks were poor substitutes for Welsh mountains. He disliked the college routine of early rising, miserable meals and long lectures many of which he scamped. The talk into the night was better; 'why should I spend precious days at the lectures,' he would taunt his more studious fellow students, 'when I can find out what you fellows have learnt all the week in a couple of hours?' Sometimes on Sundays an invitation came for the young miners to visit the homes of well-to-do semi-Socialist hosts. 'The principal hoped for tamed rabbits' – so runs the impression of these occasions which one of his friends still remembers – 'instead Aneurin walked in and behaved like the Duke of Northumberland's brother.' The surprising fact was how little he had to say or recall about those first London days. No doubt the stark shortage of cash oppressed his spirit much more than it ever did in Tredegar. And his stutter got better only slowly. He took elocution lessons from Miss Clara Bunn who recalls him reciting William Morris under her instructions. His own real remedy was to hurl himself into speeches or arguments. To the question – 'how did you cure the stutter, Nye?' – he replied, 'by torturing my audiences.'

He said the whole London adventure was a waste of time.[8]

8. When the first edition of this book appeared no statement in it was more strongly criticized by those who were generally sympathetic to Bevan's outlook than this apparent judgement about what he learnt or felt about the Labour College. The view expressed here was strongly contested by some of those who had been with him at the time, and it may well be that Bevan's own verdict, quoted here, was overlaid by subsequent events. However, the whole picture is certainly assisted by the contrary opinion expressed to me by George Phippen who obviously did know Bevan well and which I happily quote:

'I am reading with great interest your biography of Aneurin Bevan – and especially the section dealing with Aneurin's residence at the Labour College, London. However, I am puzzled by your obvious dislike of the College and, to me, your under-estimation of its influence on Nye.

'Before I detail my criticism let me give my credentials. I shared residence with Aneurin at the College from 1919 to 1921 having, like him, obtained a scholarship from the South Wales Miners' Federation. During the second year he occupied a room next to the one I and another student shared. During the whole of these two years I had a lot of contact with him, heightened by the fact that I acted as secretary for the Welsh students in our relations with the S. Wales miners. From then on and until his death I had fairly continuous contact with Aneurin and have arranged many annual dinners before and since the last war, most of which Nye attended, including one that took place a week or so before he fell ill.

'Let me first deal with the material side. You say that the College was situated "in the gloomy backstreets of Earl's Court". I have not visited Penywern Road for some years and it may be that many of the houses need repainting, as is the case with so many buildings in London. However, the street is rather spacious and structurally imposing and can hardly be termed gloomy. Then you refer to the College's "crowded bed sittingrooms". During the first year Aneurin shared a very large room with two other students and had a single room for the second year. This latter room was

But, almost certainly, he had sharpened his debating skill and his understanding of Marxism. Some of his fellow students were opposed to and even shocked by his allegiance to syndicalist

bigger than the one I had left in the Rhondda and which I had shared with three brothers. And I know that Aneurin was no better off. In any case I have never heard any complaint about the crowded state of the College rooms. You say that Nye "disliked the early rising" at the College. It is true that he liked getting up late, but the rising hours at the College were much later than we were used to at home, when some of us had to get up at 5 a.m. I mention these points to show that you seem to be at pains to present life at the College in the worst possible light.

'Then on the educational side you are hardly fair to the College. You refer, rightly, to the fact that when Aneurin entered the College he was tinged with the syndicalism engendered by *The Miners Next Step*, etc. This was true of practically all of us. But you do not seem to know that the tenor of the teaching at the College was to play down this line and to stress the role of the State as taught by Marx and Engels.

'In general you suggest that Aneurin got very little of value from the Labour College. I am quite sure that was not so. Aneurin came to the College very young and raw, though with much debating verve and ability. He had been used, like the rest of us, to a homogenous environment, where those he met differed in knowledge and experience mainly in degree. At the College he met and lived with miners from other parts of the country, with railwaymen, dyers, engineers, etc. He had to discipline himself, even if only to a limited degree, with his reading, his discussions and his lecture listening. And it should be noted that the teaching covered not only the basic subjects of Sociology, Economics, Philosophy and History. Outside lecturers were brought in to deal with Local Government, The French Revolution, Literature, History of London, etc. The inside staff was therefore supplemented by Frank Horrabin, Tommy Jackson, Ray Postgate, Walton Newbold and many others. Further, those students who wanted to study other subjects could attend the L.C.C. evening classes at the expense of the College. In this way, Aneurin and I attended a number of classes in Fulham on finance, banking and foreign exchange.

'During the second year a number of students agreed to conduct evening classes in parts of London. Nye agreed to take one in North London. When he was about to leave for the second meeting he came into my room and looked very despondent. He said: "George, I don't think I'm fit for the class. I've a good mind to give it up." I assured him that he could manage the class all right and that he'd better drop his pessimism. He went to the class and got along all right. I merely mention this incident to show that the College did help him a great deal. It gave him much greater knowledge, a wider horizon and much confidence.

'To sum up, I am quite sure, and I know the survivors of the forty students who attended the College with Nye would agree, that you have underestimated the influence that residence at the College had on Aneurin and I am surprised that you have treated this part of Nye's life so scantily. I am surprised, too, that you did not refer to many other co-students of Nye who, whether we agree with their later attitudes, or not, have played an important

doctrines. He would not budge to gratify them; rather he would
state his argument in especially outrageous terms to test the
calibre of his opponents and see how easily he could drive them
from their apparently well-fortified strongholds. In 1921 he
contributed to *Plebs* an essay on Marx's 'Communist Manifesto', the first of his published writings now traceable and one
which he would scarcely have chosen to alter in after years. The
Manifesto, he wrote, 'stands in a class by itself in Socialist
literature. Not an idea of value is fermenting in the revolutionary
movement today but can be traced in its few pages, if only in
germ. No indictment of the social order ever penned can rival it.
The largeness of its conception, its profound philosophy and its
sure grasp of history, its aphorisms and its satire, all these make
it a classic of literature, while the note of passionate revolt which
pulses through it, no less than its critical appraisement of the
forces of revolt, make it for all rebels an inspiration and a
weapon.' But coupled with this eulogy and the exposition went
a warning. 'The Manifesto affords the best example in political
literature of the combination of theoretical principles with
tactical needs, and because tactics must always be sought in
the conditions immediately at hand, the Manifesto is today
tactically valueless, except in so far as persistent stress on first
principles is of tactical importance.' Here was a glimpse of the
manner in which Bevan would always seek to apply his Marxism.
'Like all historic documents,' he continued, 'it is at the mercy of
the march of time. It did not attempt to take its stand upon any
"eternal" principles, but based itself on the shifting scenes and
fleeting forms of the society in which it had its birth. The extent
to which the theories outlined in the Manifesto are still true of
society today is the proper measure of the long-sighted pene-
tration of its authors. If the value of a theory depends upon the
time it endures, then one can say that the Manifesto is a permanent contribution to the science of society. Nevertheless,
we should be misunderstanding the spirit of its authors if we

---

part in the British working-class movement. I refer to Jim Griffiths, Ness
Edwards, Will Coldrick, Jack Williams, Charlie Brooks, Bryn Roberts – all
Labour M.P.s. This is apart from the later products of the Labour College
– Morgan Phillips, Len Williams, Jack Bailey, etc.'

attempted for one moment to give its findings the rigidity of a dogma or to make it anything like a touchstone for all time. Its limitations, though they be the ones to which all science is subject, are very real ones. It was circumscribed not so much in what it said as in what it was unable to say.'

Bevan could always talk better than he wrote, and if these were the thoughts he elaborated with scintillating, stuttering eloquence to others in the crowded bed-sittingrooms at the Labour College it is not surprising that his colleagues could never fit him into any easily tabulated category. He had no faith in the Marxist tactics devised at a time when revolution on the streets of Paris was a familiar phenomenon, even though comparable tactics had proved successful in Leningrad and Moscow. He looked for the place where the workers had real power in Britain and could see it only in the vastly strengthened trade unions;[9] hence his syndicalist application of the Marxist science. And always he detested dogma. He liked to take a great classic and masticate it, never to swallow it whole.

The best reason for studying Marx's Manifesto was 'to catch some of the fire which still glows in its pages'. Bevan had caught it, and all the events he saw around him enflamed him the more. One day he went to Golders Green to hear Jimmy Thomas, the railwaymen's leader, explain to a great meeting why the trade unions had capitulated in the recent clash with the Government. Clustering round the speaker afterwards, he heard Thomas remark in an aside: 'When the buggers are giving you trouble, give 'em a mass meeting. That gets it out of their system.' Bevan needed no fresh incitement to question both the tactics and the purposes of the orthodox Labour leaders whom Thomas represented. He may have learnt little directly from the Labour College. But he had had during the years 1919 and 1920 and early 1921 a good seat from which to watch at close quarters the most painful, tragic and instructive drama in modern Labour history. All his life the memory was indelible.

During the last two years of the war the mines had been placed under the direct national control of the Government; it was not

9. Trade union membership was four million in 1914; 5.5 million in 1917; 6.5 million in 1918; and eight million in 1919.

safe to leave coal production and labour relations in the coal-fields in the hands of the coalowners. The post-war problem of the coalowners and their backers in the Lloyd George Coalition, therefore, was how to prise what they considered to be their property out of the reluctant grip of the Government without provoking a national upheaval. Their chances looked poor. The miners had been promised full consideration for their point of view before decontrol was operated and they were now in a more rebellious mood than ever before. In January 1919, the Miners' Federation, urged on by militant pressure from almost every coalfield, particularly South Wales, presented *their* demands – a reduction in the working day from eight hours to six, a thirty per cent increase in wages and the nationalization of the mines. When these proposals were met with a derisory reply from the Government, the miners balloted in favour of strike action by six to one. Confronted with this challenge, the Government appointed a Statutory Commission, headed by Mr Justice Sankey and empowered to inquire into the nationalization proposal along with the question of hours and wages. Only with the greatest difficulty were the miners persuaded to suspend their strike notices – they had had experience of Commissions before. But this was a Commission with a difference. In March it produced an Interim Report, proposing an immediate increase in wages and an immediate reduction in hours to seven and containing the famous declaration: 'Even upon the evidence already given the present system of ownership and working in the coal industry stands condemned, and some other system must be substituted for it, either nationalization or a method of unification by national purchase and/or by joint control.'

At once the name of Sankey became honoured in every coalfield. If one Commission had gone so far, why not accept the other which the Government suggested to examine the nationalization proposal? Something good *had* come out of Nazareth. Both Lloyd George and Bonar Law, the Tory leader in the Coalition, gave the most specific promises that they would stand by whatever Sir John Sankey's further Commission recommended: Bonar Law wrote to Robert Smillie, president of the Miners' Federation, assuring him that the Government would carry out the recommendations 'in the spirit and the letter'. In the largest vote ever recorded the miners voted by thirteen to one to accept the Interim Report and await the further recommendations. During the weeks that followed the Commission did its work so well that the whole system of the private ownership of the pits was subjected to deadly exposure and in June the Majority Sankey Report recommended the nationalization of the mines. Yet in August Lloyd George rejected it. Every pledge was thrown to the winds. The miners had been duped. The Government was prepared for battle in much more favourable circumstances than the previous February.

Bevan, like many others, drew simple conclusions from this sequence of events. In a crisis property would always lie and cheat to preserve its interests – precisely as Marx had foretold. The State would rally to the aid of the property-owners – again in precise accordance with the Marxist prophecy. As for the public interest, what comparison could there be between the role of the miners and their enemies? 'They (the miners),' wrote Bevan, looking back on these events, 'put insistence on the application of new social principles to coal mining. They lifted their heads above mere material considerations and strove to persuade the nation that the coal industry could not be organized as a prime national asset in the hands of men who looked upon coal only as a means of swelling their bank balances. The miners had a vision beyond that, and they made the mightiest effort in the history of British politics to prevail on the nation to listen to their advice. The poor, under-educated miners were inspired by an idea. But the products of our public schools, of our universities, the "cream" of society, buried their snouts in the swill of the trough. And they won.'[10]

They won the first battle at Westminster in 1919 and, when the moment was propitious, the coalowners pursued their victory in the merciless lock-out of 1921. Soldiers were drafted into South Wales and the sailors manned the pumps in the pits. The miners were forced to crawl back to work almost on their knees; price lists were slashed; victimization followed in every Welsh valley.

10. Quoted from Bevan's own book, *Why Not Trust the Tories?* which also contains a full account of the Sankey Commission episode.

It is not surprising that Bevan could not endure London. A college in Earl's Court, even a special college for the working class, was no proper place for him at times such as these. He was itching to get back home where at least he could meet his enemies – in particular, the Tredegar Iron and Coal Company – face to face.

3 The Agitator 1921–29

I wanted to see him mastering men in discussion, the war-note in his voice; to see him in all his certitude and strength shattering their complacency, shaking them out of their ruts of thinking. What if he did swashbuckle? To use his own phrase, 'it worked', it produced effects. And, besides, his swashbuckling was a fine thing to see. It stirred one like the onset of battle – JACK LONDON[1]

HE was twenty-three years old when he returned from London to Tredegar – strong, zestful, soaked in the potent doctrines of Marx, Connolly, Daniel de Leon and Noah Ablett, enraged by the deceit he had seen practised from Westminster and ready to argue with anyone and everyone. Yet this abundant vitality must have made the homecoming the more bitter. Tredegar was smitten like every other colliery town. All the dreams of 1918 and 1919 had perished; now the coalowners had the miners by the throat. Even the Combine Lodge, proudly established a few years before, was powerless to withstand persecutions which the miners had hoped were ended for ever. And added to the general distress were personal problems. His father's health was failing; the choking cough made him so weak that for a while he had had to leave the pits and work as an insurance agent. He himself went from colliery office to colliery office in search of a job. Owing to his nystagmus there were doubts about the wisdom of his returning to the coalface. In any case the Tredegar Iron and Coal Company had no vacancy for him either above or below ground. The suspicion, confirmed by all the apparent evidence, accepted by his friends but not easily provable, was that he was black-listed. At first the union would not take up his case, arguing that his membership had been broken by his stay at the Labour

1. *The Iron Heel.*

College. At a full meeting of the Combine Lodge in the Workmen's Hall he proved his claim. But for him, as for a growing multitude of others, there was still no work to be found, and in his case the injury must have been especially galling; for what became of his strategy of power now? Both among the men at work and in the queues at the Labour Exchange the first result of unemployment was to sap the spirit of militancy. Later, new forms of political action to meet the new phenomenon were devised. Immediately, the sudden appearance of any army of unemployed seemed to give to the coalowners the deadliest of weapons.

His first spell of unemployment lasted nearly three years, broken only by a six-week period of work as a labourer for the Tredegar Council. The job consisted of trench-digging and pipe-laying and was partly improvised and operated on a rota basis among the unemployed to enable them to earn the necessary stamps to qualify afresh for unemployment benefit. For a while Aneurin's gang was set to dig up Charles Street; he talked, argued, laughed, got his mother to bring out jugs of tea and generally transformed the operation into an extra-mural course in capitalist economics. But he also worked. 'Nye slogged so hard at the job,' says Bill Hopkins, who was with him, 'that the blood from his hands ran down the handle of his pick.' For all the sardonic conviviality which he could spread whenever he wanted, it must have been an agonizing few weeks. He had, says his sister Myfanwy, 'hands like satin'; they were beautifully shaped and he could use them expressively, if unconsciously, to match the eloquence of his tongue. Hard physical labour he gloried in, but the raw, blistered hands he would never recall without a curse.

During these three years he was receiving an average of ten shillings a week in unemployment pay. The close-knit family, with the mother disposing all the available resources, bore the brunt. His own personal hardship during that period left no special scar, but one incident stabbed sharply. His sister Arianwen returned from college in Newport to get a job as a stenographer at a salary of two pounds a week. According to the unemployment benefit provisions of the time, eleven shillings out of this grand total would be available to keep his mother and another eleven shillings to keep him; therefore his own extended benefit was stopped and he had to return one night to tell his mother that 'in future we live upon my sister's earnings'. No bitterness was provoked between brother and sister but for years afterwards he never ceased to imagine what aching humiliations, spoken or unspoken, must have been endured in countless working-class homes. The pitiless, all-powerful State was not content with injuries inflicted in the pits and on the streets; it probed into the bosoms of families to enforce its decrees.

Unemployed himself, he rapidly became an expert on the ramifications of the insurance system and poor relief. More and more people knocked at number 7 Charles Street to seek his advice. His own father fell ill again and was at first denied any sickness benefit. Aneurin conducted the argument with the authorities so skilfully that they reversed their original verdict. Mrs Bevan was impressed. She shuddered to hear of rows at the lodge meetings, reports of which he gave to his father or the other accounts reaching her of her wild son's antics. Sometimes she warned that he would finish up in gaol. But the sickness benefit victory and his skill in debate prompted other thoughts. She wanted him to become a barrister; all the resources of the family could be mobilized to make the idea feasible. The motherly intuition was justified; if he had ever got his foot on that ladder Aneurin Bevan could have soared to the top of the profession. But he would not listen. Those who knew him at the time confirm his own autobiographical claim that the questions 'How can I get on?' or 'What career shall I choose?' never arose. 'I don't mean by this,' he wrote, 'that we were necessarily less selfish. It was merely that the texture of our lives shaped the question into a class and not into an individual form.'[2] Not 'what shall *I be*?' but 'what shall *we do*?' was the spur to his energies. Only his mother vainly urged that he should calculate for his own future.

Much more influential were the long discussions late into the night with his father. Many of the long-term unemployed in South Wales thought of emigrating; many thousands or tens of

2. *In Place of Fear.*

thousands pulled up their roots and left for England, Australia, Canada or elsewhere. Aneurin considered this possibility seriously. Once he devised a scheme for working his passage on a boat from Cardiff to South America and had even written the letter to be given to his sister Arianwen, informing her of his secret departure. Yet always in the end, with his father's sympathetic approval, he reached the same conclusion. He knew little enough about what went on in the faraway lands advertised in the emigration posters but no Marxist would suppose that the misery and the struggle could be conjured away by a passage across the seas. Above all, he did not wish to escape the struggle. Nothing in the apparatus of capitalism infuriated him more than the enticement or economic pressures employed to drive men from the half-derelict hometowns they still loved.

He himself has described the moment – a conversation with his friend Jim Minton from Blaina, following a demonstration outside the Tredegar workhouse – when he made the final choice. 'He was as fine a man as I have ever known. Intelligent, well-read and entirely self-educated, he was one of the best of the finest generation of workers that Britain has ever produced. We were standing in the workhouse yard watching the guard we had set up outside the main building. It was a lovely day. The white clouds were drifting across a high blue sky. The hills lifted towards the rim of the Black Mountains, faintly etched in the far distance. "Aneurin," he said to me, and to this day I can hear the sad undertones of his voice, "this country is finished. Come with me to Australia. I've sold my house and I can just manage to pay my debts and make the passage money. My home cost me six hundred pounds. They gave me one hundred and fifty for it. You and I can do better for ourselves in a new country than here, where all that seems left to us is to rot in idleness." His words moved me profoundly, for he was a man for whom I had an affection amounting to love, and I felt my eyes flooding. For a while I said nothing, for I wished to be clear about my own position, and I hated saying anything that might hurt him. Then I replied. "Jim," I said, "I hate to see you leave us, but if this is how you feel about it then you must go, and I wish you all the luck in the world. For myself, I'm going to stay here and fight it out You're an older man than I am and you've lost your home, and it must be difficult to go on living here with old memories. But if all the young men were to leave, who is to continue the fight? And I can't bear the thought of seeing them win over us." I said this in no spirit of braggadacio, for all my impulses were to go with him. When I returned home and told my father of our conversation, he said, "I think you've made the right decision, but it will be a long fight".'[3]

The immediate fight confronted him with awkward dilemmas. If he was kept out of the pits too long or if he succeeded in finding another permanent job, he would lose his qualification to operate in the Combine Lodge, the Federation and the Trades Council. More than any other the union was the instrument on which he pinned his faith. To sever himself from it would be like cutting off his right arm. However, if he was never to work again as a collier, he was entitled to receive a lump sum in compensation for his nystagmus and he and his mother needed the cash. The difficulty was solved by his fellow miners who proposed that he should get a job as a checkweighman when the next vacancy occurred – selection for these posts was made by the miners themselves. At first he was nervous, fearing that his rudimentary arithmetic (higher mathematics were more in his line) might involve him in mistakes which could let the others down. Yet the task was not arduous – watching the Company weigher weigh the coal to see he didn't cheat – and he could easily combine it with all his union and political activities. He accepted sixty pounds for his nystagmus settlement, became billy checkweighman at Bedwellty New Pits and soon had enough unpaid briefs for cases against the Company and the Board of Guardians piling up on the table in Charles Street to confirm his mother's belief that a fortune would be his if he ever used these talents to make money. Financially, the world looked a little brighter. Then – some ten months after he had been appointed checkweighman – Bedwellty Pits were closed. He was back on the dole again and stayed there until early in 1926.

It is necessary now to retrace the narrative back to the summer and autumn of 1921 when he returned from the Labour College.

3. *In Place of Fear.*

Much else happened in those four and a half years. 'Freedom,' he often insisted, in talking of nations and societies, 'is the by-product of economic surplus,' or in the language of his favourite, José Enrique Rodo, whom by this time he may have encountered: 'Without the arm which clears and constructs, there might now be no shelter for the brain that thinks: without some certain conquests of materialities, the rule of the spiritualities in human societies becomes impossible'.[4] Curiously, in his own life he was able to defy this inexorable doctrine. Much to his mother's annoyance, he never seemed to worry about money. What he had he put into her till like the rest of the family – unless he suddenly decided to blow the lot on a new gramophone record for his father. If he had a few shillings extra he spent them without a twinge. When he had none he happily resorted for his amusement to the Workmen's Institute Library or the mountains. The reading, reciting and self-education continued on a more extensive scale than ever. Meantime he threw his main energies into the life of Tredegar. 'Society presented itself to us,' he wrote, 'as an arena of conflicting social forces and not as a plexus of individual striving'[5] Tredegar was his arena where he could see the world struggle in microcosm. Even Ebbw Vale, two miles away across Waunpound, was to be treated as a distant province, to be left for a while to its own undirected devices.

During the winter of 1921-2 about a dozen young Socialists in Tredegar, with Bevan as their guiding spirit, decided to form their own club, adapting the idea from the work which the Plebs League or Labour College groups sponsored by returned Labour College students were doing in several of the Welsh valleys and his own pre-College experience in Blackwood. After the lodge meetings were over or on the other nights of the week, little Marxist or Left-wing Socialist groups were springing up in every mining town, and where they had their own 'professor', straight from the Labour College, a further incentive was added. Some formed branches of the Independent Labour Party or Connolly's Socialist Labour Party. Others were tempted by the newly formed Communist Party. Bevan was urged to throw in

4. *Ariel*, by José Rodo. See page 194 for more on Rodo's influence.
5. *In Place of Fear*.

his lot with the Communists by some of his comrades in the lodge. Oliver Jones, a close companion at that time, recalls the words with which he rejected the proposal. No edict had then been issued by the Labour Party forbidding association with Communists or making membership of both Parties incompatible; but Bevan insisted to those who thought of becoming Communists: 'You will cut yourself off from the main stream of the Labour movement'. He was a firm Marxist but his Marxist training taught him never to freeze his own mind in rigid attitudes. 'Remember, Oliver,' he would say, 'much of that stuff was written a long time ago.' Thanks largely to Bevan's influence, therefore, the Tredegar club followed a different course from that traced by its counterparts elsewhere.

It started as a discussion circle with each member in turn expounding the latest pamphlet or book he had read. The general tone was Marxist-syndicalist in the Noah Ablett tradition, yet within that framework there was plenty to argue about. G. D. H. Cole had recently elaborated his version of Guild Socialism; William Mellor published a book examining the possibilities of 'Direct Action'. Tredegar liked to add ingredients suited to its own taste. And there, as elsewhere, political debate easily shaded into philosophy; the aim was to set South Wales and the world aright first and, after that, the universe. They called themselves the Query Club, had a home-made badge shaped as a question-mark to put in their lapels (when the curious asked them the meaning of the badge, they replied darkly 'that's the question'), paid a weekly subscription devoted to the purpose of helping any of their members in trouble, and met every Sunday afternoon first in a café and later in the Workmen's Institute. Membership was open only to those who had been strictly vetted. At the start all except Oliver Jones, a wagon-repairer, were miners in their early twenties. All were in revolt against the coalowners, the local preachers, the union leaders, the Band of Hope, the local Council, Parliament, God and every other established authority open or concealed.

'The philosophers have only *interpreted* the world differently; the point is, to *change* it,' wrote Marx. Gradually the point penetrated the collective mind of the Tredegar Query Club. Evenings which began with a debate on dialectical materialism developed into an outburst of common hate against the Tredegar Iron and Coal Company.[6] Tredegar was a Company town. All the seven collieries where Tredegar men worked were run by the Company. It owned most of the land and many of the houses. It had its representatives on the Council and the few Lib–Labs who intruded there in the 1919 elections seemed unwilling to deliver a real challenge to the Company's authority. On the Medical Aid Society, the Hospitals' Committee, even the Workmen's Institute (once an old Temperance Hall) the Company officials with their 'Lady Bountiful' wives, sisters or aunts ruled the roost as effectively as on the Chamber of Trade itself. The Company settled everything, enveloped everything. So, quite deliberately, the Query Club resolved to capture power in Tredegar before transferring their attentions to wider spheres. Their plan of campaign was to use first the instruments ready to their hands, the miners' lodges, the ward meetings of the Labour Party, the Trades Council where they already had two or three spokesmen, Bevan at their head. 'If we go to meetings and we know what we want, we'll get our way,' he urged. Secret signs were arranged so that tactics could be changed and one Query Club member could indicate to another when a resolution should be moved or a barren argument adjourned. Soon their elders were complaining of these youths who pushed and talked and argued to such purpose at every committee meeting. These small beginnings were to have large consequences for the whole town.

To win a majority on the Council was the great aim, not merely a Labour majority, but one made up of men determined to fight the Company; taking Buckingham Palace by storm could hardly have seemed a more grandiose objective. But a few, even one, on the Council could help forward the project. Bevan, although beaten, had had a good vote in the 1919 election. Approaches were made to him to stand for the County Council, but why should he go to Newport, twenty miles away, paying his own expenses as Councillors had to do at that time, when the first tocsin of revolution was being sounded in Tredegar?

6. The Tredegar Iron and Coal Company had ceased to be engaged in steel production since the beginning of the century.

Instead, he got adopted in the West Ward as the Labour candidate for the Urban District Council, the South Wales *Weekly Argus* describing him as an 'ex-student' and 'a great debater'. On 8 April 1922 the *Argus* carried the results as follows; Bevan had been elected as 'a good fourth':

Reg Jones	Independent	726
Dai Morgan	Independent	630
W. Powell	Independent	620
A. Bevan	Labour	596

Three other Labour candidates of the older generation were elected to a Council totalling sixteen. Bevan had collected a hundred votes more than three years before. The Query Club had its foot in the door.

Aneurin Bevan did not 'take his seat in the Council Chamber'; he erupted. 'Stormy first meeting of the new local Council', ran the heading in the *Argus*. For one and a half hours they wrangled about the chairmanship. D. Griffiths, one of the surviving Labour members from the previous Council, was entitled to the post on the grounds of seniority, but the Independents were eager to establish their authority at the outset. 'How long has the principle of rotation been in operation,' asked Bevan, 'and how long has it been shelved?' Everyone knew the awkward answer. Few of his early interventions won the same approval from his Labour colleagues. Almost at once he challenged the principle on which the Tredegar Urban District Council had worked for donkey's years that the rate should be fixed first and the estimates considered afterwards. His proposal to reverse the process was not seconded and his suggestion that the whole issue must be taken to the Trades Council produced cries of shocked anguish from his fellow Labour Councillors. More trouble followed swiftly. In May the Council had agreed after a long discussion to advertise for a clerk at a salary of two pounds a week – 'Mr A. Bevan suggested the amount should be £2 12s.' In July the Chairman Mr W. Stephen Davies – general manager of the Tredegar Iron and Coal Company – and Mr A. Bevan had 'a passage of arms'.[7] Bevan asked a question about the

7. *Weekly Argus*.

appointment of a foreman at the Gas Works and found himself ruled out of order. Strongly protesting, he invited the Chairman to give his reasons and when he got none did his best to create an uproar. 'The Chairman asked members to obey the Standing Orders' and Bevan retorted, 'I must ask you to do your duty as Chairman'. When the mover of the next resolution attempted to continue as if nothing had happened, 'Mr Bevan adopted a defiant attitude,' remarking, 'I won't allow him to proceed'. Thus early he gave notice of his lifelong conviction that Standing Orders were made for man, not man for Standing Orders.

Councillor Bevan applied his mind to a whole series of new interests – housing, water, health, the beauty of the town and every other aspect of Tredegar's affairs. The future Minister of Health who was to initiate the largest programme of Council building, backed by the largest subsidies, in British history first studied the problem in the backstreets of his own town. Housing in Tredegar, he said, was appalling. 'People were living in conditions not fit for criminals. No doubt horses, especially race horses, were housed much better than some of our citizens are being reared.'[8] He fought for the establishment of a proper housing committee, for the maximum use of Government subsidies, particularly following the passage of the Wheatley Act in 1923, for work by direct labour wherever it was practicable, for keeping down the rents. These were the demands of Labour Councillors everywhere, but Bevan put his own distinctive imprint on most causes he espoused. When one Council minute proposed, as a condition for accepting tenants, that they must prove their cleanliness, Bevan said it was impossible for women to keep houses clean with coalminers coming home on cross shifts. 'It is damned hypocrisy, was his dramatic declaration,' ran the report in the *Argus*. On another occasion the following exchange was provoked by a suggestion that Council tenants had contravened tenancy agreements by keeping chickens and pigeons:

Bevan: If notices are served, there will be difficulty in getting people out . . . I think you are making a mistake.
Chairman: It isn't the first time.

8. *Weekly Argus.*

Bevan: There is no need to bring up past errors. There is no intention to take serious action, is there?
Chairman: I think there is.
Bevan: Do you think you can evict tenants for that reason?
Voice: Yes.
Bevan: Well, I do not think you can, although I believe you believe you can. (Laughter).

Appealing to the Council not to enforce the decision Mr Bevan said that they would only look foolish, while if they went to court the tenant could put up a good case against such grounds. He said they didn't want the Council houses to be made unsightly by pigeons, cats, etc., but at the same time a well-kept aviary was as attractive as anything. 'I myself do not want to keep chickens or pigeons; I am quite satisfied with the natural history the Council provides.'[9]

More serious and persistent was his attack on those Councillors who were ready to sacrifice appearances for the sake of economy. Often he tried in vain to drill it into the mind of the Council, as he did into the Cabinet and the House of Commons twenty years later, that they were building for the future; ugly houses would still be there generations later as monuments to their blindness. But Councillor D. C. Jermine, for one, was not impressed:

Jermine: People are repeatedly coming to me and saying 'you are building the wrong type and kind of house for workmen'.
Bevan: I am fed up with hearing about 'workmen's types of houses'.
Jermine: That's the impression of the people themselves.
Bevan: A rabbit-warren accommodation leads to a rabbit-warren mind.[9]

Lewis Mumford, the most imaginative authority on town planning, could not have put the point better. Bevan had not then made the acquaintance of his books, but he became later a great admirer. His own instinct was his guide. Why plant the daffodils in beds, he demanded; they looked much lovelier growing amid the grass. And why so many paths in the Park? Let the people stroll where they wished without all these petty rules prescribed by those who had comfortable gardens of their own.

Remorselessly he used the Council Chamber as a platform for attacking the Company. Almost all the Independent members were unashamed spokesmen of the Company's interests and it was easy to provoke them to protests. Why was the Council

9. *Weekly Argus.*

forced to pay so much for blocked drains due to mining sub-
sidence? It was due, said Bevan, to the rapacity of the Company
in not packing the places underground properly and the short-
sightedness of previous Company-ridden Councils in their selection of housing sites. Why did the Company refuse to join with
the Council in appealing to the railway companies to provide a
decent new station? It was due to their profit-making passion
which made them interested only in railroads to the collieries.
How much money did the Company spend in keeping its water
course clear and why should it not contribute when storms
brought heavy damage? 'They call it an Act of God with whom
they find fault,' said Bevan, 'but when things are calm they
claim all the credit.' The Medical Officer of Health reported that
nystagmus was heavier in the district than in any other in South
Wales.

Bevan: Can you give us any reason?
Medical Officer: No, Mr Bevan, it is not a case of Tredegar men
    working harder under the Tredegar Company or anything like that.

It is safe to assume that Bevan's suspicions were not allayed.
Tuberculosis was one of Tredegar's terrible scourges and the
lack of accommodation for treatment was clearly one of the
causes. Since the Company owned all the property, could they
not help? 'This destructive disease would not be nearly so
alarming,' said Bevan, 'if half the resources were devoted to it
now devoted to Ascot.'[10]

Time and again on the Tredegar Urban District Council there
were rows with the Chairman. He would tell Bevan 'to sit down
and not talk so much'. Bevan would retaliate by urging the
Chairman not to make himself absurd. Often Bevan voted in a
minority of one after differences with his Labour colleagues.
And once he found himself at loggerheads (over a dispute about
women's representation on the housing committee) with the
honorary secretary of the Tredegar Labour Women's Section.
'The few led by Mr Aneurin Bevan (who had evidently made
himself the high priest of high priests),' she wrote in a letter to
the *Argus*, 'and who had the last word on any and every question
under the sun, turned the request down with ridicule and
10. *Weekly Argus.*

contempt.' Peace was restored in this controversy when the high priest deigned to employ his most guileful smile. But the Company men were less amenable. In one furious scene, after they had hinted that he had found a Council job for his sister Arianwen, he let loose his full hatred. *They* had been indulging in these nepotic practices for years. *He*, who had just endured a few months with his sister out of work as well as himself, had scrupulously refused to lift a finger on her behalf. Much of the Council business may read amusingly today. But often at the time the class-war knives were out in the Tredegar Council Chamber.

He survived it all to win again at the election in 1925. The *Argus* Election *Who's Who* described him as 'the youngest member of the Council who has done valuable work. Greatly interested in the Council's undertakings, particularly water questions. Has a great future in the political world and is one of the best local speakers'. On his nomination paper he was still 'Unemployed Miner'. On election day he topped the poll with 1,131 votes, nearly double the number he had received three years earlier.

Sometime in the early twenties he formed the most lasting friendship of his life – with Archie Lush, generally known as plain Archie or Arch. Archie's background was the same as Aneurin's; he came from a nonconformist miner's home in Georgetown at the other end of Tredegar. When they first met, on the fringe of the crowd at some argumentative meeting in the Tredegar streets, Archie was unemployed. Suspected of having a weak heart, he never considered going down the pit and eventually got a job as an uncertificated teacher at two pounds a week. He was a black-haired, irrepressible Puck, barely five feet tall, with an endless store of Welsh satire, wit, humour and relevant or irrelevant learning. At once he was captivated by Aneurin's individuality of mind, the original twist he gave to every argument, his breath-taking iconoclasm, his apparent capacity to pluck ideas out of the air like a conjurer. They had been reared on the same doctrines, and liked to look at the world with the same resolute irreverence. But Archie acknowledged his master; this new philosopher never expounded what he had learnt from others without adding his own flash of inspiration. Aneurin in turn, for the rest of his days, was always eager to test his judgements by the standard of Archie's gay wisdom. The mutual trust was absolute.

Soon they were bosom companions. They went to the same meetings and spent half the night afterwards walking the streets or arguing in doorways where the policemen flashed their torches in the faces of these sinister figures. They went to the Institute Library; Archie might leave with Bradley's *Appearance and Reality* under his arm while Aneurin carried off *Lord Jim*, the latest Rafael Sabatini and a few detective stories. No matter; next day Aneurin would expatiate on Bradley with fantastic augmentations of his own. 'You know what that's about, don't you?' he would say when Archie pounced on the very latest work of some economics professor from Oxford. By two o'clock that night when Archie was remembering that he must be off to school at eight in the morning, he had been told. Sometime or other, maybe, Aneurin did read the books while Archie was snatching his few hours' sleep. But he would rarely start at the beginning of a volume and read sedately through to the end. He would rather dive in the middle and deduce the rest or subject the book to merciless criticism chapter by chapter. Only a handful of authors gained the honour of Aneurin's unqualified approval.

The two friends indulged in sport together, both indoor and outdoor. One rule was usually enforced at the various meetings in the Workmen's Institute; no other business to be taken after nine o'clock. Then at the stroke of the clock they dashed upstairs to the billiards room where the frequent contests between the two became one of the sights of the town. Aneurin never won; or at least, although he could make a break of thirty or forty, he always found himself outmanoeuvred by Archie's allies near the scoreboard. He was outraged by his defeats, but somehow never succeeded in unmasking the conspiracy. 'Watch that man,' he would say, to both billiards markers and political confederates, shaking his finger at the diminutive Archie. Oddly, says Archie, he never took his own advice. In personal relations, he could be naïve to the point of absurd gullibility. The ever-suspicious scourge of the Tredegar Iron and Coal Company talked and dealt with his friends as if he lived in a world of no tricks. It was too big a temptation for the gently malicious Archie to resist. He could always bait Aneurin into fresh floods of eloquence and vituperation.

Tredegar did not offer a dizzy round of pleasure but whatever was going they tried – all except the pubs which never attracted them much either then or later. They went to Miorama, a kind of charade conducted with huge cardboard strips, portraying the great events of history. They went to the cinema, paying one shilling for the best seats or refusing to go at all. Aneurin was a great film fan. Only the serials in which the heroine was left poised on a precipice until the following week provoked his criticism; he called them a 'travesty on the emotions'. They went to the theatre when the Carl Rosa Opera Company made its rare visits. They went to 'the Gaffe', a place frowned on by their parents where the barnstormers performed and the audience brought their own beer bottles. They went to the fairs at the Rec – the Recreation field; Aneurin fancied himself as a coconut shyer. And once or twice, more daring, they went to the variety show in Ebbw Vale and came away complaining that they had seen too much.

But these were infrequent nights out. Much more regular were the walks across the mountains, ten, fifteen or twenty miles in a day. 'He liked to run away from Bedlam,' says Archie, 'to have all the harness taken off him.' If they were alone, he soared into the romantic realms of his father or recited great stretches of Shakespeare to help his stutter or became as simple as a child. If there was company he liked to show off his physical strength; no athlete was allowed to match the prowess of a collier. He would always accept 'a dare'; he would jump farther, walk longer or climb higher than any challenger, or, if he failed, invent the most ingenious excuses to prove that someone had cheated. Archie, in the Monmouthshire phrase, would 'uss him on', urge him to ever more elaborate feats. Sometimes, in wrath or sympathy, Aneurin would pick up his obstreperous court jester and carry him on his shoulders. Just occasionally they played a primitive form of golf; Aneurin had a wonderful, erratic drive which came off once out of ten attempts. More often they resorted to bat and catty, a crude home-made brand of baseball. Aneurin – when he won – claimed that it was a game requiring more scientific skill than any of the vulgar pastimes taught at the public schools. He would even lay down the law on the proper way to play rugby football. This at last was too much, and suddenly all his band of admirers, and not merely Archie, would recover their full nerve and voices.

They went on holidays together, to North Wales or to Cornwall, where the romantic side of Aneurin's nature broke loose altogether. He pictured odd local characters as Phoenician pirates and searched for smugglers' loot in every cave. What else did they do there? They sat by the sea throwing pebbles into the water and watched and argued and plotted. Rarely, if ever, did they talk in terms of personal ambition. 'I spoke to him almost every day for years,' says Archie, 'and never did I hear him say: "If I become this, then such and such will be the next step".' Deep in his heart, and not as a political pose, his ambitions were communal and collectivist. He wanted to rise with his class and not out of it. Indeed, for all his romantic tastes, his emotions were 'pretty well wrapped up'. He would not easily show his love. He did not like his withers wrung and would try to avoid a too harrowing drama on the stage or the screen; he had seen enough for a lifetime in the cases he had taken to the Board of Guardians. The chief lines of argument were intellectual and unsentimental and remorselessly carried to their conclusions and usually most one-sided in the acknowledgement of the victor. Archie says that he never shifted Aneurin in a single, settled opinion. But no doubt is possible about the refreshment he drew from such a companionship. They scoured the Cornish coasts as they scaled the Welsh mountains, and came back to Tredegar with new desperate projects for the discomfiture of the Company. What else did they do? Girls; what about them? *Girls*, says Archie, with the weary air of a man who cannot be expected to remember *everything*; and then he screws up his eyes and shakes his head. 'Of course, there was the girl in Pontypool and the nurses at Abergavenny and no doubt several others too.' But no feminine distraction could long compete with the call of the wide world and little Tredegar. 'Until Jennie came along,' says Archie, 'I never saw him really brood about a girl or ask inscrutable, revealing questions about such matters as the strength of the miners' union in Fifeshire.'

Archie's account compresses this part of the story and with considerable excuse. No man was ever more determined to keep his private life private, to protect his innermost personal feelings from invasion. Once when he had just turned thirty he told a reporter that he did not intend to get married. 'One cannot afford,' he explained, 'to be tied to life by one's heartstrings.' That was not the whole truth, but it was one element of it. Despite the daring flights of his intellect and his audacity in political action, he could be cautious in personal dealings. A mixture of shyness, prudence, even puritan restraint, contributed to his early attitudes. At the same time, his sensuality was very much part of him – he would quote Nietzsche on the subject, on the heights and depths of a man's personality. He had an artist's feeling for the beauty of the human body. And always his tongue was caustic. 'Righteous people terrify me . . . Virtue is its own punishment . . . Every man is less than a man if he can't be won over by the guiles of a woman.' These are phrases recalled by those who knew him in the twenties. Keats and Shelley and the modern Left-wing theorists about love and marriage displaced the precepts of his religious upbringing. He became a puritan sensualist or, maybe, a sensual puritan. Many opposite strands were woven together in him. But it is still true that, in his early manhood, his mind was developed and his wit was exercised long before he shed other inhibitions.

No doubt exists about the affection he aroused and the gaiety he spread in several Tredegar homes where he was welcomed as a favourite son or, conceivably, an eligible husband. He could be oppressed by the meanness he saw around him, but he would never allow life to be dour and dark for long. For those who knew him well then these were golden times. He was the hero who brought a tingling excitement to their firesides. It is tempting to make the comparison between the young Aneurin and Ernest Everhard, the creation of his much-beloved Jack London in *The Iron Heel*. 'He was afraid of nothing,' wrote Jack London.

'He was a natural aristocrat – and this in spite of the fact that he was in the camp of the non-aristocrats . . . he was aflame with democracy.' The opposite strands combined to make his political no less than his personal character. He was, for members of the Query Club and for a few others, like Ernest, 'their Eagle, beating with tireless wings the void, soaring towards what was ever his sun, the flaming ideal of human freedom'. In particular, they remember him stuttering out his poems, gay, impudent and grave. Several of them were especially apposite to the jingoistic mood of the time which Aneurin gained so much unpopularity in combating. 'War,' he said with Shelley:

> War is the statesman's game, the
>   priest's delight,
> The lawyer's jest, the hired assassin's trade.

He gave his thanksgiving for victory in the words of Burns:

> Ye hypocrites! Are these your pranks?
>   To murder men, and give God thanks?
> Desist for shame! Proceed no further!
>   God won't accept your thanks for murther!

Or more crudely in the language of a less famous poet:

> Simple Simon met a Slyman
>   Of an Army Corps.
> Slyman talked of scraps of paper
>   Huns and guns and war.
> Simple Simon took for gospel
>   All that Slyman said.
> Now there ain't a Simple Simon,
>   Simple Simon's dead.

More often his tastes rose far above these levels. He had all *Endymion* by heart. Keats for some years held the highest position of honour. Keats, the romantic in half revolt against romanticism, was perfect for him, and on countless occasions then and thereafter he recited the sonnet,

> When I have fears that I may cease to be
>   Before my pen has glean'd my teeming brain
> Before high-piled books, in charact'ry,
>   Hold like rich garners the full-ripen'd grain;

When I behold, upon the night's starr'd face,
    Huge cloudy symbols of a high romance,
And feel that I may never live to trace
    Their shadows with the magic hand of chance;
And when I feel, fair creature of an hour!
    That I shall never look upon thee more,
Never have relish in the faery power
    Of unreflecting love! – then on the shore
Of the wide world I stand alone, and think
    Till Love and Fame to nothingness do sink.

The teeming brain was brought to bear on every subject. He chose his own epitaph from William Morris:

Rest, comrade, rest:
    Cull we sad flowers to lay on your sad breast:
There till the world awakes to love, we leave you:
    Rest, comrade, rest.

And to make assurance double sure he wrote one of his own, still preserved in his own handwriting:

Here lieth one who with
    His last breath
Found the friend he'd sought for,
    And that was Death.

This was youthful histrionics, and the whole selection may leave a false idea. He had black moods, but was all for life. Sentiment was subdued in him; astringency and buoyancy were always breaking through. He loved to twist Swinburne round his awkward tongue and, despite the impediment, could recite with a beautiful sense of timing:

From too much love of living,
    From hope and fear set free,
We thank with brief thanksgiving
    Whatever Gods may be
That no man lives forever,
    That dead men rise up never;
That even the weariest river
    Winds somewhere safe to sea.

Most strikingly individual to him was his consciousness of urgency, which later became almost overpowering. Keats's sonnet is matched by the lines which he learnt much later and often quoted from Yeats:

> The years like great black oxen tread the world
> And God the herdsman goads them from behind
> And I am broken by their passing feet.

Not merely must the world be changed. The deed must be done this year, preferably tomorrow or today. Truly, there was not time for all the other distractions, however irresistibly entrancing they often became.

Archie Lush was made the secretary of the Query Club a year or two after its establishment. The plan was to challenge the Company not only through the union and on the Council, but in every institution where its nominees held the power. The Workmen's Institute was one of the first targets. Deep research revealed that the real power resided in the trust board rather than the general committee openly elected by the members. One after another Query members, Aneurin first in 1923 and Archie Lush and Jack Stockton a year or two later, got themselves elected trustees and then used their majority to hand back the power to the general committee. Archie became chairman of the Institute and Aneurin chairman of the Library Committee, a post which he retained for many years, insisting throughout that however great the shortage of cash, expenditure on books must never be skimped. He was hugely proud of the library, the £300 a year spent on new volumes and the special attention given to the juvenile section. 'We have discovered,' he said, 'that nearly all the successes at the secondary school are children who use our library.' [11] Five pounds was set aside every month for Oliver Jones to spend on philosophical books. One achievement certainly for which the Query Club could claim special credit was that the Tredegar Library was built up into one of the best in the country. But the other worthy aim had gone hand in hand with this high purpose. The Company nominees were squeezed out before they had really grasped what was happening by a band of young men in their twenties who had concocted their plots virtually on the Company's premises.

11. Interview with J. L. Hodson in the *Daily News*, 18 March 1930.

The Tredegar Medical Aid Society presented a different problem. This has been regarded as an embryonic National Health Service and in one sense it was. Started about 1890 by some miners and steelworkers who clubbed together to employ a doctor and an assistant, it gradually developed into something much more ambitious. By the early twenties every miner was paying twopence or threepence a week into a central fund and the rest of the population was eligible to join at varying rates if they wished; nearly everybody in Tredegar joined. Members had a choice of about five or six doctors, they could call on the services of specialists and were entitled to certain free facilities in the hospitals run by a quite separate Committee to which the Medical Aid Society made its subscription. Undoubtedly the scheme owed part of its inspiration and sustenance to working-class initiative; Walter Conway, an old radical born in the Tredegar workhouse, played a big part in its development and the Society was always run by a committee elected by the members. Undoubtedly too it did partly achieve the aim of making the cost of sickness a communal burden, thereby lifting the worst shadow which fell across working-class homes. But the picture must not be idealized too much. There were many disputes about the way the Society should be run; for example, what rights should be retained by those who became unemployed? And side by side with the working-class initiative went the pervasive influence of the Company who also had their nominees in positions of key control both in the Society itself and on the Hospitals Committee which worked side by side with it. The ambitious eye of the Query Club examined the possibilities on the controlling bodies of both these institutions. In 1923 and 1924 they started to move into the Society and Aneurin became an important member of the Hospitals Committee.

Alongside these purposive infiltrations the Query Club, enlarged to some twenty members on the same strict selective basis enforced from the start, persistently operated in the Labour Party, the Trades Council and the lodge meetings. Its existence was not secret, although many of its particular objectives might be. 'The people sitting in the best pews,' as they described the older Labour leaders, were often outraged by the pressures of the youthful activists. But it never occurred or seemed possible to the older men and women to outlaw them and forbid their manoeuvres. No excuse was given for the charge that they were merely pushing themselves. Much more often they selected the candidate they intended to back for a particular office from outside their own number; the old-stagers were excoriated and flattered by turns. Query Club members knew their own mind; the rest were not so sure. And Tredegar politics were kept in a perpetual turmoil, partly by their operations and partly by the alternate use their leader made of his savage and seductive tongue. He made multitudes of friends and many enemies, occasionally staggering the latter and even the Query Club itself by the abrupt manner in which he would propose an expedient reconciliation.

The Query Club, the Council, the Medical Aid Society, the Library Committee, the Hospitals Committee – these might be thought sufficient activities for Aneurin's superabundant energy. But there were many more. His base remained the union and in 1924 he played a leading part in reconstituting the Tredegar Combine Executive. 'The object in view is to establish and to secure simultaneous action in cases of failure of settlement at any one or more of the collieries connected and that the body of members at each colliery shall be guaranteed the co-operation of the whole of the members employed at all collieries connected in defending and demanding that justice shall be meted out by the respective companies to each and every member, individually and collectively, *by Combination of Power*.' This had always been the objective since the Combine Lodge had been first established during the war, but the time had come to restore the sense of unity and purpose so badly bruised by the events which followed the collapse of the 1921 strike. Greater powers were given to the Executive and Bevan became chairman to see the work through. He also became chairman of the Miners' Welfare Committee.

Meantime the biggest ferment among the working class in the Welsh valleys was stirring outside the scope of any Council and often outside the direct field of the union's operations. The new phenomenon of mass long-term unemployment presented a series of new problems. Bevan did his best to persuade the

Council to bombard the Ministry of Health with protests against their parsimonious provisions for the unemployed and the effects of general dereliction on the local rates. But he had little enough hope of aid from Westminster. Once a man's covenanted or extended benefit supplied under the insurance system was exhausted, nothing was left but the poor relief dispensed by the elected Board of Guardians. For generations working people had regarded this last resort as harsh and ignominious. It was begging for a pitiful charity handed out on the most haphazard terms. But times were too serious for these proud restraints. As in the other valleys, a dual campaign was conducted in Tredegar to ensure the election of sympathetic Guardians and to urge the maximum use of their powers. Most of the money at their disposal came from the local rates, but in case of desperate need they could apply to the Ministry of Health for loans which were only granted on terms giving Whitehall a decisive say in the scales of relief permitted. It was a system calculated to provoke endless recriminations between the unemployed, the Guardians and the Government. Partly to take up individual cases and partly to mobilize the general discontent, the National Unemployed Workers' Movement was started, chiefly led by the Communists. Bevan was doubtful about the need for a separate organization. He would have preferred to see the work done by the unions and thus hoped to sustain the sense of common interest between employed and unemployed. But he would make no big issue of theoretical dispute about the best form of organization. When the N.U.W.M. acted, he acted with them. At the lodge and Combine meetings he urged support for unemployed demonstrations. The most famous of these in the Bedwellty Union – the area covered by the Guardians who met in Tredegar – occurred on 27 January 1923. Unemployed and many working miners marched together from Tredegar, Ebbw Vale, Nantyglo and Blaina and locked up the Guardians in the workhouse for eighteen hours as a protest against the latest relief cuts decreed by the Ministry of Health.[12]

12. Some confusion has arisen about this incident. In his *In Place of Fear* Bevan states that he was one of the leaders of this demonstration and describes later the conversation about emigration with his friend from Blaina quoted

Probably it was these unemployment demonstrations which encouraged Bevan to extend his activities beyond the territory controlled by the Tredegar Iron and Coal Company and across the Himalayan peaks of local pride and rivalry which divided Tredegar from Ebbw Vale. Ebbw Vale at that time was already considerably bigger than Tredegar; it too depended on coal, although it still retained a fitfully operating iron and steelworks. Ebbw Vale, Tredegar and Rhymney – three proud sovereign states in separate valleys, each with its distinct personality – were joined loosely together in the federal structure of the Constituency Labour Party which sent Evan Davies, a miner M.P. from Ebbw Vale, to Westminster. Bevan quickly gained a foothold in this body and in 1923 was elected chairman. The *Weekly Argus* of 22 March 1924 reports a knife and fork tea held in Tredegar in honour of the return of Evan Davies and a Labour Government a few months before. Evan Davies was no mean orator himself but the speech of Aneurin Bevan, the chairman, seems to have attracted as much attention as anything revealed by Ebbw Vale's M.P. He said that Mr Ramsay MacDonald's position at the head of a minority Government was difficult. He needed all the loyalty the movement could give him. But – and it was a big but – 'although we believe in loyalty, a disastrous blow would be struck at the heart of the movement if the Government remains in office longer than is necessary for immediate requirements. We all realize the Labour Government is being prevented by a series of hindering influences from bringing any emancipation of any value to the country. If the Government cannot put a policy into effect for dealing with the nation's economic problems, the sooner it gives up the better. The Government must not cling to office for the sake of office; if it does so the reaction

---

on page 49. But the claim has been contested by others who were present at the demonstration and Archie Lush's recollection is that on this occasion Bevan was away attending a conference in Stoke. The probable explanation is that Bevan had mixed up in his mind two marches to the Guardians – this first one which certainly occurred on the date given and another demonstration of a similar character which took place in 1927, following the introduction of the Guardians Default Act (see page 82 below). On the other hand there seems no doubt that the discussion about emigration did take place in 1923.

on the ideals of the miners is bound to be serious.'[13] Knife and
fork teas in the presence of sitting M.P.s are inclined to induce
sobriety of speech. But clearly Bevan had no faith that the 1923
Labour Government would achieve anything. He was never an
admirer of MacDonald. Only one member of that Government
stirred enthusiasm among militant Socialists. John Wheatley
looked a man of a different fibre from the others, and his Housing Act left its mark when all else was forgotten.[14]

John Wheatley was also one of his father's heroes, and the
family remembers how eagerly in his last days, when the old
man was lying on his bed stricken by pneumoconiosis, he would
ask whether the *Daily Herald* had come, so that he could read
about Wheatley. One night in February 1925, the harsh breathing rose to its terrible climax and David Bevan died in the arms
of his favourite son. According to the *Argus*, his chief title to
fame was that he was 'the father of Aneurin Bevan, Chairman
of the Tredegar Combine Executive, leader of the Labour movement in the Ebbw Vale division and member of the Tredegar
Council'. For the rest he was 'a firm believer in the educational
side and won several prizes for translation and composition'. He
was 'a man who delighted in national tradition'. He also delighted in his son, having spent endless hours discussing with
him both his dreams and all his stratagems and strategies for
achieving them. He lived to see him, at the age of twenty-seven,
the most talked-of figure in the life of Tredegar. And Aneurin
walked with the Baptist deacons to the hill-top cemetery, believing that he could never hope to find such a friend again.

13. *Weekly Argus.*
14. Soon after the fall of the first Labour Government Bevan attended his
first Labour Party Conference, at Liverpool in 1925. He, with his friend
Harold Finch of Blackwood, was a miners' delegate. Bevan did not manage to
get to the rostrum at the Conference itself but he played a full part in the
discussions on the miners' delegation. Harold Finch remembers Stephen
Walsh, the miners' President, asking: 'Who is that loquacious youth?
Where's he from?' 'That's Aneurin Bevan from Tredegar,' replied Finch.
'Well, my God, he's a smart boy,' said Walsh, partly fascinated and partly
irritated by the lectures to which he had been subjected. The big issue at the
1925 Conference (see page 102 below) was whether a Labour Government
should ever again be prepared to accept office without commanding a majority in the Commons. Bevan at the time was one of those who wished to
prevent MacDonald from repeating the 1923–1924 experiment.

One night a few days later he was talking of his father's death to a friend. 'Does this not make you believe in an after-life?' she asked. 'I would like to,' he said. 'My heart tells me so, but my head will not let my heart be at rest.' It was his Baptist father who had taught him to think for himself. According to his brother William, the father said to all his children: 'Be courteous, be mannerly, but always try to work out what is the argument *against* what someone is saying to you.' David Bevan was one rich source of the individualism of Aneurin Bevan.

The year 1926 brought many changes for the Bevan family. They moved from Charles Street to Beaufort House in Commercial Street, where Aneurin could have the front room as an office. He was already doing an immense amount of work for the union, unpaid. Now it was agreed, following a ballot on the issue of principle (1,953 for and 621 against) that he should be appointed disputes agent, a post which the union did not recognize officially and which gave him no fresh place in the union hierarchy. What it did give was time and facilities and resources to conduct all his operations more effectively. A special levy of one penny a week was made among Combine Lodge members to provide a wage of five pounds a week. This was a princely sum compared with what most miners were then earning and there was some haggling about the figure. But, although he cared little enough about money, he insisted that if they wanted the job done they must pay for it properly. A telephone was installed and those with grievances soon got their money's worth hearing the new disputes agent tackle the colliery officials or other authorities in their presence. His sister Arianwen acted as his secretary. The Query Club was becoming high-powered. For a while, however, all else lost significance in the shadow of the national mining crisis and the General Strike.

On 15 April all the colliery companies in the land, the Trede-gar Iron and Coal Company included, posted at the pit-head lock-out notices due to expire fifteen days later. The miners were required to work longer hours and accept a severe cut in wages. Nine months before, on 'Red Friday', Stanley Baldwin's Gov-ernment had agreed to provide what it had previously refused –

a subsidy to prevent the wage reductions demanded by the colliery owners while a Commission, headed by Sir Herbert Samuel, examined the whole structure of the industry. 'This is the first round,' said Arthur Cook, the miners' secretary: 'let us prepare for the final struggle.' But the appeal went unheeded; the Government prepared, the unions did not. The General Council of the T.U.C. backed the miners' case to the hilt, encouraged them in their resistance and stumbled forward without any considered strategy or aim into the most spectacular industrial conflict ever known. The miners, with some justice, were more optimistic than at any time since 1919. They had made the Government retreat once on 'Red Friday'; the coalowners were showing a provocative obstinacy which shocked even members of the Tory Government; the whole trade union movement was united. Bevan caught the mood of optimism. He was travelling frequently to Cardiff and joined with the others there who helped to make the South Wales miners the most militant section inside the Miners' Federation.[15]

But the challenge of the General Strike on 3 May came suddenly. Tredegar, like everywhere else, had to improvise. When the instructions came through from the union a few days before, a Council of Action was formed with Bevan as the undisputed choice for chairman. For the next nine days all trade unionists in the area answered the appeal to strike in support of the locked-out miners. Tredegar was one of the places where the stoppage was complete and where for a while it did seem that the industrial weapon could be wielded with dazzling success. The Council of Action sat in well-nigh permanent session at the Workmen's Institute and Bevan was the effective ruler of the town. He had several verbal clashes with Superintendent Robert Edwards, the policeman supposedly in charge. 'If there's any trouble here,' said Edwards to Bevan, 'we'll have the place running with blood.' Bevan replied that no police officer had any right to use such language and that the matter would be raised in the right quarter when time was available. Meanwhile, if the police behaved themselves, there would be no violence. The

15. The union at that time was called the Miners' Federation of Great Britain. It became one union – the National Union of Mineworkers – in 1945.

prophecy was fulfilled; self-discipline in Tredegar worked so well that Superintendent Edwards could find no excuse for the stern counter-measures he was eager to employ.

Only once was this record nearly broken. Oliver Jones and a few other Query Club members resolved to stop the taxicab which was bringing copies of the *Western Mail*, *British Gazette* and other Government propaganda material up from Newport. So they went to the outskirts of the town where the road was being repaired and built a barricade across it. The blackleg imports from Newport were effectively stopped, at least until the police could dismantle the barricade. They started a hunt for the culprits. Oliver Jones returned to the Workmen's Institute to report to Bevan, who promptly communicated with the colliery manager. 'If any of our men are troubled by the police,' Oliver heard him say, 'we'll have the safety men out of the pits.' When the Superintendent came on the phone to ask for information, he replied: 'Seeing you are so efficient, you'd better find out for yourself.' That night Bevan and Oliver Jones were sitting up late at Oliver Jones's house when they heard some noises at the window. Throwing open the door they found two policemen crouching outside. 'You'd better come in and have a cup of tea now that Mrs Jones has just made one,' said Bevan. Superintendent Edwards might have been treated less leniently. A few months later, following pressure from the uncrowned king of Tredegar, he was removed to another district.

During the nine days Bevan made another enemy who could not be so successfully removed. The *Western Mail*, published in Cardiff, put the coalowners' case more blatantly than any other newspaper in the country, and Bevan was particularly affronted when it made a vicious and, as he believed, obscene attack on A. J. Cook. He therefore organized a huge procession to Waunpound, the mountain between Ebbw Vale and Tredegar, where copies of the *Western Mail* were solemnly burnt and buried, Bevan delivering the funeral oration. He also had the paper banned from the Tredegar Library. For the next quarter of a century the *Western Mail* sought its revenge.

Among the miners, memories of the General Strike are erased by the sequel. The nine days' wonder, ending in the surrender of the T.U.C. leaders in Downing Street, was followed by a six-month agony. The miners were still locked out. No wavering was evident in their ranks, and at the start it was still possible for them to dream of victory. Despite the collapse in London, the unprecedented display of united working-class power left a sense of pride and exhilaration. The great mass of workers throughout the country had been stunned by the declaration calling off the strike, coming as it did within a matter of hours of a fresh appeal for continued resistance. Soon in other parts of the country the air was filled with furious recriminations and attempts to probe the mystery. But the miners could not afford merely to insist on a proper inquest; that must be postponed while the fight was still on.

In Tredegar itself Bevan had a dual task to perform. As Chairman of the Combine Lodge Executive, he was largely responsible for the distribution of strike pay. 'No difficulty has been experienced in keeping order,' he told an *Argus* reporter in June. One reason was that 'at Tredegar every person in or about the mine has received money whether unionist or non-unionist, fully paid up or not. The local lodge has not made any distinction favouring any member in regard to money which was to relieve distress. The present was not the time to bring distinction between man and man.' He also took steps to transform his Council of Action into a Relief Committee. It opened feeding kitchens, sent out two choirs to other parts of the country to collect money, ran free concerts in the Workmen's Institute, arranged jazz band and sports contests and generally organized most of the activities of the town. Some prominent citizens of Tredegar were alarmed at the comprehensive powers retained by Bevan and his Committee. Negotiations between it and the Council were initiated, as if between high contracting parties, and at the Council meeting in June the argument flared into a row. Bevan described how the money had been raised, how many kitchens had been opened, how they were providing cooked meals for fifteen hundred men a day. One Councillor protested that the Chairman of the Council should have been appointed head of the Relief Committee in a proper constitutional manner, another that the Labour Party was stealing a march over the Council, a third that all precedents had been broken. 'The fact is,' said a fourth, 'Aneurin Bevan has been too smart for us; we are absolutely whacked.'[16] This at least produced a laugh and Bevan replied in his most emollient mood. The Committee had had to act at once. If they had not done so, they would not have collected the £160 already in the kitty. His Committee, he claimed, had the confidence of seventy to eighty per cent of the public. Politely, he dared the Council majority to interfere with such a beneficent, popular, well-conducted organization. The Council's prestige was sustained at the end by a proposal that two of the aggrieved Councillors should be appointed to the Relief Committee. 'Can we have some indication,' said Bevan as a last shaft, 'of the financial value of these appointments? What we want to know is: how many shekels are they going to collect?' The *Weekly Argus*, which rarely showed pro-Labour sympathies, gave its impressive testimonial. 'It is to be hoped,' it wrote, 'that the last word has been said in regard to the constitution of the local Relief Committee, for the sooner that hatchet is buried the better ... The system of feeding is admirable and ideal.'

All the evidence available now confirms that the tribute was well justified. This was Bevan's first chance to perform a real administrative job and, much to the surprise of some, he showed himself a master at it. Tredegar survived the ordeal better than many towns, thanks to his energy in organizing a whole series of activities apart from the kitchen meals. He was not afraid to show his authority to others besides the police. Some miners were in the habit of getting coal for themselves from 'the patches' on the mountain sides. A few started doing it on a bigger scale and selling it to others. Bevan decided to take the matter in hand personally. He went up the mountain and shouted down to a miner at work in one of the holes. 'You wait, you bugger, I'll come up and deal with you,' came the voice from below. 'Don't trouble,' said Bevan, 'I'm coming down,' and with that he jumped into the hole on to the back of the would-be blackleg. It was one of the very few brawls during those tense months in Tredegar. Bevan in a temper – and it could flare almost uncontrollably – sometimes showed that he was ready for a physical fight.

16. *Weekly Argus.*

During these months of the lock-out he also became prominent at the union conferences in Cardiff and London. The approach towards negotiation was a highly complicated process between the coalowners, the miners and the Government, with occasional interventions by the General Council of the T.U.C. and some self-appointed intermediaries. Inside both the miners' union and the Cabinet opinion about the proper course to be adopted was often sharply divided. Some districts among the miners, notably South Wales, were more adamant than others in rejecting any move towards compromise. Baldwin had in his Cabinet those who wished to see a ruthless fight to the finish against the miners and mostly they got their way. And with each week that passed the stubbornness and unity of the coalowners increased. They were determined to secure unconditional surrender – not merely a reduction in wages and a lengthening of hours, but a complete abolition of the system of national negotiation, left as a legacy of the war, which they had always abhorred. At first Baldwin did make a bid for a settlement partly on the basis of the recommendations of the Samuel Commission. But since the proposal included the demand for an immediate reduction in wages, it was rejected by the miners, and since it included ideas for the reorganization of the industry, it was even more brusquely rejected by the coalowners. Thereupon Baldwin lapsed into inertia. He did worse. His Government introduced a Bill suspending the seven-hour day in the mines and making eight hours possible, a proposal which the Samuel Commission had specifically opposed. This was a direct appeasement of the coalowners or at least was bound to be regarded as such in every coalfield.

In July several Church leaders took a hand. They proposed an immediate resumption of work on the conditions prevailing before the lock-out, a Government subsidy for four months pending fresh efforts to secure a national settlement, suggestions for devising a reorganization scheme, all to be governed by the decision in the last resort of a Board, presided over by an independent chairman. The attempt to secure a compromise was genuine and the miners' executive approved the terms only to find that they were rejected outright by the Government no less than the coalowners. Meantime the readiness of the miners' executive to retreat from their earlier terms brought complaints from Durham and South Wales and the demand for a special conference of the Federation which met on 30 July. Bevan on this occasion made his first appearance at a national miners' conference. He was strongly critical of the executive attitude expressed in what he called the 'defeatist' speeches of Arthur Cook and, still more, of George Spencer, the executive representative from Nottingham. Both had demanded that the conference must face facts. But the facts as Bevan saw them were that when the four months' time-limit was exhausted, no further financial assistance for the industry would be available. The coalowners would be able to enforce the closure of uneconomic pits as they wished or to spread the burden by a general cut in wages. They would have got what they really wanted – district agreements with the power of the Federation reduced to a shadow. 'Mr Spencer's policy,' he said, 'is one that will convert the Miners' Federation into a huge concessionary society conceding point after point to the coalowners and landing us into a position which we could have had on 1 May. We say there are possibilities and probabilities of more favourable terms in the near future; otherwise I'm absolutely certain we are going to so impoverish the Federation that it will never recover from the blow to its prestige.' [17] The executive, however, won acceptance of its proposal for a district vote on the issue. By a narrow majority the districts repudiated the Church leaders' memorandum.

In the light of later events Bevan's 'possibilities and probabilities' must sound absurdly unrealistic. But something must be allowed for the fact that he and the other advocates of the more belligerent policy came from areas where the spirit of resistance was unbroken and seemed unbreakable. Moreover, in the following weeks the attitude of the coalowners became so arrogant – they now insisted they would not agree to *any* form of national negotiations – that the most moderate miners' leaders were deprived of any argument, and even the Cabinet which willed the defeat of the miners became irritated. Yet indignant protests

17. Minutes of the Miners' Federation of Great Britain. Special Conference, 30 July.

were of no avail; hunger was the coalowners' weapon and so long as the Government permitted them, even assisted them, to use it they were resolved never to yield an inch. The Boards of Guardians cut relief pay to the families of strikers. The miners' funds got lower and lower. Much the biggest contribution had come from the Russian miners, but the Government did their best to stop the flow. When an appeal was made to the American miners, Baldwin intervened with a statement that there was no distress in the British coalfields. Worst of all, a trickle back to work on the coalowners' terms started in some areas, and in Nottinghamshire, George Spencer, M.P., although a member of the Federation executive, opened direct negotiations with the employers in defiance of every pledge to which he was committed. All these events naturally added to the defiance of the militants. At another special conference of the Federation in October South Wales moved a resolution calling for a much stronger policy, to check the drift back to work, to secure finance from the other unions and to intensify the struggle for such measures as the withdrawal of the safety men in every colliery and the imposition of an embargo on the import of foreign coal.

Bevan backed the South Wales resolution in one of the most bitter speeches of the conference. Despite the Nottinghamshire defection, after twenty-two weeks there were still eight hundred thousand men idle, 'I suggest to you, you public men and leaders of long standing,' he said to the platform, 'that if eight hundred thousand have no power to obtain far better terms than we have got, then I suggest we ought to go back to the districts and tell them that trade unionism is no longer able to accomplish anything.' He admitted that 'the outlook is by no means bright'. He was furious at what he regarded as 'the obduracy and cynical disregard of the other unions. There has not been much camaraderie with the other leaders. This is the most silent funeral I have ever witnessed. If we are going down, at least, in going down, let us inflict the maximum damage on the enemy inside as well as outside.'[18] Here was a cry of angry despair. Yet he was convinced South Wales offered the only way ahead. A last

18. Minutes of the Miners' Federation of Great Britain. Special Conference, 7 October.

renewed effort to stiffen the struggle was the only chance of avoiding catastrophe. He and his colleagues from South Wales expressed the dominant mood among the rank-and-file. On a district vote the South Wales programme was carried by two to one. Bevan went from the conference on a speaking tour of the Nottinghamshire coalfield where the threat to the Federation strategy was most open and alarming.

Less than a month later the executive felt compelled to summon yet another special conference. Despite their qualms about the South Wales resolution, the leaders had done their best to execute their instructions. But propaganda speeches could not repair the effects of the Spencer treachery. In Nottinghamshire especially, but elsewhere too, the threat of starvation was driving men back to work. One delegate after another seemed aware that they were attending the most momentous conference in the history of the Federation. The executive called for a free discussion, but pleaded in effect to be released from the South Wales resolution in order to be able to seek whatever terms they could get. Arthur Horner put the case for continued resistance with all his persuasive passion. Others argued that the real decision should once again be referred to the districts; a few, like the greatly respected Tom Richards from Ebbw Vale, agreed that the position was 'crumbling' so fast that every effort must be made, with the aid of the General Council of the T.U.C., to 'bring this thing to an end'.

At the height of the controversy Bevan rose to make the most difficult and painful speech of his young life. He had made his reputation at the earlier conferences throughout the year as one of Horner's allies. Tredegar was as solid as ever. 'I come from strong men,' he said. 'My own men could stand until Christmas.' But still 'a man ought not slavishly to follow a policy merely because he has said it before' and he was forced to disagree 'with my friend Horner'. His argument was threefold. First, could anyone claim that a month hence the Federation would be stronger than it was at that moment? 'I do claim it,' intervened Horner. 'Well,' answered Bevan, 'you might claim it but nobody will give you what you claim. I say that we have reached the meridian of our negotiating power.' Second, there was a real danger of widespread disintegration; some areas would stand, but the weak ones would be smashed. Even in South Wales new threats appeared: 'there are areas where the poor relief is stopped and therefore what is the use of talking about an army when it is a paper one?' He could see no other deduction to be drawn from the reports which had come from so many of the different areas. The South Wales resolution had checked the pace at which allegiance to the strike was breaking; it could not root out the disease. Maybe what he had seen with his own eyes in Nottinghamshire had convinced him. Horner's appeal was magnificent, but it was not war; it was a recipe for massacre. But most distinctive of all was Bevan's third argument. Once he had made up his mind about the ugly conclusion, he accepted the logic. Was it seriously suggested – as some of the executive speeches had appeared to imply – that all responsibility should be thrown back into the laps of the rank-and-file? That would simply be 'weakening your position which is already weakened . . . I say that we ought not to broadcast our weakness in that way. If we are leading an army, that army must be led on the basis of military principles and not on the basis of democratic principles.' The time taken in asking for the power to negotiate would destroy the act of negotiation itself. Instead, negotiate now. It was the last hope.[19]

In truth, there was little enough room left for anything which could distantly be called negotiation. The Government's terms, which were the coalowners' terms, meant that the miners must go back on the basis of district agreements, as the coalowners had long insisted, and work for longer hours at lower wages. South Wales, including the Tredegar Combine Lodge, rejected this 'offer' but this was no more than a last defiant gesture. The November conference and the failure of Horner's appeal in effect settled the issue on the miners' side. At another conference in the same month there was nothing to be done but to bow to the inevitable. Bevan once again urged that it should be done speedily before further disruption spread in the district organizations.

19. Minutes of the Miners' Federation of Great Britain. Special Conference, 4 and 5 November.

No one can ever say whether the Horner strategy would have produced better results. All the evidence points to an opposite verdict, for there is none to suggest that the coalowners were weakening or that the Government would at last have intervened against them. As it was, breakaway company unionism began to spread not only in Nottinghamshire but in South Wales and other areas too. This was Bevan's deepest fear – a real disintegration of the Federation which would take generations to repair. Avoidance of this extreme disaster was the one valuable piece of cargo saved from the wreck. But Bevan's speech caused a real shock in Tredegar. Many could not understand why he had so swiftly changed his mind about the possibilities of resistance. His enemies attacked; many of his friends were dismayed. Gradually he restored his local leadership. If retreat there must be, let that too be done as unitedly as possible. Already in September, lest the worst should befall, he had presented a detailed plan to a conference of all the lodges represented on the Tredegar Combine Executive. 'The men will be much stronger the day before than the day after the resumption of work,' he had argued.[20] Therefore let them prepare their orderly scheme in advance. At least in Tredegar the bitter feuds between fellow miners and the worst wretchedness of that hour of defeat were prevented. The army he had led went back with their ranks unbroken and their heads as high as brave men could carry them.

Yet defeat it was, crushing and unmistakable, and the lessons must be learnt. Bevan had to re-examine the doctrines he had learnt from Noah Ablett and Connolly. It was not the case that he suddenly discarded his syndicalism in the face of this apparent proof of the impotence of industrial power. 1919 and 1921 and the years of unemployment had already made him modify his earlier beliefs. The working-class movement would have to think out much more deeply what it meant by a transference of power and to prepare for it more deliberately. 1926 reinforced these conclusions – 'it was like watching a film unfold that I had already seen made'. In particular the General Strike had shown that 'the trade union leaders were theoretically unprepared for

20. Minutes of Conference of Committees affiliated to the Combine Executive, held 16 September 1926 in the Workmen's Hall, Tredegar.

the implications involved. They had forged a revolutionary weapon without having a revolutionary intention.'[21] Even if the pendulum now swung sharply from industrial to political action, the test of intention, the test of *will*, remained. The means must be reconsidered, but the end was not altered. Certainly nothing had happened to weaken the validity of the Marxist doctrine of class struggle. Once again, and more brazenly than ever, the State had acted as the servant of the most ruthless property interests. When the gentle Baldwin bowed to take their orders, who could contest the Marxist claim? Some Labour and trade union leaders deduced from these events that they must soften their ambitions. Bevan, on the contrary, concluded that what was needed was a hardened, more resolute and purposeful leadership. And yet for him hardness did not mean dogma, resolution must not be confused with rigidity. Once again he rejected the temptation to line up with the Communists. Their desire to pursue the miners' fight to its bitterest conclusion strengthened his wariness. 'It looks as if there's nothing left but to join the C.P.,' Oliver Jones said to him at the end of 1926. 'Oh, no,' replied Bevan. 'All it means is that we shall have to fight harder than ever.'

At the height of the General Strike Baldwin had appealed to the nation as 'a man of peace'. Cannot you trust me, he had said, 'to ensure a square deal for the parties, to secure even justice between man and man?' The terms of re-employment offered to many of those who had joined the sympathetic strike or the victimization practised upon them was one betrayal of that trust. The capitulation to the coalowners was another. The introduction of the Trades Disputes Bill, robbing the unions of rights which they had held since 1906, was a third. Tredegar was one part of the country which suffered a fourth, less famous and even more humiliating imposition. In the winter session of 1926 Neville Chamberlain introduced his Board of Guardians (Default) Bill which gave to the Minister of Health the power to remove Guardians who allegedly had been too generous in the distribution of poor relief and place their authority in the hands of Commissioners appointed by the Minister. West Ham was the

21. *In Place of Fear*.

first victim of the measure; early in 1927 orders were issued applying the same treatment to Chester-le-Street in Durham and the Bedwellty Union in Monmouthshire.

No action taken by Britain's rulers in the whole inter-war period implanted more bitterness in Bevan's heart than this. No doubt the whole Poor Law system with its elected Boards of Guardians and its workhouse tests, designed to inflict indignity on the individual as a deterrent to ensure that only the neediest applied, was chaotic, haphazard in its administration from area to area, and liable to corruption. No doubt Chamberlain believed he was acting to defend standards of probity in local administration. But these high-minded protestations made the offence all the worse. Corruption was the ugly name often given to the human sympathy which the Guardians brought to bear in discharge of their wretched duties. Moreover, why was Bedwellty picked upon as one of the areas in the whole kingdom which must be subjected to the new bureaucracy? One answer was clear, whatever the other excuses. Poverty and unemployment were worse there than almost anywhere else. And most offensive of all was the timing of the measure. Hopeless as may have been the odds against them, the miners had at least been able to make a fight. But the Guardians (Default) Act was a blow struck against men and women who had just been beaten to their knees and had their hands tied behind their backs.

One special feature of the situation showed how wide was the gulf of understanding between London and the stricken areas. During the long period of the strike countless families in Tredegar had piled up debts – to the Council, the landlord, the grocer and the club. It tooks months for them to extricate themselves. Yet at the moment when the hardship was most severe – and so much more painful to bear than when the fight was on – the Commissioners not only cut the scales of relief but attempted to recover considerable sums paid out in relief during the previous year. 'I want to warn members,' said Bevan at a Council meeting in June, 'that an ugly spirit is beginning to gather . . . Our people cannot stand this much longer. An appeal must be made to the Commissioners to hold their hands.'[22] The Council – even the

22. *Weekly Argus.*

Council of that year with its anti-Labour majority – could not dismiss such an appeal; they had difficulty enough in collecting the rates. Yet in July the clerk 'read a reply from the Commissioners declining to receive a deputation as in their view no good purpose would be served'. This was the persistent policy of the Commissioners. 'They are a new race of robbers,' said Bevan at one protest demonstration.[23]

Many years later, when Bevan became a national figure, journalists from all over the world went to Tredegar to discover, as they claimed, why he carried 'an outsize chip on his shoulder'. They might more profitably have examined the operation of the Board of Guardians (Default) Act, 1926, and in particular the role of 'the infamous Major Dixon', as he is still known in Tredegar, one of Chamberlain's Commissioners.

No opportunity for revenge against these distant persecutors presented itself. But something could be achieved nearer home. Bevan continued to startle the Council chamber with fresh quarrels of his own choosing. When the Council agreed that the Army authorities should be allowed to put up recruiting posters in the town, he protested violently. The Council should be

23. The human consequences of the Government action were tabulated in a special report drawn up by Oliver Harris, treasurer of the South Wales Miners' Federation. Surveying the whole operation in the Bedwellty Union he concluded that 'the average net income per person, after rent is paid in the cases cited in this report, is two shillings and ninepence per week, which includes the Poor Relief granted and any other income'. This was compared with the average weekly cost of maintaining the inmates in the workhouse which in 1927 was ten shillings and threepence halfpenny. 'The Bedwellty poor,' he concluded, 'are asked to live on less than one-third of what it actually costs to feed, clothe and shelter inmates of our workhouses. One individual case selected from several affecting Tredegar may be cited. "Husband, Wife and Two Children. The husband, an ex-serviceman, has been ill for four years suffering from tuberculosis. They were receiving relief of one pound per week from the old Guardians, but when the Commissioners took over the administration this relief was stopped entirely. The wife owned the house which they occupied, left to her by a former husband. The house, however, was mortgaged to its full value. She does some paper hanging when she can get work of that kind, which is very seldom, although this means leaving her husband in bed unattended. She gets coal only by going to the rubbish tip to pick up what she can find. During the last three weeks the Commissioners have granted twelve shillings and sixpence per week – to maintain four persons, one of whom is a hopeless invalid and an ex-serviceman".'

downright ashamed of themselves. Such action was not in 'the tradition of Tredegar . . . To attempt to exploit people's adversities to get them to spend the best years of their life in the army was despicable.'[24] On another occasion the Council resolved to give a civic reception to the Hon. James J. Davis, a native of the town who had emigrated many years before and become Secretary of Labour in the United States. Bevan would not be a party to these courtesies. Why should they honour a man who allied himself with a most reactionary régime engaged in the same indecencies which the Chamberlains inflicted on this side of the Atlantic? 'Can't we forget politics for a while?' asked one Councillor wearily. 'Our task here is to make people remember politics, not forget them,' was Bevan's reply.

The Query Club was diligently engaged in performing this duty. By 1928 it felt strong enough to organize an open challenge. All the debates about the theory of value were now suspended to make possible the concentrated effort to capture the Council and at the last critical moment the enemy was delivered into their hands. The Water Committee had always been one of Bevan's interests. Tredegar had an eternal spring and she had long sought to improve her revenue by supplying neighbouring authorities. But for months there had seemed to be something wrong with the accounts. One day the Water Committee manager came to Archie Lush, the Water Committee Chairman, with what looked like fairly definite proof that one of the Tredegar Iron and Coal Company collieries had been illicitly tapping the Council's water supplies. Archie favoured an immediate prosecution, but Bevan advised a more Machiavellian caution. No risk of war should be run with such deadly ammunition; who could tell what would happen in the capitalist courts? They held their fire and then, a few days before election day, a leaflet was distributed to every house. Under the headline 'WHO STOLE OUR WATER?', the whole shocking story was revealed. No writs followed and on the election day Labour won ten seats out of the sixteen – five of the successful candidates being members of the Query Club. 'Breezes, protests and lively incidents' marked the first meeting of the new Council, reported the *Argus*; the majority decided to

24. *Weekly Argus*.

take the chairmanships on all the administrative committees. 'The Dictator is in power'—such was the tremulous sneer of the last surviving spokesmen of the Tredegar Iron and Coal Company.

In 1928 Bevan was also elected for the first time to the Monmouthshire County Council. The election was something of a feat, for he had stood in what was regarded as 'essentially a tradesman's ward', the most difficult in the town for a Labour candidate, and still had managed to win with a comfortable majority. 'Mr Bevan's personality,' said the *Argus*, 'was probably the most potent factor in his favour. Whether one agrees with Bevan's politics or not, there is a facet about him, apart from his ability, that is appealing and this, with his platform genius, makes him a dominating force.' Others received the news less kindly and calmly. The *Western Mail* carried these headlines on 12 March 1928:

MR ANEURIN BEVAN ARRIVES!
Socialist critic of Socialists
Monmouthshire wonders what will happen.

The *Western Mail* recalled the attacks which Bevan had often made on the County Council, including what he had considered 'their ultra-constitutional attitude' in 1926 in failing to defy the Ministry of Health in the interests of the miners. 'Plenty of fun' was prophesied now that 'the iconoclast' had become a member of the Council himself.

Years later Bevan gave a light-hearted description of his pursuit of power in the realms of local government. 'Very important man. That's Councillor Jackson,' his father had said to him. 'What's the Council,' he asked. 'Very important place indeed and they are very powerful men,' his father had replied. 'When I got older I said to myself: "The place to get to is the Council. That's where the power is." So I worked very hard and, in association with my fellows, when I was about twenty years of age, I got on the Council. I discovered when I got there that the power *had* been there, but it had just gone. So I made some enquiries, being an earnest student of social affairs, and I learned that the power had slipped down to the County Council. That was where it was and where it had gone to. So I worked very hard again and I got there and it had gone from there too.'[25] The banter contains a strand of truth. By 1928 when Labour came to power in Tredegar the Urban District Council was fighting a hopeless battle against the edicts of the Government at Westminster and the economic system it sustained. Bevan quickly discovered that the County Council at Newport was grappling in vain with the same overpowering economic forces. And at Newport he had none of the young lions of the Query Club to help him turn the world upside down. He found himself embroiled from the outset in conflicts with the older men, Standing Orders and the Labour group decisions. Labour had had a substantial majority in Monmouthshire for some years past and in the 1928 elections the majority was increased. Much good administrative work was accomplished. But even in those far-off days South Wales, like the other Labour strongholds, began to suffer the most cruel of frustrations. To turn aside perforce from the industrial action denounced by opponents as illegal and improper, to use the instruments of democratic change according to all the orthodox rules, to win victory after victory, only to discover that real influence over the destiny of the working class was still denied – this surely was enough to breed sourness and cynicism. 'Some of those Councils stewed in their own juice so long they became rancid,' said Bevan in later years.

The historians of twentieth-century Britain should not forget that some of the great industrial centres of the nation, with South Wales in the vanguard, voted first through their unions and next at the ballot box for a revolution in British society in the nineteen-twenties. Democracy needs tough champions to survive such aborted triumphs, so much more painful than any defeats. County Councillor Bevan was condemned to assist in the task of seeing whether semi-derelict Monmouthshire could pull itself up by its own bootstraps. The reports suggest that the impatience of his youth, so far from abating, was growing stronger. The angry young man was getting much angrier, and no deep psychological explanation of the phenomenon is required. He was now travelling to meetings all over the county on

25. Speech in the House of Commons, 15 December 1943 (*Hansard* Vol. 395).

behalf of the miners and the unemployed. He saw the tragedy of Tredegar vastly magnified. He wanted power to change society, but the task of securing it looked much more baffling than ten years before.

Two instances of the combined fury and despair of those days may be selected from many. Despite the deep wounds which the miners bore from 1926, they were occasionally goaded into strike action, sometimes because the colliery companies refused to discuss issues which before 1926 had been freely negotiated. Moreover, many of the owners looked longingly to the example set in Nottinghamshire where company unionism had broken the power of the Miners' Federation. After a four-month strike at the Rock Vane Pit in the Sirhowy Valley, a few workers were imported from neighbouring valleys and the hostility between strikers and blacklegs produced a direct struggle with the police. Serious charges were made against the police: it was said that some of them had been drunk and that they had batoned men and women lying on the ground. At a Council Committee meeting, Bevan warned against the peril which the authorities were courting. He could not quite agree with some of his Labour colleagues who spoke of the dangers of the people being terrorized. 'No one is going to persuade me,' he said, 'that five hundred men are going to be scattered by fifty policemen. We should simply eat them up.' The real danger was that a total contempt for the law would be spread. 'If you wish to maintain that reverence,' he said, 'you will have to treat people differently from that. A spirit is brewing that will bring something other than a smile to the faces of people in this room.'[26]

On another occasion Bevan heard that a few miners from Abertysswg, a village three miles from Tredegar, had been helping work a 'black pit' at Bedwas. He went there personally early one morning to try to dissuade them from boarding the train and was greeted by a police sergeant. 'What are you doing here?' asked the policeman. 'Don't you realize you're a Justice of the Peace?' (He had been appointed a few months before.) Bevan replied: 'When you clear your people off, we'll have the peace.' Eventually, the train went empty.

26. *Weekly Argus*.

These were the wretchedest years. After 1926 the tang of defeat was everywhere. The threat was real that even South Wales might lose its richest possession – its working-class solidarity. But, thanks partly to Bevan's influence, the infection never spread to the area controlled by the Tredegar Combine Executive.

Many of the men of Bevan's generation or the previous generation who witnessed what he witnessed in the heart of the great depression areas became fanatics or what, in many instances, might more properly be described as dedicated political saints. James Maxton, for example, insisted on a stringent personal asceticism in keeping with the hardship of those he sought to aid and lead. Arthur Cook seemed to hurl his own physical frame against the evils of the capitalist system and broke himself in the process. Some joined the Communist Party and accepted the harsh discipline and mental and material self-denying ordinances of a new and ruthless religious order. Multitudes of others, well-known or now forgotten, the propagandists of Socialism, wore themselves out in a ceaseless round of meetings at street corners and in draughty halls. Some were compelled to make a sacrifice of which they themselves could not be aware; inevitably the perpetual repetition of the same propaganda themes coarsened their minds and checked the process of thought.

Aneurin Bevan was different from all these, and the individuality of his mind and behaviour was both a strength and a weakness. He followed the same path of work and advancement, through the Council and the union, accepted by most other embryo Labour leaders of his time. He did his full share on the soap-boxes and at the street corners. On the platform he was idolized and among the select few of the Query Club he was loved. But he often refused to conform to the expected routine of a disputes agent, propagandist, Councillor or County Councillor. He might fail to turn up at a committee meeting or disrupt the proceedings with a diatribe that bore no relation to the agenda or trust to his instinct instead of the papers he was supposed to have read. Or he would come forward with a startling proposed course of action quite different from one he had recommended a few weeks before and then dazzlingly argue that both his original and his new idea were consistently the best. He made friends quite outside the normal circle of a trade union agitator, even with those in the enemy camp. He would go to their homes, eat and drink with them and then return to the platform and pour out his denunciations as fiercely as ever. Jack London's Ernest Everhard had possessed the same habits. Bevan did all this in Tredegar on a smaller scale as he did later elsewhere. Personal friendship never deflected him from his attack upon the sombre capitalism all around him. He never lost his hold on a growing mass of followers in the town. But many, apart from the Company sycophants, feared him, suspected him, distrusted him. One cause of the distrust might be envy, another the natural hostility of older men whom he pushed out of the way. But partly the suspicion among his political allies was due to his apparent refusal to accept *any* of the conventional ideas and manners in which they had been reared.

He was a rebel, not only against the coalowners and their tame Council, but against the cramping atmosphere of Welsh nonconformist society. He loved the brave things about Wales – the miners' comradeship, the physical prowess required in the pits and the steelworks, above all the spaciousness and freedom of the mountains. But he did not worship all aspects of the customs and communities which the Welsh made for themselves. Much that he saw around him was detestably and unnecessarily ugly and wretched, and it was not all the handiwork of the Tredegar Iron and Coal Company. He loved the music of Wales but he believed the Welsh in their chapels could also sing themselves into a trance. Much that he heard around him was in a cringing minor key; he had no inclination for a journey through the vale of tears even when invited by the most harmonious male voice choir. He loved life too much ever to be tempted by a hair shirt or a martyr's crown. Some strong puritan streaks he retained – for example, he always detested and denounced gambling with a fervour which the Baptist deacons would applaud, and he could be suddenly and surprisingly shocked by a tasteless exhibition on the stage or screen. He had learnt much else from his dissenting father, but he was repelled by many of the restrictive precepts of his heritage. Capitalism might be the worst enemy which sought to condemn him and his people to joyless and poverty-stricken lives. But it had accompanying features in the community life of those days, which, for his taste, too many of his and earlier generations not merely tolerated but approved – a sad contentment with small mercies, a willingness to bear heavy crosses with uncomplaining fortitude, a blindness to beauty which religion sanctified almost as assuredly as it blessed an oppressive sense of sin. No one was going to tell him how he must behave and how he must kneel before all the Welsh gods. He had resolved to carve his own way to a freedom of the mind, even while he had no thought of 'seeking a career' in the ordinary sense of the term. These were heresies at a time when Welsh nonconformity, with all the conformities it imposed, was still regarded as the sturdy backbone of the Labour movement.

Another element was already strongly growing in his character or temperament – an ungovernable sense of urgency, of the shortness of time available if great deeds were to be done and catastrophe avoided. It appears in the poems already quoted. Others might be ready to watch the slow fruition of their efforts. He believed that dramatic initiatives could change the tempo of events, that their whole course could be mastered and diverted into quite different channels. If this was primarily a political belief, it also gave an impetus to his personal dealings. He had no patience with stodgy, pedestrian minds around him. He hated the idea of moving at their pace. And then, suddenly, when they were still showing their readiness for stolid application, he was off in pursuit of one of his own delights which had nothing to do with politics at all. The myths were born that he was lazy or incapable of persistence and settled aim. The truth was that he could not breathe without the refreshment of new ideas and time for thought and brooding. He chose his own moments for lashing his companions into action and his own moments, too, for withdrawing and renewing his mental energies. The combination was not easy for his associates to bear. He picked some enemies deliberately and gave to them and several others plentiful weapons and reproaches and innuendoes to use against him. Most infuriating of all, he never seemed to care what most of them said about him. He would go his own way; not overlooking, however, the necessity for taking a large army with him. He wanted to mobilize the working class for urgent tasks and liberate them; but he also wanted to train the reserves of his own brain and liberate his own spirit.

Thus Bevan, the agitator of the late twenties, was also engaged in the never-ending adventure of enlarging his own mind. At the end of 1927 he thought seriously of attempting to get a scholarship to Oxford. The aberration was only momentary. Archie Lush went to Oxford instead and Bevan completed his own education by the most novel form of correspondence course. Philosophy was Archie's Achilles' heel; so when he was presented with essay subjects he would despatch two letters or telegrams, one to his prospective brother-in-law, Bill Williams, in Tredegar, and the other to Aneurin. From Bill Williams Archie received a grounding in the facts and from Bevan something different, first a violent attack on the inanity of the subjects set and then a completely novel elaboration of the theme. Often in the vacations the three met to debate the deficiencies of the Oxford school of philosophy. After one summer Archie Lush returned with a piece on Kant's *Categorical Imperative* inspired by one of Bevan's most daring flights of eloquence. 'Tell me, Lush,' said Mr P. W. Dodd, senior tutor at Jesus College, after he had read the document, 'I don't wish to intrude on your private affairs, but were you sober when you wrote this?' Lush assured him that he was and the matter was dropped. A month later Dodd took him on a trip to the Cotswolds and after a while drew from his pocket the offending essay. 'This is the best thing on Kant I've read for years; tell me what have you been reading?' Archie explained. The agitator was also a philosopher. Archie returned from Oxford with his faith in the genius of his friend confirmed: Bevan was confirmed in his belief in the bankruptcy of Oxford.

The same routine of walks, billiards, endless argument and plotting was sustained throughout the twenties and sometimes they celebrated victories more joyous even than the trouncing of the Tredegar Iron and Coal Company. Such, for example, was the strange case of Guy Fannani. Fannani was an Italian who came to Tredegar, got a job in the pits and soon made a reputation as 'a sensible collier' by writing letters to the *Western Mail*, putting the coalowners' case. Week by week, with much statistical detail, he argued that the colliery owners were doing the best they could and would do better still with proper co-operation from the men. Fannani, in short, was a literary blackleg, but he paid his union dues and never broke the rules. One day Aneurin and Archie were to go on a trip to Hereford where Aneurin was to see an eye specialist. Rushing out of the house at the last moment Aneurin had grabbed the letters, one of which had accidentally been put through his letter box; it was addressed to Guy Fannani who lived in the house just behind the Bevans'. Before the error was detected Archie had opened the envelope. It contained a letter to Fannani from Findlay Gibson, secretary of the South Wales coalowners, thanking him for his latest contribution to the *Western Mail* and offering some data which might be useful in the following week, and it contained also – not mentioned at all in the text – two beautiful pound notes. What to do with such a prize? Fannani would deny the two pounds; Aneurin and Archie could be accused of planting them. The visit to the eye specialist was forgotten. Anxiously they paced up and down the banks of the River Wye, calculating what course duty would dictate and not omitting to consider and reject the alternative of a first-class lunch at the 'Green Dragon' on the undreamt-of windfall.

Eventually the plan was made. They found a photographer, and had their own photographs taken to establish confidence. Then Archie, claiming to be none other than Guy Fannani himself, asked for a photograph of the two notes side by side with the letter. Back in Tredegar, they dropped the real letter and the money in Fannani's postbox and proceeded at once to the lodge meeting where they made all their accusations, waved the photograph as proof and set all Tredegar buzzing with the story of Guy Fannani's corruption. At home that night, they celebrated their cunning. 'Let's have a look at that photograph again,' said Aneurin. 'But you had it last,' said Archie. The photograph had been left behind at the meeting. Back they raced to the meeting hall only to confirm that the photograph was lost. And yet charges had been made and richly embroidered which only the photograph could sustain. 'Yes and you're the one who's really getting into trouble,' said Aneurin as they returned home once more. 'There is such a thing as false pretences, Mr Fannani. And you look like a little Italian Fascist anyhow.' Yet all ended in triumph. A few days later Guy Fannani left Tredegar and never returned.

One other episode of this period deserves to be recorded. In 1927 Bevan made his first trip abroad. The *Daily News* offered a form of travelling scholarship for miners, and he went on a tour of the Polish coalfields. To celebrate the occasion, his family presented him with a large trunk which he often had to carry for long distances on his shoulders, much to the delight of his touring companions. The deepest impression left upon him of that journey was the first-hand evidence he brought back of how British financial institutions – particularly the Prudential Assurance Company – were ready to invest in Polish mines while starving South Wales of capital. Bevan, back on the platform in Tredegar, mocked the business sense of the financiers. 'The poor old Pru,' he would say, 'offers subscribers in South Wales four pounds for a tidy burial. It takes the premiums here, transfers the money to Poland and pushes up our unemployment figures. One result of its activities clearly is to increase the Welsh death rate. How many extra four pounds will they have to pay out? I warn the Pru that they will lose on the transaction.' But, of course, Bevan was serious in his attack on the patriotism of the financiers. The Prudential came to occupy a place second only to that of the coalowners in his gallery of class enemies.

Inevitably, the chief topic of political argument between Bevan and Archie Lush and at the meetings of the Query Club at that time was what strategical deductions should be drawn by Socialists from the 1926 fiasco. Syndicalist ideas had received what looked like a death blow. It would be easy to suggest that Bevan's natural reaction was to look more approvingly to parliamentary activity. Yet this would be an excessive simplification. Arthur Cook was engaged in those years in criticizing the parliamentary leadership of Ramsay MacDonald, the discussions with the employers on which the General Council of the T.U.C. had embarked, and the ideas of class collaboration which were implicit in both. Bevan's sympathies were wholly with Cook. Syndicalism might be blunted as a weapon, but the real battle with the class enemy in one form or another could not be escaped. The most natural development in Bevan's life, therefore, particularly following his participation in the miners' conferences and his work as disputes agent, would have been if he had sought advancement as a miners' official within the South Wales Miners' Federation. This might easily have occurred but for the opening which appeared, partly by accident, in the representation of the Ebbw Vale constituency.

Evan Davies, who had been M.P. for Ebbw Vale since 1922, was a capable miners' representative who might have continued as member for the division for another twenty years. He had a strong following among the miners, particularly in Ebbw Vale and in Beaufort, the township next door to Ebbw Vale where he lived. During the middle twenties there were some murmurs of criticism. His attendances at the House of Commons were not over-meticulous. Occasionally he cancelled meetings in the constituency at the last moment. A few rumours even reached the outside world that he had found himself in financial difficulties. They had some basis, for on one occasion Bevan had joined with others in a whip-round to help him. But no one at first talked in terms of displacing the sitting Member in a safe seat. The phenomenon was as unknown then as it is today. Such an idea offended against all the Labour movement's traditions of loyalty and personal affection.

Gradually, however, the criticisms of Evan Davies became stronger and were openly broached at the meetings of the Trades Council and elsewhere. Archie Lush had been appointed secretary of the constituency party – on the casting vote of Bevan as chairman, a fact which stirred the rarely latent suspicions between Ebbw Vale and Tredegar. He was instructed to intercede with Evan Davies and report to the divisional management committee on their Member's activities in the House. The reports could not allay the growing misgivings. Only rarely did Evan Davies intervene in Commons debates; in the debates on such matters as Neville Chamberlain's removal of the Board of

Guardians in the Bedwellty Union he had not participated at all. Eventually, Archie Lush was despatched on a mission to the miners' executive in Cardiff. At first he was asking for advice, but since Evan Davies was popular among the older miners' leaders and his fellow M.P.s, he got little assistance. Eventually, after two or three more similar missions, and a considerable exchange of letters, Lush's demand on behalf of the Party became more peremptory. Since Evan Davies was a miners' M.P. and Ebbw Vale was overwhelmingly a miners' constituency, the effective choice of a candidate depended on the miners' nominations. At last the South Wales Miners' Federation agreed to conduct a ballot to see whether Evan Davies's nomination should be renewed. He had been ill for a few months and at one moment it looked as if he would retire altogether. But he chose to fight against what some of his supporters in Ebbw Vale were starting to brand as a conspiracy against him. Doubtless the idea of Bevan's candidature had crossed the mind of Archie Lush early in the proceedings. Bevan played no part in the first representations to the miners' executive, and even if Evan Davies were removed there was no certainty of securing a substantial pro-Bevan following outside Tredegar itself. A few of the younger spirits in Ebbw Vale had joined in the criticisms of Evan Davies and had even gone so far as to make the unheard-of proposition that Ebbw Vale might enlist behind the banner of the foreigner across the mountain. But Ebbw Vale and its neighbouring townships, Beaufort and Cwm, could outvote the rest of the constituency and when the ballot was ordered it became known that the third independent state of Rhymney had their own candidate to put forward – a young and brilliant miner, rapidly rising in the union, called Bryn Roberts.

At last in the early months of 1929 all the formalities had been completed for the miners' vote. Six candidates in all were nominated, Bevan, Davies, Roberts, one other from Ebbw Vale and two from neighbouring constituencies; all received from Tom Richards, the aged and respected general secretary of the South Wales miners, himself a Beaufort man, a letter advising them not to engage in canvassing or propaganda, but to let the miners decide of their own free will. How scrupulously the injunction was obeyed is still a matter of some argument. 'I doubt,' says Lewis Lewis of Blackwood, 'whether the election was conducted with due regard for the principles of the Sermon on the Mount.' Local suspicions were aggravated by the fact that the ballot at one lodge had to be scrapped and taken again. However, what had really occurred was not so incriminating. One of the ballot boxes had been found accidentally open and the ballot was taken again. Thereafter the voting went as follows:

First Ballot

Aneurin Bevan	3,066
Bryn Roberts	1,816
Evan Davies	1,533
George Davies	1,061
T. Rowley Jones	328
W. G. H. Bull	225

Second Ballot

Aneurin Bevan	3,809
Bryn Roberts	2,208
Evan Davies	1,859
George Davies	730

Third Ballot

Aneurin Bevan	5,097
Bryn Roberts	2,626
Evan Davies	1,710

Seemingly, the deed had been done. Once the miners had voted, nomination by the constituency party followed automatically. Yet there were still hazards to be encountered when the hero of Tredegar crossed the frontier officially to consolidate his conquest of Ebbw Vale. His first meeting was in Beaufort. It started in dead silence and ended in dead silence. He stammered badly, and, according to Archie Lush, made the worst speech of his life. That night the two friends went on one of their favourite walks across the Llangynydr mountain, with Aneurin wondering whether it was wise to persist against the icy blasts which the turmoil of the previous few months had stirred among Evan Davies's backers. 'Try Cwm first,' said Archie and a few nights later he had recruited Alderman Mike Murphy, the most respectable, moustachioed citizen in the place, to preside. At that meeting, says Archie, Aneurin took the roof off; he talked as if he would tear down the Tory Government with his own hands that very night. During the next few months he spoke everywhere in the constituency, developing the style which he always preferred on election platforms and which all the later intrusions of extensive election tours, radio and television would never make him willingly depart from. He liked to have the meeting to himself, to speak for an hour and a half or more, to elaborate his theme with the broadest philosophical sweep, to relate the immediate problem of his audience to the history of working-class struggle and to his own individual vision of a new society. No doubt remained about the outcome of the election itself against his Tory and Liberal opponents. But he needed to build a base of firm support outside Tredegar and to heal if he could some of the wounds inflicted on the political susceptibilities of the Ebbw Vale miners. During these months the Ebbw Vale constituency received the first lessons in its unique political education. But others, farther away, who could not see and hear and study the prodigy for themselves, nurtured their suspicions. In particular, the older miners' leaders in Cardiff and London had a grudge against the young upstart who had diverted the stars in their courses and displaced Evan Davies.

On 1 June 1929 the result was announced as follows:

BEVAN A.	(Labour)	20,088
GRIFFITHS W.	(Liberal)	8,924
BRACE M.	(Unionist)	4,287

Harold Finch saw him off at Newport station on the train to London and recalls Bevan saying: 'Who are those people up there? What's the matter with you? We're as good or better than they are.' And the *Daily Herald* reporter wrote: 'There are about fifty miners' Members in the New Parliament, but I do not think Mr Aneurin Bevan will be exactly lost in the crowd. He has a reputation for exceptional platform ability.'

4 The Young M.P. 1929–31

Oliver Cromwell: 'If they that have no goods and chattels make the laws equally with them that hath, they will make laws to take away the property of them that hath.'

Thomas Rainborough: 'If it be that all Englishmen cannot be free and some Englishmen have property, then you have said it, My Lord General, not me.' – *The Putney Debates*[1]

ANEURIN BEVAN took his place in 1929 in the first British Parliament ever elected on universal suffrage. The fact added point to one of his own frequent reflections. So far from having failed, parliamentary democracy was still a largely untested institution in the land of its origin. Full democracy was the youngest of the political creeds; not until 'the flappers' got the vote in 1928 was the development complete. The Cecils and the Churchills had been there for centuries in the old undemocratic Parliaments; the Bevans had only just arrived. He had to make up for lost time.

He brought with him a fiery message of protest from one of the most impoverished areas in the whole country. He brought, too, an acquaintance, almost sophisticated in one so young, with the timorous ways of the official Labour leaders. None the less, the victory at the polls in 1929 was, in part, a revenge for 1926 and the long agony of 1927. No revolutionary triumph could yet be celebrated, but at least the member for Ebbw Vale could look for relief and first aid for his beleaguered townships. 'The first function of a political leader,' he once wrote, 'is advocacy. It is he who must make articulate the wants, the frustrations and the aspirations of the masses.'[2] Never did an advocate hold such a brief. Desperate poverty, afflicting people of his own flesh and bone, was the great issue in politics. Nothing could count beside it.

1. Quoted in *Why Not Trust the Tories?* by Aneurin Bevan.
2. *In Place of Fear.*

And yet, mingled with the ever-present sense of urgency and passion were other qualities and awakening interests – a political intuition which taught him that he must study his new environment, an incipient curiosity about the relationship between the institution of Parliament and his Marxist theories of the class struggle, a more acute insight into the dilemmas of the Labour Government and the Labour Party than that displayed by many of his more obvious Left-wing allies. In one sense, he was a solitary figure in that 1929 House of Commons. Almost from the start he stood squarely on the Left of the Party against the leadership. But he wanted to select his own terms for the argument; he could not suppress his reservations about the courses prescribed by the acknowledged leaders of the Left. Despite temptations which at times became almost overpowering, he warily refused to tread the paths which might cut him off from the bulk of the Labour movement. All the hopes of his own people were intertwined with the spirit of that movement. Whatever the failures of individuals, it could not be kicked aside. A mighty human structure, so painfully and sacrificially established, must be given the benefit of all the doubts.

According to the official Labour mythology, the fiasco of the 1929–31 Government was chiefly due to the act of treachery perpetrated by Ramsay MacDonald, Philip Snowden and Jimmy Thomas. Admittedly, that Government had the ill-luck to be confronted with the most serious fall in world prices and the most perplexing financial collapse ever experienced in all history. It had to meet this tornado at a time when the new Keynesian techniques for dealing with such phenomena had not even been fashioned, much less popularized. Even so, the storm might have been weathered – so runs the myth – had it not been for the perfidy and pusillanimity of the men at the top: MacDonald's taste for the favours of the duchesses and his deep-laid plot against his own Party, Snowden's acid nature and inflexibility, their aloofness from and contempt for the good-hearted and well-intentioned people they claimed to lead. The scapegoat theory is now firmly established;[3] it bears small relation to the truth.

3. Much the most formidable attack on this theory is contained in Mr R. Bassett's book *1931, Political Crisis*. But Mr Bassett is striving to rectify the

In fact, the MacDonald greeted with such a swelling round of cheers at the first meeting of the Parliamentary Labour Party after the victory was not an empty, mouthing rhetorician as he is sometimes portrayed. His health was somewhat impaired, but his faculties of speech, charm and industry were still considerable. He was a skilled parliamentarian and a towering platform and conference orator; he stood head and shoulders above all rivals, the clear master of his Party. Snowden was the essence of rectitude; even his old Left-wing colleagues from whom he had drifted never dreamt of questioning his honour. Thomas possessed no comparable attributes, but his amiability, cunning and knock-about ebullience combined to make him an astute parliamentary performer and an expert negotiator. Joined with them in apparently firm trust and alliance was Arthur Henderson, the man of the machine and a big man too, helping by his presence and diligently cultivated camaraderie with his parliamentary colleagues to spread serenity and confidence. J. R. Clynes, another model of good faith and solidity, made up the numbers of an 'inner Cabinet'.

Together, the prestige of the 'Big Five' was enormous. All had their roots deep in the movement they had helped to make. They commanded the biggest Party in the House of Commons – 287 Labour Members against 261 Tories and 59 Liberals. True, the victory was not decisive, but it had surpassed most expectations. Lloyd George and the Liberals, with their vastly publicized 'We can conquer unemployment' campaign, were sadly disappointed by the failure to make a more spectacular comeback. For the first time, the Labour Party had established itself as the real, substantial alternative to Tory rule. A vibrant, radical mood of hope and deliverance had swept the country. 'This Labour Cabinet of 1929, unlike the one of 1924,' wrote Beatrice Webb, 'is a "pukka" Cabinet resting on a firm foundation in the country.'[4] 'At long last England has arisen and the day is here – the new day when the people of Britain shall come into their own,' wrote George Lansbury in the *New Leader*.[5]

---

injustices done to MacDonald. He takes small account of those who could not accept the story of the MacDonaldite betrayal in 1931, since they had been fighting MacDonaldism long before.

4. *Beatrice Webb Diaries 1924–1932.*
5. Quoted in *The Decline and Fall of the Labour Party* by John Scanlon.

MacDonald and the machine had fought back successfully against those within the Party who challenged their authority after 1924 and again after 1926. At the 1925 Party Conference Ernest Bevin had sought to secure a commitment that Labour would never again take office as a minority Government. But the manoeuvre had been scotched and, if Bevin himself continued to watch the conduct of the political leaders with surly suspicion, he presented no coherent opposition to their general outlook and programme, and he was always quite ready to clamp down on any signs of rebellion or disloyalty revealed in other quarters. One measure of the MacDonald supremacy was that the men who commanded the trade union movement, Bevin himself and Walter Citrine, looked small beside him. Moreover, almost all the big trade union leaders, including Bevin, had been engaged in an operation of their own designed to soften the ferocity of class antagonisms experienced between 1919 and 1926. In 1927 Sir Alfred Mond, on behalf of the employers, had responded to an initiative from the T.U.C., led by Ben Turner, seeking the establishment of 'representative organizations entitled to speak for industry as a whole'. The Mond–Turner talks bolstered the reputation for more 'responsible' leadership which MacDonald sought to acquire for his Party and to which, undoubtedly, he attributed his electoral success.

MacDonald's position, therefore, was not due solely to his personal pre-eminence. After 1926 he had swung the main weight of the Party in the direction he desired. *Labour and the Nation*, the official statement of Party aims adopted at the Party Conference in 1928, was an able, intelligent but acceptably amorphous expression of Socialist ideals. The actual election manifesto, maybe, was a little too specific for his liking. It enabled candidates to promise a swift increase in the benefits paid to the unemployed, a cut of an hour off the working day of the miners without any reduction in wages and a host of other immediate social reforms. Read in the light of *Labour and the Nation*, it envisaged substantial projects of nationalization and national development. Above all, it contained 'an unqualified pledge' that Labour would deal with the great problem of the day – the scourge of unemployment. But it left a large loophole. What a

Labour Government would do clearly depended on how untrammelled was its power.

The real opposition to triumphant MacDonaldism had come from two quarters – from the Independent Labour Party, led by James Maxton, and from the miners, led by A. J. Cook. Ever since 1926, when the I.L.P. had produced its policy statements *Socialism in Our Time* and *The Living Wage*, the links with the I.L.P. of MacDonald and Snowden, who had grown up in its ranks, had become tenuous. Ever since 1926 – indeed ever since 1919 – the miners had seen that the Labour leadership offered nothing better than the palest reflection of their turbulent, near-revolutionary aspirations. Bevan would never accept the easy criticisms levelled at Arthur Cook; he had 'burned himself out in a flame of protest against the unjust conditions imposed on his people',[6] and for that life of faith and sacrifice was entitled to undying honour.

In 1928 the two elements joined forces to issue the Cook–Maxton manifesto. It was a fierce denunciation of 'class collaboration' in all forms, partly provoked by the Mond–Turner negotiations and partly by the whole trend of MacDonald's leadership. 'Much of the energy which should be expended in fighting capitalism,' said the manifesto, 'is now expended in crushing everybody who dares to remain true to the ideals of the movement.' This was very near a declaration of open war – and a general election was in the offing. The odds were too heavy against so awkwardly timed an insurgence. Maxton had to beat back a challenge to himself within the I.L.P. MacDonald denounced the 'flashy futilities' of their programme. Outside Scotland, the old power of the I.L.P. was fading. Nominally no less than one hundred and forty Labour M.P.s in the new House of Commons were I.L.P. members; thirty-seven of them were financially sponsored by the I.L.P. and theoretically bound, according to a resolution passed at the I.L.P. Conference of 1928, to support I.L.P. policies by their votes in the House of Commons. But, as events quickly proved, even this latter figure exaggerated I.L.P. strength. MacDonald's authority and – as some alleged – Maxton's wild and romantic extremism reduced the only organized

6. *In Place of Fear.*

critical opposition in the Parliamentary Party to little more than a handful.

Yet the emaciated I.L.P. did retain assets for which it is rarely given credit. It had a soundly constructed intellectual case as well as a famous heritage and a colourful appeal, glistening with the shafts from Maxton's golden oratory. Maxton himself had no pretensions as a Socialist thinker. He was content with his role as a great agitator. He could make Socialists; other leaders must make Socialism. And, more immediately, what Maxton lacked different elements in the I.L.P. could supply. John Wheatley, J. A. Hobson and Frank Wise, assisted by the most eloquent and incisive Socialist journalist of the age, H. N. Brailsford, challenged all the financial experts of the political parties, the Treasury and the universities.

Remodelling their Marxism to suit modern conditions and in a modern idiom, they exposed the debility at the heart of capitalist society which the orthodox economists were unable to discern. Before Keynes and Beveridge, they put their finger on the real cause of mass unemployment – the chronic lack of effective demand induced by the capitalist system of production and exemplified in deflationary policies with their blind subservience to balanced budgets and the gold standard. To the official leaders of the Party, the I.L.P. policy proposals, based on this analysis, sounded like double-dutch, or, at least, like Poplarism run mad, a wanton belief in the efficacy of shovelling out public money without limit. But Hobson and Wise were not fools or cranks; today their ideas stand the test of scrutiny better than any other political prescriptions of that era. At the time they gave to the I.L.P. – and to those few others in the Labour Party, like Bevan, who never scorned the need for theory – a consistent critique on which their opposition to the deflationary policies dictated by the Bank of England could be based.

Moreover, the I.L.P. had a strategy. Later, after the damage had been done, its wisdom became widely recognized. 'When the Cabinet took office,' wrote Professor Tawney, 'two alternatives were open to it. It could decide to live dangerously, or to play for safety. It could choose a short life and – if the expression be not too harsh – an honest one; or it could proceed on the assumption that once a Labour Government is in office, its primary duty is to find means of remaining there. If it acted on its principles, it could not hope to survive for more than twelve months. It could postpone its execution, but only at the cost of making its opponents the censors of its policy. It would invite them, in effect, to decide the character of the measures which it should be permitted to introduce, and to determine the issues of the next election.'[7]

This, almost exactly, was the choice presented to that first Parliamentary Party meeting by John Wheatley after the thunderous cheers for MacDonald had subsided. The victor M.P.s, fresh from the euphoria of the platform, were impatient. But Wheatley always forced attention. Despite his success as Minister of Health in 1924, MacDonald had insisted that he should have no office in the new Government, and cynics might mutter that this slight was the cause of his recalcitrance. But they still had to listen. Wheatley had a way of brushing aside the petty jealousies of politics with his earnest, remorseless debating logic. He prophesied economic crisis. He foresaw a Labour Government subjected to successive humiliations as it permitted itself to become the instrument for cutting the standards of wage-earners and the unemployed. Speaking for himself, he opposed the whole idea of forming a minority Government.[8] Speaking for the I.L.P., he recommended the Tawney doctrine of living dangerously. Let the Government first introduce some of its short-range popular reforms; let it press ahead with its more decisive measures; let the Opposition Parties take the odium of throwing it out; let a self-confident Labour Party prepare for an early, fresh appeal to the public. Thus, at that first meeting, Wheatley elaborated his whole argument. He won silence, but no conviction. MacDonald easily carried the day. Amid another roar of cheers, he announced that Labour would show the world it was fit to govern. Only one possibility

7. *The Attack* by R. H. Tawney. Essay on 'The Choice before the Labour Party', written in 1934.
8. Wheatley had backed the Cook–Maxton manifesto, but he wished the campaign to go much further. John Scanlon, author of *The Decline and Fall of the Labour Party*, who knew him well, writes: 'Mr Wheatley took the view that the worst thing that could happen to the Labour movement would be a Labour Government composed of the then leaders. He believed they would do nothing to satisfy the aspirations of the workers, and because of the disappointment and disillusionment the movement would be set back twenty years.'

marred the beneficent prospect; while Wheatley forewarned against economic catastrophe and its consequences, 'sniping from within' was the chief hazard which MacDonald saw on the horizon.

Such was Aneurin Bevan's introduction to the arena where so many of the most critical fights of his own career were to be staged. Most of his sympathies were naturally with Wheatley, but he could hardly be expected to hurl himself into the combat so precipitately. His own attitude to the I.L.P. strategy, shared by many I.L.P.ers themselves, amounted to a variation on their theme. The Government should be given a chance. Something could be done at once to ease pitiable hardship. As for the fundamental measures, if the Government possessed the necessary audacity, the revelation must be made in the early months of the new administration while the momentum of the electoral victory still retained its force. Meantime he turned to the other arena, the House of Commons itself.

Writing many years later he gave a description of a young Labour Member's initiation into parliamentary mysteries. 'His first impression is that he is in church. The vaulted roofs and stained glass windows, the rows of statues of great statesmen of the past, the echoing halls, the soft-footed attendants and the whispered conversation, contrast depressingly with the crowded meetings and the clang and clash of hot opinions he has just left behind in his election campaign. Here he is, a tribune of the people, coming to make his voice heard in the seats of power. Instead, it seems he is expected to worship; and the most conservative of all religions – ancestor worship.'[9] The words sound autobiographical. But if these were the tremors which Bevan carried in his bosom, they were suppressed or disguised.

On 10 July 1929, he asked his first question – whether the Government intended before the summer recess to introduce legislation to deal with 'the iniquities of the unemployment insurance administration'. The answer was 'No'. No legislation was possible in the next few weeks.

A few days later, the House was engaged on the Committee stage of the Development (Loan Guarantees and Grants) Bill, a general measure outlining the Government's first interim propo-

9. *In Place of Fear.*

sals for dealing with unemployment. Several of the leading figures in the House had participated, including Lloyd George and Churchill. Suddenly Bevan was on his feet, casually interpolating after he had uttered the first few sentences: 'I would not have intervened in this debate, as this is my first effort . . .' The claim was no more than the truth. If ever an entirely extempore maiden speech was delivered in the House of Commons, this was it; the proof is there on the pages of Hansard.

Winston Churchill, ex-Tory, ex-Liberal, ex-Constitutionalist, Conservative ex-Chancellor of the Exchequer, was the very first of his selected targets. Naturally he was fascinated by the speech Churchill had delivered a few minutes before; it was only the second time in his life he had heard those famous accents. 'The first time,' said Bevan, 'he was in the role of the bogy man of the country, over the wireless, and on the second occasion he was the entertainer of the House of Commons. I arrived at the conclusion that his chameleon-like character in politics is founded upon a temperamental disability. He fills all the roles with such exceeding facility that his lack of political stability is at once explained . . .' The first shot had been fired in a parliamentary duel which would last nearly thirty years.

But what, continued Bevan, was the serious intent behind the ex-Chancellor's enlivening performance? Lloyd George and Churchill had criticized the Bill from different angles. Churchill had argued that the measure would prove quite inadequate whereas Lloyd George had questioned whether sufficient parliamentary control was being retained over such extensive powers yielded to the executive. Bevan detected 'the first example of collusion between the Tories and the Liberals in obstructive tactics'. The Government had been told by the Opposition leaders that they must act within the limits of their dubious parliamentary majority. Very well, that was what Ministers were doing with these moderate proposals, and still the Opposition complained. Churchill should have a real interest in seeing the present measures succeed; if they failed, the Government would have to ask the country for a mandate to apply full Socialist principles.

Contrary to the parliamentary tradition governing the treatment of maiden speakers, Churchill interrupted. Bevan swept on.

One of his chosen opponents complained that the Government's proposals were too negligible, the other that they were too audacious; one that they were too pedestrian, the other that they were too adventurous. Neatly he knocked the heads of the two statesmen together. But who, he persisted, was really interested in these acrobatics of the old parliamentary performers? All eyes should be fixed on the needs of the people. In the country at large, there was a steady drift of new industries to London, the Midlands and the South. Workers from South Wales were forced to migrate, leaving all the high rates and standing charges in the older industrial areas to be borne by a declining industry. This was the great problem which the British Government must tackle, undeterred by 'factious opposition'.

Normally, a maiden speaker receives some polite commendation from the succeeding speaker and the world moves on with the stupendous event lost in endless oblivion. But again, on this occasion, the conventions went unobserved. Nobody realized he was speaking for the first time, for the simple reason he had not told them explicitly enough. Later that day, however, Churchill and Bevan bumped into one another behind the Speaker's Chair. 'Wasn't that your maiden speech?' asked Churchill. 'Permit me to congratulate you. It is so seldom that we hear a real debating speech nowadays.' He was to hear many more from the same quarter. Churchill became almost the first with whom Bevan established one of those curious parliamentary friendships between political opponents so little understood outside and so inevitable in the claustrophobic atmosphere of the House of Commons. A sojourn there is like going for a long voyage on an ocean liner; you can't pick your fellow-passengers and every now and again the urge to escape the company of friends and relations is irresistible. Needless to say, in this instance no hint of quarter on either side was asked or given.

Lloyd George and Churchill were two good quarries, but there was another with whom Bevan had a more serious score to settle. Neville Chamberlain is now sometimes portrayed as a constructive Minister of Health; his tenure of that office between 1924 and 1929, we are told, was marked by substantial reforms. But he was the author of the Guardians (Default) Act – to the people of Ebbw Vale and Tredegar the most hated and vindictive measure ever placed on the Statute Book. Introduced by Chamberlain to deal with what he called 'open and unabashed corruption', it had meant that the whole delicate business of administering the Poor Law had been taken from the elected Guardians in certain areas and handed over to Chamberlain's nominees. Bevan, as we have seen, had been one of the leaders of the revolt in his own area against this foreign inquisition. Now the Labour Government proposed to rescind the Order applying to the Bedwellty Poor Law Union along with a few others and to transfer the authority exercised by the people whom Chamberlain had appointed to the County Councils.

Chamberlain's resentment at the revocation of the Orders under his own Act ensured that he would appear at his testiest. He often gave the impression, to friend as well as foe, that he 'looked on the Labour Party as dirt . . .' [10] On 23 July he led the attack, in his most stiff-necked, moralizing manner, against the Government's first modest attempt to reverse his administration. 'Human nature being what it is, to show people that they can be maintained by somebody else in idleness, at the same standard of living as those who are doing an honest, full week's work, is something which might, if it were carried on, undermine and weaken the fibre and character of the people.' Read today, the icy words come from another century; they might have fallen from the lips of Thomas Gradgrind. So great was the gulf between the Parties in that not-so-distant epoch when unemployment, in the Tory calendar, was still an individual crime. How many of the workers were 'wastrels'? Chamberlain did not refrain from posing the question.

'The worst thing I can say about democracy,' said Bevan at the outset, 'is that it has tolerated the right hon. Gentleman for four and a half years.' Once the Chairman of the Bedwellty Union could hold up his head. Now the same man, as Chamberlain's nominee, had gained the reputation of being 'more barbarous than any other administrator ever known in that district'. The accusation against so-called prudent administration from Whitehall was not something concocted by agitators. It came

10. *Life of Neville Chamberlain* by Keith Feiling.

from Medical Officers of Health who had seen children collapsing before their eyes, from ministers of religion, from Free Church Councils, even from Conservative Clubs. Citing case after case, Bevan consumed his enemy in a blaze of anger.

'The last contribution which the right hon. Gentleman made to the humanizing of the Poor Law,' he continued, 'was the introduction of tests in the workhouses, and many poor people were told that they could not have relief unless they did test work. I know cases of colliers who had to walk four or five miles in the morning to do work connected with building walls, cracking stones and weeding turnips. In some cases these men worked from seven-thirty in the morning to five at night; in one case a man was paid sixteen shillings a week for doing that kind of work, out of which he had to pay four and sixpence a week rent and he had a wife and two children to maintain.' If these were the facts, how could the House still listen in patience? How had this 'merciless administration' been accepted so long? How could a man faraway in London encourage something so inhuman? Now at last, having seen the face of Neville Chamberlain, he was no longer surprised.

'Three weeks before I came here,' he went on, 'a Medical Officer of Health, representing a Poor Law authority, asked that a man suffering from asthma should be taken into the infirmary. The man was almost in a dying condition. He was taken into the infirmary at Bedwellty, and he was scarcely able to sit on the chair provided for him. That man was kept there sitting in a chair without refreshment and without anybody seeing him at all, and he received no attention whatsoever. As a matter of fact, it is now admitted in the Bedwellty district that if you go into the workhouse you had better shuffle off this mortal coil as quickly as possible. In the Bedwellty workhouse the inmates get up at eight o'clock and they are given for breakfast a chunk of bread and margarine; at twelve o'clock they have a cooked dinner, and the tea is a repetition of breakfast. It is a fact that from five o'clock in the evening until eight o'clock in the morning they receive no food at all – I am speaking of people between seventy and eighty years of age. I have known them during the winter months being driven out of the rest room into the yards to walk away in the perishing cold.'

This was the South Wales of the twenties or at least the life to which so many luckless tens of thousands were condemned that none of the other inhabitants could stop his ears against the cry of anguish and protest. A world or an underworld in which skilled colliers cracked stones; thereafter, according to the Chamberlain decrees, they or their families or their aged parents must suffer 'insult and bullying' from gentlemen who drove into the plague areas in motor cars and drove away just as fast, with their prim duties done in the interests of national frugality. Of course, a minor amendment in Poor Law administration would not meet such a case. Bevan knew that. The whole wretched apparatus whereby the poor kept the poor must be overturned and transformed. But here, as one of its first steps, the new Government had given a worthwhile token of the gains which could follow the 1929 victory. Here was an example of the practical work which the new Ministers should be granted the necessary breathing-space to perform.

Meantime, the attack on Neville Chamberlain had made his parliamentary reputation in a matter of a few weeks from the beginning of the Parliament. 'It was,' reported one newspaper, 'like some great disturbance of nature . . . a storm attacking a solitary tree.'[11] If there were more like him on the untested Labour benches, the victory of 1929 might prove to be a more volcanic eruption than any had yet reckoned. But how many others of the same breed were there? No one could tell. A new Parliament always takes several months to reveal its true mettle and quality. So many of the new arrivals are strangers to one another and yet so much depends on their estimates of each other's character.

In the Government and the Parliamentary Labour Party the rot started early, although few but the incorrigible I.L.P. rebels could be held guilty of discerning as much at the time. Outwardly, during that autumn session, the Government had its successes. MacDonald was lionized in America as a great liberal statesman. Snowden, suddenly emerging as a pocket Palmerston, went to The Hague Conference on the scaling down of War Debts and captured the applause of the whole country by his

11. Quoted in *Aneurin Bevan* by Vincent Brome.

insistence on Britain's rights. Henderson made a conspicuously agreeable appearance at Geneva and quickly impressed on the Foreign Office his intention to pursue Labour's declared policy and not something else thoughtfully left behind by his predecessor in the pigeon-holes. When the diehards screamed at his abrupt dismissal of a Tory proconsul in Egypt, he gently but efficiently rolled them in the dust as if they had been Left-wing malcontents at a Labour Party Conference. Several small but desirable domestic reforms were pushed through; others were mutilated by the House of Lords or withdrawn in face of its hostility.

Behind the scenes the picture was somewhat different. Unemployment was the great issue on which all else hinged. Hugh Dalton wrote that the Government 'ran away from its programme from the first day'.[12] Rumours reached Beatrice Webb of 'J. H. Thomas's incapacity as organizer of employment. Oswald Mosley and Lansbury, his lieutenants, report that Thomas does not see them; but he is in the hands of that arch-reactionary, Horace Wilson ... whom he calls "Orace" and obeys implicitly'.[13] 'Thomas,' she continued in her diary entry of 28 July, 'disowns Socialism in public and scoffs at the programme of the Labour Party over his cups. Snowden appeals to the banking world; the P.M. is popular in refined aristocratic circles and at the Court. Certainly Susan [Susan Lawrence, Under Secretary at the Ministry of Health] is justified in beginning to sniff.' But all these damning verdicts and rebellious sniffs were locked away in private diaries and the memoirs. MacDonald, in the debate on the first King's Speech, had given a vague hint of his inclinations. He had expressed the hope that Parliament might consider itself more as a Council of State rather than a Party arena for grappling with the nation's economic problems. Only a very few saw anything sinister in the appeal.

One considerable matter, however, which interlocked with the supreme issue of unemployment, could not be quietly side-stepped or postponed. If the Government was committed to anything, it was pledged to improve the benefits paid to the unem-

12. *Call Back Yesterday* by Hugh Dalton.
13. *Beatrice Webb Diaries 1924–1932.*

ployed and to overhaul the conditions under which the benefits were disbursed. When Margaret Bondfield, Minister of Labour, produced her Bill for fulfilling these purposes, many others beside the I.L.P.ers were aghast. The improved benefits fell short of what had been expected; worse still, two long-standing grievances about the administration of the Insurance Scheme – one affecting 'the waiting period' which a man must endure before he got any benefit at all and the other affecting the onus on the unemployed man to prove that he was 'genuinely seeking work' – had not been adequately dealt with at all. Expressions of dismay came thick and fast from all over the country. At the otherwise fairly orderly Labour Party Conference in October 1929, an attempt to stage a protest against the Bondfield Bill was only narrowly defeated.

In the House of Commons, a special Party meeting was called to discuss the series of amendments put down, not only by the I.L.P. but by a large number of trade union M.P.s. Snowden came in person to quash the revolt. 'I told them frankly,' he wrote, 'that I could not be responsible for finding the money which would be required to finance the proposed amendments. The great majority of the Labour members were always reasonable when a case was put fairly and fully before them. My speech profoundly impressed the gathering . . .'[14] Snowden wrote no more than the truth. He easily dominated the vast majority of the Parliamentary Party with his flint-like finality of judgement and speech. But all were not impressed. The I.L.P. leaders were determined to press some of their amendments on the floor of the House, even if others drew back. 'It was,' said Snowden, 'an exhibition of disloyalty and of the lack of the team spirit which has so often exposed the Labour Party to the jeers of its opponents and caused dismay among its supporters in the country.' The whole affair changed the terms of dispute between the I.L.P. and the official Party. Several I.L.P. members repudiated Maxton's leadership and nestled back into the bosom of the larger Party. Henceforward the I.L.P. rebels were reduced to 'The Group',[15] and the cry of disloyalty drowned most attempts at the

14. *An Autobiography* by Philip, Viscount Snowden.
15. *Inside the Left* by Fenner Brockway.

private Party meetings to question the course which the Government was treading.

Bevan abstained on those amendments to the Insurance Bill which the I.L.P. pressed to a vote. But he helped decisively to secure a notable victory on that Clause in the Bill which gave the gravest offence. The old 'genuinely seeking work' provision of previous Acts was the statutory embodiment of the Tory view that many of the unemployed were 'workshies' and delinquents. The Government had amended the Clause in a manner which offered no full remedy for the disease and, to get it through, the front bench had called upon the services of the Attorney-General, Sir William Jowitt. Jowitt was a master of fine distinctions. But Bevan was his equal. He gave the House its first taste of another style in his power of speech – a sinuous, serpentine reasoning in the service of his cause.

I agree [said Bevan] that, listening to the Attorney-General, anyone who did not keep his mind glued to the language of the Clause would almost have been persuaded that the Clause meant what he said it did. Unfortunately for the Attorney-General, many Members on this side and on the opposite side of the House have had a good deal of experience on the interpretation placed upon these Clauses, and I am afraid that we are not able to agree with him as to what is actually meant . . . it says that the employment shall be of an extent that the individual could reasonably have been expected to obtain. What does that mean? Supposing the individual is informed by the Exchange official that ten men had employment in the colliery the day before. All those jobs have been obtained. It is retrospective. You are not urging an individual to go for a job that he might have if he had tried to go. You are simply punishing the individual for not knowing about the job afterwards. In other words, it is merely retributive justice. All the time that the individual is told that ten men have got work, there are five hundred on the Exchange . . . If you really desire that the onus of proof shall be placed on the Exchange official, why not delete the Clause? If you say that the onus is placed, under the Clause, on the official, and there is any doubt at all about it, why not confirm your own intention by deleting the Clause? Because you know that this Sub-section is intended to do something else, and the Attorney-General let the thing out in all its naked horror at the beginning of his speech. He let the Committee understand that what he desired to do was to devise a Sub-section which would leave the applicant for benefit to understand that he was expected to seek out the employer. I never expected to listen in the House of Commons to a spokesman of a

Labour Government making such a statement as that. In my district, this is, for me, not a matter for further juggling; it is for me a matter of the greatest possible importance, because I have attended Courts of Referees every day for the last two years, and I know what happens. I saw men in the middle of last winter having to walk ten and fifteen miles in the worst possible weather in order to convince the Courts of Referees that they were properly seeking out employers.

I want to know exactly where we stand in the matter. Do we believe that as things are now in the distressed areas a single extra man will have employment if you put the onus of proof still on the applicant to seek out the employer? If a single man more will have employment under these conditions, then it must be assumed that there is an employer who could employ a man but is not doing so. But if this society allows an employer who can employ a man not to do so, it ought to keep the idle man who has not been able to get employment . . .

I hope the Committee will realize that you are not under these provisions actually finding out the man who ought to be found out at all. You are not relieving the burden upon industry. All that you are doing is trying to thrust this burden upon the shoulders of local authorities which cannot bear it. It does not matter very much about some parts of the country, where the local authorities are able to come to the assistance of the unemployed man, but it is tragic in all seriousness in the South Wales coalfield, in Durham, and in Lanarkshire. It means in those coalfields that the local authorities are not able to come to the help of the unemployed man, and it means that by depriving him of his unemployment benefit, you are literally starving him and his wife and children. While I have tried not to be sentimental, I hope that hon. and right hon. Members will realize that we are again in the middle of a dreadful winter, and that the South Wales coalfield is being attacked by floods and famine. We ought to take every step in our power to ease the burdens upon these poor people and not allow any engines of legal intricacy to try and thrust more and more burdens on the shoulders of those who are unable to bear them. I submit that this Clause does not meet the point, and I hope the Government will not ask us to go into the Lobby and support it . . .

Jowitt did not reply. An Opposition member drew attention to Bevan's 'devastating' attack and insisted it had not been answered. Margaret Bondfield retired gracefully with a reference to 'the very admirable speech from the Member for Ebbw Vale'. The Clause was withdrawn and the Tories denounced the whole Bill as a shocking surrender to the extremists.

Another notable parliamentary triumph followed within a few weeks. This time the victim was Lloyd George. Gossip writers with their eyes on the headlines or dull, envious fellow Members, incapable themselves of a flashing phrase, did not hesitate to suggest that the series of assaults directed against the biggest figures in the House was part of a deliberate campaign of self-advertisement. But Bevan's alleged personal attacks were never studied. It is doubtful if he ever delivered in the whole of his life a carefully framed, calculated piece of invective in the tradition of Disraeli or O'Connell or the other masters of the fine art. His style was his own. His strength – just occasionally his weakness also when he placed too much reliance on it – was an unexampled capacity to think on his feet, a capacity not merely to conjure up a clever retort to a casual interruption, but to develop and turn a whole argument in mid-flight. The sequence in the logic combined with a rising passion drove him on. Almost always the lethal onslaught which stirred personal antagonisms was the ordered elaboration of the previous argument. Policies and, even more, ideas and intricate theories – these were the main stuff of his speeches. But policies must be identified with persons, the persons responsible. That was what the House of Commons was for. Democracy could be legitimately excited by a drama, 'the passion play of politics', as he called it. It would never show much interest in a statistical abstract or a mutual admiration society. The so-called attack on Lloyd George was a classic example of his method.

The measure before the House was the Coal Mines Bill, a patchwork affair and certainly much less than the miners desired. Labour's declared remedy for the coal problem was forbidden by the conditions for the Government's survival laid down by its opponents which the Government had accepted. But something must be done about the industry. By a complicated system of quotas, price-fixing and subsidies it was hoped that the decay could be arrested. From the miners' point of view, from Bevan's point of view, the Bill had one advantage. By pumping some money into the industry a part of Labour's election pledge could be honoured; half an hour could be lopped off the miners' working day without a reduction in wages. However, the Liberals disliked the Bill; it offended their free trade principles. If they succeeded in killing it by an insistence on their theoretical purity, even these few crumbs would be snatched from the hungry miners.

Bevan opened softly by contradicting some of the claims presented earlier in the debate by Lloyd George's first lieutenant, Sir Herbert Samuel. He always said that Samuel was one of the very best parliamentary debaters he ever heard and he always treated him with suitable respect. Then he turned to push aside the flat-footed Tory opposition to the Bill. They had now become the upholders of the most rigid *laissez-faire* doctrine. 'Hon. Members on the Conservative benches,' he said, 'are at least consistent. It is the only merit I have been able to discover in them. They have a sort of vested interest in mystery. They say: "Leave the market alone. Let it be as vague and incalculable as possible. Keep it so. Do not attempt to introduce any calculated element into it. Let the entrepreneur go on producing for an unknown market – we shall see what the gods will send us".' But what of the Liberals, the modern Lloyd George Liberals, who had supposedly recognized the limitations of *laissez-faire* but still denied Labour the power to nationalize? Sadistically almost he fingered the most tender joints in the Liberal dilemma. Much of the speech was on this theoretical level. Much of it was devoted to an intricate defence of the Bill's detailed provisions.

But the economics of the matter shaded into politics. The theoretical outer leaves must be plucked away to expose the bitter heart of the matter. What could be the meaning of the manoeuvre on the part of the Liberals who, having forced the Government to be content with a comparatively weak measure, still upbraided the same Government by turns for its weakness in attempting too little and its doctrinaire determination to do too much? Why had Lloyd George agreed to become 'joint executioner' in a temporary re-alliance with Churchill? The result, if they succeeded, would be a first-class crisis. It would mean they were demanding that 'the sinews for the reorganization of the mining industry must come out of the loins of the miner'.

Then came the great assault, aimed directly at Lloyd George who was sitting opposite in his place waiting to speak next:[16]

16. *Tempestuous Journey* by Frank Owen.

Since the very beginning of this debate we have not been having a dispassionate examination of the conditions of the industry. We have been subject merely to a desire on the part of the right hon. Gentleman, the Member for Caernarvon Boroughs, to use his parliamentary position for the purpose of trying to put new life into the decaying corpse of Liberalism. On the Second Reading, because of his Celtic fervour, he went much further than he intended to go, and now it is impossible for him to support Part I of the Bill, otherwise he will have to eat all the words he said on the Second Reading ... We have a right to say that, if it means slightly dearer coal, it is better to have slightly dearer coal than cheaper colliers. Hon. Gentlemen here must face the issue that when they vote against this Bill, they are voting for lower wages for the colliers, and they are voting at the same time for an increase in the number of accidents in the collieries ... It is always characteristic of Liberal hypocrisy to pay lip service to these things and refuse to face the consequences that follow from them. We say that you cannot get from the already dry veins of the miners new blood to revivify the industry. Their veins are shrunken white, and we are asking you to be, for once, decent to the miners – not to pay lip service, not to say that you are very sorry for them, not to say that you are very sorry that these accidents occur, not to say that you are very sorry for the low level of wages and for the conditions of famine which have existed in the mining districts since the war, and then to use all your parliamentary skill, all your rhetoric, in an act of pure demagogy, to expose the mining community of this country to another few years of misery ...

Lloyd George was more visibly shaken than most observers had ever seen him. He said he was 'sorry to have fallen foul of a young countryman of mine'. He called it 'a very bitter personal attack'. He spoke of his admiration for the speaker, 'a very able speech marred by imputing mean motives to other people'. Despite the friendship later established between the two Welshmen, he never quite forgot; years later he was still saying: 'Nothing generous about Bevan.'[17] One reporter of the scene declared that Lloyd George had been 'confronted with the ghost of his own angry youth'. No doubt that was a part of the truth, one reason why the barbs struck so woundingly. But, indeed, Bevan was not cast in the Lloyd George mould. The comparison between them, so frequently made, had no real foundation. Apart from their power of speech, their love of their native land and their common streak of Welsh guile, there was little in the likeness.

17. *A Diary With Letters* by Thomas Jones.

Both knew how a great parliamentary duel must be brought to the kill by the flash of cold steel. But Bevan, a rarity among politicians, was also reflective, philosophical, eternally fascinated by the interplay between political principles and the point of action. Lloyd George, with all his multitude of other qualities, had little interest in political theory; he was the opportunist *par excellence*, careless and impatient of principle. What the House of Commons saw that day was not the ghost of the young Lloyd George but an entirely new apparition.

Another observer of this parliamentary scene in the press gallery put his finger on Bevan's most conspicuous quality – his courage. 'Young Members,' he wrote, 'are generally chary of provoking the prominent veterans, and if they do attack them they are inexpert and feeble. Mr Bevan fears no one, shrinks before no one. In recent years there has been no finer display of parliamentary courage than his attack upon Mr Lloyd George during the Committee stage of the Coal Bill. So well was it carried out that for the moment no one thought of its audacity. He spoke to him and against him as equals in experience and power are in the habit of doing. He faced him, separated from him only by the breadth of the unbenched part of the floor. Excitedly and angrily, with a flood of words and a profusion of gestures, yet without any loss in coherence and incisiveness, he upbraided him for his treatment of the Bill, and roundly charged him with mere demagogy. So daring, so precipitate was the assault, that it left its victim astonished and slightly breathless. Veterans are not accustomed to such attacks from youths, and when youth does assail age and experience, it does not usually do so with such weakening, even paralysing, effect and with such an absence of braggart insolence.'[18]

During the following months, the Coal Mines Bill was mangled in the House of Commons and further cut to pieces in the House of Lords. Bevan had another brush with Samuel. 'From the Liberal benches,' he said, 'we are having simply an attack upon these powers because they offend some ancient free trade principle. [Hon. Members: "Hear Hear."] On this side we are not classical Free Traders. We believe in controlled exports and

18. *A Hundred Commoners* by James Johnston, published in 1931.

controlled imports.' Hansard does not record how many of Free Trader Snowden's precious blood vessels broke at this disclosure. When 'such an effective orator and such an appealing speaker', concluded the sweetly reasonable Samuel, does not in any degree convince his audience it is merely because his case is such a bad one.

The fate of the Coal Mines Bill epitomized the decay over-taking the Labour Government. An inordinate amount of parlia-mentary time had been expended on the measure; the very life of the Government hung in the balance; the Liberals and the Lords together helped to feed MacDonald's natural timidity; just enough Liberals defied their Whips to enable the Cabinet to survive and run away another day; and, despite all the parlia-mentary commotions, nothing had been done to check the mounting economic crisis outside in the country. Only in one arena were MacDonald, Snowden and Thomas still hailed as all-conquering heroes. Upstairs in the private Party meetings they recorded nothing but victories. Maxton and his friends were becoming something near outcasts. And during that spring John Wheatley died. Near the end even his hard nerve was get-ting frayed. 'I am beginning to think,' he said, 'we politicians are all flies on the wheel.'[19] His death was a near-mortal blow to the Left. Maxton without Wheatley was a different and a lesser man.

Snowden's Budget was expected to provide the great point of controversy in the spring of 1930. It did in fact produce several alarms. Maxton and the I.L.P. denounced the failure to raise more money for the social services. The Tories and several Liberals, by contrast, mounted their frontal attack on the spend-thrift Chancellor. On one occasion the Government only saved its skin by the decision of four Liberals, in breach of their Party decision, to vote in the Government lobby. But week by week, month by month, every other aspect of politics was becoming swamped by the tidal wave of unemployment.

So far from the Government's measures mitigating the horror, the figures were leaping upwards. The Wall Street crash, the closing of the Anstalt Bank in Vienna, the world-wide deflation – these vast events are now seen in their sweeping, inexorable

19. *Beatrice Webb Diaries.*

procession. No Government in Britain could have shielded itself fully from the blast. But at the time, the problem appeared in a more parochial perspective. The Labour Party had given its 'unqualified pledge' to deal with unemployment. With Snowden and the Treasury and the Bank of England unyieldingly committed to the gold standard and free trade, the Government could not even begin to fulfil the obligation; it was compelled to do the very opposite; it had to deflate to protect the exchange rates. Instead of putting out the fire, all the while, month after month, the Treasury was pouring oil on the flames. Only a few could dimly detect what was happening. Those few in the Labour Party who appreciated the greatness and urgency of events saw the terrifying helplessness of the nation mirrored in the inertia and complacency of the Labour Ministers. Within a year the unemployment figures rose from 1,163,000 or 9·6 per cent to 1,912,000 or 15·4 per cent. Compared with this, everything else seemed a trifle. Some were not content meekly to accept the situation, Bevan among the foremost.

J. H. Thomas was the man in charge of the Government's employment policy. He had George Lansbury, Minister of Works, and Sir Oswald Mosley, Chancellor of the Duchy of Lancaster, as his assistants. The combination never worked from the start. Lansbury and Mosley pressed their ideas on Thomas who either rejected them outright himself or passed them on to Snowden to perform the obsequies. Already by December 1929 Henderson was expressing privately his concern about 'the collapse of Thomas, who is completely rattled and in such a state of panic that he is bordering on lunacy'.[20] Henderson wanted Thomas sent away for a rest, in the hope that Mosley should be installed in his place.[20] But nothing happened. Early in the New Year Mosley prepared his own unemployment Memorandum. It included proposals for expanding purchasing power at home, for 'insulating' the British economy against the bitter winds blowing from abroad, for encouraging Commonwealth trade by bulk purchase agreements, for taking control over banking and credit policy, for increasing pensions and social services and for the rationalization and development of industry under

20. *Beatrice Webb Diaries.*

public control.[21] The details were no doubt open to criticism, but the general pattern would surely, by later standards of thinking, be considered sound and acceptable. The plan partly accorded with the earlier analysis of the I.L.P., devised by Hobson and Wise. If it bore more of the character of an emergency programme than social revolution, it was creditably directed to the main aim of putting in reverse the ruinous deflation. However, Snowden rejected the whole proposition. It was an insulting attack on his three most sacred convictions – the need to maintain strict economy, free trade and the gold standard. The Government would bumble on in its own fashion. On 21 May the Tories put down a vote of censure on unemployment. Thomas 'made the same old speech – just the sort of "statement of policy" which might be made by any slow-going conservative employer who happened to be in Thomas's position'.[22] Only by fifteen votes was a Government defeat averted. Mosley was not the man to go down in a water-logged ship. Next day he announced his resignation.

All the gifts of providence had been showered on Mosley – vast wealth, a beautiful wife, endless charm, a capacity for classical oratory, a savage coruscating wit, readiness to work, dynamism, the will to be great. 'Has MacDonald found his superseder in Oswald Mosley?' asked Beatrice Webb at the time. 'MacDonald owes his pre-eminence largely to the fact that he is the only artist, the only aristocrat by temperament and talent in a Party of plebeians and plain men. Hitherto he has had no competitor in personal charm and good looks, delightful voice and the gift of oratory. But Mosley has all these with the *élan* of youth, wealth and social position added to them.'[22] So thought some others, even if they did not share the snobbery of the Webbs. Mosley's resignation, it seemed, might bring all the stresses of the Labour Government to a real crisis and a new outcome. Aneurin Bevan was among those who backed his revolt from the first day. But he gave his allegiance to the measures, not the man. Hero-worship was never part of his nature; ideas entranced him more than personality. To Bevan, the Mosley programme appeared as a better defined, more practical pro-

21. *History of the British Labour Party* by G. D. H. Cole.
22. *Beatrice Webb Diaries.*

spectus than that which Maxton enunciated, one well suited to the urgencies of the hour.

Immediately, Mosley took the fight to the Parliamentary Party meeting. There, at a debate lasting several hours into the evening, he shook the inertia of the Party more violently than anyone had succeeded in doing before. It was a meticulously prepared, massive oration acclaimed by most of those who heard it as a masterpiece of lucidity and force (and repeated a few days later in the Commons almost word perfect). MacDonald himself did not face the music; he left that to Henderson. No one could tell at first whether 'Uncle Arthur' had succeeded in his familiar task of restoring the Party to a mood of unruffled if still bewildered obedience. He had not subdued the qualms of others; maybe he could not stifle his own. But Mosley came to his rescue with a monumental blunder in tactics. He insisted on a vote there and then. His legitimate impatience began to look more like arrogance. Instead of leaving the disturbed mind of the Party rank-and-file to fructify for his benefit over the weeks ahead he thrust the challenge into their faces. At that first test he mustered no more than twenty-nine votes (including Bevan's) against two hundred and ten. And, despite the brilliance of his mind and speech, he had left a bad taste in the mouths of many even apart from the haughtiness of his demand for an immediate vote which might break the whole Government. 'He talks to us,' commented one M.P., 'like a landlord addressing his tenantry.'[23]

But Bevan was committed to the fight; he had no intention of running away. Mosley's speech in the House of Commons a few days later presented the great issue in the spacious context and manner which Bevan thought necessary. If the Labour Government was to be saved from its creeping paralysis, it was now or never. If the Mosley revolt failed, another revolt on the same theme could not be easily mounted again. So, taking his first big individual initiative in the internal Party struggle, Bevan sought to divert the argument away from a hopeless dispute about Mosley's personal merits or demerits. First he joined some sixty others in presenting a demand to the Prime Minister for the dismissal of Thomas. Next he helped to collect a hundred signatures,

23. Quoted in *Arthur Henderson* by M. A. Hamilton.

including Mosley's, for a resolution he was to move at the Party meeting – 'That this Party is of the opinion that the present unprecedented volume of unemployment in Great Britain in relation to the world crisis in capitalistic production necessitates a restatement of the Government's unemployment policy, and urges upon the Government the necessity of outlining new proposals within the framework of *Labour and the Nation*.' But by now the temperature of the Party was subsiding once more. News of MacDonald's fury against the rebels was making many quail. Most of the hundred signatories lapsed into acquiescence. Bevan was smitten down as sharply as Mosley – and no one could complain that he talked like a landlord!

Was he wrong in joining this, his first parliamentary revolt against the leadership? Just before the Mosley resignation Hugh Dalton had a talk with Tom Johnston who was also involved, under Thomas, in the administrative apparatus for tackling unemployment. Johnston gave a hair-raising account of the disarray he found behind the scenes. 'If the Party only knew,' he said, 'they'd be climbing up the wall.'[24] And soon after Bevan had moved that abortive resolution at the Party meeting, his near-namesake, Ernest Bevin, was giving a wisely alarmist instruction to the executive council of his Union. Bevin regarded the economic position as so serious that it warranted 'a state of national emergency'. 'The best brains of the country should be mobilized for the purpose of really tackling the problem instead of "footling about" in the manner we are at the moment.'[25] However, Dalton's concern was committed to his diary and Bevin's concern was committed to his executive *in private*. Those who dared to speak out in public were lambasted as disloyal, with Bevin often performing the role of lambaster in chief.[26]

The scene of combat changed from Westminster to the Party Conference at Llandudno. Gone were all the easy delusions and soaring hopes of a bare twelve months before. Maxton and the

24. *Call Back Yesterday* by Hugh Dalton.
25. *Ernest Bevin* by Alan Bullock.
26. Bevin's private ideas were very close to Mosley's but the world was not to know until Mr Alan Bullock wrote his biography. Meantime the jeers against those who had followed Mosley at this time were to serve their purpose at many a rowdy Party Conference in the thirties.

I.L.P. could count on much more support from the rank-and-file workers than they could ever enlist among the M.P.s. Many beside the traditional rebels were eager to conjure with the name of Mosley or, at least, to back his proposals. Ernest Bevin's growling discontent must have been known to the leaders, if not the public. By that October of 1930 the unemployment figures had sailed past the two million mark and showed no sign of being halted. MacDonald at Llandudno faced the test of a lifetime and, despite his assumed air of a weary Titan, it is hard to deny that he rose to it superbly. Even when his speech is read today – and MacDonald's speeches were very much intended to be heard, not read – its force is apparent. Picture the full scene with the presence, the gestures, the beautiful accent, the whole elegant swaying and lilting integration of voice, mind and body which is what a great MacDonald oration was, and it is not difficult to imagine the spell he cast. Maxton himself was deeply affected, especially as MacDonald made a touching reference to the recent death of Mrs Maxton. Fenner Brockway, sitting next to him in the Conference Hall as MacDonald spoke, was alarmed to see tears pouring down Maxton's cheeks and even more amazed to hear him muttering all the while the incongruous imprecation: 'Oh, the bastard, the bloody bastard.' Maxton's stomach for the fight had been knocked out of him by MacDonald's peroration. Called upon immediately afterwards to move the I.L.P.'s resolution attacking the Government, he could make little headway. Nor could any of the others who followed. Bevin was equivocal. Frank Wise struggled manfully to bring the debate down to earth. But soon MacDonald was on his feet again, exploiting his triumph to the limit. The real threat to the Government, it might be supposed, arose, not from economic crisis and palsied administration, but from 'internal criticisms blazoned abroad'. 'I have gone into the House of Commons again and again,' he cried, 'and found the back benches putting questions to the front bench with blazing eye and a wild violence which puts to shame all the ardour which comes from the Tory Opposition.' For a few hours the Conference seemed ashamed of its doubts.

But the magic did not last. MacDonald and his clouds of glory returned to London. Mosley, more fortunate in the hour chosen for his attack than Maxton, still got his chance. Two days after MacDonald had gained one of the most spectacular Conference victories of his career, Mosley outdid the Conference master. Declaring that his Memorandum was 'in direct conflict' with Snowden's policy and calling for 'a great policy of permanent reconstruction', he revived with greater relevance than before the plea for the old, rejected I.L.P. strategy. Let the Government throw down the gauntlet to the Opposition Parties. If it must die let it be, not like an old woman in a bed, but like a man in the field. And, indeed, the great national crisis they were living in need not be a menace to the movement; it could be their supreme opportunity. Mosley, according to Fenner Brockway,[27] received the greatest ovation he had ever seen at a Party Conference. The resolution backing his unemployment policy was beaten only by 1,046,000 against 1,251,000. Those figures meant that he had the overwhelming majority of the constituency parties behind him and the fact was emphasized when Thomas was removed from the Party Executive with Mosley taking his place. Despite the MacDonald *tour-de-force*, Mosley looked the real victor of Llandudno.[28]

27. *Inside the Left* by Fenner Brockway.
28. During this parliamentary recess, just before the Llandudno Conference, Bevan went on a two weeks' visit to the Soviet Union in a party that included John Strachey, George Strauss and Jennie Lee. He kept a diary which, curiously, at first sight seems valueless; it is stuffed with pig-iron statistics and contains not a single Bevanite flash of comment or insight. But it was never his way to write general impressions; he stored them in his amazing memory. And the pig-iron statistics were significant. He was always ready to apply the test to a nation's industrial or military strength; how much steel does it produce? When he was a member of the 1945 Government he confronted spokesmen of the General Staff with this same question. In 1930, apparently, he came away from Russia with his Marxist faith neither diminished nor greatly fortified. What he did learn – or, rather, what he confirmed in his mind – was the doctrine which played a big part in his interpretation of world events for years to come; that 'freedom is the by-product of economic surplus'. Writing in *In Place of Fear*, he recalled his visit to Russia in 1930: 'On my return I was asked by a trade union leader of international repute what my impressions were. I said my visit had been too short to admit any final conclusions, but one impression I had gained: whereas in Britain we were slaves to the past, in Russia they were slaves to the future.'
    However, perhaps one of the most important results of the visit to Russia, from Bevan's personal point of view, was the strengthening it gave to a friendship which was certainly close at the time even if it became weaker

Mosley's aim was to carry the insurrection into the Parliamentary Party while continuing to win backing in the country at large. Bevan fully supported these objectives. In the King's Speech debate he made what he described as his first criticism of the Government on the floor of the House of Commons. Against the demands of the time, against even to proposals of the Liberals, the Government had a case to answer. That duty was not discharged by the 'little provincial debating speech' which was all they had been offered by Herbert Morrison from the front bench earlier in the day. The King's Speech showed no apprehension of the reality of the crisis and 'it is merely Party cheering on this side' to pretend otherwise. Altogether he struck a more sombre note than ever before. The spectacle of the army of two million unemployed, with so little done to help them, was bringing about a condition of 'cynical indifference to the House of Commons'. Those devoted to the cause of parliamentary government should be exceedingly anxious. 'We who have not been in the House very long have been listening to speeches of the elder statesmen with a good deal of helplessness and despair

later. The evidence is provided in a letter which Bevan wrote to Strachey (on 17 October 1930) and which was first published in Hugh Thomas's *John Strachey* (Eyre Methuen 1973):

'I have looked through the draft [of Strachey's Russian-visit] report with my usual carping mind and jaundiced eye, but regret to say that I can find nothing wrong. The best I can say of it is that I could not have done better myself. Perhaps – having had a somewhat more fastidious education – I could improve on the English, but I am afraid my over refeened style would arouse your virile disgust. Seriously, John, I think you have made a damned good job of it. For the life of me, I can't see anything to alter. It read a bit breathless, but that is due, obviously, to constriction of space. Breathlessness is not altogether a fault . . . I shall not be in London until next Monday and so shall not be able to avail myself of hospitality. You are very good to me John. It hurts me a little that you give so much and I can give nothing in return. So few people have given me anything that I feel a little strange and bewildered. I count our friendship as the one thing of value that membership of parliament has given me. And yet, as this friendship grows, and becomes more and more a part of me, I find myself becoming fearful. I am so conscious of bringing to our relationship nothing of value, and, therefore, am frightened of trusting so much of my affection in so ill balanced a vessel. Please forgive me for exposing so shy a feeling to the peril of words. It is your generous nature that moves me to speak, even though I know that speech would bruise where it would caress. Give my love to Esther. Aneurin.'

... I hope we shall try to get rid of that cynicism which comes over people in this House, try to destroy the atmosphere of enervation and tackle the problem in the spirit the country expects.'

His hopes could not have been very buoyant. After the fierce breezes of Llandudno, he quickly found himself half-choked in the stifling atmosphere of the private Party meeting. There all discussion was compressed, no proper rules of debate protected a minority, a closure could always be enforced by the cry of the impatient majority 'Vote, vote', and the sway exercised by the patronage in the hands of the Prime Minister was more effective even than in the Commons itself. It was there, wrote Jennie Lee, that she witnessed 'the crowning ignominies of that unhappy time'. The sheer negation of the Government 'drove everyone under forty to the verge of madness'.[29] But what could they do? Mosley took no pains to hide his blistering contempt for the Party yes-men and his arrogance merely rallied them ever more solidly to the leadership. To defeat Mosley, not unemployment, became the all-consuming common interest.

MacDonald himself had been influenced by the Mosley revolt to search out new stratagems for securing the survival of his Government. He appealed to the two Opposition Parties to sit down with his Ministers and try to devise a 'national' policy for meeting the economic blizzard. Baldwin, on behalf of the Conservatives, refused; he had troubles of his own engineered chiefly by Lord Beaverbrook. If he appeared to be abandoning the Tory nostrum of Protection in the interests of reaching an accommodation with the Government, he might be unseated from the Tory leadership. But Lloyd George was more willing and by the beginning of the autumn session something approaching a bargain had been struck. If the Government agreed to give the Liberals the Electoral Reform Bill, which they hoped would salvage their fortunes in the constituencies, the Liberals in return, or a majority of them, might be more ready to spare the Government the agonies of suspense which it had suffered in the previous session over such measures as the Coal Mines Bill. The storm outside was blowing more tempestuously than ever but inside the walls of the Palace of Westminster MacDonald

29. *Tomorrow is a New Day* by Jennie Lee.

and his Cabinet could breathe a little more freely. This unwritten and fragile agreement with the Liberals merely added to the fury with which the Party loyalists watched the growingly overt pressures of Mosley and his backers. Just at the moment when they were offered a little peace, the rebels were declaring war.

Bevan was now a marked man; he was openly allied with the rebels. One day, walking into the Smoking Room with a fellow conspirator, W. J. Brown, he met Churchill. 'Well, you young members of the Suicide Club,' said Churchill, 'what have you been up to?' Bevan replied: 'Well, for that matter, what have *you* been up to? We haven't seen much of you in the fight lately!' 'Fight?' asked Winston. 'Fight? I can't see any fight. All I can see in this Parliament is a lot of people leaning against each other . . .'[30] The picture was more accurate than that glowingly painted in the meetings upstairs of great men manfully overcoming great odds, while a small band of curs yapped at their heels.

During the winter of 1930–1 both the internal struggles within the Labour Party and the economic crisis itself seemed to be moving towards a climax. By December the unemployment total had passed two and a half million. The clash between the I.L.P. and the official Parliamentary Party looked more intractable than ever, with the I.L.P. leaders insisting that their members in Parliament must accept the instructions of the annual I.L.P. conference, while the official Party retorted by insisting on the observance of a tighter discipline to be enforced on the authority of the Party meeting. Meantime, the Mosley rebellion, with Bevan's eager assistance, proceeded apace.

Early in December 'a Mosley manifesto' was published. It recapitulated many of the ideas in his earlier Memorandum but included some startling additions affecting the reform of Parliament and the whole administrative machine. It proposed a supreme Cabinet of five and a National Planning Organization armed with the power to act much more swiftly than normal parliamentary procedure allowed. It was signed by seventeen Labour M.P.s, including Bevan, and by A. J. Cook; no proof exists, but the likelihood is that Bevan was responsible for securing the allegiance of the miners' leader. The whole programme

30. *So Far* by W. J. Brown.

was pitched on a high note; it talked of a national emergency and demanded emergency measures to deal with it. But the proposals for the supersession of orthodox parliamentary methods made more difficult any co-operation between Mosley and the I.L.P.; Maxton and his friends were not eager to contemplate any infringement of their rights to vote freely in Parliament at the very moment when they were engaged in a fight with the official Party on this issue.

Undeterred, Mosley and his backers went ahead, at the end of January, with a demand to the Party meeting that the National Executive should summon 'a special national conference to consider the unemployment crisis'. Had such a conference been arranged, it is conceivable that the narrow vote against the Mosley programme carried at the October Conference might have been reversed. The resolution at the Party meeting was to be moved by Bevan; when the news spread through the House of Commons corridors, he was summoned to MacDonald's presence. MacDonald asked for the resolution to be withdrawn. During the conversation, the Premier explained how his economic advisers had told him that the crisis had passed its peak, how the unemployment figures would soon be turning the other way, how 'recovery was just round the corner', how if the Party avoided these internal embarrassments it might soon be able to face the country with renewed prospects of victory.[31] Bevan left the interview in despair. MacDonald seemed to regard the crisis as something beyond the range of his Government to influence one way or another. At the subsequent Party meeting the Mosley–Bevan resolution was crushingly defeated – by ninety-seven votes to thirteen. On this particular occasion, Bevan was picked out as the special victim of MacDonald's ire. A few days earlier had come the news that he had been defeated in a County Council election;[32] MacDonald used the event to impress upon his fol-

31. *In Place of Fear.*
32. Bevan's defeat in the County Council election was seemingly due to over-confidence and a swing in the Catholic vote. His ward was the most difficult for a Labour candidate, but no one believed that, having won in 1928, he could now be defeated. Archie Lush concentrated his exertions in a neighbouring ward and Bevan's refusal in the Commons to vote against the Government on the issue of provision for Catholic schools was used against him.

lowers the inconsiderable quality of his opponents. Yet he had no real need of such adventitious aids. The overwhelming majority of the Parliamentary Party was eager to respect the appeals to loyalty and to huddle closer together for protection under MacDonald's banner. Just after this meeting, Beatrice Webb was writing in her diary: 'In home affairs it [the Labour Party] has no policy – it has completely lost its bearings. What I am beginning to doubt is the "inevitability of gradualness" or the practicability of gradualness . . .'[33] Yet, at the last count, only thirteen members of the Parliamentary Party had voted to do something to recover a sense of urgent purpose. Most of the others seemed content to tolerate the inertia implicit in the confession made at the same time by the arch-Fabian Sidney Webb. How could the transition to a Socialist State be accomplished? 'All I know,' he said, 'is that I don't know how to do it.'[33]

Snowden's advisers seem to have made a different impression on his mind than upon MacDonald's, although they were the same men – the panic-stricken masters of the paralytics in office. During a momentous debate on 11 and 12 February, Snowden chose to give the broadest of hints that a new departure in policy – or rather an intensification of the old policy – was being prepared by the Treasury and the Bank of England. The Tories had put down a motion calling for strict economy and the Liberals embellished the demand with a proposal for an independent Committee to examine the nation's accounts and to make proposals for immediate reductions in public expenditure. Snowden seized on these propositions as a life-saver. He spoke in frightening accents of the menace of financial collapse. 'An expenditure which may be easy and tolerable in prosperous times,' he said, 'becomes intolerable in a time of grave industrial depression.'[34] This, if he only knew it, was Keynesianism stood on its head, the very deflationary doctrine which had served to deepen the crisis the world over. It is fashionable now to suggest that few but Keynes himself, and he only with early diffidence, appreciated the folly of the Treasury's great theory. But this does less than justice to what was said and done at the time by both the

33. *Beatrice Webb Diaries.*
34. *An Autobiography* by Philip, Viscount Snowden.

Maxtonites and the Mosleyites, whatever their other aberrations.

At once the I.L.P. protested; they saw that a major attack on the social services was now the order of the day. Snowden, as if to epitomize the hopeless I.L.P. approach to financial problems, derisively quoted one of them as demanding: 'It's bigger, not smaller, Budgets we want'.[35] – in other words, the precise remedy which a later age was to approve. As for Mosley, his speech on this occasion at least deserves some sympathetic study from those Labour leaders who, so much later, became the excoriators of Snowden's economics. Snowden's call for sacrifices, he said, was 'a panic shout; the suggestion of an old woman in a fright'. The Prime Minister's complacency was a danger to the nation. Together, MacDonald and Snowden were 'like chickens running in front of a motor car and cackling the economy slogans of their opponents'. If they got their way they would 'put the nation to bed on a starvation diet'.

But Mosley's wiser understanding of the economic situation availed no more than his furious declamation. The Liberal motion was carried by four hundred and sixty-nine votes to twenty-three[36] and Snowden was 'able to induce' Sir George May, who had recently retired as head of the Prudential Assurance Company, to preside over the independent committee of inquiry.[35] The Government had put in pawn its command over the economic affairs of the nation and it might have been expected that so flagrant an abdication would at last arouse the Party from its torpor. Yet next day Snowden scored another victory at the Party meeting. The rank-and-file was unutterably depressed, but incapable of protest, much less action. 'What I was totally unprepared for,' wrote Jennie Lee in her judgement on the mood of her colleagues, 'was the behaviour of the solid rows of decent, well-intentioned, unpretentious Labour back benchers. In the long run it was they who did the most deadly damage. Again and again, an effort was made to rouse them from their inertia. On

35. *An Autobiography* by Philip, Viscount Snowden.
36. Bevan did not vote in this division, although it is clear he strongly shared the I.L.P.'s objection to the setting up of the committee. The explanation seems to be, either that he was away ill or that he felt, at the height of the Mosley revolt, that he would be unwise to invite the criticism of the Whips for another offence.

every occasion they reacted like a load of damp cement. They would see nothing, do nothing, listen to nothing that had not first been given the seal of MacDonald's approval.'[37]

Two days after the critical vote setting up the May Committee, Mosley and his followers issued a new interim statement warning of the fresh threat to wage standards and the social services. Following their defeat at the Party meeting in January, a more comprehensive document was in preparation. Its chief authors, apart from Mosley, were John Strachey, W. J. Brown, Aneurin Bevan and Allan Young, a Mosley recruit from the I.L.P. who for some time had helped to shape Mosley's ideas and instil into them much of the former J. A. Hobson–Frank Wise doctrine. The document was published on 24 February. But on the day before, an apparently well-informed leakage in the *Observer* made the sensational revelation that Mosley intended to break with the Labour Party and form one of his own. To the outside world it naturally seemed that the two announcements – the new Mosley manifesto and that proposing the formation of a new Party – were part of the same manoeuvre and that Bevan was implicated in both. That Sunday he was travelling up to London with Archie Lush. 'Well, boy, you're at the crossroads now,' said Archie, 'what are you going to do?'[38] According to his account, there was never any doubt. And when Bevan was met by the reporters a few hours later he gave the reply that of course he supported the manifesto, being one of its signatories, but that he never had any intention of leaving the Labour Party.[39] Mosley in his impatience had jumped the gun on some of his closest colleagues.[40] Before the official announcement of the formation of the New Party was made a week later, strong pressure was brought on Bevan by Strachey and the few others who had resolved to go with Mosley to get him to join them. There was in any case the

37. *Tomorrow is a New Day* by Jennie Lee.
38. In conversation with Archie Lush.
39. Reported in the *Daily Herald*, 24 February 1931.
40. Bevan was often taunted in after years about his association with Mosley. On one occasion, in May 1932, Walter Elliot was claiming that a proposal advanced at that time should commend itself to a man who had backed Mosley's Memorandum; he accused Bevan of 'deserting Sir Oswald in his adversity'. Bevan replied: 'I would point out that his adversity started when he deserted me. He was quite prosperous until then.'

difficulty about his signature to the document already printed and ready for publication. Bevan agreed that the document should be issued; what he had signed he did not wish to retract.[41] But on the much bigger issue of a breach with the official Party, he was adamant and indeed played a leading part in dissuading several I.L.P.ers who were tempted to approve the New Party manifesto. His suspicions of Mosley personally were now fully, if belatedly, aroused, despite his commitment to and approval of Mosley's policy declarations. 'Where is the money coming from?' he demanded, 'Who is going to pay? Who is going to call the tune? I tell you where you will end up. You will end up as a fascist party, I tell you—.' Mosley's breach with the Party could not have been made more clumsily. In a matter of hours he tossed away the massive support he had been accumulating throughout the country. His deep disability as a would-be leader of the Labour Party was exposed. He had no love for it, no roots in it, no compunction at the breach with old comrades. He could leave as easily as he had joined, without a twinge of conscience or regret.[42]

41. Bevan received the following letter from Allan Young, dated 28 February: 'I wanted to write you a note after the last group meeting to say that although I had been a little cross with you on other grounds, I very much appreciated your kindly and well-intentioned effort to help us over a difficult situation. I did not send this to you the next morning because, as you will guess, I have been very busy indeed. I send it to you now in order that I may have the opportunity of saying that we part good friends and I hope to be able to welcome you into the new organization at a later stage. Whatever happens, it was nice of you to help your friends in adversity, and I like to mark these things down to a man's credit.'

42. Readers may judge for themselves from this record how accurate was the verdict on Bevan's conduct in that Parliament supplied by Lord Attlee in his *Daily Herald* obituary. 'He did not realize,' said Attlee, 'the inevitable restrictions on possible action and was eager for quick results. He might indeed in those days have been considered an angry young man. He was not a very good judge of the character of those with whom he associated and fell, as did people of more experience, for Oswald Mosley.' When Mosley resigned, Attlee succeeded him as Chancellor of the Duchy of Lancaster. Certainly no 'quick results' followed this change. One of the reasons was given by Attlee in a conversation with Dalton *after* the fall of the Government – 'Snowden,' he said, 'had been blocking every positive proposal for two years.' Which is exactly what the angry young man had been complaining about throughout most of the two years. The suggestion that Bevan 'fell for' Oswald Mosley is an absurd allegation which takes no account of the great

The Mosley defection, done so brusquely and ineptly, blunted the effect of what might otherwise have been a more serious exposure of the gangrene affecting the Party leadership. Amid all its other trials the Government had suddenly found itself confronted with a first-class crisis in the Commons stemming from the old religious quarrels about education. John Scurr, one of the most loyal of the 'loyalist' M.P.s – indeed he was chairman of the consultative body between the Party and the Government which for months had been busy devising new methods to discipline the I.L.P. – moved a pro-Catholic amendment against the Government's Education Bill and pressed his opposition to a vote. The Government was defeated and although MacDonald – 'the greatest living master of falling without hurting himself', said Churchill – did his best to pretend that nothing much had happened, the incitement to the House of Lords to wreck the whole Bill became overpowering. For Sir Charles Trevelyan, the radical and respected Minister of Education, this was the last straw. He had thought it right to stay in the Government while there was still a chance of getting through a Bill for raising the school leaving age, particularly as this measure had only been kept on the Government's agenda by a persistent invocation of support from the Party rebels. But Trevelyan's sympathies had always been with those who saw where the Government was leading the Party. Now he resigned, insisting that he did so as a protest against the whole temper of the leadership. The leaders must be changed if anything was to be accomplished.[43]

However, at the Party meeting, Trevelyan was greeted with stony silence while MacDonald's appeal for 'a loyal team' raised full-throated enthusiasm.[44] Almost the last effort to stage a revolt in the arena where constitutionally and theoretically the great matters of Party policy could be soberly argued out had failed. Maxton, Wheatley, Mosley, Trevelyan – all in their several ways had tried to sound the alarm. Against them, the authority of 'the Big Five' remained to the end unshaken, almost undented. A

unemployment controversy about which the Mosley revolt was concerned. The allegation comes ill from one who gave consistent support to MacDonald.
43. *The Tragedy of Ramsay MacDonald* by McNeil Weir.
44. *British Political Parties* by R. T. McKenzie.

few in minor offices, the Attlees and the Daltons, might mutter their doubts behind cuffed hands, but at the Party meetings they played loyally in the team and pledged their support to the irre-placeable captain. A few intellectuals and trade unionists, led by G. D. H. Cole, at this time formed a group dubbed by one of its number the 'Loyal Grousers'.[45] The loyalty was more effective than the grousing. Bevan chose a different part. Having joined with others in the attempt to change things from inside and seeing after many months no prospect of success, he preferred to fight in the open, on the floor of the House of Commons and in the country. He was not to be easily forgiven for the crime by some of those who helped to sustain MacDonald's supremacy and Snowden's economics to the eleventh hour of the last day. Right at the start of his parliamentary life he felt the full force of the hatred which internal Party strife can engender. 'The essence of 1931,' says Jennie Lee, 'is that the orthodox members of the Party were blind and deaf, but far from dumb in repeating the doctrines of the leaders. Their chief sport, then as always, was persecuting anyone who tried to tell them that the Emperor was stark naked.'

The closing weeks of that parliamentary session before the summer recess ended with scenes of piteous humiliation. The bane of the Government's life was that to meet the rising bills for unemployment benefit it had to secure fresh borrowing powers from Parliament. To secure these powers, it was necessary in turn to win the approval of the Liberals, many of whom were already prepared to line up with the Tories for the destruction of the Government and almost all of whom were insisting on econ-omies, in particular a stricter administration of the insurance funds and kindred reliefs. The result was the so-called Anomalies Bill which, crudely summarized, meant that some two or three hun-dred thousand of the unemployed would have their benefits cut.

45. The group was formed on the initiative of G. D. H. Cole and his wife, and had among its number C. M. Lloyd, G. R. Mitchison and W. R. Blair of the Co-operative Wholesale Society. It began to meet at Easton Lodge, the country house of the Countess of Warwick. It formed a Society for Socialist Inquiry and Propaganda and recruited Ernest Bevin as its Chairman, Attlee, Cripps and several others, including a group of ex-University Socialists, headed by Hugh Gaitskell. So he started as a 'Loyal Grouser'.

Maxton's rebels and a few others fought the Bill line by line in a last, forlorn rearguard action. Bevan joined them, backing several of their amendments with his vote in the division lobbies in defiance of the Whips. By this time nearly half his own constituents were out of work and the attempt to reduce their standards or impose fresh conditions on their entitlement to benefit seemed to him an outrage, especially when this might on occasion be done by a regulation issued by a Minister who would no longer require precise sanction from Parliament for his conduct. He appealed to 'members of this Committee who have a regard for parliamentary institutions which young members like myself have not yet acquired and which experience over recent years has made it increasingly difficult for us to acquire'. If he had come to Westminster half-unconsciously wondering whether his old Marxist beliefs would be softened, here instead he was witnessing the class war in the raw. 'The duty of a democratic party,' he said, 'is to expose the rich to the attack of the poor.' But here was his democratic Party launching a fresh attack on the poor while the representatives of the rich man's Party smirked their approval. At four o'clock in the morning during an all-night session he fell foul of some of his colleagues from mining constituencies who, as he fiercely remonstrated, seemed to be viewing the proceedings with 'bovine complacency'. A few minutes later he apologized for the outburst but by now his patience with the whole political prospect was near breaking-point.

Nothing remained for that second Labour Government but to go out with its final whimper. The great August crisis of 1931, the long and ignominious wrangle in the Cabinet about the cuts they would accept, the intrigue with the Opposition Parties, the Cabinet's resignation and the emergence of MacDonald next morning as a Prime Minister in a National Government – all these events came upon the public, if not as a bolt from the blue, at least with a startling suddenness. To those in the Parliamentary Labour Party who had voted for MacDonald and Snowden so faithfully, such events could not be explained except as monstrous acts of treachery. But Bevan never subscribed to that smug delusion. To suppose that three men of such contrasted temperaments as MacDonald, Snowden and Thomas had been capable of the same evil in their hearts and the same selling of their souls at precisely the same moment was too absurd and convenient a coincidence for any literate Socialist M.P. to accept.

Much more revealing of the true nature of the Government's failure were the circumstances which surrounded the report of the May Committee, issued on the morning after Parliament had been packed off for the summer. It was, said Beatrice Webb, the report of 'five clever hard-faced representatives of capitalism and two dull trade unionists'.[46] The two dull trade unionists, to do them credit, dissented from the draconic economy measures demanded by the Committee. But who would notice? The sensational report was issued without any breath of dissent from the Treasury; the natural and foreseeable result was a renewed pressure on the exchanges, a fresh and staggering blow to capitalist 'confidence' in the Labour Government. The May Committee's report was the mere fulfilment of the Treasury doctrine which Snowden, the Government and the Parliamentary Party had approved. From the publication of the report on 31 July to the overthrow of the Government four weeks later was but a short, logical step. Some like Dalton and Attlee, who had voted for setting up the May Committee, later had the grace to acknowledge that the Committee should never have been appointed[47] without offering any congratulations on their perspicacity to those who had opposed its appointment at the time.

To those, like Bevan, who had attacked the policy of the banks for months, 'the Bankers' Ramp' of 1931 did not come as quite so much of a novelty. During the week or two after the publication of the May Committee report Bevan was on holiday with Archie Lush at Llanfairfechan in North Wales. He was profoundly depressed by his experience of the House of Commons, but even before the change of Government he was convinced that the report must alter the whole course of the struggle. The leadership of the Party stood condemned. A greatly sharpened fight against it must be organized outside the House of Commons and, of course, the same moral applied with even greater force when MacDonald became the head of a National Coalition. Yet

46. *Beatrice Webb Diaries.*
47. *Call Back Yesterday* by Hugh Dalton, and *1931* by R. Bassett.

he also became persuaded at the same moment that another conclusion was unavoidable. If such deadly blows could be struck at the power of the Labour movement and working-class standards by parliamentary leaders and their followers, Parliament must be recognized as one essential arena in the fight for power. To seek escape from it was to abdicate.

When Parliament met again, after the ministerial revolution engineered in the City, Downing Street and Buckingham Palace, both the Labour ex-Ministers and their followers had recovered their voices. Their rage was unloosed against the men who had sold the pass in fact abandoned so long before. Now some of the most silent accomplices of the previous régime had become raucous revolutionaries. MacDonald, Snowden and Thomas were to hang on a sour apple tree, while the cause of Socialism marched to triumph. Bevan would not strike the same note but he eagerly took part in two of the principal debates of that time. The first was on the Economy Bill which incorporated the economy measures designed to protect the exchanges, make borrowings from foreign bankers possible and enable the country to stay on the gold standard. The second, a few days later, was on the Gold Standard Amending Bill, giving the Government the authority to go off the gold standard!

On the first occasion he did not disguise that he 'felt happier that at last we have a chance of opposing policies in which we do not believe'. But he did not envisage a relaxed and formal opposition at Westminster. The Government need not think they would be faced only with a 'sterile parliamentary Opposition when they are making use of the most ruthless class policy they have ever carried out'. If Ministers supposed that their measures would be received with 'the docility of 1921-9 they must think all the guts have gone out of Englishmen'. When the patriotic appeal was made Labour could now give the only answer – a class answer. It was good that the class issue had now been exposed in all its harshness.

These may sound today like wild words – absurdly romantic words if they are taken to mean that yesterday's tame prisoners of MacDonaldism might suddenly summon their followers to the barricades. Bevan, of course, distrusted the new leadership hardly less than the old. He knew how deeply they had sunk in the same mire. It was the conjunction of events in South Wales and Westminster which inspired him to speak in revolutionary accents. For those Labour M.P.s returning from areas of mass unemployment to find that in their absence a Labour Government had been given notice, like some flunkey suspected of stealing the spoons, it did seem that parliamentary institutions might soon be facing a crisis more severe even than that in which the nation's mysterious financial mechanism was enmeshed. The period between 1929 and 1931 had done nothing to shake Bevan's Marxist analysis of the world he saw around him. When other Labour spokesmen talked of the collapse of capitalism as the cause of the crisis, Mosley, outside in Trafalgar Square, jeered. Yes, indeed, it might be, but how had Labour dealt with it? Was not this the moment which Socialists had been waiting for? 'What would you think of a Salvation Army which took to its heels on the day of judgement?' Mosley despaired of the Labour movement and despised it. Bevan's reaction was quite different. He believed that its forces could now be rallied for the truly desperate battle he saw ahead. Like so many others at the time, he had no inkling of the full scale of the defeat awaiting Labour at the polls. But if Parliament was transformed into a naked class dictatorship, Labour would have to look to other weapons. This, along with the 'patriotic' fever, was also part of the hectic mood at the time.

The second debate in which Bevan participated – on the gold standard or rather the necessity of going off it – was calculated to inspire awe in the most irreverent minds. Members talked as if the end of the world was at hand. Snowden appealed to all speakers to mark their words, lest an incautious phrase might start a new run on the exchanges. Bevan protested against 'the funeral chant' designed 'to close our mouths and drug our brains'. Discussing the gold standard in Snowden's presence was like making a bad joke in a cathedral. He did not claim to know much about the technicalities of the gold standard, an ignorance he claimed to share with almost every member of the House. What he did claim to know was the purpose behind the Government's measures – it was to secure a breathing space for private enterprise and 'my class will subsequently be asked to pay the price'. Often the House had been told that the crisis, caused by deflation, would be solved by international conferences. Now the French and the Americans had killed that hope; they had 'rubbed the lion's nose in the dust'. Next the House was told by the pundits that the deflation must be intensified, but 'you cannot have a recovery in trade if the real purchasing power of your people is brought down'. Finally, the Ministers pleaded that the normal surveillance of Parliament must be abrogated to make the economy drive possible. But, concluded Bevan, if the financial masters of the country, with Snowden as their spokesman, were saying that their operations were incompatible with democratic rights then – in the words of his old favourite, Thomas Rainborough – 'it is you who have said it, my Lord General, not me'.

The financial analysis may have been crude, but it was fundamentally more discerning than Snowden's. Having endured all the humiliations which Wheatley had prophesied to sustain the gold standard, the House was told in tremulous whispers that nothing would save the country but the immediate abandonment of the totem. The exchanges quickly began to look healthier, as Frank Wise had often foretold they would. And as the last pitiful epitaph on the servility of that Parliamentary Labour Party, its great Fabian mentor, Sidney Webb, declared, when told that Snowden's advisers had actually recommended the fatal step: 'No one ever told *us* we could do that.'[48]

The attempt to trace the contribution of an individual back-bench M.P. to parliamentary controversies may tend to exaggerate his influence and, at the same time, to give a falsely limited impression of his range of interests.[49] The debates in which he

48. *Call Back Yesterday* by Hugh Dalton.
49. An example of the freshness with which Bevan approached some other problems is given in the notes which are preserved for a speech he delivered to a meeting of teachers in his constituency at this time.
'For the first time in history,' he said, 'the common man steps on the stage. We insist that education is primarily concerned with the ordinary person, and not with the exceptional person. The ordinary person is asked to decide issues of far greater gravity than any exceptional person in the

speaks may be of no decisive significance while often when he wants to speak he is unable to do so. *Hansard* is a great leveller and a great deceiver. It is sometimes hard to fathom how such damp prose could have struck such fires; more rarely, gems of eloquence and wit may still gleam from those pages when in fact they were delivered to an empty House in the dinner hour. Aneurin Bevan in that first Parliament was obviously not one of the leading figures; even the main leaders on the Left of the Labour Party, thanks to their longer experience, naturally took a more prominent part than he did. But there is no doubt about the mark he had made both by his activities inside the Party and by his half-dozen main speeches in the House itself. 'He has a keen debating faculty,' wrote a gallery reporter who had watched the whole of that Parliament. 'That is one of the first things one notes in him, and it is in these days a faculty which is too scarce. Good, however, as his debating powers are, he would not by means of them alone have made the impression which he has made. What has conquered the House is his vitality, his enlistment of all his bodily as well as mental powers in the expression of his argument. He thinks quickly, and he does not think quietly. His thought seems to take possession of him. Some speakers are gestureless, others make use of gestures, but he seems to be all gesture, involuntarily turning his whole muscular machinery into a means of expression. His gestures are both profuse and vivid. They combine vigour with picturesqueness and significance. He is the most vitalized speaker in the House. Yet there is nothing thunderous or overwhelming about him. He is swift and tumultuous, he has the speed, the impetuosity, even the force of the wind, but whatever metaphor of storm may be suitable to

---

past . . . When I complain about our secondary schools imitating the public schools it is because they have a different task to perform . . . In order to be on terms of equality with the product of the public schools they must be trained differently. They are already too much inclined to obedience. What we want from them is more arrogance, freedom from the trammels of tradition. These boys and girls are to be asked to wield the royal sceptre; we must therefore give them the souls of kings and queens. Otherwise it may be said of us that we took the ordinary man from the shadows of history and set him in the fierce light that beats upon thrones and he was blinded and ran away.'

him, those of the thunderstorm are entirely inadmissible. The reason is that he has the Welshman's lightness of voice.'[50]

This contemporary portrait gives an excellent impression of his manner. But there was nothing self-conscious or calculated in it. He had not set his eyes on a parliamentary career in the style hallowed by tradition. As a young miner in Tredegar, he had always wanted to rise with his class and not out of it, and there is not a shred of evidence that Westminster had altered that affinity with his own people and their aspirations as the motive power of his life. His ill-wishers were ready then, as they often were later, to accuse him of a clearly formed personal ambition. 'That nonsense,' he said, 'I leave to the writers of romantic biographies.'[51] Against him, in particular, it was always the silliest of charges. Such ambition should have quelled his outbursts and groomed at least a few of his impulses; it should have guided him to hitch his star to one of the obvious band-waggons. He did the opposite. Right from the start he showed his uniqueness. There was no one else remotely like him. As a man, a speaker and a politician he always acted in a style completely individual to himself. And one of the most obvious of those in-dividual characteristics was that, in the personal sense, he seemed to take no thought for the morrow. As a political thinker, he was fascinated to peer into the future. But the intrigue and calculation of the normal politician were always odious to him. 'A man who would rise at court,' said the great Lord Halifax, 'must begin by creeping on all fours.' Bevan resolved to stand upright on his own two feet from the outset.

In that first Parliament he was learning his trade. W. J. Brown said that in those days he possessed 'an air of enquiring innocence which was most deceptive'.[52] Perhaps W. J. Brown was among the deceived. Others noted his bashfulness. Considering what came later that may sound barely credible. But in fact, in view of his stutter and the awkward, incorrigibly individual choices for action which he insisted on making, it would be foolish to underrate what resources of nervous energy he expended in

50. *A Hundred Commoners* by James Johnston.
51. *In Place of Fear*.
52. *So Far* by W. J. Brown.

screwing his courage to the sticking place – to face the hostility of colleagues, for example, especially at those lynch-law ceremonies known as private Party meetings. For that assembly he learnt, in the era of MacDonald and Snowden and the triumphant machine which ground the second Labour Government to pulp, a lifelong detestation.

Two other lessons he appeared to have learnt. As we have seen, his Marxist principles and outlook became entrenched, rather than loosened. The memory of the awful consequences which must follow from the helplessness of an elected Government in the face of economic difficulties never left him. 'People have no use,' he wrote years later, 'for an institution which pretends to supreme power and then does not use it . . . This is the real crisis in democracy. People have no use for a freedom which cheats them of redress. If confidence in political democracy is to be sustained, political freedom must arm itself with economic power. Private property in the main sources of production and distribution endangers political liberty, for it leaves Parliament with responsibility and property with power.'[53] These words were written in 1952. But the context shows that it was the experience of 1929 to 1931 which had branded them on his intelligence.

The other lesson or intuition he had acquired was no less clear and more immediately apposite to the tasks of the moment. If the leaders had given an exhibition of helplessness, the rebels had not been much more impressive. They had certainly been more farseeing of economic events, more alive to the human misery produced by the great slump, more possessed with a sense of urgency. But they had not saved themselves from ineffectiveness in action, and Bevan remained haunted by the ease with which Left-wing Socialists could be tempted to reject all compromise, to save their immortal souls – and to condemn their cause to perdition.

During the last months and weeks of the second Labour Government this became a topic of frantic, unceasing debate between him and those with whom he was in closest sympathy. Not only the Party itself, but the Left within the Party seemed

53. *In Place of Fear*.

to be slicing itself into fragments. A few had gone with Mosley,[54] a few were tempted by the Communists, the I.L.P. was heading for a final rupture with the official Party. All through the Parliament Bevan had attended several of the private meetings of the

54. One who 'went with Mosley' but soon escaped with honour from the entanglement was John Strachey, and it was Bevan who gave what Strachey's biographer Hugh Thomas described as 'the best epitaph on this Strachey adventure'. Bevan wrote to Strachey on 29 July 1931, when he heard the news of Strachey's departure from the New Party, and the letter was reproduced in Thomas's *John Strachey*:

'The news of your resignation made me very happy. It is difficult for me to explain to you how keenly I felt the impossibility of our continued political co-operation after you joined the New Party. I am now looking forward to a renewal of that co-operation in the immediate future. The break with Mosley must have been difficult for you, but if I am to be allowed to say so without the risk of being misunderstood, I am convinced that the strength of mind and personal self-reliance which this decision involved means that you have reached your full maturity, in the use of your great powers ... I always had the feeling that your subordination to [Mosley's] superficially stronger personality was bad for you, in those subtle and self-conscious directions which are most potent in the building up of one's personality. You will remember the discussion we had some time ago about the psychic basis of your relation with Celia. I am convinced, perhaps quite amateurously [sic] that your relationship with Celia in the last analysis provided you with the necessary reinforcement for your decision about Mosley. I know that you are sufficiently objective not to take offence at these remarks of mine. It is my affection for you which causes me to look so closely into the psychical rather than the superficial reasons which led you to make the decision you have. I hope that you will not commit yourself in any way regarding your future until we have had the opportunity of talking the matter over very fully.

'It seems to me, looking at the political situation in this country, that the cards are not yet dealt with which the final game will have to be played. It would be a profound error for us to judge the pace and direction of these social and political collusions which exist independently of us, and with which we have to deal. It is the besetting sin of intellectuals to be too much influenced by the drive of their own minds. They are too reluctant to submit themselves to the pressure of events. In intellectuals, there is a tendency to want to dominate and shape these things arbitrarily. They can influence these events only by being moulded by them. Thus the profound difference between the typical intellectual and persons who, like myself, have the security of metaphysics on a social struggle upon which to rely in moments of doubt and uncertainty. [This sentence is put in as it was written, even though it does not read very satisfactorily.] I am putting these words together very incoherently and inadequately, but I know that, as usual, your mind will come three parts of the way to meet mine. As I told you on one occasion before, I value your friendship very highly, and my thoughts are with you constantly in what must be for you a time of great introspection if not spiritual suffering ... Yours affectionately, Aneurin.'

I.L.P. leaders as a kind of unofficial but trusted observer; always he had tended to advise caution in risking a full breach with the official Party, urging that the I.L.P. must not destroy in advance the role it could play when MacDonaldism was exposed.[55] Naturally he pressed this view with renewed force when the crisis came. In particular, he discussed the issue with Jennie Lee, who had kept her association with the I.L.P. despite doubts about its wisdom and objectives. She was in many respects, in that 1929 Parliament, a better-known figure than Bevan himself. She had opened fire on the decadence of the leadership earlier than he and had made her own distinctive contribution to the Party debate. She was not enamoured of the course which the combined interacting intransigence of Maxton and the official leadership seemed to be marking out for the I.L.P. remnant, but a breach with the I.L.P. would be for her a much more wounding wrench than for many others; in Scotland the I.L.P. still retained much of its inspiration while the official Party, in her eyes, bore all the marks of a self-satisfied, illiberal bureaucracy. But Bevan gave her no quarter. 'As for you, I tell you,' he said, 'what the epitaph on you Scottish dissenters will be – pure, but impotent. Yes, you will be pure all right. But, remember, at the price of impotency. You will not influence the course of British politics by as much as a hair's-breadth. Why don't you get into a nunnery and be done with it? Lock yourself up in a cell away from the world and its wickedness. My Salvation Army lassie ... Poor little Casabianca! That was a hell of an intelligent performance, wasn't it? I tell you, it is the Labour Party or

55. The evidence of the consistency with which Bevan advocated this view in I.L.P. circles has been given me in conversations with Fenner Brockway – who also confirms how strongly Bevan opposed the New Party breakaway for similar reasons. His testimony, therefore, accords precisely with Jennie Lee's. The point has some interest for the whole of Bevan's career. Some of the leaders, even Attlee-type obituarists, have been inclined to portray him as an eager rebel against the Party, indulging in one such escapade after another either through some weakness of temperament or through motives of personal advertisement. The truth is the opposite. He was a most reluctant rebel; he passionately wanted to work within the Labour Party and thought nothing could be achieved outside it. The frequency of his clashes was no psychological problem; those clashes arose rather from the objective, persistent, unresolved problem of the leadership.

nothing. I know all its faults, all its dangers. But it is the Party that we have taught millions of working people to look to and regard as their own. We can't undo what we have done. And I am by no means convinced that something cannot yet be made of it.'[56]

That burst of courteous Celtic eloquence, delivered to an audience of one as Aneurin Bevan strode up and down Jennie Lee's flat in Guilford Street, was possibly the most significant and courageous, if not the most instantaneously persuasive, speech he had yet delivered.

56. *Tomorrow is a New Day* by Jennie Lee.

5 Advocate for the Unemployed 1931–34

For really I think that the poorest he that is in England hath a life to live as the greatest he. – THOMAS RAINBOROUGH[1]

OCCASIONALLY at election time, Aneurin Bevan showed a shrewder instinct than the Party managers in gauging the movements of public opinion. But, like everyone else, he never foresaw how catastrophic was to be the extent of the Labour Party's defeat in 1931. Little evidence appeared above the surface of what was happening in the public mind. The Government's economy programme at once provoked big protest marches and demonstrations. When the sailors mutinied at Invergordon, British society seemed to tremble on the edge of inscrutable convulsions. Confronted with the phenomenon of naval mutiny, unprecedented in British history for nearly a hundred and fifty years, the Government had retreated. Bevan had pressed the point on the Prime Minister: would the same concessions be forthcoming if the unemployed showed the same rebellious tendencies? For a moment it looked as if the hint might be taken. A considerable part of the nation did give 'the class answer' which Bevan had stridently called for in the House of Commons a few weeks before. His knowledge of his own people at least was accurate. Labour held its own in South Wales against the 'patriotic' avalanche better than in any other part of the country. In Ebbw Vale no 'National' candidate dared show his face at all and Bevan was returned unopposed.[2]

1. From the Putney Debates, reprinted in *Puritanism and Liberty*, selected and edited by A. S. P. Woodhouse.
2. The truth about the 1931 election, partly blurred in public understanding at the time, was that Labour had not been almost wiped out as the derisory total of 46 Labour M.P.s (52, if three I.L.P.ers and three other Independents

Immediately, he hastened to North Lanark where Jennie Lee was fighting her election. A newspaper photograph of the time shows her being sustained by an unknown 'sympathizer' whose features were not yet recognized in far-away Scotland. This was the first election when Labour candidates had been required to give a prior undertaking that they would obey the Standing Orders of the Parliamentary Labour Party, and Jennie Lee, despite all Aneurin's eloquent rebukes, had accepted the same attitude on the issue as her I.L.P. colleagues. She had also offended Catholic constituents by voting against the Scurr amendment on the Education Bill. Maxton and Buchanan had urged her to abstain with them. 'You can't fight both the Labour machine and Catholic prejudice in West Scotland,' Maxton told her, 'make up your mind!' Controversy over the Scurr amendment cost Labour many seats and was the decisive factor in North Lanark.

Bevan had resolved to stay and fight it out in the Labour Party, just as he had once refused to emigrate from the island altogether. But the decision was made with his eyes open: he knew that the struggle was bound to be tough and long. A curious historical illusion of the fifties and the present day is the belief that in some way the issues of the thirties were black and white.[3] Supposedly, this simple clarity of choice was available in particular to members of the Labour Party. All they had to do was to take up their action stations in the great Socialist army assailing the ramparts of hunger and mass unemployment and, later, of Fascism and war. This was – and is – the official tale. But for the Bevan who started out in 1931 by resisting all temptation to isolate himself from the official Party and who, after a series of violent

are added) in a House of 615 seemed to suggest. The total Labour vote had dropped by two million but there were still six and a half million left. One big factor in causing the defeat was the heavy reduction in the number of three-cornered contests, meaning that Labour faced a more united opposition than at any election between the wars.

3. Cf. a review of G. D. H. Cole's *Socialism and Fascism, 1931–1939*, by C. A. R. Crosland in the *Observer* of 4 September 1960: 'Re-reading this history of the 1930s, one feels a shameful but pronounced nostalgia. Tragic as the outcome usually was, the fight itself was exhilaratingly clear-cut and righteous; one knew what to do and where the enemy was and what was the order of battle. There were no greys in the picture.'

controversies, found himself expelled from it altogether in 1939, there was obviously no easy solution to the dilemmas of that decade.

He was a convinced Marxist but never a Communist, a strong democrat who never underrated the novelty, the hazards and the unprecedented challenge involved in the task of reconstructing society by democratic means. He knew something of the Communists' methods, loathed their dogmatism and had, therefore, never been tempted to throw in his lot with them. Taxed on the issue and although despising the whole method of argument which relied on the citation of Marxist texts, he could point to the passages from Engels which helped confirm that there was no real contradiction between his Socialism and his democratic allegiance.[4] On the other hand, he accepted the Marxist stress on the need for a full theory of social change and went far to accept the Marxist analysis of the weakness and disabilities associated with social democratic leadership. His experience in the 1929 Parliament had not assisted in persuading him that the Labour leaders, the Hendersons any more than the MacDonalds, had the *will* to change anything. Obviously a man with such a political training and outlook would be unwilling, for a start, to agree that the significance of 1931 was merely a question of spitting out 'the rotten stuff' at the top, as Beatrice Webb described MacDonald and Company.

During the next three years – long before the major fights with the Labour leadership over the United Front and the Popular Front developed – three interwoven disputes arose in which Bevan participated. The first was theoretical; could the Labour Party be weaned or jolted away from its faith in Fabian 'gradualism'? The second was urgent: what was to be done about the

4. A footnote in *In Place of Fear* says: 'The following extract from Frederick Engels' Preface to the First English Translation of Marx's *Capital* gives an unequivocal summary of Marx's views: "Surely, at such a moment, the voice ought to be heard of a man whose whole theory is the result of a life-long study of the economic history and condition of England, and whom that study led to the conclusion that, at least in Europe, England is the only country where the inevitable social revolution might be effected entirely by peaceful and legal means. He certainly never forgot to add that he hardly expected the English ruling classes to submit without a 'pro-slavery rebellion' to this peaceful and legal revolution".'

injuries which the class policy of the Tory Government was inflicting on the unemployed and distressed areas like South Wales? And, very soon, the third controversy superimposed itself on the others: what transformations in working-class strategy should follow the arrival in power in Germany of Adolf Hitler in 1933 and the sweep of Fascism across large stretches of Europe? Bevan reacted swiftly to all these fresh considerations and circumstances. To say that he always did so wisely would be absurd. But he did react and act when so many others were oblivious or complacent. And the more he acted, the more he was in trouble with the machine and the official leadership of the Party.

When the Labour Government collapsed it looked at first as if the gradualist philosophy had suffered a body blow. A lurch to the Left was natural and apparently welcomed on all sides. At the first meeting of the Parliamentary Party Hugh Dalton made a vivid appeal for unity for the purpose of getting a real Labour Government in place of 'the sham thing we have known for the past two years'.[5] At the same meeting, Lord Sankey, who was joining the National Government, still urged that, whereas MacDonald had saved the nation, Henderson had saved the soul of the Labour Party. At the Party Conference, a few weeks later, a robust Left-wing programme was rushed through without dissent from any quarter. Leaders like J. R. Clynes rejoiced that they could now parade their Socialist dreams without a blush.

If the words meant the deed, the deed was done; the Labour Party had been restored once more into an aggressive force determined to accomplish a profound change in society. But the men of the Left could not forget that MacDonald had never failed to use the right language; he had done so a bare twelve months before with mesmeric effect at Llandudno. He more than most could make shine with such glitter what Professor Tawney called 'the radiant ambiguities of the word Socialism'.[6]

Moreover, it was significant that the same conference in 1931 gave a heavy trouncing to the I.L.P. rebels. On Henderson's plea, the demand that they must sign on the dotted line and

5. *Call Back Yesterday* by Hugh Dalton.
6. *The Attack* by Professor R. H. Tawney.

accept without qualification the Standing Orders of the Parliamentary Party won an overwhelming majority. According to the Henderson doctrine, a Labour M.P. was entitled to have a conscience, so long as he revealed it only in isolated abstentions. But the sin against the Holy Ghost of the Party machine was 'the organized conscience', the attempt of two or three or more gathered together to make their conscientious scruples effective in action. And the bells, books and candles, be it not forgotten, were invoked to anathematize those who had rebelled against Dalton's 'sham Government' of the MacDonald régime.

Bevan at this time wrote a cool analysis of what had happened to the Labour Government and why the lesson was of such importance for the future. It is worth study in detail, for it reveals as well as any other document the spirit of the time and a large part of the argument which was to dominate the Party for years ahead.[7]

In the first place [he wrote] of course it is necessary to agree on what has occurred. The view appears to be held that the Labour Government was destroyed by a 'Bankers' Ramp'. In the language of a member of the late Administration, 'The 1924 Labour Government was destroyed by a Red Letter; the last was ended by a Bankers' Order'. It is an astonishing charge to find in the mouths of those committed to gradualism. If a weak and innocuous minority Government can be broken by a conspiracy of finance capitalists, what hope is there for a majority Government, which really threatens the bankers' privileges? If capitalism is in such a state of organized self-consciousness that it can conspire against a Government and bring it down by moving its international financial forces against it, what hope is there for a gradual and peaceful expropriation of the bankers?

But, it may be urged, they would then have to deal with a strong Government backed by a majority in the House of Commons, which would be a different proposition. What would the 'strong' Government do, committed, as it would be, to peacefulness and gradualism? Let us remember that the conspiracy takes the form of an acute

7. John Strachey quoted this passage in *The Coming Struggle for Power*. He did not give Bevan's name, but said it was written by 'one of the most gifted of their [the Labour Party's] younger supporters'. He added at the end: 'Unfortunately, however, the writer of the analysis had to present it, since he remained one of their supporters, in the form of an appeal for reformation to his old leaders. It fell on deaf ears. How could it have been otherwise? To have accepted it would have meant a complete retreat from the position which they had held for the whole of their political lives.'

economic crisis induced by certain financial steps, taken in the ordinary course of business, by persons, most of them beyond the reach and control of the Government. In addition, it must be remembered that the new crisis would be superimposed upon an already existing one, for it is reasonably certain that there will never be another Labour Government in England except in conditions of economic crisis and consequent mass unrest. The accession of the Labour Government, charged with menace to the whole capitalist interest, will augment this condition, and the majority Government will find itself faced with another 'National Emergency'.

What will it do? Drop its gradualism and tackle the emergency on Socialist lines? Or drop its Socialism in the hope of reassuring private enterprise in order to get a breathing space? It will find itself hesitating between these two opposite courses. On the one hand, the state of the country will demand prompt, vigorous and revolutionary measures. On the other hand, it will bring to the emergency a mandate for conventional parliamentary legislation, a working class fed on pap, and a Parliamentary Party totally unprepared either theoretically or practically to deal with the crisis. A majority Labour Government in such a situation would do nothing effective, but would pause irresolutely between the two alternatives, until either Fascist power would accomplish a *coup d'état* or a new National Government would be formed on the ruins of the old, something on the lines of what we have just seen.

Therefore it would seem that, even if one takes the view that the end of the Labour Government was not necessitated by the needs of private enterprise, but was destroyed by finance seeking to profit itself, the policy of the Party needs to be drastically overhauled.

Having stated its charge against the banking interest, the Labour Party goes on to say that the crisis could have been met without resorting to the measures which resulted in the end of the Labour Government. They assert that the Budget should be balanced, but that this could be done without attacking wage standards, or the social services. And yet at the same time, they claim, they could still have stopped the run on sterling.

In short, they hold that capitalism could have saved itself without attacking the workers. This involves the assumption that capitalism can be carried on more efficiently by socialists than by capitalists: that the sacrifices demanded of the workers are the result, not of the needs of private enterprise, but of its stupidity. This, of course, is quite consistent with gradualism, which requires that private enterprise shall continue reasonably successful whilst it is being slowly and painlessly eliminated.

The difficulty about accepting this pleasant and convenient view is that there does not appear to be the slightest evidence to justify it.

Apart from the growing mechanistic friction of private enterprise, there are profound psychological reasons why the Labour Party will never be allowed to rationalize capitalism. It must never be forgotten that the mainspring of capitalist production is the individual investor. Whatever tends to make him nervous and apprehensive of the fate of a possible investment causes him to hold tight to that liquid capital, the release of which is essential to. the maintenance and expansion of fixed capital. We may rail against him, but whilst we allow him to be the prime motivator of the productive process the sensitiveness of his psychology is always a factor to be reckoned with. It is just this psychology that a Labour Party, climbing to power in circumstances of economic difficulty, not only cannot reassure, but must of necessity offend. In opposition, the Labour Party is compelled, by the nature of the class struggle, to take up an alignment which hamstrings it when in office. A Party climbing to power by articulating the demands of the dispossessed must always wear a predatory visage to the property-owning class. Thus in a society involved in the throes of an ever more heavily waged class struggle, the Labour Party must wear the face of the implacable revolutionary, although all the time its heart is tender with the promise of peaceful gradualism. It knows that the limited vision of the workers will behold only its outward appearance, but it hopes that the gods of private enterprise will look upon its heart.

In either case one must be deceived. To satisfy the workers, the Labour Party must fulfil the threat of its face, and so destroy the political conditions necessary to economic gradualism. To calm the fears of private enterprise, it must betray its promise to the workers, and so lose their support. Once again the only result will be political vacillation and economic catastrophe. There will be another crisis in the Party. Some of its leaders will take the heroic course, and in obedience to the call of a lofty patriotism will rally to the help of the nation. More in sorrow than in anger with this democracy, which cannot await the far-off interest of tears, they will cut themselves off from the sumptuous ease and lotus-eating of the workers and condemn themselves to the deserts of London society, and the company of Spartan, ascetic bankers.

Others of the leaders, thus made powerless, will cry with a loud voice, inviting all men to behold them to bear witness to their self-abnegation in refusing office and their heroism in coming to the help of the workers in this time of need. The political arena will be thick with heroes. The poor, bewildered worker will be asked to regard as heroes those leaders who have left him and those who remain. Both, he will be told, obeyed some lofty and austere sense of duty, far beyond the limited region of class loyalties. The position was put with commendable, if unconscious, clarity by a member of the recent Labour Government. 'In refusing to join the National Government,' he said,

'Mr Henderson had saved the soul of the Labour Party, and Mr MacDonald, in forming the National Government, had saved the nation.'

Thus is the fundamental and fatal contradiction of the Labour Party exemplified in the mouth of one of its most illustrious leaders.

Others thinking along the same lines decided that their challenge to gradualism must take an organizational form As a result of the decision of the 1931 Conference, the I.L.P. was now thrust into its final conflict with the official Party. One section favoured a complete breach on grounds of general Socialist policy; another and occasionally overlapping section would not accept the Party's demands about Standing Orders which they regarded as an intolerable infringement of parliamentary freedom and an M.P.'s obligation to his constituents. A third section saw the futility of destroying their influence within the Party and wanted to stay inside it, however burdensome the compromise they must make in return. Negotiations between the I.L.P. and the official Party broke down on the rock of Standing Orders. The majority voted in favour of disaffiliation on the terms required but a considerable minority, led by Frank Wise, decided to leave the I.L.P. and join forces with other Left-wing elements inside the main Party.

So, just before the Leicester Conference in 1932, the Socialist League was formed. It incorporated, apart from the I.L.P. dissentients and other Left-wingers, much of the membership and activities of another body, the Society for Socialist Inquiry and Propaganda, which G. D. H. Cole had brought together in 1930. Cole had always desired that his body should engage in research and propaganda without formulating the full alternative programme and strategy which would bring it into general disfavour with the official leadership. But with the formation of the Socialist League, first under Frank Wise's chairmanship and, on his death, under Stafford Cripps, Cole's hope was still-born.

The Socialist League mounted a big attack on what it regarded as the Party's unsevered attachment to 'gradualist' ideas. At the Leicester Conference in 1932 it gained a swift success. With the aid of the miners and the railwaymen, the Executive was defeated on its proposals about currency and banking. Spokesmen from the League successfully insisted on a commitment to nationalize the joint stock banks as well as the Bank of England. The victory was one symbol of the powerful Leftward trend in the Party. 'The Party leadership,' wrote Cole, 'remained gradualist though not so gradualist as MacDonald.'[8] This was the core of the controversy.

Bevan's general sympathies were naturally with the League, but he was dubious about the prospects of the organization and unwilling at first to give it his open support. When Frank Wise pressed him strongly to become one of its original founders, he refused. Partly his motives were personal; he felt he must be careful in engaging in a new forlorn enterprise so soon after the Mosley adventure; and he felt too that it would be wiser to hold himself in reserve for the opportunities which soon must come. It might be better if he were untrammelled by fresh associations, if, when the moment came, he could be free to choose his own line of action. The long private letter to Frank Wise in which he explained these hesitations contradicts the usual judgement passed on his seemingly unpremeditating character. He had obviously given deep thought to this particular proposition, just as he had also thought about the advisability of following the orthodox course, for one who was quickly gaining parliamentary aptitude, of seeking election to the Front Bench. 'I feel it in my bones,' he wrote, 'that the "great days" of the Labour Party are yet to come . . . I want to be as free as possible from personal entanglements and those obligations arising out of associations which tend to obscure one's vision and limit one's freedom of decision.' This letter offers one of the rare concrete proofs of the care with which he brooded on many of his tactical decisions; often what he seemed to do by impulse was the result of considerable private consultation, chiefly with himself. 'It may be,' he concluded, 'that it is only a balance of consideration which causes me to take up the stand that I have, but not having been blessed with a black and white mind I am afraid all my decisions will bear a shade of grey.'

This was a private communication to Frank Wise. Few observers would have supposed that the Bevan of 1932 would have analysed himself in such terms. The fact that he did so and that

8. *History of the Labour Party* by G. D. H. Cole.

he was still prevailed upon to cast in his lot at a later stage with Cripps is proof of how reluctant he was to play the rebel, if the role could honourably have been avoided. The clear truth is that, if he had wanted the sweets of advancement to the leadership, they were there for the tasting. With all the parliamentary opportunities open to him, he could easily have stepped rung by rung up the ladder. This course he rejected, quite deliberately, even at the moment when he could not subdue his forebodings about the role of the Socialist League. Measures, not men, remained his guiding motto, particularly since the Mosley episode. In all his life he never subjected his own mind to anyone else's. And yet one factor perhaps which pushed him later towards the Socialist League, despite his original caution, was his appreciation of the character of Cripps – in his estimate a cleaner and more wholesome influence in the Labour leadership than any of his competitors who had so readily accepted MacDonaldism and still connived at its survival while all the time turning to rend Mac-Donald himself with an exaggerated pretence of outrage. Cripps's approach to Socialism might be crude, but was not a crude vitality greatly preferable to cynicism and lassitude?

Stafford Cripps was the name which quickly became almost synonymous with that of the Socialist League. He was one of the few members of the old Government who kept his seat at the election and was quickly hoisted into parliamentary and national prominence. His prodigious brain-power, energy and delight in hard work, his stamp of mastery and confidence, made him within a matter of months the most magnetic figure in the Party; many were already talking of him as the obvious future leader.[9]

Today, in most of the memoirs of the orthodox leaders, Cripps's speeches of those days are smiled or frowned upon as the ravings of a political juvenile who had fallen among bad advisers – notably William Mellor, the granite-like Socialist conscience of the Socialist League, or the allegedly volatile Bevan, or the last man who had captured his ear. Cripps talked of the need for emergency powers, for superseding the slow procedures of Parliament, for abolishing the House of Lords; one day he dropped dark hints about the sinister influence of

9. *Beatrice Webb Diaries.*

Royalty and the next day he was apologizing. 'To ring the front door bell of Buckingham Palace and to run away – that is not what we expect of our revolutionaries,' wrote the *Morning Post*, in one of its last gasps of wit before it expired into amalgamation with the *Daily Telegraph* and in a more equable tone than any forthcoming from the Labour leaders in their strictures on the new upstart Robespierre. Cripps was becoming 'a dangerous political lunatic', wrote Dalton in his diary in 1933.[10] Plenty of others cursed his indiscretions and envied his soaring notoriety.

In one minor sense, the charges had some validity. Cripps *was* a political innocent. He knew little of the Labour movement, less of its history and amid all his other preoccupations had little time or inclination to repair the deficiency by a reading of Socialist literature. His Marxist slogans were undigested; he declared the class war without ever having studied the contours of the battlefield.

Yet, when all this much is admitted, the portrait of him painted by Attlee, Dalton and the others amounts to a mean falsification. They were discomfited by his virtues more than his vices, for he possessed in abounding measure the very attributes they lacked – the faculty to stir great masses by his burning sincerity combined with an even more evident capacity to subdue other assemblies by sheer intellectual power. More successfully than any great political lawyer of that age or most others Cripps carried his skill undiminished and his reputation untarnished from the Courts to the Commons. And, at the same time, ordinary men and women – especially miners – could see for themselves (what Attlee saw in 1945) that the Cripps who put the coalowners in the dock at the Gresford Colliery Disaster Inquiry was a giant and one too precious to be lost among so many pygmies. No one did more, in those dismal years after 1931, to revive the fighting spirit of Labour; the later beneficiaries of his exertions should not be so patronizing.

Moreover, the Cripps of the Socialist League had a formidable case to present which was never answered at the time and which is certainly not answered now by the plea that in the entirely unforeseen and exceptional circumstances of 1945 Labour came

10. *The Fateful Years* by Hugh Dalton.

to power without having to meet the capitalist reprisals prophesied by Cripps in the early thirties. Writing in 1934, Professor Tawney presented that case in more incisive English than Cripps ever learnt to employ. 'Onions can be eaten leaf by leaf,' he wrote, 'but you cannot skin a live tiger paw by paw.'[11] If Labour was serious in its determination to challenge capitalist society, it must show *in advance*, and in a style apparently beyond the reach and temper of the official Party leaders, a will, an awareness of the nature of the enemy and a readiness to act intrepidly during the first weeks after attaining office. This was the crux of the Socialist League's rejection of gradualism, the same in essentials which Bevan had presented in his post-1931 analysis.

The two men, Cripps and Bevan, became firm political friends and allies. A sharp contrast in temperament and tastes forbade a full intimacy; Savonarola and Benvenuto Cellini, embarked on the same ship in the Renaissance age of adventure, could still not be expected to seek out each other's company every night of the voyage. But both were in politics for a high purpose. Contrary to the Attlee fable that they were both poor judges of character, each saw in the other rare qualities of political honour and intelligence, and who now will say that either was mistaken in his perceptions?

The Socialist League's ideas were pressed at the Hastings Conference in 1933 and again, more deliberately, at Southport in 1934. At Hastings the Executive appeared to make several concessions. At Southport, armed with their own carefully drafted policy declarations, the Executive felt themselves on stronger ground and the mammoth list of seventy-five amendments put forward by the Socialist League was thrown out by large majorities. It would be unfair to say that 'gradualism' was restored in its full panoply; the Executive's declarations were more precise, practical and Socialist in tone than most of those approved in the last years of the MacDonald epoch. But the Leftward surge of the immediate post-1931 period was subsiding. True, Cripps was elected to the Executive for the first time. The argument about 'gradualism' had not ended in conclusive victory for one side or the other. And the further complication

11. *The Attack* by Professor R. H. Tawney.

was that during the years between 1931 and 1934 other developments pushed into the background the whole debate about the
Party's programme and its intentions on achieving office. In the
first Socialist League fights Bevan was on the sidelines, intervening only spasmodically. Elsewhere he was in the thick of the
battle.

Mass unemployment (in 1931 and 1932 the figure hovered around
the three million mark) and real hunger for tens of thousands of
men and women, more especially in South Wales – this was the
great presiding fact of those bitterest winters of the early thirties,
and out of it emerged the hunger marches, the clashes with the
police, the arrests and imprisonments, and the whole turbulent
spectacle of a bewildered but brave people refusing to be trampled into the status of a sub-species – the spectacle which has
stamped itself on our memories as the epitome of those ugly and
heroic days.

The other fact, so readily forgotten, is that most of these
demonstrations of protest with which liberal England tries retro-
spectively to salve its conscience were organized by the Communists. It is not true, unhappily, that the Labour Party and the
T.U.C., inspired by their anger at the MacDonald betrayal,
turned with revived energy to lead and guide the passion of revolt.
Trade union membership had sunk to less than four million, the
lowest figure recorded between the two wars. Trade union
officials were forced into a series of wage negotiations where every
hard-fought victory in mitigating the cuts bore the semblance of
a defeat. Fighting a losing battle for their own members, they
felt unable to shoulder heavy fresh responsibilities on behalf of
the unemployed.

Moreover, the attack upon them by the Communists was then
being conducted with unexampled venom. John Strachey put the
theoretical Communist case against social democracy in language
a good deal more sedate than that employed in the workshops
and outside the Labour Exchanges; even so the condemnation
was clear enough. 'The truth is,' he wrote in 1932, 'that those
very organizations of working-class revolt, which the workers
have painfully created over nearly half a century, have now passed

over almost completely to the side of capitalism. Far from being an assistance to the workers in their life-and-death struggle, they are today by far the most formidable obstacle in the way of an early victory. They force upon the workers the immediate task of recapturing these organizations, or of freeing themselves from them and developing new and reliable organs of struggle.'[12] Against such a threat it is not surprising that the union leaders developed an iron-clad hostility. Yet, whatever the reasons, the fact is indisputable. Official Labour was sluggish, wary and bureaucratically pedantic in providing leadership for the great protest against poverty and industrial decay.

From the earliest days after 1931 the National Unemployed Workers' Movement, a Communist-led body, captured the field as the leading champion of the unemployed and showed no signs of being dislodged by the feeble and tardy efforts of orthodox Labour organizations. For Aneurin Bevan, the dilemma was obviously a baffling one. To have allied himself wholeheartedly with the Communist leadership, even if he could surmount his deep-seated antagonism to their methods, would have been to invite political extinction and condemn himself to total ineffectiveness. On the other hand, to have set his face against the whole unauthorized agitation, as advised by the stream of circulars from Transport House, would have been to outrage his own political instincts and to affront and injure the large numbers of militant Socialists who were caught up in Communist-led demonstrations for lack of any other means of expressing their boiling discontents. What he did was to back many of the protest marches in South Wales and elsewhere, to speak frequently on their platforms and to give his name to petitions presented at Downing Street and Westminster; all the while he sought to keep open the channel of protest on the floor of the House of Commons and to make articulate there the furious resentment outside. He got no thanks for his pains either from the Communists or the rigid constitutionalists; each suspected and half-feared him. To Ernest Bevin, he appeared as a man who had no stomach for the fight against the usurpers in the unions. And the Communists often turned on him a fire even hotter than that

12. *The Coming Struggle for Power* by John Strachey.

directed against the orthodox; they wanted no rivals but a monopoly of Left-wing leadership.

Bevan's chief contribution to the House of Commons in those years, therefore, was a sustained onslaught on the Government's treatment of the unemployed. He was a member of the Monmouthshire Public Assistance Committee and apart from his own experience he was in intimate touch with the way the administrative machine was working or being compelled to work by the Government decrees. Several others in Labour's depleted team in the Commons had a similarly close knowledge of the problem, but none was more persistent in attack and none could relate so effectively the connection between the individual case histories and the general principles by which the Government was actuated. And always he returned to his own central theme. If Parliament washed its hands or continued to deal so meanly with 'the biggest human problem it has ever had to handle', it was not only the unemployed, but Parliament which would suffer. 'If Englishmen,' he said on one early occasion in November 1931 (and by that term he presumably meant Welshmen in particular), 'have still the courage and self-respect that have been extolled from the benches opposite, they may be driven to seek some remedy for this distress before the winter is out.'

At first, the attack was centred on the Means Test, the Government's extension of the principle from the old Poor Law that family incomes must be taken into account in deciding what help was to be given to the growing number of long-term unemployed people who had exhausted their entitlements to insurance benefit and were then moved to the 'transitional payments' category. 'The purpose of the Means Test,' he said, 'is not to discover a handful of people receiving public money when they have means to supply themselves. The purpose is to compel a large number of working-class people to keep other working-class people, to balance the Budget by taking £8 to £10 millions from the unemployed.' What a mockery it made of the Government's appeals for thrift! So meagre was the amount of a family's wealth which the Public Assistance Committees were allowed to disregard in estimating its capacity to help its unemployed members that the only result must be to make whole communities of paupers.

He himself, as we have seen, had had the experience of seeing his allowance cut because of his sister's earnings. 'If the income of sisters and brothers is to be taken into account,' he was saying on one occasion, 'it will undermine the foundation of home life in this country as nothing else will.' At this a Noble Lord opposite dared to laugh. Bevan pounced on him, recalling his own case history. 'I do not want to threaten the Noble Lord,' he cried, 'but had he been near me at that time, I would have wiped that grin off his face. We know the Noble Lord has no need to pass a means test. He and his family have thriven on the proceeds of banditry for centuries.' The words were considered unparliamentary, although even the Noble Lord did not trouble to question their historical accuracy.

The biggest parliamentary fight of all on this issue started in the autumn of 1933 when the Government at last introduced its comprehensive measure for bringing order into the inhuman, chaotic apparatus for dealing with the different categories of unemployed. Hitherto Governments had wishfully thought that huge, deep-seated unemployment might be a passing phenomenon and that patchwork devices for relief might therefore suffice. They could think so no longer and the new Bill was presumably intended to supply society's considered verdict on the proper treatment to be accorded to those who could find no work because there was none to be had. Bevan thought this measure was 'the crowning infamy', for it proposed to make permanent the worst evils of the old system and added another into the bargain. Its chief feature was the fresh legislative confirmation which it gave to the division between shorter-term and long-term unemployed. The first would still be covered by their insurance contributions, the second would come under the care of a new body, the Unemployment Assistance Board. The excuse for the differentiation, said Bevan, was insupportable; what it really meant was that, on the pretence of sustaining the insurance principle, 'you punish a man for being idle longer than his fellows'. Moreover the hated Means Test was to remain. The Bill said a man must first look to his family for support – 'a principle that eats like an acid into the homes of the poor. In the small rooms and around the meagre tables of the poor hells of personal acrimony and wounded vanities arise'. And yet, even this was not the worst of it. The new provision setting up the Unemployment Assistance Board meant that an individual objecting to harsh treatment would not be able to have his case raised by his M.P. in the House of Commons. 'This is a Bill,' said Bevan, 'to take poverty out of politics and to make the poor dumb . . . The only way for a man to protest will be to throw a brick through the window . . . You want to suffocate the unemployed man's cries in a maze of bureaucracy.'

Increasingly through his life Bevan became suspicious and jealous of bodies set up by Parliament to remove power from Parliament, and when he established his own National Health Service he insisted that the Minister in charge must be directly answerable for everything connected with the Service across the floor of the House of Commons. The strength of his devotion to that principle is revealed in the long debates over the Insurance Bill in 1933 and 1934. 'If you close the avenues of appeal between the citizen and the State in between elections,' he said, 'then you must realize that human beings are not going to have the patience to sit down in resignation for five years until they have another chance.'

The turmoil outside gave one proof of what he meant, and he coupled his attack on the Bill with many complaints about the methods used by the police in their increasingly rough exchanges with unemployed demonstrators. When the Government proposed a measure for recruiting a special type of policeman, he spoke of the dangers of transforming the police into 'janissaries who could be relied upon to carry out orders from the Government'. It was a form of Fascism to make them 'amenable to orders from the Carlton Club and Downing Street'. In November 1933 he was calling for the removal of Lord Trenchard as head of the Metropolitan Police Force.

One incident in the debates over the Insurance Bill must be recounted in some detail because of its later repercussions. Under the provisions of the Bill a man coming within the ambit of the Unemployment Assistance Board had rights of appeal first to a court of referees and finally to an umpire, but this final right was limited to persons who were members of an association of employed persons on the last date of their employment and had continued to be members. In other words, members of official unions had a special status and the union leaders were not inclined to cavil at the limitation. But some M.P.s did, a few Liberals, the three I.L.P. members and Bevan.

He riddled the whole proposition. If the existence of trade unions was necessary to protect a man's rights, then the law should protect the man who organized or joined a trade union. Yet in Nottinghamshire at that moment the mineowners were fighting a savage war against trade unionism; very few trade unionists managed to survive at the Morris works in Oxford. What became of a man's rights in such places under the Bill? In fact, there were some eight million workers in employment outside unions; were they to be denied the legislative protection accorded to others? 'I hold no brief for the National Unemployed Workers' Movement [the body most likely to be excluded from representing unemployed persons under the Bill] but I stand for the rights of a British subject to join whatever organization he likes.' Let the man himself choose who should speak for him. When Mr R. S. Hudson, the Tory Under-Secretary in charge of the Bill, explained that the Government's proposal was approved by the T.U.C. General Council, Bevan's tone changed from argument to disdain. Hudson did not cut a good figure as a defender of trade unionism and, come to that, the General Council had 'fallen pretty low' in relying on Hudson as their bulwark. It seemed that the Tories were so satisfied with the docility of the T.U.C. that they were content to give them rights denied to the N.U.W.M. But no good could come of it. 'The more the National Government smiles on the unions, the more they wither away.' The unions would do better to stand on their own feet without such sinister support.

Thus Bevan, Buchanan, Maxton and others pressed what may appear to many to have been an irrefragable case. But a few days later an ominous story was published in the *Daily Herald*. The speeches of 'two prominent trade union M.P.s' – that is, Bevan and Buchanan – had been sharply criticized by the Social Insurance Committee of the T.U.C. General Council and some action followed the criticisms. Walter Citrine, on behalf of the T.U.C., did not hesitate to report Bevan's offence to the executive of the Miners' Federation and they in turn asked Bevan for an explanation. They got a sharp answer. Bevan first repudiated the charge that he had ever voted contrary to any decision of the Miners' Federation or the T.U.C.; then he carried the war into the camp of his assailants. Did the General Council intend to ransack every Labour M.P.'s speeches and ensure their conformity with the Council's policy? If so, the issue would cut very deep; there was such a thing as parliamentary privilege. Bevan offered to appear before the Miners' executive. The hot brick was politely handed back to Citrine who promptly dropped it.

However, this for the moment was no more than a minor scuffle in comparison with the great debate which occupied the bulk of the time in the whole of the 1933-34 session. Bevan's speeches in that period took up more space in *Hansard* than those of any other Member. He translated the ferment of the distressed areas into a *tour-de-force* of parliamentary opposition.[13] Anyone wishing to study the art could find few better models than Bevan's sustained performance at that time.[14]

Unemployment and the unemployed – this remained Bevan's paramount political interest, but he branched out into many other

13. A letter in his own handwriting from his absent leader, George Lansbury, then in hospital, showed that Bevan's parliamentary performance was appreciated by some, even if the General Council of the T.U.C. was ill-informed about events at Westminster. 'I am so glad,' wrote George Lansbury, 'you have been doing your bit and doing it splendidly. All through this session you and the others made me feel very proud. I hope you will continue carrying the fight into the enemy's camp ... I do want you to know your work and that of Willie Cove and the rest has cheered many a lonely vigil ...' Bevan, for a short period, had acted as George Lansbury's Parliamentary Private Secretary. It was not his role. He was probably the worst P.P.S. in the history of Parliament.

14. It was one evening after a debate on this Bill that I first met Aneurin Bevan. Thereafter I knew him as well as almost anybody else for the rest of his life. He was never a hero-worshipper; but I was. All I can recall of that first meeting is a diatribe against the newspapers for the manner in which they were reporting – or failing to report – the detailed, but important, debates on the Committee Stage. How could Parliament be the national sounding board that it ought to be when its voice was drowned by the vulgar cacophony preferred by the popular press? I did my best to defend the journalistic profession, invoking the sacred but irrelevant names of Swift, Cobbett, Hazlitt and Blatchford. But it wasn't easy. And in those days the press reported Parliament more fully than today.

fields and the opportunities in that Parliament were much greater than ever come the way of most young M.P.s. Members of the little band of fewer than fifty Labour M.P.s could speak almost whenever they wanted. The leadership was in the hands of a triumvirate. George Lansbury proved a more successful Mark Antony than anyone could have expected, Cripps was the perfect Octavius, cold, remorseless in the pursuit of his enemies and never deflected from his argument, while Lepidus, in the guise of Major C. R. Attlee, performed his errands with such peremptory agility and despatch that he soon seemed to make himself indispensable. It was probably the happiest collaboration that Labour had ever known at the top, and the example of full-scale aggression against the Tories helped to induce a spirit of comradeship along the back benches. Bevan might have difficulties with the authorities outside, but inside the House of Commons he had every encouragement to choose a wide variety of topics.

He mocked the Liberals who had helped to present the façade of national unity by joining the Government and prophesied their fate: 'the Liberals will be kicked out into the political wilderness and no man will want to know whether they have anything to eat or drink or wear; the job will be done and Great Britain will be handed over to the most reactionary Conservative Government of modern times.' He talked about agriculture, excusing himself on the grounds that he couldn't know less about the subject than the agriculturalists who talked about coal; Walter Elliot, the unorthodox Minister of Agriculture, he described as 'a man walking backwards with his face to the future'. On the affairs of the countryside and the drift of industry to the Midlands and the South, he could argue more feelingly. He hated 'the red rash' of London and 'the architectural leprosy' that was devastating areas once green and lovely. Big cities were always one of his *bêtes noires* – 'huge ulcers which are gradually sucking in the whole population and making a wilderness of meaningless streets'. Steel was another of his leading interests; with the old Ebbw Vale works still silent and motionless it was bound to be, but his concern always embraced the national as well as the local interest. Steel must surely be one of the pillars of a thriving economy; yet, to his mind, it was always discussed as a field for pillage. When the Tories produced their plan to give the industry protection, he was quite unimpressed; 'you are simply building a wall around chaos and there will be as much chaos inside the tariff wall as there is in the wall itself'. On one occasion when he had foretold the failure of the Government's policies in terms even more doleful than usual, a young Tory M.P. described him as an ungenial Cassandra. 'He enjoys prophesying the imminent fall of the capitalist system,' said Harold Macmillan, 'and is prepared to play a part, any part, in its burial, except that of mute.'

Mostly he returned to his grand theme – the economics of democracy. Either poverty would use its newly gained democracy to subdue the rights of property or property would strangle democracy amid its failure to abolish poverty and its fear of the demands of the poor. The real disease was here at home in their midst, a disease of British society. When he was invited to look abroad for remedies, to World Economic Conferences and the possibilities of creating order by international confabulations, he asked in return: how can you have order abroad and anarchy at home? 'If you want to find the cause of your modern difficulties, you must look for it in the relationship between the modern employer and the modern wage earner.' That challenge was as old as Karl Marx but still more up to date than Maynard Keynes. When presented with the latest measures to bring special aid to the Distressed Areas (renamed 'Special Areas' in a flight of inspiration by the House of Lords), he was contemptuous. It was impossible to solve the problems of Wales or Durham independently of the economy as a whole; the solution must involve a control over property rights on the roads out of Birmingham and London. Without that, Special Area Bills did little more than 'colour-wash the tombstones in the cemeteries which the Distressed Areas have become'.

Above all, he could not tolerate the piety and the preaching of those who voted so effortlessly to sustain the system which produced these palpable inhumanities. 'I have never regarded politics as the arena of morals,' he said. 'It is the arena of interests.' Nothing he saw in the Parliament of 1931 was likely to alter that old Marxist conviction of his youth. When bankers or finance houses as far away as Newfoundland or Austria were in difficulties, loans were voted for their salvation in a matter of hours; but night after night he had had to argue about every penny due to the people drawing transitional benefits. 'The Tories,' he said, 'always hold the view that the State is an apparatus for the protection of the swag of the property owners. They are true to that today in this House, and they instruct the Minister of Labour to punish the unemployed person, to depress his standards of livelihood, to pursue him and ship him abroad whenever possible by the most malignly conceived regulations, but they put the whole resources of the State behind the bondholders and the rich when they get into difficulties. Christ drove the moneychangers out of the temple, but you inscribe their title deeds on the altar cloth.' Often he was confronted with the plea that the society which tolerated these injustices must be sustained in the name of freedom. Was it not Aneurin Bevan and those who fought with him against the Insurance Bill who had the truer faith in freedom and a truer knowledge of how the bureaucracy of the Unemployment Assistance Board so gravely invaded it? 'It is the individual, not the mass, who desires to be defended,' he cried, 'it is the individual who is oppressed, it is the individual who is helpless, it is the individual who has no appeal. It is that very individual who appeals to a tribunal – which meets in camera and has none of the force of public opinion raised against it – a helpless man, who has no chance of presenting his case to the public or of mobilizing public opinion, and you call that protection.'

That speech was made in December 1934. A few days later the newly established Unemployment Assistance Board produced its first regulations. Having worked coolly and objectively on the task, freed from ignorant parliamentary pressure, it brought forward proposals which – almost unintentionally, perhaps – meant a cut in benefits for a large number of applicants. The last state was to be worse than the first.

It is necessary to retrace our steps over the years 1933 and 1934. Nothing could diminish the dominance which the unemployment problem played in Aneurin Bevan's life at the time. By 1934 the figures were falling in many areas; in the Ebbw Vale constituency they remained obstinately stuck at just under fifty per cent. But other events were now merging with the economic crisis itself. Interweaving with the controversies about the domestic and industrial situation they helped to impel him into another row with the leadership – this time with Ernest Bevin wielding the full weight of his formidable hammer.

In January of 1933 Adolf Hitler came to power in Germany; in February the Reichstag was ablaze; within a matter of weeks the evil news was spreading across Europe. Communists and Socialists were falling beneath the same lash, being kicked by the same jackboots, and the old, oft-debated, oft-spurned proposal for a united front between them to resist the onslaught suddenly appeared in a new context. A formal approach was made by the Communist International to the Executive of the Labour and Socialist International. In Britain the Communist Party and the I.L.P. came close to agreeing on a programme of common action and both approached the Labour Party. They were promptly given the dustiest of answers. Labour's Executive issued a special declaration, *Democracy versus Dictatorship*, not merely rejecting the Communist approach but insisting that no real distinction could be drawn between the Soviet and Nazi forms of totalitarianism. Both must be covered under the same sweeping clause of ban and anathema.

But this edict did not satisfy many of those in the Labour Party most deeply shaken by the news from Germany. All over the country *ad hoc* meetings of local parties and trades councils were called to discuss the new situation – one of them in Cardiff in May. Bevan was a chief speaker. 'The triumph of reaction in Germany,' he said, 'was made possible by bitter rivalries and competing organizations among workers. I don't believe we are bound to go through Fascism here because the governing class will be helpless against an organized and courageous working class.' But did the leaders contemplate the necessary organization and had they the courage? That meeting in Cardiff, like others elsewhere, broke up in disorder. The official directive from Transport House was bitterly contested. Bevan had a quarrel with the chairman and after the official meeting in the Cory Hall had ended led a band of delegates, including Communists and I.L.P.ers, in a march across Cardiff to find somewhere else to meet and discuss more militant action for the future. Several projects for action outside the ambit of the official machine were considered. The man who took the minutes at this rebel gathering was Mr Len Williams, later General Secretary of the Labour Party.

The immediate result of this row was that Bevan took the initiative in organizing what he called, somewhat pompously, the Workers' Freedom Group. The Query Club which had turned Tredegar upside down in the twenties had continued to operate in the early thirties, and now the plan was to extend its influence on a more ambitious scale. Starting at Tredegar and spreading to a few of the neighbouring towns Query Club members helped to organize small groups of young people who came together at the week-ends for the combined purpose of political instruction and physical training. The idea derived some of its inspiration from the *Schutzbund* in Vienna, the workers' para-military organiza- tion which was drilling to resist the menace of Fascism. The Tredegar Workers' Freedom Group acquired no weapons; it rented a room above an old tavern and performed its physical training in long route marches across the Welsh mountains. Bevan strode ahead, exhorting and expounding his own brand of Marxism to his young disciples. Needless to say, he had not worried about associating with young Communists in these bizarre activities and he, therefore, brought down on his head a rebuke from Transport House. 'The National Executive Com- mittee,' he was told, 'is charged by the movement to apply the organization laid down in our rules and it naturally must take interest in the creation of machinery not provided for in the rules and which may, or may not, conflict with it.' Bevan brushed aside their protests and the groups continued to operate for several months. The Workers' Freedom Group played no decis- ive role in British history. But it does give a glimpse into the gulf which divided South Wales from London.[15] Socialists in

15. The atmosphere of the time may perhaps best be indicated by quoting the document which Bevan devised as the Groups' manifesto:

South Wales really did believe that they might see Fascist jack-boots in operation within a few years. No imagination is needed to realize how they must have scoffed at the warnings from the National Executive.

Bevan also participated in more orthodox conferences with unorthodox associates during the next few months and the same issue emerged at the meeting of the T.U.C. in September which he attended as a miners' delegate. Walter Citrine presented the General Council's report on events in Germany. It was a well-marshalled tabulation of the facts, repudiating any idea of association with the Communists and hinting at the theory which became a feature for a period of official Labour's attitude to the new phenomenon in Europe. Extremism on the Right was the response to extremism on the Left; hence, in one sense, extremism on the Left was the source of all the trouble. The theory fitted nicely with the General Council's previous predilections;

WORKERS' FREEDOM GROUPS
(Provisional Title)

To form workers' groups in every locality under a group leader who will dedicate themselves to the following causes:

1. To defend liberty in every form in the certain belief that capitalism is the enemy of liberty and that as the workers learn to use the instruments of democracy more effectively, capitalism will use force against democracy and that the workers will be called upon to defend it by force.

2. To make war on the second enemy of democracy, corruption and negligence, and to cleanse and keep clean all those democratic organizations by means of which the workers hope to achieve the New Society.

3. To keep a vigilant watch on the liberties and rights won by a century long struggle for the workers and to defend them against the encroachments which are already taking place.

4. To promote all forms of working-class resistance to a lower standard of life and to vitalize all institutions which serve the workers, such as trade unions, co-operative societies, etc.

5. To encourage and organize physical training among the workers in readiness to meet any demands that may be made upon them.

6. To form First Aid Units in every group whose duty it will be to succour all workers, victimized, persecuted or in distress, and to ensure that no worker is defrauded of his or her legal rights.

7. To organize working-class resistance to war for war is the death of liberty, and with the death of liberty the worker loses life.

8. To organize clubs in association with every group, or federation of groups, and to raise funds for all group purposes.

9. To encourage the dignity and self-reliance of all workers in the conviction that they, and they alone, can redeem human society.

not merely did it underline the menace of Communism but it also seemed to offer a plausible defence for comparative quiescence. By the same reckoning, might not diffidence on the Left encourage diffidence on the Right? Fascism could not happen here in our relatively stable society – in a country where we all played football together.

Bevan admitted the plausibility of Citrine's speech and then denounced it as 'the most dangerous' he had 'ever heard'. Citrine, he alleged, was taking his stand on the ability of capitalism to recover. He himself was much more alarmist. As unemployment and poverty grew, democracy would be attacked from the Right, not the Left. It was capitalism which was incompatible with democracy, not Socialism. 'Hitlerism is the defence of capitalism by violence when democracy threatens capitalism.' He called on the Congress to send out a message to the working classes of the world that here in Britain we were going to defend democracy by using democracy. That meant the repudiation of the gospel of quiescence; indeed, the leaders, if they looked, might find in this gospel the reason why union membership had fallen to the pitiable figure of three and a half million. If young men kicking their heels in idleness at street corners – in Britain as in Germany – were getting cynical about democracy, the right answer was not to offer academic lectures about its virtues in comparison with dictatorship but to use the weapon to win economic gains; then democracy would win an affectionate place in the people's hearts.

It was more an argument about moods than precise policies. Bevan had not defined what he meant by industrial action and militancy and Citrine made the most of the omission. Bevan had not specifically declared for the United Front which was defeated overwhelmingly on another resolution. He knew the doctrine of quiescence was defeatist yet saw no clear opening for an effective assault upon it. To him the touching faith of working-class leaders in their rulers – particularly the authors of the Unemployment Bill – was an abomination. Their phlegmatic reaction to mighty events was a sign of decadence, the same streak of decadence which had helped to produce the horrific outcome in Munich and Berlin. 'Political toleration,' he had said in the

House of Commons a little while before, 'is a by-product of the complacency of the ruling class. When that complacency is disturbed there never was a more bloody-minded set of thugs than the British ruling class.' He would not abate by one jot his hostility to the domestic foe he had been fighting all his life. Hitlerism in those days, to him and to most other militant Social-ists, was seen, not as a military menace from abroad, but as a warning of what might happen here if British democrats showed the same meekness as the German democrats.

The new year brought another warning and an example. The heroic battle of Vienna, when the Austrian Socialists went down fighting before the Dollfuss dictatorship, awakened a bigger response on the Left than even the German catastrophe. And, in July, French Socialists and Communists agreed to establish their United Front, with the Spanish Socialists and Communists following suit in September. The mood was changing on the Continent and might do so here, despite the insignificance of the British Communist Party compared with its continental counter-parts. In any case what Bevan was looking for was not so much a formal unity with the Communists but the new upsurge of fighting spirit which might come from an unqualified recognition that the only real enemy was on the Right – and a more desperate enemy than the leaders seemed to appreciate. He could get no comfort from a new edict from the Executive that spring, issued for the purpose of checking the *ad hoc* joint activities between Labour Party members, Communists and I.L.P.ers then sprout-ing up in so many parts of the country. The National Executive was convinced that 'loose association with the Communist Party is just as dangerous to the interests of the Labour Party as is Communist membership itself'. It therefore promulgated the decree: 'That United Action with the Communist Party or organizations ancillary or subsidiary thereto without the sanction of the National Executive Committee is incompatible with membership of the Labour Party.' It gave warning that it would seek authority at the next Party Conference for 'full disciplinary powers' for dealing with 'any cases that may arise'.

Bevan had become more and more implicated in these activi-ties. He had written specially to Arthur Henderson, Secretary of the Party, and Walter Citrine, Secretary of the T.U.C., urging that they should take the initiative in organizing demonstrations. When these proposals were turned down, he felt more than ever that he could not be confined by official edicts. He had given his full backing to the hunger march organized earlier in the year. He joined with those who were forming anti-Fascist organizations. That summer, immediately after his gruelling session in the House of Commons on the Insurance Bill, he went to America to raise money for a body called the Committee for the Relief of the Victims of German Fascism. The Committee had been formed by a number of people of different political complexions, including Communists. Jennie Lee was a member of it and she had persuaded him to go. Instead of a short visit to New York, as originally intended, he found himself travelling from coast to coast. He found too that the American branch of the organization was more strongly controlled by the Communists than its British section. But no matter; the cause was good and he raised plenty of money. He returned to England more persuaded than ever that the attitude of both the National Executive of the Party and the General Council did not match the level of the events in Europe any more than it reflected the growing exasperation in the valleys of South Wales.

The issue became the first point of clash between the Left and the leadership at the Southport Conference in 1934 – the same Conference at which Cripps and the Socialist League had decided to challenge with their seventy-five amendments what they considered to be the 'gradualist' philosophy implicit in the official policy. First, Harold Laski challenged the action taken by the Executive in proscribing the Relief Committee for the Victims of German Fascism as a Communist body. He was sharply rebuked by Herbert Morrison whom he had described as the 'High Archbishop of Orthodoxy'. Bevan's speech on this occasion is worth studying, not as a piece of oratory, but for the evidence it offers of the Left-wing's frustrated attitude towards the leadership outside Parliament in the era of the hunger marches and the first years of Hitlerism. He spoke thus:

I want to draw the attention of delegates to the language of the Executive's recommendation. You will see that it says: 'The power of the National Executive Committee in dealing with members of the Labour Party who are also members of the listed organizations is quite clear, but it is felt that the Committee should be able to take action where members of the Labour Party associate themselves with the Listed Organizations in "United Front" or other agitations without authority from annual Party Conference or the National Executive Committee to do so.'

In the past the Party has limited itself to saying what a man shall not do. In the future, the Party is going to decide what he shall do. You have not merely a negative limitation of certain activities, but you have a positive statement that men shall not undertake any propaganda on their own initiative without first of all getting the permission of the National Executive.

Now that is an intolerable situation for any member of any political party. We are informed that in the future it is not membership of an organization which is wrong, but *association* with members of pro-scribed organizations.

I am not a member of any of the proscribed organizations, but I have associated myself in *ad hoc* activities – in activities for special matters from time to time. Where an organization has invited me to go on the platform for a special job in which I have believed, I have felt it my duty to co-operate with them. In the future, however, if I speak on the platform with a member of the Communist Party, then I am immediately associating with a proscribed organization; but if I speak on a platform with a Tory I am not.

There is no mention in this document of the League of Nations Union. The members of the Executive, the leaders of the Party, can – to use Mr Morrison's words – confuse the minds of the rank-and-file by appearing on the platform with leading members of the Conservative Party, and nothing is done. But if we appear on the platform with members of the Communist Party in the carrying out of Labour propaganda, we are to be subject to expulsion without even a Party Conference considering the matter at all.

Where is the Executive going to stop? Are they going to expel Mr Lansbury and Major Attlee and Mr Wall for associating with Communist members on the Council for Civil Liberties? Are they going to expel themselves from the Second International for associating with the French Party which has formed a united front with the Communist Party?

I ask myself, what has happened in the course of this year to warrant a change of this kind? I have heard from nowhere what has happened to cause such a drastic change in the policy of the Party. There was in the beginning of this year, quite rightly, a hunger march. I associated myself with that hunger march, and I say quite frankly that it would not have been necessary for me to have associated myself with a demonstration against the Unemployment Insurance Bill if the Executive had done its job.

I want to put on record my view about this, and to say to comrades that a great deal of activity which is being undertaken by many of these committees, in which some of us are participating, would never have been necessary were it not for the inertia, lack of enterprise and insipidity of the Executive between Conferences, and I express what is the point of view of the rank-and-file of this organization.

I have been asked frequently at meetings in this country, why is it that the Executive Committee are always falling behind the Communist Party in the organization of demonstrations? The same was true of the Dimitroff Committee. There was not a more splendid example of working-class courage than the courage of Dimitroff. Who organized the Committee of Inquiry in London? The organization which has been banned this morning.

Our case is that these organizations are not being banned, that our activities are not being frowned upon by the Executive because we associate in the carrying-out of them with members of the Communist Party. These activities are being frowned upon because they bring into bold relief the incapacity of the Party leadership in the face of the situation.

What is the purpose of the disciplinary measures – this government by caucus and cabal instead of by democracy? It is not for the purpose of preventing us from associating ourselves with members of pro-scribed organizations, it is in order to bring about in the Party itself a goose-step, to prevent us from engaging in any form of activity which has not first of all received the blessing of the Executive Committee.

I tell you there is no difficulty with men like me at all. I have not caused embarrassment to any Labour candidate or member, but I do say to you most solemnly that the responsibility for many things that are happening in Great Britain at the present time, and within our Party, rests upon the Committee, because they have not faced up to the problems of the workers of this country.

In conclusion I beg the Conference not to give these formidable powers to the Executive; they are too vague and ambiguous. If you are going to expel a man from this Party merely because he meets Gibarti, or Muenzenberg, or talks to Harry Pollitt, as Mr Morrison said this morning – if you do that then this Party will get itself laughed out of court.

Ernest Bevin was not a member of the Executive, but he quickly rushed to their aid, if they needed it.

A previous speaker [he recalled] had said that the Communist Party was an insignificant party. It would not have been if you gentlemen had had your way; we would have been split like Germany was split. And if you do not keep down the Communists you cannot keep down the Fascists. It is no use criticizing our friends on the Continent when they failed at the critical moment to maintain discipline as we propose to do now. That is where they went wrong, and they got eaten out and undermined; and when they had to take action, half their members were in one party and the other half were in the other party. Bevan tells us we did not do right on the Unemployment Act. Did he do right when he got up in the House of Commons and tried to let the Fascists in and supported everybody going to the Courts of Referees to the detriment of the trade union movement?

This, of course, was a reference to controversy in the Commons, of the previous February, when Bevan had supported the right of every unemployed man to choose his own spokesman before the umpire. 'Trying to let the Fascists in' was a somewhat tendentious description of the support he had given to a Liberal amendment at that time. Bevan rose on a point of order. He challenged Ernest Bevin to debate the issue with him on any public platform in Great Britain. 'This *is* a public platform,' cried one delegate and Bevin pounded on:

Apparently my namesake – spelt differently – can get on this platform and denounce the National Council of Labour, he can denounce the Labour Party and he is so thin-skinned that he cannot take his medicine back again. No, in this Conference, Aneurin Bevan, you are not going to get the flattery of the gossip columns that you get in London. You are going to get facts. I am stating the case – that when the trade unions had fought their damnedest to try and deal with this unemployment problem, had carried more responsibility than any other body in the country, that was the moment when in the House of Commons this loyalty was displayed . . .

Soon the fur was flying. Emanuel Shinwell, at that time candidate for Seaham, rallied to the support of the Executive. 'I know,' he said, 'that much of the confusion that exists in the minds of the rank-and-file is due to the innuendoes and insinuations of men like Aneurin Bevan. If Bevan or anyone else believes that the Party is insipid and lacking in courage . . . then in my judgement they ought to join the party or organization which they believe has got the attributes that the Labour Party ought to have.' When others replied to these dissentients, 'they squeal about personalities, forgetting that they are insulting us all the while'. Then he put his finger on 'the real trouble' – 'the inferiority complex, as I understand it, of certain would-be leaders of the Party'.

Herbert Morrison wound up the debate with his verdict on 'individuals in the Party who think they are greater than the Party as a whole'. The Executive must be armed with the necessary authority to 'prevent individuals really being disloyal to Party decisions and prevent them doing things that they ought not to be doing on their own initiative'. He won a huge majority against the reference back of the Executive's report – by 1,820,000 votes to 89,000.

The scene could stand by itself without comment.[16] But undoubtedly it played its part in the course of action which Bevan chose over the years ahead. Bevin's reply, whatever the provocation, might seem gratuitously boorish; that could be borne; it was Bevin's way. But he also showed an ignorance of the real temperature in the Welsh valleys and a complete unawareness of the long contested battle in the House of Commons. Bevan had been the foremost spokesman of the Party against the Government's Unemployment Bill through all its stages; but that counted for nothing compared with his single trespass against official trade union wisdom – a point on which the opinion of most democrats might favour Bevan rather than Bevin. A curiosity of the dispute was that Ernest Bevin, the stickler for constitutionalism and parliamentary democracy

16. Mr Alan Bullock, in his official biography of Ernest Bevin, describes Bevin's Southport attack – 'he had not forgiven Bevan for cutting across the lines of the trade union case in the House of Commons debates on the Unemployment Bill' – without mentioning the cause of the dispute or Bevan's role on the rest of the Bill. He quotes a part of Bevin's speech, but omits the sentence: 'Did he [Bevan] do right when he got up in the House of Commons and tried to let the Fascists in . . . ?' This no doubt makes it easier for him to pass judgement that 'Bevin spoke roughly, but Aneurin Bevan's intervention had invited it . . .' The point has some importance, because Bevan was often accused of being anti-trade union. He was a strong trade unionist all his life, but he was opposed to trade union bureaucracies arrogating to themselves privileges which infringed the most elementary rights of the citizen. To insist that an unemployed man must be denied his right to appeal to the Umpire about his benefit if his trade union membership had lapsed he considered to be just such an unwarranted assumption of privilege. What, I wonder, does Mr Bullock think?

against totalitarian methods, often revealed such a contempt for Parliament. Bevan believed in vigorous opposition in Parliament and vigour to sustain it outside. Bevin, it seemed to him, believed in neither and yet offered no coherent alternative; he was much too perpetually obsessed with the maintenance of power within the bureaucracy of the unions and he overlooked the fact that it was this obsession, pursued to the point of excluding more positive action, which was a chief cause of the threats to the leadership from the Left.

So Bevan, to understate the case, derived no inspiration from the great men at the head of the Labour movement. His irreverence extended even to them. During the fiasco of the 1929–31 Parliament they had mostly sat mute and contented themselves with berating those who dared to speak out. Subsequently their chief interest seemed to lie in reaching for their disciplinary daggers as if they were Excaliburs for exorcizing the dragon of Fascism. Neither Ernest Bevin's bombast nor the card-index mind of Walter Citrine ('poor fellow,' said Bevan, 'he suffers from files') could awaken the national response which the times required. And with the heavy defeat of the whole alternative programme advanced by Cripps and the Socialist League, the prospect looked the more gloomy. Worst of all was the revelation of Ernest Bevin's mind about the causes of the disaster in Germany. Could anyone really believe that it was due to a failure to maintain discipline within the social democratic parties? That is what he said. But was it not much more due to the pettiness of the rigid disciplinarians who could think of little else?

6 The Man

Be ye conscious possessors of the blessed power you contain within yourselves. But do you never forget that this power is no more exempt than other virtuous impulses from weakening and disappearing if it be not carried into action.

That which humanity needs, to be saved from all pessimistic negation, is not so much a belief that all is well at present, as the faith that it is possible through life's growth to arrive at a better state, hastened and discovered by the actions of men. Such faith in the future, belief in the efficacy of human energy, are the necessary condition of all strong action and all fecund thought.

Try, then, to develop so far as possible not any single aspect, but the plentitude of your being . . . Be attentive spectators where you may not be actors.

Even in material servitude, there is a way to keep free one's inner self, the self of reason and feeling. So never do you try to justify, by your absorption in labour, the enslaving of your soul.

Believe me, an educated sense of what is beautiful is the most efficacious collaborator in the forming of a delicate sense of justice. No better instrument exists to dignify, to ennoble the mind.

Care for one's own independence, personality, judgement, is a chief form of self-respect.   JOSÉ ENRIQUE RODO[1]

ANEURIN BEVAN might have become embittered by his early frictions with the Labour leaders, and it would be foolish to say that he never did. His most natural propensity always was to question authority, to test the dogmas of the experts, to expose 'the mandarins', as he called them, who presumed to dictate to their fellow human beings. There was no reason he could see why Labour leaders should be excluded from this astringent scrutiny. When they hit back, he was not surprised and he did not whine. He was merely confirmed in his suspicion about their general

1. From *Ariel* by José Enrique Rodo (published by Houghton Mifflin Company, 1922).

inadequacy. He did not bear long grudges; often he restored excellent relations with those who once had been his firmest opponents and might become so again. Occasionally, he unleashed his invective in a style which could make an enemy for life or turn away a friend. More frequently, with his friends, he employed a ferocious, satirical banter; 'he was the only person I ever knew,' said one, 'who could make a curse sound like a caress.' But often he was bitter, bitter at what he considered to be wonderful opportunities for leadership lost. It was not a small, waspish acrimony; it was more a splendid scorn.

In those early days in Parliament, however, he had little enough time to spare for personal irritations. While he always carried with him the knowledge of what was happening to his own people and never allowed any company he was in to forget it, he could not help finding the world a most exciting place. His own prodigious self-education had prepared him to make the most of it. And now new realms of gold in literature, in art, in music and philosophical argument, the most developed of his tastes, were spreading before him. He took an almost sensuous pleasure in exercising his own mind. His secret then which remained with him throughout his life, the cause of his perpetual imaginative freshness, was that he could escape from the thraldom of politics to other quite unsuspected fields. He wanted a world of light and gaiety and beauty for everyone else and he wanted it for himself.

So he was unlike most people who make politics their profession, and many resented it. He never kept press cuttings. He made no effort to ingratiate himself with a potential ally in Fleet Street. The eager hand-shake, the ever-ready smile of the perpetual election candidate were no part of his equipment. When a disciple urged him to give some thought to winning friends and influencing people, he retorted: 'What do you want me to be, a political gigolo?' All the hundred little ways in which politicians seek to push themselves another rung up the ladder, he despised and derided. To another friend who reported that he had spent a heavy week in his constituency involved in Rotarian lunches and Chamber of Commerce dinners, he exclaimed, '—, my boy; you're not an M.P., you're a gastronomic pimp.'

Some called his fascination with interests outside his profession indolence; others called it arrogance. Both accusations were wide of the mark. He could do no other; this was how he was made. All the minutiae of politics bored him. His mind was formed in an entirely different mould and you could no more change it than persuade him to disown his working-class ancestry. His eyes were fixed on the horizons of politics. He was obsessed by the broad, tumultuous movements in society and the world at large. Marxism had appealed to him, not only because it seemed to explain accurately the politics on his own doorstep, but also because of its sweeping and spacious visions. Ideas were his passion and he was interested in power as the vehicle for ideas. Ernest Bevin might condemn him as an intellectual; Bevan could win the interchange by refusing to despise the intellect.

Very few others with a comparable mental outlook, not merely from working-class homes but from the whole range of society, find their way to Westminster, much less succeed when they get there. They become instead painters, musicians or poets. Bevan had politics in his blood, but he could not live on it. Increasingly, he had to turn for sustenance to painting, music and poetry, to the theatre and ballet. Before his arrival in London, José Rodo, the great South American philosopher, little known in this country, had first opened his eyes to the aesthetic world. Now, charged with the task of buying books for the library back in Tredegar, he could expand his own reading and guide the instruction of the young at the same time. He could explore the museums and libraries and often remarked on the many desirable activities which could be had for nothing. 'Knowledge,' he said, 'is the one armoury they can't deny us.' He read to equip himself for the battle. And, more and more, he read for sheer delight.

He made some curious friends too or at least curious to those who thought that so adamant a Socialist should have no dealings with people outside his own Party. One was Frank Owen, the young Liberal M.P. for Hereford whom Bevan had first met as a reporter on the *South Wales Argus*. The two matched one another in zest, curiosity and a love for life. Soon after they became M.P.s in 1929, they set up house together in a mews above a garage in the Cromwell Road. Their landlord happened to be a Conservative Member of the House, who liked to complain that they were sometimes late in paying their two pounds a week rent. He would send a note to them across the Smoking Room, and they would retaliate by accusing him of being guilty of a breach of privilege. The exchange was not serious. Bevan might behave in a lordly manner, but 'keeping the tradesmen waiting' was never one of his vices.

Frank Owen, from intimate knowledge, was always ready to deride those who made the charge of laziness. True, Nye hated getting up early in the morning. One simple reason, says Frank, was that he had often been up all night devouring books. True, also, he liked a first-class meal occasionally and was ready to pay for it by going short the rest of the week. Often he joked: 'You can always live like a millionaire for five minutes.' The Café Royal became one of his haunts when he could afford it. There he tested his individual knowledge against all comers and cultivated his taste for companions quite outside the battlefield of politics. Jacob Epstein and Matthew Smith were two among this number; Will Dyson, the most savage and compassionate of modern cartoonists, was a third. When Will Dyson died Nye was grief-stricken. Standing at his own fireside he took a glass in his hand, toasted his friend and then threw it in the dying embers. The gesture might be false in another man but sprang naturally from his temperament. Sometimes Jennie Lee went with him on these carefree jaunts. 'Going around with Nye in those early days when we still hardly knew one another,' says Jennie, 'was at times like surf riding on Niagara Falls. You had to be agile or you would be drowned in the sparkling, tireless movement and ebullience.'

Another early friend was Edward Marjoribanks, the Tory stepson of the first Lord Hailsham, who so tragically committed suicide a few years later. It was he who introduced him to Lord Beaverbrook just after Bevan had made his famous attack on Lloyd George in 1930. Marjoribanks recognized genius when he heard it and rightly believed that Beaverbrook would be fascinated by the phenomenon. The association with Beaverbrook quickly grew into a friendship lasting for many years, and when the rumour spread that Bevan frequently dined with Beelzebub in person, many grave eyebrows were raised and many whisperers were ready to mock him as a hypocrite. But there was no real mystery. Beaverbrook's household bore little enough resemblance to what the outside world thought of as West End society; it was rather a private Hyde Park Corner, with many of the best debaters and arguers in the land proclaiming their contradictory creeds from well-upholstered soap-boxes.

Few holds were barred; no one was ever expected to speak anything but his mind; that was the only law. Beaverbrook and Bevan, although occasionally exchanging political advice offered and accepted with mutual caution, agreed politically about nothing – except the right of free speech. But there Bevan met in the flesh some of the heroes of his youth, H. G. Wells, Arnold Bennett and more, for Beaverbrook's company was the most catholic in the kingdom. Wells and Bevan got on like a house on fire; they were fellow crusaders in that foreign land, ever ready to lay their sacrilegious hands on Beaverbrook's sacred cause of Splendid Isolation, or, more agreeably for their host, to sound the trumpet of Covenanting Republicanism to the consternation of Cavalier guests. Once Bevan and Wells found themselves together when a truly peppery empire-building colonel had just left the room. 'I've written about that type,' said Wells, 'but I never really believed they existed.'

One in that company who loomed larger than life was Lord Castlerosse. Since wit could recognize no class distinction, Bevan became friends with him too. Another frequent visitor was Brendan Bracken, Churchill's Man Friday, who would stride up and down the room, waving his arms like a partly domesticated orang-outang and pouring out his abuse on the unbowed head of Bevan. 'You're just a *Bollinger* Bolshevik,' jeered Bracken one night as they sipped Beaverbrook's champagne. 'Why shouldn't I like good wine?' answered Bevan. 'The best I ever had from *you*, by the way, Brendan, I'd call bottom lower-class *Bolshevik* Bollinger.' Bevan could enjoy all the good things rich hosts could provide. He had his own paraphrase of a verse from Ecclesiasticus about the rich men who 'eat up the poor': 'Stand not too near the rich man lest he destroy thee – and not too far away lest he forget thee.'[2] It was all part of his gleeful mockery.

Certainly it was strange company, the most bizarre, incongruous and combative in London. Bevan learnt a lot from what he called 'slumming in the West End'. But no one in his senses who witnessed the scene ever suggested that he was being seduced by the aristocratic embrace; the few real live aristocrats who ever crossed Beaverbrook's threshold had to take pot luck in the polemics, and Bevan's adventures in those quarters were more like forays in proletarian espionage.

That no public compromises were implied or fostered by these private courtesies was shown in an article which appeared in Beaverbrook's *Daily Express* in July 1932. It described Bevan as 'brilliant, bitter, proud, class conscious, boastful of his ancestry and his family'. He was held to be guilty of 'a kind of class consciousness quite as objectionable as it is in the man who boasts of his Norman blood'. He was 'a dangerous fellow ... with every intention of tearing down the pillars of society if he can. He can hardly enter a railway train because there is no fourth class.' Bevan replied in an article a few days later. He admitted 'my heart is full of bitterness. For when I see the well-nourished bodies of the wealthy I see also the tired, haggard faces of my own people.' Yes, he was proud of being born the son of a miner. 'But there are better reasons for being proud of belonging to the working classes. It is better to have a future than a past. There is no imposing future for the present rulers of England. Too many hungry generations tread them down.' As for the charge that he was 'a menace to the capitalist system', his ambition was to prove it true. Clearly neither Beaverbrook nor Bevan was ever foolish enough to suppose that he could deflect the political faith of the other.

But this attachment and others he formed in widening circles were trivial compared with a quite different influence which now moulded his life. On 11 September 1934 the announcement was made that he had become engaged to be married to Jennie Lee.

2. The actual verse reads thus: 'Beware that thou be not deceived, and brought down in thy jollity ... Press thou not upon him, lest thou be put back; stand not far off, lest thou be forgotten.'

Both were sceptical of the institution of marriage with all the enveloping conventions which bourgeois society imposes; but both were eager not to offend the nonconformist susceptibilities of families and constituents. Hence the formal engagement announcement. 'So she's accepted you at last,' said Archie Lush, when Aneurin broke the sensational news to his old friend and prospective best man. 'Where's the wedding going to take place?' 'Where do you think?' answered Aneurin. 'You don't suppose we could take *you* to a church, do you?' On 24 October 1934, the ceremony took place at Holborn Registry Office.[3] Reporters noted that both arrived hatless and gloveless and that the bride was given no wedding ring. Nye enjoyed teasing Jennie even many years later that she had cost him two guineas; he had bought a special licence in the hope of avoiding press photographers. But they were there in force. Then and throughout the whole of their lives they both waged incessant war against the attempt of the press to intrude into matters of no public concern. Bevan always believed that along with all the other Rights of Man and Rights of Woman should be enshrined the right to privacy. Of course, a public man's public life and conduct should be the subject for perpetual scrutiny and criticism; that was essential. But his home should be his castle, protected from prying eyes by the same wide moats and drawbridges which guarded the mansions and manners of newspaper proprietors.

At first Aneurin and Jennie were afraid to trust too completely. Each was aware of his or her vulnerability and hardly dared to believe that the happiness together could last. 'I recall murmuring

3. One letter of congratulation, from W. E. D. Allen, an old associate in the Mosley rebellion, gives a quick sideglance on the Bevan of those days. 'I hasten to offer my congratulations. It was really most surprising and enjoyable news and I am sure you will both suit each other, and I hope that you will both be as happy as your natures (which are happy ones) allow. No doubt we shall see you both together in a Cabinet – postponing, once again, that terribly tardy Revolution . . . I see very few of the old 1929 gang these days – sometimes Oliver [Baldwin], and once Bill Brown . . . What has happened to John Strachey – is he still wrestling with that enormous conscience? I now have a theory that the world is saved from insanity and mass suicide by the few sane people who do not take life seriously. You are one of them, although you probably would not admit it. Do you still talk as much as ever? I hear you are now the Playboy of the Westend World . . .'

to myself, *La joie de la rue, la douleur de la maison,*' says Jennie. 'I was waiting for the snag. Very likely, Nye too had these same reservations.' For a while they could still be amused and flattered in their different worlds. They were in different political parties. Jennie spent part of the year lecturing in America or touring trouble spots in Europe in search of freelance copy. Later on separation became unbearable. They both believed that real marriages were made slowly; certainly this was the way in which two turbulent independent temperaments grew together into a union of utter trust and devotion.

When they first met in the 1929 Parliament, Jennie was not impressed. She shuddered at his black suit and striped trousers, what she took to be the uniform of a Welsh nonconformist parson or an imitation stockbroker. 'Quite soon afterwards,' says Jennie, 'I learnt that nothing could have been so completely out of character. His mother, with the help of the local Co-op tailor, had concocted an outfit deemed suitable for an M.P. Nye with blissful indifference had hardly noticed. His head was in the clouds. He was absorbed with other matters.' But, in addition to the frustrations they endured under the MacDonald régime, they had much else in common – the miner's home, the youth of struggle, the memories of 1926 and 1927, access to the same books, the same rich heritage of working-class pride and dignity. 'We might be brother and sister,' said Jennie the first time they really talked together. 'Aye,' replied Nye with an appraising, mischievous grin, 'but with a tendency to incest.' When all the other barriers to the engagement had been broken down, Jennie still imposed one final condition. He must get rid of the purple-brown overcoat that she particularly detested. A day or two later he bounded up the stairs of her Guilford Street flat with a brand new one of exactly the same colour and style as the old. He had completely missed the point. Jennie gasped, laughed, but since he looked so pleased with himself – and her – had enough sense just to say that the coat was fine. All else had been agreed, and his idea of marriage accorded with hers. 'The best way to keep a bull in a field is to take the fence down,' he would quip.

To escape from all the fuss, they went on a trip to Spain; 'we were both as nearly carefree as the circumstances of our lives had ever allowed us to be.' Jennie Lee's own description cannot be bettered: 'If you live most of your years,' she writes, 'in a Scottish or Welsh colliery district, then one day find yourself breakfasting out of doors in January (in January, mark you) with orange groves around you, the Sierra Nevada on the skyline and a brilliant blue-green sea at your feet, you rediscover all your childhood's faith in miracles. Aneurin, who when he is among Englishmen always seems to me an alien figure – he is much too unequivocally alive to suit staid English ways – looked utterly at home in Andalusia. He loved it all. The vivid colouring, the smell and flavour of the place, the warmth, the dark, proud-spirited people . . . It was a great lark the day Aneurin got himself a magnificent Spanish cloak, a sombrero, a scarlet *facha* to wind round his waist, and because we had dared him to do it, went swaggering dressed like this along the winding village street that leads down to the sea . . . I am sure those Andalusian peasants thought we were quite mad. But I am also sure they trusted us.'[4] The sense of that trust was to have considerable political consequences.

Back home, they lived for a while in Jennie Lee's flat in Guilford Street. But Nye dreamed of escaping from the smoke and rattle of the London he had always loathed. They spent two years searching for a home in the country. At last, having been deceived by numerous advertisements, they found an old, ramshackle, but genuine, Tudor cottage on Brimpton Common in Berkshire. Could the dinginess be banished by knocking down walls; could the surrounding entanglement of weeds, wire netting and general chaos be cleared; could the place be made habitable? Jennie said 'Yes'. At first Nye was doubtful; then he probed deeper and became excited, and the thrill never left him during the nine years they lived there. They pooled all their resources and managed to buy Lane End Cottage, bringing the furniture from the two-roomed London flat to spread it around the four bedrooms and three public rooms. Then they haunted the Caledonian Market in search of bargains to complete their furnishing. Nye devoted every minute he could spare from political activities to the task of reconstruction. He was no good, says

4. *Tomorrow is a New Day* by Jennie Lee.

Jennie, at weeding or smaller outside jobs, but let him loose on uprooting a hedge or knocking down a wall and rebuilding it, and he came into his own. By sheer hard labour matched by imagination, they made their own special kind of home.

Through the years the gossip-columnists liked to nudge their readers with tales of Aneurin Bevan's opulent tastes and habits. They could not understand that the richness came from within himself and that he carried it wherever he went. They had no inkling of how he and Jennie had made this, the first and most treasured of their homes, with their own hands and when they had very few shillings to spare. And soon something even more precious was added. Jennie's mother arrived to take charge. She was, says Jennie, 'our secret weapon as everyone knew who knew anything about us at all'. Nye loved telling people that he had to marry Jennie to get his mother-in-law. He never tired of the joke.

The portrait of that mother is painted in all her glory in Jennie Lee's own book about her early life and upbringing.[5] Ma Lee is the heroine of the book just as she became the light of Aneurin Bevan's home. One day, two years after their arrival at Lane End, Jennie Lee's father fell ill and they both went up to Lochgelly, returning sad and worried. 'If your father has to go underground again,' said Nye, 'it will kill him; you know that, don't you?' Jennie's mother was aching to come south and look after them, but her father was shy, dignified and not the type to take easily to a corner seat at another man's fireside, however loving and tactful his hosts might be. Moreover, there were financial implications. Nye had nothing but his £400 parliamentary salary and was still helping his widowed mother; Jennie was earning about the same or a little more. They took on a burden in love and duty. But, says Jennie: 'almost from the start "the burden" was carrying both of us, leaving us freer than ever before and having the time of our lives. Ma danced through the days, cooking, cleaning, organizing, adored by all our friends as well as by us. In those days I could go off to America or Russia or elsewhere for a month or more at a time with a completely easy mind. Nye would always go home to a good fire, every comfort and mother and father would be just as happy. And in these

5. *Tomorrow is a New Day* by Jennie Lee.

years we were still young enough to feel indestructible.' Ma Lee's devotion to her daughter was absolute. At first Nye was a stranger and his ways and requests were sometimes bewildering and unfamiliar. But he won the heart of both parents. Ma Lee became a central figure in his whole life. Not merely did she cook superbly, with the aid of Nye nipping in and out of the kitchen to take charge of the sauces and the general strategy (sometimes he cooked the whole meal himself with excellent results); never could there have been a more tender relationship between a man and his mother-in-law.

No one who was a frequent visitor to Lane End or their later establishments ever forgot the magic of those evenings. No one who was present at a session when he really talked ever forgot the experience. No one who knew him in those moods ever expected to meet anyone else who could spread the same enchantment by his gaiety, his originality, his laughter and his matchless powers of reasoning and argument. He was always probing; the brain was rarely inactive; the tongue was always searching for new phrases and formulations to awaken the imagination. Those sharp-edged aphorisms which studded his conversation and his speeches were not fashioned to impress; they were the genuine sparks from some fiery debate. Out of the topics of the day he could spin a wonderful, delicate web of theory, a grand perspective on the forces shaping society; you went away from one of those evenings feeling rich, rich in the belief of what could be achieved if his creative intelligence and the ideas it generated could be given full rein.

Not that politics always or even usually played a predominant part on those occasions; he would talk about everything and anything with varying degrees of knowledge and unvarying assurance. He was an encyclopaedist, fervently holding that all branches of knowledge were parts of the same tree; the interrelationship between them was his perpetual source of interest and inquiry. Partly he had learnt this from Rodo and from Marx, and for the same reason he extolled Lewis Mumford. He was always on the alert to find a new facet of the truth which could cast light on his theory. He noticed the idiosyncrasies of his guests and could flatter them into believing that they too had struck a vein of original gold. Alternatively he would challenge them in the fortress of their most dearly held conviction or expertise and come off best in the contest, at least in the eyes of the audience, against some leader of his profession. University professors or artists went down like ninepins, only to be reassured at the end of the night that he had been doing it for fun. A would-be mogul or a rising scriptwriter might be laid low with the startling intelligence: 'When I was a film exhibitor in Tredegar, we solved all that problem.'

Only one unspoken rule prevailed about those dinner conversations; it must be a full concerted orchestra, not a series of duets. At the head stood the conductor with his carving knife and the whole company responded, including Ma Lee in the kitchen. Benn Levy and Constance Cummings were among the most frequent visitors in those days. 'Everything was laughter and fun and larger than life,' says Constance. 'Everything was words and talk and flamboyance. I remember so often being at their home and hearing Nye in the kitchen with Jennie's mother arguing over the way to cook something. There would be the wild gabble of excited Welsh and Scots accents, debating and arguing and talking each other down all at the same time and then uproarious peals of laughter.' These nights among his friends were some of his happiest moments. Only on rare occasions were visitors invited for a political purpose; most politicians might regard as outrageous flippancy this preference for the company of those who did not know the latest manoeuvre at Westminster. But those who were there warmed their hearts and minds. 'He was like a fire in a room on a cold winter's day,' says Constance Cummings.

Physical surroundings conformed exactly with the atmosphere; it was hard to tell whether the dwellers in the house had devised the rooms or whether somehow subtly the process had happened the other way round. Apart from anything else, what Jennie Lee gave to Aneurin Bevan, with the aid of her beautiful mother and gentle father, was a series of perfect homes – at Lane End Cottage, at Cliveden Place and finally at Asheridge Farm in Buckinghamshire. Both Jennie and Nye had strong views on taste, and their home-making embodied, consciously or unconsciously, William Morris's ideal that everything should be both useful and beautiful. They abhorred fakes, bric-à-brac, and possession for display or possession's sake. No photographs or portraits of themselves were to be seen anywhere; this habit they regarded as the last word in vulgar egotism. Neither would tolerate anything bogus – such as reproduction furniture, imitation antique china or, horror of horrors, electric fires with imitation coal. Not that they were against mixing the old with the new, but anything modern was selected for its simplicity of line, whether it was Swedish glass, an electric fire or a thermos flask. Jennie had a knack of combining elegance with great comfort. Her sumptuous easy chairs were upholstered in white, the curtains were velvet, the furniture mostly antique, the lighting soft, the paintings (when in later years they could afford a few) modern, and, if the slightest chill was in the air, the fire was roaring. And yet, especially at Lane End Cottage and Cliveden Place, all this was achieved in defiance of one of Jennie's sharp sayings – 'things are as expensive as they look'. None of the antiques were collector's pieces; mostly they had been picked up at bargain prices. The same was true of the sofas and the chairs, but these were upholstered with professional skill by Ma Lee. It was Ma also who made and, whenever they moved, remade the curtains. Nye surveyed the whole scene, not with a sense of property, but with a joyous sense of living. He had love affairs with places. The mountains round Tredegar provided the tempestuous first love, but Lane End Cottage and later Asheridge Farm captured his heart hardly less, and he cagerly shared his enthusiasm with others.

The food, the wine (at Lane End Cottage more usually beer was brought in a jug from the nearby pub), the talk, the caprices, the wonderfully equipped brain, relaxed and yet expanded to the limit – this was a feast fit for the gods. And while he replenished the minds of others, he helped renew his own physical and spiritual resources. He did not need a wife to protect him from the outside world. But he did need protection in the sense of being able to withdraw, to think, to argue, to be as capricious as he wanted to be – 'to go star-tapping' was his phrase for it. Often, the trials of politics bore down on him. Never did he escape entirely from his old sense of the pressures of time. 'But always,' says Jennie, 'he had the heights and the depths, the profound enjoyments as well as the moods of utter depression. It was a mountain landscape. There is more rain than sunshine in the hills but the totality is, for those of us who are Celts, at home in the mountains and drawing strength and peace there, most beautiful and exhilarating.'

Jennie Lee also says: 'Nye was born old and died young.' The phrase tells much about his whole life and not least about the Aneurin Bevan who at the age of thirty-six had married Jennie Lee, then twenty-nine. He had come to London to help change the world, with the cries of his own people drilling in his ears. He never forgot and he never betrayed. He had seen the harshness and squalor of the world before he was in his teens. But he grew younger in zest and spirit. It was the youth partly denied him he wanted to experience, not the ways of the London world. His critics called him immature and irresponsible. But how much thought, compared with his, did they apply before boldly making up their minds to stay in the obvious rut and follow the accepted routine of political advancement? The most precious possession of a politician is time; to squander it on apparently unassociated pursuits looks too lighthearted and wayward. Bevan gave all the appearance of waywardness; the accusation against him recurred throughout his life. But he knew that his real treasure was his mind; he was resolved to keep it fresh and young and never to bury it in a cemetery of blue books and committee meetings.

It remains to add a few words on José Enrique Rodo, the influence which became interwoven with his whole character. When Aneurin Bevan first picked up one of Rodo's books cannot be precisely stated. The one big volume published in English in this country, *The Motives of Proteus*, appeared in 1929. Bevan was already talking about him then so he may have read it first that year. Conceivably he may have read the little volume, *Ariel*, containing the pith of Rodo's ideas, which was published in America in 1922, but there is no trace of this edition in his own library. What is certain is that he went on reading Rodo all through the thirties and indeed all his life. He could recite favourite passages or, more usually, would take the book from the shelf and read aloud several pages. Next to Marx, and in a few respects superseding Marx, Rodo had the most powerful effect on his intellectual outlook. He employed with Rodo particularly the method he adopted in all his reading that really mattered. He would not swallow the whole book at one gulp, but instead digested sections of it. Then he was off to the mountains or the fields to think and argue with himself about the new discoveries. In the end, the new find became his own for ever. It was not so much facts or doctrines he had assimilated but the author's full system of reasoning and development.

To attempt to summarize what he learnt from this source would be to perpetrate a travesty, for the beauty of Rodo derives from the carefully balanced qualifications, the fine tones and the veiled syntheses enveloped in his rich, languorous sentences. His 'message' could certainly not be compressed into a few paragraphs; if the flavour, the relish, the compassion and the loveliness are lost, all is lost. Moreover, it is obvious that part of Rodo's attraction for Bevan was that he expressed in wonderful language thoughts to which he was stumbling on his own account, and, further, that he never surrendered his own judgement to his new prophet. Just as Marx had appealed because he seemed to describe so faithfully the world as it looked from the Tredegar coalpits and Labour Exchange and just as he had refused to become a blind adherent of Marxist texts, so with Rodo. For all his reading, Bevan was no book-learner. What he read had to be moulded with his own experience and he hated Marxist dogmatism and Rodoesque dogmatism (not that there is such a thing) along with all other dogmatisms. For all these reasons, to quote – if by quoting it is assumed that the essence of what Rodo gave to Bevan is indicated – would be to falsify.

Two generalizations, however, may be made. Aneurin Bevan was profoundly critical of many of the most spectacular developments in modern industrial civilization and he was critical in terms which are rarely employed by Socialists who have forgotten or never read William Morris. Rodo freshly revealed or freshly expressed those criticisms for him. 'An organized society which limits its idea of civilization to the accumulation of material abundance, and of justice to their equitable distribution among its members, will never make of its great cities anything that differs essentially from the heaping up of ant-hills.' Rodo's theme was, in part, an indictment and a warning about the civilization of the United States. Bevan could never see the United States except partially through Rodo's eyes; anyone who feels this to be a proof of an illegitimate prejudice should first consider how apposite to the America of today is what Rodo wrote half a century ago.

The other feature in Rodo has a more personal significance. It could be called a book of wisdom, collected from all the ages and addressed especially to the young, on how to live and how to have life more abundantly. Aneurin Bevan followed or was already following several of those instructions. 'Antiquity,' wrote Rodo, 'had altars "for the unknown gods". Consecrate a part of your soul to the unknown future. As societies develop, thought for the future becomes more and more a factor in their growth and an inspiration to their labours ... We are only capable of progress in so far as we can adapt our actions every day to the conditions of a more distant future, to countries farther and farther away. Assurance of our part in bringing about a work that shall survive us, fruitful in time to come, exalts our human dignity and gives us triumph even over the limitations of our nature. If unhappily humanity had to despair definitely of the immortality of the individual consciousness, the most religious sentiment that it could substitute would be that which comes of the thought that even after our dissolution into the heart of things there would outlast, as part of all human inheritance, the very best of all we had felt or thought, our deepest and purest essence – just as the beams of a long-extinguished star go on indefinitely and still cheer us mortals, albeit with a melancholy light.'

Such loftiness of imagination may seem far removed from the preoccupations of a happy but deadly serious class-warrior embroiled in a savage struggle with the Governments of Baldwin and Chamberlain. But it was part of him.

7 Anti-Fascist 1934-36

Yet, Freedom! Yet thy banner, torn, but flying
Streams like the thunderstorm *against* the wind.
                                        – LORD BYRON

THE rulers of Britain who meekly reclined before the ravages
of the Great Depression were not likely to stand like lions across
the path of potential aggressors in Europe. Their policies at
home and abroad were two sides of the same coin; both were
coloured by the same inertia and absence of imagination, the
same theories of what was thought to be required for the survival
of capitalist society. At least, this assumption about the quality
of their opponents guided the minds of the men on the Left at
the height of the Baldwin era, between 1934 and 1936, and their
attitudes cannot be understood without a recognition of it. For
Aneurin Bevan certainly, the belief that a nation's foreign policy
must be shaped by domestic necessities, that the two could never
be disentangled, was an axiom of politics. And he never dismissed Stanley Baldwin, the director of Tory strategy, as a lazy
amateur, always regarding him as the most cunning defender of
his class and the most consistently adroit of parliamentary
leaders. Whatever else he neglected, Baldwin took the trouble
to study the House of Commons as a man must study a hard-to-
get, self-reliant mistress. Bevan watched with mingled admiration and contempt the seduction practised on several of his
wilting colleagues.

It is necessary to insist on the point involved since most
historical judgements on the era, like the controversies at the
time, have come to centre upon it. Many of the Left, Bevan
among them, were swiftly and deeply stirred by the terrible

197

events on the Continent. How should they not be? Their comrades were the first victims; they could almost feel the Nazi lash
across their own backs. But why, then, did these men, blindly
or factiously, deny the need for arms to withstand the menace?
That common gibe of the pre-war years is now exalted as a
decisive indictment against the Left. We are invited, by contrast,
to admire the Churchillian wisdom which kept its eye fixed
steadily on the changes disrupting the balance of power among
the European States; Baldwin's crime, in Churchill's estimate,
was his refusal to acknowledge the phenomenon or his incapacity
to rouse the nation to an awareness of the peril. But to ask that
British Socialists, particularly those from the depressed areas,
should have regarded the issue in this light is to ask for an
absurdity. How could they see the tormentors of their people
suddenly translated into stout defenders of working-class
liberties? For Bevan, that would have implied a betrayal of a
whole lifetime's experience and struggle. British capitalism, not
German Fascism, was the enemy on his doorstep, as ancient as
the industrial revolution itself, as modern as the latest Means
Test infamy. It was Tory rule which decreed that there should
still be two nations and it was doing so as brutally as in the days
of the Chartists. To suppose that the nation could overnight be
made one, by a patriotic cry, was the most cruel of frauds; all
the camouflage of Baldwin's shrewd eloquence merely made the
trickery more intolerable.

Indeed, to many Socialists, the rise of Fascism appeared as a
staggeringly accurate fulfilment of the Marxist prophecy. Had it
not always been foretold how ruthlessly the ruling class would
rally to the defence of its privileges, how contemptuously it
would sweep aside all liberal pretensions in the hour of its
extremity? More specifically, 'the rise of Fascism in each and
every country in the world is the quite inescapable consequence
of the faltering of the workers' parties before the supreme task
with which history now confronts them'. This was John
Strachey's formulation in his book, *The Menace of Fascism*,
published in 1933; his forecast of a Fascist *putsch* in Britain,
resulting from the combined decay of capitalist society and the
official Labour leadership, followed with all the exactitude of a

geometrical theorem. Bevan rarely lapsed into the same dogmatism, but he shared the mood. The question uppermost in the minds of most Socialists was not how Germany could be thwarted, but rather how soon and in what form would the pattern be applied in Britain and how could it be resisted. 'It is impossible to be a supporter of capitalism and world peace,' said Bevan. 'Our enemy is here,' said William Mellor with Cromwellian rigour and simplicity. During all the first years of the Hitler epoch, Bevan's attitude was governed by this conviction.

Thus both Socialist philosophy and working-class experience made it hard for the Left to allow itself to be diverted from the menace at home. And this attitude was only fortified by the cringing posture which Britain's rulers adopted towards the Nazi horror, their apparent eagerness to concede to a barbarian Germany what they had denied to her when she seemed civilized.[1] The generally complacent, even approving, reception given to the news from Europe by the ruling circles in London

1. Mr A. J. P. Taylor, in his chapter 'Between the Wars', included in his book *The Troublemakers*, argues powerfully that a major factor throughout the thirties in determining Labour's attitude, particularly on the Left, was the deep-rooted pro-German, anti-French sentiment dating from their opposition to the Versailles Treaty and the 1914-18 war itself. But this played little part in shaping Bevan's approach. In a Commons debate on 28 November 1934, he delivered a strong attack on Lloyd George, who had spoken almost as an apologist for Hitler. He denied Lloyd George's view that 'the reason why the present régime was established in Germany is because the disarmament pledge in the Peace Treaty has not been fulfilled. That is an utterly superficial judgement.' He continued: 'For practically fourteen years the German national eagle did not feel itself outraged by either the War Guilt Clause or the subordinate status to which it was reduced by the Peace Treaty. These became flags which the Nazis waved for their own propaganda when the economic situation presented them with their opportunity.'

Bevan, indeed, was never a pro-German sentimentalist before the war any more than he became an anti-German fanatic in the years of German rearmament after 1950 – as his opponents in the Labour Party falsely alleged. Usually, he swam against the tides of pro- or anti-German hysteria. He was anti-Hitler from the first day. He assailed Vansittartism at the height of the war and denounced the folly of unconditional surrender. He backed the attempts to save Germany from starvation after 1945 and bitterly opposed the Anglo-American policy of dismantling German factories. Then, when the dismantlers, the Vansittartites, the Churchillites, the Bevinites and the Morrisonians turned in unison to rearm their old enemy, he opposed that too. Germany, in his view, must be allowed to live, but not to dictate. It was the attitude of a good Socialist and a good European.

offered a further confirmation of the Marxist analysis. Nothing in the demeanour of the Baldwin régime suggested that it could ever become the standard-bearer of popular resistance to the new sweep of tyranny across the Continent; rather it appeared as the willing abettor of the Fascist counter-revolution.

And nothing, be it added, in Churchill's record during those first years of the thirties marked him out as the exponent of an older and more honourable British tradition which might set national interests above those of class. He was no Gladstone hurling thunderbolts against the perpetrators of the atrocities and summoning the nation to a great moral crusade. Churchill, indeed, was the class warrior *par excellence*; memories of the General Strike were still sharp in working-class homes; plentiful other evidence was there to prove that his role had not changed. Had he not extolled Mussolini as the scourge of Bolshevism, approved Japan's 'civilizing mission' in Manchuria, hailed Hitler as a German patriot, and even, in one admittedly isolated moment of aberration, applauded the spirit of Mosley's black-shirts? His most recent exploit was his long, bitter, rearguard campaign against Indian freedom, and never once, amid these other preoccupations, had his words touched the hearts or articulated the hopes of South Wales or Durham. The Churchill of 1934 was not the man of 1940. He had made his contribution to the crushing, near-fatal impediment of national division, myopia and industrial decay which Britain bore, as she stumbled forward towards the greatest war in history.

The Labour Party, and the Left within the Labour Party, groped and stumbled too. But many within its ranks did discover the sense of urgency which the crisis called for; according to their lights, they exerted themselves to fend off the catastrophe, and not all the lights were dim. Aneurin Bevan was one of the few who staked and nearly wrecked his whole political life in the process.

According to the economic historians, the year 1934 was a year of economic recovery. No one noticed this at the time – except possibly the Government's diligent statistical experts and pro-pagandists. The figures can be cited to prove that trade had taken an upward turn, that a check had been imposed on the ever-mounting unemployment totals. But these marginal improvements meant little or nothing in the areas most sorely afflicted. For the unemployed man and his family, each fresh year of agony added to the despair and the bitterness, and in South Wales especially the process of decay persisted, even if its pace could be said to have slackened. 'It is,' said Bevan, 'like living in the middle of a graveyard and spending most of your time reading the inscriptions on the tombstones.'

For those unwilling to submit, political agitation was the honourable resort and that in turn meant association with the Communists who had been the first and were still the foremost to carry the struggle on to the streets. At the Southport Conference of the Labour Party in October 1934, Bevan had been fiercely rebuked for his appearances on the platforms of the National Unemployed Workers' Movement; these heretical flirtations had been condemned by a huge majority. But the politics of discontent were not to be kept in strict channels by card votes and cardboard leadership. All over the country, within a matter of days, the decrees of Ernest Bevin and Conference were being flouted. Bevan went straight from Southport to address a meeting in Manchester organized by the Manchester Trades and Labour Council; there, sitting on the platform beside him, were Arthur Greenwood, a member of Labour's National Executive, and Willie Gallacher, the Communist leader. A few days later he was on the plinth in Trafalgar Square joining a mass demonstration against the Government's Sedition Bill. Labour Party, Trade Union, I.L.P. and Communist banners sailed together in the breeze and no one, not even Transport House, dared invoke the Southport proscriptions to check the contagion.

Two events raised the agitational temperature to a new pitch of intensity – the first a clumsy and insulting attempt by the Government to secure the opposite effect. The Distressed Areas (Development and Improvement) Bill was introduced in November as an obvious sop, a Chamberlain umbrella to ward off a hurricane. Apparently in full seriousness, it was proposed that two commissioners (unpaid), one for England and Wales and the other for Scotland, should be charged with the task of touring the stricken areas to find out what was wrong; £2,000,000 were to be made available as a grant if they should eventually discover any worthwhile projects to spend it on. At this, something stirred even on the Tory back benches. Chamberlain lamented his lot, whining in his diary about 'the frightfully sudden slump in the Government's stock, and the continual nagging and carping by the young Tory intellectuals.'[2] One chief carper was the young intellectual member from Stockton-on-Tees, Harold Macmillan. It was on this occasion that, recalling and moderating the language of Disraeli, he saw on the Treasury Bench, not a range of extinct volcanoes, but a few disused slag-heaps who might well be tidied up. The real problem, he charged, was not in South Wales or Durham, but in Whitehall and Westminster.

Spokesmen from the Labour benches struck the same note more fiercely. Bevan affected to discern the ineffable MacDonald touch in the whole proposition. 'It has been suggested,' he said, 'that the Prime Minister is the prisoner of the Conservatives; it is entirely untrue. The Conservatives are the prisoners of the Prime Minister, because he has now succeeded in enveloping the whole Cabinet in the misty, murky twilight in which he usually moves.' Then he poured contempt on the idea of travelling commissioners to whom M.P.s must take their pleas and complaints instead of to the responsible Ministers. The elected representatives of the people would have to go down on their knees to 'an amateur appointed by the Government as charity-monger'. As for the young, would-be rebel Tories,[3] the lions in the debating chamber and the lambs in the voting lobby, could they not understand why the Government restricted its interventions to such miserable palliatives? 'Make-believe measures'

2. *The Life of Neville Chamberlain* by Keith Feiling.
3. On a later stage of the Bill, when Macmillan seemed momentarily more enthusiastic about it, Bevan began: 'I have tried on many occasions to explain why an hon. Member of the obvious talent and qualities of the hon. Member for Stockton has not received greater notice by the Government of which he is a supporter.' Now he understood better. Macmillan's quick change gave no assurance of stability. At this Macmillan interrupted to defend his consistency. 'We are to understand,' retorted Bevan, 'that the disused slag-heaps have produced a valuable measure.'

were the only ones acceptable. If the Tories grappled with the real problem they would have to discard their Tory principles; they would have to intervene on a massive scale, knocking the great god, private profit, off his pedestal altogether. 'The real planners of the basic industries of Great Britain at this time,' he said, 'are the banks, and the banks are doing it quite irresponsibly, without having to answer to anybody. They exert governmental powers, sentencing some areas to death and giving a reprieve to others.'

Much more serious was the other event – the publication of the new regulations by the Unemployment Assistance Board established under the Act against which Bevan had led the parliamentary fight during the previous session. Chamberlain himself, it seems, had always reckoned on trouble in South Wales, where, according to his belief, the disbursements made by the local authorities under the existing dispensation were shockingly 'lavish'. Yet even he found the first proposals of the Board too tough; in consultation with the Minister of Labour, Mr Oliver Stanley, he had tried to work out 'what seemed a golden mean'[4] (in the words of his biographer). But the last-minute patchwork made quite insufficient improvement. The bureaucratic Board, deprived of the assistance which M.P.s could give in scrutinizing its edicts, failed hopelessly to take account of variations in rent all over the country and a whole vast complex of other anomalies. Bevan's persistent forecast during the long nights of argument when the Bill was going through its Committee stage was now fulfilled to the letter. The regulations were scheduled to come into operation in January and February. But during the first five or six weeks of the New Year the Government was confronted with the biggest explosion of popular anger in the whole inter-war period, second only to the General Strike itself.

South Wales took the lead, with the South Wales Miners' Federation brushing aside all the restraints of Southport and demanding and securing united action. Soon the revolt spread to almost every industrial area. Marches, demonstrations, riots, baton charges, arrests – these were the items of news from

4. *The Life of Neville Chamberlain* by Keith Feiling.

North, South, East and West. Undoubtedly, the leadership of the movement in many areas was Communist, but this was no plot deeply laid by scheming agitators. All other considerations were swamped in the spontaneous wave of protest. 'The spirit of 1926,' said the trembling *Times*, 'is showing itself again.' Within a matter of days the all-powerful Government with its 500 majority in the Commons had issued a standstill order, revoking the cuts and yielding to tumult what it had refused to reason. Not until fourteen months later would a new Minister of Labour be willing to permit the Board to promulgate its revised regulations. One cannot but wish, wrote Chamberlain privately, 'that the Board, since they had this discretion all the time, had used it more effectively to ease the transition'.[5]

One cannot but wish, too, that Ministers had heeded the debate of the previous twelve months. Bevan perhaps had more right to mock the Government's surrender than anyone else, for whereas the other critics, quite properly, had ranged over the whole field of the treatment of the unemployed, he had concentrated his chief attack on the irresponsible Board and the curtailment of the rights of Parliament. 'People are inclined to jeer at this House as a deliberative assembly, but I know of no more comprehensive pool of public knowledge than this,' he said when Parliament debated the new situation after the February days of uproar. Considering the circumstances, the impeachment was a soft one; but then, for the moment at least, a great victory had been won, and he wanted no mistake in the harvesting of it. He hoped that these events 'will convince hon. Members that it is not safe to legislate in such a way as to deprive the executive of the advice and experience of Members of the House of Commons'.

Yet still the victory was no more than defensive. Somehow or other Labour must discover the means of going over to the attack. Something possibly could be achieved on the industrial front; a new militancy there could shake the politicians.[6]

5. *The Life of Neville Chamberlain* by Keith Feiling.
6. The new militancy produced a new excuse for Tory Ministers. One of them dared to hint that difficulties about labour relations were a contributory cause in preventing the movement of new industries to Wales. 'We are tired of waiting,' said Bevan; 'we have waited ten or fifteen years and have tried

All through these years Bevan had naturally kept his close association with the Miners' Federation. Often at their Conferences the miners' leaders received an overspill of his brimming invective. At their Conference in December 1933, for example, he ridiculed the hopeless outcome of the attempt to secure national negotiations with the coalowners, while the National Government, protesting its goodwill, would never left a finger to rebuke the coalowners' obstinacy. 'The Miners' Federation,' he said, 'has fallen so low in the estimation of the Government that you are met only by the permanent officials of the Mines' Department. We shall soon be meeting the charwoman and the office boy to take notes. That is where the dignity of the Miners' Federation lies.' But the miners' leaders faced problems which audacity alone could not solve. The dream of *one* miners' union which could frustrate the colliery owners' tactic of playing off one district against another and compel national negotiations was still no more than a distant hope of the visionaries. Apart from the weakness of the miners arising from persistent massive unemployment in the industry, there were many areas, including South Wales, where company unionism was still a formidable force, crippling every effort to secure united action. During these years of deepest depression this other agony was piled on all the rest; mining valleys were the scene of internecine conflict, as bitter as anything the coalfields had known in their long ferocious history. However, by the beginning of 1935 – except in Nottinghamshire – the worst of these battles had been won. The curse of company unionism was rooted out. In April 1935, after nearly ten years of retreat, the Miners' Federation felt able to formulate a wage claim – 'the miner's two bob' – and resolved

---

every conceivable way open to us, only to be told at the end that one of the reasons why industries do not come to South Wales is that South Wales miners and steelworkers are too bellicose, and that they frighten employers away. So employers now have to be *tickled*. We have to be good boys, in order to persuade the good, kind employers to put a factory down among us.' The situation at that particular moment, he added, had a touch of comedy. Sir Arthur Pugh had just been given a knighthood in the Jubilee Honours, and he was the boss of the bellicose steelworkers. Was this the proper way to reward irresponsible militancy? Bevan's irony was likely to be better appreciated in Ebbw Vale than in the House of Commons. No one before had unmasked the red-hot revolutionary side of Sir Arthur Pugh's nature.

to back it with the readiness to strike.[7] Bevan threw himself eagerly into the campaign. 'The miners,' he cried at one demonstration in Cardiff, 'are being crucified on the cross of rabid profit-making, and the Miners' Federation must lift that cross high enough for all to see.' They did their best, but more was required.

Bevan no longer believed that the weapon of industrial action could by itself wrest power from his enemies. Only through political action and parliamentary action could the real heights be scaled. He had not been seduced or cowed into this more orthodox attitude, but partly no doubt his thoughts were influenced by the achievements of the tiny band of Labour spokesmen in the House. It was the most congenial Parliament of his lifetime; the leadership was fighting the enemy and there was therefore no need to fight the leaders.[8] But what of the machine outside and what if that machine succeeded in clamping its grip on the Party within, according to the full 1929–31 precedent? Bevan, as we have seen, had already had a few clashes with the General Council and the National Executive. He knew how jealously many

7. *The Miners. In Crisis and War* by R. Page Arnot.
8. An entirely false picture has been painted of Labour's role in the 1931–35 Parliament, largely owing to an uncritical acceptance of the views of the two chief leaders of the movement outside the Commons, Bevin and Dalton. For example, Mr Henry Pelling writes in his *Short History of the Labour Party*: '. . . Obviously the Parliamentary Party was a poor and nerveless thing in this Parliament of the early 1930s. Lansbury himself was already 72, and was in any case a poor leader because of his tendency towards a woolly-minded sentimentality. His two ablest assistants, Attlee and Cripps, both seemed to be suffering from the shock of electoral defeat, and inclined to advocate policies of extreme and barren militancy. Cripps, for instance, made speeches about the "sinister influence of Buckingham Palace" and the need for a temporary dictatorship by the Party if Labour should win a general election.' In fact, Lansbury surprised many by the astuteness of his leadership; Baldwin, who – unlike the Bevinite historians – saw it at first-hand, paid his perceptive tribute. To confine the characterization of Cripps to a few quotations of this nature is to make an absurd caricature of his persistent brilliance as an Opposition spokesman. Meantime, on the back benches, Bevan acted closely with George Buchanan and James Maxton, the three together revealing a parliamentary skill which the Daltons were never able to emulate. But undoubtedly Mr Pelling has faithfully represented Bevin's view of the parliamentary scene which, however distorted and unjustified, played its part in affecting the relations between Right and Left within the Party.

members of those bodies frowned on the loose-reined parliamentary leadership of Lansbury, Attlee and Cripps. And yet he still knew better than the hard-headed realists, the Bevins and the Daltons, what had *worked*. Much the biggest single Labour victory of the thirties (never, unhappily, to be repeated on the same scale) was the defeat of the Assistance Board's regulations. The deed had been done by a combined operation; by deadly parliamentary manoeuvre and attack in the face of vastly superior numbers, with the infantry from the back benches let loose in support of Cripps's cavalry charges; and, more important still, by the mobilization and unleashing of a united working class, marching and demonstrating on the streets. Why could a Labour leadership not conduct the same dual operation on a broader front?

The great domestic issue was surely glaring enough, and more and more Bevan elaborated it in his speeches in Parliament and outside. It was never for him solely a question of pleading first-aid for the stricken areas. He saw the whole country – the countryside no less than the huge sprawling cities – being subjected to a monstrous distortion by the whims of the private profit test. It was not merely that homes and communities were being broken and great industries left derelict in South Wales and the North; new horrors were being constructed in London and the Midlands, with men and women and their families shunted from one to the other like cattle. And all this was happening when electricity and transport and modern techniques and planning could make industry much more easily mobile than the men.[9] A wanton, unthinking sabotage of man's productive

9. Compare his speech in the Commons on 23 July 1935: 'The other day we were asked – and the Government staggered me by taking credit for it – to vote a sum of £40,000,000 – I am not objecting to it – for the electrification of railways in North London. We were asked to vote that sum because the traffic problems of London have grown so enormously that it is not possible to move the vast population through its environs every day unless there is speedier transport. Many of us thought that the Government were doing a remarkably courageous thing and advancing boldly and intelligently in asking the country to find £40,000,000 for that purpose. At the same time that the country is spending £40,000,000 merely as a consequence of the fact that people are all huddled together here, nobody seems to pay any attention to the economic disutility of promoting a system of society in which nearly 8,000,000 people

powers, an all-enveloping ugliness, a degrading obsequiousness before stupidity in smooth accents – these, along with the wan faces of Tredegar children and the indignities of the family Means Test, were some of the features which made him hate the whole visage of capitalism. He saw it all so clearly and believed a real Labour leadership could make the rest of Britain see it too. It was theme enough for a life-time. In season or out of season he returned to it with unfailing originality. But he, like others, had to turn aside to even more urgent themes.

_____

are crowded all of a heap and then spending enormous sums of money on supplying services which are a direct consequence of the fact that they are in a heap. That £40,000,000 is being spent in London while millions of pounds are being poured in unemployment benefit in South Wales and all social activities are becoming derelict because, since the census of 1921 the population of South and South-east England has increased by twenty-six per cent, although the population of the country as a whole has increased by only six per cent.

'There is a great concentration of population in two or three large centres of the country. I suggest to hon. Members that that is not a development and a tendency that they can view with complacency. If London goes on swelling much more, it will become completely intolerable, developing as it does a kind of city intelligence which is anti-social.

'. . . The Government have not faced the fact that there is a profound revolution in the technique of industry and in the relationship between industry and society. In the past industry was less mobile than man, now man is less mobile than industry. The right hon. Gentleman has said that he distrusts plans. There has always been a plan for society, a plan imposed by natural and physical conditions. Men had to establish their industries at the mouth of rivers or on the sites of mines or in areas which were topographically suitable for them and on those sites there grew up the great centres of population. Now that state of affairs has ended. The development of electrical power, the ability to create atmospheres inside factories and the transport system, all combined, have made industry infinitely mobile, and although man has developed on the old sites of industry a complicated social apparatus, the economic foundations of that apparatus have been sapped by the movements of industry in obeying the caprice of seeking a very uncertain margin of profit.

'. . . But it is a monstrous proposition that a large community must be shifted from one spot to another, sometimes only twenty miles away – and twenty miles is as important as a hundred miles if a community has to be shifted – because the works will then be more favourably situated from the competitive point of view. That proposition cannot be defended. At any rate, if you are going to shift industry for such reasons they ought to be properly examined, and the community ought to have its say before it has to pay the price of dislocation.'

During the year 1935 the issues of foreign policy superimposed themselves on all others, transforming the terms of conflict between the political parties. Only rarely in the House of Commons had Aneurin Bevan strayed beyond the frontiers of his main domestic argument, but his general approach to the foreign scene can easily be established from his speeches outside and his political upbringing. He accepted the general Marxist thesis that capitalism caused the imperialist rivalries which in turn caused war. One of the favourite books of his youth was H. N. Brailsford's *The War of Steel and Gold*; another was J. A. Hobson's *Imperialism*, from which both Lenin and Brailsford had derived much of their analysis. These had had much more influence on Bevan than the liberal theorists who piously preached the need for the rule of law in international affairs.

Politics for him was about power and economics; good laws could provide the coping-stone for the edifice of peace, but not the foundations. 'The League of Nations,' he said in February 1933, 'is increasingly a conspiracy to maintain the frontiers imposed by the peace treaties in an attempt to keep some countries financially dead. It is bound to end in disaster.' There was only one way to protest against war: to say clearly in advance: 'We won't fight.' Again, in November 1934: 'What weapon has the working class except the General Strike? There will be only one weapon left – the determination to stop the wheels if war is declared or threatened.' This was the old remedy which the Socialist International had failed to apply in 1914. It was the 1917 Leninist doctrine of revolutionary defeatism. Little Socialist thinking had been done in the interim to bring the doctrine up to date. Labour's foreign policy stock-in-trade in the twenties and the early thirties had comprised a condemnation of the pre-1914 international anarchy, an attack on the iniquities of the Versailles settlement and a boundless faith in Arthur Henderson's efforts to secure international disarmament. To Bevan, all this looked too vapid, legalistic and un-Marxist. He never believed that the nations would throw away their arms while they felt insecure; the security must come first and the insecurity was due to capitalist pressures within the sovereign states. Yet these theories did not add up to a policy; they were little more than romantic dreams of what the working class might do if the apocalypse were fulfilled.

Whilst Socialist thinking stood still – in Soviet Russia no less than in Britain – the world was moving fast. Way back in 1930 a voice from the wilderness, and certainly one that Bevan respected, had given warning to Communists and Socialists alike: 'Should Fascism come to power in Germany,' it said, 'it will ride over your skulls and spines like a terrific tank. Your salvation lies in merciless struggle. And only a fighting unity with Social Democratic workers can bring victory. Make haste, you have very little time left!' But that was Trotsky, not Stalin. Only after the damage had been done in Germany did Communist strategy start to change and give birth to a new hope – the hope that, in the face of the common enemy, the ancient savage feud between Communists and Socialists might at last be repaired.

However, the change did come. In September 1934, the Soviet Union joined the League of Nations and the 'thieves' kitchen' began to look more respectable in Left-wing Socialist eyes. In May 1935 France and Russia signed a treaty of mutual assistance. In both France and Spain, Communists and Socialists and many others were beginning to work together in Popular Front agitations. The *ad hoc* committees in South Wales and the other distressed areas of Britain, directing united activities, seemed to have their continental counterparts on a much more significant scale. If these movements had been granted longer time to fructify – time to forget the Communist virulence of a few years earlier when all Social Democrats were branded as Social Fascists – even the rigidity of the British political structure might have been loosened.

But other events were moving even more swiftly. Mussolini was preparing for war against Abyssinia. During the summer of 1935 he made his estimate of his potential opponents in London and Paris. At the Stresa Conference in April with Sir John Simon and M Pierre Laval, neither of whom was indelicate enough to mention Abyssinia at all, he seemed to get the green light to go ahead. True, during that same summer, pro-League sentiment in Britain rose to the highest pitch, symbolized in the famous Peace Ballot. But what did it really amount to? Would the British Government act decisively? Mussolini guessed right

or maybe he did not need to guess; the secret assurances from
M Laval may have been sufficiently specific.

And, curiously, Bevan guessed right too. More and more his
own attitude had been getting out of tune with the rising pro-
League enthusiasm of the British public and the bulk of the
Labour Party. Both the Communists, directed by the switch in
the Kremlin, and the orthodox supporters of collective security
were now bent on making Abyssinia the great test case for the
Covenant. This, in their view, was no moment for academic
theories about war resistance; if Mussolini could be stopped in
his tracks, a mighty blow would have been struck against the
Fascist forces and the rule of international law would be spec-
tacularly vindicated. The case was certainly powerful. And,
momentarily at least, the pro-League enthusiasts seemed to have
captured the British Government as their champion. On 11
September, Sir Samuel Hoare, Britain's Foreign Secretary,
mounted the rostrum at Geneva. Mussolini had his armies ready
to march. He had issued the threat 'with Geneva, despite
Geneva, against Geneva'. But Sir Samuel Hoare spoke in clear,
emphatic tones. 'In conformity with its precise and explicit
obligations,' he said, 'the League stands, and my country stands
with it, for the collective maintenance of the Covenant in its
entirety, and particularly for steady and collective resistance to
all acts of unprovoked aggression. The attitude of the British
nation in the last few weeks has clearly demonstrated the fact
that this is no variable and unreliable sentiment; but a principle
of international conduct to which they and their Government
hold with firm, enduring and universal persistence.' The day
on which these words were uttered was the most exciting that
Geneva had known since Aristide Briand on behalf of France
had received Germany into the League. A wild response greeted
the speech. M Laval spoke approvingly in the name of France.
The Soviet Union, the Dominions, Holland, Belgium, the
Scandinavians, the Little Entente, the Balkan Entente, all
pledged themselves to follow the same lead in upholding 'in its
entirety' the full Covenant of the League.

Bevan remained unimpressed. Along with Stafford Cripps, the
Socialist League and the pacifist section of the Party, led by

George Lansbury, he insisted that no capitalist Government of Baldwin and Chamberlain could be entrusted with the workers' allegiance in making war or threatening war. He refused to believe that Sir Samuel Hoare's word was the deed; despite the apparent evidence from Geneva, he could not see his ancient enemies suddenly changing their political characters. Speaking at a Socialist League Conference a few days later he said: 'At Geneva, France and Britain have been negotiating to give Mussolini all he wanted without the necessity of fighting for it.' Whatever verdict may be passed on the deductions he drew, the insight was undeniable; both the event and the memoirs are there to prove how nearly he had stumbled on the truth. But this, admittedly, was not the core of the case put by Cripps and Bevan. More fundamental was their fear that the Labour movement would be sucked into a full bi-partisan defence and foreign policy with a capitalist Government whose purposes they could neither share nor control. Britain's policy, said Bevan, in the same speech at Birmingham, is that of 'the successful burglar turned householder. If I am going to ask workers to shed their blood, it will not be for medieval Abyssinia or Fascist Italy, but for making a better social system.' A few days later he received the backing of his local party in Ebbw Vale. The issue in the Labour Party was to be settled at the Conference in Brighton. Soon after, as everyone knew, the country would be plunged into a general election. Bevan went to Brighton declaring his intention to give full support to the Socialist League's line.

In fact, he played no overt part in those proceedings – the most dramatic of all Labour Conferences, where for once, with Ernest Bevin's assault on Lansbury, a Labour leader was stabbed to political death in the open forum. Possibly Bevan failed to catch the Chairman's eye. Possibly he had doubts about the line to which the Left had committed itself. For Lansbury's brand of pacifism he had no sympathy and no great respect; sometimes Cripps would present a theoretical Socialist case with an arid simplicity which offended his intellect. In any case, he, along with many others, must have cursed the fates which were enabling the authors of the Unemployment Insurance Act and the

Means Test to invite the verdict of the electorate in an atmosphere of war crisis.

Brighton, we are often told, marked the watershed between Labour's post-1931 indulgence in pacifist and emotional extremism and the preparation for the responsibility of 1940.[10] No such glimmering of enlightenment was apparent at the time. Brighton looked more like a tragic confusion. It did mark the reassertion of the trade union machine's authority, in the person of Ernest Bevin; but in the process some of the most vital elements in the Party, Lansbury's idealism and the militancy which Cripps could awaken, were heavily bruised; and in the years to come how much inertia was that strengthened machine to be empowered to impose!

The dilemma at Brighton had certainly been painful. It was asking too much – and both Cripps and Bevan must have known it in their bones – that the Party should abandon its long-expressed allegiance to the League at this hour of critical challenge. On the other hand, the best that could be done, Labour's pleadings to the Government to stand by their obligations, merely played into the hands of Stanley Baldwin who won an election on the promise that he would do exactly that. After it was all over, Mr Attlee pathetically delivered his indictment of the arch-culprit. 'The people of this country,' he said, 'trusted the right hon. Gentleman and really believed that he stood for peace. He wantonly threw that confidence away, and he will not get it again.' But Left-wing leaders, even more than unsuspecting maidens, do not cut a bold figure when they pronounce themselves betrayed. It is their business to discern traitors, to expose them in advance and to fight against their wiles. Altogether, no stranger episode had occurred in Labour history. The Ernest Bevins, for once, had the idealistic policy and it ended in total disillusion. Cripps, Bevan and Lansbury, for whatever

10. The well-publicized theory is that at Brighton Bevin's hammer started to knock the nonsense out of the thick heads of the obstreperous rank-and-file; thereafter he and Dalton and a few other unsung national heroes, who have had to wait for their biographers (or autobiographers) to bestow the proper meed of recognition, were slowly able to open the eyes of the movement to the realities of the Fascist peril. The authors of this fairy tale have conveniently forgotten Edinburgh, a year later; but of that, more follows.

curious reasons, were the hard-headed realists who had put their finger on the kernel of truth; the Baldwin Government never had the slightest intention of upholding the Covenant 'in its entirety' and it was a fraud on the nation to pretend that they ever had.

Thanks partly, therefore, to the confusions of Brighton, but thanks much more to the fact that Baldwin had kept the initiative firmly in his hands, Labour went into the election well beaten before the start. Baldwin fought on a clear policy of supporting collective security and building the necessary arms to sustain it. Neville Chamberlain declared that if the Abyssinians were betrayed we should deserve to be handed down to the shame of our children and our children's children. When ugly rumours circulated of a deal behind the League's back, Sir Samuel Hoare self-righteously scotched them in an election speech at Chelsea. The whole wardrobe of Labour's foreign policies had been stolen. No doubt, also, memories of the 1931 fiasco continued to influence the mood of the electorate. Labour regained some of its lost territory in the industrial areas, raising its parliamentary representation from 50 to 150, but no real challenge had been delivered, and the election passed off more placidly than any other of the inter-war period.

With the votes safely harvested, Sir Samuel Hoare proceeded to make his deal with Laval in Paris. Baldwin first approved the action of his colleague and then jettisoned him in the face of the national storm of protest. Yet that was a protest with a difference. There were no marches, no riots, few demonstrations; it was a more sedate revolt; in one sense led by *The Times* and the archbishops. The Hoare-Laval episode, for all its affront to standards of morality, and despite its quick repercussions in the House of Commons, did not shake the political fabric of the country, nor was the long-term policy of the Government diverted. Some consequences for the Labour Party were more persistent. What the whole commotion did do was to harden the belief on the Left that Baldwin and Chamberlain were utterly untrustworthy in meeting the Fascist menace. The substantial case of the Right wing at Brighton had been that the Government *must* be trusted if the League was to be saved. Baldwin had shattered that claim and the battle of Brighton would have to be fought out again on different terms.

During the winter of 1935 and the New Year of 1936, the Socialist League and the Left within the Labour Party were bandaging the heavy wounds inflicted upon them in October. The Left looked weaker than at any time since 1931. It had little enough distinctive to say when Hitler was marching into the Rhineland in March and could do no more than watch the scene with the same impotence shown by everyone else. In June, Léon Blum's Popular Front Government took office in France; here was the first clear success for the spirit of democratic resistance in Europe, and once again the Left-wingers who had argued that they must never contaminate themselves by association with non-Socialist allies were forced to question their purist theories. Then, in July, came the news of the outbreak of war in Spain. No other event of that epoch made such an impact on the mind of the British Labour movement. Henceforward the whole tone of the argument was altered.

Despite the predictable character of the 1935 election, it had a special interest both for Jennie Lee and Aneurin Bevan which deserves to be noted. Particular events intruded in North Lanark and in Ebbw Vale which greatly influenced their future.

Soon after her defeat in 1931, Jennie Lee had received an invitation to accept nomination as the prospective Labour candidate for North Lanark. After anxious consideration she refused, for the invitation was conditional on her readiness to accept the recently approved Standing Orders of the Parliamentary Party. She explained in a letter why she took 'this difficult and unpleasant stand'. 'I have no personal grievances whatsoever against the Labour Party,' she wrote. 'It has showered kindnesses and opportunities of every kind upon me, and if at this moment I were consulting my own comfort and convenience, I should most certainly remain with the larger and more powerful organization. But, as a Socialist, it is quite impossible for me to give the written promises that are being demanded by the Labour Party as a condition of endorsement. I am more than willing to promise to support any future Labour Government so far as it is carrying out our Socialist policy. But that promise will not be accepted by Party Headquarters. They are demanding that here and now I pledge myself to give unqualified support to any future Labour Cabinet, irrespective of who may compose that Cabinet or what its policy may be. That I cannot do . . . If a Labour Cabinet or any other Cabinet produces legislation that means reduced wages or worsened conditions for any section of workers, no Socialist has the right to remain neutral. I must be free to support the Socialist alternatives in keeping with pre-election promises and propaganda. That right I am definitely and categorically denied . . .'

This letter, it must be remembered, was written at a time when the 1931 fiasco was still sharp in every Socialist's mind. It was the votes of the I.L.P. rebels against the MacDonald Government which were provoking Labour's disciplinarians to demand the enforcement of rigorous Standing Orders. That naturally made those on the Left suspicious about the future. Yet there was an awkward and powerful argument on the other side. 'Once my letter was in the post,' wrote Jennie, 'I felt very naked. The door-bell rang. When I saw Aneurin Bevan outside I had half a mind to pretend that I was not at home. But I had better get it over. I knew what I was in for. Pedant, bigot, Salvation Army lassie – all the familiar abuse flowed over my head. I myself had quite a command of invective. The bullying was by no means all on one side.'[11]

That scene occurred in 1932. Aneurin had no more respect for the Standing Orders than she had, but he was not prepared to be driven out of the Labour Party by the calculated pedantry of his opponents. So on this issue they simply agreed to disagree. In the 1935 general election Jennie was once more I.L.P. candidate for North Lanark and there was every expectation that she would regain the seat – if the Labour Party could be persuaded not to put up an official Labour candidate against her. It was now Aneurin's turn to feel outraged by the operation of the machine. Despite the fact that it attempted elsewhere to give a clear run to a few Liberals – for instance, Megan Lloyd George in Anglesey – it worked overtime to ensure that an official Labour

11. *Tomorrow is a New Day* by Jennie Lee.

candidate was nominated in North Lanark. The machine hated the Left much more than the moderate middle; to keep Jennie Lee out, it was willing to hand a seat to the Tories.

A few days before the poll she received a letter from Tredegar. 'I cannot say how sorry I am,' he wrote, 'that McAllister is standing, but I was afraid of it all along. It was difficult to believe that you would have no Labour opponent in the midst of the welter of bitterness and backbiting which is probably going on in the Scottish constituencies. You must be having a terrible time.' Then he added a comment about his own contest. 'Probably the Scottish press contains no information about political events in Wales, but I can assure you that things are none too easy in the Ebbw Vale division. Richard Thomas and Co., big tinplate producers, have bought the Ebbw Vale steel works. The announcement has been made recently, and Lady Firth, the wife of the managing director of Richard Thomas, is spending her time in Ebbw Vale stirring up as much trouble as she can. It is much more difficult than we expected.' He went on to say jokingly: 'In the event of my being defeated in Ebbw Vale, I am looking forward to being supported by your £400 a year for North Lanark, and in case we are both defeated I have arranged for a barrel organ. That would be O.K. for us. You look all right with a shawl over your head, and your gipsy blood will come in first class.'

The official Labour candidate in North Lanark forfeited his deposit but collected 6,763 votes, enough to put the Tory in with a majority of 5,034, despite Jennie Lee's respectable 17,267 secured against both Party machines. Aneurin on this occasion had really to fight, not simply to take victory for granted – he eventually secured a majority of 17,862 over his Conservative opponent, Miss F. E. Scarborough – but the Richard Thomas story had many long-term repercussions.

The old Ebbw Vale steel works had been closed, putting some ten thousand steelworkers out of work, just at the time of Bevan's first election in 1929. Ever since then he had battered at the doors of Government departments, headed deputations from the local council and the unions, brought Ministers to Ebbw Vale and generally pulled every string he could to get the works reopened.

He even submitted to what, for him, was the indignity of ingratiating himself with the Special Areas Commissioner appointed by the National Government, Sir Malcolm Stewart. Nothing was left undone that could be done, both in Parliament and by private negotiation. Then, in the summer of 1935, they got 'a nibble' – the prospect that Sir William Firth might make a bid for the old steel works on behalf of Richard Thomas Ltd. Just at the moment when the deal was tenderly balanced, Bevan's temper was not improved by receiving a letter on crested notepaper from Quiet Court, 92 Bedford Avenue, Barnet, Herts. Miss F. E. Scarborough, his recently adopted Conservative opponent, asked him to join a Central Petition Committee she was arranging, designed to secure the signature of 'every grown person in Ebbw Vale and surrounding districts' in support of Government aid to get the steel works reopened. Bevan replied that since the Government had already been deluged with demands from Ebbw Vale, it was difficult to see what purpose could be served by Miss Scarborough's manoeuvre. 'The assumption behind your proposal,' he wrote, 'is that the Government is able to start the works, but won't. If that be the case, I suggest that what the Government requires is not a petition but penal servitude.'

When the election was over Miss Scarborough returned to Quiet Court. But Sir William Firth, a champion of expansion among the restrictionist leaders of the steel industry, came and saw and conquered. He laid the foundations of the renovation of Ebbw Vale and his monument still stands today. Yet long after his death his remains the most controversial name in the history of British steel. The old steel masters would never forgive him. Two years after his purchase his enemies exploited his financial difficulties to try and put him out of business – in his own words: 'in very dirty weather some pirates pushed us on the rocks and boarded us.' [12] Three years later again, in 1940, the pirates made

12. Mr Duncan Burn, the historian of the steel industry, who is certainly not favourable to Sir William Firth in his judgements, describes the incident thus: 'He [Firth] was forced to seek additional financial support from the City, and this was only granted on condition that he "co-operated" with the Federation on terms which may have been dictated by some of his principal rivals.' (*The Steel Industry* 1939–1959.)

him walk the plank. No inquiry into the affair was permitted by the Government of the day.

This is not the place to re-examine the Firth saga. But Sir William's arrival in Ebbw Vale certainly left its mark on Aneurin Bevan. Despite the first interventions of Lady Firth, the two men became firm friends, and even Aneurin's hardened eyes were opened wide by the methods of warfare employed between the steel masters and by their financial overlords. By comparison, political infighting resembled a preparatory school pillow-fight. Sir Henry Spencer, later the managing director of Richard Thomas and Baldwins, has given his verdict of the episode. 'It was,' he says, 'Sir William Firth – who was a restless rebel with an original, non-conformist, unconventional outlook and power-ful personality – who shook the industry from top to toe by his imaginative, spectacular, controversial modernization of derelict Ebbw Vale into an integrated iron, steel, and continuous hot and cold reduction sheet and tinplate mill – the first of its kind out-side the United States. He did this against the wishes and against the bitter hostility of the whole of the steel industry, and with no sympathy from banking. Indeed, at the end, when money ran short, both the industry and the banks combined to try and ruin him and his company, and to prevent the completion of Ebbw Vale.'[13]

Sir William Firth was condemned as 'hopelessly unco-opera-tive', a perpetual trouble-maker; he was clearly a rebel against the Standing Orders of the steel industry. Not that the steel men had much use for such soft weapons of reproof. But the steel he produced saved Ebbw Vale and, when the war came, helped to save the nation. The quickly established kinship between the two men was not surprising. Ever afterwards Bevan *knew* about steel; he got his brief from experts and incorporated it in his own political philosophy. What a politician learns in his own con-stituency, if he also has the imagination to see the parish pump in a national perspective, becomes an integral part of himself. Even while he was increasingly involved in the controversies about foreign affairs, Bevan resolved to have his revenge on the

13. Speech, *Steel and the Nation*, delivered by Mr Harry F. Spencer, later Sir Henry, 20 January 1961.

steel masters and the bankers who thought they could treat Ebbw Vale and the gold which started pouring from its once-derelict works as their playthings.

Spain cut the knot of emotional and intellectual contradictions in which the Left had been tangled ever since Hitler came to power. Suddenly the claims of international law, class solidarity and the desire to win the Soviet Union as an ally fitted into the same strategy. These subconscious releases no doubt played their part in swelling the mood of sympathy for the Spanish Republic which swept so swiftly through the British working class. But no complicated explanations are required. The spectacle itself was stirring enough.

On the morning of 18 July, General Franco issued his *pronunciamento* of revolt from Las Palmas in the Canaries: that day the signal was given for a rebel uprising in almost all the leading Spanish cities. Quickly enough, on the Madrid radio, came the authentic note of Republican resistance which was to serve for long months ahead. 'It is better to die on your feet than to live on your knees! *No pasarán!*' Butchery on both sides was let loose; for a few days, even weeks perhaps, statesmen in London might be pardoned if they thought the confusion too great for any general pattern to be discerned. Yet the first truly remarkable feature of Spain's civil war was how speedily the uprising was crushed over so wide an area. Despite the hesitancies of the Government and the mass desertion of the Army to the rebel cause, the Republic was victoriously defended in a matter of days in Madrid and Barcelona and over more than two-thirds of Spanish soil. This was the result of Spain's plebiscite when, admittedly amid immense violence and confusion, men had to vote with their own right arms instead of at the ballot box. The outside world knew little of the ancient Spanish feuds which had helped to produce the crisis. Too swiftly and crudely perhaps but none the less correctly, many observers regarded the event as part of the Fascist plan for the conquest of Europe. In their eyes the heroic Republic was legitimate and liberal. By every standard of law, interest, comradeship and honour it had the right to call upon the aid of friends of peace and freedom everywhere. And here, moreover, a real victory could be won. If democracy triumphed on Spanish battlefields, the cause could be invigorated all over Europe. Men and women across the whole Continent might believe once again that the entire Fascist onslaught on civilization could be checked and rolled back.

Aneurin Bevan was one of those in Britain who at once saw the new event in its full setting. The note struck in his speeches was deeper and stronger than any he had sounded before in dealing with the foreign situation. 'Should Spain become Fascist, as assuredly it will if the rebels succeed,' he said, 'then Britain's undisputed power in the Mediterranean is gone. We shall be too weak to offer any formidable resistance to the Fascist Governments of Germany, Italy and Spain who will form an alliance. We must form an alliance with France, Spain, Russia and Turkey so as to become so powerful that we shall never have any fear of the Fascists breaking the peace.' Henceforward the Spanish struggle must dominate the whole arena of domestic and world politics. Both idealism and realism prescribed the same remedy.

However, the barely credible fact is that neither the British Government nor those critics within the ruling class who had claimed to be most alarmed by its feckless conduct in face of the Fascist menace caught even a glimpse of these clarities. From the earliest days the British Ambassador to Spain, Sir Henry Chilton, was sending back information 'intended to cripple the Government and serve the insurgents'.[14] Spain was dismissed either as an irrelevant sideshow to the main drama or as the victim of a devilish Communist conspiracy. Britain, said Sir Samuel Hoare, had no concern in this 'faction fight'. Baldwin, according to the report of his most confidential secretary, Thomas Jones, 'was much affected by the Spanish troubles. "I told Eden yesterday [said Baldwin] that on no account, French or other, must he bring us into the fight on the side of the Russians." I reminded him of Bullitt's prophecy made to me two months ago that Moscow looked forward to a Communist Government in Spain in three months.'[15] This was Jones's entry

14. These are the words of the American Ambassador. Quoted by Hugh Thomas in *The Spanish Civil War*.
15. *A Diary with Letters* by Thomas Jones.

in his diary on 27 July, only ten days after the outbreak of the war when there was certainly no sign, much less proof, of Russian intervention. Thomas Jones, who moved easily between Downing Street and Cliveden, was ready to admit that he hoped for a Franco victory and no doubt his preference was widely shared in the same circles. 'In this quarrel, I was neutral,' wrote Winston Churchill,[16] omitting to recollect that his first reaction was open support for the insurgents delivered in the same strain in which he had once denounced 'the foul baboonery of Bolshevism' way back in 1918. 'I was sure,' he insisted, 'that with all the rest they had on their hands the British Government was right to keep out of Spain.' Baldwin and Churchill were at one; they had their United Front on this issue if on few others. Most of the so-called non-Party elements which had been shaken by the Hoare-Laval deal showed the same complacency. The archbishops were silent. And when General Franco's armies appeared to be closing on Madrid, *The Times*, ever strong on the stronger side, pronounced the Republican Government 'helpless and discredited'. Mussolini had declared that it would all be over by November; the Churchills and the Edens, no less than the Baldwins, the Chamberlains, the Simons and the Hoares, were content. It is important to recall how swift and resolute was the British Government in rejecting any idea of assistance to the Spanish Republic, how much its attitude and that of the bulk of its supporters veered towards ill-concealed sympathy with the Fascist revolt. This played its part in shaping the temper of the Left.

The authoritative bodies of the British Labour movement did not hesitate to express their view about the rights and wrongs of the quarrel. If the régime in Madrid was Communist or Communist-infiltrated, the fact went undetected by Sir Walter Citrine and Mr Ernest Bevin who could normally scent a Communist conspiracy before Churchill had even got a whiff of it. Within two days a resolution had been passed, confirmed within a week by both the National Executive of the Party and the General Council of the T.U.C., affirming the warmest support of British workers for their Spanish comrades. An immedi-

16. *The Gathering Storm* by Winston Churchill.

ate appeal was launched to raise funds for the distress which must follow the fighting. For the moment it looked as if the whole movement had swung into action with united fervour. On 28 July an emergency meeting of the two international bodies – the International Federation of Trade Unions and the Labour and Socialist International – was held in Brussels. There, the full promises of support were reaffirmed and it was agreed that representatives should be sent at once to Spain to get first-hand information of what was required. Citrine himself was about to leave Paris on this mission when an urgent message from Madrid suggested that his services might be even more urgently needed in Paris and London. However, the other delegate, de Broukère of Belgium, continued on the journey. He soon sent back the simple message that much the most pressing need of the Republic was for arms. Most of the army had deserted to Franco, taking their weapons with them. A new army had to be improvised and war materials of all kinds must be secured from somewhere. However, even at the meeting in Brussels in July, this proposition met with difficulties. There were rumours that the French Government was hesitating to make the decision to supply the Spanish Government. Even so, at the Brussels meeting the Internationals did not equivocate. They issued a clear declaration insisting on the right of the Spanish Government to buy arms.

At the beginning of August French policy took a more specific form – all the Governments concerned on both sides were to be invited to sign a Non-Intervention agreement, declaring their readiness to maintain an embargo on the supply of arms both to the Republic and to Franco. What had really happened behind the scenes to produce this initiative is crucial to the whole story. One of the first acts of the Spanish Government was to appeal to the French for arms and originally there was no doubt about the sympathy and the resolve of the French Prime Minister, Léon Blum. Although he had only been in office since June and had plentiful troubles of his own, he at once consulted the two leading Radical members of his Cabinet – the Foreign Minister, Yvon Delbos, and the War Minister, Edouard Daladier – and agreed to the Spanish request. Very soon the first despatch of arms was on the way. But soon, too, the British Ambassador in Paris was sounding the alarm in London. An urgent telephone call was received at the Quai d'Orsay from the French Ambassador in London. An Anglo-French meeting in London had previously been fixed to discuss other matters. Baldwin now urged that Blum should accompany his Foreign Minister to London. This was the first step in the application of British pressure on the French. 'Are you going to send arms to the Spanish Republic?' was the question put by Anthony Eden to Blum in London. 'Yes,' said Blum. 'It is your affair,' replied Eden, 'but I ask you one thing. Be prudent.'

Blum returned to Paris to find that, in face of the British advice and some sensational revelations in the French Right-wing press about the proposed aid for Spain, his Radical colleagues were wavering. His own intentions, fortified by the first evidence of Italian assistance for the rebels, remained unaltered. But at a stormy meeting of the French Cabinet on 2 August, Delbos, 'in consideration of the British position', proposed an approach to 'interested Governments' to secure 'a Non-Intervention Pact'. Blum was still unconvinced. He argued powerfully to Mr Philip Noel-Baker who had just arrived in Paris that a Nationalist Spain would be a threat to Britain no less than France. He despatched Admiral Darlan, French Chief of Naval Staff, to London to argue in the same sense. But all these appeals were of no avail against the firm conclusions already reached in London. On 7 August the British Ambassador in Paris presented Delbos with what was little short of an ultimatum. If France did not agree to ban the export of arms to Spain and a war with Germany ensued, Britain might consider herself absolved from the obligation to help France under the Treaty of Locarno. Darlan had returned from London to confirm the news about British official opinion. So, on 8 August French policy was changed. All exports of arms to Spain would be stopped the next day. The reversal of view was said to be due to the 'almost unanimously favourable' response forthcoming to the idea of a Non-Intervention Pact. In fact, only Britain had agreed at once; most of the other countries were 'studying' the proposition. Blum was utterly downcast and near resignation.

Once, when the Spanish representative in Paris described to him the young militiamen fighting Fascism in the sierras, he buried his face in his hands and wept. He was still ready, with the aid of his Air Minister, Pierre Cot, to connive at surreptitious supplies of aircraft to the Republic. But no amount of tears or devious manoeuvres could alter the fateful nature of the step he had taken. Henceforth, the Non-Intervention scheme could plausibly be presented to the world as the brain-child of the widely-respected Socialist Prime Minister of France.[17]

These exchanges, of course, were not public knowledge at the time. Only one fact was incontrovertible; it was on the authority of the French Government that the Non-Intervention scheme had been officially put forward, and British Ministers were content that their own role in the affair should remain modestly concealed. This was their trump card with the Labour leaders, and they played it mercilessly. The spokesmen of the Labour Party were still extremely conscious of how frantically the Spanish Republicans opposed the idea. On 18 August, they went on a deputation to Anthony Eden at the Foreign Office. They put the Spanish case, only to be informed how imperative it was that the French plan should be backed if European peace was to be preserved. Moreover, they were assured that the agreement would be rapidly initialled and could be made to succeed. It was in fact signed at the end of August and the first meeting of the Non-Intervention Committee, to enforce the embargo, was scheduled to meet in London on 9 September. Beneath all the pressures the Labour leadership was yielding. Spain was to pay dearly for their credulous faith in the word of Anthony Eden. A more astringent leadership might at least have begun to unmask the truth about the comings and goings between London and Paris. But not a particle of it was uncovered. Baldwin and Eden themselves could not have improved on the manner in which the tale was told by Labour leaders to their followers.

Special measures were considered necessary if the unpalatable doctrine of Non-Intervention was to be approved by the Labour

17. These facts about the origins of Non-Intervention are taken from *The Spanish Civil War* by Hugh Thomas, the most detailed and authoritative book on the subject.

movement. On 28 August an extraordinary Joint Meeting of the T.U.C. General Council, the National Executive, and the full Parliamentary Party was summoned. Blum's dilemma and the way he had solved it, supposedly of his own free will, supplied the main argument of the leadership. A declaration was proposed and carried 'expressing regret that it should have been thought expedient, on the ground of the danger of war inherent in the situation, to conclude agreements among the European Powers laying an embargo upon the supply of arms and munitions of war to Spain, by which the rebel forces and the democratically elected and recognized Government of Spain are placed on the same footing. While such agreements may lessen international tension, provided they are applied immediately, are loyally observed by all parties, and their execution is effectively co-ordinated and supervised, the utmost vigilance will be necessary to prevent these agreements being utilized to injure the Spanish Government.' The National Council of Labour was instructed 'to maintain its close watch upon events'. Such quavering accents certainly did not match the mood outside. Bevan and a few others objected to the resolution, calling instead for a return to the earlier doctrine which the International had enunciated a month before. He had one ally, Herbert Morrison, on the Executive itself. Bevan, indeed, guessed the truth; he made the open challenge that the Non-Intervention idea had been born in London. But Bevin, Citrine, Dalton and their supporters had no great difficulty in swaying the meeting to their policy – which was also Baldwin's and Eden's policy.

Early in September a Labour delegation was despatched to Paris to seek confirmation of the French view in preparation for the Trades Union Congress which was to meet in Plymouth on 7 September. Among its number was Hugh Dalton who has since confessed that he 'was a good deal less enthusiastic than many of my political friends on behalf of the Spanish Republican Government'.[18] He was eager to sustain the French view and he got

18. *The Fateful Years* by Hugh Dalton. Dalton's insistence on how Blum reiterated that Non-Intervention was *his* policy, not Eden's, reads strangely in the face of the known facts of the agony Blum had endured in the last weeks of July and the beginning of August. Dalton, it seems, found out only what he wanted to find out. He made no effort to unravel facts which, if

from Blum the assurance he desired – Non-Intervention was *his* policy, not Eden's. Possibly Dalton might have drawn a somewhat different inference from Blum's other piece of information – that the French Government was secretly supplying aircraft to the Republic at that very moment. But that was a titbit for his diary, not an argument for the T.U.C.

Citrine and Bevin were able to put their case at Plymouth with Blum as the chief witness for their wisdom. 'Your General Council,' said Citrine, 'believe that this policy, distasteful as it is to them and it will be to you, is the only practical policy which can be followed in the present position. We do not accept the gibe that we are following the British Government. We are not even taking our policy from the Socialist-led Government of France, which was the initiator of this. We decided our policy, unpopular though it may be with large masses of our own people who do not perhaps understand the niceties of the question, because we believe that policy is right, however distasteful, and the policy which your wisdom will commend.' Ernest Bevin said that 'we have not fallen head over heels into the business; the Non-Intervention agreement would have to be honoured; the National Council of Labour will have to watch every step'. He called for a unanimous vote and he almost got it; in the end, after considerable debate, only 51,000 votes were cast against 3,029,000 for the General Council. Opposition had been flattened by the note Bevin struck in his winding-up speech. 'The choice before us,' he said, 'was whether or not we would take a step which in our view would lead to war.' Then he sailed into one of his most admired perorations: 'It is not a question of calling men out on strike and paying them strike pay, when the worst you have to face is defeat and loss of membership – it is an issue of life and death, an issue of the road that humanity is going to take for the next hundred years. Peace is not determined by an incident that happens at a moment. A writer once said that the seed of all future wars is sown in the settlement of previous wars, and Europe today is at the crossroads. Cool heads, cool judgements, combined with fearless courage in facing the

divulged at that time, might have proved extremely damaging to the British Government.

situation, settling it with our heads and not with our emotions, may indeed prove that in the end, notwithstanding the black cloud of dictatorship at the moment, this democracy may yet again set the feet of men upon a road that our children may call us blessed for having taken.' And with these proud words ringing in their ears, the British trade union movement put its seal on the Non-Intervention policy.

But the decisions of Plymouth could not dampen the flame of anger in the country. The news was too bitter. Although the deeds of Spanish Republican heroism were already beginning to echo round the world, free Spain seemed to be crumbling beneath the weight of General Franco's metal. Franco swore that he would be in the capital by October. Evidence of a concerted conspiracy by the Fascist powers poured in from all sides. Opposition was growing in France to the declared policy of the Blum Government. The stage was set for the Edinburgh Conference of the Labour Party – a more significant assembly than the more famous Brighton. It was at Edinburgh that Bevan's course was set for the remaining years of the peace, and the fact must be understood. Since the orthodox histories and biographies of the age reduce the Spanish war to a secondary status, they conceal the real reasons why Socialist suspicion of the Government was so deep-rooted and why a suspicion hardly less deep was nurtured on the Left about the fibre and courage, if not the purposes, of the official Labour leadership.

Nothing at Edinburgh mattered beside Spain, although the Executive had produced a statement on international and defence policy, designed, albeit in ambiguous terms, to confirm their victory at Brighton and to wean the Party away from its rigid opposition to the Government's rearmament programme. For Bevin and Dalton, the leaders of the view that it was hopelessly inconsistent for Labour to demand collective security and still to vote against the arms estimates, this was the major item on the agenda. But the Spanish experience did not assist them in countering the argument of their Executive colleagues, and the overwhelming majority of the Party, that votes against arms were votes against a Government whose policy could not be trusted. If some Tories regarded Franco as a gallant Christian gentleman, why should they not soon detect the same saintly qualities in Hitler and Mussolini, and if all these holy crusaders were acting in unison, why should infidels assist in fitting on their armour? Moreover, the plea that academic theories must give way to the urgencies of the hour now fortified the thesis of the Left. How to save Spain? That was the only test. Tempers at the Conference were not improved when the rumour circulated that special delegates were coming from Spain, but that the Executive had decided to put the issue to the vote before they had been heard.

On the Monday afternoon, Arthur Greenwood opened the case for the Executive. He agreed that the Non-Intervention policy was a very bad second best, but he pressed hard the points argued by Citrine and Bevin at Plymouth. 'If you established free trade in arms,' he said, 'believe me, it could only be done over the body of Léon Blum and the Popular Front Government in France.' Even more serious was the wider issue. 'Is this Conference prepared to have the battle between dictatorship and democracy fought over the bleeding body of Spain? That is a question you have to answer. I say it is a very serious decision. Is anybody in this Conference prepared to suggest action which, if it were taken, might mean that a lighted match was dropped into the powder barrel?' He asked for trust in the National Council of Labour which had lived night and day with the problem and which felt 'exactly as you feel about it'. At the end a delegate from the floor intervened. Had the National Council of Labour been in touch with the Spanish Government and what line of action had that Government asked for? Greenwood answered with commendable and damaging candour. 'Of course we know what they want – what we should want in the circumstances. They want arms. That is what the argument is about today.'

Greenwood had been defensive and shaky in the face of some angry interruptions, but the big union battalions came to his aid – Ernest Bevin, Charles Dukes of the General and Municipal Workers, George Hicks of the Building Workers and finally Attlee, leader of the Party. But this was not the walk-over of Plymouth. Sir Charles Trevelyan, William Dobbie, M.P., just back with first-hand news from the Spanish front, and Philip

Noel-Baker all rounded on the Executive. 'You are beggared of policy at this moment,' said Trevelyan. 'When the last great war that is looming comes, and when Japan and Germany crash in to destroy Soviet Russia, I hope then the Labour Party will have some other policy to offer than their sympathy, accompanied by bandages and cigarettes.' A huge derisive cheer from the Conference hit the platform. 'God help the Labour movement,' commented Bevin, if that was the basis on which the decision was to be made.

It was Aneurin Bevan who most stirred the Conference that morning. He came to the rostrum soon after Charles Dukes had explained that the National Council of Labour had not been 'able to secure a tittle of evidence' that arms were pouring into the rebels. 'We have been told by Mr Bevin,' he started, 'and we are told by Mr Greenwood that those of us who were critical of the official policy of the Party were being governed by our sentiments and not by our heads. I listened to Mr Dukes with great care, and if Mr Dukes is representative of the cool, cold, calculated and well-informed manner in which the official policy of the Party is being decided, then I am all for sentiment and emotion. He told us there was no evidence before the National Council of Labour as to the supply of arms to the rebels in Spain. Every reputable visitor from Spain informs us that the Government of Spain is without arms from outside and the rebels are getting all they need to support them. Every newspaper office in London is full of information about arms pouring in through Lisbon. Del Vayo has made statements at Geneva and laid a document before the League to the effect that arms are pouring in to the rebels and that now the rebels are superior in the air. Everybody in the world knows about the rebels getting arms – except the National Council of Labour. Mr Bevin told the Conference that the reason why the rebels were getting arms in Spain was because the Fascists were ignoring all the claims of international law.'

At this Ernest Bevin rose to his feet in protest: 'On a point of correction,' he insisted, 'I did not utter the words, or anything akin to the words, that Mr Aneurin Bevan is attributing to me. What I said was that the Fascist Governments are now ignoring international law and I indicated that the only alternative to prevent them recognizing the Burgos Government was some form of action of this character by M Blum.' But Bevan struck back: 'I do not know what Mr Bevin means by that, because if the reference in his speech to the Fascist Governments ignoring international law did not relate to the issues before the Conference, then they were entirely irrelevant. What we are discussing and what Mr Bevin was discussing was the fact that the rebels are receiving arms and the Government is not receiving arms, and that the rebels are receiving arms because the Fascist nations ignore the obligations of international covenants.' One observer recorded the exchange thus: 'I have seen Bevin many a time hammer his way through a Conference successfully. Watching this scene from the press table, I have never seen him so disconcerted by an opponent as on this occasion. Frowning heavily, his big form sank back into his seat and he made no more interruptions.'[19]

Bevan swept on, turning his fire on Greenwood. 'I want to point out to Mr Greenwood that he ought not to come to this Conference and make statements about what occurs in private conferences of the Party, especially when he makes wrong statements. Mr Greenwood said this afternoon that we had met in Transport House, London – members of the Parliamentary Party, the National Executive and the General Council – and that no alternative suggestion was made. Mr Greenwood knows very well that there were many people at that conference who opposed the policy, and the alternative to the policy suggested by the National Council of Labour is obviously that the embargo should be raised, and the Spanish Government obtain arms. That is why we opposed it. We have had a dreadful picture painted to us of what would be the consequences if free trade in arms took place. Will Conference consider for a moment the consequences that will occur in Europe if the present situation is allowed to work out to its logical conclusion? Is it not obvious to everyone that if the arms continue to pour into the rebels in Spain, our Spanish comrades will be slaughtered by hundreds of thousands? Has Mr Bevin and the National Council considered the fate of the Blum Government if a Fascist Government is established in Spain? How long will French democracy

19. *Labour's Big Three* by J. T. Murphy.

stand against Fascism in Germany, Fascism in Italy, Fascism in Spain and Fascism in Portugal? How long will French democracy stand if the French Fascists attempt a *coup d'état* against the French Popular Front Government, and are supplied with arms by friends in Spain? We have the suggestion that for the sake of avoiding a European war we must maintain a neutral attitude. If the Popular Front French Government is destroyed and democracy in France is destroyed, then the Franco-Soviet Pact will soon be denounced, and democracy in Europe will soon be in ruins. That is the consequence of this policy. And what is going to be the effect upon the vitality of Socialism throughout the world if our comrades in Spain are slaughtered and democracy in Europe is on its back as a consequence of our acquiescence in neutrality in Great Britain?

'Everybody knows who has studied this matter at all, that there is divided opinion in France as to the line the French Government should take; and instead of the British Labour movement, by its policy, supporting those comrades in France who are desirous of supporting the Spanish Government, we are putting arguments in the mouths of the French Right by our support of the British Government. Comrades on the platform know very well that the original proposal of the Blum Government was not for the immediate application of an embargo; it was for the application of an embargo after all the other countries had agreed, and it was the British Government that insisted on the immediate application of an embargo. I believe that the decision of the Labour Party in this matter will have disastrous consequences for the Socialist movement throughout the world. I ask those trade union leaders here carefully to consider whether the votes they propose to give on this resolution are really representative of the rank-and-file they are supposed to represent at this Conference.'[20]

Yet on Monday the Executive survived. Their resolution was carried by 1,836,000 votes to 519,000. What Jennie Lee, who was at Edinburgh reporting the Conference for the I.L.P., called[21]

20. It may seem, from the evidence already cited, that Bevan's view of the French attitude was a good deal more accurate than that presented by Greenwood and Bevin. His argument ran along the same lines as those Blum had sent Admiral Darlan to press in London.
21. *Tomorrow is a New Day* by Jennie Lee.

'their more than usually "weighty" air', their manner 'that they knew a great deal more than it was expedient to say' had once again persuaded Labour to play the statesman. Mr Attlee, in winding up for the Executive, said Dalton, had 'as his gift is, lowered the temperature'. But this triumph was short-lived; on the Wednesday other gifts were brought to bear.

The two Spanish delegates had arrived and were at last allowed to speak. Señor de Asua spoke in French, Noel-Baker translating; the words themselves were telling enough. Here was the detailed proof of the supply of arms to the rebels which Charles Dukes had searched for in vain, and the very quietness of the reproach struck like a dagger. 'We do not ask you to change your vote of Monday last. We do not ask your country to change its policy. We do not want to mix in your affairs. But we are fighting with sticks and knives against tanks and aircraft and guns and it revolts the conscience of the world that that should be true. We must have arms. Help us to buy them somewhere in the world.' Then came Señora Isabel de Palencia, a proud Amazon straight from the Spanish battlefields, speaking perfect Scottish and recalling her own Scottish childhood when she had walked the streets of Edinburgh 'peopled to me, in my child's mind, with the characters of Walter Scott and echoing with the music of Robert Burns' poems'. No one who heard that speech was ever likely to forget it; it was a marvel of calculated passion. 'Now we are going to leave you,' she concluded. 'We are going to leave you with our hearts very comforted. We thank you, as my comrade has said, for your sympathy, for your support. We know that we are holding your hand across the distance. But let me tell you, if you wish this atrocious war to end soon, come and help us as you have been asked, whenever you can. Think of the precious gift that is being wasted – of the lives of our youth. Do not tarry. Now you know the truth. Now you know what the situation is in Spain. Come and help us. Come and help us. Scotsmen, ye ken noo!'

The Conference rose and sang the Red Flag. Isabel Palencia gave the clenched-fist salute. All the inhibitions of Monday were forgotten. And swift action followed. Dalton made the announcement at the commencement of the afternoon session. The

Executive had met in the lunch interval and agreed at once that the speeches should be published in pamphlet form. And even that was not all. It was also agreed that Attlee and Greenwood should proceed forthwith on a special mission to London to discuss the situation with the acting Prime Minister, Mr Neville Chamberlain.

On Thursday night the missionaries had returned and on Friday they reported to the Conference. They had seen Chamberlain, urged upon him the necessity of ensuring that the Non-Intervention Committee did its work effectively, and received in return the assurance 'that the British representatives were fully conscious of the dangers which would be incurred if the situation were not cleared up without delay . . .' 'We are calling upon our Government, without delay,' said Attlee, 'to establish the facts'; if the breaches of the Non-Intervention treaty continued, then the whole treaty must be abrogated. Ernest Bevin leapt in to improve the occasion, no doubt recalling how his own special brand of demagogy had swept the board at Plymouth. No one could stoop to conquer with the same agility as the rock-like Bevin, and he could do it in the same breath when he abjured the easy cheers won by the Trevelyans and the Bevans. 'We understand this statement to mean,' he said, 'that from the moment we leave this Conference, our officers will be on the doorstep [it was assumed he meant the doorstep of Number 10 Downing Street] not in a week, but every day, to get results.' Bevin was to be the watchdog who would put an end to any Chamberlain 'monkey-tricks'.

Friday's temper had certainly altered from Monday's. But Labour had still not specifically repudiated its allegiance to the Non-Intervention policy. Many could not suppress the fear that Labour leaders who scurried back and forth to London with Chamberlain's assurances had no imagination to grasp the greatness of the occasion and little stomach for the fight. 'It was very silly of Mr Bevin to talk in that way,' wrote Jennie Lee. 'He ought to have known better. But British Labour leaders have a monotonous willingness to trust promises made to them by Conservative politicians, and the equally monotonous aftermath is the air of hurt surprise with which they later return to tell us that we have all once again been let down.'[22] Hugh Dalton derisively passed a different verdict which helps to indicate why suspicion of the leaders had cut so deep. The delegates, he wrote, 'were wildly excited. They were wallowing in sheer emotion, in vicarious valour. They had no clue in their minds as to the risks, and the realities, for Britain of a general war. Nor did they, even dimly, comprehend how unrepresentative they were, on the issue, of the great mass of their fellow countrymen.'[23] Gallup polls had not been invented then, but if they had been the latest findings would doubtless have confirmed how wise was the conclusion of such a leading member of Labour's Executive that nothing could or should be done to save the Spanish Republic.

At the end, the whole Conference sang the *Internationale*. 'Then comrades, come rally' – that was too much for Jennie Lee. She 'crept miserably out of the hall and stumbled into Aneurin. He looked haggard and careworn. He was ill anyhow at the time and in no condition to stand punishment. He looked as if he had just dragged himself from the torture chamber. And he was not the only delegate who felt like that. Out they came, singly and in groups, the most unhappy, guilty-looking collection of people I have ever seen. Their very misery made me hope again. If they felt like that something perhaps could still be done.'[22] A short while later she strayed into the Caledonian Hotel where the Executive was staying. She looked on the company, metaphorically spat and left as swiftly as she could. Walking up Prince's Street, just by the Scott Memorial, she heard footsteps behind her and turned to face Aneurin. 'Jennie,' said Nye who had witnessed the scene at the Caledonian, 'you really must cultivate the gift of social hypocrisy.' Then, despite the hurt they both felt at the whole spectacle of Labour subservience, they could not help laughing at so strange a remonstrance from such a quarter; he was not the best of tutors in this part of the political curriculum. They walked off, comforted to be together again, but not in the direction of the Caledonian Hotel.

No concealment was possible about the mood of the Left after Edinburgh. It was, said Professor Laski, 'the worst annual

22. *Tomorrow is a New Day* by Jennie Lee.
23. *The Fateful Years* by Hugh Dalton.

conference in the post-war history of the Party,'[24] and undoubtedly the Executive's attitude about Spain was responsible
for the feeling of near-despair. This may seem curious, since on
paper the distinction between the Executive and its critics was a
fine one. The Executive had eventually agreed that the Non-
Intervention agreement must be denounced if its provisions were
being violated and eventually they had agreed also that it *was*
being violated, whereas the critics on the other hand had called
for a clear admission of the known facts and outright denunciation. Was there any firm ground here for basing a quarrel? But
all had witnessed how the Executive's concessions had had to be
extorted, and, despite all Bevin's bombast, where was the
assurance that the will of the Conference would be translated
into a full-blooded campaign in the country? H. N. Brailsford,
who was then busily engaged in helping to organize the British
contingent of the International Brigade of volunteers to fight in
Spain, expressed a general reaction. 'Thirty years ago,' he
wrote, 'as a young man I joined the I.L.P., for under Hardie it
had courage and faith. Were I as a young man to read of the
record of this Edinburgh Conference, would anything it had
done fire me with a wish to join the Labour Party? This slouch-
ing leadership, this parasitic attitude towards the Government
of the other class, would attract no young man.'[24]

The division between Right and Left was as much one of tone,
temper and temperament as about precise differences in policy.
The Left was convinced that the crisis in Europe was moving
towards a climax in which the role played by Britain's National
Government was both contemptible and dangerous. But the
Right-wing leadership always had some fresh reason for *not*
acting, some excuse why British politics must be kept in the old
hopeless rut. They had even chosen this very moment to qualify
their opposition to the Government's rearmament programme,
thus, as the Left believed, injuring one of the few effective
sanctions which Labour could apply to enforce a change in
foreign policy and the overthrow of the Government itself. This
timorous approach had been expressed at the Conference in the
general resolution on international affairs introduced by Dalton

24. Quoted in *The Post-War History of the British Working Class* by Allen Hutt.

and carried by 1,738,000 to 657,000. Moreover the Conference had voted by heavy majorities against the proposal for accepting the affiliation of the Communist Party and against any United or Popular Front. These were propositions which as yet commanded no full assent even on the Left. But the Right seemed to be setting its face more stubbornly than ever against the new trend which had changed the aspect of politics in France and Spain. During the closing stages of the Edinburgh Conference, Cripps, Bevan, Laski, William Mellor, George Strauss and a few others met to discuss what they should do to meet the new and, as they thought, desperate situation.[25] Among other matters, they decided to proceed with a project they had considered before – the launching of a new Socialist weekly. It was at Edinburgh that *Tribune* was conceived.

All eyes were still on Spain. Would Madrid fall, as Badajoz, Talavera and Toledo had fallen to the Franco offensive? General Mola boasted that he would be drinking coffee in the Puerta del Sol by 12 October. A bout of bad weather made the General wait for reinforcements; the twelfth came and General Mola was still some thirty miles from his cup of coffee. And in Madrid they put out a café table in the street, poured out the coffee, added a garbage can, and left the notice: 'Reserved for General Mola'. But soon bravado had to give way to other qualities. In the last week of October, six bombs had dropped in the centre of the city. Moorish troops were only a fourpenny tramride away. The great battle for Madrid had started. No one could have believed that it would still be in Republican hands three years later. The people of Spain and the first contingents of the International Brigade who marched into the beleaguered capital that October made it so.

25. Oddly, Ernest Bevin shared the dismay about the Edinburgh Conference, but for entirely different reasons. His biographer, Alan Bullock, writes: 'Bevin came as near to despairing of the Labour Party after the Edinburgh Conference as he ever did, and several times that winter he remarked to Francis Williams that the trade unions would have been in a stronger political position if they had not committed themselves so completely to one party.' It was a curious moment for him to consider the attractions of flirtation with other parties. Spain, it seems, left him quite unmoved. Señora Palencia had not touched his heart. What had really angered him was the equivocal speech of Herbert Morrison on the arms debate – 'one of the worst pieces of tightrope walking I have ever seen in this Conference', as he called it.

Bevan went from Edinburgh to Paris, to a hastily-called conference of Socialists from several countries determined to assist the Republic. He was able to confirm that French Socialists were not so unanimously behind the policy of Non-Intervention as the all-knowing experts at Edinburgh had suggested. Non-Intervention, in any real sense, was already collapsing. On 7 October the Soviet Union complained of violations of the agreement of the Non-Intervention Committee and two weeks later announced its decision to send aid to the Republic. On 29 October, the Labour Party leaders, in a Commons debate, formally revoked their support for the Non-Intervention policy. According to Ernest Bevin's great speech at Plymouth, this should have meant that the Party was making the choice for European war; but Labour leaders now argued alternatively that only by rejecting Non-Intervention could European peace be preserved.[26] Early in November an official delegation of the French Popular Front parties came to London, with Léon Blum's approval, to enlist support in Britain, if France too should denounce the Non-Intervention Pact. Thus, within three weeks, not a shred was left of the formidable case presented by the official leaders at Plymouth and Edinburgh. None of them dared argue it further. Unfortunately, the indelible impression remained of leaders trailing behind events. The British Government, no less than the Labour Left, could take their measure. For history records no ugly scenes between Baldwin and Ernest Bevin on the Downing Street doorstep.

During that November the country witnessed the biggest hunger march of the thirties and one which had more official backing from the Labour Party than any of its predecessors. It was odd

26. How much wiser was this second view than that with which the leaders had bemused both the T.U.C. at Plymouth and the Labour Party at Edinburgh is now proved. All the evidence confirms the case which Bevan and the Left pressed from the start and continued to press afterwards, in the teeth of all the warnings from the Government that aid for Spain would increase the danger of general war. A. J. P. Taylor writes in *The Origins of the Second World War*: 'It was widely believed at the time that Germany and Italy would themselves fight on the rebel side, if their intervention was challenged. Strangely enough, this was not true. One of the few well-documented facts of the time is that both Hitler and Mussolini were determined not to risk war over Spain. If challenged, they would have withdrawn.'

that this display of unity should occur just after the disillusion of Edinburgh. But, of course, the march had been prepared long before and the contrast offers a fitting proof of the different tempo at which events were moving within the Labour hierarchy and among the rank-and-file.

Just before Parliament had risen for the summer recess, Bevan had delivered one of his most vitriolic attacks on the Government's treatment of the unemployed. He could not listen with patience to the new Minister of Labour who explained the decisions of the Unemployment Assistance Board. 'All we have got,' he said, 'is a puppet, an incompetent hack who comes down to the House to make a disgraceful speech for an administration over which he has no control.' Once again he returned to his favourite theme of the relations between Parliament and the poverty outside. 'The House of Commons,' he continued, 'has reduced my people to such impotence; what are we to do? You have deprived them of any voice anywhere. You have established seven thousand officials without the slightest responsibility to the people and we cannot control them here. What do hon. Members opposite suggest that they should do? Vote every four or five years? I hope if the Regulations worsen the conditions of the people in my district, they will behave in such a manner that you will require to send a regular army to keep order.' The cries of shame which greeted this declaration merely spurred him on; for most Tory M.P.s were showing precious little interest in the condition of South Wales. 'If income tax is under consideration,' he said, 'those benches are packed. If electricity is under consideration, those benches are packed. If there is some opposition to a little Municipal Bill, for which hon. Members opposite have been subsidized by private concerns, those benches are packed. If it is a sugar subsidy, those benches are packed. If it is swag, those benches are packed, but if it is the poor, they are empty. I am filled with contempt and disgust for the House of Commons.'[27] There was only one way to bring Tories to reason – by trouble outside.

27. Bevan's disgust was also illustrated in that same speech by individual cases. It is desirable to quote further, perhaps, to show what was happening in this country – a bare twenty-five years ago. 'One officer in a division

So Bevan was heartily in favour of the new hunger march and he was not to be subdued by Transport House proscriptions. The momentum behind the march swept others along too. On 8 November a huge demonstration in Hyde Park, two hundred thousand strong, greeted the marchers from all over the country. On the platform with Bevan were Wal Hannington, Communist leader of the unemployed, and Clem Attlee, leader of the Labour Party. 'The hunger marchers,' said Bevan, 'have achieved one thing. They have for the first time in the history of the national Labour movement achieved a united platform. Communists, I.L.P.ers, Socialists, members of the Labour Party and Co-operators for the first time have joined hands together, and we are not going to unclasp them. This demonstration proves to the country that Labour needs a united leadership.' He eagerly drew the same moral for the Spanish campaign. 'We have to move quickly. This is a matter of life and death. We must demand that the British Labour movement insists on arms for Spain.' On 10 November he presented the hunger marchers' petition to Parliament. On Armistice Sunday in Trafalgar Square, he was again the chief speaker. 'Our message to King Edward,' he said, 'is that the people cannot rejoice, they are sad at heart. We could bring to London next year a poverty army that could make the Coronation look like a hollow sham. We are not here just to give honour to the dead, but to bring life to the living.'

A whole world seemed to separate the spirit of the hunger marchers in Trafalgar Square and the spirit of the majorities at Edinburgh. Bevan had no doubt which inspiration the age required. At a meeting in December he said: 'There is only one answer to the National Government of the Right and that is a National Government of the Left.'

---

actually boasts, in discussing the Means Test,' he said, 'that he was able to disclose to the parents that their sons and daughters were earning much more money than they had told their parents. There exists a system of domestic espionage subsidized by the State. What a splendid way of keeping a family together. What happy homes this will make. The assistance officer goes along to the mother and father and says: "It is not true that your son is earning £2 a week; he is getting £2 10s. a week and has not told you of the ten shillings." This mighty nation is paying £1,500,000 a year to employ officers to sneak on sons and daughters.'

The year ended on a note of comedy, when King Edward VIII crossed his path. The popular young monarch made his famous tour of South Wales. Bevan was outraged by the whole escapade. To organize an expedition to Wales as if it were an unknown, barbarous and distant land 'much in the same way as you might go to the Congo' seemed to him an affront. He said that the King was being used to mask persecution and that Ernest Brown, the Minister of Labour, who accompanied him on the visit, was 'the instrument of that persecution'. Of course, when Brown travelled with the King, he did not have to meet the full blast of protest. Let him try going there 'without the shelter of the royal purple'!

However, Edward, during his tour, was paying a visit to the social centre at Rhymney in Bevan's constituency. One women's organization felt that their Member ought to be present. 'I cannot,' he wrote, 'associate myself with a visit which would appear to support the notion that private charity has made, or can ever make, a contribution of any value to the solution of the problem of South Wales.' The reply was phrased in temperate terms, but this particular section of his constituents was not mollified. Then, a few weeks later, the news of the abdication crisis broke. Bevan received another letter from the women's organization in Rhymney; well, now we know, it said, why you wouldn't accompany Edward and how proud we are to have a Member with such foresight, good taste and discretion. Honour could not really require that he should offend his puritan constituents further by rallying to the defence of the fallen monarch.

Bevan certainly did not share the high-minded but, as he believed, mistaken constitutional theories of most of his Labour colleagues on the issues raised by the Abdication. Attlee backed Baldwin; a constitutional king must accept the advice of his Cabinet. But the real point, insisted Bevan, was whether the Cabinet had given the right advice. That was an entirely different and more arguable proposition which the Labour leaders had not even stopped to consider. In any case, Bevan was horrified by the statesmanlike judgements brought to bear in this Ruritanian affair, while South Wales was starving and Spain fighting for her life.

His heretical outlook became known in the House of Commons and one day he received a private communication from the monarch himself. Lord Beaverbrook was the intermediary; Bevan was invited to go round at once to Stornoway House, Beaverbrook's London establishment, as His Majesty wished to consult him on a certain matter. There Bevan was greeted by one of the King's aides-de-camp: 'I remember,' he recalled in private conversation years later, 'a slight little figure in satin breeches with a toy sword at his side.' Bevan was asked to say what he thought would be the reaction of the Parliamentary Labour Party if His Majesty insisted on marrying Mrs Simpson. His reply was that his own feelings were entirely neutral, but if the King wished to understand the feelings of the members of the Party, he could not do better than ask himself what would be the reaction of 'a typical middle-class woman in Surbiton'. A few minutes later Bevan was shown to the great room upstairs. There, he said, 'was a single figure walking up and down under a brilliantly-lit candelabra – tears streaming down his cheeks into his whisky – Winston Churchill,' Edward's chief defender. The figure turned round and said: 'I never thought the time would come when a Churchill must desert his King.' 'Oh, it is only the second occasion in history,' replied Bevan, tactlessly recalling the far-off day when the great Duke of Marlborough had marched out of London at the head of King James's troops and returned at the head of King William's.[28]

But the crisis had its serious aspect. According to Bevan's belief, royalty 'in the propaganda apparatus of society as it is', had four functions: to foster the illusion of national unity; to preserve the hierarchy of honours and titles by which representatives of the workers are subjected to the most insidious form of corruption; to supply a fertile source of diversion; and, above all, to intervene in a time of acute political crisis and exert its influence in favour of the existing social order. Naturally the Tories were upset by the failure of Edward to play the game by the traditional rules. But why should the Labour leaders have fallen into their trap? They allowed the problem to be presented

28. Ironically, Bevan perhaps had gained his knowledge of politics in the age of Queen Anne from the presentation copy of Churchill's *Marlborough* which the author had sent him in October 1934 with the inscription: 'To Aneurin Bevan with every good wish for a lifetime's happiness.'

as one of Parliament versus King. But Parliament from the beginning to the end had not been allowed to discuss the matter at all. Bevan's description of the parliamentary scene when all was settled reveals how deep was his discontent with his Party.[29]

The gladiators of the parliamentary arena [he wrote] faced each other across the table adorned by the mace, symbol of the authority which was supposed to be in issue. The trembling accents of the Speaker fell into a well of awed silence as he read the Royal message. Surely never have sentiments so meagre been arrayed in language ennobled by great usage and sanctified by awful deeds. A mean wine in a goblet of old gold. Here indeed was the great past mimed by the ignoble present. 'History repeats itself,' said Marx, 'first as tragedy, second as farce.' And here was farce. The pathetic can never be epic, and here was bathos affecting to speak in accents of the heroic. The Prime Minister, who has a natural gift for the counterfeit, surpassed himself. He spoke as a pilot who had guided the ship of State safely to harbour through stormy seas, past jagged rocks, and in the teeth of the buffeting winds. The winds, indeed, were boudoir hysteria, the rocks threatened to wreck only his own career, and the official Opposition had not blown even a zephyr across his path. But what of that? He was fighting one of the great tourneys of history and he laid about him dauntlessly with his wooden sword. So satisfied was he that the words of another might mar the page he had added to history that he expressed the hope that no one would do other than imitate what he had done so well. True enough, when the Leader of the Opposition came to speak, he stooped obediently in order to preserve the level which had been reached...

The Labour Party missed a great opportunity. From beginning to end it raised no distinctive voice, made no gesture of independence. It held its hand when it might have struck with deadly effect... Against the cant and hypocrisy of the Court scandals, the Parliamentary Labour Party should have limned its own message ... It has shown that when it likes it can put the workers at the centre of the parliamentary stage. But from the beginning to end of the monarchical crisis it revealed one grave defect. *The Labour Party has too much reverence*.

This was a good epitaph, not merely for 1936, but for a whole unfinished epoch.

29. This report appears in the first issue of *Tribune*, dated 1 January 1937, in the column 'Inside Westminster', signed 'M.P.' Bevan wrote this parliamentary sketch for *Tribune* for several months.

8 Revolt 1937

The hour is great; and the honourable Gentlemen, I must say, are small. – THOMAS CARLYLE

IN January 1937, the Unity Campaign was launched – the most ambitious bid made by the British Left throughout the whole period of the thirties to break the stultifying rigidity of party alignments. The overwhelming bulk of both the Conservative and Labour Parties believed that Party loyalty must take precedence over all other virtues. Many were aghast at the mounting horror in Europe, but all, or almost all, believed that any move against the Parliamentary or Party machines was either undesirable or impossible or both. Aneurin Bevan was one of the few Members of Parliament who were not prepared to accept tamely this paralysing dispensation. In 1937 and again in 1938 and 1939 he sought an escape from it. He was just turning forty years old and was rising to the height of his intellectual and debating powers. Spain had vastly lengthened his horizons. Increasingly he saw events in their wide historical perspective. But his anger was growing too. His patience with little minds, never an outstanding quality, was becoming perilously thin.

The spur to the new Campaign derived from the Party leadership's display of impotence at Edinburgh. Soon after the Conference was over Stafford Cripps took the initiative in opening talks between representatives of the Socialist League, the Independent Labour Party and the Communist Party. The negotiation was not easy. For years past profound cleavages of principle, arising chiefly from the policies of the Soviet Union, had made the I.L.P. and the Communists appear more as rivals than as comrades in the same Socialist cause. Occasionally, on specific activities like the hunger marches or resistance to Mosley in the East End, they had managed to co-operate; much more often they had been at each other's throats in fierce theoretical disputes, enflamed on the I.L.P. side by the knowledge of what many good Socialists (and good Communists) had suffered at Communist hands. Within the Socialist League, there were similar qualms; some shared the distaste for associating with the Communists at all, some foretold that the Communist aim was merely to destroy the Socialist League as a competitor, others were alarmed by the warning issued from the National Executive of the Labour Party when news of the 'Unity' talks became known. Consequently, the vote at a special delegate conference of the League in favour of proceeding with the Campaign was only carried by 56 to 38, with 23 abstentions.

But the persistence and persuasion of Cripps, backed by William Mellor and Aneurin Bevan, pushed the project forward. Naturally they were much assisted by the tug of events in France and Spain. The field for a wide measure of agreement *did* exist – all the elements involved in the negotiation were agreed on implacable opposition to the Government's rearmament programme, its foreign policy and, above all, its betrayal of the Spanish Republic. No great difficulty was encountered in devising a list of immediate demands for helping the unemployed, for fighting unemployment and rescuing the distressed areas. So the Campaign was presented as one 'to revitalize the activity and transform the policy of the Labour movement', to seek, as the manifesto said, 'Unity within the framework of the Labour party and the trade unions'.

Other domestic developments over the previous months had helped to make the moment seem propitious. The Left Book Club, started by Victor Gollancz, Harold Laski and John Strachey in the summer of 1936, had proved a spectacular success; thanks largely to its efforts, the seed for the United Front had been widely sown. Another organization set up soon after Edinburgh, the Constituency Party Association, was working for the limited objective of securing a bigger and more direct representation of local Labour Parties on the National Executive. At Edinburgh, the difference in outlook between the unions and the constituency parties had emerged more sharply than ever before and there were many, including a few of the official leaders, who were persuaded that the rift could only be healed by deliberate constitutional action to enhance the power of the local parties. And at the beginning of January, the first issue of *Tribune* appeared. The project had been planned for some months. Cripps and George Strauss supplied most of the capital, about £20,000 between the two of them. The hope was to establish a 50,000 sale for a twopenny weekly in a matter of weeks on the crest of the enthusiasm generated by the Unity Campaign. Only after months was it painfully and expensively learnt that founding a newspaper and conducting a political campaign were two different operations.

William Mellor was editor; Bevan was a member of the controlling Board, along with Cripps, George Strauss, Ellen Wilkinson, Harold Laski and Noel Brailsford. The combination of Mellor and Bevan marked one minor victory for unity. Mostly their ideas were in accord; they had the same Marxist training, the same deeply-rooted doubts about the official Party leadership. But their mental processes jarred. Working with William Mellor was like living on the foothills of Vesuvius. On slight provocation the molten lava would pour forth in protest against the imbecilities of the world in general and anyone who dared cross him in particular. All who might be suspected of betraying the Cause were in peril of being consumed by his private supply of hell-fire. A wonderful gentleness and generosity mingled with these ferocities but both the lowly and the great went in dread of his wrath – all except Bevan. He was quite ready to bait the endearing ogre with his wildest flights of theory. He would arrive at Board meetings late, sweep the agenda into the wastepaper basket with a first rhetorical flourish and launch into a discourse which either embraced the whole future of the cosmos or, alternatively, made the political issue at stake appear delicate as gossamer. Mellor had no patience with these dazzling performances; he would growl his resentment for hours afterwards. Somehow he had managed to transfer the instincts of his own raw puritan upbringing from the field of personal morals to political action. He was shocked by Bevan's intellectual richness and laxity; could not such a man be tempted by the political equivalent of the whore of Babylon? Yet Mellor now persuaded Bevan to apply his talents to journalism more assiduously. Week by week, under the pseudonym 'M.P.', he wrote a parliamentary sketch which provided the paper with its most original feature. Sometimes his writings, so different from his speech, were laboured and lacking in pith and euphony. But these contributions to the early *Tribune* were among the best he ever wrote. They were delivered every Wednesday morning to the *Tribune* courier (usually myself), to the accompaniment of violent curses against the taskmaster Mellor by a dishevelled Bevan who had often been up all night at his typewriter in his room in London. But the copy was never late. Perhaps he did faintly share the awe which Mellor inspired in others. Each was resolved to work with the other; they joined forces to exert their influence on Cripps, and he in turn suffused the whole enterprise, both *Tribune* and the Unity Campaign, with his own exalted optimism.

A vast overflowing meeting in the Free Trade Hall, Manchester, on 24 January gave the Campaign a spectacular start. A platform bringing together Mellor, Cripps, James Maxton and Harry Pollitt was certainly formidable. With the aid of the other principal signatories of the Manifesto – Harold Laski, George Strauss, Aneurin Bevan, H. N. Brailsford, John Strachey, William Gallacher, Fred Jowett, Fenner Brockway, Tom Mann, Jack Tanner, Arthur Horner, Palme Dutt, G. R. Mitchison and Frank Horrabin – a series of mass meetings was organized all over the country on a scale that dwarfed anything known for years. Cripps called the Manchester meeting 'the most remarkable experience of my short political career'. It really did seem conceivable in those first electric weeks that the miracle could be worked; that the Labour Party could be taken by storm.

Bevan backed the Campaign to the full, speaking at a large number of meetings in South Wales and elsewhere. 'We have not come to make discord,' he said, 'but to bring peace to Labour and a sword to our enemies.' On the day after the Manchester meeting the *Daily Herald* read the Riot Act on behalf of Transport House, sternly rebuking the Socialist

League for its breach of the anti-United Front resolution passed at Edinburgh. Bevan replied. 'The fact that a minority fails to carry its view,' he said, 'surely does not mean it stops advocating it.' If so, what was the position of Hugh Dalton, the Party Chairman? He claimed the right to advocate support for the Government's rearmament programme in defiance of the Conference. As for the technicality about appearing on platforms with Communists, it had been broken time and again by leaders of the Party – by Greenwood, by Attlee, even on occasion by Ernest Bevin himself, and by anyone who dared associate with the South Wales Miners' Federation, that 'old criminal in the prosecution of United Front activities'. 'I trust,' wrote Bevan to the *Daily Herald*, 'that all these distinguished persons will not cause you to falter in the pursuit of virtue. Please don't be deterred in the fanatical application of your sterile logic. Let a Labour Conference be called and declare its own expulsion!' As the weeks passed his attack became fiercer. He challenged the Executive to offer itself for election by the rank-and-file, forecasting that not twenty per cent of them would be returned. To those who warned that he was risking expulsion he replied that he did not see why an M.P. should sacrifice his principles to keep his job any more than a miner or other worker. 'One of the dangers of the sort of machine we have created,' he said at Cardiff on 31 January, 'is that we have made it comparatively easy for a large number of people to acquire prestige and status. Our machine is more bureaucratic than democratic. The principle of selection from above has taken the place of election from below. If you get selection from above you always get the Yes-men.'

This outburst may sound splenetic, but once again it is necessary to insist on the conflicting conceptions of political strategy accepted by the leadership and a great part of the rank-and-file. To the leaders opposition meant a more or less sedate presentation of their case in the House of Commons, coupled with the development of a practical programme to be offered at the next election. Care must be observed not to give offence to special sections of the community; weighty considerations about the Catholic vote had not been absent from the Executive's approach to the Spanish situation.[1] During these same months, under the energetic chairmanship of Hugh Dalton, the Executive was busy preparing an *Immediate Programme* and conducting its own expert survey into conditions in the distressed areas. Dalton himself, in close collaboration with Ernest Bevin, then Chairman of the T.U.C., was also working hard to secure a reversal of the Parliamentary Party's attitude to the arms estimates; to remove, as he thought, a fatal disability from Labour's electoral appeal. But few believed at the time that Labour would win the next election on these lines. Meantime a mighty tide of emotion and anger and exhilaration was swelling in the distressed areas, on the hunger marches, at the United demonstrations, at the universities, in the Left Book Clubs, in literature, in the very spirit of the age. To people on the Left, it seemed to penetrate almost everywhere, only to lap in vain against the locked doors of Transport House. One sentence in Bevan's Cardiff speech expressed the contrast precisely. 'A Labour movement,' he said, 'which lies dormant for four or five years could not, when the general election comes, have the strength of a giant to succeed at one blow.' A great gulf seemed to be fixed between the politics of the streets and the politics of the Westminster committee rooms. Bevan's whole striving in the thirties was to find a bridge between the two. For one unleashed the necessary spirit of revolt while the other looked too much like a docile surrender to the fates, a repetition on the international front of Labour's submission in 1931. Bevan was especially suspicious of those Labour leaders who appeared to think that little more than a shift in diplomatic attitude was required and that Anthony Eden, regarded in some Labour circles as 'a very Daniel among the lions', could perform the trick for them. 'When Labour leaders,' he wrote, 'substitute the role of courtier for that of agitator, they fail at both.'[2]

---

1. Cf. *The Fateful Years* by Hugh Dalton, page 103. 'Nor could we [Labour's National Executive] ignore the fact that the Catholics, both in Britain and in France, were on Franco's side.' As a matter of fact, to their credit, many of them weren't.

2. This quotation, like most others from Bevan in this chapter, is taken from his weekly *Tribune* article.

Further evidence of how vast was the difference in mood between the leaders and the led is revealed in some of the diaries and private letters of the time. What was Cripps 'nattering' about, asked Dalton. 'It was a piece of clotted nonsense anyhow,'[3] – a shocking interference with the Executive's steadily constructive work. The great Fabian seer, Sidney Webb, wrote to Cripps's father, Lord Parmoor, to express his disapproval both of the world prospect and Stafford's antics: 'I try to remember,' he said, 'that those who are not actually "in the saddle" or "at the wheel" are necessarily unaware of very important considerations. We cannot expect to be able to form a valid judgement about complications about which we are necessarily ignorant.'[4] To say that this gospel of quiescence and abdication represented the considered view of the leadership would be too severe. But that is what their performance looked like and felt like, while Spanish democracy was fighting and bleeding. Dalton and Bevin certainly were not moved to seek new political initiatives by events in Spain and to many they appeared, not unjustifiably, as the effective leaders of the Party. Attlee himself leant more to the Left. He looked with greater favour on the activities of such bodies as the Left Book Club and was persuaded, in the spring of 1937, to contribute a volume of his own to its list. One of his laconic sentences was much quoted at the time as an illustration of how the leadership was completely failing to reflect the impatience of the rank-and-file. 'I would not myself,' he wrote, 'rule out such a thing [a move towards a Popular Front] as an impossibility in the event of the imminence of a world crisis.'[5] For the rank-and-file and for Bevan the world crisis was already imminent. The enemy was at the gates, but seemingly the British Labour movement was still constricted by the edicts of the Edinburgh Conference. It was the authority of Edinburgh, forbidding any association with Communists, which was now invoked to quell the Unity Campaign.

Bevin, Dalton and the full Executive moved promptly to crush the rebellion. On 27 January, the Socialist League was dis-

3. *The Fateful Years* by Hugh Dalton.
4. From a letter in *Stafford Cripps* by Eric Estorick.
5. *The Labour Party in Perspective* by C. R. Attlee.

affiliated. Ernest Bevin replied brusquely to a private appeal from G. D. H. Cole. 'You talk about driving Cripps out,' he wrote. 'Cripps is driving himself out. The Annual Conference came to certain decisions. If I did not accept the decisions of the Conference of my union I know jolly well what the members would do with me.'[6] In public his language was less delicate. He first compared the ringleaders of the new movement with MacDonald, Snowden and Thomas, advancing the curious historical thesis that the 1931 crash was somehow due to MacDonald's refusal to accept majority decisions. In the next sentence he hit on another contradictory comparison. 'I saw Mosley come into the Labour movement and I see no difference in the tactics of Mosley and Cripps.'[7] But these broadsides did not injure the Campaign. In March the Executive decreed that individual membership of the Socialist League would be made incompatible with membership of the official Party. Either the Campaign would have to end or there would be wholesale expulsions; the Socialist League would have to choose at its Whitsun conference. Dalton enlivened the controversy with a more direct attack on Cripps. The Socialist League, he said, was little more than a rich man's toy. The so-called Unity Campaign was being financed by one or two rich men. If it were deprived of these plutocratic props the whole agitation would collapse.[8] *Tribune* replied to these allegations by publishing the records of the large sums raised at the Unity meetings. William Mellor was fully capable of giving blow for blow. Bevin and Dalton indeed had their own special reason for wishing to smother the Cripps offensive. They believed that the moment was coming when they could change the Party's attitude about defence; suspicion of what was afoot gave fresh impetus to the Campaign.

No one urged more forcibly than Aneurin Bevan that the Government's arms programme must be relentlessly opposed. When in February a new Defence White Paper was issued – proposing much the steepest increase in arms expenditure yet contemplated – he believed that the choice before the Party had

6. *The Life and Times of Ernest Bevin* by Alan Bullock.
7. Quoted in *Tribune*.
8. *The Fateful Years* by Hugh Dalton.

become critical. It would be 'a crime of the first magnitude if the Labour Party helped to deceive the workers into believing that the war machine now being built either guarantees the peace, or may be used to defend the interest of the workers.' In the light of subsequent events, these words may read strangely. At the time many jeered that Labour was always calling for strong action abroad while denying the means to support it. Dalton's claim was that the dilemma could only be resolved by reversing the Party's whole attitude to the arms estimates; the Party's policy, he said, was 'Arms for Spain', but the plain man interpreted Labour's votes in the Commons as meaning 'No Arms for Britain'.[9] Most historians have seen the issue in the same simple terms: arms or no arms – that was the question. How long did it take the Labour Party to shed its near-pacifist traditions in face of the European reality? This is the manner in which developments within the Party are described by Churchill, Dalton, the biographer of Bevin and most other authorities on the period. The case appears conclusive.

Yet so hackneyed an analysis bears little relevance to Bevan's reasoning. He was no pacifist; he did not underrate the Fascist menace; he was now calling ever more insistently for a mutual defence pact in Europe embracing Britain, France, the Soviet Union, Czechoslovakia and all the other threatened States. But he saw the whole question of the arms programme in terms of political strategy. If Labour tacitly agreed to the defence plans of the Government, its case on foreign policy would go by default. It would be telling the public, by implication, that the Government which stolidly refused to mobilize the peace forces of the world could be relied upon in the last resort to perform this essential task: and that would be 'black treachery'. Moreover, he had his retort to those who pleaded that the arms must be voted to the Chamberlain Government since a Labour Government would require them. 'It is no argument,' he wrote, 'that because I may need a sword in the future that I should therefore put a sword in the hands of my enemy now. We shall be told that if our opposition proves successful the nation would be without arms. The answer is obvious. If we are strong enough to prevent the

9. *The Fateful Years* by Hugh Dalton.

Government from arming we are strong enough to form the Government and so the problem would not arise. Is it that we are strong enough to betray the workers, but not to save them? The Government could not live a day after a defeat on the arms question.' Bevan believed that any softening of the criticism of the Government, necessarily involved in concessions about the arms programme, would merely encourage it to pursue its desperately dangerous diplomacy.

This prophecy at least was fulfilled, and the Commons debate on the new Defence Estimates offered a striking confirmation of his fears. Chamberlain was asked the direct question how he conceived his obligations to the countries bordering on Germany, particularly Czechoslovakia. His reply, wrote Bevan, would be well received in Berlin. For Chamberlain answered that while Britain was bound to defend the frontiers of France, Belgium, Egypt and Iraq, her obligations elsewhere were defined by nothing more binding than the Covenant of the League which he more than most had been ready to relegate to the dustbin. 'In other words,' Bevan continued, 'we are back where we were in 1914 – a race in arms in a world of anarchy . . . We do not escape entanglements in Central Europe, because France conceives herself bound to support Czechoslovakia, so we can be drawn into a quarrel there. At the same time, we throw away the protection that might be afforded by an all-in confederacy of peace-loving States, which would include Soviet Russia.' During these weeks he became increasingly alarmed by the feebleness of the Opposition in the Commons. He was irritated when front-bench speakers framed so much of their case in legal terms. 'We were treated to long dissertations on this and that article of the Covenant of the League, more like Egyptologists reading from the Book of the Dead than Labour men dealing with issues of life and death for millions of workers.' He scorned the mild accents in which Labour's case was delivered. 'Beachcomber,' he wrote, 'once described Mr Ramsay MacDonald as "a sheep in sheep's clothing". It applies to many of the front-bench men with whom the Parliamentary Labour Party is cursed.'

It was the continuing Spanish struggle which stirred him most, reinforcing his distrust both of the Government's purposes and of the official Opposition's readiness to give it the accommodation on the arms programme which Ministers most desired. Ever since Madrid had been saved, it had been legitimate to hope for a real Republican victory: 'had Spain been left to herself,' reported the *Times* Correspondent on the spot on 7 January, 'the war would have been over long ago.' All the more galling was the impotence imposed by the Government policy. In the middle of March, at a meeting of the full Socialist and Trade Union International in London, the appeals from the Spanish Socialists were clamantly renewed. The response was embellished in flowery resolutions, but no assurance was forthcoming of a concerted attack on the Non-Intervention agreement, and Ernest Bevin in particular had seemed to favour caution. Bevan construed the British Labour attitude as a return to the discredited temporizing of Edinburgh.

This might be an exaggeration, but a debate in the House soon confirmed his suspicion. The Government introduced a Merchant Shipping (Spanish Frontiers Observers) Bill, allegedly designed to tighten the controls preventing the passage of supplies to both sides. Conceivably, the truer intention was to minimize the possibility of embarrassing incidents and, in any case, an acceptance of the Bill implied a willingness to give the Government the benefit of the doubt in interpreting its motives. At first Labour's Parliamentary Committee suggested that the Bill should be allowed to go through unopposed, but a revolt led by Seymour Cocks, Cripps, Bevan and a few others defeated this line at the Party meeting. After the initial attack on the Second Reading, however, the leadership wilted again. The fight was kept going from the back benches. Cripps, said Bevan, showed himself a master of opposition. Bevan himself railed in *Tribune* against 'the irresponsible caucus who hold power'. The most eloquent leader of the rebellion on that occasion was Seymour Cocks, who joined with Cripps and Bevan in sustaining the debate to the early hours of the morning. 'If there is anybody in this House,' he said, 'who has a sense of chivalry or a feeling of fair play, who loves liberty and cherishes democracy, I ask him to vote against the Bill on the Third Reading. The Spanish people are fighting for liberty and freedom. Liberty and freedom are precious flowers. It is our duty to see they are not trampled down.

> O native land; let not these only flowers
> Of God, be desert strewn and withered now.

If anybody will help me, I will divide the House.' Bevan was one of the sixteen who responded to his appeal and defied the Whips.

Such incidents as these are never now recalled by the biographers and autobiographers of the official Party. They would have us believe that, after the momentary hesitations at Edinburgh, the Party leaders quickly exposed the hypocrisies of Non-Intervention and thereafter sought to rally the nation on the side of the Spanish Republic as one part of their effort to withstand the general Fascist onslaught in Europe. Ernest Bevin in particular is portrayed as the Coeur de Lion of this crusade. But the record speaks differently. Another Spanish debate took place in the Commons on 14 April. Labour put down a vote of censure, condemning the Government for its failure to protect British vessels trading with Bilbao from the pirate ships of General Franco. Unfortunately, the Foreign Secretary was able to quote a leading article from the *Daily Herald* powerfully defending the continuance of Non-Intervention.[10] 'My paper,' as Ernest Bevin liked to call it, had succeeded in 'stabbing in the back' (to quote one of Bevin's own favourite phrases) the Labour spokesmen in the Commons. It was these revelations of Bevin's mind which accentuated the bitterness of the internal Party dispute. On the test of Spain – and what could count against it in urgency and

10. *Hansard*, 14 April: Mr Eden: 'If the Non-Intervention scheme were torn to pieces who would benefit? Not the Spanish Government. I have here some very wise words which were written on the subject: "It is suggested that Non-Intervention should be thrown over . . . that the Spanish Government should be provided with arms . . . But in view of what has actually happened these last eight months can it be reasonably doubted that the results would not be these but the very reverse? . . . And if Non-Intervention were now abandoned, is it not certain that the Fascists would pour men into Spain until a Government defeat were assured?" That is the *Daily Herald* of March 15th.'

Mr Cocks: 'He will get a peerage for that.'

Mr Eden: 'It is very sound sense; whether that deserves a peerage I do not know.'

drama? – the Bevin–Dalton leadership looked feeble almost to the point of deceit. How could the nation be roused to the menace of Fascism if the immediate Fascist challenge in Spain was to be sidestepped or soft-pedalled? The biographers have solved the dilemma by concealing it. At the time no such effective remedy was available.

A few weeks later Bevan was involved in another parliamentary scene which resulted in his own suspension from the House of Commons. He was always fascinated by the way the conventions of Parliament itself appeared to reflect the class requirements of the Government. The very time-table for debates, during one week in April 1937, indicated the scheme of priorities accepted by Ministers. In his Budget, the Chancellor of the Exchequer had introduced an Excess Profits Tax; this, for the City and the London newspapers, became the principal topic of the hour, pushing all else into the shadows. In particular, it took precedence over a new Bill concerning the Special Areas. Bevan was maddened by the contrast between the lively, packed benches which discussed the complaints of the financiers and the swift relapse into weariness when yet another Special Areas Amendment Bill had to pass through all its stages. He was maddened still more by having to deal with Ernest Brown as the chief Government spokesman on the issue which touched his own people most sorely. Oliver Stanley, the aristocrat, had been swept out of the Ministry of Labour by the U.A.B. Regulations storm. Ernest Brown, the lay preacher – 'the immunity of the pulpit has deprived him of the disciplines of intellectual integrity,' wrote Bevan – was an inspired choice for his successor. He had no other interest but to serve his masters; they would smirk at his conceits and his gaucheries while contentedly profiting from the way in which he would use his big voice and his bravado in rough-and-tumbles with the Labour benches. He was the brawny butler employed to keep the lower servants in their place. On the night of 22 April tempers broke. An all-night sitting had been the only resort left to the Opposition for securing a full discussion of the Special Areas Bill. Several brushes with the Chair had occurred and at 3.42 a.m. the Tory Chief Whip moved the closure. A dozen Members were on their

Above 1908: The butcher's boy (left in the white coat), earning two shillings and sixpence a week.

Below 1945: Jennie Lee and Aneurin Bevan.

Above Aneurin Bevan Minister of Health.

Below 1935: Unemployed demonstration at Port Talbot.

Left 1934: Mr Aneurin Bevan and Miss Jennie Lee whose engagement was announced recently, out walking together at Southport.

Below Aneurin Bevan.

Above   Labour Party Conference at Blackpool.

Opposite above   1938:   Off to Spain with Emanuel Shinwell, Jack Lawson, Edward (Ted) Williams and W. Paling.

Opposite below   1935:   Unemployed demonstration at Port Talbot.

Above 1937:   Aneurin Bevan at Labour Party Conference at Bournemouth.

Opposite above 1934:   Nye and Jennie married, with Archie Lush best man.

Opposite below 1936:   Addressing a Trafalgar Square hunger march demonstration.

1945:   On the way to his first Cabinet Meeting.

feet with points of order for Sir Denis Herbert, the Chairman of Ways and Means. *Hansard* reports the incident thus:

Maxton: I am putting a point of order. It is I who hold the Floor and not you, Sir.

Chairman: Clause Four.

Hon. Members: No.

Bevan: Leave the Chair. Your conduct has been abominable.

Chairman: I must ask the hon. Member to withdraw that remark.

Bevan: I say I have been in the House for seven years and your conduct is abominable. I have never seen anything as bad.

Chairman: I must again ask the hon. Member to withdraw that.

Bevan: I say your conduct has been abominable in the Committee tonight and I refuse to withdraw what is true.

Chairman: I name the hon. Member for Ebbw Vale for disregarding the authority of the chair.

Bevan was suspended by 119 votes to 43. Next day, the *Daily Express* invited the silenced Member to state his case to the world. He told once again the story the country would not hear, the story of South Wales and the other distressed areas where 'men and women are rotting to death in the midst of industrial graveyards'. No one cared to heal the wounds of these victims of economic lunacy; instead acid was poured into them. How many people knew that the poorest of the poor had to suffer from the only cut still in force of those imposed in 1931? That was the meaning of the Means Test. 'One little collier boy fifteen years of age went home to his parents the other day and proudly announced that he had an increase of three shillings a week; the following week the Board reduced the allowance of his un-employed father. This is the modern version of "Feed my lambs!" What satisfaction it must be to the Chancellor of the Exchequer that he is able to transmute the stunted bodies of white-faced collier boys into dreadnoughts.'

Bevan's rage at the contemporary scene in 1937 and official Labour's all-too feeble response to it was not something which merely exploded fitfully in Parliament or on the platform. It suffused the whole of his outlook. His intimate knowledge of the plagues afflicting South Wales, his Marxism, his vision of the European struggle and his horror at the British Government's treatment of it, all combined to give him a rooted obsession with the decadence of British society. The comprehensive nature of his indictment is evident in all his writings and speeches at the time. It coloured his estimate of the leading parliamentary figures of the day.

Stanley Baldwin was then at the peak of his authority and reputation. For all Bevan's reluctant admiration of him as a parliamentary strategist, he was infuriated by the 'audible reveries' which were Baldwin's substitute for oratory on grave occasions. Where others marvelled at these philosophical flights, Bevan saw in them 'a shambling gait of pedestrian thought'. 'It is medicine man talk,' he said. 'It lifts the discussion on to so abstract a plane that the minds of the hearers are relieved of the effort of considering the details of the immediate problems. It imposes no intellectual strain because thought drifts into thought, assembling and dissolving like clouds in the upper air, having no connection with earthly obstacles. It flatters, because it appears to offer intimate companionship with a rare and noble spirit. It pleases the unsceptical, because it blurs the outline of unpleasant fact in a maze of meaningless generalities. Over and over again I have been amazed by the ease with which even Labour Members are deceived by this nonsense. Murmurs of admiration break out as this second-rate orator trails his tawdry wisps of mist over the parliamentary scene.' This verdict on Baldwin may now be readily approved; the accepted history of those times has been written in Churchillian terms. But in the spring of 1937, on the eve of his retirement, Baldwin was seen in another light; he was ecstatically hailed as one of the greatest of British Premiers, and those perorations, which grated on Bevan's ears, were thought to distil the very essence of the spirit of England.

In June, Baldwin handed over the premiership to Neville Chamberlain. 'In the funeral service of capitalism,' wrote Bevan, 'the honeyed and soothing platitudes of the clergyman are finished, and the *cortège* is now under the sombre and impressive guidance of the undertaker.' At the Conservative Party meeting when the appointment was made, Churchill seconded the nomination and used the occasion, while underlining his essential Conservative loyalty, to vindicate his independence. 'We have to combat Socialism,' he said, 'and we can do it more effectively as a pack of hounds than as a flock of sheep.' (Transport House, please note this advice of an experienced politician, urged Bevan.) Of Chamberlain, Bevan also gave a character sketch, in defiance of the popular opinion of the time, from which history will hardly dissent. 'He has the lucidity which is the by-product of a fundamentally sterile mind . . . He does not have to struggle, like Churchill has for example, with the crowded pulsations of a fecund imagination. On the contrary he is almost devoid of imagination. He never suggests a rich hinterland of knowledge ready for recruitment at need and informing his utterances with the undertones of ripened reflection. No, his ideas march like soldiers on a bare plain, compact and mobile – and often formidable . . . He is wholly incapable of seeing a universal significance in the seemingly trivial, as distinct from Mr Baldwin, who is always able to prove to the satisfaction of the Tories that the gods give their benediction to the meanest inspirations of the Conservative Central Office.' 'Listening to a speech by Chamberlain,' said Bevan, was 'like paying a visit to Woolworths; everything in its place and nothing above sixpence.' Of another figure in that administration his contemporary judgement may be considered perceptive. He begged his colleagues not to be too much entranced by the new 'juvenile lead', Anthony Eden. 'He is more pathetic than sinister. He is utterly outmatched by his international opponents. Beneath the sophistication of his appearance and manner he has all the unplumbable stupidities and unawareness of his class and type.'

Enough has been quoted to prove that Bevan was not overawed by the great men of that parliamentary epoch. The comment, to later generations, may seem hardly worth making. Today the Baldwin and Chamberlain régimes have few defenders. An exertion of the will is required to remember that those administrations were, in parliamentary terms, the strongest of the century. Churchill could score no victories in the 1922 Committee; he was as much an ineffective maverick there as Bevan was in the private Labour Party meetings. The great Churchillian philippics in the Commons made hardly a dent. First Baldwin and then Chamberlain reigned supreme. Captain

Margesson, at the Whips' Office, executed their behests with an undeceptive ease, and men like Halifax, Simon, Samuel Hoare and Kingsley Wood were able to fortify the impression of unshakable competence and solidity. Bevan was merely the more provoked by this smooth, well-oiled apparatus of government and he wanted a Labour Party which shared his boundless irreverence. In one sense his real complaint, more all-embracing than any particular dispute over policy, was that the Labour leaders pitched their criticisms too low. 'It is the whole spirit of the leadership which is at fault,' he wrote in July. 'It refuses to fight desperately and heroically on matters of big principle. It refuses to arouse the electorate on burning day-to-day issues, such as the Means Test, the forty-hour week and Spain. It is too ready to compromise with existing conditions. It is too respectable and too statesmanlike; too frightened of offending the middle class.'

During these years, by observation and by practice, Bevan himself acquired the cunning and the style which was to make him the prince of parliamentary debaters. He studied the procedures of the House and was often to the fore in the disputes over Money Resolutions and the other inscrutabilities which are normally left to a few pedantic specialists. Many of the minor parliamentary occasions which play a considerable part in shaping an M.P.'s standing with his colleagues are unreportable, even if the press was avidly eager to give a true portrait of parliamentary proceedings. They are concerned with precedents, the rulings of previous Speakers, fine distinctions which are well-nigh impossible to learn from the published authorities. Bevan built up in his mind a store of this abstruse knowledge. Unlike some others, he quickly appreciated that he could not influence the Commons by waiting for the great debates. Parliamentary opportunities are seized, not bestowed. The *Hansard* of the thirties contains numerous examples, too intricate for exposition, of how, in the company of other exponents of the art like George Buchanan and James Maxton, he helped to turn apparently trivial disputes into serious controversies.

But these chances provided only a small part of his interest. The open forum of the Commons chamber perpetually fascin-

ated him as much as the intrigues in the committee rooms upstairs repelled. Only in the rarest cases have men who have made
another reputation outside succeeded in securing an equal
mastery in the House of Commons. Bevan was already winning
fame far outside South Wales for his ability as a speaker, but he
did not conform to the traditional pattern of a Socialist rabble-
rouser. He was often called a great orator. He himself hated the
description, and if that slightly archaic word summons up the
idea of conscious grandiloquence, it was certainly inapposite.
The outrageous ranter started so softly; his wit was delicate;
he dealt in paradox and satire. His sentences were uttered with
the perfect, if unconscious, timing of an actor. He seemed to
wrestle with the problems of his audience and, as the argument
mounted in intensity, the language became direct and simple.
As he spoke, a glowing clarity pierced the clouds and the story
ended in a blaze of sunshine. That was Aneurin Bevan on the
platform, and his success did not depend on the demagogue's
trick of telling the public what it wanted to hear. Often at a
crowded election meeting, he would turn aside to explore the
most awkward and obscure of themes. This was no rehearsed
recitation. The wonderfully equipped brain was exerting itself
to the limit to seek out fresh departures and conquer undis-
covered territories. Thus, while others needed to transform their
platform manner to suit parliamentary requirements, Bevan
could use the same technique in both places. He was always
primarily a debater; his perorations might rise to a tremendous
emotional climax, but the argument always came from the intellect. The House of Commons, it has been said, is like the trunk
of an elephant; it can fell an oak or pick up a pin. The analogy
applies well to Bevan's versatility. He did not neglect the lesser
parliamentary openings, yet more and more he sought to enlarge
the frontiers of political thought in a fashion distinguishing him
from all his contemporaries.

Once, many decades ago, a critical foreign observer commented on the routine conduct of British parliamentary discussion, which, seemingly, has persisted over the centuries. 'It
is rarely possible for the English, in their parliamentary debates,'
wrote Heinrich Heine, 'to give utterance to a principle. They

discuss only the utility or disutility of a thing, and produce *facts*, for and against. With facts there can be no quarrel, but no victories either. They produce nothing but physical blows on one side or the other; and the spectacle of such strife reminds me of the celebrated *pro patria* quarrels of the German students, the result of which is that so and so many passes are made, so and so many *quarte* and *tierce* thrusts – and nothing was proved.'[11] No more apt description was ever written of the formal Party tit-for-tat which so often prevails in the House of Commons. To Bevan this method of combat was anathema. One of his favourite jeers would certainly have been approved by Heine. He often poured scorn on the speakers who appeared to believe in 'the democracy of facts'; all facts were equal in their elaborate tabulations. He was always striving to transmute the small change of politics into large principles. He had done so in his criticisms of the Government's treatment of the unemployed and of its economic policies. Now, as he intervened more often on many other topics, he increasingly introduced into his speeches the wider philosophical interests drawn from his reading and his endless private polemics with his friends and himself. There was in one sense, a likeness between his taste and Baldwin's; with the essential difference that while Baldwin mused on his grandiose dissertations Bevan was always piercingly astringent. Other debaters would concentrate on the weaknesses of an opponent's case; Bevan usually preferred to address himself to its strength. Indeed, if an opponent had failed to present the real core of it, he would often supply the deficiency for him, before the demolition work began. This was one chief secret of his success as a debater. He was not content to win a few outposts; he wanted to capture the whole citadel. Because he did not choose to equip himself with a carefully prepared set of statistics and quotations, he was often accused of flippancy and laziness. But, unconsciously no doubt, he was reaching out for a bigger and rarer prize – the capacity to sway the assembly with a spacious argument.

Possibly it was the absence of this broad backcloth to their minds, symbolized in the thin, threadbare accents of an Attlee,

11. Quoted from *The Poetry and Prose of Heinrich Heine* by Frederic Ewen.

which, as much as their particular policies, provoked his discontent with the Party leadership. Men and women, particularly young men and women, could only be stirred by a daring philosophy, a design for living. Too often all they could hear from the great sounding-board of Westminster was the clatter of parish pumps, the screech of personal egos, the grinding gear of intrigue. The purpose of oratory, said Bevan (not that he used the word), was to make people *do* things. Deeds were the test in his unsentimental creed. But who, with his hand on his heart, could say that the Labour leaders of 1937 looked like *doing* anything? Parliament tamed them if they were not tame already. The spectacle might easily have induced an hostility to Parliament itself, reinforcing the old semi-syndicalist theories of industrial action which he had brought with him to Westminster in 1929. But curiously the effect was the opposite. Even in the years of the Baldwin–Chamberlain hegemony, even while the institution was failing so pitiably to mirror the turmoil outside, he acquired a deep respect, almost a love, for the House of Commons. He saw it as the place where, given a proper use of its possibilities, poverty could win the battle against property without bloodshed. Not that he enjoyed, as a substitute for political action, the cosy conventions of the parliamentary game. He never shut his ears to the storms outside; a large part of his complaint was that so many did. An M.P. on Monday, fresh from his constituency, he often said, was a better man than the one who had escaped from the foetid corridors on Friday. Yet gradually and imperceptibly – and the fact was of considerable importance for his own future and the Labour Party's – he came to regard Parliament as the most precious potential instrument in the hands of the people. Doubtless his own prowess in the arena influenced his view. It would be harsh to blame a great matador for upholding the virtues of bull-fighting.

Frustration inside the House of Commons merely added to the vigour of activity outside. Week after week the Unity Campaign held its massive demonstrations. Many trade unions were showing renewed signs of militancy, on the industrial front if not in political action. In May the London busmen came out on strike,

synchronizing their action with the day scheduled for the beginning of the celebrations in connection with George VI's coronation. Cripps made the charge that the affair was being run as a
political stunt by the Conservative Party. 'In all this coronation
bunting or bunkum,' he said, 'the Government appear to have
overlooked the essential nature of the struggle which is proceeding in this country.'[12] And so it appeared on that brilliant May
Day of 1937 when thousands of busmen in their white coats led
the vast procession through a London whose traffic had been
reduced so conveniently near to a standstill. The strike, like the
earlier Fascist and counter-Fascist activities in the East End, had
brought militancy from the depressed areas to the streets of
London. It resulted too, despite its official character, in a mortal
clash between rank-and-file members of the union and its
leadership. It was still not altogether fanciful to believe that a
break-through might come, that the Labour hierarchy might be
shifted from its stubborn postures. Yet the momentum of the
first few months' campaigning began to falter. Only one big
union, the shop assistants, voted at union conferences on the
'Unity' ticket. If Bevin was tough enough to fight and defeat
his own rank-and-file in the bus section, he was not likely to
tolerate any yielding on the political front. Huge public meetings,
however enthusiastic, were no match for Labour's machine, so
long as all or almost all the union general secretaries and executives were acting in league together and in concert with the
leadership of the Parliamentary Party. On specific issues, like
Spain, the Bevin–Dalton combination might be shaken. It
remained immune to the broader, more diffused assault,
especially when it could invoke on its side all the deep and
natural suspicions of Communist purposes.

At its Whitsun Conference in Leicester, the Socialist League
had to decide how to meet the Executive challenge that all its
members would be liable to expulsion if they continued the
Unity Campaign. It chose to dissolve, thus dispersing the target;
the drive for unity must take precedence over the League's own
existence. Many were to regret that decision in later years when
the Left in the Party, robbed by their own act of any effective

12. *Stafford Cripps* by Eric Estorick.

organization, found themselves hopelessly pitted as individuals against the Executive machine. But Cripps, with the full support of Bevan and Mellor, dominated the League and got his way. Even in the short run, however, the policy had no success. Soon the Executive insisted that any individuals appearing on platforms with the Communists would be expelled. Fresh defensive dispositions must be made. The Campaign for Unity would still continue, but henceforth it would be conducted by a Committee solely composed of Labour members; advocacy for unity was now substituted for unity in action. These were retreats, but some compensations appeared. The Executive itself made proposals, to be presented to the next Party Conference, for altering the Executive representation in favour of local parties. And in July, on the first anniversary of the outbreak of the Spanish Civil War, the National Council of Labour called forthrightly for an end to the long-standing farce of Non-Intervention and made plans for its first official Trafalgar Square rally on behalf of Spain. Labour's Executive was engaged in its familiar midsummer manoeuvres – the yielding of a few inches to the Left in preparation for holding the main field at the autumn Conference. But, in truth, there was another wound nearer the heart which was sapping the strength of the Unity Campaign. During the summer came the news of a fresh bout of Stalin show trials in Russia and during those months, too, information trickled through from Spain of the furious strife between the Communists and the Anarchists or the P.O.U.M. Cripps, Mellor and Bevan did their best to prevent these events from shattering the whole British Left into sectarian fragments, but they could not counter the numbing effects of the inconvenient horror on their followers, nor suppress the anguish in their own hearts.

One other defeat for the Left was unmistakable. In July Hugh Dalton at last succeeded in persuading the Parliamentary Party to alter its attitude to the Defence Estimates. This was as skilful a piece of backstairs intrigue as even Dalton had ever executed. He lobbied his own friends without putting his opponents – they included a majority among the Party leaders – on their guard. None but the eventual victors knew that so momentous a decision was to be taken at the meeting. Thus, by 45 votes to 39, Dalton secured agreement that the Party should henceforth not vote against the Estimates, and in the subsequent Commons vote only a handful defied the authority of the Party meeting. Bevan reported that the decision had 'brought consternation' to the Parliamentary Party. He quoted the unequivocal statements made by Attlee and Morrison at the Edinburgh Conference that no such departure in policy was contemplated and denounced 'a patent breach of Conference decisions'. The forthcoming Bournemouth Conference, he said, 'will be the proper place to rectify this monstrous betrayal of principle'.

But Bournemouth did not bring the open trial of strength which the events of the spring and summer had foreshadowed. Once the campaigners for unity had decided not to risk mass expulsions it was evident to all that the Executive held the whip hand and would be able to pick off any offenders one by one. No breach had been made in the solid, concerted power of the big trade unions. The Executive felt strong enough, not only to threaten action against anyone who still dared to appear on a platform with a Communist but even to refuse endorsement for William Mellor as a Labour candidate at Stockport. Bevan condemned this act as 'malicious, vindictive and out of all accord with the traditions of the Party'. He accused the Executive of using its giant's strength to 'convert the Party into a mass of sycophantic robots'. On the unity issue itself, at the Conference, all the forty-three resolutions advocating a United Front were ruled out of order in accordance with the three-year rule forbidding a repetition of matters previously decided. Cripps, Laski and Strauss could make little headway in presenting the narrower question of their right to argue for the new strategy inside the Party. Herbert Morrison was able to sweep the Conference with some brilliant mockery of the Communist incapacity to provide comfortable bedfellows for anybody, and the Party's opposition to the United Front was in effect reaffirmed by 2,116,000 votes to 331,000.

Even more decisive was the support for the Executive in the debate on international policy and defence. But here at least Bevan was able to rescue something from the wreckage for the Left with a speech which won the biggest ovation of the week.

First he ridiculed Ernest Bevin's claim earlier in the debate that the rearmament programme had already given reassurance to peace-loving countries in Europe, like Czechoslovakia. That was a most dangerous plea, words which would be quoted by the Government all over the country. 'I hope,' said Bevan, 'that Czechoslovakia will not take them at their face value.' Then he elaborated his fundamental case. 'You cannot deny arms to any Government until those who are able to deny them are themselves strong enough to form a Government; and when that happens the movement has declared – and I support it and my friends support it – that we are prepared to provide whatever support is necessary to carry out a Socialist international policy. But what we are not prepared to do is to tie the movement behind a National Government which will betray our policy. That is the real issue before us.' Moreover Ernest Bevin's argument for a strongly armed Britain to sustain the Government might soon be extended to an argument for a united nation behind them. Labour would be led from one surrender to another. 'Therefore, the Conference is not merely discussing foreign policy; it is discussing the spiritual and the physical independence of the working-class movement in this country.' As for the alleged parliamentary difficulties of such an attitude, they had good precedents. 'When a King in the past tried to carry out policies which did not receive the support of his subjects, the monied classes denied him the necessary means to carry them out. Our whole Constitution has been built up on that basis. The Government is not carrying out the policy in which we believe, any more than Charles I carried out the policy of Hampden and Cromwell. We should therefore deny to the National Government our bodies, our consent, where the capitalist class denied their money. Mr Bevin is a successful trade union negotiator and Mr Walker is an official of the Iron and Steel Trades' Federation. If they took the same conduct into industrial negotiations that they are taking into politics, they would be sacked and they would deserve it, because the movement is handing itself over to the National Government without even having its price.' Against this whole doctrine of surrender, Bevan proposed a quite different course of action. 'We should conduct throughout the country such a campaign against the National Government, against its armament programme and against its foreign policy, as will make our position clear; we should say to the country we are prepared to make whatever sacrifices are necessary, to give whatever arms are necessary in order to fight Fascist powers and in order to consolidate world peace, but we are not going to put a sword in the hands of our enemies that may be used to cut off our own heads. There is no other way in which the movement can save its soul.'

This, the issue of political strategy, not the bald question of arms or no arms, was the argument on the Left in the thirties on which the real controversy turned. Looking back, Dalton and Bevin may claim that they were the realists, approving the provision of the arms which were later shown to be so essential and which, incidentally, the National Government claimed to be supplying in the abundant measure that would make the Fascist powers pause. But the historians who adopt this thesis as if it were unarguable omit to mention the accuracy of Bevan's forecast. For two years more, after Bournemouth, the National Government was able to pursue its disastrous course. Labour could not claim to have deflected it by one jot, and that too must be held the responsibility of a leadership which gained such overwhelming majorities for such meek and unadventurous aims.

These two heavy defeats, on the Unity Campaign and the arms programme, might have been expected to pulverize the Left completely. In dealing with the rebels, the leadership had shown itself more purposive and effective than for some years past; it had also succeeded in carrying unanimously its *Immediate Programme*. But the Left could also boast its victories at Bournemouth and delegates left the Conference in no downcast mood. One reason was the resolution about Spain, unanimously adopted; gone were all the uncertainties of Edinburgh, Non-Intervention was roundly denounced, a National Campaign was to be launched by official Labour. A second reason was the alteration in the Party's Constitution, giving seven instead of five places upon the National Executive Committee to the constituency parties and ensuring that all the constituency spokesmen should be elected by the constituencies without trade union participation; this had only been achieved after fierce debate and narrow votes and following the defeat of a last-minute effort by Ernest Bevin to postpone the operation of the reform for another eighteen months. Jubilantly the local parties seized the chance, in the elections to the new Executive, to show how strong had been the sentiment for unity. Cripps, Laski and D. N. Pritt were among the chosen seven for the constituencies, while Ellen Wilkinson secured her place in the women's section. The Left still retained real positions of strength within the Party.

Oddly both Right and Left found the verdict of Bournemouth agreeable. 'I believed,' wrote Dalton, 'that our movement at the end of this Conference did feel itself worthy of great deeds in days to come.'[13] It is notable that his record of the Bournemouth triumphs did not even mention the unanimously agreed resolution about Spain. 'We have definitely put behind us the disillusionment of 1931,' wrote Cripps.[14] In view of subsequent events, his enthusiasm may sound like an absurd aberration. But others, including the Communist theoreticians, shared it. Bournemouth, they darkly revealed, despite all its outward defeats, marked a new, more hopeful stage in the struggle for working-class unity. At least it was true that a new zest had been imparted to the campaign in support of the Spanish Republic. The National Executive, with Cripps in the lead, set about organizing a series of mass demonstrations. And Major Attlee went to Spain and gave the clenched fist salute and returned to defend himself against his bourgeois critics in the columns of *Tribune*.

Bevan himself was not quite prepared to cast aside all inhibitions in these carousals of unity. Back at Westminster, he reported a general improvement. On both the foreign and domestic fronts[15] the Government was on the defensive. The

13. *The Fateful Years* by Hugh Dalton.
14. *Tribune*.
15. When Oliver Stanley deplored the talk of a slump, asserting that industry lived by confidence and the talk would impair it, Bevan commented with a typical Bevanism: 'The position of the Government is, therefore, that it is not the coming depression which causes the fear of it, but the fear of it that causes the depression. The assumption apparently is that the more ignorant one is of the future the better it is likely to be.'

initiative was passing to Labour; 'it was a tremendous responsibility and a great opportunity'. But would Labour take it? One sign gave him little encouragement. This year for the first time he stood for the election to the front bench. He was one of twenty-six nominated and the *Daily Telegraph* remarked: 'The House in past sessions has listened to more of his oratory than to that of almost any private Member. Possibly Right-wing Members may support his candidature in the hope that the responsibility of the front bench will induce him to keep his weapons for attacking the common enemy on the other side of the House.' But Bevan came far down the list of defeated candidates. Scorning the charge of disappointed ambition, he did not refrain in his *Tribune* article (now under his own name) from passing judgement on some of those elected. 'Age and long service,' he wrote, 'may be, and unquestionably are, good reasons for respect and gratitude, but they are not by themselves the best grounds for selecting the firing line. Some of those the Party thought fit to elect to front bench positions are too old, and some of them obviously too ill to perform their duties. Those who voted for them acted with frivolous irresponsibility and it is a pity that the secrecy of the ballot prevents them from being called to account. It is difficult to believe that the Parliamentary Labour Party seriously intends to fight for Socialism when it selects leaders whose battles are obviously behind them.' These words helped to instil an undying hatred against their author in some quarters at Westminster.

Yet part of his crime was that he truly believed the world crisis was mounting to a new point of intensity and peril. The new-found unity at Bournemouth was supposed to reflect this awareness. Clearly it had not penetrated the cloisters of the Parliamentary Labour Party. There the worship of infallible, ineffective leadership was hardly less devout than in the years of the MacDonald era. And the vast majority of its members felt their front bench to be so rich in talent and experience that they could well afford to do without the foremost debater of the age.

9 Expulsion 1938-39

The dogmas of a quiet past are inadequate to the stormy present. The occasion is piled high with difficulty and we must rise with the occasion. As our case is new, so we must seek anew and act anew. We must disenthral ourselves. – ADRAHAM LINCOLN

DURING the first two weeks of January 1938, Aneurin Bevan, with a few other Labour M.P.s, went to Spain on the invitation of the Republican Government. Henceforth, his own political mood responded more closely than ever to the rise and fall of the Spanish tragedy.

He truly loved Spain; it was his favourite among all European countries. Driving along the Mediterranean coast from France, he remarked that 'the place names read like chapter headings in a book of old romance. Gerona, Barcelona, Tarragona, Castellon, Valencia. To our northern ears these names have a gracious sound, and an association redolent of sunshine.' This road was now in daily peril of bombing raids by 'the Black Planes' despatched from the Balearic Isles. They came in from the sea at a great height, swooped down and did their worst before there was any chance of defence. In any case, such fighter aircraft as the Republic possessed were needed at the front to protect the troops from machine-gunning. In Valencia he witnessed his first air raid and was greatly impressed by the concrete air-raid shelters, 'commodious, strong and even elegant' and capable of providing refuge for half the population of the city, which the Government had had the energy to construct amid all its other preoccupations. He saw no signs of panic. But he had a full taste of the fury felt by those who must face danger with no power to strike back.

From the sunshine of Valencia he and Tom Williams M.P. were taken, through blizzards and along the slippery mountain roads, to Teruel, the coldest place in the whole country and the scene a few days earlier of one of the Republic's most famous victories. On the climb upwards his driver had to swerve desperately to avoid the lorry-loads of Italian prisoners whose presence in Spain Tory Under-Secretaries were so adept at denying in the House of Commons. In a railway carriage behind the front he talked with General Rojo, one of the defenders of Madrid and then in command of the Government forces. Rojo could not conceal his doubts about the future; suspected of war-weariness or lack of resolution, he was removed from his post a few weeks later. For the moment, the victory of Teruel was widely acclaimed as a turning-point in the war.

So Bevan and Tom Williams drove back to Valencia in gay spirits heightened by the beauty of the night. 'The moon was at the full, an incandescent circle of light. The Mediterranean was on our right, and on our left the foothills of the coastal sierra stepped up to form a ribbed silhouette against the clear sky. It was all so lovely and for the moment we felt happy. But not our driver. He kept glancing up at the moon and muttering under his breath. He was obviously cursing with an eloquence that might even have educated two old colliers like Tom and me if we could have understood him. When we questioned him he explained his bad temper. There was too much light, he said. Too much moon.' They were on the road which Franco's Italian allies were bombing so frequently, and the moon was an enemy, not a friend. The scene epitomized the feelings Bevan brought back from Spain, a mingling of exaltation and presentiment for the future. He came home proud of the Spanish working class, ashamed that Britain had done so little to help them, but convinced that the men he had seen furiously clearing the ice-packed roads to Teruel could never be beaten. The fight to assist Spain, he insisted, must 'be given precedence over all the other activities of the Labour movement'.

Yet at Westminster Spain was still treated as an intrusion into the main drama. The Non-Intervention Committee was engaged in interminable discussions about a plan for the withdrawal of volunteers on both sides. Lord Halifax boasted that Britain had no Spanish blood on her hands. And a new twist was given to the official doctrine approved since the outbreak of the war; if embroilment in the conflict must be avoided at all costs as the governing British interest, only one short step was needed to reach the conclusion that the best way to secure the desired result was the speediest possible ending of the war by the encouragement of an outright Franco victory. Neville Chamberlain was ready to accept the logic; Anthony Eden was not. Bevan had brought back from Spain the rumour that a new deal with Mussolini was in the making; the accusation sounded like a fantastic Left-wing *canard*. But Eden's resignation produced the proof. Chamberlain, placing his confidence in Mussolini's 'perfect good faith', was ready to proceed with the negotiations for an Anglo-Italian treaty to settle all outstanding issues, even though, as Eden knew, all Mussolini's promises about the withdrawal of Italian legionaries from Spain remained blatantly unfulfilled.

The day when Eden was to make his resignation speech promised to be, according to Bevan's description, the most exciting sitting which the Commons had known since 1931. This was no melodrama, with the verdict agreed in advance. No one could be sure who would emerge as the victor – the determined Premier with 'the rather sinister, repellent appearance' or 'the youngest, the most colourful, the most controversial, the most important and at the same time the most popular Minister of State'. However, with Eden's own speech, the tension relaxed. The favourite gladiator of the Tory garden parties, the d'Artagnan of the drawing rooms, unsheathed his wooden sword and the House subsided as he proved once again how much there was to be said on the other side of the question. Instead of widening the issue to embrace the realities of the European scene, he narrowed it almost to a point of diplomatic finesse. None of his backers, not even Lord Cranborne with his charge of 'surrender to blackmail', could recover the initiative. 'If Eden had been big enough,' wrote Bevan at the time, 'he could have ruined Chamberlain.' Instead, it was the most polite resignation of modern times and left not a ripple on the political waters.

Some time later, Bevan was taunting the would-be Tory rebels with their tameness. 'The hon. Member for Ebbw Vale,' said Eden, 'will perhaps forgive me if I do not follow him in the definition of what he is pleased to call "yes men". I do not know that I should be accepted as an unexceptionable authority on that subject.' Bevan interrupted: 'The right hon. Gentleman is not a "yes man", but he still wears the same tie.' Eden replied: 'The hon. Member seems to suffer from a complex on that subject.' Today, the exchange offers a fitting insight into the pre-war Eden; Bevan's 'complex' seems justified. Heralded on his appointment to high office as the gallant crusader for collective security, Eden discharged the role so successfully that, by the time he resigned four years later, Hitler had marched into the Rhineland, Mussolini had conquered Abyssinia and the Fascist invader was in control of more than half Spain. In private, Eden lamented to the Spanish Republic's Ambassador his incapacity to persuade his Cabinet colleagues to adopt bolder courses; in public, even after his resignation, he came to heel as meekly as Captain Margesson, the Tory Chief Whip, could wish.

His departure from office did have one small effect: Chamberlain could pursue more brazenly his aim of a settlement with Mussolini. 'We must not try,' he said in the resignation debate, 'to delude small weak nations into thinking that they will be protected against aggression, and acting accordingly.' The hint was taken in Berlin and Rome. Coincidentally, in the first weeks of March, Hitler seized Austria, and Franco launched a great offensive on the Aragon front. Not merely was Teruel recaptured; soon the territory of the Spanish Republic would be sliced in half and the last links severed between Barcelona and Madrid. It was the Austrian crisis, however, which commanded the world's attention, and Bevan did not approve the disproportionate significance attached to the two events. In the subsequent Commons debate, Chamberlain seemed quite unmoved by the mounting European tumult. 'He does not so much rise to the occasion as reduce it to his own stature,' wrote Bevan. 'No sooner does an idea look like taking fire than he promptly quenches it, for the strict formalism of his mind profoundly distrusts the sprawl of vigorous ideas.' By contrast, Churchill shook the Commons with one of his most powerful philippics. 'Chamberlain puts in the organ stops so that only a thin, listless trickle of sound is allowed to issue forth. Churchill on the other hand pulls out all the stops and allows the argument to speak through him in a diapason of majestic harmony.' Bevan was vastly impressed by Churchill's summons to the free democracies to make their stand against the onrush of Hitlerism.[1] All the more deplorable and revealing, therefore, was the absence from his speech of a single reference to the Spanish conflict; so deep, thought Bevan, was the allegiance to Franco's cause within the ranks of the Tory Party. Yet it was only in Spain that something could be *done*. So long as Churchill refused to relate his grand appeal to the struggle before their eyes it remained woefully inadequate. Attlee, in Bevan's view, made the speech of his life in this debate; he spoke like a man who knew that the Aragon front was the front for all freedom. But for Chamberlain, for Eden, even for Churchill, Spain was still no more than an inconvenient sideshow.

The barely credible fact was that collapse on the Aragon front did not break the Republican resistance; rather its vigour was renewed. Juan Negrin, the Spanish Premier, flew to Paris in a desperate effort to get the French frontier opened to the flow of arms. Léon Blum had just formed his second Popular Front Government and was himself ready to deliver an ultimatum to Franco.[2] But the French General Staff and a few members of Blum's Cabinet advised caution; Britain would certainly not back a far-reaching departure in French policy. Even so, the French did agree to the opening of the frontier. Arms from the Russians,

---

1. Bevan's relations with Churchill in the pre-war days were much more friendly than their subsequent war-time antagonism might suggest. When a little while later, at the time of the Sandys Privilege case, the Tories howled down Churchill, Bevan came to his defence. He was particularly irritated by the manner in which 'the Government-inspired press' would not permit a fair deal for Churchill, much less the Labour Opposition. 'There has never been a time,' said Bevan, during one of the debates on the Sandys case, 'when the Prime Minister of the day had more support in the popular press than the present Prime Minister. There never was a time when the organs of the press goosestepped behind the Government more than some of them do today.'

2. The evidence is provided in Hugh Thomas's book *The Spanish Civil War*.

from private sources, and some even from the French Government itself began to pour across the Pyrenees. It was still imaginable that the Spanish disaster could be retrieved. Yet this was the moment selected by Chamberlain to sign his Anglo-Italian Mediterranean Treaty. Italy graciously agreed to withdraw her troops from Spain once the war was over! And by the middle of June the French, under pressure from Britain, decided once more to close the frontier.

During this spring and summer of 1938 the Labour Opposition assailed the Government almost as forcefully as Bevan himself could have wished. Day after day, at question time and in debate, the Government spokesmen were bruised and battered. Tempers were raised by the ever more frequent Italian attacks on British ships trading with the Republic; in the two months following the signature of the Anglo-Italian Treaty twenty-two were attacked and eleven were sunk; twenty-one British seamen and several Non-Intervention observers were killed. British merchant ships went down in full view of British warships. But still no patriotic outcry stirred in the Conservative Party; Chamberlain and Margesson retained their unruffled command.

Typical of others was the debate on 21 June. Philip Noel-Baker produced formidable evidence of the Italian complicity in the assault on British ships. A few murmurs of discontent could be detected along the Tory back benches. Lloyd George demanded reprisals against the Italian air bases in Majorca. Churchill was moved to break his silence on the Spanish issue: 'I fear this abjection is woefully misunderstood abroad.' A Captain Evans rushed to the support of his Premier. The British seamen, he said, did not deserve protection; were they not only engaged in the trade for profits? Bevan unloosed upon him a torrent of wrath. 'I understand,' he said, 'we are to defend British citizens abroad only if the man attacking them is smaller than ourselves. If it is a couple of helpless Negroes, down with them,[3] but if it is the Duke of Alba, back him up. I never heard

---

3. Just prior to this Spanish debate the Commons had discussed a report on the recent disturbances in Trinidad. Nothing would have been heard of the island's troubles, said Bevan, had it not been for the rebellious activities of Uriah Butler, 'an inspired Negro genius' who was however treated as the

a more disgraceful suggestion. If the hon. and gallant Gentleman's principles had been applied in the past, Clive, instead of being honoured and his descendants enjoying large estates, would have been clapped into prison, because if anybody was after loot Clive was.' Why did the Government refuse to address a protest to Mussolini? Why could they not even invite him to mediate with Franco, if Franco was still regarded as an independent agent? Such courses were said to be injudicious. 'So it is the assumption of the Conservative Party and the British Government that one of the conditions for peace with Italy is that Italy shall be allowed to murder British seamen.' Mussolini, in fact, had two objectives: to enforce afresh the closure of the French frontier and to blockade the Spanish ports. British policy was assisting the accomplishment of both. And the real cause of it all was that 'there is on the Government side of the House a deep sympathy for Franco, a deep desire for him to win ... We are now witnessing no other than a piece of naked class policy by the other side.' Mr R. A. Butler, Under-Secretary at the Foreign Office and the rising hope of the pliant, appeasing Tories, dismissed all these intemperate charges; his appeal for 'calm sagacity' brought easy victory in the voting lobbies. And yet, by an ironic twist in the diplomatic process, the suggestion of Bevan and others that a protest should be sent to the arch-culprit, Mussolini, did save the lives of a few British sailors. Lord Perth, the British Ambassador in Rome, was constrained to warn Ciano that Chamberlain 'might fall if the raids continued'![4] So, to parry this mortal blow to Italian interests, they were called off for a few weeks.

At last, if sadly late, Labour in the Commons was making policy towards Spain the central target of its attack. But was

---

criminal of the piece. Bevan was outraged by the whole tone of the report which criticized the Governor for daring to open negotiations with Butler, 'a fugitive from justice'. His disgust was all the greater since the report had been signed by Sir Arthur Pugh, the T.U.C.'s representative on the Commission. 'The T.U.C.,' he said, 'should repudiate Sir Arthur Pugh's signature and I hope that next time they are asked to elect representatives for Commissions of this sort they will not select them from the most conservative-minded and reactionary-minded trade unionists.'

4. Ciano's diary. Quoted by Hugh Thomas in *The Spanish Civil War*.

parliamentary action enough and could more be done? After the Bournemouth Conference a special Spanish Campaign Committee had been appointed by Labour's National Executive 'to launch a nation-wide campaign to compel the Government' to abandon Non-Intervention. But following the first mammoth meeting in the Albert Hall – 'the beginning not the end', the audience was assured – little else had happened. The special Committee did not even meet for the next seven weeks. According to the Bournemouth decrees, all ideas of United or Popular Fronts were supposed to be buried for ever. But the demand was soon revived, on Spain in particular and against the Fascist threat generally, in new quarters. *Reynolds News* urged the formation of a 'United Peace Alliance', and appeared at first to have considerable backing inside the Co-operative movement. The *News Chronicle* appealed on much the same lines. Popular Front Councils were formed on a local basis in many areas. Labour's National Executive thundered out its response to these unofficial agitations somewhat more swiftly than it had reacted to many developments in Spain. While Franco was driving hard towards the Catalan coast, a circular was issued (with no mention of Spain) urging all sections of the movement 'to defend the party's traditional independence'. 'Affiliated organizations are reminded' – so ran the clarion call from the official leaders – 'that in the Parliament of 1929 Labour was only nineteen seats short of a bare majority'. To prepare for the next election, to allow no distraction – that was Labour's grand strategy. As the bitter news filtered through from the Aragon Front many read these stupefying edicts in a frenzy of desperation.

This was the true origin of the revived campaign for the Popular Front – not a conspiracy contrived by a few disgruntled, would-be Left-wing leaders, but a swell of discontent and frustration from below.[5] Inevitably, the implication of the cam-

5. Hugh Dalton, in his memoirs *The Fateful Years*, writes: 'On my return from Australia and New Zealand in April, 1938, I found that Cripps was at it again. He was now campaigning for a Popular Front, or "United Peace Alliance", not only with Communists and the I.L.P., but with any Liberals and other political nondescripts who would join.' Such sentences are designed to bolster Dalton's other charge that Cripps was concerned with a publicity stunt for himself; that he ran *Tribune* as a paper dedicated 'to the worship of

paign was that Labour, to secure new allies, might have to make some sacrifices in its Socialist domestic programme, and the taunt of treachery came readily to the lips of those uncompromising revolutionaries, Hugh Dalton and Herbert Morrison. Bevan might have been expected to insist on the purity of his Socialist faith more credibly than they. All his life he had been suspicious of any dealings with 'the class enemy', however disguised. A bare three years before he had joined with Cripps in opposing what he regarded as the bogus appeal of a 'collective security' programme peddled by capitalist governments. One year before, in the Unity Campaign, he had agreed with his fellow-campaigners that they should collaborate only with non-capitalist allies. He needed no instruction about the dangers of association with the Edens, the Churchills and the Sinclairs. But the force of events, especially in Spain, clamoured for a re-examination of these deeply-entrenched convictions.

Electorally, the Executive's case did not hold water. The relevant arithmetic was not the nineteen seats by which Labour fell short of a majority in 1929 but the one hundred and sixty-four additional seats Labour must add to its existing strength in the Commons. To win on that scale, Labour must be victorious in every constituency where the Tories held majorities up to six thousand. No one seriously believed the feat possible; none of the recent by-elections had shown a turn-over even remotely approaching this figure. Even, therefore, if Chamberlain graciously agreed to order a premature dissolution or even if the world could wait to 1939 or 1940 when the election was due, Labour's official strategy offered not a glimmer of hope. And, in any case, the Popular Front idea was never immediately concerned with elections, however its impact might be expected

---

One Leader, the projection of his Unique Personality and the promotion of his Personal Policy'. These ludicrous falsehoods would not be worth mentioning were it not for the fact that Dalton's book purports to be an accurate contribution to Labour history, and Dalton certainly was the second or third, if not the most powerful figure in the Party at the time. He conceals the fact that the campaign for the Popular Front and the United Peace Alliance was launched before Cripps was ever associated with it. And he never mentions Spain as an issue which helped to inspire the pressure for the Popular Front. Indeed, after 1937, Dalton's book never mentions Spain at all.

later to reap rewards at the polls. The aim was to produce such a ferment of opinion, such hostility to the appeasement policy of the Government, such a pressure in Parliament that British policy could be diverted from its dangerous course before more damage was done. The truth was that no one could gauge what would be the magnetic effect of a re-alignment of forces on the Left; the claims of both the official leaders and the rebels were unprovable. Maybe the Popular Front was always a desperate, forlorn bid. But what other card in the Socialist hand was there left to play? Better this than the infuriating inertia of official Labour in the face of calamity. For Bevan, at least, one consideration was paramount: when he said that all must be subordinated to the necessities of the Spanish struggle, he meant it. 'We must accept the implications of the Popular Front alliance,' he said at a May Day demonstration in Pontypool. 'If the National Government remains in office another two or three years we shall rue in blood and tears that we did not take action earlier. The country is faced with two alternatives – the establishment of a Popular Front in this country, under the leadership of the Labour Party, or drift to disaster under the National Government.'

This conclusion had been reached in close consultation with Cripps.[6] However, he, like Bevan, still bore the scars of Bournemouth; none knew better how rooted was the official objection to any such new departure. Both men, therefore – and even *Tribune* – attempted to put their new appeal with marked moderation.

6. William Mellor had ceased his close political association with the others. More wary or doctrinaire than they about the idea of combination with Communist or capitalist allies, he could not support the Popular Front strategy. But there was another cause of the quarrel. The *Tribune* Board had decided on a much closer association with the Left Book Club and both Cripps and the controllers of the Left Book Club were agreed that a different editor was required to make *Tribune*'s fortunes prosper in the new circumstances. So Mellor was fired by Cripps in a brusque manner which left many hard feelings. Thereupon, Cripps had to depart on a long-arranged tour to Jamaica. Bevan was left in charge to carry through the change-over. Two months later, a new editor – Mr H. J. Hartshorn – took over. Thereafter, until the signature of the Nazi-Soviet Pact in 1939, *Tribune* became much more uncritically pro-Communist in its political line than it had been previously or was ever again afterwards. Cripps was still the dominant influence on the paper; Bevan still wrote for it, although for a while not so prominently as hitherto. The Left Book Club influence, with John Strachey as the main contributor, became increasingly evident.

Their immediate call was for the summoning of a Special Conference where the Party could review the earth-shaking events since the previous October. The plea was a strong one. Under the rules agreed at Bournemouth changing the time of the Annual Conference from the autumn to Whitsun, no Conference at all was scheduled to take place that year, but, in case of emergency, a Special Conference had been promised. Surely the emergency had now come. First, therefore, Cripps presented his Popular Front proposal to the Executive; he got the support of Harold Laski, Ellen Wilkinson and D. N. Pritt, but no one else. Thereafter he pressed the demand for a Special Conference; week by week letters favouring the idea poured into Transport House from the miners, the engineers, several smaller unions and nearly two hundred constituency parties. 'The proposal was discussed at each meeting of the National Executive Committee' – so ran the report under the heading 'Spain' to the eventual 1939 Conference – 'but it was felt that the discussions and decisions at the Bournemouth Conference left no occasion for revision.'

Thus the British Labour Party and the British House of Commons adjourned for the summer recess of 1938. 'Who will care to prophesy,' wrote Cripps in *Tribune* at the end of July, 'what will happen in the next two months? ... As these next few weeks will be critical for Spain, so too they will be critical for Czechoslovakia and South-Eastern Europe.' Bevan was more reflective. Who could blame his fellow Members for wishing to escape from the House of Commons after that stifling July? The place was 'a combination of a law court, a public school and a medieval cloister'. But many M.P.s, he said, were filled with memories of 1914; they felt they might soon be called back to a Europe racked by war. One man retained his confidence. 'I believe we all feel,' said Neville Chamberlain, 'that the atmosphere is lighter and that throughout the Continent there is a relaxation of that sense of tension which six months ago was present.' Sir Walter Citrine and the General Council of the T.U.C. seemed to concur. They heartily endorsed the rejection of a Special Labour Conference.

Less than two months later Europe was plunged into the Czech crisis, Parliament was recalled and Chamberlain went to Munich.

For a few hours perhaps, when the Prime Minister returned to London bringing 'peace with honour', a sigh of relief swept the land. But there were many that night who shut themselves in their homes, bitterly ashamed of what had been done in their name.

Bevan's thoughts naturally turned to Spain, where the Munich compact must come as another crushing blow to the only people in Europe who were attempting to execute in deeds the Churchillian remedy of armed resistance to the Fascist onslaught. For weeks, even months, past, Negrin's hope – his only hope – had been that the Republic might sufficiently hold its territory to be able to step forward as a valued ally of Britain and France once the whole Continent was thrust into the war he expected. Now that hope was fading. Indeed, at Munich Chamberlain talked with Mussolini of a conference to 'solve Spain' as the Czech problem had been 'solved'. Hitler drew a more direct moral. Hitherto, German policy towards Spain had been careful not to go so far as to risk a complete rupture with Britain and France; the Non-Intervention Committee must be kept talking. Up till this point the Chamberlain thesis that legitimate support for the Republic meant war had never been true; Hitler had always kept open his line of retreat and had fed Franco's armies more with the purpose of sustaining the conflict than winning outright victory.[7] After Munich, Hitler felt free to abandon these nice calculations. In return for German participation in the major Spanish iron ore projects, he pledged enough arms to secure the kill. These ugly developments, of course, could only be guessed at the time. But guessing was easy. Seymour Cocks, the Labour M.P. for Broxtowe and a friend of Bevan, related a conversation he had with Churchill just after Munich. He asked, as many asked, whether Chamberlain's policy did not conceal some deeper plan unapparent to the outside world. 'No,' replied Churchill, 'in the depths of that dusty soul there is nothing but abject surrender.' One overt sign was the readiness of Chamberlain to implement at once the Anglo-Italian Agreement. The capitulation to the Fascist

7. The detailed proof about German policy both before and after Munich is supplied in Hugh Thomas's *The Spanish Civil War*.

powers seemed measureless. In Bevan's mind, as in the mind of many others, fleeting hope was giving place to despair.

A new intensity was added to the tone of his attack in Parliament and outside. Surely now the Labour Executive would call the Special Conference it had rejected in the summer; if it failed to do so it 'would be guilty of a deep disservice to the whole country'. He turned his fire on the Parliamentary Party, accused it of 'a softness which is a frightening portent for the future' and, alleging that Sir Charles Edwards, the Labour Chief Whip, was too old and incompetent for the job, demanded his resignation. This broadside – an article in *Tribune* – was bitterly resented, as Bevan knew it would be. He was castigated at the Party meeting; 'Charlie' Edwards was a most popular, even venerated, figure and the dastardly assault upon him drew a more crowded and explosive assembly in the Committee room upstairs than anything induced by the commotions in Europe. Bevan's reaction was to carry the fight more openly on to the floor of the House of Commons.

Two considerable parliamentary occasions may be selected from many. All through the year when Spain and the international situation dominated parliamentary proceedings, Bevan had not failed to press his attack on the Government's continued failure to do anything effective to assist the distressed areas.[8] That autumn the Government brought forward a measure to maintain in operation its Special Area legislation. Since a few crumbs were offered, Labour's parliamentary leadership decided not to vote against the Government proposals on the grounds that this action would be misconstrued; it would expose Labour to the charge that it had voted against a few extra pence for the hardest hit local authorities. Thus, argued Bevan, our condition is so pitiful that we are afraid of being accused of wanting to do

8. While the condition of the distressed areas and the operation of the Means Test were still the two chief domestic issues on which Bevan contributed to Commons debates, he also spoke on many others – notably housing. A rural housing Bill had been introduced. Grants were supplied to the landlord and the argument of the Tories was that plenty of it would go to the tenants. Bevan, however, believed that it was the whole landlord system which was wrong. 'It is,' he said, 'as if we saw a fellow in the street hammering another and instead of preventing him doing it, we sent for large doses of iodine so that the wound inflicted would not be poisoned.'

less for the unemployed than the National Government. The sole result of these tactics was to kill the debate in the Commons; with no vote promised in advance, the House was nearly empty; nobody listened, nobody cared, nobody reported. And yet how outrageous were the propositions Labour agreed to connive at. Ernest Brown, the Minister of Labour in charge, was not really in charge at all. He was a messenger boy for the various Boards and Commissions appointed by the Government to take poverty out of politics. Worse, he was content to recapitulate to the House the reasons why business men like Lord Nuffield preferred to open new works in Birmingham rather than in South Wales and Durham. Bevan was furious. Birmingham, he said, was 'a monstrosity . . . a maze of meaningless, impoverished, sprawling suburbs'. Yet South Wales must languish while the commercial potentates who had already done so much to deface the country added to 'the obesity' of Birmingham! 'Is there anything lacking?' cried Bevan. 'Yes, the dignity of the elected representatives of the people when faced with these irresponsible business buccaneers.' Labour could not even screw up its courage to vote against these squalidly inadequate decrees.

'People say of us,' he wrote in *Tribune*, 'that we speak too readily and act too tardily. It is a damaging charge to make against a Party which sets before itself so ambitious a task as the reconstruction of the whole social order. If we shrink from a vote now, what shall we not shrink from later?' Had Labour's leaders the nerve and resolution to perform the most difficult task politicians ever set themselves – a root-and-branch transformation of society by democratic means? All through his life this gnawing doubt could not be exorcized from his mind. It was the thought which fed his anger at every fresh example of Labour's pusillanimity in opposition. Faithless in small things, what would Labour's leaders do if the empire of real power became theirs?

Immediately, another instance of what he considered to be Labour's deferential attitude to its opponents was provided. The Government had produced a plan for a voluntary register to assist National Service recruitment. Labour agreed officially to support the scheme without attempting to secure concessions in return. Bevan was aghast, the more so since trade union leaders

agreed to share platforms with the hated Tories to boost the
project at the very moment when he was being rebuked by the
same leaders for wishing to make common cause with the Tories'
enemies. Not a word from the official leaders about the price of
their support; not a word demanding aid for Republican Spain;
not a word about the need to sign an Anglo-Soviet Pact; not a
word about nationalizing the arms industry; precious little even
about safeguarding trade union rights. All was yielded uncondi-
tionally to Ministers who 'for selfish class interests were throwing away important strategic advantages in Spain'. The excuse
was that Labour was relieved by the Government's continued
reliance on voluntary methods and must do nothing to disturb
this display of righteousness. Bevan prophesied that 'if we are
not good recruiting sergeants', the Government would introduce
conscription. 'I must say,' he said, 'I felicitate the Government
on the position they have got the Opposition into on this matter.
There can have been few examples in history of an Opposition
which so effectively abandoned its obligations and which so misled people, as to ask for the opportunity of appearing on platforms with generals and colonels and majors and lieutenants of
counties in order to implore people to put themselves under the
leadership of its opponents.' On that issue of the National
Register Bevan, with ten others, voted against the Government,
in defiance of the Party Whips.

The moment marked the climax of his whole argument about
rearmament and foreign policy. At last, the class Government
needed to appeal to the nation. It could not do so, at least with
full effect, without Labour's blessing. And yet would-be militant
Labour, smarting from all the offences which the Chamberlain
régime had committed in foreign affairs, asked nothing in return.
At the heart of Bevan's political faith was a belief in the dignity
and potential strength of the working class. Nothing could make
him angrier than the spectacle of the elected leaders of this
mighty force reduced to the status of flunkeys or, what was
worse, batmen. Yet that, as he thought, was the exhibition
Labour gave on the eve of the greatest war in history.

Many others, in the aftermath of Munich, were persuaded that
unorthodox remedies were needed to meet the extremity of the

situation. Cripps suggested to Dalton that an attempt should be made to test the intentions of the anti-Chamberlain Tories. Dalton was not averse to a behind-the-scenes approach, however intransigent he had been – and still was – in opposing any open Popular Front campaign. Conversations were arranged, but few, if any, of the Tories were ready to move. Harold Macmillan, it seems, was the only one; he talked in terms of a '1931 in reverse',[9] but none of the others believed in the possibility of a successful revolt against the Chamberlain–Margesson hegemony. Outside, two famous by-elections were fought. At Oxford, the official Labour candidate was withdrawn and the Master of Balliol, A. D. Lindsay, stood as an 'Independent Progressive', reducing the Tory majority from 6,645 to 3,434. Despite frowns from Transport House, thirty-nine Labour M.P.s, a quarter of the Parliamentary Party, gave their support to Lindsay. At Bridgwater, Vernon Bartlett, standing on the same Independent Progressive ticket with unofficial Labour backing, won a spectacular victory in the teeth of all the 'peace' propaganda of the Munichites. In the first days after Munich, all the pundits averred that if he went to the polls as the Man of Peace, Chamberlain could win on a landslide. But the national sentiment which might have brought this result quickly evaporated. Bridgwater was the proof. At the end of December, Bevan reported in *Tribune* a deep uneasiness among Tory M.P.s; at last the first cracks were appearing in the appeasement edifice. Labour should place itself in a position to be able to profit from these changes: 'it is not likely that another similar opportunity will occur this side of Armageddon.'

Cripps and Bevan now resolved on a supreme effort to transform the British political scene. At the time, if not in retrospect, the moment seemed well-chosen. During the first days of 1939, Chamberlain and Halifax were in Rome, feasting with Mussolini and raising their glasses in tribute to the new Emperor of Abyssinia; one fear was that they would grant full belligerent rights to Franco and toast him too. (Halifax told Ciano that he hoped Franco would 'settle the Spanish question'.)[10] In Spain

9. *The Fateful Years* by Hugh Dalton.
10. Ciano's diary quoted by Hugh Thomas in *The Spanish Civil War*.

itself, with the aid of the most decisive supply of German weapons received throughout the whole war, Franco's forces were unleashing a new offensive aimed directly at Barcelona. In France Léon Blum, now out of office, was bitterly assailing the Government of Daladier and Bonnet for their refusal to abandon Non-Intervention. A reopening of the French frontier was the last remaining hope of the Republic. But by now the Italian Government was able to deliver effectively the ultimatum which only British cowardice had made valid before; Ciano told the French that any move by them towards intervention would involve the despatch of 'regular' Italian divisions to Spain, whatever the risk of world war.

In London a lesser event symbolized the spirit of the time. Mr Duncan Sandys, M.P., Churchill's son-in-law, had for some months been one of the few back-bench Tories daring to show a tremor of independence. He called a meeting in London designed to rally the nation's youth in support of a new, more robust national policy. Fleet Street guessed that the move had been made on Churchill's prompting; might it not indicate that the rebel Tories were at last prepared to rebel? But the meeting ended in derision. 'I and my friends,' said Mr Sandys at the close, 'would not be here if there was any question of turning out Chamberlain.' If this was the standard of audacity among the most audacious Tories, what hope was there from them? Such futilities could only blur the issue. Leadership must come from the Left if there was to be any true national alternative to the Government of Chamberlain which still called itself National. Might not the Labour Party, despite all its past adamantine objections, be ready, at such an hour, to consider a new initiative? Neither Cripps nor Bevan had any illusions. They knew how inflexible Labour orthodoxy could be, how fierce would be the resentment against them for seeking once again to challenge the decisions of Bournemouth and Edinburgh, how contemptible they would appear if the challenge were not pressed to the limit. Whatever the arguments about the merits of the course they adopted, courage was required of the men who took it.

On 9 January, Cripps wrote to the Secretary of the Party requesting a special meeting of the National Executive at once to consider his accompanying memorandum. This was an elaborate document setting out in detail the argument for a Popular Front, the programme in foreign and domestic affairs on which it should be based, the electoral calculations implied in it and the manner in which Labour should open negotiations with other parties and groups. 'I certainly should not desire to encourage the Party to any combination with other non-Socialist elements in normal political times,' wrote Cripps. 'But the present times are not normal. Indeed they are absolutely unprecedented in their seriousness for democratic and working-class institutions of every kind. In such times it is absolutely impossible to overlook the fact that a too rigid adherence to Party discipline and to traditional Party tactics may amount to losing the substance of working-class freedom and democracy for the shadow of maintaining a particular type of organization which is, as a mere machine, in itself of no value.' The proposal was considered by the Executive four days later, when it was rejected by seventeen votes to three: Ellen Wilkinson and D. N. Pritt were Cripps's only two supporters. But Cripps had never intended to leave the matter there. A year before, when he had made a similar proposal, the Executive had circularized all constituent bodies with a full statement of the majority case, leaving the minority case unexplained to the Labour rank-and-file. On this occasion, Cripps had prepared in advance copies of his own memorandum, ready for immediate circulation in the event of defeat at the Executive. He told his Executive colleagues that he would claim the right to present his views to the whole movement. He did not tell them that the plans for this action were already in being. When next morning 'the plot' was discovered, the Executive issued to the press a full blast against Cripps. His manoeuvre in circularizing the local parties was regarded almost as a piece of sharp practice and was made to figure prominently in the controversies of the next few weeks. While the nation debated the political issues at stake and while Barcelona was falling, several Executive members chiefly complained of Cripps's outrage against constitutional propriety.

Some Executive members favoured peremptory expulsion as the only fitting punishment for so unmannerly a crime. The majority preferred to put the onus back on Cripps. They referred to 'the past campaigns waged over a long period at Sir Stafford Cripps's instigation', condemned 'the present organized effort fundamentally to change the Party's direction and leadership', and required that Cripps should reaffirm his allegiance to the Party Constitution and order the withdrawal of his memorandum. Failing compliance, he would be expelled. Many pleadings were made to Cripps by his Executive colleagues, but no mitigation of the ultimatum was offered. No doubt about the outcome was possible. At the Executive meeting on 25 January Cripps gave his answer and the expulsion decree was enforced.

That night he attended a huge 'Arms for Spain' meeting in the Queen's Hall. Franco's troops were in the suburbs of Barcelona, but it was hard to guess in London how near was the end. And there, in the Queen's Hall, it was legitimate to dream that a political break-through in Britain might be possible. The night before, Alfred Barnes, Chairman of the Co-operative Party, and Sir Archibald Sinclair, leader of the Liberal Party, had endorsed the Cripps memorandum. On the platform were leaders of the International Brigade, Ebby Edwards and Will Lawther representing the Miners' Federation, Victor Gollancz, J. B. Priestley, A. D. Lindsay, Vernon Bartlett and a host of other considerable personages who had not previously been engaged in united political activity. Bevan was one of the principal speakers. 'If Sir Stafford Cripps is expelled,' he said, 'for wanting to unite the forces of freedom and democracy they can go on expelling others. They can expel me. His crime is my crime.' He contrasted the spirit of the Queen's Hall where he 'seemed to catch the authentic voice of the British people' with the suffocating atmosphere in the House of Commons. 'From Parliament itself nothing can be expected. It is jaded, tired and cynical. It can be stirred from outside, but only from outside.'

For a few precious weeks, as in the first momentum of the Unity Campaign two years before, it appeared once again that the miracle could happen. Cripps formed an *ad hoc* National Petition Committee and the response was swift and exhilarating. Among the first petitioners were Sir Charles Trevelyan, Will Lawther, and one whose name may read strangely in a catalogue of the 'disloyal' – Sam Watson, at that time treasurer of the Durham Miners' Union. Seven M.P.s – Bevan himself, George Strauss, S. O. Davies, John Parker, Cecil Poole, Phillips Price and Ben Riley – along with many candidates and other prominent Party members – R. H. S. Crossman, G. D. H. Cole, Frank Pakenham – wrote to protest against the Cripps expulsion. 'We regard it as in keeping,' they wrote, 'with the failure of the Executive to mobilize effectively the opposition to the National Government which exists in the country among members of all parties and among those who belong to no party. There is a grave danger that this failure, if continued, will reduce the Labour Party to political impotence.'

Bevan was the most outspoken of all. Since a considerable part of the Executive's counter-blast against Cripps consisted of a lengthy compilation of quotations from his speeches delivered throughout the country over a period of years, he accused Transport House of using its money to maintain 'a sort of espionage system against members of the Party who do not find favour with the janissaries of the Party machine'. In particular, he invited the Labour Party to draw 'the last bitter drop of revelation' from what was happening in Spain while the National Executive was brandishing its disciplinary weapons. He asked his fellow Party members to mark the following sequence of events. On 27 February Labour had held a demonstration in Trafalgar Square to protest against the Government's intention to recognize General Franco; on Monday, 28 February, Chamberlain announced his decision to proceed with the recognition; on Tuesday, 1 March, Labour moved its vote of censure. But why, asked Bevan, was the Government able to act in such flagrant contempt of the Opposition's deepest emotions on a major issue of policy? It was because Chamberlain had no fear of the Opposition in the country and at the polls; so little had been done to breed the respect which an Opposition should be able to extort.

Seymour Cocks in that censure debate quoted the two terrible lines from A. E. Housman which were Bevan's inspiration too and were always present in his mind when persuasive voices urged him to moderate his passions in the face of infamy:

> Be still, be still, my soul; it is but for a season;
> Let us endure an hour and see injustice done.

The performance of Chamberlain in recognizing Franco – his refusal even to urge any proper terms of amnesty for Franco's victims – was, wrote Bevan, 'the blackest page in British history ... We have seen the ideals of our movement and the gallant workers who have fought for them harried and slaughtered all over Europe, and we have not helped them to victory or succoured them in their defeat.'

But these romantic associations and laments were not permitted to intrude into the Labour Party controversy. Soon all Labour Party members prominently backing the Cripps Petition were informed that persistence in this course would involve their expulsion along with Cripps himself. They too had committed the ultimate indecency: they had broken the Labour Party Constitution. But had they? Those participating in the Unity Campaign two years before had clearly offended by appearing on platforms with Communists; the Popular Front Petitioners had been careful to avoid this most heinous of crimes. The Petition had been launched at a meeting presided over by Sir Charles Trevelyan and supported by Will Lawther. Even if it were argued that Cripps had been guilty of a technical offence as a member of the Executive, what could be the charge against those backing him who held no official position? The argument seemed to be that a minority had no right to advocate its views or at least to organize in an effort to become the majority. 'If every organized effort to change Party policy,' wrote Bevan, 'is to be described as an organized attack on the Party itself then the rigidity imposed by Party discipline will soon change into *rigor mortis*.' The Labour Party should take special care not to transform itself into 'an intellectual concentration camp'. This was the burden of the exchanges which followed between the Executive on one side and on the other Bevan, Strauss and two Labour candidates, Lieutenant Commander Edgar Young and Mr Robert Bruce. Bevan asked the taunting question: can you please tell us how we can, constitutionally, express ourselves for the dire purpose of winning a majority? Or again: there are resolutions on the Party agenda favouring a Popular Front; are we permitted to indicate our support for these resolutions, particularly if we undertake to do so only at properly sponsored Labour Party meetings, or is it your desire that only one side of this argument should be heard? He got no answer, but instead a direct ultimatum, approved on the Executive by thirteen votes to eleven. If the offenders refused to indicate their withdrawal from the Popular Front campaign within seven days, expulsion would follow automatically.

Expulsion did follow, despite a last, vain protest. 'The refusal of the Executive,' wrote Bevan and Strauss, 'to allow us to appear before it so that we might defend ourselves; its failure to give us clear guidance as to the manner in which we could advocate our views without coming into collision with the Constitution; its rejection of the reasonable assurances which we were prepared to give in our last letter; the fact that it listened to letters read containing charges against us without giving us the elementary right of being told of them, much less the chance of defending ourselves against them; all these events force us to the conclusion that the Executive has allowed itself to become party to a controversy rather than to remain the administrative head of a great organization.' This was their case against the manner of the expulsion, apart from the direct Popular Front issue. Bevan's thoughts naturally reverted to the unfinished argument he had had with Jennie Lee in 1931; her quarrel with the Party had derived as much from her objection to its illiberal, oligarchic methods of working as from the differences on basic policy. But his fundamental belief about a Socialist's relation to the Labour Party had not altered. The justice of Jennie Lee's case was reinforced, but not the correctness of her deductions. Bevan had not courted expulsion, much less martyrdom. The desperate situation meant that greater risks must be run. In that sense, once again, he was a reluctant rebel.

So Bevan and Strauss were out. The same fate befell Trevelyan, Young and Bruce. What happened to all the others? H. N. Brailsford, the most distinguished of Socialist journalists, wrote to the papers indicating that he had committed all the same crimes and wished for the honour of the same punishment which, by some oversight, was denied him. His was a rare example. All the other M.P.s concerned, Will Lawther, Sam Watson and the rest of the leading Labour Petitioners complied with the Executive edict. Party loyalty reigned supreme in the Labour Party just as Captain Margesson had succeeded in sustaining the same virtue in the ranks of the Tories. Oddly, few political philosophers stopped to consider then and few historians have pondered since whether the elevation of Party loyalty above all other loyalties was not an expression of the same instinct in both Parties and, further, whether this widely-shared thirst for conformity was not a potent cause of the national slide to catastrophe. However, let it be recorded here since it is admitted nowhere else. Only three men in the pre-war House of Commons were prepared by their actions and their votes to defy their Party machines to such a degree that they invited full Party ostracism: Stafford Cripps, Aneurin Bevan and George Strauss. Churchill, Harold Macmillan, Brendan Bracken and one or two other members of the Conservative Party did speak and act in a manner which, if Captain Margesson had operated his discipline as vigorously as the Labour Whips, would have forced them to pay the same penalty. For the full, effective revolt on the Tory side the nation had to wait till May 1940.

The world would not stand still to enable Labour to unravel these intricate puzzles of Constitution and conscience. Undistracted by official Labour's single-minded concentration on the task of winning the next election as an independent force, Hitler marched into Prague. Even Chamberlain seemed upset. But ten days later, speaking still in the accent of authoritative wisdom, he announced to the House that he was unable to give any information about negotiations with other friendly powers; he was still opposed, he said, to setting up opposing blocs. That, if it meant anything, implied that he was still opposed to an approach to the Soviet Union. Labour's front bench sat silent. All on his own Bevan jumped up, only to be snubbed by Chamberlain. Amid cries of 'Sit down', Bevan jumped up again. There was great anxiety in the country, he said; the Premier's reply was quite unsatisfactory; it was speed the country wanted now, and then, as a final shaft, above the uproar: 'Has the Prime

Minister agreed on this delay with the Leader of the Opposition?' 'With the exception of Bevan,' reported William Barkley of the *Daily Express*, 'so far as could be established from the public attitude of M.P.s when they heard Mr Chamberlain, Parliament is unitedly behind him.' That was certainly an exaggeration, but a few days later when Chamberlain announced his Government's pledge to protect Poland, Rumania and Greece against aggression, most members were so bemused or stunned that they never paused to examine the implications. Chamberlainites still believed that Chamberlain could do no wrong. Anti-appeasers might argue that this was one step towards the Grand Alliance they desired. Bevan was one of the few who soon expressed his misgivings. He called it 'a most serious departure – we have underwritten partial commitments by the Government which fall far short of the system of collective security, for which we have urged the people to arm'.

Another debate of those days must be noted. The Government had introduced its Military Training Bill, the very conscription measure which its voluntary methods of the previous December were supposed to make superfluous. Official Labour felt itself tricked and denounced the whole proposition. Bevan was able to tell them the trickery could have been foreseen,[11] that he had in fact prophesied it in precise terms in the debate on the voluntary Register. A display of prescience was not the way to get loved, especially as he showed no compunction in rubbing his argument in the old sores. Labour had conceded all along the line. It gave up strikes; it agreed to no wage increases or improvements in the social services; it agreed to help recruitment. All it got in return was a parody of the genuine collective security system which alone could offer national defence. 'The working-class movement of Great Britain makes all the sacrifices and conces-

11. No one was angrier at what he considered to be the Government's trickery than Ernest Bevin. Alan Bullock writes in his *Life and Times of Ernest Bevin*: 'In exerting his influence with the trade union movement to secure support for the Government's preparations [the National Register of the previous December], Bevin had acted on explicit assurances from the Minister of Labour and Sir John Anderson that their scheme for voluntary recruitment was not intended to prepare the way for compulsion.' So Ernest Bevin was misled as Aneurin Bevan said he would be.

sions and not a single concession is made from the other side at any stage.'

Bevan, it may be seen, did not oppose conscription on principle; he did not deny that a Government which truly tried to defend the country might need to resort to a measure of this character. His case was based on the utter untrustworthiness of the Chamberlain administration to fulfil any purpose which Labour could approve and the failure of Labour to exert its power. Should he and the other Labour spokesmen have recognized the national peril and been ready to assist Chamberlain in making good by arms and conscription the immense strategic losses forfeited by the Government's diplomacy? The question is academic. No Labour leader of the age, even if he had wanted to, could have recommended this course and retained any influence with his followers. It would have involved a repudiation of every argument for the voluntary method which Labour had deployed, with the Government's grateful thanks, a bare four months before. It would have been tantamount to an assertion that the detested Chamberlain Government *could* be trusted with as large powers over the lives of British citizens in peacetime as were grudgingly yielded to Lloyd George and Asquith at the height of the 1914–18 war. To ask for that, was to ask for the impossible.

The only real alternative, Bevan's alternative, was that Labour should have used its power robustly to extract the necessary concessions in foreign policy and the whole conduct of national affairs. But no doubt the time for the delivery of so bold a challenge had long since passed. It is idle for hindsighted historians or party propagandists to debate Labour's delinquency in refusing to accept conscription four months before the outbreak of war. The questions they might more profitably pose are these: why was a Government with so impregnable a parliamentary majority so little capable of appealing to the nation and why could they not even enlist the support of an official Opposition ever eager to don the cloak of suburban, patriotic respectability as the hallmark of electoral credit? Put the point bluntly: on the conscription issue the Government could not get Dalton and Bevin to make a move on their behalf, much less vote for them. Why not?

These tremendous events – Hitler's occupation of Prague, the Polish pledge and the Conscription Bill – intervened between the expulsion of Cripps and Bevan and the Southport Conference of the Party in May where the expelled members hoped to make their appeal. The atmosphere had been altered from the January days when the Popular Front Petition had been launched. Few but the most blinkered appeasers or the most persistent optimists were still able to believe that European peace could be maintained on anything like honourable terms. And for Socialists another event had occurred, the most poignant of all, which left in their hearts a leaden weight of shame and sadness. The primary purpose of the Popular Front campaign had been to save Spain and now there was no longer a Spain to save. Refugees from Barcelona had streamed across the French frontier; conspiracy in Madrid had ended the war; Negrin's Government was in exile. Franco had given a pledge that his summary tribunals would only deal with criminals – 'reprisals being alien to the Nationalist movement'. Then started the vengeance which has lasted till this day. These horrors, more than any edicts from Transport House, had broken the spirit of the Left. At Southport there should at least have been a searing inquest into all that had happened since Edinburgh three years before. Some instruction might have been learnt for another decade and another generation, since nothing would avail in the pre-ordained months ahead. It was in fact the most pallid and listless Conference in Labour's history.

In preparation for Southport, Bevan had fortified himself with the backing of his constituency. He could not command then the overwhelming, emotional support which came later. He was still a young M.P. on trial, many older members of the local Party believed he had made a serious mistake, and some prominent Councillors took the precaution of being absent from his platform. But he swept aside any real opposition with the forthrightness of his appeal. He claimed to have acted on grounds of principle; any M.P. who failed to do so on an issue of such importance was not worth having; if those who had selected him as their candidate ten years before wished to change their minds, it was their right, but so long as he was their standard-bearer, he must insist on his right to exercise his own judgement and speak his own mind. The vote in his favour was well-nigh unanimous. He also won a remarkable personal triumph at the annual conference of the South Wales Miners' Federation in Cardiff. Everyone assembling at this conference believed his cause was doomed in advance, most delegates having been mandated by the branches to vote against him. Three other miner M.P.s presented the official indictment. Bevan turned his invective upon each in turn, saying to one of them: 'Are you looking for an Under-Secretaryship in a future Government? All you have to do is to go on saying "Yes, Yes, Yes".' At the end many delegates tore up their mandate and a resolution was passed, with only half a dozen dissentients, regretting the expulsion, demanding reinstatement and insisting that the victim should have the right to state his case at the Party Conference.

Yet at Southport both he and George Strauss were condemned to sit as observers in the gallery. According to the Party's rules, the suspension of the Conference Standing Orders was required to enable an expelled member to speak. On a vote of 1,227,000 to 1,083,000 this privilege was accorded to Cripps; a swift intervention from Ernest Bevin forestalled the plea that Bevan also should be allowed to the rostrum. As it happened, Cripps, on this occasion, was not at his brilliant best. His carefully prepared brief was not attuned to the one audience above all others which yearns for the glow of emotion and historical perspective. If ever Cripps needed Bevan, this was the hour. Cripps based his whole case on the constitutional right of a member of the Party to try and convert the rank-and-file to his point of view. The liberal logic was unanswerable, or at least no one tried to answer it. Dalton spoke for the Executive; he knew that an appeal to loyalty would touch chords which all the wisdom of John Stuart Mill could never pluck. Much the roughest and most effective reply, however, came from George Brown, the delegate from St Albans. Abjuring any desire to attack Cripps personally but eager to discount all the fine talk of Sir Stafford's services to the movement, he said he thought it was time someone pricked this bubble once and for all . . . 'We have spent nine blasted months in a pre-election year,' he shouted, 'just doing nothing else but argue the toss about Cripps.' Cripps's expulsion was approved by 2,100,000 votes to 402,000. Two days later a Popular Front resolution was defeated by an even more substantial majority. And that was all or almost all at the Conference whose decisions everyone did their best to forget. No doubt George Brown returned happily to St Albans to prepare for the election which never came – not at least until after Britain's Popular Front Government, formed in the extremity of war in 1940, and later including Stafford Cripps as one of its most eminent members, had saved the nation and enabled George Brown and the others to argue another day.

Southport marked the end of an epoch in the pre-war politics of the Left. The last door had been slammed in the face of any new resurgence. All that Bevan could contrive was a final epitaph on those years of degradation. Parliament adjourned for the summer recess at the end of July, not without a protest from Bevan. By the third week in August, confronted with the Nazi-Soviet Pact, the threat to Poland and the imminence of general war, it was recalled. M.P.s reassembled on that day in an atmosphere of stupendous crisis. Never had the sombre Premier spoken more sombrely. He presented a Bill giving emergency powers to the executive and appealed for a short debate. The expectation was that, after a few formal speeches, the Government would get its way. Those who have not heard it cannot imagine how awesome is the hush which descends on the House of Commons at these moments. An overpowering impatience exudes from the Government benches and if the official Opposition is a party to the compact of restraint the oppressive mood becomes more stifling than ever. To speak at all is an outrage; to attempt to argue, a blasphemy. Members imagine that a word out of place can shake continents; the ordinary back benchers cannot know what the all-knowing Ministers know; they are eager to retire to the smoking-room and the tea-rooms where indiscretions may be exchanged, safe from the prying ears of the press and the Patronage Secretary. It was at such an hour, with the Speaker testily seeking to assist the Ministers' will, but unable to suspend the procedure of the House for their convenience, that Bevan rose to his feet, alone, to continue the debate on 24 August 1939.

'I must say,' he began, 'that it is a little hard for some of us who for many years, in this House and outside, have been engaged in prophesying this moment to hear one of the chief architects of it say that he wishes to shorten the discussion.' He urged that even now talks should be pursued with the Soviet Union, emphasized the difficulties of fulfilling the Polish pledge, asked why the British discussions with Russia had taken so long and why the British Foreign Secretary had not gone to Moscow himself. The Government, he charged, had 'thrown away' the assistance of Russia. 'I think the guarantee to Poland, in the absence of an agreement with Russia, was a mistake. It was militarily silly. It should have followed and not preceded negotiations with Russia.' And yet the Prime Minister still dared to come to the House of Commons. 'The more blunders he makes, the more necessity there is for unity and for no critics to be heard.'

Murmurs of disgust were mounting, but Bevan sailed on. 'This is the same Government, its personnel is the same, as that which was the architect of Munich. The suggestion is that the people of my constituency, the colliers, the steelworkers and the railwaymen, should offer their bodies as a deterrent to German aggression.' Then he pointed his finger directly at Chamberlain. 'There is one man over there you could offer – *offer him*. Let the Conservative Party if it is in earnest call a Carlton Club meeting and get rid of the Prime Minister. He is the man upon whom Hitler relies; he is the man responsible for the situation.'

By now the Tory benches were screaming. One anguished hon. Member let loose the cry 'Be British!' 'You talk to me about being British, you Francoites,' retorted Bevan, 'there is a Brigadier-General sitting over there who, in this House, got up over and over again to defend Government policy in Spain which will throw away hundreds of thousands of lives and you people over there dare to ask for unity. It is monstrous.' A moment later he was saying: 'There is one way in which you young fellows on the front bench there . . .' The Speaker intervened. 'The one way,' continued Bevan, 'in which these young

Members can do their duty is to say that they are no longer going to remain in the team led by three or four people whose policy may plunge Europe into war in a few weeks and may result in the sacrifice of all our young people. That is why I say that no job is easier than that of the Prime Minister. No Opposition could be kinder. It has prophesied this every month for four or five years. It has fought against it at every stage of the journey, and at the end it abstains even from saying "I told you so". It is not for the sake of saying "I told you so" that I am making this statement this afternoon, but because I believe this is the most effective way in which Germany and Italy can be persuaded that the resolution of the country is united behind its obligations to get rid of the assassins of democracy in so many parts of Europe.'

But Bevan's words fell on deaf as well as scandalized ears. A flick of the Tory Whips was still sufficient to enforce obedience, even if no one could suppress the Whipless Bevan. Nine months had still to pass – nine months of measureless indignity, ineptitude, strategic loss and disaster – before others spoke in the same accents, and enough Tories would do their duty and remove Chamberlain from the premiership.

10 The Fight with Chamberlain
September 1939–June 1941

A strenuous resistance to every appearance of lawless power; a spirit of independence carried to some degree of enthusiasm; an inquisitive character to discover, and a bold one to display, every corruption and every error of government; these are the qualities which recommend a man to a seat in the House of Commons. – EDMUND BURKE [1]

These politicians suppose ... that you are blindly to follow the opinions of your party, when in direct opposition to your own clear ideas; a degree of servitude that no worthy man could bear the thought of submitting to; and such as, I believe, no connections (except some court factions) could ever be so senselessly tyrannical as to impose.
– EDMUND BURKE [1]

THE war brought for Aneurin Bevan a new fame or notoriety, to use the word his growing host of enemies would have preferred. He emerged as the foremost parliamentary critic of Churchill and the wartime Coalition, acquiring in the country at large the status of a national bogy man. His conduct was regarded in some quarters as little short of treason; for a considerable period he was watched by an employee of M.I.5 or some other secret service agency. Many, in both the House of Commons and the press, attributed his performance to a diseased ambition. Only a tiny handful of M.P.s cared to be closely associated with him and even they were often startled by the daring of his attacks. A malicious, frustrated, irascible demagogue – this is the portrait that some would paint of the wartime Bevan.

A few at the time and more in retrospect saw a comparison with the part played by Charles James Fox in the French Revolutionary and early Napoleonic wars. Fox thought those wars

1. *Thoughts on the Cause of the Present Discontents.*

unjust and unnecessary; there at least the parallel breaks down. But once the thought of this comparison is admitted at all, the likeness between the two men becomes striking. Fox revealed the same paradoxical mixture of impetuous speech and deadly debating skill, of apparent waywardness combined with allegiance to principle.[2] He too made his reputation primarily in opposition, despised the accusations of lack of patriotism since he knew how wide they were of the mark, gave a new meaning to the debased word *charm*, and aroused the same devotion from his friends. To study the life of Fox is to know Bevan better and *vice versa*. Once Fox's great antagonist, William Pitt, was told by some of his disciples that they could not explain why the Foxites followed such a man. 'Ah,' replied Pitt in a rare moment of insight, 'but you have not been under the wand of the magician.'[3] This was the spell which Bevan cast on the first Bevanites, to use the term anachronistically, and the magician somehow succeeded in capturing the ear of the House of Commons and half the nation even at the time when he was being vilified as a near-traitor. Escaping from the shadowy position of Cripps's first lieutenant, he became the undisputed, almost idolized, leader of the Left within the Labour Party.

2. Political biographies did not figure prominently in Bevan's wide reading, but an exception to this rule was Sir George Trevelyan's *Early History of Charles James Fox*. He knew the book so well that it has been hinted that he may self-consciously have modelled himself on Fox. Any such idea was quite foreign to his nature. However, Trevelyan's masterpiece contains many illustrations of Fox's style which bear a most uncanny resemblance to Bevan's. 'The orator,' he writes, 'who, when taken unawares, retorts upon his assailant with a shower of sentences so apt that they might each have been coined for the purpose of the moment, has purchased his enviable gift by many an hour of unseen and apparently objectless labour ...' This was Bevan's self-training. 'The fiercer the storm, the more completely in his element,' says Trevelyan elsewhere, 'was one who possessed, beyond his fellows, that willingness "to go out in all weathers" which Gerard Hamilton, with the appreciative envy of a vain and timid speaker, pronounced to be the quality of all others that made an inestimable debater.' Trevelyan also quotes Macaulay thus: 'Brougham is quite right about Charles Fox. He was, indeed *a* great orator; but then he was *the* great debater.' Aneurin Bevan extorted from the wartime House of Commons a comparable recognition of his debating prowess.
3. I am indebted for the idea of citing this comment to Leslie Hale, M.P., who knew Bevan well in the later years and was one of his most fervent admirers. The story was reproduced in the *Times* obituary.

What, then, is the truth about the Bevan of the war period? It is necessary to trace in detail how his views about the conduct of the war generally and Churchill in particular steadily developed. Luckily, apart from personal recollections and the parliamentary reports, it is possible to discover week by week how his mind responded to great events. From 1939 to 1945 he was intimately associated with *Tribune*. In the early days, there was a clash with the editor, Mr H. J. Hartshorn, who attempted to run a policy much too close to the Communist line for the acceptance of Bevan and Cripps. His place was taken by Raymond Postgate; Bevan, Strauss and Victor Gollancz formed the editorial board, with Bevan contributing articles almost every week. In 1942, Bevan took over more directly, becoming editor himself and recruiting Jon Kimche and Evelyn Anderson as his chief assistants So all through the war he had his pebble and sling for dealing with the Goliaths of Fleet Street even while he was day by day confronting Churchill and the other Ministers face to face in the Commons. And the development of his attitude is therefore fully documented.

Whatever verdict may be passed upon them, his views were not the result of sudden spasms of frustration or spleen. They were part of a coherent political philosophy which he considered to be as valid in wartime as it was in the pre-war era of unemployment and appeasement. He was the most *principled* of politicians – in the sense that his purpose was to apply general principles to the dilemmas of the time and in the sense, too, that to sustain his principles in practice was the motive power of his political life, the passion that absorbed him. No one who talked to him often and intimately would dispute this claim, despite its plain conflict with the popular impression. He was perpetually and consciously wary of the empiricism on which most politicians rely. He was rarely satisfied with an attitude to a political problem until he had applied a principle of which he approved to it. Political Parties, especially Parties of the Left, he believed, could not live from hand to mouth; they could only thrive on a more regular diet, and the failure to recognize this truth was a primary cause of the anaemia afflicting the Labour Party. His political opponents in other Parties or his own may legitimately argue that his principles were invalid or that his methods in applying them were unwise, ill-timed or dangerous. No one who knew him, especially in those war years when the ostracism sometimes became so fierce, can doubt that it was an innermost conviction of the justice or correctness of his case which drove him on. Again, contrary to the popular belief, he did not revel in parliamentary rows for their own sake, particularly with members of his own Party, or find comfort in the publicity they brought him. Once he was in a fight, he would give no quarter, but on the eve of many of them he endured agonies, and always he detested the hostility which so often surrounded him when he left his own home or the company of his closest associates. Nothing could be further from his calculations than a conscious appetite for the headlines. He was often wounded by what people said about him, although he did his best to pretend otherwise. For such an apparently swashbuckling warrior, he had a very thin and sensitive skin. During moments of crisis every nerve was exposed; he had none of the blessed gift of a Roosevelt or a Lloyd George, who could command sleep at will and composedly shut their minds against the trials of the hour. But he had also acquired a strong armour and a sharp sword – a breath-taking insolence of manner which his critics called arrogance and a most versatile wit which could prick a bubble or stab to the heart. The arrogance, if such it was, could be positively patrician in flavour and helped to multiply enemies. But it was excusable; for it was employed to put him on even terms with the powerful and to expose political toadying in every form.

The claim of those who would defend Bevan's conduct throughout the war must be that he was a real prophet without honour, who used his growing influence for purposes deeply beneficial for the winning of the victory and the making of the peace. On this severe test, let the record be judged. Of course, many of the controversies in which he engaged are still unsettled; the courses he followed are bound to be the subject for dispute. But his greatest quality shines through; from some source within him he could summon up, albeit with immense effort, courage without measure. During the war years especially he needed every scrap of it.

During the last days before the outbreak of war, Aneurin Bevan and Jennie Lee were at their cottage on Brimpton Common, fifty miles from London. With the assistance of Jennie's mother and father, they had made a wonderful home. Chained to Westminster during the week while Parliament was sitting and compelled usually at week-ends to travel far and wide making speeches, Nye lusted after it. His hatred of the city and his love of the countryside was no pose. Here for him were real riches. 'Aneurin,' wrote Jennie, 'was an adept at escaping to his cabbages. He could talk about them for hours, and on the strength of his three-acre garden rather fancied himself as an expert on agriculture. Then often in the evening we would ban any talk about politics and he would read to me or he would scold me for being so unmusical and do his best to share with me his own fierce Welsh love of good music.' It was always hard to tug him away from these pursuits, but, insists Jennie, particularly at that moment in 1939, real escape was impossible. 'When you read what do you read about? When you write what do you write about? When you talk with your friends where does your conversation take you? There were ghosts looking over our garden hedges, sitting beside us at our country fireside . . . the memory of the many we ourselves had known and loved who had been murdered, exiled, betrayed in the long seemingly endless night into which Europe had been plunged.'[4]

On Sunday, 3 September, they tuned into the one o'clock news for the official confirmation that the war had really begun. 'We had discussed all this so often and so much,' wrote Jennie, 'now at last it had come. Our enemy Hitler had become the national enemy.' A sense of relief mixed with presentiments about the unknown horrors ahead. Nye symbolized the occasion by playing on the gramophone some of the Spanish marching songs which he had brought back on records from Spain. These, with a few of his favourite Welsh choruses, often did service at such moments in reviving his spirit. That the war had to be fought he never doubted. The cause was just, however much it might have been tarnished by Chamberlain and the Munichites through the preceding years.

4. *Tomorrow is a New Day* by Jennie Lee.

The next issue of *Tribune* carried an article headed 'Our Duty' signed by Cripps and himself, but clearly written in the language of Cripps. Only a brief glance at the past was permitted. 'A very heavy responsibility rests on the British Government and upon those who have allowed that Government to remain in office during the last vital months. [After the Popular Front fiasco, Cripps had spent his time in a series of abortive approaches to individual political leaders.] The policy of doing nothing and hoping for the best, which many have adopted, is now seen to be one of the prime factors in our tragedy.' Then they turned to the future. It might be a long war, 'much longer than many people think now'. The aim must be the end of Fascism for ever. 'There must be no question of compromise until the world has been freed of this terrible and vicious system of force and suppression.' Much else followed – on the need to mobilize the nation's resources and avoid the evils of wartime censorship, on the peace aims to be pursued in the war, on 'the opportunity that will come for the workers to assert their power in our own and other countries'. But, immediately, one urgent demand must take precedence. If any real national unity was to be sustained, there must be a swift change of Government: Chamberlain and his closest associates must go.

Baldwin had prophesied that the bomber would always get through. In 1938 one leading expert had estimated that the German Luftwaffe could drop two thousand tons of bombs daily on London, inflicting casualties approximating to the figure of 250,000 in the first week alone. Once the wonderment at the absence of these terrors had passed, and Europe had relapsed into comparative quietude following Poland's defeat in a matter of days, men and women rubbed their eyes. Could this be war? Simply, it was not. Only one side was hardening its muscles for world struggle. After it was over, the 'phoney' war became a topic for elaborate derision. The 'business as usual' attitude in Whitehall, the leaflet raids on Germany, the punctilious instructions about the carrying of gas masks, the speeches of Chamberlain and Ironside, the Maginot line – all this and much else were to be swept aside into the same rubbish-heap. But the mockery provoked by the recollection that grown-up men had placed their faith in these futilities must not be mistaken for the prevailing opinion at the time.

The nation was fed on a different diet. 'A never-ending stream of optimistic propaganda, retailed to a censored press by a Government Department, concealed from the public every item of news that could alarm or discourage and presented a uniform picture of growing Allied strength and success. The newspapers were full of accounts of a superlatively equipped Expeditionary Force, with tanks advancing across the plains of northern France . . .'[5] The chosen commanders were paraded as military geniuses. Gort was a Prince Rupert, Ironside an obvious potential Cromwell, and Gamelin, in charge of the great French Army – the mere mention of its name could bring a mist of tears to Churchill's eyes – a Massena at least, if not Napoleon himself. The politicians were not backward in lending their authority to these romantic glorifications and receiving in reward their glow of reflected glamour. Leslie Hore-Belisha, the popular and energetic Secretary for War, spoke of the carriage of the Expeditionary Force to France as if it were the greatest feat in logistics since Hannibal crossed the Alps. He assured the nation on the news-reels that we were 'winning the war comfortably'. His Parliamentary Private Secretary, Mr Alec Beechman – the utterances of this political sub-species, the P.P.S.s, deserve an historical study all their own – said that victory was 'a mathematical certainty'. Gossip-writers were busy revealing with what resolution and administrative dynamism Chamberlain, the Man of Peace, had turned his hand to war. And Winston Churchill himself, although his speeches had an aggressive ardour to which the others never aspired, spread the same optimism in public and privately told the War Cabinet that Britain's situation was far more favourable than at the start of the Kaiser's war.[5] The politics of this period resembled what had gone before, not what was to follow. Clausewitz was amended: war was a continuation of appeasement by other means. The Chamberlain ascendancy still looked as impregnable as ever. He, like so many Premiers before and since, was regarded by many as indispensable, and the eyes of those – Stafford Cripps, for

5. *The Turn of the Tide* by Sir Arthur Bryant.

example – who cast about for an alternative alighted by some curious optical illusion on that modern Chatham *manqué*, Lord Halifax.

It would be ridiculous to pretend that Bevan, any more than the others, discerned in advance the hammer-blows by which Hitler was to shatter this scene of resolute repose. But he knew that the spirit induced by the Government's publicity machine was wrong and evil. His whole nature was insulted. 'Immediately on the outbreak of war,' he wrote, 'England was given over to the mental level of the *Boys' Own Paper* and the *Magnet*. The Children's Hour has been extended to cover the whole of British broadcasting, and the editors of the national dailies use treacle instead of ink. If one can speak of a general mind in Britain at all just now, it is sodden and limp with the ceaseless drip of adolescent propaganda.' This was the opening shot in his wartime battle with the national press. He attacked the *Daily Herald* – Bevin's Own and at that time edited by Francis Williams, Bevin's later biographer – as 'one of the worst sinners ... It has the intellectual astringency of a parish magazine and the scepticism of a Holy Roller. It snatches at every incident of the royal panoply and serves it up with the sycophancy of an eighteenth century placeman ... How can the mental sinews of our people tauten to the challenge of the modern world if it is fed on such childish rubbish?' In Parliament he put the question: 'Is the Minister aware that the impression is now universal that if the Germans do not bomb us to death the Ministry of Information will bore us to death?'

These irritations gave place to longer-term reflections. One night he stumbled home in the fog and the blackout from the House of Commons to his London rooms, glancing up at the blind windows on both sides of the street. The wardens had done their work well. Not a glint of light showed anywhere. 'Behind those walls,' wrote Bevan, 'were people I knew nothing about, thinking thoughts I knew nothing about, exposed to new influences and dependent for their communication with each other more and more upon the radio and the newspapers.' He confessed himself a little frightened by the murky spectacle. The radio was now an instrument of the Government and the newspapers were in the hands of the workers' enemies, keeping from their minds 'a whole block of social reality'. How could a Socialist movement survive when the means by which it moved – the platform, the branch meetings, the possibilities of association – were denied it? He recalled to himself William Morris's: 'Fellowship is life and lack of fellowship is death.' He was afraid of the mental blackout which war might spread. But, as he thought, he found a compensation. War excites opposite reactions at the same time. While the organs of authority might wish to instil a soporific acceptance or a drilled, unquestioning enthusiasm, it is also 'impossible to maintain an attitude of neutrality to war and the problems arising out of it. Social problems thrust themselves upon the minds of the most obtuse and compel an interest, grudging at first, but which often afterwards grows into an eager thirst for new knowledge. War opens minds that were sealed, stimulates dormant intelligences, and recruits into political controversy thousands who otherwise would remain in the political hinterland. It is with these new, eager, virgin minds that Labour must concern itself if it is to breast the tides of war and emerge from it holding the leadership of the nation.' Those were astonishing words for a man to write in January 1940, at the height of the 'phoney' war. Here was a prophecy of 1945 and the whole intellectual ferment, particularly among the young, which was to lead to it.

Much more urgent matters pressed for attention. What was to be done about the Tory Government – 'Its very existence is worth armies to Hitler'? At the beginning of the war the Labour leaders had agreed to an electoral truce, involving a ban on any election contests between official Labour and Conservative candidates and congealing the parliamentary situation so that the Tories still held their overwhelming majority. In the Commons Labour seemed content that all votes should be taken on strict party lines, insisting that their own Whips should operate as heretofore and thus helping to ensure that Captain Margesson, the Tory Chief Whip, could rely on the same passivity in his flock. Bevan quickly concluded that the agreement about the truce had been too hastily made, especially as Sir Walter Citrine was soon complaining about the 'contemptuous' treatment of the trade unions by the Government. As early as November 1939 Bevan was urging that the truce should be ended and that many more free votes should be permitted in a Parliament denied its normal means of refreshment. He was equally quick to pounce on the excuse of Ministers 'that it is unpatriotic to ventilate our grievances in public'. If 'the war deepens and hardens', he said, the excuse would be invoked more frequently. 'It will be better if it is stamped on at once.' As the weeks passed, his pressure for Labour to 'turn the heat on' became stronger. He had thought there had been an understanding in the Labour Party at the outset to fight on the two necessary fronts – against Hitler and to get Chamberlain out, as the essential preliminary to success in the main struggle. But in January he was saying that Labour had been 'blackmailed into silence'. There was a danger of 'a voluntary totalitarianism'. For good measure, he quoted a gibe of the day: that Lord Haw-Haw was the only person putting across the opposition case in Britain.

A footnote to the history of the time must be inserted here. In December 1939 both Bevan and George Strauss were readmitted to membership of the Labour Party. On the day after their expulsion at the Southport Conference in May 1939, they, with Cripps, had applied for readmission. They had agreed to accept the decision of the Conference about the Popular Front, recognizing from their own point of view that without the Labour Party such a political strategy was worthless, and they had offered to sign all the undertakings obligatory on other members of the Party, while insisting on the right to freedom of discussion acknowledged by Dalton in his Conference speech for the Executive. This letter was referred by the Executive to a sub-committee which reported in September. The three offenders were told that they could be readmitted if they signed a declaration expressing regret for their past action, accepting 'the Constitution, Programme, Principles and Policy of the Party without reservation', and undertaking in future 'to refrain from conducting or taking part in campaigns in opposition to the declared policy of the Party'.

Cripps replied to this letter in October, making apparent his sense of outrage that anyone should have dared to send him such a document. He was not prepared to apologize for the past, but instead reaffirmed his view that if his advice had been followed 'we should not be in the ghastly position we are in today'. The Party leaders who had attacked him for his lack of Socialist purity now found themselves 'under the unpleasant compulsion of supporting the most reactionary Government which has not only been largely responsible for our present plight but which bids fair to destroy the country by its continued ineptitudes and inefficiencies'. As for the demand that he should never oppose declared Party policy, this, said Cripps, 'might well form part of the credo of some totalitarian party in a dictatorship state'. The National Executive, instead of concerning itself about 'the inviolability of Party discipline' might have been better employed in trying 'to get rid of the present Government before we are finally overwhelmed by disaster'.

The tone of this letter was undoubtedly relished by Bevan; it was Cripps at his most magnificent. But Bevan himself treated the issue more circumspectly. He too rejected the Executive's totalitarian formula, but whereas Cripps had lost all patience with the leadership, Bevan was as adamant as ever in his belief that nothing could be achieved outside the Labour Party. He was eager to get back into its ranks even though at that moment he was engaged in renewed criticisms of its conduct. The South Wales Miners' Federation intervened on his behalf and his case for re-entry was strengthened by the fact that others who had left the Party to join the National Government in 1931 were re-admitted without having to sign anything more than the custom-ary pledge of allegiance to the Party's Constitution. Bevan and Strauss now agreed to sign this additional undertaking: 'to refrain from conducting or taking part in campaigns in opposition to the declared policy of the Party; but this declaration does not interfere with my legitimate rights within the Party Constitution.' Honour and pedantry were satisfied. Bevan was back in the fold – as the more sheeplike learnt to their alarm at the next Party meeting. The reality was that most of the venom had gone from this controversy, overlaid as it was by the urgencies of the war.[6]

6. The most diligent of his enemies could not refrain from comment. On 5 December 1939, the *Western Mail* carried a leading article. 'After doing

One unforeseen problem involving the risks run through what Dalton in his memoirs justly calls 'the midwinter madness' [7] of the Chamberlain Government revealed how different was Bevan's outlook from that of most of his newly-embraced colleagues. When the Soviet Government threatened and then went to war with Finland in November 1939, the sympathies of almost all British people and every democrat were with the Finns; this was a darker deed even than Stalin's cavortings with Ribbentrop over the signing of the Nazi-Soviet Pact. But sympathy and strategy could not go hand in hand; never was that harsh truth more painfully illustrated. Churchill admitted that 'any action we might take to help the Finns might lead to war with Russia' [8] – and yet he and his Cabinet colleagues were ready to take the action which could bring this calamity in its train. They were only checked in their purpose by the refusal of the Norwegians and the Swedes to provide the necessary accommodation across their territories.

Dalton asserts that the proposal to send not only arms and aircraft but also an Anglo-French Expeditionary Force to Finland struck him as 'sheer political lunacy ... It might even make quite certain that we lost the war.' [7] The readers of his memoirs might deduce that Dalton openly warned against the peril. But no; the record is silent. Since the Party was giving glib, if warmhearted, support to the midwinter madness, to speak out would

---

penance on the mat for many weary months,' it said, 'that haughty sesquipedalian, Mr Aneurin Bevan, has at last been admitted to the Socialist fold ... Will his constituents kill a fatted calf over the prodigal's return or chortle in their joy with those who slew the Jabberwock:

> Come to my arms, my beamish boy
> O! frabjous day! Callooh! Callay!'

Much followed on the whole variety of his crimes, including even an alleged preference for words of five or six syllables, and the article concluded: 'This escapade would cost him his seat in many parts of the country, but in Ebbw Vale we suppose it counts for political righteousness.' Henceforward, throughout the war, the *Western Mail* – the chief morning newspaper circulating in his constituency – conducted a vendetta against him of unexampled and occasionally brilliant virulence. Ebbw Vale was unmoved. Bevan told his constituents: 'When they stop attacking me, it will be time to get worried.'

7. *The Fateful Years* by Hugh Dalton.
8. *The Gathering Storm* by Winston Churchill.

no doubt have been 'disloyal'. But Bevan did. He was outraged as much as anybody by the Russian attack on Finland. He wrote that Stalin's excuses for the action 'smelt more of *Mein Kampf* than the Communist manifesto' – a rebuke which brought on his head a furious counter-blast from the *Daily Worker*. The Russians had 'committed a blunder of the first magnitude'. But when all this and much more was said, the course of 'all aid to Finland' which the Government appeared to accept, which Labour backed and which so few voices were raised to oppose, was fraught with incalculable dangers. Bevan denounced the hypocrisy of the League of Nations where Russian aggression could be condemned in twenty-four hours, while Albania and China were still waiting to have their cases heard and where Haile Selassie of Abyssinia was now treated as an untouchable. 'Why is it,' he asked, 'that in the middle of a war with Fascist Germany we are in a position to send planes to be used against the Soviet Union?' (Churchill, along with the rest of the Cabinet, was ready to send fifty bombers.) Instead of conniving at the operation, the Labour movement should approach the Government at once and insist that 'the immediate necessity is to concentrate on the defeat of the Fascist power in Germany, and that no particle of the resources of France and Britain should be diverted to the minor theatre of war which has sprung up in the East'. As it happened, the warning was superfluous. Soon Finland was compelled to plead for peace. But the experience did not enhance Bevan's faith in the discernment of Britain's war leaders, Churchill included.

Another crisis of the time – more a one-week wonder than a major disturbance comparable with the Finnish agony – gives a glimpse of Bevan's acute perception of the parliamentary scene. When Hore-Belisha resigned from his post as Secretary for War in January 1940, the newspapers used their biggest type: 'Great Belisha Scandal' – 'Great Belisha Crisis Grows' – 'Belisha Anger is Rising'. Almost the entire popular press ranged itself behind the fallen favourite; a tremendous row was forecast for the day when he divulged his full case to the Commons. But Bevan was sceptical; he knew his Belisha and he thought the emotional atmosphere would soon disperse. The newspapers were 'starved wolves' and this was 'the juiciest bit of news of the war', but nothing significant would emerge. And so it proved. Chamberlain 'was batting on an easy wicket because he knew the bowler was not trying to get him out'. Not that Belisha's speech was anything but highly polished and adept. Just occasionally it contained the hint of a threat. 'To vary my metaphor,' wrote Bevan, 'he pulled out just enough of the blade to show its edge.' But for the rest, it was as he had forecast. 'It is not worth our while,' he concluded, 'to expend any sympathy on Mr Leslie Hore-Belisha. He doesn't deserve it.' Either there was a profound difference of opinion about the conduct of the war dividing him from his colleagues or he was the victim of a shabby personal intrigue. He should have had the dignity to hit out, but he refused. 'He therefore stamps himself as a political adventurer, colourful and aggressive it is true, but representing no public principle of any importance.' Much more serious was the failure of the Labour Party spokesmen to exploit the quarrel for larger purposes. The impression prevailed that 'we are witnesses of a puppet show. This is not good for Parliament, nor for the vitality of democratic government in this country.'

Bevan's own parliamentary interventions through this period covered many interests and grew in intensity. He attacked Sir John Anderson, the Home Secretary, for what he regarded as the unnecessarily severe interference with civil liberties incorporated in his emergency legislation. He was bitter about the refusal of the Government to make concessions in the operation of the Means Test. He lamented the obvious failure – while more than a million men were still out of work – to grow more food at home; the problem was not really so insoluble – 'It is not clever people Britain needs. It is men with guts.' He brushed aside 'the fairy stories' of the Minister of Economic Warfare who sought to persuade the Commons that a blockade full of leaks had put a stranglehold on Hitler.

The most formidable of all these attacks came in April. Chamberlain, a few days before, had defended the record of his war administration with unforgettable emphasis. During the past seven months, he said, 'our relative position towards the enemy has become a great deal stronger than it was'. Hitler had failed to make use of his initial superiority for overwhelming France and ourselves. 'One thing is certain: he missed the bus ... I would be the last to underestimate his strength,' Chamberlain continued, 'but I say this too: the very completeness of his preparations has left him very little margin of strength still to call upon.' Sir Kingsley Wood, Chamberlain's Secretary of State for Air, was not committing the same crude error of premature readiness; rather he drew comfort from the resources that Britain might still be able to tap. Bevan fell upon him. 'We are not engaged,' he said, 'in a medieval tournament in which we try not to outnumber the enemy too much. We want maximum employment of our resources at the earliest possible time in order to save the lives of hundreds of thousands of our people ... This job has to be done, and it can only be done by a supreme national effort.' The same case was pressed by many others from the Labour side, but Bevan could give to an argument a special bite and challenge. Dismissing the occupants of the Treasury bench, he turned to the ranks behind, to the honourable members who with their vast majority had 'a great burden of responsibility'. 'I will not go into the polemics of the past or say how far they are to blame for the existing position. They will remember how docile, sheep-like and uncritical they have been of all the things done by those on the front bench for the last two or three years. It seems to be impossible to make any impression on them now when, after eight months, we have these unused resources. What are they waiting for? Are they waiting for some terrible calamity on sea or land or in the air before we can shake them out of this mood? Have thousands, it may be hundreds of thousands, of our people to lose their lives and be mutilated before these stupid Tories can be moved? Is that what they are waiting for?'

They had not to wait much longer. The terrible calamity of Norway was already in the making. It was not clear, as Churchill first claimed, 'that Hitler's action in invading Scandinavia is as great a strategic and political error as that which was committed by Napoleon in 1807, when he invaded Spain'.[9] Instead, the British Government which a few weeks before had been planning

9. *The Unrelenting Struggle* by Winston Churchill.

to divert some of its resources to rescue Finland could not retain a foothold in the Norwegian fjords. But something moved at last on the Tory back benches, and what was lost at Trondheim and Narvik was much more than regained at Westminster. Ironically, Churchill, a principal architect of the Norwegian fiasco, was its principal beneficiary, and as all the world could see a few days later, when Hitler's tanks were sweeping through the Ardennes, bypassing the Maginot defences, the 'phoney' war was ended.

It was a war without a hero, at least among the politicians. Military catastrophe was needed to achieve what Labour disgruntlement had not the power to enforce and what Tory independence had not the daring to demand. Chamberlain remained complacent to the end, appealing to his 'friends' in the House still to save him amid the ruin. Hore-Belisha had been unwilling to strike, unwilling even to wound. Eden had become a forgotten man. Churchill had given his blessing to the 'phoney' war Government and loyally attempted to perform in the final debate of the Chamberlain era the service which Lloyd George pleaded with him to withhold – 'to provide an air-raid shelter to protect his colleagues from splinters'. If any last-minute laurels are to be distributed they must go to Attlee and Morrison who decided, against the advice of many of their colleagues, to force the debate to a division; to Leopold Amery who demanded in God's name and Cromwell's words that Chamberlain should go; to Sir Roger Keyes who sailed into the engagement in his full Admiral's uniform; to the thirty-three Tories who marched into the Labour lobby and the sixty more who abstained; and, finally, to Lloyd George whose invective pierced the armour of Chamberlain's conceit and then was mercilessly twisted to inflame the wound. Even so, this final combination of factors would not by itself have been enough. Only by looking back further over the years is it possible to discern how Churchill in the end was able to step forward as the saviour. His long, lonely sojourn in the parliamentary wilderness was probably the greatest of his services to his country.

Bevan did not get the chance to be in at the kill; he was not called in the debate. But he could certainly claim that this hour of national deliverance was one he had striven for with all his heart and mind, not for minutes or months but for years.

After Churchill had replaced Chamberlain and while the battle in Flanders and France blazed so swiftly to its climax, the temper of the country changed more dramatically than that of the House of Commons. Only a few days earlier many, including the King, had considered that the proper successor to Chamberlain, if successor there must be, was Halifax. Churchill, on his entry into the Commons, was greeted with loud Labour and Liberal cheers, but with almost total silence on his own side. So deeply ingrained was the subservience to Chamberlain among the men who still retained a parliamentary majority. This fact was quickly blotted from the public memory. But it played its part in the political aftermath of the Norway debate.

To many, the establishment of Churchill in the premiership and the entry of the Labour leaders into the Cabinet was not a sufficient response to the military events of the time. Cripps and Bevan welcomed Churchill's arrival in power and joined with the rest of the Party in approving Labour's decision. But they argued that the Labour negotiators had underplayed their hand. 'The first shock,' wrote Cripps, 'was the inclusion of Mr Neville Chamberlain. What led the Labour leaders to agree to his retention? Why burden the new start with this sombre legacy? Why carry the symbols of defeat into what we all hope will be a victory Government? This is not the clean break we all longed for.' He was horrified by the continued acceptance of the Men of Munich and by some of the other appointments – notably Leopold Amery, an old ally of Churchill in the fight against Indian freedom, as Secretary of State for India; and Lord Lloyd at the Colonial Office, a man 'legitimately suspected of Fascist sympathies'. In making these strictures, Cripps and Bevan were undoubtedly expressing the feelings of many others besides Left-wing members of the Labour Party. But it is hard to believe that a stronger stand on the part of Attlee and Greenwood, the Labour negotiators, could have extracted more. The time was too short, the crisis in France too pressing, the need for an answer too peremptory. They had to take Churchill as they found him, with his sense of loyalty to colleagues, old and new, and his estimate of the need to offer some balm for the wounds of the Conservative Party. Moreover, Attlee had secured a high proportion of offices for Labour nominees, enough to ensure that they could exert immense influence, if the chosen Ministers showed the will and capacity. The real test of Labour's contribution to the power of the Coalition must come later.

Against the background of Dunkirk, the threatened invasion, the opening shots in the Battle of Britain and the exertions of the Ministers to galvanize the lethargic war machine they had inherited, all political and parliamentary events in that blazing, momentous summer are bound to look puny. Bevan's conduct can be represented in that fashion. He had, for example, a couple of rows in the House of Commons of a kind often long remembered when major speeches are forgotten. On one occasion he was in conflict with the Chairman of Ways and Means who rebuked him for introducing into a Committee stage debate an attack on the general record of the Home Secretary, Sir John Anderson. 'In these times of emergency,' said Bevan, 'we must get rid of these silly little fictions' – a remark which the Chairman described as offensive to the Chair and insulting to the House. On another occasion Bevan's fierce cross-examination of a Minister produced from Mr Ernest Thurtle, the Labour Under-Secretary at the Ministry of Information, sitting opposite, the muttered comment that questions were being pressed by certain members whose attitude to the war was 'lukewarm'. Bevan rounded on the interrupter: 'Is it not time that certain Members should not act as pimps to the Government every time?' Thurtle was on his feet demanding whether it was in order for such 'foul and offensive terms' to be employed in the House. When he got no satisfaction amid the ensuing uproar, he continued: 'I say, Bevan, if you would like to say that to me outside I will deal with you.' The exchange got big headlines next day. Bevan had made another lifelong enemy. It was easy to picture him, not as a lion of debate, but as an irritating wasp.

Such incidents, blown up out of all proportion, bore no relation to his thoughts on the stirring events of the time. The real complaint against him was twofold; first, that with a handful of others he insisted on examining in detail the emergency legislation which the Government presented and, second, that he voiced both in Parliament and outside the widespread opposition to the continued tolerance of the Men of Munich in the Government. When the leading members of the Labour Party assumed office, the formal leadership on the Opposition front bench fell upon Mr Lees-Smith. He was, says Dalton, 'very calm, sensible, loyal, experienced and, no disadvantage in his proposed new duties, a little slow'.[10] Clearly the Labour Ministers wished and maybe expected to see their followers completely docile, now that the administration was fortified by their own presence. But Bevan, obviously, would not be satisfied with this role, particularly as political apathy outside had been shattered by the Norway debate and what followed. The national mood was highly explosive. Men and women were conscious that they were witnessing huge historical convulsions. The overthrow of the Chamberlain Government marked no more than the beginning of the profound changes required in British society if the war was to be won. Bevan recalled a favourite quotation from Karl Marx. 'The redeeming feature of war,' Marx had written, 'is that it puts a nation to the test. As exposure to the atmosphere reduces all mummies to instant dissolution, so war passes supreme judgement upon social systems that have outlived their vitality.'[11] Bevan believed that Britain was to be put to a test of this exacting nature. As events were to prove, these revolutionary ideas in the air at the time were romantically exaggerated. But they were still nearer the mark than Dalton's assumption that Socialists would be content to watch admiringly the performance of the Labour Ministers, and, for the rest, to see the expression of their ardent expectations in the reliable accents of Mr Lees-Smith.

At the end of July, Bevan was already striking a strong note of criticism. He agreed that the Labour Ministers had done much essential work in the provision of labour and materials for the war effort. But he claimed that 'in the realms of higher policy they have conspicuously failed'. He urged them to be more aggressive within the War Cabinet in pressing their distinctive point of view. Had not Attlee at Bournemouth, on entering the Government, said: 'I am quite sure that our war effort needs the

10. *The Fateful Years* by Hugh Dalton.
11. *The Eastern Question, 1885* by Karl Marx.

application of the Socialist principle of service before private property'? 'Fascism,' wrote Bevan, 'is not in itself a new order of society. It is the future refusing to be born. And it is timid Socialism which refuses to give birth to the future.' As yet, his own alternative prescriptions were vague; they referred chiefly to the need for a declaration of the purpose for which the war was being fought, going much further than Chamberlain's jejune condemnation of Hitler as a 'wicked man'.

On one matter he could be specific. Dunkirk and the events leading to it had thrown a glare of light, more revealing than anything fully appreciated at the time of the Norway debate, on the incapacity of the previous Government. In most other countries incompetence on this scale would have been taken as a proof of treachery. In earlier centuries the men responsible would have been impeached. One substitute for these savageries in 1940 was a pamphlet called *Guilty Men* which sold like a pornographic classic and of which Bevan was alleged, falsely, to be the author. Yet as late as July it was still thought fitting that Chamberlain should broadcast to the nation, and the words he employed showed how little he or his associates recognized the scale of the historical disaster for which they bore so heavy a responsibility. 'I always knew,' said the oblivious Chamberlain, 'that you could not get one hundred per cent effort here until the bombs started falling . . . Every workman suddenly realized that on his individual efforts depended quick necessary supplies.' This was too much to bear and it was made the worse by the eagerness of one Labour leader to shield Chamberlain from Left-wing attack. A Gallup Poll at the time showed that seventy-seven per cent of the public wanted Chamberlain removed. But not Sir Walter Citrine; he delivered a speech deploring the whole campaign against the Men of Munich and suggesting that it was part of some sinister conspiracy. The inference was, said Bevan, that Labour must tamely accept for the duration of the war the terms of the bargain made in May, however inefficient the Chamberlainite Ministers were proved to be. Sir Walter should be repudiated by the General Council. 'When he speaks for himself he is not dangerous. His drab and colourless personality, without the fortification of his position, raises not a flicker of interest in anybody. Divested of authority his opinions are those of a political illiterate. He should confine himself to his filing system. I am told he is quite good at that.' Maybe Bevan had made another enemy, although possibly in view of past encounters the last straw was superfluous.

At this time also – in August 1940 in two *Tribune* articles – he examined the performance of Churchill upon that memorable scene. The first article took the form of a plea for the reconstruction of the Government. Churchill himself had an immense popularity; behind him was 'a united nation in a sense that has never before been achieved'. But the Premier's popularity did not extend to many of his Ministers. Partly their apparent deficiencies might arise because his 'robust and spacious personality' dwarfed them all. 'The real reason, however, goes deeper than that. It is not only that the light of the candles cannot be seen against the sun. Many people are beginning to doubt whether the candles are lit at all.' Of course, Bevan knew what would be the objection to his demand; a fresh Government upheaval could not be contemplated so soon. 'It is not necessary,' he replied, 'to see the end of the race to know that some of the horses will never see the finish. We were a bit doubtful of them when they came up to the starting post. They looked broken-winded and knock-kneed and some even seemed to have the staggers. Nevertheless we consoled ourselves with the reflection that Hereward the Wake's mare "Swallow" looked like that and yet she gave the Normans the surprise of their lives by producing a most astonishing turn of speed. It might be, we thought, these Ministers will surprise the Germans. Well they probably have, but not the sort of surprise we should have liked.' He then listed the Ministers whose services could be spared; Mr Duff Cooper, Sir Kingsley Wood, Sir John Reith, Lord Halifax and above all, Sir John Anderson [12] whose treatment of anti-Fascist aliens (he had locked them all up holus-bolus in the Isle of Man) had 'brought us to shame before decent opinion throughout the world'. Let it be conceded, said Bevan, that the

12. All these Ministers were in fact moved to other posts or discarded altogether within a few months. It is impossible to claim that Bevan's attack had been responsible; but something might be allowed for his foresight or insight.

Government had to be formed in May in great haste. 'National unity was the overwhelming consideration, as indeed it still is.' But it was also necessary to select the best men for the tasks ahead. 'The principle of coalition provides the hilt. It is the men who form the blade. We have a strong hilt, but a very blunt blade. It is Mr Churchill's job to sharpen it quickly.'

A portrait of Churchill himself followed. 'In the short space of a few months,' Bevan wrote on 30 August, 'he has grown from being a unique parliamentary debater into the unchallenged leader and spokesman of the British people.' His position and his national backing were stronger than anything Lloyd George had been able to achieve in the first world war. However, 'in a democracy, idolatry is the first sin. Not even the supreme emergency of war justifies the abandonment of critical judgement . . . To surrender all to one man is to risk all being destroyed by him. That is why dictatorship is at the same time the strongest and the weakest of social systems, and it is one of the main reasons why the Nazis will ultimately fail and the democracies will triumph. The soul of democracy can never be fatally wounded for it is never wholly exposed.'

He then glanced back to consider one source of Churchill's strength – the 'most fruitful period of his life', the later thirties when he was making speeches which are 'unsurpassed in the long annals of Parliament. Towards the end of this period he started on those long series of orations about the arming of Germany, the nature of the Nazi menace, and the necessity of collective European action to meet them, which are unrivalled for prophetic insight, for colourful imagery, for felicity of expression, for sardonic humour and biting satire.' This was Churchill at the zenith of his intellectual powers. Yet 'although he won every debate he lost every division. All the manifold gifts of the first parliamentarian of the time could do nothing against the servile limpets of the Tory Party machine.'

Conceivably, continued Bevan, Churchill had learnt 'a dangerous lesson' from those melancholy years – that 'a Party manager, no matter how stupid, was more powerful than any single individual, no matter how brilliant and accomplished'. If his own exclusion was not enough to teach him, there was the fate of

Lloyd George to reinforce the lesson – 'the most colourful personality of British history' kept out of office since 1922. 'Against the dull weight of Party organization the most dynamic personalities fight in vain.' Confronted with this knowledge, Churchill might be inclined 'to overestimate the power of political groups at a time when they are in a more fluid condition than they have been for fifty years'. There was rumour that the leadership of the Tory Party might soon become vacant. Churchill's memories, concluded Bevan, 'may tempt him to assume the tawdry purple now slipping from Mr Chamberlain's shoulders. If he does so he will become the creature of the Tory machine. It would be a national tragedy and a pitiful twist of personal irony if the years of exile taught Mr Winston Churchill the disciplines of Party obedience just at the moment when we need the audacities of freedom.'

No one can complain that Bevan's 1940 estimate of Churchill lacked insight and magnanimity. He shared to the full the widespread feeling that Churchill had expressed the national will with incomparable courage and mastery. But even so and even then he was not prepared to treat Churchill's relationship with the Tory Party as a trifle. In October the deed was done. As Bevan wrote: 'By one of those graceful and emollient acts for which the British governing class is justly famed, Mr Chamberlain was slipped inconspicuously from the political scene and Mr Churchill was unanimously elected leader of the Tory Party which for years had been seeking his political extinction.' From the Tory point of view the transaction was obviously profitable – 'once more the Tory caucus drapes itself in the national flag'. But what of the interests of the nation and the conduct of the war? 'It is a thousand pities,' wrote Bevan, 'that Mr Churchill should have chosen to take a step which must agitate dormant suspicions and awaken to life rivalries which are best forgotten when the enemy's knife is at our throat. It is a million pities that he should have chosen to give new vigour to elements in our national life which must be progressively weakened if we are to gather sufficient strength to win through.'

Churchill also did not regard the affair of the Party leadership as trifling. In fact he attached to it a significance precisely equal to that which Bevan discerned. He admitted after the war that 'there may still be various opinions' about the course he took. But he himself had no doubt at the time. Two overpowering reasons persuaded him that no other choice was possible. First, if he had yielded the office to someone else, 'he [the new Party leader] would have had the real political power. For me there would have been only the executive responsibility'. The second reason supplied by Churchill is even more revealing: 'in dealing with the Labour and Liberal Parties in the Coalition it was always an important basic fact that as Prime Minister and at this time Leader of the largest Party I did not depend upon their votes and I could in the ultimate issue carry on in Parliament without them.'[13] If Churchill found it necessary at such a time to make so delicate or brutal an estimate of parliamentary power, others were entitled to do the same. Henceforth, said Bevan, 'it will be necessary to watch Mr Churchill from two aspects: as a national leader in an unprecedented situation, and as the spokesman of the Tory Party'. Henceforth his attitude to Churchill altered perceptibly but still slowly. It is legitimate to recall that one origin of the wartime arguments between them was a decision taken by Churchill himself for the purpose of establishing his own dominance, through the Tory Party, over the House of Commons. Churchill's choice was his own; but it was clamantly backed by Beaverbrook, Bracken, Eden and others who had suffered in the pre-war years from Captain Margesson's lash. Thus, some may say, Churchill got Parliament in his grip. Or thus he bowed in the House of Rimmon; thus he acknowledged the power of the Tory machine which had made unavoidable what he himself called 'the Unnecessary War'.

Churchill might believe that the Tory machine would keep M.P.s in order for him; no doubt the Labour Ministers were confident that their own Whips would help perform the same national service. In view of all the pressures upon them, their prayers for a quiet parliamentary life are understandable. But the Commons could so easily have been reduced to the status of a Reichstag. Churchill would have gone there to deliver his great orations and his Ministers to deliver their decrees. Once Sir

13. *Their Finest Hour* by Winston Churchill.

Oracle had spoken, no dog would have barked. That this did not happen was due to a small number of M.P.s on both sides of the House. On the front Opposition bench Emanuel Shinwell and Earl Winterton, the famous 'Arsenic and Old Lace' combination, were unwilling to stifle their criticisms. Hore-Belisha began to recover his voice. On the Labour benches, Sydney Silverman and Dick Stokes quickly showed their readiness to join Bevan in his forays or to launch their own. By the end of 1940, Bevan was saying that it was the liveliest Parliament he had known since 1931. That the nation's interest was served by this vigilance is readily proved. It was, after all, parliamentary revolt which had rescued the country in 1940, and thereafter, on a whole series of issues, even the all-wise Ministers retreated in the face of parliamentary pressure, commending their second thoughts to the House as even wiser than their first. Moreover, letters were pouring into Members of Parliament, at least to those who were active, in larger numbers than for some years past. The more often Bevan spoke, the bigger the postbag he received. More than ever was it vital in his view that the safety valve of redress in Parliament should be seen to be in working order.

The fact that Parliament was kept alive made him all the more annoyed with what he considered to be the sycophantic style of the national newspapers. At one moment in 1940 there had been a hullabaloo because Mr Duff Cooper had threatened to introduce a real censorship. Bevan jeered: 'You don't need to muzzle sheep.' He then proved the reasons why 'hardly a whisper' of parliamentary realities 'ever reaches the arid pages of the "kept" press'. Lord Beaverbrook was in the War Cabinet; 'an astonishing amount of latitude has been allowed his papers, but it is obvious there are limits beyond which they will not be allowed to go'. The Rothermere press was chronically reactionary anyhow. 'Sir Walter Layton is in America on Government war work, so that ties up the *News Chronicle* and the London *Star*.' The *Daily Herald* is 'dominated by Lord Southwood and if that isn't enough Sir Walter Citrine is hardly likely to develop any skittishness'. The Astors ran the *Observer* and *The Times* and 'we all know how they are yearning to lead us into the promised land'. The *Daily Telegraph* was controlled by Lord Camrose, 'dull, dim and diehard'. There was the *Daily Worker* – 'unfortunately its peculiar sense of hearing only enables it to distinguish the voice of William Gallacher'. As for the 'solitary but ambiguous isolation' of the *Daily Mirror*, 'where it wants to go I cannot tell. What I do know is that the authorities view with irritated anxiety this somewhat undisciplined member of the Fleet Street flock.' Fleet Street might retort that Bevan was squealing because his own speeches were not more fully reported. 'Of course I complain,' he said, 'why shouldn't I?' He was not asking for favours for himself. He wanted a square deal for all the back benchers who 'are trying to raise a critical voice above the loud bleating of the official fold'.

Ministers did not share Bevan's view about the amenable nature of the press. The editor of the *Daily Herald* was constantly rebuked by Labour Ministers. Warnings were given to the *Daily Mirror*. Beaverbrook received many complaints from his Cabinet colleagues – and from Sir Samuel Hoare, far away in Madrid, who plaintively appealed via Lord Halifax in the vain hope of altering David Low's line on General Franco's profile. And early in 1941 Herbert Morrison, by now Home Secretary, took direct action against the *Daily Worker*. 'I arranged with Scotland Yard,' says Morrison, 'to go along to the *Worker* offices one evening and stop the presses then and there.'[14] He used powers given to his predecessor under regulations supposed to deal with circumstances arising from physical invasion, thereby robbing the victim of any chance of stating his case. No doubt the provocation was considerable. The *Worker* had insidiously attempted, ever since the Communist line had been switched at the beginning of the war, to oppose the war effort. But Bevan was not prepared to let such an abuse of the powers granted by Parliament pass without protest. He knew that he would have almost the whole House against him, but he took the lead in proposing a motion condemning Morrison's action.

He detested the policy which the *Worker* had followed, but the suppression of opinions which could only secure so pitiful a following was a sign of weakness, not of strength. 'The Prime Minister,' he said in the debate, 'uses unexampled eloquence

14. *An Autobiography* by Herbert Morrison.

over the radio and talks about freedom and democracy. What does freedom mean if not that men may not be yanked off to prison by policemen without having a chance of defending themselves, and that a newspaper will not be suppressed without having a chance of being heard in its own defence? These are not idle forms; they are the citadels of our democratic institutions.' If the *Worker* had been guilty of incitement to sabotage, Morrison could have taken them to the courts. He and some of the other Labour Ministers were allowing themselves to be made the catspaws of reactionary policies. Bevan appealed over their heads to his own fellow back benchers. 'For Heaven's sake, take care where you are going. A few years ago we were accusing Members on the other side of the House of leading us to disaster and to war because of loyalty to their Party and to the old school tie. They put loyalty to their Party above loyalty to their country. Today they are asking us to do the same thing, to go into the lobby, not because we believe the Government have done the right thing, but because our Ministers are involved.' But his appeal won small response. Only seven Labour Members voted with him against the Whips.

Soon after this first wartime revolt against official Party decisions Bevan was involved in another of greater significance which led him to elaborate his ideas of the proper relationship between an M.P. and his Party. The conclusion he reached was to govern his parliamentary conduct for the rest of the war and indeed was to shape his whole career. The immediate issue which gave rise to the controversy may seem far removed from the great battles then proceeding in Africa and the menace of invasion which still dominated the nation's thoughts. But the war was a war for democracy, and Bevan was unwilling to put democracy in cold storage for the duration. Moreover, he believed that the people's morale in fighting the war depended partly on the proof which the Government gave that it was acting justly. Men could not live in an atmosphere of exalted patriotism; they were entitled, not only for themselves but for others, to see some evidence that the new Government had shed the old class motives of the Chamberlain régime. To secure this assurance in deeds, not words, was peculiarly the duty of the Labour Ministers. Churchill had other commitments and other dreams. 'His ear is so sensitively attuned to the bugle note of history,' wrote Bevan, 'that he is often deaf to the more raucous clamour of contemporary life, a defect which his Conservative upbringing and background tend to reinforce. The seven-league-boot tempo of his imagination hastens him on to the "sunny uplands" of the future, but he is apt to forget that the slow steps of humanity must travel every inch of the weary road that leads there.' Labour Ministers should be able to understand better; it was one reason for their existence.

The issue concerned the most acid memory retained by Socialists from the pre-war era – the Means Test. In November 1940, the Government announced that the Household Means Test for old age pensioners was to be abolished in a Bill soon to be presented to Parliament. Bevan's rejoicing at this declaration can be imagined. He acknowledged how difficult it was to turn from the arresting drama on the world stage to the prosaic business of the disbursement of insurance benefits. But he asked his readers in *Tribune* to be patient and imaginative. 'Progress crawls on a thousand feet', he quoted. Victory in the apparently interminable fight to end the infamy of the Means Test was something worth celebrating. He cited an example to illustrate what he meant. He had received in his postbag the case of an old lady, eighty years of age, who left London on account of the air raids. She went to live with her son-in-law, who was sixty-five, and retired on a small State pension. The old lady, who got nineteen shillings and sixpence in relief in London, was reduced to twelve shillings and sixpence because she was alleged to be partly kept by her son-in-law. 'Can anyone,' asked Bevan, 'imagine anything more likely to embitter the relations of these two people than that?' But now at last, thanks to the pressure of the Labour Ministers, the Churchill Government was to concede what the Chamberlain Government had refused. The wretched system would soon be 'nothing but a bad memory'. The details had still to be declared; the Treasury was no doubt fighting a rearguard action over the anomalies which might arise; 'we shall have to keep our eyes open', said Bevan. But for the moment he rejoiced as he more than most had the right to do and paid full tribute to the Labour Ministers responsible.

However, when the Bill was examined it did not fulfil the Prime Minister's promise that 'the test will become one of personal need'. A considerable advance had been won, but elements of the old family test remained. Despite a decision at the Party meeting to support the measure without qualification, therefore, a number of Labour M.P.s, including several of the Party's chief experts on the Means Text and including Bevan, put down an Amendment to the Second Reading of the Bill. They made it clear that they would vote for their own Amendment but not against the Bill as a whole. This statement provoked from Mr Pethick-Lawrence, the front-bench Labour Party spokesman, a severe attack on the Members who had signed the Amendment. 'They want to pose as champions of the oppressed,' he said, 'while they are playing politics and doing their best to sabotage an agreed solution.' It was not fair fighting; it was cowardice. 'They have allowed themselves to be made tools of by others less ingenuous than themselves.' The accusation was clearly directed against Bevan. He had recruited a few innocents to join in his heresies against the infallible private Party meeting.

Some of the rebel M.P.s spoke for themselves. No pledge they had ever given in their lives was more specific than their hostility to the Household Means Test; they were trying to redeem it. Then Bevan took the floor. He called Pethick-Lawrence's speech 'hysterical and splenetic'. It was the first time in his life he had been called a political coward. His vote would mean that he wanted the Bill, but he wanted more. What was wrong with that? Pethick-Lawrence had suggested that if the compromise was rejected, the matter could not be raised again until the end of the war. Was he serious? 'Yes,' interrupted Pethick-Lawrence. 'Then he is stupid as well as serious,' answered Bevan. If the Amendment were carried the Cabinet would have to think again and do better, as the Labour Ministers should already have persuaded it to do. Then Bevan revealed, amid the fury of all the Party loyalists, that the Parliamentary Labour Party had decided to hold a special meeting a few days later to bring to book those who insisted on fulfilling their pledges in the House. To expose these backstairs manoeuvres in the broad light of day is the ultimate indecency. But Bevan did not care. Why were the parliamentary thumbscrews to be applied? 'Why?' insisted Bevan. 'Why? Because your constituents will want to know why you had not voted [for the Amendment] and you do not want the unpleasantness of having to reply. Why should you be allowed to bury your consciences secretly? Why should you be exempted from the obligation to make a public explanation of your public conduct, and be permitted clandestinely to violate every pledge you have given? It is not in keeping with the honour of a Member of Parliament that he should seek in a closed and secret room upstairs an excuse for betraying the people he represents.'

Nineteen Labour Members voted for the Amendment, and the battle was transferred to the torture chamber upstairs. There furious charges and counter-charges were made for three hours. Some called for the withdrawal of the Whip, others for the most severe reprimand. But as the afternoon wore on more and more did not relish the prospect of explaining in public why the Government, with their assistance, could not muster up enough courage to end the Household Means Test. Would they not be asked in the country why Labour Ministers and Labour M.P.s could not stand up to the Tories on a matter which touched Labour's honour so sorely? 'That's a dirty question,' Bevan was told when he posed it in the Commons. Dirty or not, it won the day. At the Party meeting the 'previous question' was moved. The rebels had escaped without a bone broken and without a hair scorched.

The moral which Bevan drew from these growing asperities was that the Party should be prepared to reconsider its whole attitude to parliamentary discipline. The majority theory that the first duty of M.P.s was to uphold the policies of Labour Ministers with binding decisions at secret Party meetings was a recipe for making Parliament a rubber stamp. 'In this fashion,' he wrote, 'political parties become the enemies of parliamentary democracy. To allow Ministers to assume that they need never face hostile criticism in the Commons would help to produce a steady and insidious undermining of the war effort. It is better that Ministers should be embarrassed than that Parliament should die ... In Germany democracy died by the headman's axe. In Britain it can be by pernicious anaemia.' Bevan's argument was principally addressed to the wartime situation where absence of a formal Opposition meant that Labour's disciplinary theories would make Parliament a mere register for the private compacts between the Party leaders in the Government. But his alternative theory also had larger and longer implications. 'Party discipline,' he said, 'should end where it impinges on parliamentary liberty.'

Apart from its parliamentary implications, the Means Test dispute illustrated another of his constant themes – the need for a much bolder approach to social change and the need for the Labour Ministers in the Government and the Labour movement outside to press for it. Indeed, the theme was not his; it was part of the exhilaration of the time. As he had foreseen, but more swiftly and buoyantly, men and women engaged in the heroic or mundane tasks of the war were also ready to think adventurously about the future. It was not true, as Churchill seemed often to imply, that one interest might elbow out the other; the two marched together. The huge response to J. B. Priestley's postscripts on the radio was one evidence of the spirit of the age; they seemed to provide a complement to Churchill's glowing war reports. Film producers began to recognize that the real life of the people was more exciting than bedroom farces in historical fancy dress. Publishers suddenly discovered that they could sell vast numbers of books on political and sociological topics. Soldiers were reading in their camp beds and airmen at their depots. They were not content to study the contortions of Jane in the *Daily Mirror*, but once that daily ritual was performed bombarded the editor with their grievances and their expectations. Community life, so far from being disrupted by bombs and blackouts, was being richly renewed. Throngs of young people, home on leave or at work in London, attended lunchtime concerts in the National Gallery or crowded to the War Artists' Exhibitions. Many an Air Raid Precaution centre became a miniature mock Parliament, with class barriers broken, tongues untied and accents forgotten. Men and women became true neighbours, even comrades, and England caught a glimpse of what a co-operative Commonwealth might be.

With this new spirit went a political ferment directed partly against the squalor of the past and partly in excited hope towards the future and the peace when it came. Harassed Ministers might suppose that this mood and the awkward pressures it aroused were all the work of sensational journalists or agitators. Their own concentration on the immediate requirements of the war was natural enough, but they often appeared out of touch with the people they aspired to lead. As Bevan tirelessly reiterated in the Commons and outside, the demand for a declaration of war aims or the demand for present tokens of the coming revolution should not be regarded as signs of disgruntlement or war weariness; here was a rich source of popular energy and resilience. He had his finger on this pulse of national awakening and he preferred to trust the intuitions it gave him than abide by the weary precepts of the Party managers.

In particular, he wanted to see the Labour leaders infected by the new political zest. The more he felt disappointed in that wish the more he revealed his frustration. In January 1941, he wrote that the collapse of the Chamberlain Government had restored the political initiative to Labour; now 'it had lost it again'. In February he persisted that 'the present policy of the Labour Party gives the Party no work to do except to take poison, and that poison is to accept the obligation of defending the policies of the Tory majority in the Government'. Almost the only other Party activity encouraged from headquarters was the expulsion of Party members who had been foolish enough to take part in the Communist-run People's Convention – 'The inquisition is brought in because the crusade is over'. In March he was urging that there must be a resumption of political agitation in the country; that, plus free voting in the Commons, would be necessary to give some real thrust to the Labour Ministers in the Government. The case was copiously illustrated by examinations of the Government's alleged failure to take sufficiently radical measures in dealing with coal, the railways, the land and the production effort generally. By May – just prior to the Labour Party Conference of that year – he was complaining that 'the Labour leadership insists upon regarding itself as a junior partner in the Government when in fact it is alone the custodian of those inspirations and policies through which victory can be achieved'.

However, the Whitsun Conference of the Party in London gave him no cause to alter his verdict. Almost the only lively moment in a leaden week was when the Kings Norton Party, with Frank Pakenham[15] as their rebellious spokesman, claimed the right to be heard in protest against an Executive edict against them for breaking the electoral truce; their offence was that, when a by-election occurred in Kings Norton, they had issued a circular explaining why they could not support the Conservative candidate allowed a free run under the terms of the truce. Bevan suggested that 'the Party could well afford to have a little more democracy at the bottom and a little less manipulation at the top. Our Conferences are rapidly becoming collections of Labour Party Storm Troops.' But Kings Norton was not heard; so black a crime could be condemned without ceremony. After the Conference was over, he said the Labour Party was becoming 'ossified'; 'in the guise of loyalty to Party and in the name of discipline the Labour Party has poisoned its own vitals'. How could young people see their inspiration expressed in the operation of pedants and inquisitors? For the past ten years the Party had been committing 'political infanticide'. Some on the Left suggested that the position was so bad that they must write off the Labour Party as hopeless and build afresh from the foundations. This Bevan rejected. The only hope was to act independently of the machine, to seek to mobilize in unofficial groups and activities the huge swell of opinion outside which could so easily be canalized in a Socialist channel, to teach Labour to speak the language of audacity, to choose to lead instead of to bludgeon.

Such, then, were the types of wartime controversies in which Bevan had participated up till midsummer 1941. All these interventions together, it may be seen, did not add up to a deep or consistent critique of the conduct of the war. *How could the war be won?* Few at the time dared to think about this presiding question; if they ever did realistically, their conclusions might be too near defeatism. Most people were prepared to accept on faith the strategic conceptions of the Government so regally

15. Later Lord Pakenham, now Lord Longford.

expounded or concealed in the great Churchill orations. Except for the attempted Finnish escapade, none of the disputes about strategy had emerged as major questions of the day. Bevan had had a few brushes with Churchill on secondary matters, but that was all. When in April the nation was struck by the treble blow of disaster in Greece, the setback in Libya and the fall of Crete, he was not inclined to join the rare critics who said that we should never have challenged the German Army so far from our own bases and so near to its own. 'It was a most noble impulse,' he said, 'which impelled us to land in Greece.' Judgement about the reverses in Africa must be suspended until more facts were known. Churchill had broadcast his conviction that, with our successes against Italy, the threat to Egypt had been removed; 'this streamlined war makes prophecy unwise', said Bevan. The reproof was mild. In short, so far Bevan approved Churchill's strategy; the only conquest – or surrender – which aroused his suspicion was Churchill's acceptance of the Conservative Party leadership.

Like others, too, Bevan looked half sceptically and half longingly to the great neutrals. It was obvious, he wrote in February 1941, that we could not defend ourselves effectively against the Nazis without full American aid; he did not underestimate the importance of the closest ties between Britain and America. But he had a fear and a hope. 'Great Britain was, to a large extent, responsible after the last war for maintaining the old social framework on the Continent. Is America going to perform the same hideous task for us and the rest of the world, when this war is over?' He dared to believe not. 'For America, in many respects, contains more vital and energetic democratic strains than older Great Britain.' As for the other great neutral – the Soviet Union – Bevan, like his friend Cripps who had been sent to Moscow by Churchill as Ambassador (despite surly objections from some Labour Ministers), could not believe that the Nazi-Soviet Pact had spoken the final word on Russia's role. That was why he had been so determined in his opposition to the proposed policy over Finland. He could not believe, moreover, that Hitler would be able to make permanent the adjustments in his ideology necessary for a lasting compact with the Russians. In a speech in October 1940, he had appealed for a 'diplomatic offensive', since military offensives were impossible. He believed that the moment was favourable for establishing closer relations with Russia. 'I am not suggesting that the Russians are anxious to go to war; I am not even arguing that Russia will come into the war; but I am suggesting that circumstances today are far more favourable to a *rapprochement* with Russia than they have been since the war began.'

These wishful thoughts about the Soviet–German relations were premature, although, oddly, Hitler just at this time was making his fateful decision.[16] But on 22 June 1941, came the news that Germany had invaded Russia. Bevan's war, like the war itself, was now to be fought on many more fronts.

16. Hitler gave his War Directive No. 21, code-named Barbarossa, incorporating his decision to attack Russia, on 8 December 1940. 'Since I struggled through to this decision,' wrote Hitler, 'I again feel spiritually free. The partnership with the Soviet Union . . . was . . . often very irksome to me, for in some way or other it seemed to me to break with my whole origin, my concepts, and my former obligations. I am happy now to be relieved of these mental agonies.'

11   The Fight with Churchill I: June 1941–July 1942

Churchill on the top of the wave has in him the stuff of which tyrants are made. – LORD BEAVERBROOK[1]

ANEURIN BEVAN shared the belief of many others that the German invasion of the Soviet Union had revolutionized the character of the war. Before 22 June 1941, victory had been an elusive dream; thereafter it was brought within the range of practical calculation. His attitude and that of most Left-wing Socialists was powerfully influenced by their sympathies with the Russian Revolution. They had spent twenty years defending the Soviet régime against those who hated it more for its working-class base than its totalitarian practices. Despite the crimes and blunders of the Soviet rulers and the chicanery of Communist Parties in other lands, they believed that Communist revolutionary achievements would be vindicated. For them, the Nazi-Soviet Pact and the Finnish war were appalling aberrations; unity between the Soviet people and other peoples engaged in a war against Fascism was a restoration of the proper historical process. And dominating this strong sentiment was a deep sense of relief about the war itself and Britain's chance of survival. Churchill might speak bravely about victory through bombing raids, Mediterranean campaigns and the eventual rising of the European peoples against their Nazi overlords. But these vague and distant prospects were now dramatically transformed.

Churchill in his first broadcast on the Sunday night of Hitler's invasion rose to the occasion. 'If Hitler invaded hell,' he had said the night before, 'I would make at least a favourable reference to the Devil in the House of Commons.'[2] But he excelled

1. *Politicians and the War* by Lord Beaverbrook.
2. *The Grand Alliance* by Winston Churchill.

his own best, and Bevan in the Commons debate two days later congratulated him. 'It was an exceedingly clever statement, a very difficult one to make, but made with great wisdom and strength.' He had only one criticism. 'I was a bit worried by the use of one sentence in which he [Churchill] said he would give all economic and technical assistance to the Soviet Union. I thought that was an understatement which might be misunderstood in some quarters ...' Momentarily Hitler had secured his aim of a single-front war on the European Continent, but no one could doubt that the establishment of a second land front must be the aim. A 'mere air offensive' would not satisfy people for long. Bevan foretold 'a dreadful sense of frustration if the German military machine marches into Russia and subdues the Soviet Union, as it has subdued other countries, and all we can do in the meantime is to send bombing planes into Germany – a dreadful sense of frustration which will carry with it a more deadly menace to the war resolution of Great Britain.'

This became Bevan's paramount thought. On 27 June in *Tribune* he proposed that the British and Soviet Governments should sign a treaty of alliance forbidding a separate peace. On 4 July he wrote: 'there is only one question for us in these swift days: what can we do to help ourselves by coming to the aid of the Soviet armies?' He recognized that if he talked of the need for a new Continental expeditionary force, he would be accused of playing with men's lives. His reply was: 'We *do* envisage a land attack on Germany at some time. It seems to me that a decision to engage in no land venture of any kind at this moment is to admit the impossibility of victory in the event of Russia being beaten.' Moreover, Churchill had taken pride in the warnings he had given to Stalin months before. What preparations had been made to exploit the supreme opportunity foreseen and now granted? 'The people of Great Britain are not content to play a passive role at this moment.'

These invocations to action were likely to rouse bitter reproaches, particularly as they came from an 'armchair strategist'. To add to the offence, he did not confine his pressure to speeches in the House or articles in *Tribune*. He joined with others, including Communists, in an 'Aid for Russia' campaign which later developed into a full-scale demand for the opening of a Second Front. The first meeting took place in the Stoll Theatre in London. Bevan appeared on the same platform with Harry Pollitt, the Communist leader who had now been restored to favour in the Communist hierarchy following his temporary deviation in September 1939 when he had supported 'the imperialist war'. Many criticized Bevan for his readiness to associate with 'the saboteurs' of a few months earlier, but he would not listen. If Churchill could embrace Stalin in the interests of the war against Nazism, must he keep Pollitt at arm's length? A series of spectacular meetings followed all over the country. They were organized by the Soviet Today Society, a Communist organization, and their vitality and success were partly due to the exuberant spirit of Communists released from the ordeal of explaining the sterile pre-22 June Party line. But, even more, the response reflected the profound instinct of all the most politically active sections of the British working class that if Russia were allowed to be destroyed all else and all hope of victory would go down in her defeat. The huge meetings of the Second Front campaign smashed any remaining traces of political apathy, proving that political agitation need not be abandoned in wartime. Bevan's action in appearing on platforms with Communists was a plain breach of Labour Party rules. But the fact that no letter of rebuke came from Transport House was the surest proof that the temper of the times was changing.

The Labour machine would indeed have made itself ridiculous – not always a deterrent to action – if it had sought to proscribe Second Front activities; it would have been offending against the whole ethos of the time; moreover, the Communists, Bevan and *Tribune* had one ally in a high place. Beaverbrook's newspapers, particularly the *Evening Standard*, at that time edited by Frank Owen, were campaigning in the same cause. Many suspected with some justice that these journals would not have been so forthright and clamorous in their pro-Russian enthusiasm if Lord Beaverbrook himself had not looked with favour on their efforts. Beaverbrook as a member of the War Cabinet had to relinquish the detailed day-to-day supervision over his property which was his normal custom, but telepathic communication was fully maintained. He had been the first British Cabinet Minister to visit Stalin after Russia's entry into the war and the two men embraced like long-lost revolutionary comrades. Beaverbrook, in or out of the Government, became the driving force behind the pressure for the supply of arms to Russia and a principal critic of official strategy. Occasionally, with this new common interest, he and Bevan renewed their conversations and arguments of pre-war days.

One organization remained anchored to the old belief that any association with Communists smelt of treachery. It was at this time and in the following year that an agent from M.I.5, or possibly some other secret service agency, was set to shadow Bevan on his travels and at his meetings throughout the country. He wormed his way into the confidence of the campaigners and was once or twice a welcome visitor to Lane End Cottage. Gradually Bevan's suspicions were aroused about the trustworthiness of this ardent supporter of a Second Front and critic of His Majesty's Government. He had a habit of disappearing for weeks on end and one night at a dinner party in London, where both were guests, casually remarked that he had recently been in Sweden. Bevan realized that no one was allowed to go outside the country without Government approval and he resolved to put the matter to the test. So he followed his pursuer into the cloakroom, seized him by the throat and extorted a confession. Jennie and Aneurin often smiled to themselves at the thought of what this master mind could have discovered at Lane End Cottage. For there in a drawer beside Aneurin's bed was a German Iron Cross and an old German revolver – the property which Bevan had taken for safe keeping from one of his old German refugee friends who might have been packed off to the Isle of Man in Sir John Anderson's clumsy roundup of aliens in 1940. An Iron Cross kept as a loving memento by the unpatriotic Bevan would have been a fine trophy in this otherwise barren feat of espionage! But all ended well. The spy was released from the Bevan stranglehold with the warning that he must report Bevan's meetings more accurately than the press to whatever authorities he served and that it would be agreeable in future if he could perform his duties less obtrusively. He was also informed that since Stalin wanted a

Second Front and since Hitler was anxious to know whether one was to be launched the campaign could only be beneficial in encouraging the one and raising doubts in the mind of the other. This intelligence too, it was hoped, would be passed on to higher quarters.

No doubt it was absurd to suppose that a Second Front, in any real sense of the term, could have been launched in 1941. (The argument about 1942 and 1943 is in a different category and will be treated later.) Hitler's Europe at that time was not fortified as strongly as Churchill claimed in his notes to Stalin[3] and Churchill himself played with the idea of extensive raids on Norway and elsewhere. Even so, the case against such action on the facts available now is overpowering; the resources, the landing craft, men in sufficient numbers were just not there. But this does not end the debate about the change wrought by Russia's entry into the war. Bevan's demand was that the whole strategy of the war should be remodelled to take account of the new, stupendous event. Incredibly, that view was not shared either by Churchill or his advisers. They were convinced that the Russians could not survive. Cripps was reported to have said, on his return from Moscow, that the Germans would go through the Russians like a hot knife through butter and the phrase was popular in some circles at the time. Was it not only two years previously that the War Office had regarded Poland as a more valuable ally than the Soviet Union? A profound anti-Soviet prejudice coloured their whole outlook. 'Almost all responsible military opinion,' says Churchill, 'held that the Russian armies would soon be defeated and largely destroyed.'[4] He himself took 'a more san-

3. *Winston Churchill and the Second Front* by Trumbull Higgins (New York; Oxford University Press).
4. *The Grand Alliance* by Winston Churchill. 'The War Plans Division and the G.2 Section of the U.S. Army also agreed with the British that the Soviets would be defeated in a few months ...' – Trumbull Higgins in *Winston Churchill and the Second Front*.

A different view about the Soviet capacity to resist was expressed in a pamphlet by Jennie Lee called *Russia Our Ally* which she started writing just after Hitler's invasion and was published in August 1941. It was based chiefly on the extensive tour which she had made through the Soviet Union in 1937. She was strongly critical of many features of Soviet society and Communist policy, but she refuted with detailed evidence the supposition of Britain's experts – Stafford Cripps included – that the Russians would collapse.

guine view' of the Russian powers of resistance. The claim may be correct, although he offers no proof – a most uncharacteristic oversight. In any case, since all the others were utterly despairing, it is a poor boast of Churchill's superior foresight. They wanted as little interference with their previous plans as possible. The diversion of supplies to Russia was for the Service Departments 'like flaying off pieces of their skin'.[5] Churchill's memoirs are littered with the indications that in his heart he regarded the Russian war as a temporary affair; for example, he wrote to General Auchinleck in Cairo on 19 July: 'If we do not use the lull accorded us by the German entanglement in Russia to restore the situation in Cyrenaica the opportunity may never recur.' But there is no need to press the point. Churchill himself unwittingly admits the whole case (and it may be noted that the admission covers a long period): 'It is right to make it clear,' he writes, 'that for more than a year after Russia was involved in the war she presented herself to our minds as a burden and not as a help.'[5] When President Roosevelt stated in September that the Russian front would hold and that Moscow would not be taken, he was, says Churchill, 'considered very bold'.

The Second Front campaigners took the same bold view derided by the military experts, and they were discontented with a strategy of keeping fingers crossed to ensure that their hopes were not dashed. Bevan guessed accurately the attitude of the British military chiefs and his criticism was directed against it. Had he known then the full measure of their refusal to contemplate any alteration in strategic concepts in the light of the developments on the Eastern front his invectives would have been the more scorching. For the reaction of the British strategists, Churchill included, was an example of military blindness without parallel in the history of war. It was pardonable, however gross the error, to under-estimate Soviet strength; Hitler made the same miscalculation. It was myopic not to recognize the immensity of the conflict; Hitler and almost everybody else could see that. Yet the British experts remained stubbornly wedded to four sterile propositions: (1) The Russian front – comprising the biggest battles ever fought – did not matter

5. *The Grand Alliance* by Winston Churchill.

341

greatly; (2) if anything, it was a distraction and Africa was more important; (3) the Russians would be beaten anyhow; (4) somehow or other we could win the war after Soviet defeat, irrespective of the consequences on Nazi power or British morale. Fortunately, this grand strategy of Churchill and his advisers had never to be implemented because their prophecies went unfulfilled. And, whatever criticisms may be made of the Second Front demand in 1941, Bevan and his fellow armchair strategists had a wiser understanding of the scale and significance of what had happened. The new war in the East was not a flash of lightning; it was a flaming sun which would never sink so long as the war lasted. A second Marlborough would have been able to mark the distinction.

Faced with what he considered to be the Government's quite inadequate response to the new situation, Bevan's whole scale of criticism altered. In particular, he scrutinized Churchill himself with more sceptical eyes. A great war debate had been fixed for the end of July 1941, primarily on the issue of production. The newspapers at the time were filled with stories of the failure to secure maximum output. Much Tory hostility was directed against Ernest Bevin at the Ministry of Labour; he had not been doing properly his primary job of keeping the workers in order. Instead he countered with the charge that private industry was not sufficiently controlled and that a Minister of Production was needed to co-ordinate the war effort more efficiently. At least these were the rumours in the Westminster corridors. And just before the debate the Prime Minister announced Government changes; there was to be no Minister of Production, but posts had been found for Mr Brendan Bracken, Churchill's Parliamentary Private Secretary, and for Mr Duncan Sandys, his son-in-law. Churchill's speech, however, was another masterpiece of oratory; 'if speeches could win a war,' said Bevan, 'then we have as good as won.' But what of the content? First the all-powerful Premier made a savage attack on his critics – 'apparently,' wrote Bevan, 'it was a greater offence to point out the defects in policy than to be guilty of them.' Next Churchill gave his reasons for rejecting the proposal for a Minister of Production.

'Ernest Bevin lost,' wrote Bevan. 'The House of Commons lost. Every shop steward lost. The country lost. The only victory was the Prime Minister's and that was won by exploiting his own personal position and by the natural reluctance of his critics to impair the unity of the nation by going all out against him.' One trouble was that we have 'a Prime Minister who is completely illiterate in all matters connected with industry'. But the real disease went deeper: 'This is a one-man Government.' Had the Prime Minister been subject to proper pressure and guidance from his colleagues,[6] he could never have made the appointments which brought upon him 'the furtive derision' of the House of Commons. And, finally, what was the strategy of the one-man Government? Churchill had turned from the production front and the Eastern front to give warning of the continued possibility of an invasion of the British Isles that year. Such an idea, said Bevan, was 'infinitely defeatist'. Was Churchill assuming that the Soviet armies would be wiped out before the autumn or was he expecting Hitler to invade while he still had the Red Armies on his hands? The explanation was that Churchill 'is bound to talk of the risk of the Germans invading us because we cannot invade them', and that in turn might be due to failures on the production front. Bevan called the article in *Tribune* in which these strictures appeared: 'The Problem of Mr Churchill.' It was the most open assault on the war leader made since May 1940.

During the last months of 1941 while the German armies were engulfing European Russia, Bevan sustained his attack. In September he taunted the Government once more for its renewed talk of the dangers of invasion, condemning this as no more than 'the worn-out alarmism of our own discredited Brasshats'. The Government kept on crying ' "Wolf, Wolf" at the very moment when the people can see the wolf engaged in a life and death struggle with the bear at the other end of the field. The

6. Roughly at this time I paid a visit to Lloyd George at Churt. He too was complaining of the subservience shown by the members of Churchill's War Cabinet and the high-handed manner which Churchill displayed towards them. 'Now *my* War Cabinet was different,' said Lloyd George. 'They were all big men. I was never able to treat *any* of my colleagues the way Churchill treats *all* of his.' Then the old man paused and his eye twinkled. 'Oh, yes,' he added, 'there was one I treated that way – Curzon.'

general view is that the best way to deal with the danger from the wolf is to give the bear a hand.' In October he was raising more general doubts about the competence of the war direction. Looking back on Dakar, Libya, Crete and Greece, were there not legitimate anxieties about the management of the nation's military affairs? Who could believe the Government propaganda that bombing raids on Germany would achieve the victory, especially when the men in command seemed to regard the Russian war as no more than an 'unexpectedly advantageous sideshow'?[7] And was the country to sit quiet beneath such speeches as that which Lord Halifax had delivered in Washington, just after his return from a meeting of the War Cabinet in London? Halifax had gone out of his way to declare that the shortage of shipping and equipment made any landing in Europe not feasible, thus giving Hitler all 'the comfort, consolation and reassurance' he needed. What was to be done, asked Bevan in an angry clash with Churchill in the House, about 'this irresponsible person with a bad record? ... How far removed from treason is a statement like that? ... The Prime Minister should realize that unless he gets rid of some of these men, they will drag him down with them.' Halifax's offence was in a special category; it should have led to instant dismissal. But Bevan's fire ranged over others on the Treasury bench. Many of them were infected by 'the deepest nostalgia for a dying order, and from nostalgia nothing comes but inertia and self-pity'.

By now several Labour M.P.s were showing signs of rebellion. In December, forty-two of them voted against the Government and against the Party Whip, thereby provoking the sharpest crisis the Party had known since the formation of the Government; they opposed a Government plan for the extension of conscription, insisting that much sterner measures must be taken to conscript property before the concession was granted.

7. Bevan's view of the attitude of the British 'Brass-hats' to the Eastern war is strikingly confirmed by a letter which Lord Beaverbrook, who had seen them at close quarters, wrote at this time: 'There has been no attempt to take into account the new factor introduced by Russian resistance. There is today only one problem – how to help Russia. Yet on that issue the Chiefs of Staff content themselves with saying that nothing can be done.' Quoted in *The Private Papers of Harry Hopkins* by Robert Sherwood.

On the Tory back benches too, for quite different reasons and purposes, there were rumblings of discontent against the war leadership. Just occasionally these elements of opposition joined forces. It happened when Herbert Morrison, the Home Secretary, stepped in to ban a broadcast on the wartime Regulation 18B which permitted the locking up of suspected citizens without trial. Bevan on this occasion called the Cabinet 'a little caucus communicating between themselves against the public interest ... We have allowed Ministers in the last two years to have an exaggerated sense of their own importance. We have allowed them to get away with things they ought never to have been allowed to get away with. Plutarch has said: "When a man's powers are equal to his passions, he becomes a tyrant." The Home Secretary has become irresponsible because he has not been sufficiently kicked in this House. If he had been restrained more he would have been a better man.'

By now also particular grievances were being welded in Bevan's mind into a more comprehensive criticism. He, and his friend Dick Stokes, the Member for Ipswich, were receiving detailed evidence about failures in the quality and quantity of British tank production. The information put at their disposal fortified the general accusations in the press which had led to the abortive demand for the appointment of a Minister of Production a few months earlier. He was more than ever convinced that a new reconstruction of the Government was essential. Above all, added to these older doubts, was his new and deeper doubt, induced by the Government's reaction to the events in the East, about the general strategy of the war. How could so broad an indictment be delivered without challenging the leader who presided over the whole scene? Bevan was not afraid of the logic; not to accept it would be an act of cowardice. Some of his friends pleaded that his attacks on Churchill would only weaken his general case; the man was impregnable and indispensable; better for any would-be critic to direct his arrows at less well-shielded targets. But Bevan was impenitent and resolved. In a one-man Government the one man must be held responsible.

In December 1941, the one man went to Washington. Japan's attack on Pearl Harbor and the entry of the United States into the war transformed the whole perspective once more. Churchill might be dubious about the survival of his Russian ally, but he recognized at once, with an unbounded sense of relief, the towering significance of the American involvement. On the way to see the President, he was able 'to pass in review the whole war as I saw it and felt it in the light of its sudden vast expansion'. His chief fear was that the Americans, enraged by the Japanese attack and under popular pressure for revenge, would be tempted by an 'America First' policy, a diversion of strategic interest to the Pacific. But the fear proved groundless. Before the Japanese attack, the top American leaders had argued to themselves that nothing must be allowed to stop them concentrating their strength against the enemy whose defeat would be decisive and against whom it was possible to combine the resources of Britain, the United States and Russia. Pearl Harbor did not make them waver in this clear strategic creed. This decision, as far-seeing as any in the whole war, was made by those who were often to be patronized as headstrong amateurs by the British experts. Instead of finding an American war leadership obsessed by the requirements of the Pacific, Churchill was confronted with men who talked of a Second Front in Europe as 'irresponsibly' as Aneurin Bevan. Churchill, on his journey across the Atlantic, wrote: 'Hitler's failure and losses in Russia are the prime fact in the war at this time . . . Neither Great Britain nor the United States has any part to play in this event, except to make sure that we send, without fail and punctually, the supplies we have promised. In this way alone shall we hold our influence over Stalin and be able to weave the mighty Russian effort into the general texture of the war.'[8] But at the Washington meeting the American generals and the American War Minister were speaking a different language. The only way to win the war, said General H. H. Arnold, was simply to hit Germany 'where it hurts most, where she is strongest – right across the Channel from England, using the shortest and most direct route to Berlin'.[9] For the moment,

8. *The Grand Alliance* by Winston Churchill.
9. Quoted in *Winston Churchill and the Second Front* by Trumbull Higgins, which also contains a wealth of other quotations from American generals to the same effect.

these ambitions had to be put aside as impractical. Churchill's general prospectus – for a holding operation in 1942, for the conquest of North Africa in that same year and for eventual landings on the European continent in 1943 – won approval. But it is necessary to note that there was from the start a sharp divergence in strategic outlook between the British and the Americans.

The effect – and the intention – of Churchill's 1941 review of the war situation, as embellished with the advantage of hindsight in his memoirs, is to show how closely the development of the war accorded with his ideas and plans and thereby to underline how febrile and inapposite were the strictures of his critics, whether American generals or parliamentarians at home. We are asked to believe that a master mind was in command throughout and that the courses prescribed were prophetically correct. But things looked very differently at the time and not only to a sceptical Labour back bencher. A new Chief of the British Imperial General Staff had just been appointed – General Sir Alan Brooke. 'I remember well,' he wrote, 'being appalled in those early days . . . to find the lack of a definite policy for the prosecution of the war. We worked from day to day a hand-to-mouth existence . . . that swung us like a weathercock.'[10] His anxieties were not those of the Americans. Brooke was even more dubious than Churchill about the Russian powers of resistance, more rootedly opposed to the diversion of supplies to the Eastern front and yet convinced that it was to *his* plan rather than Churchill's that the development of the war conformed. Churchill was perpetually interfering with sober military planning and played with ideas for raids on the Continent which would make absurd demands on non-existent resources. After one explosive scene in December 1941 Brooke wrote in his diary: 'God knows where we should be without him, but God knows where we shall go with him!'[10] What Churchill would have said if he had discovered that his chief military adviser was piling up these adverse verdicts on his strategic judgement in an elaborate diary passes imagination. He was outraged enough by 'the naggings and snarlings' in Parliament. 'I am pointing out to the

10. *The Turn of the Tide* by Sir Arthur Bryant.

President,' he wrote just before his return to London, 'that we can no more control the expression of freak opinion by individual Members than he can those of Congress backwoodsmen.'[11]

Bevan had now come near to attaining the status of 'snarler' in chief.[12] Churchill would undoubtedly have regarded as 'a freak opinion' the spacious review of the world scene which Bevan made in the opening days of 1942. He had just taken over the editorship of *Tribune*[13] and he set out his beliefs and aims in the broadest philosophical terms. Churchill had recently told the Conservative Party that the nation was fighting the war in defence of the values of traditional England. Bevan loved England and, more particularly, Wales, but his whole being revolted against such parochialism. 'The time has come,' he wrote, 'to insist upon the acceptance and application of a truth which a century and a half of experience has established with all the authority of science and of political philosophy. It is this – that mankind has progressed in all the arts and crafts, has achieved dignity and learning, the certainty of peace and the benediction of security, just to the extent that ordinary men and women won freedom and pushed their way into the central citadels of power.' Two great forces had been unleashed by the destruction of medieval Europe – the natural sciences and the emancipation of the common people. 'They are not separate forces. They inter-

11. *The Grand Alliance* by Winston Churchill.
12. Bevan's snarlings provoked the *Western Mail* to frenzied protests and some sentences may usefully be quoted to reveal the public image he was given by the press. They called him 'a flamboyant egotist' and when one Minister in Parliament chided Bevan with developing an inferiority complex, the *Western Mail* commented: 'We confess we had not observed any symptoms . . . Every mannerism that he cultivates, every speech he delivers, even the expression he wears in the most familiar photographs, bear witness to a profound consciousness of his own superiority. Socialists may believe in the equality of other folk, but Mr Bevan always conveys the impression of living at a greater intellectual altitude than the rest of the miners' leaders.'
13. Bevan quarrelled with Raymond Postgate, who had edited the paper since 1940. The difference was much more one of temperament than of policy. Postgate agreed in the interests of the paper that no public statement about their disagreements should be made. During his editorship the standard of the paper had been greatly improved, despite the meagre resources available, and a notable list of new contributors had been secured, most of whom continued to write in the following years.

weave and reinforce each other . . . Both the grandeur and the limitations of the Soviet Union are explainable in these terms. We are convinced that the Soviet Union will re-establish her connections with the main democratic inspirations of the twentieth century.' Bevan then applied his general principles to the immediate tasks ahead. 'Week by week,' he continued, '*Tribune* will show how our propaganda reflects the distrust of our spokesmen in the democratic ideal. We shall expose every example of the failure to apply the principles of a dynamic democracy to the problems of war. We shall show how the inefficiency of British industry, the failure of our military intelligence, the flat-footedness of the Army command, the debility of our propaganda to enemy countries and the shortcomings of our grand strategy are due, in one form or another, to the fact that Britain is still controlled by those who think, consciously or unconsciously, that ordinary men and women are there to be governed and not to govern.'

The solution, said Bevan, was that 'the people will have to take charge of the war and this, of course, means the peace as well'. To this end the widest possible free discussion of the facts was required; an endless battle would have to be fought against the censorship of opinion. His scepticism embraced most existing institutions. 'Even the parties of the Left seem to be mentally muscle-bound and repeat old phrases with less and less conviction. It is from the unencumbered minds of ordinary people that vigorous ideas will emerge.' One conclusion from this ferment of debate he dared to anticipate. 'Complex the society of the future is bound to be, as complex and subtle as the mind of modern man. But one solution will have to be found if it is to endure. It will reconcile the needs of an ordered economic life with the fullest efflorescence of personal liberty. Without an ordered economic life the individual frustrates himself in a morass of fears and insecurities. Without personal liberty an ordered economic life is like a plant that never flowers.'

This definition of his democratic Socialist faith marked a development of the views predominant in his mind when he had entered Parliament thirteen years before. He had then leaned more towards a less qualified Marxist interpretation of events, but both his own pre-war clashes with the Labour hierarchy and the suffocations imposed by war propaganda and the prevailing worship of the new god, Churchill, tilted the balance of his mind towards a deeper recognition of the liberal and democratic virtues. He was always tempted to swim against the stream. It was typical of him that he should express his doubts about Soviet society at the moment when most Left-wingers were bowled over by the spectacle of Soviet heroism, typical too that he refused to make obeisance to Churchill when this appeared to be the new national religion.

He infused the same iconoclastic spirit into *Tribune* for the rest of the war and a little later he secured a literary editor who could out-match himself in incorrigible irreverence. '*Tribune* is not perfect, as I should know,' wrote George Orwell, 'but I do think it is the only existing paper that makes a genuine effort to be both progressive and humane – that is, to combine a radical Socialist policy with a respect for freedom of speech and a civilized attitude towards literature and the arts.' Aneurin Bevan was the only editor in Fleet Street who, in those days before Orwell's reputation was sure, would have given him complete freedom to offend all readers and lash all hypocrisies, including Socialist hypocrisies. Bevan did it at the moment when elsewhere he was being denounced as something near a Soviet agent. A close companionship between the convivial Bevan and the dour, discerning Orwell was never established; but the editor would defend his colleague along with every other comma and semi-colon in his rebellious weekly against all-comers. Often in those days, there were rowdy scenes, with Bevan in their midst, at El Vino's, the Fleet Street bar. Some came to jeer and argue and stayed to be flayed or captivated. He was thrilled with the task of saving *Tribune* from financial collapse. 'I shall edit the paper myself without salary,' he wrote excitedly to Jennie Lee, then in America, 'and I shall scour Fleet Street giving journalists with good information and bad consciences the privilege of burning candles for their souls on the same financial terms as myself.' Often on a Thursday the proud editor was ready to sell copies of his paper or expound its contents all the way from El Vino's to New Palace Yard. The liberty he believed in was not something to be pickled in the preserving juices of a peroration; it was a weapon to be used.

When Churchill returned from America he demanded to be sustained by a Vote of Confidence in the House of Commons. The Japanese were sweeping all before them on land and sea and a desperate battle was being fought in Libya. Criticism in the press was provoked both by the events themselves and by the optimistic statements of military spokesmen on the spot whose prophecies were so quickly overtaken by the onrush of disaster. Churchill was determined to secure a parliamentary shield in advance against the worse disasters which he believed must come. 'If we have handled our resources wrongly,' he proclaimed boldly, 'no one is so much to blame as I.' He would not find scapegoats among the generals or among his 'loyal and trusted colleagues'. He taunted his opponents, particularly those who favoured more dramatic action to help the Russians. 'I suppose there are some of those who were vocal and voluble, and even clamant, for a Second Front to be opened in France who are now going to come up bland and smiling and ask why it is that we have not ample forces in Malaya, Burma, Borneo and Celebes.'[14] In particular, he was ruthless in demanding a vote. Any Member who thought the Government ought to be broken up 'ought to have the manhood to testify his convictions in the lobby . . . No one need be mealy-mouthed in debate and no one should be chicken-hearted in voting. I have voted against Governments I have been elected to support, and looking back, I have sometimes felt very glad that I did so. Everyone in these rough times must do what he thinks is his duty.' Bevan might have been prepared to respond; he had voted against his own Party when he thought it necessary more consistently than Churchill. But, apart from the consideration that he would probably have found few other Labour members to join him, Bevan's aim was not the destruction of the Government, but its reformation. Churchill got his Vote of Confidence by four hundred and sixty-four to one; only the three I.L.P. anti-war Members either acted as tellers or voted against him.

Then followed the flood of calamity, culminating in the fall of Singapore, in Churchill's description 'the worst disaster and largest capitulation in British history'. In Libya the British forces

14. Quoted in *The Hinge o Fate* by Winston Churchill.

suffered a severe rebuff. In the Atlantic the U-boat attack was pressed to a new pitch of intensity. To add insult to injury, the German battle cruisers, *Scharnhorst* and *Gneisenau*, escaped up the Channel. 'It was certainly not strange,' wrote Churchill, 'that public confidence in the administration and its conduct of the war should have quavered.'[15] Certainly it was not strange that Bevan in *Tribune* renewed his onslaught. The defeat of the Army of the Nile was the most inexplicable event of all, since Churchill had claimed in the recent debate that through five months it had been equipped for the offensive with weapons at least equal to anything possessed by the Germans.[16] Still 'they' lost. '*They*,' said *Tribune*, 'is the War Office and the Ministry of Defence: Churchill, the strategist of the war and Margesson, his welfare officer ... The continuance of War Office misrule remains the outstanding scandal of the Churchill administration ... The French Revolution had its Carnot; the last war produced Lloyd George; the Russian Revolution a Trotsky, and we have Captain Margesson. Could fate be more unkind? ... We don't blame Margesson. He merely took the job Churchill gave him. Margesson's absurdity for the job is the measure of Churchill's failure as Defence Minister. That failure is costing us precious lives and will cost us more yet.' During the next two weeks *Tribune* clamoured for a reconstruction of the Government. It was not Churchill's resignation which was demanded. He would

15. *The Hinge of Fate* by Winston Churchill.
16. On 11 December 1941, Churchill had said in the House of Commons: 'On November 10th General Auchinleck set out to destroy the entire armed forces of the Germans and Italians in Cyrenaica. And now, on December 11th, I am bound to say that it seems very probable that he will do so. The foundation of everything was supply and mechanized transport, and this was provided on what had hitherto been considered a fantastic scale. At the beginning of the offensive I told the House that we should for the first time be fighting the Germans on equal terms with modern weapons. This was quite true.' Whether it was quite true is another question. Sir Arthur Bryant in *The Turn of the Tide* writes as follows about the position which Brooke found at this time: 'Nor were the British yet the equals of the Germans in tank and mechanized warfare. Their tanks were weaker in fire power and armour, they lacked mobile front-line workshops for servicing damaged vehicles and were short of anti-tank and anti-aircraft weapons and spares of every kind – points which Brooke had been trying to impress on his political chiefs for the past eighteen months.'

still stay Prime Minister. But he must appoint a real Minister of Production and a separate Minister of Defence. His hold on the two offices was one conceivable reason why he refused all proper inquiries into our military reverses. 'They might disclose that he has meddled in operational decisions.' It is comical to recall that the verdict on this point of the Chief of the Imperial General Staff concurred with *Tribune*'s; Brooke was busy writing in his diary Bevanite strictures on Churchill's meddling.

Despite Churchill's Vote of Confidence a bare three weeks before, a new political crisis, sensed by Churchill himself, was in the making. One contributory cause of it was the return of Stafford Cripps from Moscow. He had received from the British public an extraordinary hero's welcome, as if almost single-handed he had first enticed Hitler to invade Russia and then inspired the Russian armies to fight back. Only the Labour leaders and their satellites remained churlish; when Cripps addressed a private meeting in the Commons on his mission it was noticed that no Labour Minister or Under-Secretary came to hear him. But outside, in the public mind and in the press, his stature was swollen to legendary proportions. Possibly it was the bleakness of the surrounding countryside which contributed to his eminence. And, whatever his Labour ex-colleagues might think, the Prime Minister had an immense respect for Cripps's intellectual powers. Churchill first made an offer to him to serve as Minister of Supply; Cripps refused, partly on the advice of Bevan who urged him to accept no office outside the War Cabinet.[17] Then under 'external pressure',[18] as Churchill admits, he embarked on a general overhaul of his Government. Cripps was made Leader of the House of Commons and given a place in the War Cabinet of seven. Oliver Lyttelton became Minister of Production. Among several other consequential changes, Captain Margesson was removed from the War Office. It was not the full reconstruction which Bevan had pleaded for, but he was entitled to rub salt in the wound. 'The political story of the war,' he wrote, 'is a record of the Government slowly making

17. *Stafford Cripps* by Colin Cooke.
18. *The Hinge of Fate* by Winston Churchill.

concessions to the critics when the latter have been proved right by events. But the loss of an army in Singapore and the sequence of disasters is too high a price to pay for the education of a Government. It is no comfort to us to win the argument and to lose the war.' It had been a slow process weeding out the Men of Munich, but now at last none remained in the War Cabinet. How exhilarating it would have been if a new broom could have swept clean long before!

For the moment a less momentous quarrel than any concerned with Cabinet making or military planning intruded. The *Daily Mirror* published a brilliant cartoon by Zec of a merchant seaman lying exhausted on a raft in a stormy sea; underneath was the caption: 'The price of petrol has been raised by a penny (official).' Most people took this to be a fine tribute to the courage of British seamen, one obvious interpretation being that customers should not squeal too much about the increased price of petrol when such heroism was needed to transport it across the Atlantic. A more sophisticated view might be that the cartoon was also making an accusation; while sailors were being drowned, the petrol companies were making profits (as they no doubt were). But the assembled War Cabinet and its advisers believed that something much more sinister had happened. Many complaints about the *Daily Mirror* had previously been received from the War Office and other quarters. It was no more critical than some other journals, but it expressed these criticisms with a raucous effectiveness. Now, in the Cabinet's eyes, the paper had gone too far. Herbert Morrison believed that the cartoon was 'wicked'.[19] So did Ernest Bevin. Churchill was for suppression on the spot, and Lord Simon, the Lord Chancellor, agreeing that the cartoon was 'cruel and deplorable', informed the Home Secretary that he possessed the power to act. Eventually calmer counsels prevailed. Beaverbrook, with a sound vested interest in free printing to protect, argued that the *Mirror* should be let off with a warning and Morrison agreed with him. Morrison was instructed to see Guy Bartholomew, the effective controller of the paper, and the editor. They were told they were endangering the war effort.

19. *An Autobiography* by Herbert Morrison.

'If you go on,' said Morrison, 'we can suppress you at a speed that will surprise you. There must be more responsible control.' In fact the *Daily Mirror* was threatened with Regulation 2D which gave authority to suppress a newspaper instantly.

When knowledge of this action became public, almost every newspaper in the land from *The Times* to the *Daily Herald* protested. Lord Camrose's *Daily Telegraph* was almost the only exception. 'Mr Morrison's action,' wrote *Tribune*, 'has done more harm to the morale of the country than all the cartoons and leaders of the *Mirror* put together – if these have had a harmful effect.' The Commons debate which followed was one of the stormiest the wartime Parliament had known and, as in the case of the *Daily Worker* suppression, Bevan took the lead in opposing Morrison's action. 'I do not like the *Daily Mirror*,' he said. 'I do not like that form of journalism. I do not like the strip-tease artists. But it is not because the Home Secretary is aesthetically repelled that he warns it . . . He likes the paper. He has taken its money.' At this point, Bevan held aloft a bunch of articles written during the war by Morrison himself. Morrison, he insisted, was the wrong man to be Home Secretary. For years he had been 'the witch-finder of the Labour Party, the smeller out of evil spirits'. One of those evil spirits was sitting beside him at that moment, the Leader of the House of Commons, an honoured member of the War Cabinet, Sir Stafford Cripps. However 'suave' Morrison's utterances, 'his spirit is really intolerant'. Bevan professed himself 'deeply ashamed' that a Labour Home Secretary should have made himself the instrument of this work. He was not surprised that Morrison had been unwilling to take the *Mirror* to the courts. His case was too bad and the *Mirror* would have been able to put Morrison in the dock as one of its principal witnesses. 'The Government,' he concluded, 'are seeking to suppress their critics. The only way for the Government to meet their critics is to redress the wrongs from which the people are suffering and to put their policy right.'

The onslaught brought uproar on the Labour benches. The Member for Ebbw Vale, replied Morrison, is never happier than when he is having a shot at his own political friends. 'And you are never happier,' interrupted Bevan, 'than when you are attacking your own principles.' One trade union M.P. and a member of the T.U.C. General Council thought to calm the furious scene by declaring that the General Council was seriously considering whether it was worthwhile spending money on M.P.s who spoke as Bevan had spoken. Bevan was on his feet at once suggesting to the Speaker that such a threat might involve a breach of parliamentary privilege. No more was heard of the matter – for the moment. And Bevan certainly was not gagged either inside the House or out of it. At a mass London meeting called to condemn the Government's move against the *Mirror*, he gave a beautiful example of his capacity for playful abuse. 'I have never met,' he said, 'a less judicially minded man than Morrison. He was for years the chief whipper-in of the Labour Party [*pause and the first ripples of laughter*] – and the chief whipper-out [*real laughter*]. Our traditions are too great and too precious to be stolen from us by a little Cockney [*a few gasps and loud laughter again*]. I apologize to the rest of the Cockneys [*laughter and general contentment all round*].'

The Government had made a gaffe and mockery was the best cure. But the incident did have its serious aspect. It revealed into what a hypersensitive state Britain's war leaders had got themselves; they were living in a 'cocoon' of their own, to use one of Bevan's favourite analogies. If Churchill had had his way and the paper had been suppressed a first-class crisis would have been created for no reason whatever. (Morrison claimed later that he would have resigned rather than agree to this course which had been so strongly urged upon him.) As it was, the action achieved the desired result. 'We had no further cause for complaint about the *Mirror*,' wrote Morrison justly, adding not so justly that the paper 'managed to continue with its forthright outlook'.[20] In fact, Cassandra, its foremost critic, was sent off to fight other wars elsewhere. The editor of the *Mirror* softened his criticisms and some others may have been encouraged to follow his example. And yet Bevan, never a lover of the national press, was compelled to agree that most of the newspapers were reflecting the curious movement away from Party which seemed a feature of the times and which found expression most dramatically in the

20. *An Autobiography* by Herbert Morrison.

way men and women looked to a solitary individual, Stafford Cripps, to provide what the great organization of Labour had failed to do: to lead the country. 'With the exception of the Tories, with their ever loyal yes-lord of the *Daily Telegraph*,' he wrote, 'there is not a Party that can boast of the unqualified support of a national newspaper. Unless, of course, Lord Beaverbrook can be taken as a Party by himself.'

It was an odd sensation for the all-powerful War Cabinet to be laughed out of court, with Bevan winning approval in the most unlikely quarters. It did not endear him to the men in office. But on another subject, too, they were compelled to listen. The coal industry had always remained one of his prime interests. During the early months of 1942, the country faced a coal crisis which threatened to impede the whole war effort. The development gave a sharper spur both to Bevan's growing disillusion with the way the nation's productive machine was organized and his discontent with the pressure exerted by the Labour Ministers.

Ever since 1940 he had pleaded for drastic action; the exigencies and vagaries of war added a fresh argument for the nationalization of the industry but David Grenfell, the Minister of Mines, had no chance against his superior, Oliver Lyttelton, then at the Board of Trade – to whom, wrote Bevan, 'you have only to mention nationalization . . . to paralyse his brain'. During 1940 some of the coalfields – in Yorkshire, Leicestershire and Nottinghamshire – made fat profits by feeding the war industries of the North and the Midlands whereas others – in Durham, Northumberland and South Wales – languished owing to the collapse of foreign markets or the breakdown of coastal shipping. The whole situation cried out for a national scheme, but all the Government would offer was a levy on coal prices. Meantime, Ernest Bevin, the Minister of Labour, decreed that if a miner under thirty years of age was idle for six weeks or more, he would immediately be called up for the forces. Apart from the failure to reallocate mining labour where it was needed, this involved putting a formidable weapon in the hands of coalowners who wanted to deal with troublesome miners. 'And if I am told,' said Bevan, 'that coalowners won't do that, then I say you don't know the coalowners.' On top of these other muddles, there was chaos in distribution. At one moment the Minister was appealing to the better-off to stock their cellars; at the next he was warning against the evils of hoarding, if the poor were to be allowed to buy at all.

That was in 1940. In May 1941, Grenfell made what Bevan called 'a slightly hysterical S.O.S. to the House of Commons'. He, like the miners' union, knew what was coming, but, said Bevan, 'the House of Commons did not respond. Why? Because the House of Commons has got into the wicked state of imagining that economic problems can be solved by emotional crusades. The Prime Minister's special gifts have hypnotized the whole administration.' By August 1941, the danger was deepening. Some 50,000 men from the industry had been called to the colours. The chief culprit, said Bevan, was Churchill. 'Unfortunately we have a Prime Minister who listens to the generals more than to the industrial people inside the Government. In fact the Government are the only enemy up to now which the generals have been able to defeat.' Ernest Bevin must also share the responsibility. He appealed on the radio to men who had left the coalfields before the war to go back. Did he really think it would work, asked Bevan – especially when 'in my district there are men working at the pits for less wages than women get in the filling factories near by'? No: exhortation was no substitute for a plan. A Government which wanted to deal realistically with the problem would have taken over the pits at once. Even if that could not have been done, some effort should have been made to establish unified control. Some obstacle blocked the path to so obvious a measure and the Labour Ministers had not had the energy to remove it.

That was the speech – one among several – which he had delivered in August 1941. In December, when forty Labour Members revolted against the Government's refusal to take larger powers over property, Ernest Bevin produced what was called the Bevin formula – he gave an assurance that the Government would consider taking over any industry if it could be shown that the step was necessary for the successful prosecution of the war. The 'essential silliness' of that test, said Bevan, was only later understood by those who were duped by it. It threw the onus back on the critics and ensured that the Labour Ministers would run away from their principles. For it gave a handle to Tory Cabinet Ministers to argue that any proposal for nationalization was an unwarranted attempt to push Party nostrums. And all the while, when the mineowners joined with the unions in demanding a release of miners from the army, Churchill obstinately resisted. In February, March, April and May of 1942 the situation deteriorated. Hugh Dalton, the newly appointed President of the Board of Trade, found that coal was far the biggest and most urgent of his problems. In March he had to appoint a Committee to draw up a plan for the rationing of coal. And then at last, after detailed examination and with Bevin's backing, he made to the Cabinet the proposal which Bevan had urged in 1940 – the pits must be requisitioned for the period of the war.[21]

Ernest Bevin's boast that such a proposal would be considered on its merits was quickly exploded. For, says Dalton, 'we met with great resistance, some from most surprising quarters, and had to fall back on a second-rate compromise'. Dalton's plan was an adaptation of a half-baked scheme produced by the miners' leaders in deference to Ernest Bevin's reluctance to advocate full-scale requisitioning in the previous December. Bevan could not be expected to be enthusiastic. The central feature of the scheme was the appointment of Controllers who were to have sole charge of the industry, while the owners continued to draw the profits. 'The State steps in,' said Bevan, 'not in substitution of private interests but as their guardian.' If the Controllers made a mess of the job, State interference would be blamed. If they succeeded, the owners would still be drawing their dividends, while the miners were subject to the Controllers with imprisonment the penalty for resistance. 'Do the Government really believe the British miner will work willingly for this new type of Gauleiter? ... The first requirement of any scheme for the mining industry is that it secures the goodwill of the mining community. This the Government scheme lamentably fails to do. It may secure the support of a few leaders at the top. But they don't cut the coal. Until the mining industry is made a national possession we shall not even begin to approach the solution of the coal problem. So much has been clear for more than a decade.'

21. *The Fateful Years* by Hugh Dalton.

However, these warnings were for the future. Immediately, Bevan was not prepared to press the demand for the recall of the seven thousand miners from the forces needed to stave off the crisis. If, as Churchill now claimed, the pulling out of these trained men would disrupt several units, it might be too late for this obvious remedy. 'Better run the risk of going cold next winter,' wrote Bevan, 'than letting Hitler escape this year. Some scheme of coal rationing, therefore, seems inevitable. Those who complain at the thought of it might spare a moment to reflect on the sufferings of the people of Leningrad during the past winter.'

The episode classically illustrated a considerable part of Bevan's general case. In the instance of coal at least, the argument for Socialist measures to help win the war was overwhelming, as both Bevin and Dalton had been belatedly forced to admit by their proposition to the Cabinet. But they were poorly supported by some of their Labour Cabinet colleagues; what else can be the meaning of Dalton's unusually cryptic confession about resistance from 'some surprising quarters'? Moreover, the Labour Ministers had made quite insufficient effort to enlist substantial backing from the Labour back benchers and the movement outside; their earlier reticence had been partly responsible for the timidity of the Miners' Federation. And in the result, what happened? Dalton's coal rationing scheme was killed by the Tory 1922 Committee which exerted itself more robustly than Labour M.P.s. The seven thousand miners had to be withdrawn from the forces. Altogether, a serious injury was inflicted on the nation's capacity to make war and the country stumbled on to face a few more coal crises. Anyone who questions Bevan's charges about Churchill's 'illiteracy' on industrial matters and the price the nation paid for it must study the story of coal.

Coal – and the political balance between the Parties revealed in the politics of coal – figured prominently at the Labour Party Conference held at the end of May. Of course, the delegates knew nothing of Dalton's rejected proposition to the War Cabinet, less still of the resistance to it from surprising quarters. Those revelations would have taken the roof off. Instead, the miners' representatives recommended a Labour variation of the Government's scheme, claiming that it was the best compromise

– a bad one, they admitted – which could possibly be extracted from the coalowners and the 1922 Committee. Grudgingly, the Conference accepted Attlee's dictum: 'We cannot dictate to others the acceptance of our Socialist programme.' Morrison put a better face on matters. He rallied the Conference with a powerful appeal for the necessity of sustaining the Government at so critical a moment of the war. As for nationalization, why were delegates so downcast? Had he not nationalized the Fire Service?

No considerable body of opinion in the Party wanted to break the Coalition; and here was the effective card which the Executive could always play. Yet it was not an exact answer to Bevan's argument; he believed that Labour could exert a much greater influence *within* the Coalition. At the Conference a more adventurous spirit was stirring beneath the surface. When Attlee protested that the Government 'accept the principle that vested interests must not stand in the way of our war effort', he was received with ironical cheers. And the place woke up when one delegate, Rhys Davies M.P., cried, 'While our Party is crawling to the Right, the workers are marching to the Left.' One sign of this movement had been the success of independent candidates at three recent by-elections in destroying big Tory majorities. The Executive gazed with horror on the phenomenon; a touch of discipline was needed before the contagion spread further. So Morrison introduced an addendum to the resolutions passed at previous Conferences requiring local Parties to co-operate with other Parties in the Government in promoting the return of Government candidates. Bevan opposed the whole idea. He foresaw the Conservative and Labour Parties becoming more and more fused together 'so that the Party machine will get further and further out of relationship with social and political realities'. He prophesied a huge crop of independent candidates. Soon the Executive might ask that there should be no by-elections at all in wartime and the growing selection of candidates at the top would transform the British Parliament into a Reichstag. He almost won the vote; Morrison's proposal was carried only by 1,275,000 votes to 1,209,000. And on another resolution the Executive was actually defeated; a demand for the removal of the ban on the *Daily Worker* was carried, against Morrison's opposition, by a narrow 9,000 majority. Conferences in wartime were naturally much less elaborate and representative gatherings than in peace. The Executive had on its side all the prestige of the War Ministers. But the stir in the country had penetrated and Bevan, expelled only two years before at Southport, was now the leading figure on the Left.

However, in that spring and summer of 1942, neither coal nor domestic politics nor any other matter could compete for public attention with the war itself. Within less than four months, Japan had conquered most of Britain's Far Eastern empire and had plunged deep into Burma. Soon she might be threatening India and Ceylon; the Indian Ocean might become a Japanese lake and Japan would be reaching out to establish a direct link with her German ally. The U-boats were taking a terrible toll and the poised battle in Libya might soon flare up afresh. Brooke confessed in his diary at the end of March 'a growing conviction that we are going to lose this war unless we control it very differently and fight it with more conviction'.[22] It was only a momentary spasm of dejection, but it showed the mood in those disastrous days. And overhanging all else was the prospective renewal of the vast campaign in Russia. Could the Russians survive the same battery again? If they succeeded, all might be retrieved. The American strategists, despite all the Japanese victories, had not abandoned their belief that Germany was the principal enemy. But what if the Russians failed? Britain could then expect a devastating reinforcement of Rommel's army in Egypt and a reapplication of Germany's strength in the West. A German victory in the East would make real the peril that the Germans and Japanese might join hands across the Caucasus. To many – to Stalin naturally, to the top American strategists and to the ignorant Second Front campaigners in Britain – the outcome of the Russian campaign took the central place in the whole strategic picture. And Hitler shared the same opinion. His armies in the East had suffered a million casualties; the Russian winter had enclosed upon them, spreading a fearful gloom. 'It is nothing short of a miracle that we stood it,' wrote Goebbels. 'Sometimes

22. *The Turn of the Tide* by Sir Arthur Bryant.

the Fuehrer said it simply would not be possible to survive.'[23]
The Fuehrer was determined to repair the disaster in 1942. All
else was subordinate. Compared with Russia, Egypt was a minor
affair; Rommel could beg for major reinforcements in vain.

The continued curiosity was that Britain's strategists, Churchill at their head and his advisers even more resolutely, held a
quite contrary view. Their settled opinion was that, apart from
the provision of supplies by means of the hazardous Arctic
convoys, little or nothing could be done to influence the Russian
struggle; the decision rested in the lap of the gods. Brooke in
particular held to this doctrine with unshakable devotion. It is
hard to believe that he did not expect a Russian 'crack-up', as he
called it. 'The steps in his graduated strategic policy,' writes his
biographer, 'were first to hold the enemy's drives – in the Indian
Ocean, the Atlantic, the Mediterranean and the African desert,
and, if necessary in the Caucasus – and then, when the requisite
force had been assembled at the decisive point, to defeat Rommel
and clear the North African coast preparatory to using the shipping so released to threaten Europe's southern shore. Every
successive stage demanded the most far-sighted planning, not
only of military effort but of industrial production and sea
transport. For in the light of Axis strength, the margin between
success and failure was so narrow that no resource could be mis-
directed or applied at the wrong place.'[24] This was a workable
strategy but only on one condition: that the Russian front held
and of that Brooke had little hope; his first 1941 estimate had not
been revised. The margin between success and failure was
narrow on the Russian front too; but Brooke never applied his
doctrine there. However, Brooke claims that the imposition of
his strategy first on the obstreperous Churchill and next on his
American allies was his chief claim to fame. Churchill, alternatively, claims that the strategy was his. Victory cancels everything and puts old strategic controversies in the dustbin. But,
once again, it must be insisted, it was luck, the gods, or the
Russian resistance, whichever term is preferred, which ensured
that Brooke's strategy was never put fully to the test. The fact

23. Goebbels' *Diary*.
24. *The Turn of the Tide* by Sir Arthur Bryant.

that some strategists prove fortunate is no reason for dismissing out of hand the wisdom of others who made different calculations at the time.

These preliminary comments are needed to put in their proper perspective, first the grave American doubts about the Churchill–Brooke strategy, and second, the reaction to all these events of Aneurin Bevan, a lonely back bencher who was not prepared to surrender his mind and responsibility into the keeping of the experts. On 9 March, Roosevelt wrote to Churchill: 'I am becoming more and more interested in the establishment of a new front this summer.'[25] On 27 March Henry Stimson, the United States Secretary for War, wrote to the President to fortify his resolve: 'The rate of construction of a number of landing barges should not be allowed to lose the crisis of the World War. And yet that is the only objection to the offensive that, after talks with British critics here, I have heard made.'[26] At the beginning of April Roosevelt sent to London a high-powered delegation, consisting of Harry Hopkins, his principal private emissary, and General Marshall. 'Your people and mine,' wrote Roosevelt to Churchill, 'demand the establishment of a front to draw off the pressure on the Russians, and these peoples are wise enough to see that the Russians are killing more Germans and destroying more equipment than you and I put together.'[25] Marshall brought with him a more detailed memorandum, proposing preparations for a massive attack on the Continent in 1943 and an emergency plan for 1942, either to take advantage of a sudden German disintegration or to help avert an imminent Russian collapse. The document, said Churchill, was 'masterly . . . The conception underlying it accorded with the classic principles of war – namely concentration against the main enemy'.[25] It seemed that the American plan had won British acceptance. 'At long last,' said General Eisenhower to Stimson in Washington when the news came through, 'we are definitely committed to one concept of fighting . . . and we won't just be thrashing around in the dark.'[26] This is no place to follow the stubborn rearguard action

25. *The Hinge of Fate* by Winston Churchill.
26. Quoted in *Winston Churchill and the Second Front* by Trumbull Higgins.

of Brooke, with Churchill's eventual acceptance, against any project for attacking the European continent in 1942 and the gradual awakening to the facts in Washington. Suffice it to say that the idea of some Second Front in 1942 was not merely the mad dream of a few armchair strategists. It was a project which the British and American high commands had discussed with such purpose that on 11 April Roosevelt felt entitled to cable Stalin that he was putting forward 'a very important military proposal involving the utilization of our armed forces in a manner to relieve your critical western front'.[28] And this was only one of the many heartening messages which Roosevelt sent to Stalin in the subsequent weeks.

All these confabulations between London, Washington and Moscow were of course secret at the time. Bevan and his Second Front campaigners were derided as a bunch of irresponsible cranks. What did they know about war? In fact the case for the Second Front elaborated by *Tribune* on 13 March would have been approved by General Marshall; that very week he had presented his major memorandum on the subject to the President. Bevan too accepted the classic principle of war – concentration against the main enemy. The question was: did Churchill? And the question was provoked not only by the venom with which the pro-Churchill press denounced the Second Front campaign, but by many other facts about previous military operations which were now becoming known and discussed in the Smoking Room of the House of Commons and the military clubs. On 1 May *Tribune* launched the first of a series of sensational articles. 'Why Churchill?' was the title. Thomas Rainsboro was the author; he was said to be 'a brilliant and unusually well-informed writer'. Some suspected that Bevan himself was hiding under this suitably modest pseudonym. But in fact the author was Frank Owen, Bevan's old Liberal friend of the 1929 Parliament, recently editor of the *Evening Standard* and at that time training for the Tank Corps near Andover. Frank Owen had a considerable acquaintance with several of Britain's leading soldiers. He also had a pen like a dagger. Certainly no other

28. Quoted in *Winston Churchill and the Second Front* by Trumbull Higgins.

newspaper at the time would have printed his articles. For Owen's attack was directed at the centre of the target – on Churchill as the Captain-General, the supreme strategist and war leader.

First Finland: when the Red Army failed at first to break the Mannerheim Line, had not Churchill passed his judgement: 'Thus does Communism rot the soul of its victims in peace and make it abject in war'? Next Norway: had not his prophecies gone equally unfulfilled then and had he not been directly responsible for the failure of the naval operations? Next France: two or three times as First Lord of the Admiralty he had visited the Maginot Line and pronounced it and the French armies good – 'Mr Hore Belisha, then War Minister, showed unusual restraint in refraining from returning the call by inspecting the Scapa Flow defences, which stood in equal need of scrutiny!' Next 1940: no criticism; 'I concede his ancient glory'. Next Libya and Greece: 'In five weeks his [Churchill's] interference had thrown away the full fruits of Wavell's brilliant effort and had furthermore committed Britain to the disastrous Balkan campaign of April–May 1940.' Next the *Repulse* and the *Prince of Wales*: 'had not Churchill insisted on sending them to Malaya, getting Admiralty consent to his demands?' Next Crete: Churchill said he would hold it at all costs, but it was lost in four days. And finally Russia, the crowning question: what was Churchill's policy? All honour to him for pledging 'full aid' to the Russians on the day of the invasion. But what did 'full aid' mean? 'It is no Cabinet secret that but for vast public pressure and a hell of a row in the Government itself the supplies which we have sent to Russia would have fallen far short of their present volume.' As for the Second Front, 'the Churchillized press have pretended that Stalin never asked for a diversion in the West last autumn. I declare that this is a plain lie.' Then came the final blast: 'On Sunday last, Churchill after carrying out a campaign of intimidation against the Second Fronters without recent parallel in British politics, joined the Second Front. He welcomed "the aggressive military spirit of the British people" which for several weeks he had denounced as ill-informed and ill-conditioned armchair strategy ... And will he act before 1943? Churchill has made up his mind to win this war ...

Therefore no risks, until overwhelming strength is ours. It is not a dishonourable ambition. The question is: is it a reasonable proposition? If we could go on piling up arms and men till 1943 and then crack Hitler on the snout, it would be admirable. But what is Hitler going to be engaged in till 1943? War is not an addition sum but an equation in time. *Have we time to afford Churchill's strategy?*'

That last question by itself was near enough to the bone to justify Rainsboro's articles; it was the great question then being debated between London and Washington, and if the rest of the press would not discuss the issue *Tribune* would. Yet a howl of rage was let loose and, since no one had penetrated Rainsboro's disguise, it descended on Bevan's head. He made no apologies. 'The concentration of hero-worship on one individual,' he wrote, 'is always full of sinister consequences for the nation which indulges it. It is all the more dangerous when that statesman has made himself the leader of one Party in the State; exposed himself wholly to the pressure of vested interests; and speaks only the voice of tradition and not the hopes and aspirations for the future which are stirring in every breast.' Moreover, Churchill was also Minister of Defence; that must never be forgotten. Some papers, like *The Times*, inquired plaintively whether it was desirable to have a different form of defence organization, without ever mentioning Churchill's name. '*Tribune* will have no part in such cowardly obscurantism. It insists on laying the charge where it belongs. If the Prime Minister insists upon making himself responsible for all questions of higher military strategy, then he must be ready to face accusations directed against that strategy.' Rainsboro's list of charges showed that there was a case to answer about the past. And for the future the great question remained: have we time to afford Churchill's strategy?

As the weeks passed, no real accord on this supreme matter had been reached between the British and the Americans, although the divergence was concealed by something near a deception – not, be it noted, a deception which baffled the enemy but one that was to breed bitterness between the allies. In May, Molotov, the Soviet Foreign Minister, came to London, went to

Washington and returned to Moscow via London again. The outcome of these journeys, apart from the signature of a twenty years' treaty between Britain and the Soviet Union, was the famous declaration of 11 June: 'In the course of the conversations full understanding was reached with regard to the urgent task of creating a Second Front in Europe in 1942.' That seemed plain enough. Molotov went on his way rejoicing and Stalin received further encouraging messages from Roosevelt. Yet, as far as the British were concerned, the words were never intended to mean what they appeared to say. Sir Arthur Bryant, Brooke's biographer, writes: 'thanks to the firm front of the British Chiefs of Staff Molotov failed to obtain any promise of a landing in 1942.'[29] This emphatic claim is based on the *aide-mémoire* which Churchill presented to Molotov on his departure and the document does indeed include the words: 'We can therefore give no promise in the matter.' Yet these words alone do not contain the full burden of the *aide-mémoire*, as Bryant goes near to implying. It opened with the declaration that 'we are making preparations for a landing on the Continent in August or September 1942' and it closed with an assurance that provided that 'it appears sound and sensible we shall not hesitate to put our plans into effect'.[30] Moreover, Molotov discussed the preliminary arrangements for the projected 1942 expedition as well as those for 1943[31] and Washington's first understanding of the meaning of the 11 June statement did not differ greatly from Molotov's. And yet it appears to be the fact that on the very day – 11 June – when the agreed declaration was made public the British Cabinet took a specific decision *against* a landing in 1942 unless it could be launched with overwhelming strength.[31] In the light of this decision, urgent consultation with the Americans was necessary and on 13 June Churchill left for Washington. One reason why he went was his alarm at the reports that the American President *was* seriously pressing for a 1942 operation. It is no part of the argument here whether the projected operation was right or wrong, feasible or unfeasible. What is indisputable is that all

29. *The Turn of the Tide* by Sir Arthur Bryant.
30. *The Hinge of Fate* by Winston Churchill.
31. *The Turn of the Tide* by Sir Arthur Bryant.

these nuances, concealments and misunderstandings were constructing a perilously thin ice for the statesmen of the Grand Alliance to skate upon.

Churchill did not wish to be away at that moment, since the great battle in Libya on which he had set so many of his hopes had been unleashed by Rommel at the beginning of June and was still raging. Through March, April and May Churchill had been 'very ill-content'[32] with his Commander-in-Chief in Cairo, General Auchinleck. Auchinleck was constantly pressed to take the offensive earlier than he deemed prudent, occasionally receiving from Churchill bitter messages sent in defiance of Brooke's advice. Auchinleck did his best in his reply to set out both strategic and tactical reasons why the early Libyan offensive which Churchill urged might be dangerous. It could have little effect on the coming Russian campaign; it might imperil the northern front along the Turkish and Persian frontiers for which he was also responsible; without the requisite superiority in cruiser tanks, it might be an extremely risky operation. But all his formidable arguments were of no avail; Churchill was more 'furious' than ever. In May, with Brooke wilting under Churchill's pressure, definite orders were sent to Auchinleck; he must either obey or be relieved. 'This,' Churchill admitted, 'was a most unusual procedure on our part towards a high military commander.'[33] And the result was that Auchinleck, against his better judgement, so altered his dispositions that he was better arrayed for an offensive than to meet the attack which actually came.[34] Throughout the days that followed, the hectoring interference from Downing Street ranged from high strategy to lesser matters. 'It is such a pity,' wrote General Sir John Kennedy one night when the battle was reaching its climax, 'that Winston's fine courage and drive cannot be harnessed to the war effort in a more rational way . . . A more dangerous matter at the moment is his pressure on Auchinleck to hold Tobruk.'[35] The pressure could not succeed where all Auchinleck's frantic efforts to obey

32. *Auchinleck* by John Connell.
33. *The Hinge of Fate* by Winston Churchill.
34. Cited in *Auchinleck* by John Connell.
35. *The Business of War* by Sir John Kennedy.

his furious master failed. Tobruk fell; thirty-five thousand British, Indian and South African soldiers were taken prisoner. In place of the early expectations of a Second Front in Europe, encouraged by the communiqué after Molotov's visit and Churchill's high hopes of an offensive campaign in Libya, British arms had suffered another, unforeseen, inexplicable, immeasurable disaster.

The fall of Tobruk was for Churchill 'one of the heaviest blows'[36] of the war; no words are needed to emphasize how cruel was the news which reached him in Washington while he negotiated with men already dubious about his direction of Britain's strategy. But the blow was cruel for the nation too and during the next few days the headlines in the New York newspapers conveyed alarmist reports from London: 'ANGER IN ENGLAND', 'TOBRUK FALL MAY BRING CHANGE OF GOVERNMENT', 'CHURCHILL TO BE CENSURED'. 'I do not think,' said Churchill later, 'any public man charged with a high mission from this country ever seemed to be barracked from his homeland in his absence – unintentionally, I can well believe – to the extent that befell me while on this visit to the United States.'[36] His irritation was natural. But what did he expect his countrymen to do? What sort of people did he think they were? All his own prophecies about the desert campaigns appeared to be confounded. First-hand reports from the front by highly-qualified war correspondents criticized both the quality of the weapons supplied to British soldiers and the manner in which the battle had been fought. These seemed to give the lie direct to the claims Churchill had been making only a few days before; and they pointed to a more general pattern of inadequacy in the nation's productive and military effort. Moreover there were suspicions about Tobruk itself. Bevan in *Tribune* put the question point-blank: 'Who was responsible for the decision to hold Tobruk? Was it Ritchie?[37] Or was the command direct from London? There is a cloud of doubt about it. If it was Ritchie, then he appears to have under-

36. *The Hinge of Fate* by Winston Churchill.
37. General Sir Neil Ritchie was the commander of the Eighth Army, under Auchinleck.

estimated stupidly the mobility of his agile opponent. If it was London, then it is another example of the romantic frivolity which has directed too many of our military failures.'[38] Churchill in America did his best to pour scorn on the clamour. He explained to his hosts that 'I doubted whether I should be able to provoke twenty Members into the lobby against the Government on an issue of confidence' and that 'those who were voluble in Parliament in no way represented the House of Commons'.[30] The coolness and the courage were magnificent. But other accomplishments in addition – the right organization and the right strategy – were needed to win the war. Had a brave people no right to inquire into past failures and to demand better service for the future?

Churchill mistook the public mind. The widespread criticism of the Government was not the result of 'the chatter of the press', 'the shrill voices' outside and the machinations of 'the would-be profiteers of disaster' in the House of Commons.[39] No doubt it was agreeable to the men in command, even inevitable, that they should attribute the public outcry to unworthy motives. They may be pardoned also for not stopping to consider what sinister developments might have occurred if the deep anxieties of the people had found no expression in the House of Commons or the press. One glory and one strength of the British people throughout the war was that they were not prepared to put all their democratic habits in pawn for the duration. As it happened, polling-day in a by-election at Maldon occurred a few days after the fall of Tobruk; Mr Tom Driberg, an Independent candidate, critical of the Government but pledged to support the full prosecution of the war, defeated the official Government candidate by a spectacular majority. And Churchill was wrong too about the

38. Auchinleck's biographer, John Connell, concurs with the question Bevan put at the time. He writes, after the most exhaustive discussion of the whole affair: 'An important aspect of the tragedy of Tobruk was that Churchill, both at the time and later, was incapable of recognizing that he himself was one of the principal instigators.' Brooke proposed to Churchill that 'in fairness to Auchinleck', he should include a paragraph in his subsequent speech to the Commons explaining how they had both expressed 'the strong hope' from London that Tobruk would be held. Churchill refused to do so. (*The Business of War* by Sir John Kennedy.)
39. *The Hinge of Fate* by Winston Churchill.

'contemptible' nature of the opposition in Parliament. Soon after his return from Washington Stafford Cripps presented him with a report stating 'that there is a very grave disturbance of opinion both in the House of Commons and in the country'.[40]

Thus the stage was set for – next to the Norway debate – the most critical parliamentary occasion of the war. Of course, Churchill possessed enormous reserves of strength both in the country at large and in the House of Commons as a whole. All his principal Ministers, representing three Parties in the State, stood unwaveringly beside him. None of the press critics was suggesting *his* removal; they were careful still to aim at lesser figures. But now at last others besides Bevan in the House of Commons were ready to recognize that oblique attacks on the administration would no longer suffice. On 25 June a motion was placed on the House of Commons Order Paper: 'That this House, while paying tribute to the heroism and endurance of the Armed Forces of the Crown in circumstances of exceptional difficulty, has no confidence in the central direction of the war.' The first name on the motion was that of Sir John Wardlaw-Milne, possibly the most powerful of Tory back benchers. Allied with him was the greatly honoured Admiral of the Fleet, Sir Roger Keyes; everyone could recall how his intervention in the Norway debate had helped to kill Chamberlain. A third signatory was Leslie Hore-Belisha, sometimes regarded, chiefly by himself, as a potential Prime Minister. No full concerted plan was agreed between these three and the few Labour M.P.s who might be expected to vote with them. Bevan had a few private talks with Belisha, that was all. But clearly he could not refuse to back such a challenge without denying everything he had said and written for months past. Once the motion was published, the Westminster corridors were agog. The Whips worked overtime, although probably their efforts were superfluous. Confronted with the stark possibility that a vote might do real damage to the Churchill Coalition and confronted, too, with the motley character of the opposition, the vast bulk of M.P.s rallied to the Government before the debate ever started. Moreover, the battle in Libya was still at its peak; no one could guess the out-

40. *The Hinge of Fate* by Winston Churchill.

come and many feared that a Cabinet crisis at such a moment might increase the chances of military catastrophe.

Sir John Wardlaw-Milne, sensing the hostility around him, put to the War Cabinet a proposal that the motion should be deferred until the battle was over. For the task of challenging Churchill he had other disabilities besides cold feet. He represented the old, never fully submerged current of Chamberlainite opinion within the ranks of Conservative back benchers. How could a man who bore so heavy a responsibility for the deficiencies of the past now step forward as a saviour? But Sir John could not draw back; the Cabinet would not let him. There on the morning of 1 July he stood with a red flower in his buttonhole to open the attack, 'looking', as one reporter said, 'like a *Punch* drawing of a statesman'. Sir John was no orator, but he started well. Gradually, a reluctant House was compelled to listen to his grave recital of grave facts. Then, without warning almost, he stuttered out a digression: 'It would be a very desirable move – if His Majesty the King and His Royal Highness would agree – if His Royal Highness the Duke of Gloucester were to be appointed Commander-in-Chief of the British Army – without of course administrative duties.' At first there was a gasp, followed by a noise which that assembly has not heard before or since, a loud, long, excruciating cacophony, half-groan, half-guffaw. The House of Commons can be the rudest place in the world. Sir John's gaffe, wrote Churchill, 'proved injurious to his case, as it was deemed a proposal to involve the Royal Family in grievous controversial responsibilities'.[41] This matchless meiosis may be taken as the final proof of Churchill's romantic loyalty to the throne. The House had other thoughts. It dearly loved dukes, but it could not see Royal Gloucester as Britain's answer to Rommel.

Sir John never recovered, and Sir Roger Keyes, who followed him, completed the damage. Churchill had once been his hero and as he stumbled through his prepared notes and the interrupters goaded him, his old love could not be constrained. Whereas Sir John had argued that Churchill was interfering too much with the detailed conduct of the war, Sir Roger boldly argued that he interfered too little. What was needed were more Gallipolis,

41. *The Hinge of Fate* by Winston Churchill.

with the timorous hand of the Admiralty removed to enable the brave Churchillian adventures to succeed. 'It would be a deplorable disaster if the Prime Minister had to go,' he cried. Never was there such a vote of censure! That night the debate continued till three o'clock next morning, the longest sitting of the war. But the interest flagged. The great anti-Churchill motion was being blown out in a gale of derision.

Next day Bevan rose to continue the debate in an atmosphere of freezing hostility, with his cause already doomed. The benches were packed; a Bevan speech was always worth hearing and it may be guessed that his many enemies relished the prospect of seeing him trapped in a corner. Often before, in their belief, he had come near to cutting his own political throat; now, with his embroilment in the Wardlaw-Milne–Keyes fiasco, he had succeeded. Some newspapers which had joined the hunt against the Government a short while before were now jeering. Never did a man speak in the House of Commons on so great an occasion with fewer sure friends at his side and so solid a weight of opinion against him.

He began quietly, as always. It was the duty of Members to represent opinion outside. The real disservice to the country would have been if the motion had been withdrawn. As for the morale of the troops, it was not speeches in Parliament which might injure it; 'it is what they experience themselves in battle'. It would be serious if the soldiers in the field could not hear any voices raised on their behalf in the House of Commons. He then complained about the Prime Minister's tactics in the debate. Why had he not been prepared to give an account of what had happened on the first day? Why must he reserve his statement to the end? This procedure might ensure his triumph in the division lobbies. But 'the country is beginning to say that he fights debates like a war and the war like a debate'.

Some might still suppose, with the detailed comments which came next on the Minister of Production's speech of the previous day, that he would be content to stress the contradictions in Ministerial utterances. But that was rarely Bevan's way. He was never a snapper-up of unconsidered trifles; in his reckoning the bigger the parliamentary occasion, the more substantial must be the argument. His attack was three-pronged; the main strategy of the war was wrong; the wrong weapons had been produced; and those weapons were being managed by men not properly trained in their use. On his second count – about the weapons – he got the ear of the House. Where were the British dive bombers? The Germans believed in them, but not apparently the Air Ministry. Where were the transport planes? They and other forms of Air Force co-operation with the Army could help win battles more than long-range bombers over Cologne and Bremen. Neither Bevan nor the House could know of the agonized appeals which had come from Cairo and elsewhere for fuller air support, but enough had filtered through about the controversy over the Air Ministry's obsession with victory through bombing to induce respectful silence.[42] Bevan pressed home his advantage. 'If the House of Commons refuses to exercise its independence against the Government, the House of Commons must accept responsibility for the result . . . It is *we*, not the party machines, not secret meetings upstairs of Members on any side of the House, who are responsible for sending British soldiers on to the battlefield with improper weapons.'

By now he was in full command, but he turned aside to commit what many considered a serious error. It was outrageous enough that this amateur should presume to talk on military matters. Yet suddenly he launched a full-scale assault on the high commanders of the British Army.[43] They too must bear the

42. On 12 April General Wavell, from India, wrote to the Chiefs of Staff: 'It certainly gives us furiously to think, when, after trying with less than twenty light bombers to meet attack which has cost us three important warships and several others and nearly a hundred thousand tons of merchant shipping, we see that over two hundred heavy bombers attacked one town in Germany.' (Quoted by Churchill in *The Hinge of Fate*.) On 16 June, Casey, Minister of State in Cairo, wrote to Churchill to 'put to you again the case for a force of modern high-speed heavy bombers in this theatre . . . Looking around to see what can be done to help Auchinleck in his hard fight in the desert and to help Tedder and Harwood in their hard struggle to save Malta, it seems to me that the only way in which we can strengthen our position here in the immediate future is by giving them a substantial force of these aircraft. May I ask you once more to give this your sympathetic and urgent consideration.' The help was not forthcoming, the telegram was not acknowledged. (Quoted by John Connell in *Auchinleck*.)

43. Churchill sometimes spoke of his generals in terms not so different from Bevan's. Brooke wrote in his diary a few weeks earlier: 'He [Churchill] came out continually with remarks such as: "Have you not got a single General in

guilt for the lack of proper co-ordination between land and air forces.[44] 'We have in this country five or six generals, members of other nations, Czechs, Poles and French, all of them trained in the use of these German weapons and this German technique.' Why not put them in the field in charge of our troops?[45] Did not the Prime Minister know the taunt: if Rommel had been in the British Army he would still have been a sergeant? 'The fact of the matter is that the British Army is ridden by class prejudice. You have got to change it . . . If the House of Commons has not the guts to make the Government change it, events will. Although the House may not take any notice of me today, you will be doing it next week. Remember my words next Monday and Tuesday. It is events which are criticizing the Government.' This outburst was to be quoted against Bevan for months, even years, afterwards. Not merely had he insulted the men in command; was he not prophesying fresh defeat in the field?

Yet, error or no error, at the time the muttered anger was quickly subdued. He was back on his main attack – on the principal strategist of the war. No one had misconceived the nature of the war more than the Prime Minister; no one was more Maginot-minded. And *why* was the strategy wrong? The Prime Minister had 'qualities of greatness'. But he had too much to do. He had a wrong instrument of Government. He mistook 'verbal felicities for mental inspirations'. He could in the course of an evening produce a whole series of brilliant improvisations, but he has not the machinery to carry them out.

---

the Army who can win battles, have none of them any ideas, must we continually lose battles in this way?"'
44. How near this was to reality is shown in the letter written by Brooke to Wavell in May: 'We are now reaping the full disadvantage of an all-out independent air policy directed towards the bombing of Germany. As a result we are short of all the suitable types of aircraft for support of the other two services. It is an uphill battle as the Air Ministry at once takes cover behind the War Cabinet's continual desire for an all-out policy of bombing directed against Germany.' (Quoted by Sir Arthur Bryant in *The Turn of the Tide*.)
45. Oddly, a comparable thought had once occurred to Churchill. 'I cannot tell you how angry the Prime Minister has made me,' said Sir John Dill, at that time – December 1941 – C.I.G.S. 'What he said about the Army tonight I can never forgive. He complained he could get nothing done by the Army. Then he said he wished he had Papagos [commander-in-chief of the Greek Army] to run it.' (Quoted by Sir John Kennedy in *The Business of War*.)

He would go to the War Cabinet, having seen the Chiefs of Staff, to defend his own decisions. 'That is not true,' interrupted Churchill. But Bevan was not to be stopped and the angry House still stayed to listen. 'The Prime Minister has been fighting rearguard actions against the House of Commons all the time, making concessions all the while to buy off the political situation, not to create a machine for war-making.' The charge could not be shouted down. Members could recall the long struggle to establish a Ministry of Production.

Yet, if this had been all, the speech would not have lingered in the memory. In his last minutes he looked to the future. 'If this debate,' he said, 'resulted in causing demoralization in the country in the slightest degree, I would have preferred to cut my tongue out.' Nobody mocked. Our weapons were not what they ought to be, but Hitler was not going to call off the war till we produced better ones. 'The country expects, and declarations have been made – I can speak freely about this, though I understand the Prime Minister cannot – that in a very short time, at a time and place decided by the Government, we shall launch an attack upon the enemy in a theatre of war nearer to this country. I do beg and pray the Government when they make that decision to make it as a consequence of strategical propriety and not as a consequence of political propaganda. Nevertheless we have to do it. We cannot postpone it till next year. Stalin expects it; please do not misunderstand me, for heaven's sake, do not let us make the mistake of betraying those lion-hearted Russians. Speeches have been made, the Russians believe them and have broken the champagne bottles on them. They believe this country will act this year on what they call the Second Front. Molotov said so; they expect it and the British nation expects it. I say it is right, it is the correct thing to do, and the Government have practically said so. Do not in these high matters speak with a twisted tongue; do not use words with double meanings; do not use sentences with hidden purposes. On these high matters, speak truthfully and simply, so that the people can understand and trust . . .'

This was the passage that brought the hush. Next morning the newspapers were acclaiming the massive concluding speech of Churchill and his massive majority – four hundred and seventy-five to twenty-five. He called for the rout of 'the naggers and the snarlers' and there was never any doubt that he would have his way. But many Members, including those who helped form the majority, were not prepared to dismiss Bevan's 'diatribe with its bitter animosity', as Churchill called it, as contemptuously as he. Walter Elliot, who spoke after Bevan, called his speech 'the authentic voice of the Vote of Censure – a powerful speech, a well-informed speech, a cogent speech. I rejoice,' he said, 'in having been able to ring my lance against his shield and in being able to say: "Here is an adversary against whom anyone will be proud to tilt in the House of Commons".' Every other speaker that day – except Churchill – paid his willing or unwilling tribute. 'Never before,' said one M.P., 'have so many Members entered a division lobby with so many reservations in their minds.' No report or description can convey the effect of a speaker who relies on spontaneous inspiration. It was on this day that Bevan stepped into his place as a debater of the first order, the only living rival to Churchill in the parliamentary art.

The great debate of July 1942 had its accompaniment and its aftermath. While Churchill was speaking, someone else was coming to his aid. Auchinleck was saving Egypt. 'Our policy has been,' said Churchill, referring to the generals on the spot, 'not to worry them but to leave them alone to do their job. Now and then I send messages of encouragement and sometimes a query and a suggestion, but it is absolutely impossible to fight battles from Westminster and Whitehall. The less one interferes the better.'[46] Auchinleck, above all men, could have proved that this wise doctrine, which won such general approval in the Commons, had been shockingly disregarded in the treatment he had received at Churchill's hands. However, in the first days of July

46. Compare this statement with one incident, selected from many. On 17 March, the Prime Minister sent the following message to Auchinleck: 'I ought to have added the following to my message of March 15th. If as a result of all discussions, it is decided that you must stand on defensive until July, it will be necessary at once to consider the movement of at least fifteen air squadrons from Libya to sustain Russian left-wing in the Caucasus.' Brooke advised the Prime Minister not to send this telegram but Churchill insisted, saying (according to General Kennedy) 'it will be a whip to him'. (Quoted by John Connell in *Auchinleck*.)

he fought his own battle – the first battle of Alamein, although that name was not to become famous for several months yet. The world was never to be told the truth about that decisive engagement until long after Auchinleck had been made one of the scapegoats for the desert failure and long after Churchill had pilloried him in his memoirs. Thus, too, Bevan's forebodings of bad news on the Monday or Tuesday were falsified. His charges against the generals may be considered unwarranted and unfair – although the accusation cannot lie in Churchill's mouth since he himself moved swiftly to secure their removal. He wanted to go at once to the Middle East but Brooke recruited Brendan Bracken's aid to stop him. Brooke 'dreaded the impact of the Prime Minister's presence in the middle of a battle'.[47]

Meantime, on the other and greater front Hitler's gigantic armies were plunging eastwards towards Stalingrad and 'the urgent task of creating a Second Front in Europe in 1942' had become more urgent than ever. Could it really be true, as Bevan half-hinted, that Britain might be speaking with 'a twisted tongue' on such a high matter? He himself would not believe it but he had touched the nerve centre of the central strategic controversy of the war. Not only Stalin expected it. In Washington Marshall was 'very stirred up' and talked of 'a showdown'. 'As the British won't go through with what they agreed to,' wrote Stimson in his diary, 'we will turn our backs on them and take up war with Japan.'[48]

Meantime also the Parliamentary Labour Party was performing its traditional rites. Bevan and the other seven Labour M.P.s[49] who had voted for the Censure motion were 'carpeted' by the Deputy Prime Minister, Mr Attlee. They had acted in defiance of the secret Party meeting. In the crisis of war, that remained for some the cardinal sin.

47. *The Turn of the Tide* by Sir Arthur Bryant.
48. Quoted from Stimson's diary in *The Turn of the Tide* by Sir Arthur Bryant.
49. The Labour members, apart from Bevan, who voted against the Government were: F. J. Bellenger, F. G. Bowles, Dr L. Haden-Guest, B. V. Kirby, S. S. Silverman, R. R. Stokes and Neil Maclean.

12 The Fight with Churchill II: July 1942–April 1944

It is a great and special part of our duty and office, Mr Speaker, to maintain freedom of consultation and speech . . . I desire you from the bottom of your hearts to hate all messengers, tale-carriers, or any other thing, whatsoever it be, that any manner of way infringe the liberties of this honourable Council. Yea, hate it or them, I say, as venomous and poison unto our Commonwealth, for they are venomous beasts that do use it. – PETER WENTWORTH, speaking in the Parliament of 1576[1]

'Why do you keep on attacking Churchill? What do you think happens if *he* goes?' asked Archie Lush on one occasion at the height of the war. 'All right,' replied Aneurin. 'Suppose he fell under a bus. What should we have to do? Send a postcard to Hitler, giving in?' On another occasion he was talking about the House of Commons with Lewis Lewis of Blackwood. 'There's only one man there who counts – Winston Churchill,' said Aneurin. 'It's necessary for us to show we're not afraid of him, that we can fight him on his own ground.'

Churchill's own ground, particularly in the latter months of 1942, following the famous censure debate in July, had a special meaning. Bevan persisted in attacking Churchill as the grand strategist of the war – at the very point where, supposedly, his authority was most unchallengeable and where, certainly, his pride was greatest and his skin the thinnest. This, according to Bevan's enemies at the time and his detractors since, was his most grievous and inexcusable error. Here he plunged head first out of his depth and the miracle was that he ever scrambled back to political safety and repute. For Bevan *did* believe that Churchill's strategy might result in the nation's defeat or at least a stalemate, and when the prophecy was disproved he still main-

1. Quoted in *Elizabeth and Her Parliaments* 1559–1581 by J. E. Neale.

tained that the Churchill strategy had lengthened the war by many months, if not years. And yet the war was satisfactorily won. Against Churchill's victory no defence may seem possible for Bevan's thesis and the anti-Churchill diatribes which derived principally from it. For undoubtedly, whatever other mistakes or follies Churchill might acknowledge – he acknowledges none in his memoirs – he would be content to rest his case before history on his title as the presiding, triumphant world strategist. And if the Churchillian boast is accepted, Bevan was the 'squalid nuisance in war' whom Churchill denounced.

Oddly, although for very different reasons, Bevan's judgement on Churchill as the war leader accords with that of Churchill's most intimate adviser, Alan Brooke. 'Winston never had the slightest doubt,' wrote Brooke after the war, 'that he had inherited all the military genius of his great ancestor, Marlborough.' Yet this is the very claim which Brooke will not concede. His memoirs portray Churchill as the indispensable political leader and cheer leader. As a strategist, Brooke rates him low, if not as a positive menace. 'Perhaps the most remarkable failing of his,' Brooke wrote at the end of 1942, 'is that he can never see a whole strategical problem at once. His gaze always settles on some definite part of the canvas and the rest of the picture is lost. It is difficult to make him realize the influence of one theatre against another ... This failing is accentuated by the fact that often he does not want to see the whole picture, especially if the wider vision should in any way interfere with the operation he may have temporarily set his heart on.'[2] A failure to see the whole strategical picture may be thought a considerable deficiency in a would-be world strategist.

However, Bevan's case cannot be left to rest on the testimony of Brooke and those who have written in the same tone, especially as his quarrel was also with Brooke's strategy. The controversy must be fully probed, remembering throughout that the two contestants were never evenly matched in weapons and armour. Churchill had all the stupendous cares of office on his shoulders, but he was surrounded in Government circles, in the House of Commons and in the country at large by massive

2. *The Turn of the Tide* by Sir Arthur Bryant.

support. Bevan was almost alone – much more so than Churchill himself had been in the thirties. He had no military experience. He had no access to Government files. Except on the subject of tank production he had no secret informants in high places. Yet in the teeth of all the jeers he compelled the House of Commons to listen. His case concerned the argument about the Second Front in a new and altogether more significant guise.

During the summer of 1942 Hitler launched his second great attack on Russia, the mightiest mechanical offensive in the history of the world. Bevan believed as many others believed – and as they were entitled to believe on the basis of the public assurances given following Molotov's visit to London – that the response of Britain and the United States sometime during the year would be the opening of a Second Front in the West. He took a leading part in a fresh series of Second Front meetings all over the country and week by week in *Tribune* urged the necessity of giving the fullest support to the Russian armies. He did not underrate the dangers or the exertions required to execute the task. In *Tribune* of 17 July he argued that the nation should be put on a siege basis to enable the maximum diversion of supplies to the war. Two weeks later he wrote: 'The country provides a curious spectacle. It is united at the top and divided from there down. The three main political Parties lean against each other in the Government which in its turn is surrounded by a House of Commons now far on the way to creating a record for spinelessness and sycophantic docility. At Westminster all is self-admiring peace – but nowhere else. The country seethes with discontent against the military conduct of the war, and everywhere where men gather together one subject is fiercely debated – when are we going to back up in Europe the Homeric resistance of the Soviet Union?' This outburst was prompted by an article in the *Daily Telegraph* which had hotly denounced the Second Front agitation. *Tribune* accused the *Telegraph* of preaching defeatism; for how did Lord Camrose think victory would be possible if the Soviet Union was crushed?

On 7 August *Tribune* wrote of 'the mounting anger' of the British people. Let not the Government imagine that the House of Commons expressed adequately the popular feeling. There it could rely on 'bloated majorities and well-paid servility'. At the end of August came reports of Churchill's meeting in Moscow with Stalin. Since the communiqués gave no hint of dissension between the war leaders, the Government press invoked them as a further reason for countering the Second Front demand. But *Tribune* refused to be mollified by so patent an excuse. It declared, as was easy to prove, that there had been no abatement of the Russian appeal. It called on Parliament to express 'the Leftward current of opinion in Britain which is deep, constant and strong . . . No consideration of mere Party loyalty must be allowed to stand in the way'.

Churchill had returned from Moscow to deliver one of his great orations, enriched on this occasion by a flattering tribute to Stalin. 'Churchill has spoken, up goes the Government stock; the critics are silenced,' wrote *Tribune*. 'After all, it will be said, if Churchill has come back with an arrangement with Stalin, we must do nothing that will hold up or disarrange its execution. This, of course, is the infantile basis of our present-day politics which has kept us so persistently near the abyss.' Bevan's own speech in the Commons on this occasion exceeded any that had gone before in acid directness. He dismissed Churchill's speech as a 'turgid, wordy, dull, prosaic' contribution to the chapters in the book he was writing. He mocked the secret press conference which Churchill had given to the editors of London newspapers just before the debate where the Premier had allegedly appeared in 'some sort of uniform or other'. 'I wish he would recognize,' said Bevan, 'that he is the civilian head of a civilian Government and not go parading round in ridiculous uniforms.' He would be more dignified if he was content with 'ordinary fustian'. But his concern about the press conference had a more serious point. Churchill, he alleged, had used the occasion to 'rail against the representatives of the press for giving so much space to his critics'. Here was a Prime Minister, the head of one Party in the State, who held formidable powers over the press, engaging in 'political intimidation without any precedent in the history of this country'. Here was evidence of the Prime Minister's 'increasing paranoia . . . The time has come when we should make this man realize that the House of Commons is his master.'

After this introduction, he turned to his major theme about the conduct of the war. He dismissed 'the efficacy of long-term bombing as even a principal weapon with which to win the war'. Germany would stand up to the bombardment as Britain had done. 'This idea of sending out thousands of bombers every night just will not work . . . it belongs to the realm of rhetoric.' The crucial test was on land, and what was the Government doing or planning? 'We had in December of last year the longest notice that any nation could have of a major war event. The whole world knew that this spring and this summer the German army was going to be locked in conflict on the Russian front. War is full of unpredictable facts, but that was a predictable one. The Government had nine months' notice to make their preparations . . . I want to know from the Prime Minister and the Government what military preparations this Government took to deal with that fact . . . Here we have Stalingrad besieged and almost fallen, with forty-five German divisions in the West. I say that this year, fought with imagination and courage, the Germans could have been beaten . . . The ordinary working-class people believe that it is the intention of this Government to launch a Second Front in Europe. If that is not done and if Stalingrad falls and the Russians are driven behind the Urals, the working-class people of this country will be asking why. It will be no use for the Prime Minister to tell them that military considerations make it impossible, because unfortunately for the Prime Minister, British people have more confidence in the sagacity of Voroshilov and Timoshenko than in that of Winston Churchill and they know that the Russian generals have declared that a Second Front is possible . . .' Much else followed on the threatened coal shortage due to the Prime Minister's 'absolute ignorance of the elementary facts of industrial life', on the failure of the Prime Minister to speak in fresh accents either to the people of Britain or Europe. He called Churchill's continuance in office 'a major national disaster'. And he concluded. '. . . It [the nation] gets nothing from the Prime Minister. It gets neither courageous disposal of our material and physical forces nor does it get intellectual and spiritual inspiration. It gets nothing but nostalgia over ancient battles and old ways that are dead.'

This comprehensive onslaught brought on Bevan's head the full torrent of abuse from the newspapers which many had been itching to let loose upon him. 'These sour, snarling attacks,' wrote A. J. Cummings in the *News Chronicle*, 'must tend to destroy whatever status Mr Bevan may have acquired as an honest parliamentary critic. I do not suggest that he should follow Mr Hore-Belisha's inspiring example and enter a Cistercian monastery ... but if he were to return to some quiet Welsh village for a spell of hard thinking, he might be less apt to talk so violently through his hat.' Cummings also produced a rhyme sent him by A. A. Milne:

> Goebbels, though not religious, must thank Heaven
> For dropping in his lap Aneurin Bevan;
> And doubtless, this pious mood invokes
> An equal blessing on the trusty Stokes.
> How well each does his work as a belittler
> Of Germany's arch-enemy! Heil Hitler!

The doggerel reflects accurately the flavour of controversy at the time. The *Western Mail* worked itself into a frenzy of denunciation. It described this speech as 'the most disgraceful exhibition of peevishly offensive cussedness that has been heard for a long time ... Free speech is a jewel, but this is not freedom. It is unbridled and intolerable licence ... For him Parliament is a platform for self-advertising performances, and as he is usually tedious and uninteresting on the rare occasions when he tries to talk sense he can only attract attention to his vain and egregious self by offensive audacity and by throwing mud and bricks at the nation and its leaders struggling in dire adversity.' The *Western Mail* prophesied that the electors of Ebbw Vale would welcome the first opportunity of getting rid of their Member.

But Bevan was only incited afresh by these jeers. 'I was hoping,' he said in early October in a debate on coal, 'to be able to make a speech without saying anything about the Prime Minister, but he is so much in the centre of the picture that you cannot fire a shot and try to hit the target without his being somewhere on the horizon.' Then he broadened the indictment to include most of his fellow M.P.s. 'There are over two hundred Members of the House,' he said, 'directly concerned in the administration, either holding jobs or sweating on the top line for jobs. The result is the Executive has been allowed to make muddle after muddle and to have escape after escape because the back-bench private Members do not realize that they are as much responsible for carrying this war to a successful conclusion as the Government themselves.' He had made a mistake a few months before, he insisted, when 'I seconded a motion to the effect that we had no confidence in the central direction of the war. I assumed that there *was* a central direction.' And at a Second Front demonstration in Trafalgar Square, attended, according to the *Manchester Guardian*, by more than thirty-five thousand people, he claimed that the conquered people of Europe were holding down a greater German army than the whole of the British Empire forces. 'That represents,' he said, 'a dispersal of British strength amounting to criminal folly.'

Within a few weeks he was faced with facts which appeared to damage his reputation more than all the venom of the newspapers. Montgomery launched his offensive at Alamein in October and the combined British and American conquest of North Africa was started in the early weeks of November. This, the nation was told, was the real Second Front. While Bevan had been shouting, Churchill had been preparing for action. When the Commons met to debate the new situation on 12 November, Churchill had every reason to be jubilant. One of the Tory back-bench sharpshooters, Commander Braithwaite, sought to ensure that Churchill's chief antagonist should not be allowed to escape his humiliation. Churchill, he said, was honoured as a fighting man, but in the forces 'there is nothing but withering contempt for certain advocates of the Second Front. They have come to be known as the "Fireside Fusiliers". I am authorized by certain ratings to say that they would be only too happy to provide facilities at the earliest possible moment for the Member for Ebbw Vale to be landed on a hostile coast.' Loud laughter greeted the sally, and Bevan rose to face the ridicule which he knew could destroy an M.P.'s standing with his colleagues in a matter of minutes. Never in his belligerent parliamentary career was he more nearly on the ropes. He could expect no mercy from a House of Commons which he had by turns upbraided and insulted.

Yet he was not to be subdued. Did they sneer at him for being 'an amateur strategist'? Well, so was Churchill himself; so were Roosevelt and Stalin; so Lloyd George had been, all amateur strategists. All M.P.s were there as amateurs, not experts. Representative government itself was government of the experts by the amateurs and always had been. 'It is the obligation of this House,' he insisted, 'to discuss major strategy, and for hon. Members to say otherwise means that they are undermining the very foundations of representative government.' So much for his title to speak on the whole conduct of the war which he would concede to no one. Was he really asked, then, to apologize for the criticisms he had made in the censure debate in July? They had been threefold; about the weapons, the generals in command, and the absence of proper co-operation between the Army and the Air Force. On each of those counts, Churchill's defence now was that big changes had been made. It was not the critics who needed to withdraw. As for the victories – which the newspapers called defeats for the critics – he welcomed them joyously. 'The Government can keep on confounding me by winning victories and I shall be delighted if they can beat me ceaselessly with such sweet chastisement.' Even at the climax of a battle, he could still charm his enemies.

But he made no concessions. The Prime Minister, he continued, was now remedying some of his earlier mistakes. 'He always refers to a defeat as a disaster as though it came from God, but to a victory as though it came from himself.' Yet the great victory of Alamein itself must be seen in proportion. It had been won against fifteen enemy divisions; the Russians were facing one hundred and seventy-six divisions on the Eastern front. Thus he strove to restore the debate to his own perspective. In the circumstances little but a defensive speech was possible. Yet in the last minutes he counter-attacked and, according to one reporter, roused the Tories to a higher pitch of fury than ever before. 'At the Mansion House the other day,' he said, 'the Prime Minister guaranteed the British Empire. What we have we hold. Hon. Members dare not say that in the Rhondda Valley or on the Clyde. The British Army are not fighting for the old world. If hon. Members opposite think we are going through this in order to keep their Malayan swamps, they are making a mistake. We can see the Conservatives crawling out of their holes now. In 1940 and 1941 they would not have dared to say these things.'

This was a foretaste of a deeper controversy which was to follow in the months ahead. Immediately, he refused to abandon his criticism of the central direction of the war. At the beginning of January 1943, in *Tribune*, he underlined his objection to the whole Mediterranean strategy. 'A long and wasting battle' would have to be fought in North Africa, with the enemy enjoying easier supply routes. Churchill had called the southern shores of Europe 'the soft underbelly' of the Axis. When we get to Italy, said Bevan, we may find that it has acquired 'formidable armour'. 'It is still for the Government and its military experts to explain how it will be more practicable to invade Europe at the end of a three thousand-mile supply line across eighty miles of water than it is to do so from our bases in this country.'

During that month Churchill went to Casablanca to meet Roosevelt and concert plans for the future. *Tribune* almost alone of all the newspapers was unimpressed. Was there any intended irony, it asked, in Stalin's statement that he was too busy fighting to find time to attend the conference? Churchill, of course, had shown no reluctance in going. 'He has a fully developed sense of the theatre and an almost juvenile appreciation of the unusual and the garish.' But who could believe that the vast, complicated assessments required for the planning of modern war were best conducted 'in a hastily improvised hidey-hole' in Casablanca? 'The whole thing smells more of a boy scout's tent than it does of the council chamber of statesmen in the midst of world war.' Such impudence found no backing elsewhere. Casablanca, in the eyes of the rest of Fleet Street, was another Churchill triumph. The fighting in Africa, East and West, filled the headlines. After the long years of withdrawal and defeat the taste of victory satisfied most palates. And Viscount Simon in a House of Lords debate scolded those who dared to meddle with the higher conduct of the war. The call for a Second Front, said the Lord Chancellor, was 'a seriously misleading catch-penny phrase'.

Viscount Simon was not the best choice of an authority to give the verdict of history, and it is not recorded how his remark was received in Moscow. Yet he did represent the entire weight of British official opinion at the time – Beaverbrook had been the only British Cabinet Minister who took a different view – and if the later judgements of both Churchill and Brooke in their memoirs are to be accepted the derisive tone of Simon's condemnation was abundantly justified. On this test, Bevan was guilty of gross ignorance of the military affairs in which he presumed to interfere and an even grosser irresponsibility. If the Government had heeded the clamour he helped to foment, a futile slaughter on the Western front would have been substituted for the well-conceived Mediterranean strategy and the Western Allies would have embarked on the one major course which – according to Brooke – could have lost them the war. On this same test, Bevan's attacks on Churchill can only be dismissed as outrageous and intolerable. Those in his own Party who sought to outlaw him not merely at this time but throughout his career are thereby provided with a vindication. The man's irresponsibility was incorrigible; his role in the Second Front controversy provides the proof. The best service of a biographer, it might be thought, must be to draw the thickest veil across the whole episode.

Aneurin Bevan himself would have ordered no such cowardly retreat. Indeed if his wartime debates with Churchill on this dominant issue were thus to be dismissed, his stature as a man and a political leader would be fatally diminished. And no apologies are needed. Contrary to the popular assumption, the strength of Bevan's case can be illustrated from those parts of the story of the war either suppressed, concealed or unwittingly revealed in Churchill's and Brooke's own records. The bare outline of the facts – secret at the time, but since uncovered – must therefore be recited.

Early in July 1942, Churchill told Roosevelt that the operation across the Channel that year which the United States Joint Chiefs of Staff had been urging on both war leaders was rejected by the British. He urged instead consideration of the North African venture. But Roosevelt was not content. He despatched Marshall, Admiral King and Harry Hopkins to London on what proved to be one of the most decisive missions of the war. The first charge imposed by the President on his emissaries was to try to rescue the possibility of the 1942 cross-Channel operation; in the event of a Russian collapse, he said, this became 'not merely advisable but imperative'. The official American draft, supported by General Eisenhower and General Spaatz of the American Air Force in London, proposed an attack on France in October. But Churchill and Brooke produced their powerful arguments against it and, since the British would have to bear the brunt of the burden, their voice prevailed. Eisenhower that night said that the moment might come to be called 'the blackest day in history'.[3] At this time Bevan was conducting his Second Front campaign in the country. If on this count he was guilty of gross irresponsibility, the guilt must be shared by the American President and the American Joint Chiefs of Staff.

The second decision reached at the London conference was even more far-reaching. Gradually and against the wish of many of his advisers, Roosevelt accepted Churchill's and Brooke's proposal, which Churchill subtly disguised as Roosevelt's own, for the attack on North Africa. Henry Stimson, the United States Secretary of State for War, came near to resignation in protest. General Marshall was extremely dubious. General Mac-Arthur called the operation 'absolutely useless'. Bevan also, as we have seen, had his doubts about the Mediterranean strategy. The amateur strategist was in better expert company than he knew. None of these American objectors believed that the North African operation would do much, if anything, to relieve the Russians. Rather, Eisenhower specifically argued that the best argument for doing it was the assumption that the Russians were certain to be defeated; the capture of Africa would improve the Allied defensive position later. Brooke concurred in this assessment. If only Bevan had known, his severely qualified tributes to the North African venture might have been that much less glowing!

Two grave consequences were feared by the American opponents of the North African expedition. They thought that the

3. Quoted in *Winston Churchill and the Second Front* by Trumbull Higgins, the most complete exposition of the argument presented here.

diversion of supplies and shipping would forbid any chance of mounting a real Second Front in 1943, and that this in turn would involve a clear repudiation of the United States (and British) commitment to the Russians. Churchill cavilled at the objection both at the time and later and was quite prepared to promise Stalin during his Moscow visit in September 1942 'a very great operation in 1943'.[4] But it was the Americans who were proved right in this prophecy by the event. And, conceivably, the other consequence was graver still. With the pressure for the major attack in Europe removed, the huge transfer of American power to the Pacific started. Heavy cuts were made in the construction of the landing craft so essential for a Western front assault. The men at the London conference had played into the hands of the 'Pacific-First' strategists in the United States High Command, chiefly Admiral King who had been the first of the American experts at the London conference to accept the abandonment of the 1942 operation against France. Gone was the full efficacy of the great decision recognizing Europe as the paramount theatre which Churchill had secured with apparent ease on his first visit to Washington in 1941. Hypothetical calculations cannot be clinched. But it would require some hardihood to claim that this most serious departure from the doctrine which Churchill himself had once enunciated did not greatly lengthen the war – as Bevan alleged. Right up till the spring of 1944 the military power of the United States was to be used more against Japan than against Germany.

Another expert witness may be consulted. Hitler frequently expressed his anxieties about the opening of a Second Front in the West. After the abortive raid on Dieppe in September 1942, he declared: 'I must freely admit . . . that a major landing of the enemy in the West would bring us to a generally critical position.' He thought Dieppe the prelude to a larger enterprise and gave orders for the construction of the Atlantic Wall as a means to alleviate the severe pressures on his manpower in the West. When the Allies invaded North Africa he despatched one hundred and twenty-five thousand men to Tunis and lost them all. Churchill called this a strategic error on Hitler's

4. *The Hinge of Fate* by Winston Churchill.

part, but it was not necessarily too heavy a price to pay for immunity in the West for another twelve months. In the months after the Allies had shown their hand in North Africa, Hitler was able to move big reinforcements from Western Europe to the Eastern front – twenty-seven divisions, according to Stalin's estimate; less, according to Churchill; but the movement itself is not disputed.

Such faith, then, did Churchill and Brooke show in the endurance of their Russian ally! They disregarded Stalin's warnings, broke their qualified commitment for 1942, repeated it more emphatically for 1943 and then broke it again, and, for the benefit of the North African expedition, cut the promised supplies by the Arctic route to Russia at the height of the battle of Stalingrad. Brooke in any case regarded British supplies to Russia as 'absolute madness'.[5] How great must have been their confidence that Russia would survive without their aid and that Hitler would be prevented from recoiling westward once more with massive, victorious armies – the spectre feared by Bevan and so constantly portrayed by him to the Commons as the consummation Britain must at all costs forestall!

And yet neither Churchill nor Brooke revealed any such conviction about Soviet capacity. True, they had abandoned the crude knife-through-butter prophecy approved by the experts a year before. But they still kept their fingers crossed. 'My own feeling,' wrote Churchill in Moscow in August, 'is that it is an even chance they will hold, but C.I.G.S. will not go so far as this.'[6] The two British war leaders had a bet on the subject and, fortunately for Britain's strategy, Churchill won. But how can it be disputed that the strategy itself was the most colossal of gambles? If Stalin had lost the battle of Stalingrad, North Africa would have weighed as a trifle in the balance and Churchill would never have been able to describe the battle of Alamein as the turning of 'the Hinge of Fate'. The essence of Bevan's strategical opinions was that he considered Stalingrad and the whole Russian campaign of such supreme significance that supreme exertions and sacrifices should be made to influence the

5. *The Turn of the Tide* by Sir Arthur Bryant.
6. *The Hinge of Fate* by Winston Churchill.

outcome. It accorded with what Clausewitz and Churchill himself had once described as the highest principle of war – concentration against the main enemy.

One addition to the military argument must be made. Bevan, in the censure debate of July 1942, had talked of the dangers of the Allies speaking to one another with 'a twisted tongue'. Whatever the view about the exact nature of the commitment to a Second Front in 1942, no shred of doubt is possible about the commitment for 1943. Churchill in Moscow had spoken of 'a deadly attack upon Hitler next year'. Stalin and everyone else concerned knew what he meant. 'We have given Stalin to understand that the great attack on the Continent will come in 1943,' wrote Churchill himself to Roosevelt in November 1942.[7] Brooke has many revealing passages on 'the great difficulties in getting out of Winston's promise to Stalin, namely the establishment of a Western front in 1943'. Few undertakings between allies were ever more solemnly avowed and re-avowed.[8] Yet at Casablanca at the beginning of 1943 no firm decision was reached about the fulfilment of the pledge. The old debate between the Anglo-American strategists had broken out afresh. General Marshall was opposed to 'dabbling wastefully' in the Mediterranean and wanted all landing craft transferred to England for an attack in 1943. And by now another recruit, untainted by American or Russian strategic notions, had been won over to the Western front idea. General Montgomery wrote from Cyrenaica to Brooke advising a cross-Channel attack as the best hope for 1943. 'This obviates all difficulties of shipping, air support and

7. *The Hinge of Fate* by Winston Churchill.
8. Since Churchill himself in his memoirs seeks to argue that he did not mislead the Russians, it may be desirable to adduce the additional evidence offered in *British Foreign Policy in the Second World War*, the official history by Sir Llewellyn Woodward. On 1 July Sir Archibald Clark Kerr, probably the best Ambassador Britain ever had in Moscow, wrote a long memorandum explaining his view that the weakness in the British case, from the Russian angle, was 'not in our inability to open the Second Front, but in our having let [Stalin] believe we were going to'. In August Clark Kerr had a long discussion with Maisky in Moscow. Maisky complained that 'we were still not treating his people as equals, as, for instance, we treated the Americans'. Clark Kerr wrote: 'Again I protested, but in my heart I felt that he was right. I feel that we are still holding these people at arm's length.'

so on,' he wrote as if he were a contributor to *Tribune*; 'we should be developing the offensive from a firm base.'[9] It is not known whether Commander Braithwaite was tempted to denounce the victor of Alamein as a 'Fireside Fusilier'.

Altogether, the debate about the military implications of the Second Front can never be proved one way or the other. Churchill and Brooke present their formidable case on one side; Stalin, Hitler, Marshall and Bevan on the other. Whatever else the discussion was about, it concerned something more than a catch-penny phrase. And one political conclusion is unavoidable. The absence of a Second Front in 1942 and 1943 fed Soviet intransigence and helped to sow the seeds of a more widely embracing world contest in the future. It is sad for the reputation of the West that in that early quarrel with the Soviet Union its leaders *did* speak with a twisted tongue.

The war itself necessarily overshadowed the whole political scene, but other connected problems jostled for attention. During the last six months of 1942 and the early months of 1943, when he was pressing his Second Front argument most strongly, Bevan engaged in parliamentary activities every week while Parliament was sitting and often almost every day. In October, at the beginning of the 1942–3 session, he stood for election to the Administrative Committee[10] of twelve which directed the affairs of the Parliamentary Labour Party. Those at the head of the poll received just over a hundred votes. Those at the bottom, unelected, received less than forty, and they included Bevan and Dick Stokes. Emanuel Shinwell scraped into the eleventh place on the Committee and the names of some of those elected above him included 'docile old-stagers', as *Tribune* reported, who had played little or no part in the Commons at all. Here was a gauge of the general temper of the Labour Party in Parliament which thrust Bevan into violent conflict with his colleagues.

Of course, part of his quarrel with them arose from their adulation of Churchill, whom Bevan regarded as an incurable

9. Quoted in *The Turn of the Tide* by Sir Arthur Bryant.
10. Later renamed the Parliamentary Committee, colloquially known as the Shadow Cabinet.

romantic, 'a man suffering from petrified adolescence'. Having a strong romantic streak in his own nature, he did not offer the analysis solely as a reproach, and when he suggested that Churchill's perorations were too much imbued with the values of the *Boys' Own Paper* he was not making the comparison in ignorance; he too had studied that field of literature. Winston Churchill's romantic faith in England – and Winston Churchill – had been a rich source of strength in 1940 and 1941. But was the same man fitted for the different tasks of 1942 and 1943? How could his romantic outlook, particularly since it appeared to derive its inspiration from distant centuries, qualify him to understand the requirements of industrial organization and revolutionary war in Europe? And, looking farther ahead, how could it be supposed that the Churchill of the General Strike and the gold standard and the India Bill could illuminate the problems of post-war Britain and what Bevan believed and hoped would be a revolutionary world? The *Boys' Own Paper* offered no sure guide here.

Bevan never withdrew his tribute to Churchill's incomparable services to the nation in the very worst days of the war. He was usually ready to admit that those services could be retained while other features in his political character were counteracted. But two conditions were essential. Churchill must be surrounded by Ministers capable of resisting his whims and impulses; he must be confronted by a House of Commons which refused to be cowed. Bevan did not believe that the first of these conditions was fulfilled by Attlee, Bevin, Morrison, and the others. Indeed his rage against them became stronger than against Churchill himself. He could not know what happened around the Cabinet table, but he could make his guess from the measures presented to the Commons. On a long list of domestic issues – coal, old age pensions, workmen's compensation, the Beveridge report, town and country planning, and problems connected with post-war planning generally which became prominent in political debate in 1943 – he was angered by what he considered to be the submissive attitude of the Labour Ministers in the Cabinet.[11]

11. On 2 April 1943, Bevan wrote in *Tribune* a review of S. K. Padover's life of Thomas Jefferson, in which he described what he believed to be the

Yet in 1942 and 1943 other questions upon which the Labour Ministers were in duty bound to speak pressed more urgently. Had they anything distinctive to say about the nature of the revolution in Europe and the post-war settlement to be encouraged by British and Allied policy? If so, no one could hear it. Churchill's voice filled the whole amphitheatre of national politics. Throughout the remaining years of the war Bevan sought to make articulate the fervent striving for a new world which he felt all around him and which Churchill and the Cabinet, Labour Ministers included, appeared to treat with impatient incomprehension.

The House of Commons was his main forum; *Tribune* was used to fill in any gaps or oversights. He more than any other Member was resolved to keep the place alive. Sometimes he acted in conjunction with a considerable number of Labour

qualities required in a political leader in an age of great social change – qualities which he thought were sadly lacking in Britain at the time.

'The first quality necessary in a revolutionary architect seems to me to be an irreverence for traditional ideas. Without this attitude of iconoclasticism all the other qualities are bound to operate on a lower level of consciousness ... If the past shouts too loudly in our ears, how is it possible to hear the first whispers of the future? ...

'The second quality in our society builder must be a certain intellectual arrogance: what I like to call the courage of reason ... If Jefferson, being the child of his time, ascribed a power to human reason more optimistic than events have justified he did not fall into the bottomless quagmire of believing that a better guide could be found in intuition and "blood-thinking".

'The corruption of thought which accompanied the steepening decline of the existing social order has infected even the Left with its deep distrust of the efficacy of rational thinking. Towards the end of a definite type of society the defenders of it are unable to discover a rational justification for its continuance. This naturally occurs first in the most sensitive and gifted of them, and these have to make a hard choice. They must either accept that reason has condemned their society to extinction and work for the new one, or cast doubt on the instrument of reason itself. The strain of this crisis produces many strange phenomena, usually of a semi-religious nature like Buchmanism, which is essentially a disease of the declining middle class. Thus the material crisis which is taking place in society outside them is staged within the minds and hearts of the more aware of the ruling class as a spiritual and mental torment.

'It is at this moment that the third important quality of the society builder exerts its decisive influence. He must be capable of an embracing imaginative sympathy with the drama of mankind, which lifts him above preoccupations with personal consequences, and tunes him in, as it were, to the contemporary purpose of which from then on he becomes the instrument.'

Members or, on one or two important occasions, a majority of them. Sometimes he found himself competing or consorting with other prominent but less persistent critics such as Emanuel Shinwell. More often he was supported by a few, of whom Dick Stokes, Sydney Silverman, George Strauss, Tom Driberg and Frank Bowles were the most effective. Frequently he was alone or almost alone. His closest friend in the Commons during these years was Frank Bowles, who had been returned for Nuneaton in 1942 and who gave him a staunch comradeship which he never forgot. What he achieved in this period was to help cut Churchill down to size – a fact which played its part in the post-war history of Britain.

Coal was one of his perennial interests. He had prophesied that the compromise enforced upon and accepted by the Labour Ministers in the spring of 1942 would not solve the problem, and in October he went farther and prophesied for that winter a serious fuel shortage which could affect the whole war effort. He jeered at those who complained that absenteeism in the pits rather than the absence of any real planning for the industry was the main cause of the trouble. 'You could eliminate absenteeism in the pits altogether,' he said, 'if the miners had brass lungs, iron muscles and wooden heads.' That winter, however, was exceptionally mild and his worst forebodings went unfulfilled. But in the following spring he could return to the charge with his case reinforced. The output of coal continued to fall. The atmosphere in the coalfields became uglier. 'The situation,' he wrote in *Tribune* on 23 April, 'condemns not only the Government but also the cowardice of the Labour Party and the Trades Union Congress.' Both bodies, after making their pious references to the traditional policy of the Party favouring nationalization, had tamely approved the Government's unworkable scheme. 'The Government has tried everything,' he continued, 'to solve the problem of the mining industry. Semi-starvation, imprisonment, exhortations, threats, the supplications of the miners' leaders, and what is almost the omnipotence of Churchill's oratory – all have failed. No, we are wrong. There is one thing they have not tried. They haven't tried getting rid of the coalowners. For there is one truth the Government have not learned. You can get coal without coalowners, but you cannot get coal without miners. Let us not lose heart. The miners will teach it them one day.'

Coal continued to provide the clearest illustration of the injury inflicted upon the war effort by the readiness of the Government to accept the dictation of vested interests, and of the Labour Ministers to be content with the role of junior partners. The Government spokesman in the Lords, Lord Munster, explained as the reason for the Government's opposition to any form of nationalization measure that it would be 'disastrous to introduce a Bill of such a highly controversial character'. Bevan in *Tribune* drew the deductions from this plea. 'It is not controversial to conscript labour, break up family life, force young lads into the pits under threat of imprisonment, but it is controversial to conscript the property of the coalowners. It is dangerously controversial to touch the rich, but the poor can be kicked around with impunity.' Was this not an invitation to the miners, if their voice was ever to be heard, to create more trouble than the coalowners? 'The Prime Minister surrenders to the blackmail of the coalowners and asks the miners to be satisfied with a circular letter.' Bevan prophesied that this 'pretty study in democratic politics' was piling up a real explosion for the future. The explosion when it came was to involve him in one of the biggest fights of his life.

India was another topic on which he found himself at logger-heads with both Conservative and Labour leaders. He and other leaders on the Left had been inhibited by the fact that Stafford Cripps had headed the mission to India in April 1942 which had failed to reach accommodation with Gandhi and the Congress Party. Cripps had doubtless done his best; Gandhi had been obdurate and showed little understanding of the military requirements for resisting the threat of Japanese invasion. However, in August, Gandhi, Nehru and the principal leaders of Congress were arrested and interned; a grandiose plot of sabotage and subversion had been unearthed; the police had seized documents from Congress offices revealing the seditious debates which had proceeded between Gandhi and his confederates. Most of the British newspapers were prepared to take these documents at their face value. Here was the evidence of the 'treachery' of the Indian leaders. But *Tribune* underlined the contribution which Nehru in particular had made to these debates; it was clear that he wished passionately for an Allied victory and was searching for the best way to protect Indian freedom. That men with these views should have been driven into apparent hostility to the Allied cause was a pitiful failure of statesmanship. 'The Imperial Lion has roused himself,' wrote *Tribune*. 'Invoking the spirits of Clive and Hastings and Dyer, he roars again. Gandhi arrested, Nehru arrested, two hundred and fifty other Congress leaders arrested, and seventy-two year old Grandma Gandhi is also arrested lest her trembling whispers might rock the foundations of the great Raj ... The Kuban Cossacks gallop sword in hand in a vain endeavour to halt the Panzered invader; plea follows plea and hope battles against suspicion that Britain will sustain her Soviet Ally; military experts and Tory stooges declaim upon the practical difficulties of a Second Front; China fights on in desperate isolation, and the world resounds with demands for democratic solidarity. Now comes our answer. Our armoured cars are going into action – against Congress supporters in Bombay! Our political warfare has reached new inspiring heights. We have proclaimed *A Whipping Act* for the people of India ... The root trouble is that our rulers have never really believed what many themselves have said a hundred times; that this is a People's War.'

Before this language is dismissed as exaggerated, it should be noted that Churchill, in making his first announcement on the subject to the reassembled Commons, seemed to relish the chance of reviving his old rhetoric of the thirties when he had denounced Gandhi as 'a naked fakir'. He was confident, he said, that Gandhi did not represent 'the Hindu masses'. Gandhi and his associates had been prepared to embark on 'horrible and criminal courses'. The activities of the Congress Party may have been aided 'by Japanese fifth-column work on a widely extended scale'. He was sure that the real reliance should be placed on 'the martial races' of India. The manner of his statement even more than the matter shocked the Labour benches. Bevan interrupted to ask whether Attlee and Cripps had approved it. When Churchill replied guardedly that Attlee and he had worked on the actual words until a late hour the night before, Bevan shouted: 'Then they ought to be ashamed of themselves. They do not represent us.' 'The hon. Member,' said Churchill, 'is a merchant of discourtesy.' (Better, commented Bevan afterwards, than being a wholesaler in disaster.) Next day Arthur Greenwood, speaking officially on behalf of the Labour Party, came down heavily against the Government's Indian policy.

Bevan was saddened by the tragic course which events in India were taking. Before the war he had met Jawaharlal Nehru on his visits to London. After the war they became close friends. Bevan was well aware in September 1942 of Nehru's real attitude; he was horrified that so true a friend of freedom was being kept behind prison bars. He urged a fresh exertion to secure a rapprochement. Above all, it was necessary to kill the Churchill charge, trumpeted damagingly at the time in the British press, that the Indian leaders were scarcely distinguishable from fifth columnists. 'There is an impression here in some circles,' reported *The Times* Delhi correspondent on 15 September, 'that Mr Churchill's assertion that there was deliberate fifth column activity is rather a surmise based on the nature of the disturbances than a conclusion based on evidence that Japanese agents were actually at work.' Fortunately the Japanese did not approach as close to Indian territory as had been feared. Had they done so, Britain and the world might have paid dearly for the vast superstructure of misunderstanding which Churchill erected on 'a surmise'.

Nearer home, the controversy stirred Bevan into a direct attack on his leader. 'Mr Attlee,' he wrote in *Tribune* on 2 October, 'is loyal to the point of self-effacement – but Mr Attlee is no longer the spokesman of the movement which carried him from obscurity into the second position in the land. This is a political fact, not a personal issue ... He remains loyal, but only to Mr Churchill. If Mr Attlee has gained some of the toughness which comes with high position in politics it has been reserved for the members and policies of his own Party ... Now in the name of Labour and Socialism he has underwritten one of the blackest documents which imperialist bigotry ever devised – Mr Churchill's India effusion.' A few days earlier the National Executive of the Labour Party had a long and abortive discussion on what could be done about Labour Party members who persisted in attacking their leaders. Bevan, Laski and Shinwell were said to be the chief offenders. Nothing could be done about their conduct on the Indian issue, for the critics, not the leaders, were leading the Party. And a few days later Bevan and Attlee clashed in the House of Commons. 'The hon. Member,' said Attlee, after a Bevan interruption, 'is so adept at pursuing lines, he pursues them so far that he generally finds himself back where he started. He is apt to become airborne in the last five minutes of his speech.' To which Bevan replied: 'The right hon. Gentleman is usually sunk at the end of his.'

Attlee might regard the general conduct of the war as beyond criticism – the chapters in his autobiography on the subject sound one long squeak of approbation – but there was one Minister who did not. Stafford Cripps came to the conclusion that the War Cabinet was not really in command and he proposed a drastic overhaul of the whole apparatus. He presented a memorandum to Churchill and the two men argued strenuously about it all through September 1942. But neither could persuade the other; so Cripps offered his resignation from the War Cabinet, accepting instead the post of Minister of Aircraft Production. Herbert Morrison took his place in the War Cabinet and Anthony Eden succeeded him as Leader of the House of Commons.

The outside world assumed that Cripps's removal had been due to his comparative failure in that position, but Bevan, in a *Tribune* article entitled 'The Art of Political Assassination', had a darker explanation of the deed. 'The Prime Minister did not take long,' he wrote, 'to make full political use of the renewed prestige which came to him as a result of the victories in North Africa. He used it cynically, brutally and irresponsibly.' Cripps himself was partly to blame, for he had shown a too uncritical fidelity, thus weakening his position in the country. 'He was, therefore, ripe for political assassination, and who more likely to drive the dagger home than the master in whose service he had exposed himself?' There was the advantage too that Cripps, having no Party at his back, could be removed without protest; 'lonely men are easiest murdered'. Churchill now appeared to arrogate to himself the right to move Labour Ministers in and out of the Cabinet as he wished. It was part of the illicit dominance over the whole administration which he had been allowed to assemble into his hands. 'May we suggest that the Labour leaders should read the history of John Churchill, the first Duke of Marlborough? If they do so they may then take the precaution of wearing whatever may be the modern equivalent of the medieval mailed vest.'

This may be cited by his critics as a typical essay in Bevanite extravagance. On all the evidence available now it is clear that Churchill had not been guilty of conspiring against Cripps, that the initiative which resulted in the change came from Cripps himself. However, Bevan's brazen attack contained one strand of poetic truth. Churchill had shown much persuasive skill in warding off the political uproar which would undoubtedly have followed a Cripps resignation, and by the same stroke he had succeeded in putting Cripps as a political figure in cold storage for the rest of the war. It was more an act of political anaesthetization than assassination, but it served the same purpose even more effectively. Moreover, Cripps's criticisms of the conduct of the Government from inside accorded closely with those which Bevan was making more flamboyantly outside. Cripps in his argument with Churchill had been primarily concerned with the absence of what he considered real control by the War Cabinet over major strategy and the production machine. Hardly less severe were his strictures on Churchill's brusque attitude to any preparatory proposals for dealing with the post-war settlement. However, Cripps, no doubt conscious of his political isolation, felt he could do little outside the Government to further the causes in which he believed. He was content to accept a purely administrative post, thus abandoning the advice which Bevan had urged upon him at the time of his appointment that he should only agree to serve in the War Cabinet itself. Bevan always concurred with Macaulay's adage that 'a man in office, and out of the Cabinet, is a mere slave'.

One of Cripps's arguments with Churchill – as it had long been one of Bevan's – was that the prospect held out for the future of Britain and Europe must affect the actual prosecution of the war. Churchill's insistence that nothing must be allowed to divert attention from the pursuit of victory was a false distinction. Suddenly in the late autumn of 1942 events in North Africa placed this controversy – in the shape of the Darlan episode – at the centre of the stage.

Britain and the United States had long followed divergent policies towards the Vichy régime of Marshal Pétain which claimed to be the legitimate and independent Government of defeated France. Britain had given hesitant encouragement to the forces of Fighting France led and organized by General de Gaulle as a resistance movement to Vichy and all its works. The United States had maintained close relations with Vichy throughout and hoped to make profitable political use of this connection at the time of the North African landings. In deference to President Roosevelt's view, Churchill agreed to exclude any association of de Gaulle's forces with the North African expedition and to refrain even from informing him of the event till it happened. General Giraud, who had made a spectacular escape from a German prison camp, was to be brought to Algiers as the French leader favoured by Anglo-American diplomacy to conduct French affairs in North Africa. The plan always had two substantial defects: it underrated the calibre of de Gaulle and the significance of the resistance movement which he and his companions had been able to arouse in France. An accident – as the Americans first thought, a lucky one – enforced an alteration in the agreed arrangements. Admiral Darlan, Pétain's Minister of Marine and one who had proved himself a savage enemy of all those who had helped to sustain the war against the Nazis in France, happened to be in Algiers on the day when the Americans landed. The American military commanders on the spot were speedily convinced that Darlan carried much more authority than Giraud and could assist their military operations. They made a deal, recognizing Darlan as the effective French authority in North Africa, which General Eisenhower, in charge of the expedition, Roosevelt and Churchill were quick to confirm. The expedient was said to be temporary; but how temporary and how expedient? Overnight the detested Darlan was embraced almost as an ally.

Bevan played a leading part in the storm of protest that followed. Immediately on receipt of the news of the trafficking with Darlan he wrote in *Tribune*: 'What kind of Europe have we in mind? One built by rats for rats? It may appear to some people a very clever idea to seduce and beguile these men who owe their power to hurt us to their having been the jackals of our enemies; but it does not bear that appearance to the millions of oppressed men and women in Europe to whom we look for help in our offensive against Germany. Are they to be expected to face torture, imprisonment and death so that the authors of their calamities may be fêted by us? It is not good diplomacy to beguile your enemies and lose your friends.' Then he quoted one of his favourite aphorisms of the German Socialist, Ferdinand Lassalle: 'You cannot be clever in big things.' The episode seemed to confirm his fears that the Churchill régime failed to understand – or, conceivably, understood too well and was determined to thwart – the revolutionary impulse in Europe. His suspicions were naturally deepened when it became known that the B.B.C., on Government instructions, had refused facilities for de Gaulle to speak to the French people. Bevan put a motion on the Order Paper of the House of Commons reading as follows: 'That this House is of the opinion that our relations with Admiral Darlan and his kind are inconsistent with the ideals for which we entered and are fighting the war; furthermore that these relations, if persisted in, will undermine the faith in us among our friends in the oppressed and invaded nations and impair the military, social and political prospects of the final and complete triumph of the cause of the United Nations.' He demanded a full-scale debate, and protested violently when Eden told him that discussion of the subject would take place only in secret.

Churchill himself has admitted that the action of the American commanders 'raised issues of a moral and sentimental character of cardinal importance' and that 'many of my best friends' regarded the affair as 'a base and squalid deal with one of our most bitter enemies'. Almost certainly there were members of his own Cabinet, possibly Anthony Eden, who disagreed with him about it.[12] 'Mounting pressures' forced Churchill 'to seek

12. *Unity 1942–1944, War Memoirs* by General de Gaulle.

refuge' in a secret session.[13] There he delivered a speech, which, according to his own account, changed opinion more palpably than any he had ever delivered. The claim is probably true. It was a brilliantly devised recital of the military necessities on the spot and of the paramount need to do nothing to injure the Anglo-American partnership. As far as can be ascertained Bevan did not speak in this debate, he regarded secret sessions on political issues as a waste of time and an offence against the whole spirit of Parliament. But it is hard to believe that Churchill's concluding words were not directed principally against him. 'I must say,' said Churchill, 'I think he is a poor creature with a jaundiced outlook and disorganized loyalties who in all this tremendous African episode, West and East alike, can find no point to excite his interests except the arrangements made between General Eisenhower and Admiral Darlan ... I ask them [the House] to treat with proper reprobation that small, busy and venomous band who harbour and endeavour to propagate unworthy and unfounded suspicions . . .'[14]

With the debate safely won, Churchill believed that the crisis was over. He and Roosevelt had by now received the unexpected support of Stalin; in his eyes the devious conduct of the affair seemed to bestow on the Western leaders an unaccustomed lustre. But the crisis was not over, and the fact that Churchill thought so goes far to justify the attack upon him. Darlan was still there and the whole case of the critics was that his presence would have profoundly evil consequences for months ahead. If he was able to consolidate his authority with Anglo-American aid, the French people would be engulfed in a continuous civil war while Britain was held guilty of a most flagrant act of treachery to the forces of Fighting France. One well qualified to speak had used

13. *The Hinge of Fate* by Winston Churchill.
14. Most Members were under strict obligations to tear up any notes they might have used in a secret session debate; Churchill kept his and published them in a special volume after the war. From the historian's point of view the disadvantage of this arrangement is that Churchill is enabled to present his case to posterity while his critics in the Commons continue to be silenced. A post-war dispensation permitted Members to recall and make public what they had said in secret sessions. But Churchill was one of the few who had taken the precaution of keeping his own private *Hansard*.

language not very different from Bevan's. When de Gaulle had been informed of the Darlan arrangement by Churchill and Eden he had replied: 'You invoke strategic reasons, but it is a strategic error to place oneself in a situation contradictory to the moral character of this war. We are no longer in the eighteenth century when Frederick the Great paid the courtiers of Vienna in order to be able to take Silesia, nor in the Italian Renaissance when one hired the myrmidons of Milan or the mercenaries of Florence. In any case we do not put them at the head of a liberated people afterwards.'[15] *Tribune* could not have put the point better.

In fact, Churchill and the Allied cause were rescued from the long-term dangers of the deed by the hand of the young assassin, Fernand Bonnier de la Chapelle, who shot Darlan as he drove to his villa in Algiers on Christmas Eve. Churchill in his memoirs has the grace to admit that 'Darlan's murder, however criminal, relieved the Allies of their embarrassment at working with him'. At the time an official howl of denunciation was let loose against the assassin who was secretly and anonymously tried and shot by a form of lynch-law two days later. 'Such an act [the assassination] could benefit only the enemy,' said the *Daily Telegraph* with practised and adventurous, if imbecile, servility. *Tribune* was one of the very few journals in Britain which paid tribute to the courage of 'the nameless warrior'. 'How could we fail,' asked General de Gaulle, 'to recognize and understand what inspired this young man's rage?' To understand that, was to understand one aspect of the character of the war which Churchill, Roosevelt, and Stalin disregarded with increasingly serious results. If Bevan was one of 'a small, busy and venomous band' on the Darlan episode, his company, which included the whole resistance movement of France, was not to be despised.[16]

15. *Unity 1942–1944, War Memoirs* by General de Gaulle.
16. One minor aftermath of the Darlan affair was a fresh quarrel between Bevan and Churchill in the Commons. A few months later Mr Randolph Churchill, at that time M.P. for Preston and serving in North Africa, had written a letter to the *Evening Standard* defending the conduct of the military commanders in dealing with the ex-Vichy authorities. Bevan put questions to Churchill and later forced an adjournment debate on whether other serving soldiers were permitted the same freedom to express their views on

The majority of Labour M.P.s preferred not to trespass into the realms of strategy and diplomacy. However, one domestic issue came to the fore which temporarily ended the parliamentary isolation of the few rebels. In June 1941, Arthur Greenwood, at that time still a member of the Government, had appointed Sir William Beveridge to produce a report on 'Social Insurance and Allied Services'. In December 1942, his comprehensive plan for overhauling the nation's social security system was published. Probably few members of the Government, least of all Churchill, guessed the impact which the Beveridge Report would make on the public mind. But for a few days and weeks the document did appear to have the backing of the Government; the B.B.C. broadcast its general provisions to Europe in twenty-two languages; only one or two Conservative newspapers and a few notoriously diehard Tory M.P.s dared to dissent. Here, it was said, was a charter for abolishing poverty. Moreover, the Report contained a date when the new heaven was to be ushered in; its author proposed that the scheme should start on 1 July 1944, and that 1945 should be the first year in which the new benefits should be disbursed. Sir Walter Citrine spoke of 'the public conscience recognizing at long last what the Labour Party has stood for'. Within two weeks of its publication, the National

---

political topics. Would they be allowed to present the opposite case? Churchill said that the question had been put to him by Bevan 'no doubt from those motives of delicacy in personal matters which are characteristic of him'. Bevan said that he should have been 'exempted from this cheap sneer', since he had tried to raise the matter with another Minister. The issue, in his view, was one of principle. The end of the adjournment debate was marked by a remarkable denunciation of Bevan from the motherly Miss Eleanor Rathbone. She accused him of being actuated by 'a malicious and virulent dislike of the Prime Minister' and concluded: 'It is with disgust and almost loathing we watch this kind of temperament, these cattish displays of feline malice.' Mr A. J. Cummings, of the *News Chronicle*, carried these sentences of comment: 'Not within my recollection has any Member of Parliament received so severe a castigation as that administered by Miss Rathbone to Mr Aneurin Bevan. It might almost be described as a maternal spanking; and the House seemed to appreciate it to the full. Perhaps Mr Bevan will learn one day the difference between pointed parliamentary criticism and the wild cat's snarl.' Mr Cummings, in fact, had misrepresented the views of large numbers of M.P.s on this issue. Deeply as they resented Bevan's attacks on Churchill, they knew that other serving officers would not easily be able to engage in political controversy in the newspapers.

Council of Labour backed the whole Beveridge plan, particularly stressing the need for legislation before the end of the war. A Gallup poll showed that nine out of ten of the public agreed with them.

From the outset Bevan was unwilling to believe that the walls of the Tory Jericho would fall so easily. He was convinced that the Report would become a focus of conflict between the Parties, however much liberal enthusiasts might suppose that all men of goodwill would combine to make the dream come true. Like everything else the workers had ever achieved, the Beveridge Report would have to be fought for. Incidentally he could not regard it as the last word in social wisdom. Like many other Socialists, he had always been reluctant to agree to basing social services on insurance schemes, holding that the non-contributory principle could have the double advantage of avoiding unnecessary bureaucracy and a poll tax which masqueraded as an insurance premium. Yet the Report did challenge the niggardly conception of the social services approved by the Tories in the twenties and the thirties; it held out the promise of substantial, early improvements in benefits; and to cast away the massive support for it roused in the country would be an act of madness. A fresh opportunity was offered for exposing the real nature of the British political conflict.

Who could believe that the Tory-dominated Government intended to make Beveridge a reality, especially as in January 1943 Churchill reconstructed his Government in a manner which increased the Tory dominance? The War Cabinet was enlarged which meant that the three Labour Ministers within it were hopelessly outnumbered. It could not be overlooked that Arthur Greenwood, the originator of the Beveridge inquiry, had previously been removed from the Government altogether. Three men had been charged with the work of post-war planning, two of them Tories – Lord Portal and Mr W. S. Morrison. As for the third, Sir William Jowitt, he must be described, wrote Bevan in *Tribune*, as 'slightly mottled. Even if he turned over a new leaf and showed signs of embarrassing the Tories, they have already drawn his immature fangs by leaving him without a department.' Bevan derided the idea that a concerted, purposeful effort was now to be made to plan for the peace with Tory assistance. 'The Beveridge Report which was the one egg laid for post-war planning,' he wrote, 'the Tories are now doing their best to addle. They have entrusted further egg laying to a number of carefully selected and hopefully infertile hens. We must await their boastful if sterile cackle . . . There is one thought haunting the Tory Party and that is how they are going to cheat the progressive forces in the country. All the accumulated experience and craft of centuries of governing class rule are being devoted to this question.'

Today the warning may sound superfluous or banal. The Beveridge Report was not implemented until some five and a half years later and then only after Tory Chancellors and ex-Chancellors had delivered doleful prophecies about its cost and after the whole Tory Party had fought a long campaign against one part of it in particular, culminating in their last ditch fight to prevent the introduction of the National Health Service on 5 July 1948. At the time – in early 1943 – Bevan had discerned the truth about the political balance within the Cabinet which many were inclined to smudge or conceal. Unbeknown to the outside world, Churchill had in January and February circulated two memoranda to his Cabinet colleagues stating that he would not seek to implement Beveridge during the war or even make any firm promises about the post-war period.[17] He was tempted to dismiss ideas of planning for a better world as 'airy visions of Utopia and Eldorado'. In the light of these Churchillian decrees, it is evident that, consciously or unconsciously, his Ministers *were* engaged in a delaying action not so different from that which Bevan attributed to them.

The clash between Churchill's obduracy and the radical temper in the country – with the Labour Ministers unhappily placed as shock-absorbers in between – came in February 1943, when the Beveridge Report was first debated. The opening Government spokesmen spoke with such chilly vagueness about the possibilities of legislation that the Parliamentary Labour Party, despite their eagerness to avoid embarrassing the Labour Ministers, felt compelled to condemn the Government's attitude

17. *The Hinge of Fate* by Winston Churchill. Appendix F.

409

in what amounted to a vote of censure. Efforts were made by the Party leaders to avoid this indignity and a strong rumour ran through the lobbies that Ernest Bevin had threatened to resign if Labour M.P.s pressed their critical resolution to the voting lobbies. But threats could avail no more than Herbert Morrison's concluding speech in the Beveridge debate. Ninety-seven members of the Party – in other words, almost all those who were not directly or indirectly associated with the administration – voted against the advice of the Labour Ministers.

The Beveridge Report should have created a crisis for the Tories, not Labour. The chance was lost because the Labour Ministers so consistently underrated their strength in the country. It was the old disease in a new manifestation. By their compliance in the Cabinet, they created a situation where either they must be repudiated by their followers or the Labour Party must cut itself off from the swelling tide of national opinion. On this occasion the Parliamentary Party had refused to take the fatal course so strongly recommended by the men in the Government. Here, at least, was one merciful deliverance, and it pointed the course which Bevan more and more followed in the remaining years before 1945. The attitude of the Labour leaders was treated as a wretched, awkward irrelevance; with them or without them, the major task was to keep stoking the fires of public controversy.

Churchill himself came to his aid. Recognizing at last how irrepressible was the public interest in post-war reconstruction and hoping perhaps that the sentiment might be canalized in the direction he desired by his own intervention, he made a broadcast outlining in suitably opaque terms a Four Year Plan to be adopted after the war for providing food, homes and jobs. The appeal had some success. But wrapped in the rhetoric was a stick of political dynamite. Churchill envisaged that his plan would be presented to the country at the polls ' either by a National Government, formally representative, as this one is, of the three Parties in the State, or by a National Government comprising the best men in all Parties who are willing to serve'. Here was a direct revelation of Churchill's hope – or his plotting, if the hope should fail. 'Mr Churchill gives us plenty of notice,' said Bevan.

Churchill wanted a post-war Coalition in one form or another and believed he would be able to manoeuvre effectively to get it. He might think that the Tories by themselves, even with his own prestige, would not be able to win the election. He needed, as Bevan said, 'a few Left decoys', and some Labour Ministers were being groomed for the part, even if they were unconscious of it. The result, if Churchill got his way, would be 'the destruction of the forces of the Left'. Bevan gave plenty of notice too. A few days after Churchill's broadcast he made it clear that he would use all his energies to prevent Labour accepting any proposal in any form for a post-war Coalition with the Tories.

Hardly a month passed without some fresh illustration in the Commons of the painful dilemma in which Labour was placed. In May another row arose over a Pensions Bill. Forty Labour Members, led by Bevan, put down a motion condemning it since it offered no increase and rejecting the Ministerial plea that piecemeal increases would jeopardize the larger vision of Beveridge. Once again all the pressures were employed to persuade them to withdraw. When that failed, a Labour Minister was produced to repeat the appeal in the name of national unity. Bevan expressed his alarm at the gulf being dug not merely between the leaders and the rank-and-file in the Labour Party but between Parliament and the people. Had the Labour Ministers in the Cabinet pressed for the increase which every Labour M.P. believed to be justified? If not, they should be ashamed of themselves. But if they had, was this not yet another case of their being blackmailed into submission by the Tory majority in the Cabinet which reflected no Tory majority in the country? And if this was the Tory attitude, what faith could be placed in *any* of their post-war promises? On this occasion fifty-nine Labour M.P.s voted against the Government. Once more the Party meeting rebuked the rebels and reaffirmed the Standing Orders. The logic of the leaders' demand was that every agreement reached by them in the Cabinet should be underwritten at the private Party meeting. But who would dare call that parliamentary government?

Bevan looked to the Party Conference in June 1943 for one release from the parliamentary impasse. 'It is characteristic of

British Labour,' he wrote, 'that it never examines the assumptions on which it acts. It is therefore always the servant and never the master of events.' Maintaining the electoral truce and joining with the Tories in producing post-war plans might easily mean that a Coalition would be thought advantageous for carrying through the plans later. Moreover, in all the Cabinet discussions, Labour had no sanction; what trade union leader would go into negotiations assuring the employer that in no circumstances would he contemplate a strike? Bevan's remedy was *not* that Labour should withdraw from the Government; the effect on the war effort might be too serious. But he urged an absolutely clear declaration by the Party that it would fight independently of the Tories at the first post-war election and meantime that it would hold itself free to break the by-election truce on a particular issue if the Tories continued their delaying tactics on Beveridge and other questions. His idea could not be put in this precise form to the Conference. There, a direct vote on the ending of the electoral truce was defeated by 2,243,000 to 374,000, a much bigger majority for the platform than the one they had secured on a similar issue the year before.

Bevan came away from this Conference greatly disturbed. He could see no reflection at it of the eager, adventurous spirit sweeping through the country, particularly among the young, nor even of the more robust attitude beginning to stir among a minority of Labour M.P.s. The Party's real dilemma had never even been faced. In the Commons, Labour's tenuous hold on the public feeling had only been sustained by a repudiation of the Labour Ministers. In the country, candidates put up by the new Common Wealth Party formed by Sir Richard Acland had been breaking the truce and winning spectacular victories, with the evident approval of the bulk of Labour voters and against all the advice of the Labour leaders. Yet at the Conference, after perfunctory debates, Common Wealth was made a proscribed organization, unqualified allegiance to the electoral truce was renewed, and approval was bestowed on policy statements of bewildering ambiguity. On the Beveridge Report, Attlee protested that the Government had accepted its principles, and that 'every phase of it, every aspect of its assumptions, is being pursued day by day with the utmost vigour'. Complete, uncritical support of the Government was all he and the other Ministers asked for. If such leadership had its way, the national awakening would be shackled by discipline and drenched in complacency.

Bevan's analysis of what had happened at the Conference was significant since it included the most explicit statement he had yet made about a quarrel he was to pursue, intermittently, for the rest of his life. He had enemies enough already, but he now challenged another – the most formidable and apparently impervious and irremovable force in the Labour movement. In his pre-war battles he had often protested against what he regarded as the baneful and bureaucratic power granted by Labour's Constitution to the leaders of a few big unions. Increasingly, in the House of Commons, he had complained of the practice whereby Ministers consulted with outside bodies, including the General Council of the T.U.C., and then confronted Parliament with something near a *fait accompli*.

During the weeks just prior to the 1943 Conference the General Council had committed what he considered to be two other offences. After the Beveridge vote, the General Council had stepped in to throw its cloak of approval over the Labour Ministers whose attitude had been repudiated by the Parliamentary Party. It had been the chief bulwark upholding the caution of the leadership. And yet when the General Council had its own quarrel with the Government – over the operation of the Trade Disputes Act of 1927 which forbade certain unions from joining the T.U.C. – it threatened to defy the Government and take action which might lead to the withdrawal of the Labour Ministers from it without consulting the Parliamentary Party at all. The latest T.U.C. pronouncement in this dispute had been read to the Party Conference in a hushed accent by the Chairman who also appealed to delegates not to discuss at all the affairs of the all-wise General Council. Needless to say, Bevan's case was not that the General Council had no right to quarrel with the Government and less still that the unions had no important role to play in wartime. His charge was that all too often the union leaders failed to represent their members and revealed little understanding of 'the problem facing us – how so to manage our affairs that the industrial strength of Labour is reinforced by the idealism which resides in the political awakening of the younger generation'.

Once Bevan had decided to make the challenge he delivered it with characteristic audacity. Some trade union leaders, he said, show 'a contempt for Parliament which is only equalled by the leaders of the German Labour Front'. In their action over the Trade Disputes Act, they had shown a similar contempt for the Party Conference. They seemed to imagine that both M.P.s and Conference delegates had no other duty but to take their orders. 'Of course, the Executive of the Party connived at this affront to the Conference because its majority is composed of stooges of the trade union leaders. Can anyone wonder why it is that in these circumstances the local Labour Parties are unable to recruit considerable numbers of young men and women? Why should young people pour their energies into a Party where they would be the marionettes of a clique of trade union bosses who owe their power to the cunning with which they manipulate the social democratic machine.' In short, Bevan suspected, with much justice, that several of the union leaders had no faith in a great Left-wing victory after the war;[18] they were more attracted by the increasing influence they could exert behind the scenes with Ministers from all Parties. The General Council might easily become the foremost advocate of a continuance of the Coalition. Bevan believed that the danger could best be averted by exposing it to public scrutiny. And despite his depression at the Conference, he was still exhilarated by the trend of opinion outside. 'The country,' he said (this was 18 June 1943), 'is moving and will continue to move Left. The Tories need us. We don't need them. They have only one asset, and we are partly responsible for it. That is Churchill. But he is already an old man, and we shall witness quite a number of changes yet which will tend to reduce the glamour of his name to rational and manageable limits.'

18. Sir Walter Citrine, General Secretary of the T.U.C., was one of the union leaders who was convinced that Churchill and the Tories would be elected easily after the war. He freely expressed this view in private right up till 1945.

He had his own remedies for the disease which he thought was afflicting the Labour Party and they went deeper than any prescriptions to be applied to the immediate tactical situation presented by Labour's minority position in the wartime Coalition. The first, adumbrated in an article in *Tribune* in August, was concerned with the role of the trade unions. Of course, he was never anti-trade union, as his enemies were quick to allege. 'The broad industrial basis among the masses,' he said, brought to the Labour Party 'invaluable advantages of traditional loyalties and the refreshment of practical urgencies in everyday life.' The unions would be an indispensable instrument in securing further social changes. But somehow the trade unions no longer brought the impact of the masses to bear on the making of Labour policy. Each union was affiliated to the Labour Party as a national body and this gave to the official apparatus of the union an exaggerated power. 'The union as an institution is enfranchised within the Labour Party, but the union membership is not.' Bevan proposed that trade union affiliation to the Labour Party should be exclusively through their local branches to the local divisional Labour Parties. This would distribute power instead of concentrating it in the head offices. It would depress the political status of the leaders and elevate that of the rank-and-file. It would produce immediate democratic invigoration. 'It would make the Labour Party a mass party at one stroke.' The reform, which Bevan advocated at intervals for the rest of his life, still looks a long way off.

His other remedy could be applied more swiftly; it was to make Members of Parliament recognize their individual responsibilities in the face of pressures from Ministers, General Councils, private Party meetings or anybody else. A concrete example of what he meant occurred in October 1943 when after long delay the Government produced a Workmen's Compensation Bill, the detailed provisions of which had been agreed in advance by the employers and the General Council of the T.U.C. When Labour members moved amendments they were told, first at the Party meeting and later in the Commons, that they should not disturb a compromise so carefully arrived at. Bevan accused those responsible for the negotiations of being guilty of 'the gravest constitutional impropriety'. Or must all Labour Members have a stereotyped election address reading as follows: 'I promise that at any time when a matter comes before the House I shall act in such matter as the T.U.C. instructs me'? Bevan defined his own constitutional doctrine in defiant terms. 'I do not represent the F.B.I., nor do I represent the T.U.C. I happen to represent constituents in Ebbw Vale. When I go back to my constituents I expect them to hold me to account for what I have done, and I do not expect, if they disagree with anything I have done, to be able to explain it away by saying that I did it on the instruction of some outside body. I do not want to adopt that alibi. I think it is dishonourable and dangerously subversive of parliamentary institutions.'

Herbert Morrison, in charge of the Bill, hit back as hard as he could. When a group of miners' M.P.s persisted with their amendment, he said that it would wreck the compromise and threatened to withdraw the Bill altogether. Bevan counterattacked unmercifully. It was, said one reporter, 'a real old-time row'. Describing Morrison's attitude as that of 'a squalid backstairs Tammany Hall politician',[19] Bevan accused him of 'wallowing in self-pity' over the plight in which he had placed himself. He should have known better. 'We represent the rank-and-file far more than do the trade union leaders.' As for Morrison's threat, M.P.s could not be 'bullied and blackmailed' for ever. A threat must be answered by a threat. If the Home Secretary did withdraw the Bill, Bevan promised he would stump the coalfields and back strike action. One young Tory, Quintin Hogg, leapt to Morrison's defence.[20] Bevan, he said, had shown himself 'an

19. This is the phrase as reported in *Hansard*, although in the popular recollection Bevan was thought to have described Morrison as 'a third-rate Tammany Hall boss'.
20. Bevan had several exchanges at this time with members of the Tory Reform Committee which had just been formed, with Viscount Hinchingbrooke as its chairman and Quintin Hogg (now Lord Hailsham) as one of its principal members. 'The reformists in the Conservative Party,' said Bevan, 'have always been progressive young men walking backwards with their faces to the future. They always say to us "Look where we are looking" and we should say to them, "Look where you are going" . . . I have watched with surprise the gnarled old oak (of the Conservative Party) sprouting and budding with considerable promise, but the leaves have been blighted and have in the past fallen from the tree long before it came to fruition.'

enemy of democracy, an enemy of his country, an enemy of the organized working-class movement'. Was not his talk of strike action a repudiation of the very parliamentary principles of which he claimed to be the guardian? But Mr Hogg did not go unanswered. Why should the workers respect a decision of Parliament which had been 'rigged' before it ever reached Parliament? 'Trade union leaders and Ministers of the Crown,' said Bevan, 'set the Constitution on one side and expect ordinary workmen to pay more respect to it than they do themselves.' On this particular occasion forty-two Labour rebels were excoriated at the Party meeting for daring to vote five shillings extra for miners under the Workmen's Compensation Bill.

Mr Hogg could not be expected to appreciate the special inhibitions in performing their parliamentary duties suffered by Labour M.P.s. On other occasions Bevan attacked on a wider front. Nearly two hundred M.P.s were tied by their jobs to support of the Churchill administration. Churchill had encouraged younger Members to go into the forces and in addition had introduced a system whereby certificates of absence from the Commons were granted by him to those he wished to send abroad on diplomatic or military missions. The Disqualification Act which permitted this system provoked Bevan's ire whenever it came up for renewal. 'The Prime Minister,' he said, 'distributes his certificates like confetti. He uses them to relieve himself of political embarrassment.' Even more questionable was the manner in which expense accounts were allowed to M.P.s on Government duties; Bevan had asked the Treasury for details, but none had been forthcoming. 'When a man gets up on those benches to support the Government, you do not know what Government money is in his pocket. That is a very serious state of affairs ... The power of the executive to confer financial benefits upon members of this House should be carefully scrutinized. It affects the very citadel of the British Constitution.'

These insinuations were denounced as wild and disgraceful. Bevan's outburst was compared unfavourably with the intervention in the same debate of James Maxton who declared that the House of Commons in his experience was 'a pretty clean place'. So no doubt it was. But Bevan's major charge could not be so easily parried. Increasingly the executive established its hold over the wartime House of Commons, whereas, in Bevan's view, the chief function of the House of Commons was to control the executive. A Churchill certificate permitting an M.P. to absent himself from the House of Commons for months, even years, was a wartime convenience; it was also a constitutional monstrosity.

Few of Bevan's speeches during the war – not even his most violent onslaughts on Churchill – caused more anger than the series he delivered on the status of Parliament. He seemed to be deliberately insulting his fellow Members. Yet it is hard to see how the three-pronged attack – on the failure to keep a sufficient number of Members independent of the executive, on the illicit deference to outside bodies, and on the invasion of Members' rights by the secret Party meetings – can be confuted on grounds of parliamentary principle. He saw the Churchill régime as one that by 'the unobserved accretion of malpractice' was reviving some of the worst features of eighteenth-century parliamentary methods. He recalled the long battles against allowing Members to hold offices of profit under the Crown, how in order to guard against this peril the framers of the American Constitution had decided that no member of the executive could retain a seat in Congress. 'The power of the people over the Government,' he wrote, 'is preserved by the vote at election, but that power is taken away again if those they elect fall under the control of the Government.' The sentence carries a flavour of John Wilkes or Junius whom he was reading at the time. And when Anthony Eden replied to his speech on the Disqualification Bill with the claim that high office was a burdensome, badly-rewarded occupation, Bevan in *Tribune* treated him to a reply which Junius would have applauded.

If [he wrote] we could only penetrate the veil which conceals from us the privacy of their [the Ministers'] lives, we would be able to understand and sympathize with a situation so different from what we had been led to expect. Here is a man going about his dimly lit but enviable activities as an ordinary private Member of the House of Commons. If he is not careless, at least he is carefree. He has nothing to furrow his brow but an occasional embarrassment from a constituent, and even here he has erected between him and them the political benediction of the electoral truce. So here we have this happy man, secure, comfortable and mainly passive. Suddenly, without warning, a message comes from Number 10 Downing Street demanding his immediate presence. With a sinking feeling, and invaded by a dread of things to come, he obeys the summons, as indeed he must, for is he not dedicated to a life of self-sacrifice? When he arrives with lagging steps, he finds his worst fears are confirmed. He is called to high office in the Government. It is this point which calls for special attention. It is remarkable and inspiring testimony to the kind of men who serve us in our political life, that despite the circumstances described by Mr Eden last week there is hardly an example on record of any man having refused the Prime Minister's call. Nor, except for the well-upholstered crown of thorns which Mr Chamberlain thrust on Eden's own brow, is there any instance in recent years of one of them having given up office voluntarily. In face of this selfless devotion, the voices of the critics should now be silent in reverence.

More serious from the point of view of Bevan's own career were the particular accusations he made against his own Party's connivance at practices derogatory to Parliament. An attack on the General Council of the T.U.C. was a form of Labour *lèse-majesté*. His disrespect for the Party meeting, apart from the constitutional aspects of the case, was intimately associated with the general debate about Labour's and the Coalition's future. There, in secret, the leaders held the whiphand and they wanted to permit no weakening of it. All power to the Party meeting was the watchword of the leadership throughout most of Bevan's political life. In wartime the slogan was especially insidious. Twenty of the leaders held Ministerial posts; their Parliamentary Private Secretaries felt obliged to vote with them; and those hopeful of future favours might be expected to be at least equally compliant. The leadership started each debate with an almost automatic majority on its side, a fact which made the Beveridge revolt all the more remarkable. There too the private Member could escape from his public accountability by pleading that, whatever his own judgements or the demands of his constituents, he had acted loyally in conformity with his Party.

Herbert Morrison, as Bevan admitted, did have his solution for the problem presented to Labour by the wartime Coalition. He argued that only a tighter discipline within the Parliamentary Party could avoid the persistent divisions which might cause people to distrust Labour's capacity to govern. 'He was bitterly angry the other day,' wrote Bevan, 'because a number of Labour M.P.s exposed the shortcomings of his Workmen's Compensation Bill. His solution is not a better Compensation Act, but silent M.P.s. Naturally, if you are doing something you know you ought not to do, then you would like to do it as unobtrusively as possible. That would be nice for harassed Ministers, but neither the Labour Party nor Parliament itself could survive such a "solution".' Bevan's solution, on the other hand, was that Labour must accept the impossibility of the Coalition Government agreeing on satisfactory measures for post-war Britain, that it must prepare and present to the country its own programme, and that Labour M.P.s worth their salt must exercise their independence to help secure this result. Subsequent revelations by Labour Ministers go far to confirm his view about the whole Beveridge controversy. Whatever assurances Attlee might use to sway the Party Conference or the Party meeting, the Cabinet, under Churchill's direction, was engaged in a deliberate stalling action about all major proposals for post-war reform.[21]

At first Bevan seemed to win few adherents for the course of action he advised. After the sharp spasm of revolt over Beveridge, the Parliamentary Party relapsed into acquiescence once more. His diatribes against the Ministers no doubt contributed further to his unpopularity.[22] At the beginning of the autumn session

21. Hugh Dalton writes in *The Fateful Years*: 'Following acrimonious debates and votes in Parliament about Bevin's Catering Bill and the Beveridge Report, Churchill became still more allergic to post-war policy. He was concerned to hold his Government together. He skilfully encouraged irrelevance and delay.' And Herbert Morrison writes in his *Autobiography*: 'My feelings were that the Government were being half-hearted about the way to prepare for post-war problems. It is true that some gestures were made, as with the Beveridge Report. And in November, 1943, Lord Woolton left the Ministry of Food to become Minister of Reconstruction. He was, I think, beset by opposition from the Tories. Churchill was not going to tolerate any possible division within the Conservative Party because of alleged pressure by the Labour Party to prepare schemes of reform when the war was over.'
22. Another controversy at this time broke out over Herbert Morrison's decision to release Oswald Mosley from detention on grounds of his ill-health. However, this revolt was more respectable, since Ernest Bevin and his henchmen were seen deliberately encouraging it in the Commons lobbies. Morrison claimed to have acted in a judicial capacity, but this did not prevent him from invoking Party discipline to help make up the minds of Labour

in 1943 he stood again for the Administrative Committee and received only twenty-nine votes, several fewer even than the year before. Shinwell, elected the year before, was thrown off. 'Mr Aneurin Bevan,' wrote the *Manchester Guardian*, 'has sustained his reputation as the most fluent and telling speaker on the Labour benches, but a copious vocabulary does not make a statesman.'

Few people in 1943 would have dissented from the *Manchester Guardian*'s verdict; no one saw Aneurin Bevan as a statesman. Even those compelled to acknowledge his brilliant gifts tended to dismiss him as a man of no judgement. Yet during that same period when he was pursuing his argument with the Labour leaders about post-war policy he was expressing views on the development of the war – mostly in defiance of orthodox or popular opinion – which can bear scrutiny today.

He was, for example, a strong opponent of the demand for the 'Unconditional Surrender' of all the enemies of the United Nations made by Churchill and Roosevelt at Casablanca. He admitted that this declaration might be regarded as 'a desirable war-whoop outlawing the more obvious types of appeasement' and designed to reassure Stalin. But a moment's consideration revealed serious disadvantages. Bevan feared that the formula would be used to injure the encouragement of the revolutionary forces in Europe, specifically mentioning Italy as one country where a political weapon more delicate than a sledge-hammer might be wielded. A British policy which embraced Admiral Darlan while keeping Italian revolutionaries at arm's length might need the cover of 'Unconditional Surrender' to conceal its lack of astuteness. Bevan and the others who protested against the Casablanca declaration were branded, sometimes by ex-Munichites and apologists for the Darlan deal, as men who had no stomach to see the war through to the end.

M.P.s if unhappily they did not reach the right conclusion on the merits of the matter without this assistance. Bevan played no leading part in this dispute, but he was sceptical about the bouquets offered to Morrison for his courage. He wrote: 'It is almost becoming a definition of courage in a Labour leader that he defies his followers.'

But, in the light of what Churchill and others have since revealed, the 'Unconditional Surrender' story now looks rather different. The declaration was produced on the final day at Casablanca by Roosevelt after vague consultations but without Churchill's precise prior agreement. Many years later, Ernest Bevin, in an interchange with Churchill, complained both that the policy itself had aggravated post-war problems in Europe and that the War Cabinet at the time had never been properly consulted. Churchill was able to disprove this second accusation; he showed that the only point at which the War Cabinet had cavilled was Churchill's own preference for the exclusion of Italy from the declaration's scope. Today it is evident that the criticisms about the 'Unconditional Surrender' policy which Bevan voiced at the time were shared in the highest quarters. Another reason why he opposed the idea so clumsily concocted at Casablanca was the support it appeared to give to the racialist campaigns conducted by Lord Vansittart, assisted at times by some prominent trade union leaders. British opinion during the Second World War remained remarkably unaffected by the crude anti-Hun propaganda which had been prominent and influential in the First World War. Some people, however, did seek to beat the racialist drum. Bevan and *Tribune* consistently denounced a form of demagogy which they believed could only lengthen the war and injure the chances of securing a healthy peace. 'To talk at the moment,' he wrote in June 1943 'of the general guilt of the German people, as a whole, for the behaviour of the Nazis is both unwise and inexpedient. Nor is it a decent spectacle to see certain people indulge their blood pressure at the expense of the young men who have to do their will in the plane, the battleship and on the battlefield. Let us do what we must. But no more, lest every excess be paid for in the suffering and bloodshed of the innocent.' Hitler, he said, was the best witness that there were some good Germans; if there had not been, why was it necessary for him first 'to gag, bully and intimidate the German people'? 'It is essential to grasp firmly the principle that men and women are more the creatures of their social institutions and their political machinery than they are of their bloodstreams and of their remote history.' Of course, Germany must be kept disarmed; nobody disputed that. But she must be allowed to live; otherwise the disease would fester again. Bevan particularly urged in this article that the duty of Socialists must be to encourage their fellow Socialists in the post-war Germany. 'The City will look after its own. Cannot we look after ours?'

This was one of the issues debated in June 1943 at the Labour Party Conference which had left Bevan so disheartened. A resolution opposing 'the imposition of a treaty of revenge' upon the German people was defeated in favour of a much tougher one backed by some of the big trade union leaders. A meeting was called immediately after the Conference by some of the delegates, including Bevan, where a resolution was passed expressing 'indignation that the Labour movement should be made to appear to share the detestable views which have come to be known as "Vansittartism".' Bevan's association with this resolution provided another fine opening for his enemies. 'All his perverted rhetoric,' wrote the *Western Mail*, 'is directed towards mitigating the retribution that is awaiting the enemy. He sheds crocodile tears, but views the ghastly spectacle of their ravaged victims without protest.' The accusation of demagogy so frequently made against him appears especially inapposite to his thought and utterances on the German question. He upheld the same view about Germany both during the war and after: keep her disarmed and let her live. He did not need to eat his words later. Some statesmen were not so fortunate.[23]

More urgent and acute than these controversies about the post-war world was another which Bevan initiated on the treatment of Italy, after the fall of Mussolini in July 1943. Since Churchill himself had wished to exclude Italy from the terms of the 'Unconditional Surrender' formula, it must have been galling

23. During the debate at the Labour Party Conference Mr Lincoln Evans (now Sir Lincoln) quoted with evident approval a speech by Mr Herbert Morrison. 'After this war is won,' Mr Morrison had said, 'Europe will be in a state of great confusion and Germany cannot be permitted to take advantage of it. We must sit on the Germans' necks militarily, and control them, but not for two years only. The control ought to be applied for twenty years, and even for one hundred if necessary.' Mr Morrison in the fifties became the leading Labour supporter of German rearmament. Bevan still argued that Germany should be kept disarmed.

for him when Bevan criticized the inhibitions imposed by it on making a speedy and fruitful peace with the Italians. But this was only one small aspect of a great argument. Churchill saw in the overthrow of Mussolini by the Fascist Grand Council, King Victor Emmanuel and Marshal Badoglio a convenient palace revolution which, exploited with diplomatic delicacy, could be used to expedite his Mediterranean strategy. Bevan saw an awakening of revolutionary ardour among the Italian people which could help to instil the same spirit across the whole Continent. The romantic streak in both men coloured their judgements. Churchill was a royal romantic, Bevan became at times a revolutionary romantic. 'Think of it; a free Italy!' For him, as for Byron, it was 'the very poetry of politics'. And his swift intuition about the Italian resurgence was largely confirmed by events, whereas Churchill's nostalgic allegiance to the Italian monarchy was to bring in its train many painful defeats for British diplomacy. The case is crucial for an appreciation of Bevan's conduct in 1943 and 1944. He believed that Churchill's blindness to the revolutionary impulses at work in Europe might lengthen the war, add to the toll of slaughter and maim the new society struggling to be born. These were charges too serious for an honest man to deliver in tentative and muffled language.

Churchill spoke in the House of Commons two days after Mussolini had been overthrown and imprisoned on the instructions of King Victor Emmanuel. He gave his own verdict on the great event and deprecated any comment by others. His advice was that the Italians should be left 'to stew in their own juice for a bit until we obtain from their Government, or whoever possesses the necessary authority, all the indispensable requirements we demand for carrying on the war against our prime and capital foe, which is not Italy, but Germany'. The appeal for statesman-like restraint rarely fails to win a reverent response in the House of Commons. The men presumed to know unpublishable facts are thought to be wiser than those who seek to apply first principles. But Bevan and a few others pressed for a full debate.

They might have pressed even more strongly if they had known of the communications between Roosevelt and Churchill on the subject a few days later. Roosevelt told Churchill that the same people who had made 'such a fuss' over the deal with Darlan were threatening to 'make a row if we seem to recognize the House of Savoy or Badoglio'. Churchill replied that he had no worries on that score. He would recognize the House of Savoy or Badoglio if they served 'our war purposes' – purposes which could be only injured by 'chaos, Bolshevization or civil war'. He believed that these authorities offered the best instrument for maintaining order. True, he did envisage that the Crown Prince Umberto and a new Prime Minister might have to take over if the King and Badoglio 'sank under the odium of surrender'.[24] So small was his comprehension of the true situation in Italy. The chief odium to fall on the King and Badoglio – apart from that arising from their earlier crimes in the service of Mussolini – was to be due to their failure to make the swiftest possible surrender, an act urged upon them at the time by the Italian revolutionaries and one which could have been of immense benefit to the Allied cause. After an interview a few days later with Badoglio, Ivanhoe Bonomi, the aged ex-Premier who had come forward as a spokesman for the revolutionaries, said: 'he [Badoglio] does not understand democratic necessities'.[25] Nor, on this occasion, did Churchill.

It should not have been so difficult to decipher what was happening. Churchill claims that he had 'long pondered' (starting some eight months before) on the measures that would be necessary in the event of an Italian collapse. These ponderings, it seems, took no account of the huge strike wave which had swept Milan, Turin and other parts of Northern Italy in January, February and March. Nor were they assisted by news from the Italian underground of the formation of an Anti-Fascist United Freedom Front in April and the decision of groups representing this body in July to take insurrectionary action if the plotters against Mussolini in the Court and the Army failed to move. Churchill's own memoirs make no mention whatever of the influence of the underground movement. Often still today in

24. *The Closing of the Ring* by Winston Churchill.
25. Quoted in *Mussolini's Enemies, The Italian Anti-Fascist Resistance* by Charles E. Delzell (Princeton University Press), the most detailed description of the role of the Italian resistance from which many of the facts in this section are taken.

other accounts the myth is sustained that the famous debate at the Fascist Grand Council, when Grandi, Ciano and other Fascist leaders turned on their Duce, was the single effective stroke in the *coup d'état*. Yet the revolutionaries had been exerting their pressure long before by strike action and through Bonomi's representations to the King. If the Fascist Grand Council had never met, a move against Mussolini could not have been long postponed. This background, apart from the news about the strikes, was not known in Britain at the time. But when the great day of Mussolini's destruction came, all the world could see and hear what happened in Rome, Milan and other Italian cities. Huge crowds swept through the streets singing patriotic songs and shouting 'Down with Fascism'. The clandestine parties quickly produced special editions of their newspapers. Badoglio's slogans – 'let everyone return now to his post . . . the war continues' – were drowned in the din. 'This is an Italian Revolution', wrote *Tribune* on 30 July. Certainly it was one of the historic moments of the war. And the moment was lost.

The British Parliament was preparing to adjourn for the summer recess. Bevan pressed urgently for a debate and, when Anthony Eden said that the Cabinet had unanimously decided not to have one, coolly announced that he could not accede to their wish. He gave notice that a debate on the forbidden topic would take place on the Consolidated Fund Bill a few days later – the annual Bill on which Members are entitled to raise any grievance they wish before supplies are voted. So the House of Commons did discuss the Italian crisis in its very first days. Bevan was called 'mischievous' and 'irresponsible' for initiating the debate and even more mischievous and irresponsible after he had spoken. At the time such charges sound portentous. Yet none of the annals of the war – not even Churchill's – record that Bevan's intervention produced any of the dire effects on the war effort and the peace negotiations with Italy forecast in that debate by grave, minatory and aspiring back benchers or Parliamentary Private Secretaries.

Bevan's case comprised a criticism, an analysis, a warning – and another frontal attack on Churchill. After the Government's treatment of Darlan and de Gaulle ('the gentleman has awkward corners, like we all have') he was deeply suspicious of the Government's attitude to the resistance movements in Europe. Parliament had no right to leave the political decisions to generals on the spot. Much too much was at stake. In Sicily and Italy, it was evident, the political arm was as important as the military arm. The real blow against the Fascist dictatorship had been struck by the Italian workers; that was a source of great gratification and hope for the future. Yet all the advantages of the situation could be squandered if the wrong decisions were made. Were the King and Badoglio to be the British and American Quislings in Italy? If so, millions of potential allies in Europe would be thrown away. How shameful and disastrous it would be if Britain accepted responsibility for shooting down Italians quarrelling with their masters. And who could trust Churchill to deal with such a problem? 'The Prime Minister has got very many virtues and when the time comes I hope to pay my tribute to them, but I am bound to say that political honesty and sagacity have never been among them.' Bevan then recited, amid ever angrier interruptions, the speech which Churchill had delivered on a visit to Rome in 1927 when he had paid tribute to Mussolini's 'gentle and simple' bearing, his statesmanship, his services not only to Italy but to all Europe in rescuing his country from Bolshevism. Does anyone think, said Bevan, that Socialists could go away for the summer recess 'leaving the political architecture of Italy to a mind that reasons like that? ... There are Members in this House who have no complaint against Fascism, except when it is strong enough to threaten them ... But the people of Great Britain are hoping, desperately hoping, that in Italy the ordinary people of Italy will overthrow the existing régime.'

These warnings and aspirations might be condemned as outrageous in the House of Commons. In Rome they would have sounded more relevant. There, Badoglio was busy suppressing the underground newspapers, banning 'disturbances', firing on demonstrators, attempting to forbid the operation of political parties and establishing a Ministry which reflected not at all the hopes and ambitions of the ordinary people of Italy. On 5 August Churchill transmitted to Roosevelt a report which an Italian emissary had brought to the British Ambassador in Lisbon and which Churchill pronounced to be of 'substantial' worth. The report included this account of the social upheaval in the country: 'Italy turned Red overnight. In Turin and Milan there were Communist demonstrations which had to be put down by armed force. Twenty years of Fascism have obliterated the middle class. There is nothing between the King, with the Patriots who have rallied round him, who have complete control, and rampant Bolshevism.'[26] It is not fanciful or unfair to suppose that Churchill accepted this delineation of the Italian scene; at least it fed his prejudices. Yet the picture was completely false. Communist influence among the revolutionaries was strong, but certainly not predominant. The so-called Patriots around the King were not in complete control; they were attempting to stultify the revolution and were impeding the swift achievement of a peace, thus giving the Germans precious time to prepare their counter-stroke. It is dangerous for a statesman to accept and act upon assumptions so grotesquely at variance with modern realities. And that was the core of Bevan's accusation.

Some two months later, when the House of Commons debated the same subject again – on 22 September – the Italian situation had deteriorated swiftly and tragically. In August the Allies bombed Milan and other of the northern cities, ostensibly to speed the Armistice negotiations with the Badoglio Government. But these were the centres of the revolution ('Must we do Badoglio's dirty work for him?' asked Bevan). On 1 September the Armistice was secretly signed and on 8 September it was publicly announced. On 9 September the King and Badoglio left Rome for Brindisi, making no provision for the administration of the city and leaving anarchy behind until the Germans took over. Some Italian soldiers argued that Rome could have been defended.[27] However questionable the claim, what is certain is that the panic-stricken King gave no thought to the possibility. On that same day – forty-five days after the overthrow of Mussolini – the Allies made their landings at Salerno in the teeth of fierce German opposition. Thanks to the failure of the Badoglio Government to declare peace at once on 25 July, the military

26. *The Closing of the Ring* by Winston Churchill.
27. See *Mussolini's Enemies* by Charles Delzell.

situation had been transformed in a manner most injurious both to the Allies and to the Italian revolutionaries. Four German divisions had been able to escape from Sicily. Others had been ordered southward. Meantime, in Rome and the northern cities, the revolutionaries formed Committees of National Liberation on a basis openly hostile to the Badoglio régime. These were to provide the soul and sinews of the Italian resistance.

Churchill's main aim in the Commons debate was to rebut the charge that the military operations against Italy had been unconscionably slow. In fact the Salerno landing had taken place six days before it was originally planned and Churchill ridiculed those who 'talked of throwing armies ashore here and there as if they were goods to be dumped on a beach and forgotten'. The protracted peace negotiations, he claimed, had not adversely affected the position; 'the truth is that the armistice was delayed to fit in with the attack, and not that the attack was delayed to fit in with the announcement'. Even so, criticism of the military operations was at least arguable. They had appeared to take no sufficient advantage of the internal collapse in Italy, evident before the fall of Mussolini and confirmed by it.[28] Much more vulnerable, however, was Churchill's political case. He gave wholehearted backing to the King and Badoglio and urged that 'all surviving forces of Italian life should be rallied together round their lawful Government'. When one Member interjected: 'You will not get the people to rise behind the banner of turncoats,' Churchill replied that the critic had not given sufficient importance to diminishing the burden falling on our own soldiers. This was the stock-in-trade of the Government's apologists. Military expediency dictated their political arrangements.

Churchill claimed that this speech 'convinced the House' and that there was no 'effective challenge'.[29] But Bevan's reply accorded with the facts in Italy, if not with the temper of the House. 'On the Prime Minister's own statement he does not

28. Churchill himself acknowledged, much later in a speech on 24 May 1944, that Allied military action after Mussolini's fall 'might have been more swift and audacious . . . it is no part of my submission to the House that no mistakes are made by us or by the common action of our Allies.'
29. *The Closing of the Ring* by Winston Churchill.

understand what is happening in Italy. The right hon. Gentleman says that he knew nothing about the Badoglio régime.
Political myopia could not be greater.' The British Government
had completely failed to realize the revolutionary nature of the
Italian rising.[30]

But Churchill was not to be budged, particularly as none of
the Labour Ministers in the Cabinet and so few in the House of
Commons dared to raise their voices. He bombarded an increasingly sceptical Washington with demands for full support for
the King Victor–Badoglio régime, did his best to ban demonstrations of protest in Italy and, when Roosevelt and Cordell Hull
became more insistent that some modest Leftward changes must
be made in the personnel of the Italian administration, played for
time with tireless ingenuity. 'Be careful,' he wrote to his Minister
in Algiers, Harold Macmillan, 'that nothing is done to make the
King and Badoglio weaker than they are. On the contrary, we
must hold them and carry them forward with our armies.' Any
talk of reconstruction of the Government must be held up till
Rome was captured. 'In Rome lie the title deeds of Italy and of
the Catholic Church. Badoglio and the King reinstated there will
have a far better chance of rallying such elements of Italian
strength as exist.'[31] But the title deeds of the Italian revolution
were not in Rome; that was a city handed over as a shambles by
this same King and his Minister to the mercies of the Nazis. The
real title deeds were in Milan and Turin and in countless towns
and villages and mountainside retreats where the Committees of
Liberation were gathering the elements of Italian strength. They

30. An indication of the role being played by King Victor Emmanuel is
given in an extract dated 31 October 1943, from the diary of Benedetto
Croce – *Croce, The King and the Allies*, translated by Sylvia Sprigge: 'I spoke
with Sforza and then with Sforza and Badoglio together. We showed
him that it was desirable to induce the King to abdicate because there is no
other way out. Badoglio seemed to me to be already persuaded of this; he
says the King will not hear of it, and Badoglio who is an old military man and
is bound by his oath, would certainly not take violent action. He referred
to the long struggle he had had to wage with the King to induce him to
declare war on Germany. Badoglio fears that if he withdraws and, seeing the
refusals of all those who have been asked, no political Ministry can be
formed, the King will begin thinking of some other military personality with
whom to make a military dictatorship.'
31. *The Closing of the Ring* by Winston Churchill.

had already saved the lives of thousands of British prisoners; they were to make a splendid contribution to the Allied cause.

In December, in another big war debate, Bevan drew a broader moral. 'The Italian people gave us Italy,' he said, 'we failed to take advantage of it.' How much longer were we to bolster up the tottering Badoglio régime? And where else were we to suffer from similar delusions about the popular feeling in Europe? Was it true that we had entered into obligations to perform for King George of Greece the same services we had rendered to King Victor of Italy? And what was the reason for the interminable delay in recognizing the power of Marshal Tito in Yugoslavia? 'The purblind adherence to reactionary forces in Europe is costing thousands of British lives.'

By this time, however, the Allied armies had become bogged down south of Rome. If the point of going to Italy was not to exploit the Italian revolution with the utmost speed, what was the real purpose behind the whole campaign? Bevan reverted to his general criticisms of the Mediterranean strategy. 'The whole of this country wants to know what strategical conception behind the war put the British and American armies to fight their way right up the whole peninsula in the autumn and winter ... Does anybody suggest to me that is a wise strategy? It is nonsense. Is that the "soft underbelly of the Axis"? We are climbing up the backbone.' This was one of Bevan's retorts to Churchill which became famous. Hitler, continued Bevan, had for three years been allowed to put our forces in a series of concentration camps and immobilize them. He was tying down our armies much more than we were tying down his. We were engaging considerably less German forces than the Yugoslav underground. General Eisenhower had boasted that in Italy we were getting much closer to the vitals of the enemy. But in fact the Germans had been able to transfer divisions from Italy to Russia at the height of the battle raging at Kiev. 'Indeed, I am bound to say, if the House will forgive the metaphor, that the Allied High Command have approached the Italian mainland like an old man approaching a young bride, fascinated, sluggish and apprehensive.' The whole House rocked with laughter. Even Mr Cummings of the *News Chronicle* acclaimed the whole speech as an outstanding performance. It sought to relate the Italian campaign to the much larger picture of the war which Churchill and Eden had just returned from discussing with Stalin at Teheran. Churchill was as stubbornly wedded to his Mediterranean strategy as he was to the Badoglio régime. But whatever its virtues and however much the Italian revolution had seemed to open up unforeseen advantages, 'climbing up the backbone' was a highly dubious procedure. Churchill was infuriated by these criticisms whether they came from Bevan, Stalin or General Marshall. That winter they came strongly from all three.

One anticipatory footnote on the Italian episode must be added. When the Allies did finally reach Rome in May 1944 there was no question of reinstating King Victor Emmanuel, according to Churchill's wish of the previous October; instead he was kept out of the city lest he attempted to repudiate the pledge of abdication which the Italian Parties had extorted from him. Marshal Badoglio was forced to depart from the scene, too, despite a momentary and Machiavellian switch in his favour by Stalin and the Italian Communist Party in the previous March – a move heartily welcomed by Churchill and condemned by Bevan. Thus the two figures whom Churchill had cherished as men who commanded allegiance and could therefore sustain order in the post-Mussolini Italy were removed as soon as the Committees of National Liberation had established their freedom to act. Churchill was furious over Badoglio's removal, but on a visit to Rome derived the last morsel of comfort from 'the powerful and engaging personality and grasp of the whole situation' displayed by the Crown Prince Umberto – who was also removed with popular approval a few months later.[32] Churchill on that occasion (August 1944) said he hoped the people of Italy would 'recapture the ideals of freedom which inspired the Risorgimento'. He was still unaware that the Second Risorgi-

32. Churchill used his authority in the Commons to deride his few critics, even when he was making political judgements which were, later, shown to be grotesquely wide of the mark. In a debate on 28 September, referring to his Italian visit, he said: 'I had the advantage of an interview with the Lieutenant of the Realm [Umberto], whose sincerity and ardour in the Allied cause and whose growing stature in Italian eyes are equally apparent. [Interruption.] I give my opinion and I dare say it will weigh as much as a mocking giggle.'

mento – and one as glorious as the first and even braver – had started in the streets of Milan and Turin eighteen months earlier. Bevan had told him at the time.

No gift of insight was needed to see that the prospect of peace after the war would depend on the relations between the victorious powers. As the Russian armies rolled back westward the political battlefield assumed an entirely new aspect. Bevan's contribution to this new debate was individual and farseeing.

'We must not lose sight of the fact,' he wrote in September 1943, 'that the assistance of Russia played little or no part in the calculations of British strategy. This must therefore be judged in the absence of that assistance, and in the light of that conclusion our strategy stands wholly condemned. Tory Britain was leading us straight to defeat.' Thanks chiefly to the Soviet resistance, the scene had been transformed, but once again Tory Britain was incapable of meeting the new situation. 'It is a revolutionary Europe which confronts them, and they are frightened by the apparition.' This should have been the crucial moment, said Bevan, for Labour in the Cabinet to exert its influence. Why were the Labour Ministers content to leave the great decisions on European policy to Churchill and Eden?[33] 'It is not national unity we have now,' wrote Bevan, 'it is a silent conspiracy against the future.' And the absence of any democratic Socialist voice in the highest councils was the more deplorable when anxieties were growing about what role would be played by the great power returning victoriously to Europe from the East.

33. During the latter years of the war Bevan was engaged in more frequent controversies with Eden. He wrote in *Tribune* (15 January 1943) a brief character sketch of the Foreign Secretary. 'Attractive in the narrow, conventional sense. Always a possibility as a stop-gap Prime Minister. League of Nations society at Geneva introduced him to a whole range of ideas strange to a Tory. There he acquired a progressive vocabulary, and this, allied to the amiability that flows from weakness of character, deceives many people into thinking that his political intentions are honourable. Actually there is nothing in his conduct to justify such a conclusion. His resignation from the Government of Mr Chamberlain over our Italian diplomacy provided him with a balance at the political bank on which he has drawn generously ever since. His behaviour during the civil war in Spain proves conclusively that whenever he has to choose between his Tory instincts and his progressive inclinations his instincts can be relied upon to win every time.' Premonitions of Suez!

Bevan traced a hardening in the Soviet attitude back to the Casablanca Conference. It was a legitimate surmise. In the weeks or months following Casablanca Stalin must have guessed, even though he was not specifically told, that no Second Front in the West was to be launched in 1943. More and more he made his own dispositions about Poland, Germany and much else. (In March he announced that Poland could have no claim on the Ukraine and White Russia. In July he appointed his own National Committee of Free Germany. In August he replaced Western-minded diplomats, Litvinov in Washington and Maisky in London, with two younger, tougher characters.) Russia, wrote *Tribune* (on 27 August 1943), is embarked upon 'a strong, national self-centred policy'. The differences between the Allies were already sufficiently marked to justify a supreme effort to resolve them. 'There is hardly a price that is too high to attain this end. Failure will mean to lay the foundation of a third world war.'

In October 1943 Bevan analysed the post-war prospect more fully. The central issue would be the adjustment of relations between the three principal victors. Yet of the Big Three, Britain would be very definitely the weakest, 'a fact which instinctive patriotism deters us from accepting, but nothing is to be gained by the refusal'. What then would be the role of the Big Two? American isolationism, said Bevan, was dead and would never be revived. 'The United States will inherit Nazi Germany's position as bulwark and protector of world capitalism in the West.' The real relationship between the United States and 'the great rival system championed by the Soviet Union' would be one of acute hostility, jealousy and suspicion, with occasional moves towards hard bargains driven at the expense of third parties. 'This polarization of international relations between Moscow and Washington,' he continued, 'would be nothing short of a world catastrophe. It would petrify the existing systems in both countries and make genuine co-operation between them impossible. It would make a third world war an eventual certainty. It would reduce all other nations, including Britain, to a satellite status of depending upon one or other of these two great Powers. It would crush all hopes for the emergence of a democratic Socialism, cherished by the progressive movements on the

Continent and in Britain who do not wish to model themselves either on the capitalist democracy of America or the totalitarian Socialism of Soviet Russia.'

The solution he prescribed, both in the interests of British independence and to mitigate the lethal 'polarization', was that Britain should 'gain the support and provide for the mutual help of the nations of Europe'. That was another reason why a good relationship between Britain and the European resistance movements was essential. It could be achieved only by a British Government embarking on adventurous reforms at home and proving its trust in the revolutionary peoples abroad. 'We shall not get that; we shall not expect it from our present rulers. Our chief task, therefore, in this coming year is to revive the international conscience of the Labour movement. Labour must have its own diplomacy, a diplomacy that enacts its own faith.' (*Tribune*, 24 December 1943.)

In January 1944 the Red Armies reached the borders of Poland. Everyone, in particular the world of Labour, wrote Bevan, would watch 'with painful anxiety' what Russia would do; 'her conduct will have the most profound consequences for the authority of Socialist values all over the world'. If she sought to mould small nations to her ways of thinking and mode of life by force of arms and coercion, 'she will dim the lustre of Socialist principles everywhere'. And of course it was necessary that the Western Powers should show a similar recognition of the limits upon their proper influence. The small nations had the capacity for a great rebirth. Under the domination of the Nazis they had rediscovered the meaning of personal liberty, and defeat had discredited their own ruling classes with their traditions and institutions of exploitation. It was in the profound interest of all that these nations should be allowed 'to experiment with mutations of political and social organization'. However, the Russian arrival in Poland sparked off the most overt political crisis between the Soviet Union and her Allies. The conflict between the Polish Government in exile in London and the Soviet Government looked irreconcilable. Bevan was not prepared to give unqualified backing to one side or the other. 'As Socialists,' wrote *Tribune* in an editorial, 'we are bound in duty to support

Soviet Russia when it acts as a progressive Socialist power. But it is equally our Socialist obligation to raise our voice against any attempts of the strong at trampling over the rights of the weak. As Socialists we fight the reactionary ambitions and claims of the Poles; but we must also defend Poland's right to self-determination and independence just as we defend the rights of any other nation oppressed or threatened by oppression.' The shadow fell beyond Poland. In the First World War, *Tribune* recalled, the Soviets had adopted the democratic slogan: Peace without indemnities and annexations. 'Is it conceivable that Russia should now drop that programme and adopt as her slogan: Peace *with* indemnities and annexations? If so, it will not be peace.'

The attitude of the great Powers to the small nations made Bevan sceptical about the high-level meetings between Roosevelt and Churchill or Roosevelt, Churchill and Stalin. He protested against 'the secret diplomacy of Quebec, Teheran, Cairo and Moscow'. The declarations issued after them bore little relation to the real decisions made. Nothing more could be revealed, the world was told, for reasons of military expediency. Yet the future of Europe was being shaped behind those closed doors where democratic pressures were locked out.

At Teheran in December 1943, Stalin had sat at the table with Roosevelt and Churchill. So far from Soviet influence being used to pierce the veil of secrecy, the danger had been infinitely worsened. Stalin sought secret compacts to enable him to enlarge his frontiers. Bevan urged that the Soviet leaders should read what Lenin had to say about 'growth by conquest'. If any of the Soviet military leaders believed that Russian security could be guaranteed by the arrangement of frontiers, by the construction of geographical Maginot lines, 'they had better go back to school again. For if history proves nothing else, it proves the foolishness of relying on them as defences against the changing methods and instruments of war.' (*Tribune*, 18 February 1944.)[34] He was

34. Bevan returned to this theme on many different occasions. For example in the House of Commons on 29 September 1944: 'I do not believe that Russian security will be based on this or that frontier. In these days of fly bombs, does anybody imagine that the peace of the world can depend on this chain of mountains, or that river line, or that line of fortifications? Those

equally forthright in his attack on the Soviet manoeuvre in March when they recognized Marshal Badoglio. Stalin had as little sympathy with the new Europe as Churchill and Roosevelt. The hugger-mugger contrivances of these three eighteenth-century autocrats threatened to introduce a new Age of Metternich. 'The conclusion we draw,' he wrote, 'is that Labour in Europe and in this country must guard the full independence of its policy. To win our battles we must look to our own forces and our own principles. *We* must not bow to expediency.'

The European scene, as much as any domestic calculations, made Bevan passionately eager to see Labour in Britain preparing for power. So much could be achieved and so much was being squandered. Little real inspiration was being offered from across the Atlantic. American foreign policy was merely British nine-teenth-century foreign policy in the modern medium. 'But if America gives us headaches, Russia gives us heartaches.' Natur-ally the achievements of the Red Army, coupled with Russia's revolutionary tradition, obtained for her a special place in Social-ist affections. Some, therefore, were inclined to accept all her judgements on international relations. But Russia's assumed interests could not be allowed to 'sterilize all progress elsewhere'. Her diplomacy seemed to be aimed at keeping Europe in an atomized condition, consisting of a number of weak nations of varying political complexions in the West, with a fringe of small nations on her borders, under her political and economic domina-tion. 'I cannot believe,' wrote Bevan (on 7 April 1944), 'that Russia will find her safety on the edge of an unstable Europe. Her main interest is an economically progressive Europe, satisfied with a future of material advancement and therefore not likely to become a prey to militarist adventurers . . . In the absence of the Socialist alternative, Western Europe in particular will become a ground of contention between Russia on the one side and American and British capitalism on the other, with inevit-able inflammatory consequences.'

Bevan proposed his own alternative. He rejected any attempt to partition Germany as 'not only uncivilized in its intent, but

---

ideas belong to the last century and have nothing to do with the necessities of the modern world.'

sinister in its consequences'. It was natural and inevitable that Russia should influence preponderantly the life of the nations immediately on her borders, that she should seek to prevent them from forming combinations that might be aimed against her. That was the price to be paid for the bitter recent past, and only time and normal intercourse could assuage its evils. (This was his melancholy acceptance of Poland's fate.) 'But – as a first stage – ' he added, 'an organic confederation of the Western European nations, like France, Holland, Belgium, Italy, Spain, the Scandinavian nations along with a sane Germany and Austria, and a progressive Britain, is the only solution likely to lay the foundation for peace and prosperity in Europe. It is this solution that Russia, because of her fears, cannot initiate, and that America and Britain, with their present policy of reaction, will be unable to bring about. It remains, therefore, for British Labour to show the way.'

Despite the crowding shadows, Bevan had his gleams of optimism. He foresaw a renewed arms race between the Soviet and American war machines, but believed that a new and enlightened power could be interposed between them. The British ruling class, relegated from its world power status, had become paralysed in its efforts to devise a modern substitute, and the Labour leaders had been afflicted by the contagion. But he drew sustenance from the mood of the British people who were showing that they would reject 'the pursuit of illusory power adventures' and that they were ready for 'a more enlightened approach to social problems than at any time in their history'. In this article on 14 April 1944, he plainly prophesied that Labour would have the opportunity to show its stature. The election after the war would be won. 'The British Labour Party will come to power when the whole world will be looking for a lead. That is to say, it will have a world audience listening to its guidance.' More than ever was it important, he urged, that Labour should not compromise its freedom of action in advance by commitments to the barren policies of the Coalition.

This confident and spacious vision of Labour's potentialities did not, however, succeed in reconciling him with his leaders. A few weeks later they were taking steps to throw him out of the Party altogether.

13 The Fight with Bevin April–June 1944

I will speak so loud that I will be heard outside the House.
— HENRY FOX[1]

ANEURIN BEVAN'S new antagonist – an old one reincarnated –
was Ernest Bevin, the toughest of trade union leaders and
incomparably the most powerful Labour figure in the wartime
administration. However apt some observers may have thought
Bevan's strictures on the submissiveness of the Labour Ministers, none could believe they applied to Ernest Bevin. He did not
look like a man likely to be browbeaten by anybody. As Minister of
Labour in charge of mobilizing the nation's manpower resources,
his reputation had grown immeasurably in the war. His
knowledge of industrial matters was supposed to exceed that of
any rival. While Attlee's most frequent contribution to Cabinet
discussions was a swift 'I agree, I agree' or a laconic aside, Bevin
insisted on having his say. The words rambled but the mind
could be imaginative and resourceful. His unblushing egotism
had an attractive candour about it; he had a ruminating shrewd-
ness; but he was also suspicious, cunning, and often vindictive.
If anyone was capable of feeding Aneurin Bevan's flesh to
the fowls of the air and the beasts of the field – the fate desired for him by so many – the person best qualified to do it
was this Goliath of a man, Ernest Bevin. And he very nearly
did.

The origin of their quarrel was coal. Ernest Bevin might know
a great deal about dockers, busmen, and all the other vast company of workers represented in the Transport and General
Workers Union (Bevan was quite ready to contest this proposition

1. Quoted in *The Early History of Charles James Fox* by Sir George Trevelyan.

439

too), but one boast he must not be allowed. According to Bevan, he knew little about miners while making the error of thinking he knew a lot. This lack of faith in Ernest Bevin's omniscience was not just a Bevanite idiosyncrasy. It was shared by many other miners. D. R. Grenfell M.P., a miner who had also been Minister of Mines, had revealed to the House of Commons how in 1940 Ernest Bevin, as Minister of Labour, had been responsible for the fatal dispersal of mining manpower which bred the subsequent crises in coal production. Grenfell made the accusation which was never effectively rebutted that Bevin would have injured the industry irreparably by his policies if his headstrong ignorance had not been checked.[2] However, Bevan's critical attitude did not rest on these revelations alone. The two men, as we have seen, had had many pre-war conflicts. And Bevin (with Churchill) was pre-eminently responsible for what Bevan called the 'domestic neglect, political cowardice and romantic thinking' which made coal the most intractable of industrial wartime problems.

The prophecies which Bevan and other miner M.P.s and the miners' union made in 1940, 1941 and 1942 were confirmed in 1943. Output and manpower were steadily falling. Ernest Bevin, therefore, went to the conference of the Miners' Federation in July, told them that at the end of the year there would not be 'enough men and boys in the industry to carry it on' and concluded that he would have to resort to 'some desperate remedies'.[3] He had already provided an option for men to go to the pits instead of the Army; the pitiful number of three thousand had chosen the pits. Conscription for the mines was now to be adopted; 'the Bevin boys' were to be directed there. This was soon supplemented by an appeal by Bevin over the radio for thirty thousand miners and an announcement that mining would take priority over all other Services. He sought to make the appeal succeed by painting in bright colours how attractive mining could be as a career after the war.

Bevin was supposed to be the hard-headed trade union leader, Bevan the impractical phrasemonger. But it was Bevan who did

2. *Hansard*, 13 October 1943.
3. Quoted in *The Miners In Crisis and War* by R. Page Arnot.

his best to bring Bevin down to earth. He pointed out that the most recent wage award, particularly affecting juveniles, offered quite inadequate increases, still leaving rewards in the mining industry well below those in most other trades. Mining remained the hard, dirty, dangerous occupation it had always been. Of course there had been some minor reforms and some modest wage increases, but the industry was still cursed by a wage structure and district agreements which aroused fierce antagonism. In one sense the war deepened the gulf between mining and the other communities. If it had not been for the Essential Work Order, tying men to the industry, there would have been a wholesale exodus. The miners were now compelled by force to submit to the conditions against which they had been rebelling since 1918. No patriotic appeal could wipe away these smarting memories and indignities. Indeed all the sermons preached to the miners by Cabinet Ministers and union leaders about the vital nature of their work merely added to their resentment. So what right, asked Bevan, had the Minister of Labour to promise good conditions after the war? Would the coalowners still be in charge? If so, Bevin had no right to promise anything. If not, the condition for the fulfilment of Bevin's pledge was that the Tories should be thrown out. And if that was what Bevin meant, why didn't he say so? His reticence was a deception. He found it, said Bevan, 'easier to deceive the people than to offend the Tories'. And a depressing consequence was the divorce of the utterances of Labour leaders from reality; it reduced their stature in the eyes of the people. 'For after all the people know the facts. They have to live with them.'

In 1943 there were more individual strikes in the mining industry – all of them unofficial – than in any year since the beginning of the century. Considering that the miners were as much in favour of the war effort as anybody and that the official line of the Communist Party was at that period rigidly opposed to all strikes, this figure was a striking testimony to the stark economic conditions in the coalfields and the unworkable nature of the system of dual control by the Government and the coalowners imposed on the industry in the previous year. Yet Ernest Bevin, with all his experience, could not believe that these were the real sources of the trouble. In a speech at the end of September he talked darkly of disturbances arising 'not from a wages dispute but in order to embarrass the Government in the political field'. He referred to 'one or two cases' where opposition had been organized to stop the officers of the union from being heard and claimed that these were deliberate plans to impede the war effort. 'We cannot tolerate it,' he said. Commenting on this speech, Bevan said that any idea of strengthening the union officials against the strikers was 'Gauleiter reasoning'. One of the troubles already was that too many trade union officials had become as much a part of the apparatus of the State as the civil servants. 'It is not a healthy situation for the unions when their members have to strike both against the union and the employers before they can obtain redress. That is not a situation which calls for the legal strengthening of the unions. It is rather one which demands that the unions should resume their proper functions as advocates and champions of the workers.' Bevan's urgent advice to Bevin and his Labour colleagues in the Government was that they should turn their minds away from thoughts of coercing the workers and seek remedies for the real disease.

He was by no means alone in giving these warnings. In a House of Commons debate in October 1943 one mining M.P. after another tried to explain to the rest of the House and the nation that the situation was getting out of control. It is impossible to read the debate without hearing the drum-beat of alarm. Yet it is also apparent that the warnings were not really believed. The Minister in charge, Mr Gwilym Lloyd George, who had no new proposals to offer, appealed for 'a placid debate'. Seymour Cocks, M.P. for Broxtowe, gave the reply. 'The state of feeling among the miners at the moment is not placid,' he said, 'it is developing into a raging maelstrom, a foaming Niagara of discontent . . . Unless the causes of discontent are removed grave events are possible; unless they are removed I think it is the duty of Labour Ministers to leave the Government.' Seymour Cocks was especially scornful about talk of fresh discipline. In Nottinghamshire, he said, 'discipline, if you can call it discipline, is maintained by a system of organized and authorized bullying in

an atmosphere of noise, dust, heat, sweat and blasphemy.'
Bevan's contribution to the debate was a demand that a member
of the War Cabinet should speak. It was unfair to leave the
apologia for policies breeding such perils to a Minister without
power. Next day Churchill himself came forward to perform the
task and he did it with grace and skill. He grasped the nettle of
the miners' demand for nationalization or real national control.
His principle, he said, – the principle which held the Coalition
together – was 'everything for the war, whether controversial or
not, and nothing controversial that is not *bona fide* needed for the
war'. Judged by this test, he claimed that 'a permanent great
change' in the mining industry could not be justified. That door
was slammed once more. However, this flat rejection of the
demand which Bevan had been making since 1940 was sweetened
by a most eloquent tribute to the miners. If oratory could bring
peace to the coalfields, Churchill had done it.

But among the miners' M.P.s in the Commons debate, at a
special conference of the Miners' Federation a few weeks later
and above all in the mining villages and union branches, it was
evident that Churchill's writ did not run. The executive at the
miners' conference ran into great difficulties with the rank-and-
file for appearing to accept for a while, however reluctantly, the
rejection of the miners' own proposals. Two of the districts,
South Wales and Lancashire, voted openly against the advice of
the Federation leaders. And one of those leaders, the highly
respected vice-chairman, James Bowman, expressed the anger of
his members in words which should have penetrated Downing
Street. 'We have passed the phase in this war,' he said, 'when
slogans and appeals are of any use. The speech of the Prime
Minister in the House of Commons in the recent coal debate was
one of the greatest disservices to the mining industry . . . Men in
the coalfields have seen, as a result of the statement by the Prime
Minister, that anything which involves major political changes
cannot be done during this war, and the capitalists are now
crawling out of their funk-holes and claiming their position for
the post-war world.' Bowman used some further words which do
not usually fall from the lips of a trade union leader. He prophesied that if something dramatic was not done to meet the

miners' demands, 'men will continue to correct their grievances by guerrilla tactics at pit after pit and district after district'.[4]

But nothing was done. Churchill doubtless believed that a victory in the Commons was also a victory in the coalfields, and Ernest Bevin, who had also suffered many bruises in the debate, took no visible step to stir his colleagues. Indeed, one step was taken which greatly worsened the situation. During the winter there took place a complicated series of wage negotiations designed to alleviate the position whereby the wages of miners were falling still further behind those in other industries. Under the final award the miners got much less than they had asked for, but district by district some advance had been achieved. Then suddenly a Government announcement suggested that the improvements secured would not be supported by the Government subsidy required to pay for them. Overnight it appeared that the belated and inadequate concessions made to the miners were to be snatched from them. The result, on top of all that had gone before, was an explosion. Strikes broke out – particularly in South Wales and Yorkshire – on a scale much bigger even than the year before. The exact number of men involved was not published at the time. In fact more men were out than at any period since 1926.

A violent press campaign was conducted against the miners. Everyone knew that preparations were being made for the great cross-Channel operation which, it was hoped, would bring the war to an end. Coal was a tedious topic by comparison. Heroes were risking their lives in the air and on the seas while the miners were perversely fighting for a few shillings. Only the slenderest reports had appeared in the newspapers of the miners' long argument with the Government and the steady accumulation of grievances. The strike wave at such a moment looked like a stab in the back. Only a few voices were raised to counter the general hysteria and Bevan's was naturally one of them. On 17 March 1944, he wrote an article in *Tribune* entitled 'Are Miners Different?', which attempted to deal with the allegation implicit in the general press campaign that 'half a million miners suffer from a kind of mental malady which isolates them incurably

4. See *The Miners In Crisis and War* by R. Page Arnot.

from the rest of the community ... Is it really conceivable that half a million men and their women folk can get so much out of step with the rest of society as to earn the reputation of social lepers?' He then recited the record of the Government's handling of the coal industry, culminating in Churchill's October declaration rejecting nationalization: 'there is no crisis in the mining industry which would justify such action.' Churchill's rooted refusal to contemplate the abolition of private property in coal-mines was the deep cause of the crisis. And one of its ugliest accompaniments was the undermining of the credit of the miners' own leaders with their followers. Perforce they often came to their followers empty-handed. But they had spent so much of their time, in Bevan's words, 'exhorting, rebuking and even abusing' the rank-and-file that 'the miners have come perilously near to a morbid distrust of their leaders'.

A part of Bevan's charge at least could not be contested. One hundred and twenty thousand men unofficially on strike in Yorkshire, one hundred thousand in Wales and several thousands in addition in Lancashire, Staffordshire, Durham and Scotland were, whatever else they were doing, expressing lack of confidence in their leaders. Moreover, the strike action achieved what the leaders had failed to achieve. In March the Government tumbled over itself to repair its crowning blunder of mid-February. A complete overhaul of the wage structure was offered on 24 March and finally approved by the Government, the unions, and the reluctant owners on 20 April. The main demand of the miners was still denied, but they had been appeased. The strikes abated. Bevan himself had been to South Wales to urge the men first to accept the original award, whatever the anomalies, and later to call off their unofficial strike action. He went to the second round of meetings following a pressing private appeal from Ernest Bevin himself. Other M.P.s from the mining areas had done the same.[5] The South Wales strike ended on 18 March

5. The *Western Mail*, in pursuit of its vendetta against Bevan, accused him of failing to participate in these appeals to the unofficial strikers when other South Wales M.P.s did so. There is no basis for the charge. Frank Bowles, M.P. accompanied Bevan to a meeting in his own constituency and to another in the neighbouring constituency at Blackwood. Frank Bowles has also provided the recollection – which he clearly remembers Bevan telling

and the Yorkshire strike on 11 April. These dates are relevant to the story that follows. Both the timing of the men's coming out and the timing of their return show that the strike wave was intimately associated with substantial grievances. Action in Whitehall directly set off the explosion; a revival of wisdom there brought almost instant relief. The coalfields might not respond to oratory from Westminster; deeds helped.

Yet this was not the end of the tale, but the beginning. Ernest Bevin naturally watched the strike movement with growing alarm. Some other smaller unofficial strikes were taking place in other industries, among engineering apprentices and gas workers. Newspapers reported that bands of Trotskyites, who rejected the Communist line of full support for the war effort, were among the instigators. Bevin said later that the nation was living on the edge of a volcano which might affect three million workers. On 5 April he attended a luncheon where he underlined the peril – but chiefly the peril in the mines. The stoppage in the Yorkshire coalfield, he said, was far worse than if Sheffield had been bombed. That morning he had attended the Cabinet and that afternoon he called in at a meeting of the General Council of the T.U.C. He told them that as a result of the strikes, 'which in his judgement were being incited by persons outside the industry concerned',[6] a paralysis was developing in some of

---

him at the time – that Ernest Bevin had appealed to him to assist in ending the strikes.

Bevin's appeal to Bevan may read strangely in view of their public antagonism. There was another similar and even more curious incident. Sometime in 1943 or 1944, after informal approaches from members of the Government, Bevan and Dick Stokes went to Ireland on a secret mission in an attempt to persuade De Valera to alter or mitigate his attitude about the use of Irish ports by British ships. Not a hint of this strange assignment to two of the leading parliamentary rebels was made public at the time. Bevan asked De Valera whether, if an approach was made by the United States and Britain, Irish facilities could be provided for submarines. De Valera, red with anger, said that if the British tried to use the Irish ports, the Irish would fight them. 'I will take a gun myself,' he cried. 'And what if the Germans land?' asked Bevan. 'Then we'll expect you to send us arms,' retorted De Valera. He adamantly insisted on Irish neutrality. 'For the first time in five hundred years,' remarked Bevan, 'a sense of guilt has crossed the Irish sea.'

6. According to the report later given by Sir Walter Citrine to the Trades Union Congress. Report of Proceedings at Blackpool T.U.C., October 1944.

the major industries of the country. Under the existing law he had no effective power to deal with *incitement* to strike. That was the power he must have.

At first some members of the General Council demurred. They pointed out that it was often difficult to discover the exact cause of a strike and that undoubtedly there were occasions when they were provoked by 'the precipitate and autocratic action of employers'. But eventually unanimous support was won for providing penalties against persons inciting men to come out on unofficial strike. Trade union representatives meeting the employers under the auspices of the Ministry of Labour were empowered to agree with Regulation 1 AA. 'No person' – ran its essential clause – 'shall declare, instigate, or make any other person to take part in, or shall otherwise act in furtherance of, any strike among persons engaged in the performance of essential services, or any lock out of persons so engaged.' Trade unionists operating through the normal machinery were protected; instigating unofficial strikes was the offence aimed at. The penalty was five years' penal servitude, or £500 fine, or both. The new regulation was issued on 17 April – as it happened, six days after the Yorkshire strike had ended.

Leakages in the press had revealed what was afoot before the 17th. Bevan at first treated the whole idea as a gruesome joke. 'William Le Queux, John Buchan and Phillips Oppenheim and similar fiction writers,' he wrote in *Tribune* on 14 April, 'have always been favourite authors of ours in our off-moments. Part of their charm lies in their juvenile attitude. Everything becomes conspiratorial . . . We always knew that it is this refusal to grow up which is part of the Prime Minister's attraction for the general public. But we never suspected Ernest Bevin of a boyish gusto for the sensational and romantic. It appears we were quite wrong. Behind that stolid and somewhat unprepossessing exterior is a romantic and elfish spirit.' Bevan refused to believe that the actions and proposed orders against the Trotskyites were to be taken seriously. He hoped that cooler heads would prevail before the House of Commons was 'hauled in' to endorse what its masters, the Employers' Federation and the Trades Union Congress, had decided.

If unhappily the plan *was* serious the proposition was, said Bevan, that an organization inspired by the teachings of Trotsky had not only plenty of members and money, but 'more influence among certain sections of the workers than His Majesty's Government and the trade union leaders combined'. Of course 'the jackals of the Yellow Press' had been in full cry to put across the story to the public. A reporter from the *Daily Mail* claimed that he had headed a special team of investigators all over the country tracking down the Trotskyites. He had interviewed a former Assistant Commissioner of Scotland Yard, Sir Wyndham Childs, who had said that the strikes were being financed from America by the International Workers of the World and that their chief agent had been a certain Mr Albert Inkpin who had recently died. 'Find his successor,' Sir Wyndham had solemnly told the *Daily Mail*, 'and you will find the man who ought to be arrested.' But Mr Albert Inkpin had been secretary of the Friends of Russia Society and an orthodox Communist. 'The suggestion that Inkpin was a Trotskyite,' commented Bevan, 'has produced high blood pressure in Communist headquarters.'

Yet the *Daily Mail* was not alone in purveying these fantasies. William Lawther, President of the Miners, had also suggested that the Trotskyites were a real menace. 'To suggest,' replied Bevan, 'that the miners went on strike in opposition to the advice of their own leaders as a result of the agitation of an outside body of obscure political pedants is either to insult their intelligence or ours ... The miners' leaders who use such language know they are talking nonsense. They dare not tell the South Wales miners or the Yorkshire miners that they went on strike at the instigation of Trotskyites. The men would laugh them off the platform.' Then he brought the counter-attack home to the principal miscreants: 'Mr Ernest Bevin and the rest of the Government are obviously looking for scapegoats for the mess they have made of the mining industry. They won't blame themselves, and they can't blame the trade union leaders who have so faithfully followed them. They can't blame the Jews this time because most of the industry is in the hands of Aryans of unimpeachable stock. So they must perforce elevate a poor little band of political sectarians to the status of an organization powerful enough to throw a dangerous spanner into the war machinery. Do Mr Bevin and his friends really hope the country will swallow that rubbish?'

But Mr Bevin and his friends did not doubt they could get their way. The Order was framed and promulgated at a time when Parliament was not sitting. The General Council had agreed and that was good enough for most Labour Members of Parliament. A few newspapers expressed concern. The *Manchester Guardian* agreed that there were 'questions to be put to the Government about the regulation', but regretted that the only M.P.s showing any interest were 'Mr Aneurin Bevan and his associates, who have worked so hard to gain their reputation of being soured critics of the Government'. Bevan himself was too 'splenetic'. Yet without the splenetic Bevan it is unlikely that any debate would have been forced. He saw Regulation 1 AA as a cowardly resort by union leaders and Labour Ministers who were prepared to be tough with their political friends because of cowardice in face of their political enemies. The timing of the Order merely added to the offence. 'We know,' he said, 'that we are a military base for the forthcoming operations and that the Government must give the armies what is known as an assured base. But are we seriously asked to believe that these people of ours who have comported themselves with so much calm, dignity and quiet determination during more than four years of war, cannot now be trusted in the final and critical hour of the battle? What nonsense – and what an insult to our people!'

Outside the House of Commons and outside Fleet Street, considerable numbers of people agreed with him. The South Wales Miners' Federation called on M.P.s to amend the Order. The Scottish T.U.C. took much the same view. A considerable number of Labour M.P.s, outside the normal band of rebels, were disturbed. But the machine worked remorselessly. This was Ernest Bevin at war, not one of his shadows. Every M.P. who had signed the 'prayer' against the Order put down by Bevan was threatened with disciplinary action. Bevan himself was approached by some of the miners' leaders and told that he would be in trouble if he persisted. And at the Party meeting it was agreed that the Minister of Labour should receive whole-hearted backing.

When the debate came, Bevan delivered one of the most devastating speeches of his life. Had it not been for 'the hush of painful expectancy' induced by the pending military operations, which, as he himself said at the start, overhung their proceedings, it is hard to believe that he would not have rallied many supporters to his cause by his detailed analysis of the Order and the way it had been made. But it was also a ruthless speech and many of his closest companions shuddered as he piled one onslaught upon another. He was not fighting to win in the House; he knew he was beaten there. But he was determined that the men in Yorkshire and South Wales should know that their case had been put on the floor of the House of Commons.

It was not the first time, he said, that the Government 'had slapped the House of Commons in the face', but this was a 'peculiarly vicious' example. The outside bodies consulted by the Minister had no special knowledge to offer. Bevin had no excuse 'for conspiring behind our backs and making laws in our absence'. Moreover, the outside bodies were the chief beneficiaries under the Order. The Government went to the employers and the union leaders and said: We propose to confer special privileges upon you; we propose to raise you above the law. Bevin was reducing parliamentary procedure to a farce, and to that customary offence he had added another. He had incited the newspapers to embark on a campaign of calumny against the miners. 'Are we seriously asked to believe that the stolid Yorkshire miners came out on strike because of a number of evilly disposed Trotskyites? This is the suggestion made by the Minister of Labour. Otherwise why did they strike? Why did not the newspapers discharge their proper function to the public and make the nation aware of the grievances of the Yorkshire miners?' They came out both in Yorkshire and South Wales because of 'the incompetence of the Minister of Fuel and the Minister of Labour'. Many of the strikes were about grievances subsequently remedied. Anomalies had arisen under the wages award, but they were not rectified until the men struck. And had not he and his friends been warning the Government for three years that a serious situation was arising in the mining industry, that there might be a stoppage at a critical moment in the war?

The press did not report these warnings and protests, but when the miners struck made them the victims of 'scurrilous abuse'. Could not the House and the newspapers stop to consider why men went on strike? 'Last week there was a bus strike in London. A military bus went in and the men came out. Do people not realize that exactly the same purpose, exactly the same capacity for generous indignation, exactly the same stalwart courage that our men display on the battlefields they also display in bus garages? Do we expect men to be lions on the battlefield and sheep at home?' This was the absurd expectation of the newspapers which maligned the men whose case they would not even report. And they had stooped to even more disgraceful methods in dealing with the handful of Trotskyites who had been arrested in Newcastle a few days before, without the invocation of Regulation 1 AA. The alleged Trotskyites had been kept in remand for twenty-one days and tried *in camera*, the explanation of the secret trial being that the police had not been able to complete their investigations into their alleged offences. The newspapers had piled up public hatred against them and committed contempt of court on a fantastic scale. Yet no action was taken by 'this venal Government' to protect them in any way.

Under the Order itself, who would be safe? Suppose some boys in a gang from the pits decide to go home? 'I did it myself when I was a nipper. Is it to be five years' penal servitude because the boys have a nostalgia for sunshine?' Would shop stewards not incorporated under the rules of the Amalgamated Engineering Union be safe? Many trade union officials did not like shop stewards because they were nearer the men. Did Bevin propose to operate the Order against them? 'If he does he will create more strikes than the Trotskyites have been able to do in five years of war. In fact we shall have to get rid of him, because he will be a public danger if he operates the Order.'

All this was fierce enough. The finger was pointing directly at Ernest Bevin. Yet it was in the few following minutes that the speech was transformed into a political crisis. A sharp distinction was drawn under the Order between what a man could say at a trade union meeting and what he could say in the street; there was to be one law for the trade union official and another for the unofficial agitator. That was the essence of the Regulation. Bevan continued thus:

There are over thirteen million workers in this country who are not in the trade unions. Not one of them will have any protection whatever under this Regulation. It may be said that they can all go into the unions. Of course they can, but are we now setting out to recruit trade union membership by threats of five years' penal servitude? It is the trade union officials who are invoking the law against their own members. Do not let anybody on this side of the House think that he is defending the trade unions; he is defending the trade union official who has arteriosclerosis and who cannot readjust himself to his membership. He is defending an official who has become so unpopular among his own membership that the only way he can keep them in order is to threaten them with five years' gaol. Whenever you get the rank-and-file at trade union meetings this Regulation will be opposed. The General Council at the top supports it but the worker at the bottom opposes it. The farther you get away from the trade union official to the rank-and-file, the less support the Regulation gets. The more you move away from reality, from the robust, dignified, normal worker, to the jaded, cynical, irresponsible trade union official the more support the Regulation gets. That is the situation. Is that an exaggeration? . . . I say this Regulation is the enfranchisement of the corporate society and the disfranchisement of the individual. It gives status to the organized body and destroys the status of the individual citizen. It elevates the irresponsible trade union official – and I use the word irresponsible in the constitutional sense of the term, because a trade union official *is* irresponsible. He is not subject to election, as we are; he is not exposed to pressure, as we are. George Bernard Shaw said in *The Applecart* that the person in this country who is in the most strongly entrenched position, next to the King, is the trade union official.

This was the passage that spread cold horror along the Labour benches. Many in Bevan's audience had been trade union officials themselves. Yet they were backing Bevin, and Bevin by his Regulation was branding the hundred thousand Welsh strikers as block-headed dupes or near-traitors. Bevan was not prepared to see his people condemned in this style by men who ought to know better. He would hurl the insult back in the faces of those who dared make it. The rowdy meeting he had addressed in his own constituency urging the men to go back merely made him the more enraged at the spectacle of Labour M.P.s who would sit silent and vote obediently when Ernest Bevin and the General

Council of the T.U.C. wrested authority from them. Thereafter he cooled. He said he had an argument which he hoped would appeal to his 'trade union friends'. If the protection of all citizens was to be handed to the unions, then the State would have to survey the rules of the unions. Did the T.U.C. want that? Soldiers were civilians in uniform. They hoped to come back to enjoy their liberties. Yet after putting them in uniform and handing them their orders, the Government stabbed them in the back. At last his tone became softer. 'I ask the Government, for Heaven's sake, to consider the mood of the people. If they are big men they will say: "We have made a mistake. We will take it back. We will trust the people. We will trust to conciliation and self-discipline, because we know it is not necessary to bludgeon our workers into efforts required to win the war".'

The rest of the debate was largely a comment on the wounds which Bevan had inflicted. His prayer was seconded by David Kirkwood who said that the Clydeside was as much up in arms against the Order as South Wales. Many workers called it 'a licence to employers to continue their provocation'. His own union, the engineers, was split from top to bottom. He accused Bevin of 'letting down the working class' and 'betraying all the good work he has done throughout his life'. But most speakers backed the Government, some Tories saying it was high time to 'stamp out agitators'. The strongest reply came from Arthur Greenwood, the acting leader of the Labour Party. Bevan, he said, 'made a speech today of an anti-trade union character the like of which I have never heard from the most diehard Tory in this House or outside the House. My hon. Friend gibbeted the trade union movement, gibbeted its leaders, frowned upon its officials and even said the elected representatives of the people were nobody ... I believe the hon. Member for Ebbw Vale is going to risk a fall on this and I ask my friends to oppose the prayer in the national interest.' These were severe words from the kindly Arthur Greenwood; in the light of the disciplinary threats issued throughout the previous week, they gave the hint of action.

The House waited for Bevin himself to complete the slaughter. He did not usually speak to persuade. A speech from Ernest Bevin on a major occasion had all the horrific fascination of a public execution. If the mind was left immune, eyes and ears and emotions were riveted. Yet on this day he fumbled with the axe. He called Bevan a liar and had to withdraw. He spoke vaguely of the industrial volcano on which the nation had been living. He expatiated irrelevantly on his own relations with the press. What he certainly did not provide was any detailed evidence of how the strikes had been instigated or why, if there had been real subversive activities, he could not deal with them under powers already at his disposal.[7] Bevin did not even trouble to answer the case. He was dealing with what he called 'a little, tiny, semilegal, rhetorical minority'. Big votes were the instruments for extirpating small minorities.

Bevin was followed by George Buchanan, one who could capture the ear of the House in a manner which Bevin never learnt. Bevin, he said, had talked of 'wide and airy things', but hardly at all about the Regulation. He did not understand and should not sneer at the House of Commons, and the Labour Party as a whole must 'never make the mistake of being merely a trade union Party subject to the trade union movement'. It was a Friday afternoon. In the last hour of the debate while Sydney Silverman was concluding the case for Bevan's prayer, large numbers of Tory M.P.s, rallied by the Whips, who had not listened to a word of the discussion crowded behind the bar of the House and noisily chattered and catcalled. Time and again there were calls for order. 'May it not be,' asked Maxton, 'that long absence has made them forget the courtesies?'

Disraeli said once: 'a majority is the best repartee'. At four o'clock Bevin got his majority – by three hundred and fourteen votes to twenty-three – and next day the newspapers celebrated

---

7. The nearest Bevin came to a reply on this point was in answer to an interruption by S. O. Davies who had asked: 'What is the hon. Gentleman talking about?' Bevin retorted: 'I mean that at one moment everything is peaceful; then suddenly in the most mysterious way these activities come – and the people who make the bullets do not fire them. We find activities going on in workshops, first from one source, and then from another. That is why we have set out to deal with this instigation business . . . I am not prepared to accept the coincidences of this development. Why was it in gas and coal; why was it all that three weeks, in the most vital thing affecting vital production? What is the answer to it? Why were certain districts selected and why suddenly did the circus fly off here and there?'

a mighty Bevin triumph. 'An overwhelming majority,' said the *Daily Telegraph*. 'All but a handful of Labour Members supported the Government against Mr Aneurin Bevan' – this was the embroidery of 'Bevin's Own', the *Daily Herald*. But in fact something somewhat different had happened. Only fifty-six Labour Members out of a total of one hundred and sixty-five had voted for Regulation 1 AA; twenty-three of these were Ministers, Whips or Parliamentary Private Secretaries. Bevin had used all his powers of persuasion and compulsion; one hundred and nine out of one hundred and sixty-five Labour M.P.s, for one reason or another, had failed to respond to his summons. It was a remarkable result which all the trumpetings of the pro-Government press could not conceal from Labour Members themselves.

A major dilemma now confronted the Party leadership. While strict parliamentary discipline works smoothly – that is, usually, when it is superfluous – Party leaders may regard it as a most delicate device for achieving their ends. But when discipline cracks, it exacerbates every controversy within the ranks into a major Party crisis. Having delivered such fierce prior threats against any rebels who dared vote in opposition to Regulation 1 AA, some action was required by the parliamentary leadership if their authority was not to be impaired. But what action? Were David Kirkwood, D. R. Grenfell, and thirteen other Labour M.P.s who had voted with Bevan also to be drummed out of the Party? And if so many had abstained from voting, would a motion for withdrawing the Whip and expelling the offenders be carried at the Party meeting? And what of the rebels outside – the South Wales miners, the Scottish T.U.C., Harold Laski, the Vice-Chairman of the National Executive, who had come down heavily against Bevin's Order? A literal application of the unworkable disciplinary code would cause a first-class split in the whole movement. The great weapon of Standing Orders had broken in their hands. Yet the trade union leaders, urged on by a bellicose speech by Bevin at Bristol on the day after the Commons debate, cared little for these awkward calculations. They wanted blood. Tom O'Brien, general secretary of the Theatre Employees and a member of the General Council, said that 'the war record of Aneurin Bevan is one of damaging irresponsibility, cowardly and disgracefully carried out. It is time he stopped his political buccaneering and realized that he cannot be mutineer and monarch at the same time'. John Brown, of the Iron and Steel Trades Confederation, and Will Lawther, of the Miners' Federation, delivered full-throated attacks on the political wing of the Party. Bevin at Bristol accused Bevan of denouncing the trade unions and kicking away the ladder on which he had climbed to position.

But the ladder was still there, as Bevan quickly pointed out in a speech at Tredegar. Apart from his own constituency, he was backed by the South Wales Miners, the executive of the Distributive Workers and a host of trade union branches and shop stewards all over the country. 'When Mr Bevin says that I attacked the trade unions he is accusing me of the dirt that sticks to his own fingers.' In the House of Commons debate 'he had won the vote and lost the argument'. Why was Bevin so angry? 'I suspect the reason is that he knows my twenty-three [votes in the Commons] represent more trade unionists in the country than his three hundred and fourteen.' *Tribune*, not altogether surprisingly, concurred with this verdict. 'There is little doubt,' it said, 'that a free vote throughout the trade union movement would kill the Regulation and dispose utterly of the claim of Mr Ernest Bevin, which he has palmed off on the credulous Churchill, to speak as the Labour Emperor whose lightest whims are honoured law among the working people of this land.' *Tribune* also widened the argument. The attempt to crush Bevan, it said, was part of the effort to demoralize the thrust for the eventual overthrow of the Coalition. And Harold Laski did the same. 'It has been the unstated assumption of all his [Bevin's] activities that to doubt the wisdom of the policy he supports is a kind of political blasphemy.' On a host of matters, the Labour Party was 'profoundly dissatisfied with the record of their leaders'. Some were content to act as Bevin camp-followers. 'It would be a poor kind of Labour Party if its members confined their effort to the humble receipt of whatever he and his colleagues thought satisfactory concessions from Mr Churchill and the Tory Party.'

The parliamentary leadership adopted a crude solution to their problem. Bevan alone from the sixteen who had voted against the Regulation was selected for burning; the blaze might be sufficient to scorch the others into obedience. According to the declaration made by Arthur Greenwood to the Party meeting, Bevan had been a persistent obstructor and non-co-operator with the Party; he did not carry out Party decisions; he had used shocking language about the unions and union officials in the debate. These offences distinguished him sufficiently from his companions. The Administrative Committee proposed that he should have the Whip withdrawn, with the almost certain consequence that he would be expelled from the Party altogether by the National Executive of the Party, while the others should be reported with, in effect, a recommendation to mercy. However, at the Party meeting, despite a strong muster of Cabinet Ministers, including Bevin, no decision was reached. Bevan defended himself strongly and the issue was postponed for a week.

That week-end there was much speculation. On one side some members of the Administrative Committee dropped hints that they would resign if the full penalty were not imposed on the next occasion. The executive of the South Wales Miners urged that steps should be taken to avoid the expulsion and the resulting split. Conciliators were at work, notably Mr Shinwell who suggested that the whole matter should be shelved by the Parliamentary Party pending discussion between the leaders in Parliament and the National Executive. And Bevan himself, at packed meetings in his constituency, said that if he were expelled he would still fight 'to retain the Ebbw Vale seat for Socialism'. He denied that it was a quarrel between himself and Ernest Bevin alone, challenged Bevin to hold a ballot vote of the unions on the issue of Regulation 1 AA itself, and declared that the real quarrel went much deeper; it touched the whole question of the post-war aspirations of Socialism. 'Had the Labour leaders fought the Germans as hard as they have fought me,' he added, 'the war would have been over long ago.' He also drew attention to a consideration which he thought weighed with the leaders. A few weeks hence the 1944 Labour Party Conference was to be held. Not merely was Bevan a candidate for the Executive, but he might also have a chance there to defeat the Party leadership on the Regulation 1 AA issue. The question, wrote the *Observer*, was whether 'Mr Bevin is going to roll up Mr Bevan on the question of discipline as he did Mr Lansbury a few years ago on the question of pacifism'. The old pre-war conflict between Left and Right in the Party seemed to have emerged in a new guise, but the Bevan of 1944 had much bigger battalions on his side than the Bevan of 1939.

The meeting of the Parliamentary Party on the following Wednesday was the largest for years. Not since the Labour Government of 1929 had there been a fuller attendance. Among the others, fifteen Ministers were present and Attlee spoke, bestowing all his authority on the Administrative Committee's recommendation for expulsion. But once again the leaders could not get their way. By seventy-one votes to sixty the Shinwell amendment was carried against the wishes of the platform. 'In view of the probability of a general election in the next twelve months', it was agreed not to proceed with any expulsions but to refer the matter to a joint meeting of the Administrative Committee and the National Executive, 'with a view to preventing a recurrence of the incident'. Everyone took this to be, as the *Daily Herald* admitted, 'a complete rebuff' for the leaders. Bevan claimed that the two factors which had influenced the decision were the forthcoming Party Conference and the 'refreshment' which Labour M.P.s had received over the intervening week-end by contact with their constituents. The rank-and-file had proved wiser than their leaders. He urged in *Tribune* that the joint meeting of the Party leaders should consider not only 'the incident' but the way in which the enthusiasm of the movement could be recovered. 'Disciplinary action is the resort of a Party made introvert and therefore beginning to decay.'

But the happy ending had not yet come. At a meeting of the Party's National Executive a week later two decisions were taken. The first which was claimed to be entirely unconnected with the second cancelled the Party's Whitsun Conference, in deference to the railway authorities who wanted to cut down rail travel. The British Legion and some fifty-nine other organizations failed to cancel their conferences, but the Labour decision was swiftly made. On the same day, in the words of the *Manchester Guardian*, 'the Bevan affair took an entirely unexpected turn'.

Following the joint meeting with the parliamentary leaders, the National Executive passed a resolution 'profoundly deploring the action of Mr Aneurin Bevan in deliberately flouting decisions of the Parliamentary Party and thereby causing disunity within its ranks' and demanding that he should give an assurance in writing within seven days that he would in future loyally abide by the Standing Orders of the Parliamentary Labour Party. Many members of the Parliamentary Party were angered by this *diktat*. They thought, as the Political Correspondent of the *Manchester Guardian* thought, that the leaders had 'rudely ignored' the sense of the Party meeting the week before. Some vainly tried to raise the issue at a further meeting only to be ruled out of order by the Chairman. Bevan himself toyed with the idea of proposing a vote of censure on Greenwood for failing to sustain the independence of the Parliamentary Party. But no escape from the ultimatum was available. He was cornered.

To sign or not to sign: it was a wretched choice. He believed that the principles he had enunciated about the rights of M.P.s against the Party meeting went to the roots of parliamentary government, but all his efforts to explain this doctrine by word and action met with little response. Tighter discipline was the remedy prescribed by the leaders and, despite wariness and concern about the longer consequences which might follow Bevan's expulsion, the bulk of the Parliamentary Party agreed with them. Of course Bevan was never opposed to the institution of Party. Democracy was impossible without it. But who was to bestow the Party label? Was it to be done by a central caucus or by the management committees which selected candidates? If the answer was the first there was a real danger of creeping totalitarianism; if the second, democratic vigour could be recaptured. But he had made no headway in securing converts to his constitutional theories. He must wait for another day.

And his argument about Parliament merged into another. 'Recent events in which I have been involved,' he told his constituents, 'were the result of attempting to force Tory policies down the throats of Socialists.' Some of his own friends and backers could not see that it was partly the exaggerated authority accorded to the Party meeting which made this process easier.

It was there in the Party meeting that Labour M.P.s were required to underwrite the bargains and compromises made between the employers' organizations and the General Council of the T.U.C. or the agreements in the Cabinet, for example over Beveridge. Only by stripping aside the secrecy and speaking – and speaking loudly and even raucously – in the House of Commons could the people outside be enlisted in the struggle. Only thus had Regulation 1 AA been prevented from passing through Parliament on the nod. 'Either we restore the healthy vigour of Parliament which comes with independence, discussion and criticism,' he wrote, 'or we submit to the corporate rule of Big Business and collaborationist Labour leaders.' One final thought clinched his decision. More than any other prominent member of the Party he had sensed the Leftward mood of the public inspired by the war. 'It will not be stifled, and it will not be silenced,' he wrote. 'No Standing Orders can do that.'

So he made up his mind, as he told his constituents, to 'swallow his pride' and reply to the Executive accepting the conditions and regulations governing the Party as they applied to other members. He called the seven-day ultimatum 'vindictive and malignant' but he had to comply. 'It is because I believe that there are elements in the Party which wish to continue association with the Tories when the war is over that I refuse to allow myself to be manoeuvred out of the Party and thus leave them with a clear field in which to accomplish the ruin of the Labour movement.' The Ebbw Vale Labour Party passed a unanimous resolution congratulating him on his stand against Regulation 1 AA and expressing confidence in his conduct as M.P. The expulsion crisis was over – or almost over.

Some of his opponents, it seems, were nettled by his choice. The General Council of the T.U.C. still wanted Bevan's head on a charger. After a heated discussion they resolved to approach the Miners' Federation; what did that body propose to *do* about Bevan's attack on trade union leaders in the 1 AA debate? The chairman of the General Council was instructed to write to Mr Ebby Edwards, secretary of the Miners' Federation, urging fresh disciplinary action. When Bevan heard of this move he telephoned Ebby Edwards to ask him whether the

Miners' Federation wanted a privilege case raised in the House of Commons. If they did not, they would be well advised to drop any talk of sanctions against him. The advice was taken. The Miners' executive issued a statement supporting the attitude of the T.U.C. and the Labour Party on the Regulation, deploring Bevan's unprovoked attack on responsible union officials and asserting the executive's right to negotiate with Government departments. But that was all. The knife was restored to its sheath.

There were other signs that the penitent had not lost his resilience. When Charles Dukes, secretary of the General and Municipal Workers' Union and another powerful figure on the General Council, described Bevan and others as 'opposition-minded', he retorted: 'Of course we are, and we shall continue to be until the working classes have got power. Why is not Mr Dukes still opposition-minded? Has he joined the British ruling classes?' When the T.U.C. issued a statement defending its whole record on 1 AA, Bevan invited every worker to read it – 'the clearest exposure of the General Council's case it is possible to imagine'. And when Jack Tanner, the president of the Amalgamated Engineering Union, confessed he had made a mistake in not opposing the Regulation from the outset, Bevan said that he would be as much honoured by the rank-and-file as he would be reviled in official circles. 'He has violated the free-masonry among the leaders, now so developed as to create a new code of loyalty. The code operates in a curious fashion. It requires the leaders to rally to each other's defence whenever danger comes from a revolt of the membership.'

Several of the leaders did rally to Bevin's defence at the Trades Union Congress in October of that year. Sir Walter Citrine presented the General Council's statement, including its condemnation of 'a most amazing attack on the trade union movement delivered by Mr Aneurin Bevan'. By this time Ernest Bevin's tiny, semi-legal rhetorical minority had become quite an army, nearly three million strong. The motion for the reference back of the General Council's statement was defeated by no more than 3,686,000 to 2,802,000. But by this time too the controversy which had come so near to dismembering the Labour Party,

461

twelve months before its most spectacular victory at the polls, was dying a natural death.

No one was ever prosecuted under Regulation 1 AA. Three different theories explaining this phenomenon are conceivable. Either the firm hand of Ernest Bevin had cowed the ubiquitous saboteurs who plotted to wreck Britain's war effort in March and April 1944, or the Regulation was quite superfluous, or Bevin dared not use the weapon he had caused so much trouble in fashioning. Only the first and most improbable of these explanations would be a tribute to Ernest Bevin's statesmanship and insight into the mind of British workers. Aneurin Bevan at least knew the mind of the miners better than Ernest Bevin and better than most of their own leaders. And this was the reason why he survived to fight another day.

14 The Fight against Coalition
April 1944–March 1945

You do assist the storm . . . Out of our way, I say. – THE BOATSWAIN
to the passengers at the beginning of *The Tempest*.

ONE night when London was being blitzed, Jennie Lee, George Strauss and a few others were anxiously waiting at Strauss's home in Kensington Palace Gardens, where Jennie and Aneurin often stayed throughout the war. Aneurin was on the way to join them when he was caught in the raid and nearly hit by an explosion in Oxford Street. He had saved himself from splinters by the miner's habit of falling to the ground in the presence of danger. As he picked himself up and walked on, counting his luck, he also felt pity and pride for the great wounded animal of a city he saw around him. When he arrived, still brushing the glass from his shoulders, he remarked: 'I could have loved London to-night.' London beneath the bombardment had been transfigured into one brave community, and Aneurin, like the rest of her citizens, was deeply stirred. The press might picture him as a malevolent saboteur of the war effort, and the chronicle of his public life necessarily stresses his continuous and violent criticisms. But anyone who knew him could testify that he shared to the full the nation's thrill at the spectacle of courage or the news of victories. As much as any boastful patriot, but after his own individual style, he loved his country – on that evening, even benighted, sprawling, monstrous London.

Normally he agreed with William Cobbett about the Great Wen; he ached for the countryside. However, in 1944, he and Jennie reluctantly made up their minds to sell Lane End Cottage and move to London. They were preparing, quite consciously, for the fresh political struggle which they knew must come at the end of the war. They needed a base near to the House of Commons. After much searching Jennie discovered that an eleven-year lease of a house in Cliveden Place, off Sloane Square, was available for £170. Hating to leave the country, Aneurin drew what consolation he could from their resolve that the money received for Lane End should be set aside for the time when they could move once more out of London. Aneurin's new idea was to find a farmhouse in the Welsh hills. But the practical difficulties proved too great. Asheridge Farm on the top of the Chilterns, which they bought seven years later, was as far away from London as they could go while still heavily engaged in political activities. Moving there was never the resort of a weary statesman seeking semi-retirement, as the gossips chose to insinuate. The dream of escaping from what H. G. Wells called London's inky catarrh of a climate and, more still, from the claustrophobic political atmosphere of the city was reborn almost as soon as he moved into 23 Cliveden Place in June 1944 – just in time for the flying-bombs to start. His new home was badly shattered and for a while they lived like troglodytes in the cellar.

One of their early visitors in those first days was Jack McElhone, a young trade union journalist from Detroit who had joined the Canadian Air Force and made Cliveden Place his home-from-home until he was shot down during the last raids over Berlin. To celebrate Jack's arrival, when they had just moved in, Aneurin got out his one bottle of vintage wine which he had been cherishing and a cheese from France, then the last word in luxury. Only later did Jack pluck up courage to reveal that he had no taste for wine or highly flavoured cheese. Jack was one of many whose names were not well known but whose friendship was intimately treasured.

Cliveden Place became, like all the Bevan households, a sanctuary from the dark corners of the political workshop, a secluded realm of light, conviviality, spacious argument and imagination. His enemies might imagine him plotting with his few close associates in Parliament, but House of Commons 'shop' was never tolerated for long. A few M.P.s – Frank Bowles was the most intimate in the later war years – came there. More often the visitors were playwrights, actors, artists, journalists, professors, those whose friendships were sustained solely for the freshening interest they could awaken over a whole range of topics. Cliveden Place itself, with the whole evening and half the night ahead to explore the planet and the universe, was the best setting for these feasts. But now and again he and his visitors went out to the restaurants. Aneurin had three favourites where he was always assured of a jubilant greeting from the proprietor – from Barry Neame at the Hind's Head at Bray in the Lane End Cottage days; or Abel, one of London's leading anti-Fascist Italians, at the Ivy; or René de Meo at the Pheasantry in the King's Road, Chelsea. René on those evenings would welcome them with his own Italian cooking and a wide smile like a brilliant Italian sky. There Aneurin argued with Italian Socialists one week and Italian tenors the next and acquired his loving and lasting interest in the whole Italian scene.

Thanks largely to Jennie's frequent tours in the United States, American trade unionists and American journalists were included among the regular guests at Cliveden Place. Walter Reuther, Victor Reuther and others who had organized the automobile workers of Detroit called whenever they came to London. According to the myth, Americans and journalists were supposed to figure high on Aneurin's list of *bêtes noires*. But the exceptions were so numerous they made nonsense of the rule. John Gunther and his wife, Bill and Tess Shirer, Eric Gedye, Walter Lippman, Mary and Ned Russell of the *Herald Tribune*, Ed Murrow and a large number of others whom he met on his journeys to Fleet Street came back and went away again with an impression far different from that painted in most British newspapers. Sometimes they left with an entirely novel portrait in their minds of his greatest American hero (not that he would ever use the word), Thomas Jefferson. Sometimes they would be asked, in the words of Abraham Lincoln, to 'disenthral' themselves. And often, to bait them, he would take down his copy of Rodo, read aloud Havelock Ellis's introduction to the masterpiece and ask for the modern American reply to the soft but deadly impeachment.[1]

1. The essential passage reads as follows: ' "In the beginning was action." In those words which Goethe set at the outset of *Faust*, Rodo remarks, the historian might begin the history of the North American Republic. Its

But, of course, British politics and political personalities were not banished from this domestic arena. Rodo could lead to Churchill. Rodo, for all his aristocratic proclivities, was a philosopher of democracy. 'He is altogether out of sympathy,' says Havelock Ellis, 'with the anti-democratic conception of life often associated with Nietzsche's doctrine of the Superman.' So was Bevan. Tirelessly he told his astonished visitors that Churchill's personal ascendancy would fade. 'It is a wasting asset! Victory will puff it into a brief blaze and, no doubt, he and the Tories associated with him will try to use it to light their way to victory at the polls before it dies down in diminishing smoulderings. But those who do not belong to his political and personal entourage would be foolish to imagine they can warm themselves at that fire for long.' These words were written in February 1944, when hardly a single other voice was raised to

---

genius is that of force in movement. Will is the chisel which has carved this people out of hard stone and given it a character of originality and daring. It possesses an insatiable aspiration to cultivate all human activities, to model the torso of an athlete for the heart of a freeman. The undiscriminating efforts of its virile energy, even in the material sphere, are saved from vulgarity by an epic grandeur.

'Yet, asks Rodo, can this powerful nation be said to be realizing, even tending to realize, the legitimate demands, moral, intellectual and spiritual, of our civilization? Is this feverish restlessness, centupling the movement and intensity of life, expended on objects that are truly worthwhile? Can we find in this land even an approximate image of the perfect city?

'North American life seems, indeed, to Rodo, to proceed in that vicious circle which Pascal described as the course of the pursuit of well-being which has no end outside itself. Its titanic energy of material aggrandisement produces a singular impression of insufficiency and vacuity . . . So it is that we find in the United States a radical inaptitude for selection, a general disorder of the ideal faculties, a total failure to realize the supreme spiritual importance of leisure. They have attained the satisfaction of their vanity of material magnificence, but they have not acquired the tone of fine taste. They pronounce with solemn and emphatic accent the word "art", but they have not been able to conceive that divine activity, for their febrile sensationalism excludes its noble severity. Neither the idealism of beauty nor the idealism of truth arouses their passion and their war against ignorance results in a general semi-culture combined with languor of high culture. Nature has not granted them the genius for propaganda by beauty or for apostolic vocation by the attraction of love. Bartholdi's statue of Liberty over New York awakens no such emotion of religious veneration as the ancient traveller felt when he saw emerge from the diaphanous nights of Attika the gleam of Athene's golden spear on the height of the Akropolis.'

question the continuing authority which Churchill was expected to exercise in the years ahead. And it was not malice but long-considered conviction about the working of democratic societies which enabled him to make the estimate. 'This is merely the immortal tragedy of all public life,' he wrote at the same time, 'that the *hero*'s need of the people outlasts *their* need of him. *They* obey the pressures of contemporary conditions whilst *he* strives to perpetuate the situation where he stood supreme. *He* is therefore overwhelmed by a nostalgia for past glory whereas *they* are pushed on by new needs, impelled by other hopes and led by other nascent heroes.' This was the clear-sighted appraisal made by Labour's outcast while his contemporaries were still dazzled by the Churchill sun.

Throughout the spring, summer and autumn of 1944 the mind of the nation was naturally concentrated upon the preparation for and the launching of the Second Front in the West. But citizens of a democratic State, including the servicemen themselves, could not live on an exclusive diet of war news. More and more they turned their thoughts to what would happen when victory was won. Bevan responded to this mood more purposefully than any other leading figure in Parliament. Newspaper attacks helped to make his name a household word; whenever he addressed public meetings the halls were jammed, often with hundreds waiting outside. His postbag became totally unmanageable; it included stacks of letters from soldiers all over the world. For him the portents were plain, and he strove diligently to make them come true.

Yet many obstacles presented themselves. It was natural for many to believe that Churchill could step forth as the Man Who Won the War, as Lloyd George had done in 1918. Most of the Labour leaders, as has been shown, were by no means clear about the course they wished to follow in the years ahead. They showed no sympathy with Bevan's attempt to relate each issue as it arose to the paramount aim of preventing a continuance of the Coalition and preparing the way for a radical reconstruction of British society. Inevitably, he was involved in fresh conflicts with Churchill who was using all his authority and guile to guide British politics along a quite different channel. Hindsight may suggest that Bevan had the easier task, since the spirit of the age was on his side. But that spirit was not reflected in the stale Parliament originally elected in 1935 at the height of the Baldwin era. Throughout 1944 and the early months of 1945 the contest about the future of the Coalition wavered back and forth, and few could prophesy the outcome. The series of incidents and controversies in the last period of 'the Long Parliament' must be followed in detail. For if public feeling outside had failed to win any victories in that arena, the Leftward tide might either have threatened parliamentary institutions themselves or become lost altogether in the sands.

Despite his preoccupation with the war itself, Churchill increasingly intervened in the detailed direction of parliamentary skirmishes. One minor scuffle arose over a by-election at West Derbyshire, a constituency which had been represented since the sixteenth century by someone connected with the family of the Duke of Devonshire. The reigning Duke, an Under-Secretary at the Colonial Office who was chairman of his local Conservative Association, called an emergency meeting and announced the resignation of the sitting Member. Somehow it had been arranged that his son, Lord Hartington, should have been conveniently on leave from the army in time to be adopted as the Conservative candidate on the same day. The Tory Whips in the House of Commons acted with equal speed. The writ for the new election was moved on the very afternoon when the vacancy was first announced. The war itself had not been conducted with quite this same clockwork precision. 'There was a Hartington in Parliament,' wrote Bevan, 'before there was a democracy in Britain. Why should the divine conjunction of Parliament and the Hartingtons be ruptured by the voice of democracy?' That voice insisted on being heard. Mr Charles White stood as an Independent Labour candidate, defying the truce, and, despite the rushed election, succeeded in expelling the Devonshires from Derbyshire by a handsome majority.

Mr White took his seat in the House of Commons on a day when Churchill was about to make one of his great war orations. The contrast between the almighty Premier and the latest evidence of his evanescent majority was marked by a few, although most observers still chose to dismiss as freaks the frequent Government defeats at by-elections. Churchill could not refrain from sneering at the 'little folk, who exist in every country and who follow alongside the juggernaut car of the God of War to see what fun or notoriety they can extract from the proceedings'. He was infuriated by the successful breaches of the electoral truce. When another Independent stood at a by-election in Brighton, he sent two splenetic letters to the Tory nominee denouncing as 'a swindle' any attempt by intruding candidates to claim that they opposed the Tories while still supporting the war. 'Churchill has thrown his political reputation into the arena,' wrote Bevan. 'It is likely to become quite considerably tarnished in subsequent by-elections.'

More spectacular was Churchill's attitude to the parliamentary crisis which blew up in March when a clause insisting on Equal Pay for women teachers was inserted into the Education Bill. The Government had been defeated by one vote. Tories had joined with Labour back benchers in rejecting ministerial advice but few at first believed that anything but a minor incident had occurred. After all, this was the first time in the whole war when the Churchill Government had suffered a parliamentary setback. The members who had voted in the majority were merely expressing their view on the merits of the issue and had no wish to undermine confidence in the Government as a whole. But Churchill rejected all these excuses. He demanded that M.P.s should turn a somersault and restore the clause in its original form, threatening that the Government would resign if his whim was not respected. His temper was not improved when Bevan outmanoeuvred him in parliamentary tactics. Churchill had supposed that he could deliver a massive speech on the whole constitutional situation. Bevan informed him that this would not be allowed, since Churchill himself had required that the debate must take place on the particular clause; he would be permitted by the rules of order to discuss only the virtues and vices of equal pay about which he was gloriously or ingloriously ignorant. Bevan also noted that the Labour Ministers had connived at the indignity of the whole affair. 'They have run away in this instance as in others.' In *Tribune* he added further comments on

'Mr Churchill's morbid pre-occupation with his own ascendancy'. The result of the Premier's intervention was 'to hold up Parliament to the derision of the world'. For Churchill to insist that every vote in the Commons must be one of confidence; for him to insist, further, that every vote against him at a by-election was 'a swindle'; and for Labour to condone this situation was to permit the Prime Minister to indulge in 'the megalomania of totalitarianism'.

However, the Equal Pay crisis had no long-term repercussions. It was effectively closed when scores of Members who had not been present at the original debate turned up to do Churchill's bidding, and when other Members agreed to reverse their verdict of a few hours before. Bevan voted with the small minority of twenty-three who refused to accept the Churchill decree.

Soon a much bigger source of strife and, in particular, of strife within the Labour Party, appeared. It derived from the most urgent domestic problem of the day and yet was suffused with the visions of a new world which had captured the public mind. Hitler's bombs, pre-war neglect and the wartime hold-up in building had combined to create a housing shortage of excruciating severity. 'Homes for heroes' was the most emotive phrase in Britain's political vocabulary; it summoned up all the memories of the post-1918 betrayal and gave edge to the resolve that the experience should not be repeated. Moreover, the physical state of the blitzed towns made it feasible for men and women to consider the pattern of reconstruction in quite novel terms. A number of brilliant experts in the field – Patrick Abercrombie, Thomas Sharp, Donald Gibson, William Holford, Charles Reilly and many more – had lifted the debate to a plane where it seemed to touch every question of how people were to live together in civilized, democratic communities. Charles Reilly, in particular, had the kind of mind which could impress and was impressed by Bevan's. As fellow students of Lewis Mumford, they saw town and country planning in its most capacious context. The chance for a new start linked with the social themes which had absorbed Bevan in the thirties when he had pilloried the haphazard drift of industry from the old industrial areas to the Midlands and the South. He naturally saw the national ownership of the land, especially in the big cities, as the fundamental instrument required to make planning effective. The challenge to property could not be dodged.

Most Socialists at the time shared these dreams and aspirations, and many others were forced to similar conclusions by a consideration of the hard facts of the case. Much work covering the whole field of the use of land, land values and the distribution of industry had been done by three Commissions or Committees of Inquiry, and their recommendations were incorporated in three documents – the Scott, Uthwatt and Barlow reports. A running fire of questions and debates complaining of delay in dealing with these matters had been sustained from 1941 onwards, not only by Labour M.P.s but also by eminent authorities in the House of Lords. Lord Astor, at that time Lord Mayor of Plymouth, came out in favour of land nationalization. At one stage, Lord Reith, the Minister in charge, appealed to the blitzed cities to 'plan boldly'; some months later he was removed from his office, perhaps because he appeared too awkwardly in earnest. By 1944 the situation had become desperate. Some of the blitzed cities had prepared their plans, but could make no headway without powers of compulsory purchase and some sure guidance about the prices they would have to pay. At last, in June 1944, the Government presented to Parliament its Town and Country Planning Bill for dealing with the problem.

Mr Justice Uthwatt and his fellow investigators appointed by the Government to examine the question of land values had been among those who recognized the merits of public ownership. But the Uthwatt Report itself, fearing that nationalization 'would arouse keen political controversy' and working within limited terms of reference, proposed instead a complicated scheme for the acquisition by the State of the development rights of undeveloped land coupled with proposals, reasonably favourable to the local authorities, for compulsory acquisition. The big property organizations regarded Uthwatt as concealed nationalization. Lord Brocket of the Property Owners' Protection Society denounced it as unprovoked aggression. The tussle behind the scenes ensured that the Town and Country Planning Bill offered no fulfilment of the ardent hopes of experts and the public alike.

Lewis Silkin, Labour's chief authority, called it 'a miserable and mean measure which represents a victory by the land-owning interests over the public interest. If the Labour Party accepts it, even in principle, it will be guilty of having betrayed the hopes of all who have placed their trust in our movement . . . It will have passed a sentence of death upon comprehensive planning for many generations to come.' These were strong words from a respectable Labour leader, for clearly the Labour Ministers *had* accepted the measure. Presumably they hoped that, armed with their recently sharpened disciplinary weapons, the Party meeting would approve the agreement they had reached in the Cabinet.

Bevan sat back and enjoyed the fun. Often when only a small minority opposed the leadership at the Party meetings, big decisions were rushed through in less than an hour, with an effective closure applied by the majority. No 'guillotine' in the Commons itself worked with quite the same undiscriminating expedition. But when the Labour Ministers found themselves in a minority, lengthy meetings were adjourned and recalled to ensure that grave issues were explored with due deliberation. Four such meetings were found necessary to reach the conclusion that Labour would abstain on the Second Reading of the Town and Country Planning Bill while seeking to improve the measure drastically on the Committee stage. A few rebels still voted against the decision and the Party leaders had not the heart or nerve to reprove them. The Ministers themselves – under the special wartime dispensation included in the Standing Orders – voted *for* the Government against the decisions of the immaculately wise Party meeting. Meantime, some Tory rebels were showing themselves more recalcitrant and determined than the well-Whipped Labour Members. Their concern was that the Planning Bill was too harsh on the property owners. On the Committee stage of the Bill, Churchill himself had to intervene once more. By dropping the crucial compensation clauses, he sought by the same stroke to avoid continued storms in the passage of the Bill and to appease his own followers.

Bevan naturally exploited the new situation. The Prime Minister, he said, had allowed his reputation to be used for 'squalid ends'; he bowed to pressures from the Right while never acknowledging the all too feeble pressures from the Left. The Coalition was 'spiritually dead'; to expect good legislation from it was 'to expect a large family from a mule'. The town and country planning debates had shown that the Coalition could only be kept together if there was no town and country planning. All that Parliament could do was to wait for the army to defeat the Germans in order 'to get back to real politics once more'.

Altogether, the long-forgotten intricacies of parliamentary manoeuvre over the Town and Country Planning Bill cast a gleam of light across the whole field of British politics. The question of the ownership of land was the real rock on which the Coalition was broken. Here was where property stood its ground against the prevailing sentiment of the age and political accommodations were forbidden. Thereafter neither Churchillian rhetoric nor the reticence of the Labour Ministers could prevent the resumption of the Party struggle. A few weeks earlier Bevan had been tried by drum-head court martial and nearly shot at dawn as a deserter. Soon the whole army, with the exception of a few of its commanders, was moving in his direction.

However, the truth about what was happening was partially concealed at the time. For, concurrently with the town and country planning controversies, another occurred which showed how persistent was the temper favouring Coalition policies in the higher reaches of the Labour leadership. Among what Bevan called 'the tired, turgid and tepid documents flowing from the muddy waters of the Coalition' was one sponsored by Ernest Bevin and hailed in many quarters as a State paper of historic importance – the White Paper on 'Employment Policy' issued in May 1944. Churchill undoubtedly regarded this document as the cornerstone of his post-war policy, the means for fulfilling the hope he had expressed in his broadcast of March 1943 that 'the best men of all Parties' would stay together after the war to carry through a Four Year Plan. Lord Woolton called it 'the Government's salute to the ex-soldier'. Ernest Bevin looked upon it with pride as an acceptance by all Parties of the expansionist economic policies he had sought to urge on Governments in the thirties. In view of the uninhibited blast with which he blew his own trumpet, it was not fanciful to fear that the Labour leaders had still not made up their minds to end the Coalition. If Churchill and Bevin had agreed on a common policy to secure the all-important objective of full employment, why should they suddenly choose to go separate ways? Or if the Labour Ministers did eventually make the breach, would they not leave Churchill with the claim that he had an employment policy which Bevin had blessed? Bevan attempted to tear up the Employment White Paper as mercilessly as he had torn up the others on other topics. 'Miguel de Unamuno, the Basque philosopher and scholar, remarks in his work *The Tragic Sense of Life*,' he wrote, 'that expression is death. Is that what the Government is after? Death by White Paper! . . . What is in the Government's mind except playing for time? The whisper is going round Whitehall that these White Papers are the blue-prints of the Coalition programme at the next general election. White Paper carrots! The donkey should watch out.'

The Employment White Paper was a tentative, aridly over-simplified essay in Keynesian economics. Its chief practical proposal amounted to little more than the suggestion that public works programmes should be available to be turned on and off as the signs of slump appeared or disappeared. But it did contain the admission that private enterprise left to itself would produce unemployment and an acknowledgement that it was the duty of the State to sustain 'a high and stable level of employment'. These were the innovations in Government thinking which Ernest Bevin wished to see hailed as revolutionary strides forward. Aneurin Bevan was more shocked than angered by such naïveties. If the admission was evidence of anything it merely proved the absurdity of the economics taught in the schools and universities. There students were taught how the economic system ought to correct its own defects by automatic readjustments. 'The system of private enterprise,' he wrote, 'went on producing unemployment, whilst the schools went on proving it ought not to do so.' In the Commons debate he spread his iconoclasm to cover both the economics professors and the top civil servants. 'The great British Treasury,' he said, 'has caught up with the soapbox orators in Hyde Park. That is all the White Paper is . . .' As for the much vaunted pledge accepting the

Government's responsibility to provide jobs, he asked: 'Do you think young men coming back will listen to a lot of doddering old gentlemen saying the Government will have *no* responsibility whether they worked or not?' The proposition was absurd. The White Paper was 'shallow, empty and superficial, bearing all the stigmata of its Coalition origin'.

In the first few days after the White Paper's publication only those on the Left of the Party spoke out in condemnation of it as sharply as Bevan. But opinion moved steadily along this channel. The White Paper gave monopolies and cartels no more than a warning scold and then remained silent on the main body of principles which had identified the Labour Party since its inception – the demand that the main industries and services of the nation must be national property. Could Ernest Bevin really regard the concealment or disparagement of this great argument as a victory? The Parliamentary Labour Party refused to do so in the manner he desired. As in the case of the Town and Country Planning Bill, the Labour leaders found themselves limping far behind their followers. 'Soon,' said Bevan, 'there will be no escape from the grim alternatives looming up before the Labour Party. It will have to abandon either its principles or its leaders.'

Bevan's belief at the time was that with some reluctance throughout 1944 the Labour leaders were making up their minds to reject the Churchill proposal for a post-war Coalition. Today all concerned who are still able to do so would doubtless condemn as quite unwarranted his suspicion that they had ever contemplated the idea at all. The claim may be correct, although no evidence has been adduced to prove it. What is incontestable is that well into 1945 Churchill still thought his project feasible. Attlee and Bevin, it seems, did not take the precaution of warning him privately in a contrary sense. In September 1944, however, the Party's National Executive did make a decision that Labour should fight the election as an independent Party and in October a public statement to this effect was published. But this statement did not remove all doubts. A few eminent and possibly inspired political commentators still argued that a Coalition might be re-formed after an election had been fought on a Party basis. Some leaders seemed to envisage a considerable intervening period between the ending of the war with Germany and the appeal to the electorate, in which, presumably, the Coalition would continue in office. Confusion was added when Arthur Greenwood, speaking for the Labour Party in Parliament, urged in the autumn of 1944 that the existing Parliament should continue to carry through all the social legislation projected in the previous few years. Bevan attacked all these varied arguments for delay. He urged instead that the Labour Party Conference – which was to take place in December – should make a clear declaration of Labour's determination to fight the election as an independent force, unfettered by any of the compromises agreed in the Coalition, as soon as conceivably possible after the ending of hostilities in Europe. However, other events intervened which were to make the Conference of 1944 one of the most truly decisive in Labour's history.

The crisis in Greece burst on the British public with shattering suddenness one Monday morning in December 1944. While the great battles were raging in France little attention could be spared for events in Athens. Churchill himself had been deeply implicated in all the major decisions governing Greek affairs. A small band of critics, led by Bevan, had vainly sought to discover what those decisions were. Both Churchill and Bevan from their very different viewpoints – Churchill privately, Bevan publicly – had expressed forebodings that liberated Greece might be plunged into serious domestic conflict. When British troops, backing the Government of Papandreou, landed in October it seemed for a few weeks that the worst fears were not to be fulfilled. The soldiers were garlanded with flowers and hailed everywhere as liberators. Then, on 4 December, came the news which startled the world. The report of the *Times* correspondent on the spot was typical of most others. 'Seeds of civil war were well and truly sown by the Athens police this morning,' ran his opening sentence, 'when they fired on a demonstration of children and youths.' He described how, when a vast demonstration of protest against the Greek Government had wheeled into Constitution Square, the police had opened fire. The crowd fell flat, but the police continued firing. When they stopped, the demonstrators got to their feet and started to pick up their wounded. Then the police fired again. A few more sentences from that famous despatch must be quoted, for the reports in *The Times* and from other, including American, journalists became an important element in the political reaction in Britain. British armoured cars, reported the *Times* correspondent, had been patrolling the roads before the shooting began. 'The presence of our troops served only to associate Britain with what is everywhere condemned as "Fascist" action . . .' His immediate verdict was that 'a grievous injury' had been inflicted on Anglo-Greek friendship.

Throughout the whole subsequent discussion about Greece no satisfactory excuse for this action, which resulted in eleven demonstrators being killed and sixty-six wounded, has ever been offered. Churchill told the House of Commons that he was not prepared to say, 'on the evidence so far available', who started the firing. When he described the event in his memoirs he achieved the notable meiosis that the demonstrators 'collided with the police'.[2] Most of the accepted histories of the period reduce the incident to minor proportions. But no doubt is possible about the effect of it on public feeling at the time. In the estimate of those who chose to believe eye-witness reports in the most responsible newspapers the Greek police, supported by the Greek Government and the British army, appeared as the aggressors in the bloody events that followed. Hostility to Britain's Greek policy was certainly not confined to jaundiced critics in the House of Commons. The United States Government pointedly expressed its lack of support for British policy. Relations between the White House and Downing Street, says Mr Harry Hopkins, became 'more strained than ever before'.[3]

It is necessary to look back over two or three years on the events which led to the December crisis in Athens. Subsequent discoveries reveal much more than was known then to any of the parliamentary contestants. Churchill has sought to defend in every detail his conduct both before and after 4 December. His claim is that he was suppressing a brutal Communist attempt to seize power. But the real sequence of events suggests more subtle

2. *Triumph and Tragedy* by Winston Churchill.
3. *The White House Papers of Harry Hopkins* by Robert Sherwood.

explanations. Before 4 December Churchill was partly responsible for strengthening the monster he feared. After 4 December he
only escaped from the worst consequences of his error by partially
yielding to the advice of his critics, headed by Bevan. The charge
against Bevan, on the other hand, is that in the Greek crisis he
played the demagogue, in the interests of the Communists. The
record must be examined.

For eighteen months or more, prior to the events of December,
Churchill had been increasingly alarmed by developments among
the guerrilla forces in Greece and their strained relationship with
the exiled Government of Greece, headed by King George II.
Much the most powerful of these forces was the National
Liberation Front (known by the initials E.A.M.) which in April
1942 had formed the People's Liberation Army (E.L.A.S.).
E.A.M.-E.L.A.S. gathered together various parties and individuals representing the Left and Centre, but reports accepted
by the Foreign Office indicated that the whole combination was
dominated by the Communists who increasingly used their
supplies of weapons less against the German occupying forces
than for the purpose of destroying other guerrilla bands and
establishing their hold on the Greek countryside. Moreover,
E.L.A.S. and originally all the other guerrilla forces were
strongly republican and bitterly hostile to the King.[4] A widening
gulf grew between the King, who Churchill believed had the
right to return to his country with an Anglo-Greek army, and
the forces which were likely to be dominant in Greece when the
Germans were driven out. Grudgingly Churchill and the King
were compelled to make concessions to the pressure of E.A.M.-
E.L.A.S. which found their republican reflection inside the
exiled Government itself. All the detailed journeyings and
manoeuvres between Cairo, London and the Greek mountains
cannot be recited here. By the autumn of 1944 the King had
agreed not to return to Greece with the liberating armies and had
promised to leave the decision about the monarchy to the free

4. King George had broken his oath in establishing the Metaxas dictatorship
in Greece in 1936; he himself was German without a drop of Greek blood in
his veins; most of the Greek Quislings in power in Athens were ex-
monarchists.

choice of the Greek people. A Coalition Government, headed by Papandreou and including representatives of E.A.M., was formed, E.A.M. in return agreeing to accept the orders of General Scobie, the British commander in charge of the expedition.

Meantime, Churchill had cleared his decks with Stalin. On his visit to Moscow in October 1944 he had seized the moment which he described as 'apt for business' to 'settle about our affairs in the Balkans'. The idea was to prevent the Allies 'getting at cross-purposes in small ways'. So Churchill put the question: 'So far as Britain and Russia are concerned, how would it do for you to have ninety per cent predominance in Rumania, for us to have ninety per cent of the say in Greece, and go fifty-fifty about Yugoslavia?' This percentage arrangement, written on a half-sheet of paper, was pushed across the table to Stalin who placed a large tick against it. 'It was all settled,' says Churchill, 'in no more time than it takes to set down.' He himself had qualms that this method of decreeing the fate of millions of people might be regarded as 'rather cynical' and wanted to burn the piece of paper. 'No, you keep it,' said Stalin.[5] Throughout the weeks and months that followed Churchill was insistent that Stalin had held to his bargain. He had virtually agreed that Britain 'in accord with the U.S.A.' should do what they wanted in Greece and he did not lift a finger to assist or encourage the Greek Communists.

The 'rather cynical' arrangement, so casually made, was a potent political document. It was never revealed to the British House of Commons. There, on frequent occasions, Bevan challenged Churchill and Eden for making secret agreements which went far beyond anything justified by military security and expediency. He was strongly opposed to the idea of 'zones of influence', partly in the interests of the small nations affected but also because he believed that secret compacts, shielded from democratic pressures and sanctions, would prove to be a fertile source of misunderstanding between the great Powers themselves. Bevan was always told, in Eden's best patronizing tone, that no secret political agreements had been entered into. The half-sheet of paper dividing up the Balkans remains as proof of how justified his suspicions were.

5. *Triumph and Tragedy* by Winston Churchill.

No doubt exists about Churchill's expectation when he despatched British troops to Greece. He set little store on the agreements reached with E.A.M.-E.L.A.S. His aim was to forestall a Communist *putsch*. On 7 November, some three weeks after the arrival of the British troops, he sent this message to Eden, then in Athens. 'In my opinion having paid the price we have to Russia for freedom of action in Greece, we should not hesitate to use British troops to support the Royal Hellenic Government under M Papandreou ... I hope the Greek Brigade will soon arrive, and will not hesitate to shoot when necessary ... I fully expect a clash with E.A.M. and we must not shrink from it, provided the ground is well chosen.'[6]

Bevan of course had no access to the secret advice reaching the British Government from their liaison officers in Greece. Little information about the Communist dominance of E.A.M.-E.L.A.S. was allowed to leak out, partly owing to a long tussle between the British military authorities and the Foreign Office; the military were eager to say or do nothing to discourage the most effective guerrillas whereas the Foreign Office was more and more alarmed by the potential post-war Communist threat. Like most other observers, including *The Times*, Bevan was inclined to regard E.A.M. as the broad Greek counterpart to the resistance forces in Italy or France. He attributed to British diplomacy the same lack of sympathy towards the resistance movement in Greece which he detected in its dealings with other countries. Above all, he believed that Churchill's whole mind and approach were warped by his romantic love of royalty. At question-time and in speeches throughout the latter part of 1943 and 1944 Bevan sought to discover what was the nature of the commitments to King George of Greece and why he, like King Victor of Italy and King Peter of Yugoslavia, were considered such powerful military allies. Usually he was confronted by a bland Anthony Eden assuring him that he was grotesquely mistaken. The British Government had no wish to interfere with the free choice of the Greek people. King George had agreed to a plebiscite. Nothing could be more innocent.

6. *Triumph and Tragedy* by Winston Churchill.

But Bevan was never convinced. In a speech in August 1944, he delivered a full-scale attack on the Government's Greek policy. Eden's assurances might be worthless; they might be no more to be relied upon than those he had once given in the Spanish civil war. No doubt there were real difficulties; elements in E.A.M. might be exceeding their authority. But the Government had shackled themselves with one quite unnecessary handicap. They 'have approached the Greek people under the worst possible auspices by being made to appear as the special champions of King George'. The trouble was that 'the Prime Minister cannot see a king without wanting to shore him up'. Eden's smile became blander still. Bevan was accused of purveying the tittle-tattle of the newspapers. His *Tribune* made a speciality of attacking not only Churchill's royalism but also that of Britain's Ambassador to the exiled Greek Government in Cairo, Mr Reginald Leeper.

It is now possible to judge both the accuracy of Bevan's charges and the influence of the policy he criticized in preparing the way for the Greek tragedy. On his appointment as Ambassador in 1943, Mr Leeper writes: 'My instructions were to give every possible support to the King and his Government'.[7] Since many members of the Government were republican, this was not an easy assignment. Mr Leeper candidly admits that he favoured the King against his Ministers, particularly on the critical issue of the date and conditions of the King's return to Greece. The plebiscite proposals so skilfully used by Eden in debate to prove the Government's good faith had originally been presented by E.A.M. and flatly rejected by Churchill. Churchill's own memoirs are littered with references to his allegiance to 'the Royal Hellenic Government' which contrast strangely with his contempt for the 'surge of appetite among ambitious *émigré* nonentities'.[8] More significant still was the instruction sent by the British Government to the British liaison mission in enemy-occupied Greece in April 1943. It agreed that 'in view of the operational importance attached to subversive activities in Greece', all dealings with republican groups could not be severed;

7. *When Greek Meets Greek* by Reginald Leeper.
8. *Triumph and Tragedy* by Winston Churchill.

'but subject to special operational necessity you should always veer in the direction of groups willing to support the King and the Government and furthermore impress on such other groups as may be anti-monarchical the fact that the King and the Government enjoy the fullest support of His Majesty's Government'.[9] Mr C. M. Woodhouse, the recipient of this directive, was rootedly hostile to E.L.A.S.; his verdict on the British Government's attitude to the King may therefore be considered all the more weighty. He believed that it enormously strengthened the Communists, injured British influence and made a bitter division among the Greek people inevitable.[10] Churchill's obstinate backing for the King and the King's obstinate refusal to make concessions in time – it was not until September 1944 that he agreed not to return to Greece with the armies and even then he refused to consider appointing a Regent, as was urged upon him – were two factors which were to poison the act of liberation. Eden's soft answers are now silenced by the facts.

A third factor undoubtedly was the ruthless methods of E.L.A.S. Whether they had planned a full-scale seizure of the Government, and if so how long in advance the preparations had been made, is uncertain. If this was their aim, it remains a mystery why they did not take action before the British troops had been able to consolidate their position. What is certain is that they were unwilling to disarm according to their undertakings; the arrival of the Greek Brigade and the maraudings of another Right-wing force, led by Colonel Grivas, gave pretexts

9. Lecture by C. M. Woodhouse, former M.P. for Oxford and Under Secretary of State at the Home Office, reprinted in *European Resistance Movements 1939–1945*.

10. Mr Woodhouse writes in his book *Apple of Discord*: 'The loyalty of Mr Churchill, and to a lesser degree of his Government, towards the late King was thus morally justified by his conduct towards his Allies rather than by his conduct towards his people. Its practical justification is less certain, for it was one of two things that combined to keep Greece divided. The other, which might never have flourished if the first had ceased to exist, was the power of the Communist Party of Greece . . . The practical argument against the policy which Mr Churchill imposed upon his Cabinet is therefore this: that however right the King might be, he was debarred by circumstances beyond his control from being able to unite the Greek people. The policy pursued in London of supporting King George could only perpetuate the schism of the Hellenes.'

for their refusal. On 1 December, the E.A.M. representatives resigned from the Government and called a general strike. They also called a demonstration for 3 December which the Government first agreed to and then banned. Then followed the wretched massacre in Constitution Square. General Scobie ordered E.L.A.S. to evacuate Athens. Instead their forces seized police stations and for a moment looked capable of taking over the city.

And far away in London Churchill had his finger on the trigger. He sat up late on the night of 4 December with Anthony Eden; there was no time, he claims, to call a Cabinet meeting. Running in his mind, says Churchill, was the telegram which Arthur Balfour had once sent to the British authorities in Ireland: 'Don't hesitate to shoot.' Eventually Eden went to bed and Churchill stayed up to complete his instructions for General Scobie: 'Do not hesitate to act as if you were in a conquered city where a local rebellion is in progress . . . We have to hold and dominate Athens. It would be a great thing for you to succeed in this without bloodshed if possible, but also with bloodshed if necessary.' This telegram, despatched at 4.50 in the morning, was, Churchill admitted later, 'somewhat strident in tone'.[11]

That day he faced a stunned and shocked House of Commons. His tone had softened. No hint was given of the precise orders to General Scobie, but the meaning was plain enough. British troops were acting to prevent bloodshed. The menace was Communist dictatorship. 'Yes, a conciliatory policy,' he replied to one questioner, 'but that should not include running away from, or lying down under, the threat of armed revolution.' Since Churchill brushed aside the reports in *The Times*, the House appeared to be confronted with a stark conflict in testimony about the origin of the whole affair. Several members, including Bevan, sought to secure an immediate debate, but the Speaker refused. For a moment the anger on the Labour benches was so vocal and strong that the police shots in Athens appeared to have cracked the Coalition Government.

Three days later the Commons staged the first of a series of debates on Greece, the most poignant and bitter of the whole war period. Bevan joined Seymour Cocks, Frank Bowles, Richard

11. *Triumph and Tragedy* by Winston Churchill.

483

Acland and Tom Driberg to draft a motion of censure to be debated on the King's Speech which was then before the House – 'but humbly regrets that the Gracious Speech contains no assurance that His Majesty's forces will not be used to disarm the friends of democracy in Greece and other parts of Europe or to suppress those popular movements which have valorously assisted in the defeat of the enemy and upon whose success we must rely for future friendly co-operation in Europe.' Bevan himself had exhausted his right to speak, having been called earlier in the King's Speech debate before the Greek crisis had exploded. The choice for moving the motion fell on Seymour Cocks who had never previously criticized Churchill's war leadership, and who now sat up all night preparing his oration. Seymour Cocks was probably the best read man in the House of Commons. When he made a speech he polished every phrase and summoned history to his aid in a manner Churchill could hardly excel. He loved the heritage of Greece and he loved England too with a pure, burning patriotism. He had a paralysed leg and side, yet when he dragged himself to his feet, swaying on his stick, the man himself and the words he uttered achieved a perfect nobility. The shooting in Constitution Square he called 'another Peterloo'. Of Churchill, he spoke of his grief at seeing Chatham sunk to the level of Lord North. 'I would rather,' he cried, 'this hand of mine were burnt off at the wrist, leaving a blackened and twisted stump, than sign an order to the British Army to fire on the workers of Greece.' He called for a halt to 'these mad and mischievous proceedings'. But Churchill would not halt. He claimed to be dealing with armed revolution conducted by a band of gangsters and that day sent fresh instructions to General Scobie: 'The clear objective is the defeat of E.A.M. The ending of the fighting is subsidiary to this.'

In the House of Commons Churchill won the vote by two hundred and seventy-nine to thirty. Officially the Labour Party had abstained. Bevan voted with the defiant minority. On this occasion there was no talk of discipline. The mood in the country extending far outside the ranks of the Left of the Labour Party was so hot that any attempt at it might have broken the leadership itself. Moreover, the Labour Party Conference, postponed from the previous May, was scheduled to take place in the following week. The leadership feared that it might easily face defeat if it gave unqualified blessing to the Churchill policy in Greece. 'No peace without victory' – this was 'the guiding principle' which Churchill relentlessly urged on Scobie and the other authorities in Athens, apparently with the full support of his Labour colleagues.[12] But no Labour leader outside the Government dared speak in such accents. Those who abstained, like those who voted against the Government, pleaded for fresh efforts at conciliation.

The Labour Party Conference of 1944 met at the Central Hall, London, in an atmosphere of suspicion and excitement. Several big issues (discussed later) crowded for debate, yet the news from Greece overshadowed all else. Some believed that the whole character of the war was changing and that the Churchill of 1940 was reverting to type – to the interventionist of 1918 and 1919. Everyone could sense that the sentiment of the rank-and-file was overwhelmingly against the Government. The Labour Ministers looked isolated. The strain on the Coalition might reach breaking-point. After long confabulations the Executive neatly side-stepped its dilemma. It could not censure the Government directly without humiliating the Labour Ministers and possibly destroying the Coalition. It could not risk a frontal clash with the tide of opinion in the Conference without courting a defeat which might also undermine the Ministers' position. A resolution on Greece was therefore devised calling for 'an armistice without delay' and 'the resumption of conversations between all sections of the people who have resisted the Nazi invaders, with a view to the establishment of a provisional national Government'. Much stiffer emergency resolutions which had been submitted by the railwaymen and the miners and other organizations were ruled out of order by the Conference Arrangements Committee. But the Executive's proposal and even more the speeches in which it was recommended to Conference did repudiate the Churchill doctrine of 'no peace without victory'.

Ernest Bevin neither supported nor opposed the Executive resolution. He pleaded for a debate without emotionalism and

12. *Triumph and Tragedy* by Winston Churchill.

melodrama, recited the facts with many emotional overtones, boldly claimed that the steps taken in Greece were the decisions of the whole Cabinet, yet hinted that the Government's purposes might not be so different from those described in the resolution. Ernest Bevin had swayed countless Conferences before with his bluff displays of power and intransigence, but on that day he could not disguise his annoyance at the Executive's refusal to grant him the chance of unconditional victory. Bevan's speech from the other extreme, even though compressed into five minutes, came nearer to the Conference's centre of gravity. 'It would be deplorable,' he said, 'if the unanimous carrying of this resolution was regarded by the world as endorsement of Mr Bevin's speech. Mr Bevin has described what has been happening in Greece. I have no time to answer him. But there is one complete answer. Only three bodies of public opinion in the world have gone on record in his support, namely Fascist Spain, Fascist Portugal and the majority of Tories in the House of Commons.' Bevin's description of events, he insisted, had been 'garbled and inadequate where it was not unveracious'. As for the peace terms, what was intended? 'Are all Greek irregulars in Greece to be asked to deliver up their arms before any discussion can take place? Is the war to go on all the time and Greeks slay Greeks and Greeks slay Britons until the irregulars have been defeated?' Finally he came to the political issue at home. 'I do not want to break up the National Government on this issue, but remember, we cannot be carried very much farther along this road. This Conference should go on record as condemning the action of the Government and insisting that our representatives inside the Government should exercise a more decisive influence upon the conduct of our affairs or else leave the Tories to do their own dirty work themselves.'

In the House of Commons Bevan combined his strictures on the past conduct of the Government with three constructive proposals for seeking an escape from the impasse. He wanted an abandonment of any idea of a fight to a finish, argued that the disarmament of the guerrillas could only succeed if the Greek Brigade were also disarmed and called for the appointment of Archbishop Damaskinos as Regent. These suggestions were not novel, but their advocacy by Bevan must have been especially irritating for the Ministers, for they coincided closely with what Roosevelt was urging from Washington. The Regency proposal which the King had turned down months before was revived by Harold Macmillan and the British Ambassador from Athens. But Churchill opposed it. Not merely did the King persist in his refusal; Churchill also assumed – chiefly it seems because the proposition was favoured by E.A.M. – that the Archbishop was a dangerous and ambitious man of the Left, who once appointed Regent might establish a dictatorship. Right up till 19 December, Churchill was still instructing Field-Marshal Alexander that 'the Cabinet feel it better to let the military operations to clear Athens and Attica run for a little while rather than embark all our fortunes on the character of the Archbishop'.[13] If this was indeed the unanimous view of his Cabinet, Bevan's complaints about the subservience of the Labour Ministers were certainly justified.

For on 21 December – the day after Bevan had been urging his constructive proposals in the House of Commons – Field-Marshal Alexander plucked up his courage to address Churchill in a more direct manner than any of the others had dared. 'I am most concerned,' he cabled, 'that you should know what the true situation is and what we can do and cannot do. This is my duty.' He estimated that it would not be possible to crush E.L.A.S. with the forces available. 'It is my opinion,' he emphasized, 'that the Greek problem cannot be solved by military measures. The answer must be found in the political field.' This blunt warning, coupled with the King's continued refusal to contemplate a Regency, may have been the cause of Churchill's decision to visit Athens himself. Once there he made the discovery that the Archbishop was 'the outstanding figure in the Greek turmoil', participated in a conference at which E.L.A.S. delegates were present, recognized that, despite their support, the Regency proposal was the only way out, and agreed that the plan must be forced on the stubborn King. Two weeks later an agreement was reached with E.L.A.S. whereby their forces were to withdraw well clear of Athens and prisoners would be released on both sides. This was hardly 'no peace without victory'. Mr Leeper concluded that the

13. *Triumph and Tragedy* by Winston Churchill.

declaration extorted from the King 'finally scotched the legend that the British were trying to force the King back on his people'.[14] Some trouble might have been avoided if it had been scotched a good deal earlier. And at the moment of crisis in Athens, it was Alexander's message which altered Churchill's course and British policy. His appeal for a *political* solution accorded precisely with Bevan's demands in the House of Commons and at the Labour Party Conference.

Various epilogues on this part of the Greek tragedy were spoken by some of the principal performers in a notable parliamentary debate on 18 January. Churchill furiously denounced E.L.A.S., declared that they had played little part in the war against Germany and claimed that his policy had prevented 'a hideous massacre in which all forms of Government would have been set aside and triumphant Trotskyism installed'. He gave an account of E.L.A.S. atrocities, turning at the end to his chief antagonist. 'I know,' he said, 'that the hon. Member for Ebbw Vale would not stand for anything of that kind. I know that he would not, but would rather throw away great advantages in an argument than stand for one moment for inhumanity.' Mr Quintin Hogg would not let Bevan off so lightly. Whom, he asked, was Labour going to follow – their own leaders or the siren voice from Ebbw Vale? What the House had been witnessing in the Greek debates was 'a squalid conspiracy of a little clique who have deliberately exploited the tragedy of two nations in order to further their own sordid little political ambitions'.

Bevan was not to be drawn by this diversion. His quarry was Churchill, not Hogg. 'As we are talking of the Mediterranean,' he said, 'I might draw a metaphor from marine fauna and ask why, if I have a good John Dory on the dish, should I pay any attention to the shrimps?' Churchill had supported the King to the limit; and the King had only at last been removed from the arena by the pressure of the Labour Party. Churchill had opposed the Regency; it was the critics who had paved the way for that solution. The story of strong forces marching on Athens to let loose a massacre was 'a grotesque piece of Churchillian rubbish'. As for the atrocities, let the Tories not hide their own manoeuvres

14. *When Greek Meets Greek* by Reginald Leeper.

behind 'the bloody hands of a few assassins'. The spirit of Churchill's speech would still not bring peace to Greece. 'Why should we believe that a Tory is different abroad from one at home? He is the friend of the City at home and the friend of Hambros, in Athens. He is the friend of the landlord here, as he is there, the friend of the rich and powerful here, as he is there.' In short, Bevan saw the whole Greek episode as one which exposed the deep gulf of principle between the Parties. It was not his fault that the Labour leaders were left stranded on the opposite bank. At the end of the debate the leaders of the Party repudiated once again the charge that foreign policy was made on 'the impulse of the Prime Minister or on the sole discretion of the Foreign Secretary'. Then the report concluded thus:

Mr Attlee: On the record of this Government and on the known opinions of this Government we have the right to be trusted to carry out the principles in which we believe.
Mr Bevan: No.
Mr Attlee: I have stuck a great deal more closely to carrying out the principles in which I believe and in working with my Party than has the hon. Member opposite.

And with this celebrated retort the drama ended for the moment. It may be that the Labour Ministers had unitedly supported Churchill in his devotion to King George of the Hellenes right up till the last second when the Regency had to be extorted from the King by threat of an ultimatum. If so, the self-indictment is a harsh one. Not even the most distant hint appears in any of the histories or biographies that the Labour Ministers ever whispered one word of dissent. Churchill claims that his whole Cabinet supported him 'like a rock'. Mr Attlee's book of memoirs, *As It Happened*, does not mention the 1944 Greek crisis at all. 'It's a good title,' said Bevan when Attlee's book appeared. 'Things happened to him. He never *did* anything.'

Labour Party Conferences, according to modern theory, have little influence and authority. The words are spoken from the Conference platforms; but the deeds are done within the Parliamentary Party. Many instances can be cited to substantiate the claim. Yet with all the limitations upon them, Conferences can indicate to leaders who wish to survive the boundaries beyond which they will stray at their peril. They can deflect the course of leadership and block paths along which otherwise the movement might be forced to travel. 1944 was such a Conference. Much of the lassitude evident at the previous wartime assemblies had vanished. The big trade unions were not lined up in a solid phalanx to back the Executive's views. Greece came near to setting the whole place aflame. No exceptional percipience was needed to see how frayed was the Party's allegiance to the Coalition.

The new temper was symbolized most sharply in the results of the elections for constituency party representation on the National Executive. Harold Laski, a strong critic of the Party leaders outside the House of Commons, came top; Emanuel Shinwell, a strong critic inside the House of Commons, came second; and most sensational of all, Aneurin Bevan, standing for the first time, secured the fifth place out of seven. Here was the rank-and-file's answer to the attempt of the trade union and parliamentary leaders to expel him from the Party altogether a bare six months before, and here too was the proof of how deep would have been the rupture within the Party if they had been able to succeed. The leadership was given clear notice that any further dalliance with Churchill's post-war Coalition ideas would leave them totally severed from their followers. And the event also illustrated how wide was the chasm which separated the adventurous spirit in the country from the shuffling timidity of the Parliamentary Labour Party. A few weeks before Bevan had again had no success in the elections for the Administrative Committee. In the vote at the beginning of the session he had failed to secure a place and when a special election was held to fill a vacancy he was beaten by Alderman Charles Key, M.P. for Bow and Bromley. If the Parliamentary Party had had its way, he would have stayed an outcast, despite his pre-eminent debating ability. However, he had forced his way into the leadership in open defiance of his parliamentary colleagues backed by the trade union bureaucracy. No other leading figure in Labour's history travelled such a rough, precipitous road to power within the Party and many who had blocked his path waited expectantly to see him fall.

At the Conference in 1944, however, he received a tumultuous welcome. He spoke on the Executive's statement about 'Labour and the Next Election' which went almost the whole way he had wanted in forbidding any idea of a post-war Coalition. He gently pressed his advantage. The document spoke of ending the great Coalition partnership with dignity and good feeling. He had not noticed much good feeling in the recent Commons debate on Greece! Tories did not fight with dignity when their interests were at stake; Labour must learn to fight with equal resolution. Professing himself shocked by the strong language used by some speakers about Churchill, he added: 'The man has not changed. All that has happened is that people are now finding out realities they should have known before.'

On Greece, as we have seen, he fought a drawn battle. On international affairs generally, the Executive got its way, defeating an anti-Vansittartite resolution from the Left on the future of Germany. Several resolutions highly critical of Government policy on domestic affairs were carried without much argument. The most significant vote occurred at the end of the debate on Labour's future domestic policy. The Executive had presented a document on 'Economic Controls, Public Ownership and Full Employment' which made no reference to definite commitments about public ownership, and this oversight was not remedied in the speeches from the platform. It seemed that the Executive might not be committed to much more than the vague proposals outlined in the Coalition White Papers. But dozens of resolutions from the local Parties had appeared on the agenda demanding an extensive programme of common ownership. A composite resolution, moved by Ian Mikardo, required that the Party programme should include 'the transfer to public ownership of the land, large-scale building, heavy industry, and all forms of banking, transport and fuel and power' and also 'appropriate legislation' to ensure that these services should be 'democratically controlled'. The Executive asked that this resolution should be neither accepted nor rejected. It was overwhelmingly approved on a show of hands.

Bevan regarded this as a victory of cardinal importance. It would help, he believed, to kill 'the pernicious pretence that State control, nationalization of some key industries and Socialism are all one and the same thing'. Progressive Tories argued that all the advantages of planning could be secured by controls without ownership. Some Socialists were deceived by the same idea, 'although I am bound to confess I think many of them wanted to be deceived. A certain weakness of Socialist faith likes to masquerade as up-to-date "realism".' Bevan was convinced that 'attempts by the modern State to combine in one organization the merits of private and public enterprise lose both.' He cited the dual control of the wartime coal industry, with all its duplicated bureaucracy, as proof of his case. But his argument went deeper, to the root of his philosophy of power. 'In practice it is impossible for the modern State to maintain an independent control over the decisions of big business. When the State extends its control over big business, big business moves in to control the State. The political decisions of the State become so important a part of the business transactions of the combines that it is a law of their survival that those decisions should suit the needs of profit-making. The State ceases to be the umpire. *It becomes the prize.*' Either the State must be a nullity in economic affairs – the old Liberal theory – or it must be a partner which big business will work to dominate – an incipient Fascism – or it must possess Socialist power. The choice must not be blurred. Moreover, State control of private enterprises had other disabilities. 'It can never be a positive, active, operational factor. It must always be negative, slow and remote ... Planning by State control of private enterprise is therefore the abandonment of planning altogether, and without a plan we shall perish.'

Bevan's resolve was to place the argument for public ownership at the centre of the stage. 'The issue,' he wrote in 1944, 'is one of the transfer of power, and it is this issue which must be kept to the front of all our reasoning about the future. We shall be able to afford the light cavalry of private enterprise and competition in a number of business enterprises if the principal economic activities of society are articulated by means of a dominating sector of publicly owned industries.' The issue soon came sharply to the fore on the new National Executive of which Bevan had become a member. Morrison who was charged with drawing up the Party's proposed election programme wanted to exclude iron and steel from the list of Labour's nationalization measures. He lost that first engagement, but he was not easily beaten. The battle was to be endlessly fought and refought in the next ten years.

Bevan's quarrels – as for example with Herbert Morrison about public ownership or earlier about the rights of Parliament or with Ernest Bevin over Regulation 1 AA and Greece – derived from profound differences of principle. He never saw them in any other light and he never ceased to rail against the habit of the newspapers of 'personalizing' every dispute in which he engaged. Contrary to the impression they sought to purvey, he did not pursue personal vendettas. The argument, not the man, was the origin of his animosities. He himself was so convinced of this truth that he regarded the attribution of any other motive as scandalous malice. Often when the source of a quarrel had faded from prominence he would resume a geniality either to the victim's face or behind his back which made the anger of a few months before seem inconceivable. 'Fair play for Morrison,' he would say, 'he did do such and such.' 'But didn't you call him a third-rate Tammany Hall boss?' his companion might say. 'Fifth-rate,' replied Aneurin with a smile so tender that it clearly included even Tammany Hall bosses of every category in the catalogue of men. But still: 'Fair play for Morrison.' Sometimes when indulging in these unsuspected reconciliations he would quote:

> Time's glory is to calm contending kings,

occasionally adding with a hint of triumph –

> To unmask falsehood, and bring truth to light.

After the 1944 Conference, it might be noted, Morrison was one of the leaders who recognized that the Tories would have to be fought. Bevan welcomed, even if he did not exactly embrace, a powerful ally.

Yet often he could use language which scorched and left many scars. Occasionally he would round on an interrupter, especially in the oppressive atmosphere of the Party meeting, without pity or restraint. One such incident occurred in the Commons in December. Again the quarrel derived from principle, but few in the turmoil that followed were likely to remember. Anthony Eden was explaining why the British Government had told the Italians that they would not approve the appointment of Count Sforza as Italian Foreign Secretary. Amid the protests from several quarters, Bevan intervened to protest that the Italian Government did not contain any member 'of any of the parties in Italy who share *our* views'. He was speaking from the second bench when suddenly he was startled to hear falling from the lips of Mr F. W. Pethick-Lawrence, the most aged and respected of Labour front benchers, the words: 'Share *your* views, you mean.' Bevan leant forward over the bald head in front of him until he was almost looking into the face upside down, and let fly: 'That is just the answer I might have expected from the crusted old Tory who still remains a member of this Party.' Then the interchange continued thus:

Mr Montague : Do not speak for us.
Mr Bevan : I do not.
Mr Montague : Then do not pretend to.
Mr Bevan : The Socialist Party of Italy, affiliated to the International of which this person (*jabbing his finger repeatedly downwards at the trembling head below*) is supposed to be a member – (*Interruption*)
Hon. Members : Order.
Mr Bevan : I mean this hon. Member (*Hon Members :* right hon. Member). My right hon. Friend will notice who are his defenders. The Socialist Parties of Italy affiliated to the organization to which we are attached have repudiated the action of the British Government.

Bevan had put the case upon which his Socialist comrades in Italy felt passionately while his leaders sat silent or gratuitously repudiated his protest. But no one would stop to argue these niceties. Bevan had savaged the harmless Pethick-Lawrence. Many remembered that, and a few would never forget or forgive.

He also conducted at this time a long quarrel lasting over many months, chiefly through the columns of *Tribune*, with those whom the ignoramuses suspected of being his close allies – the British Communists. A year or two earlier, at the time of the Second

Front campaign, he had been their hero. But gradually they discovered what they should never have forgotten – that he was never prepared to follow their 'line'. He campaigned both in Parliament and outside against all proposals for inflicting a Carthaginian peace on Germany. When the news leaked that Churchill and Roosevelt had initialled the so-called Morgenthau plan for the 'pastoralization' of Germany, he spoke out more strongly, stressing that a policy did not become Socialist because Stalin approved it. Of course Germany must be made militarily impotent; but must she also be made economically prostrate? That, said Bevan, would be an outrage against Socialist principle. The *Daily Worker* accused him of 'speaking for the Germans' and allying with Oswald Mosley. Other grounds of quarrel appeared. *Tribune* under Bevan's direction was the first British newspaper, or among the very first, to protest against the Soviet betrayal of the heroic victims in the Warsaw rising. He condemned Stalin no less than Churchill for the cynicism with which they divided Europe into spheres of influence; this he believed was a contributory factor in the tragedies of Poland and Greece. And unlike not merely Communists but many others extending far to the Right in the political spectrum, he refused to accept at their face value the protestations of Allied unity and infallibility which followed the agreements reached at the Moscow, Teheran and Yalta conferences between Stalin, Roosevelt and Churchill.

Just before the Yalta Conference in 1945, he wrote: 'There is nothing in the situation surrounding the Conference which justifies optimism for the future. From the first the three great Powers have insisted that the problems of future security depend upon whether they can reach agreement among themselves. The small nations must await their fate at the hands of the Great Ones ... Of these three great Powers, Britain is the most foolish in accepting that logic, for she is the weakest of the three. It is in her interest, as it is in the interests of all mankind, that the power of principle should be considered at least equally with the principle of power ... The absence of representatives from the smaller nations at this particular Conference will prove the decisive factor in the peace settlement. It is they who have the most interest in asserting fidelity to principle in the making of the peace. When they were left outside the Conference door, principles were left outside also, as will soon be made bitterly clear.' At the time very few other voices were raised making the same prophecy, but not many today would question its accuracy. The British Communists were naturally hostile; Yalta for them was the 1945 Sinai and when Churchill brought back the tablets of stone agreed with Stalin they were prepared to approve the continuance of a Government with Churchill at its head. One of the oddities of politics was that when Bevan was working for the destruction of any post-war Coalition with the Tories, the Communists could or would not breathe a whisper of support.

Bevan's elevation to the Executive did not curb his style. At the Party Conference, the retiring Secretary, James Middleton, made reference to the prospect. 'I have seen forty Executives,' he said; 'I am worried to death I won't see this one. I long to see Aneurin bearing what Jimmy Thomas used to call "a full sense of his own responsibility".' There were no early signs of it. During the first months of 1945 his chief ground of complaint was directed against the leader of the Party – Clement Attlee. He believed that Attlee had pitifully failed to represent a Socialist view in the Cabinet, particularly on the issues of Greece, Italy and the future of Germany. His was the prime responsibility, and at the end of February he committed what Bevan in *Tribune* called 'Attlee's Crowning Blunder'. He had agreed to represent the British Government, along with Eden, at the forthcoming United Nations Conference in San Francisco· Was it not significant, asked Bevan, that this was the first of the great wartime international conferences which a Labour Minister had been allowed to attend? The Tories wanted Attlee as a cover, wanted to identify Labour as closely as possible with the Coalition's foreign policy at the very moment when Labour should be keeping its hands free for new initiatives in foreign affairs. Churchill openly revealed his satisfaction that the country's relations with other nations 'are now high and dry above the ebb and flow of the tides of Party controversy'. A month later Bevan's indignation was even more uncontrollable. Attlee – 'a modest little man with much to be modest about', in Churchill's phrase – had agreed to take second place on the delegation. 'We did not expect,' wrote Bevan, 'that he would affront his own followers and demean the status of the whole Labour movement by agreeing to serve as lieutenant to Anthony Eden. Much more is involved in this than a mere question of personal merits. We are not prepared to argue which of the two men is the abler. That the question should ever arise is due to the way Mr Attlee has consistently underplayed his position and opportunities. He seems determined to make a trumpet sound like a tin whistle . . . He brings to the fierce struggle of politics the tepid enthusiasm of a lazy summer afternoon at a cricket match.'

This was the last of Bevan's character sketches of the wartime Labour Ministers. That rich anthology of invective was now completed. The war was ending, the sniff of the election – what Churchill called the 'odour of dissolution' – was already in the air. Elections, even before the contest actually starts, can produce kaleidoscopic change not only across the political scene but in all political groupings and personal relations. Overnight, civilities towards opponents are replaced by rasping hatred; the deep wounds inflicted by friends miraculously heal. Hatchets are buried, even carelessly in places where they cannot be disinterred. M.P.s who have not fired a parliamentary question in anger reach for their tomahawks. Coalitions splinter; great Parties not merely unite, they congeal. Thus it was in the lovely spring of 1945. Soon – although still not too soon – even the non-playing captain, Mr Attlee, was to join the game.

I believe in the instinctive wisdom of our well-tried democracy. –
WINSTON CHURCHILL, 4 July 1945

NOT surprisingly Bevan foresaw both the temper and the
political issues which would dominate the general election of
1945. Had he not been insisting, for months and even years, that
a stupendous convulsion had taken place in the public mind and
that Labour had a potential support in the country which only
audacious leadership was needed to mobilize and capitalize?
Churchill had declared in October 1944 that the termination of
the Parliament should be settled by the ending of the German
war but that there need be no 'violent hurry' in fixing the actual
date of the election. Ever since then discussion had prevailed
about the timing and the manner of the break-up of the Coalition
and the appeal to the polls. Bevan's answer was consistent: the
sooner the better. His thrusting enthusiasm and the widespread
opinion it represented had some influence on developments.

At the time of the Party Conference in December 1944, he had
stated what he considered to be the simplicities of the situation.
Churchill's reputation as the war leader would be the chief asset
exploited by the Tory Party. Better late than never Labour must
reckon with the myth and realize their duty to expose it. The
second supposed asset of the Tories might be more subtle. They
would play upon the universal desire for privacy and freedom of
choice. 'This,' wrote Bevan, 'is the normal result of war and of
any collective effort. Human beings possess the attributes of the
cat and the dog. They want to hunt in packs at one time, and to
hunt alone at others. They are both gregarious and self-sufficient.
They need the warmth of association and the withdrawals of

sanctity. They are capable of self-sacrifice for group needs, and of sacrificing the group interests to their own immediate desires. War insists from its onset on the nature of the dog, and the cat qualities are kept in abeyance. When the war is over, the cat nature demands satisfaction, and this takes the form of romantic nostalgia for a life of freedom from the disciplines of State interference.'

The post-war danger to the Labour Party, therefore, would be 'a general lethargy of the collective will'. Since the Tory 'never addresses himself to the merits of political issues, but rather to the subjective attitudes of the electorate', the anti-social sentiment would be wildly exploited. How could Labour inoculate the people against this attack upon their emotions? Bevan described the necessary counter-emotion in a colloquial sentence. 'It is the suspicion of being had . . . Ordinary people are always suspicious of being "had". Heaven knows they are completely justified. What the Labour Party needs to do is to mobilize the *We* against the *They* . . . We are still near enough to the last war to recall how *They* had us then, and Winston Churchill was one of the *They*. Old dogs don't learn new tricks, and Churchill remembers well enough how effective the trick was then not to try any other this time.' Bevan himself had produced a powerful prophylactic against this Tory virus in his book *Why Not Trust the Tories?* which Victor Gollancz had published a few months before and which sold some 80,000 copies. It recounted the whole story of 1918, sharply drawing all the morals for 1945. One other ingredient must be added to the recipe. Since Labour had declared its determination to break with the Coalition, it was the challenger. All its acts should fit this role. It could not afford to seem wary in hastening the battle.

Such was the counsel which Bevan urged on the National Executive all through March and April when the issue was being debated. He was impatient of all excuses. When in mid-April Ernest Bevin and Brendan Bracken were provoked into a Party exchange from public platforms, some grave voices warned that those who revealed partisan passions would see the disadvantage recoil on their own heads. Bevan drew the opposite conclusion. The strong feelings existed in the country; the sooner they were provided with the normal constitutional means of expression the better. 'A firmer lid,' he wrote, 'is hardly the recipe for a boiling pot.' The advice that Labour should be cautious came from those quarters which would be most bitterly hostile when the electoral battle was joined. 'Labour has dawdled long enough,' wrote Bevan. 'The time has come to act.'

Labour did act. Under Herbert Morrison's chairmanship, the National Executive produced its statement of future policy, *Let Us Face the Future*. This programme was in effect a compromise between the statement presented by the Executive to the 1944 Conference and the amendment moved by Ian Mikardo. Bevan in *Tribune* urged that those who feared it did not go far enough should not cavil. 'At last,' he wrote, 'we are facing the right direction even if the pace of advance is not so quick as some of us would like. We must remember that only a few short months ago there was a justifiable fear that we might not set out on the journey at all. The advocates of a continuance of the Coalition were powerful and persistent, and at one time it looked as though politics in Britain would be swamped in a flood of cynicism induced by artificial alliances and shallow agreements at the top. We have escaped that danger which might have destroyed our hopes for a generation. We are slowly but surely disentangling ourselves from the embrace of the Tory Party, and in this declaration of Labour policy we have shown that the Party has found its way back to its authentic principles and allegiances.' Bevan himself had been largely responsible on the Executive for adding one item which gave spice to the dish. 'We give clear notice,' said the document, 'that we will not tolerate obstruction of the people's will by the House of Lords.' *Tribune*'s editorial welcoming the programme in April was headed: 'Into Battle'. On this occasion there were no doubts about the enemy.

It might be thought that at this stage the political armies were finally poised for the struggle. Nothing remained but to give the signal. Yet it was not so. Right till the end Churchill hankered after some contrivance which would keep the Coalition in being. His fear was not that he would be defeated at the polls; he, like his most intimate advisers, notably Beaverbrook and Brendan Bracken, was utterly confident that nothing could count in the scales against his own prestige. But he loved Coalitions; he felt that the one he had dominated had been the most successful in British history; and frequently to the fore in his mind was the thought that if fresh clashes with the Communists, as in Greece, were to occur, Labour participation in his administration was invaluable. By this means he could best assure the continuity of his foreign policies which interested him more than any domestic disputes. Thus when the great news of the German surrender came on 8 May and as Churchill paraded through the streets, he could still spare time for electoral calculations. 'Few questions, national or personal,' he admitted later, 'have so perplexed my mind as did the fixing of the date of the general election.'[1] He still desired and half-expected a continuance of the Coalition until the end of the Japanese war. That might mean a period of eighteen months or even two years. If that was denied him, less lofty decisions must be made at once. All his cronies, backed by the Party managers, favoured the speediest possible election – say in June or early July – while the victory bells were still ringing.

Eden and Attlee were away in San Francisco, Attlee having been given a promise that Churchill would not fix the election date in his absence. On 11 May Churchill cabled Eden: 'there is a consensus of opinion on our side that June is better for our Party.' Eden concurred. On that same day Churchill was visited by Morrison and Bevin. Morrison suggested October when a new register would be available. Churchill replied with his proposal for two more years of Coalition or at least an extension of its life to cover the war with Japan. Morrison expressed his strong preference for a Party Government. 'Bevin,' says Morrison, 'appeared to be on Churchill's side.' Attlee returned five days later. He was 'wobbly', according to Morrison.[2] Attlee saw Churchill just before departing for Blackpool where the Labour Party Conference was to meet. 'I certainly had the impression when he left,' wrote Churchill, 'that he would do his best to keep us together, and so reported to my colleagues.' Attlee and Bevin together constituted a formidable alliance in support of the

1. *Triumph and Tragedy* by Winston Churchill.
2. *An Autobiography* by Herbert Morrison.

Churchill time-table. They were, after all, the chief spokesmen of the political and industrial wings of the movement. And there were others who agreed with them. A. V. Alexander, the First Lord of the Admiralty, made a speech in the City of London in the same sense. And the City of London did not demur.

Attlee, therefore, put to the National Executive his proposal for backing Churchill's idea, now formally incorporated in a letter, that the Coalition should continue until the end of the Japanese war. Failing that, Churchill would undoubtedly force an election in July. Attlee, it seems, had no great confidence in a July victory. Bevin backed Attlee. Dalton sympathized with their argument, but felt the Conference would not stand for it. He proposed that Labour should agree to stay in the Coalition until November and then reconsider the matter in the light of the state, at that time, of the Japanese war.[3] Morrison stuck to his earlier view. Bevan had had talks with Shinwell before the Executive meeting. They had agreed to reject any Coalition proposal and to warn the Executive what storms it would face in the Conference next day if the Attlee–Bevin advice were approved. Party unity would be ruptured and the leadership would have cast away the greatest political opportunity of the century. It was the mood of the general Conference which settled the issue, the incipient spirit revealed at the 1944 assembly now vastly excited. Attlee and Bevin secured only three supporters on the Executive – Fred Burrows, Wilfrid Burke and Tom Williamson. Next day a united leadership confronted the most enthusiastic Conference in Labour's history. Churchill could do his worst. Rumour was stilled, intrigue at an end. The Coalition was no more. Few stopped to marvel that the two most prominent of Labour's leaders had been hauled out of it by the scruff of their necks.

'Never before,' said Ellen Wilkinson, the Conference chairman, 'was Labour so united or in such fighting fettle.' And it was true. One by one the leaders received their ovations, Morrison and Ernest Bevin vying for the biggest. Streams of young candidates mounted the rostrum. Stafford Cripps, back in the

3. *The Fateful Years* by Hugh Dalton.

fold, remarked how he found the air of Blackpool more congenial than Southport. Bevan, re-elected to the Executive in the fourth place, just a few votes behind Shinwell, Laski and Morrison, was charged with replying in the debate on full employment. He won the loudest laugh of the Conference. 'This island is almost made of coal and surrounded by fish. Only an organizing genius could produce a shortage of coal and fish in Great Britain at the same time.' But he was serious too. This was the moment he had worked for and no one could begrudge him his shout of triumph. These were his concluding words:

It is for us a question of where power is going to lie. There is no absence of knowledge, there is no lack of wisdom, as to what to do in Great Britain. What is lacking is that the power lies in the wrong hands and the will to do it is not there. We want to tell our friends on the other side that the men in the Services are not going to allow a repetition of what happened between the wars. We are not going to allow our financial resources to be sent all over the world, and idleness and starvation to exist in Great Britain. And we warn them we are entering this fight with this in our hearts. We were brought up between the two wars in the distressed areas of this country, and we have such biting and bitter memories as will never be erased until the Tories are destroyed on every political platform in this country. I went to the United States of America and Canada in 1934 and 1935, addressing meetings right throughout the Continent. Sitting before me in the cities were men with whom I had been to school, men I had known, fine men, the best men that this nation has ever produced, scattered to the four corners of the earth. By what? By any natural visitation? No; by the greed, by the stupidity, and, yes, by the lack of patriotism of British Tories and British capitalists. Homes ruined, dreams shattered! Are we going to see a repetition of that? If the Tories are sent back with a majority, all those ugly scenes will be repeated once more. There is no evidence that I can see that they have learnt anything from the past.

But we – and may I say this as one who, in the course of the last five and a half years, has had very many differences with the leaders of our own Party, and rather more with the leader of the other Party – we, at this time, are completely united on this matter. There are no differences between us now, and any memories of past differences we shall erase from our minds and from our hearts, because we have before us not only the greatest opportunity this nation has ever provided for a Party, but the greatest responsibility that any nation has ever undertaken.

It is in no pure Party spirit that we are going into this election. We know that in us, and in us alone, lies the economic salvation of this country and the opportunity of providing a great example to the world. Therefore, remember in the elections that are immediately ahead, we are the memories of those bitter years; we are the voice of the British people; we are the natural custodians of the interests of those young men and women in the Services abroad. We are the builders. We have been the dreamers, we have been the sufferers, now we are the builders. We enter this campaign at this general election, not merely to get rid of the Tory majority – that will not be enough for our task. It will not be sufficient to get a parliamentary majority. We want the complete political extinction of the Tory Party, and twenty-five years of Labour Government. We cannot do in five years what requires to be done. It needs a new industrial revolution. We require that modern industrial science be applied to our heavy industry. It can only be done by men with modern minds, by men of a new age. It can only be done by the fine young men and women that we have seen in this Conference this week.

Bevan naturally hurled himself into the subsequent campaign with gusto. Although not one of the official leaders of the Party, he travelled north, south, east and west on extensive tours, addressing huge meetings and returning only in the last few days to his own constituency for the traditional rally on Waunpound, the mountain between Tredegar and Ebbw Vale. 'Everything has gone splendidly in the campaign so far,' announced Archie Lush. 'But now we must prepare ourselves for reverses – the candidate has arrived.'

He had no love of elections. The hustling from one meeting to another, the inescapable repetitions, the lack of time for reflection did not suit his style. But for Socialists everywhere, and possibly for Bevan in particular, 1945 had a unique exhilaration and sweetness. He saw the chance of revenge for the wretchedness of the twenties and the thirties, for the Guardians Default Act, for the betrayal of Spain, for the whole pusillanimous epoch of Baldwin and Chamberlain. On his own home ground, Wales was naturally uppermost in his thoughts. 'The Tory claim to be a national Party,' he said at a meeting in Cwm, 'comes with a particular irony to the people of Wales. I don't wish to speak in any narrow Nationalist sense, but nevertheless, I believe that for a Welshman to vote Tory in this election is an act of naked treachery to his country.' Some students of the election noted that his election address struck a more hard-hitting note than most others.[4] 'What the election is about,' he wrote, 'is a real struggle for power in Britain. It is a struggle between Big Business and the People.'

A chief feature of the election was the all-pervasive presence of Churchill and, in the eyes of the Labour leaders, the fall of the great man from his pedestal. In his first broadcast he made the charge that a Socialist system could not be run without a Gestapo, that Socialism in its essence was an attack upon 'the right of the ordinary man and woman to breathe freely without having a harsh, clumsy, tyrannical hand clapped across their mouth and nostrils'. This set the tone for every Tory underling. Soon Captain Harold Balfour, for example, was saying: 'Mosley and Cripps have the same policy. The Socialist State of Cripps is to be the same as the Fascist State of the blackshirts.' No one could deny that it was Churchill who had opened up the gutters. And no one could deny that Bevan had prophesied the moment. In 1918, as Bevan reminded the House of Commons in one of the rowdy parliamentary debates which preceded the dissolution, Churchill had cheerfully joined in the indecencies of the 'Hang the Kaiser' election and then meekly apologized afterwards that he had swum with the stream; he would do the same again. 'For the past three years,' said Bevan at a meeting in Cardiff just before the poll, 'I have sought to warn the country, and particularly the Labour Party, against the danger of building him up to more than life-size by uncritical hero-worship. It was always apparent to me that some day he would capitalize all the hero-worship against the worshippers themselves.'

After the election was over and before the result was announced – owing to the count of Service votes there was a three weeks' interval between polling day and the declaration – Bevan reflected on the manner in which the Tories had conducted the campaign. The voice of Churchill dominated the ether (he broadcast four times to Attlee's one); his features, reproduced a million-fold, were plastered on the walls of every town, village and hamlet; every word that dropped from his lips was amplified, every gesture made during his tours of the country and the

4. *The British General Election of 1945* by R. B McCallum and Alison Readman.

capital was absurdly magnified by powerful newspapers sworn to his service. All this, said Bevan, was a degradation of democracy. If it succeeded the consequences could be serious, particularly since Churchill was profoundly bored by the great domestic issues with which the country would be faced.

Bevan also commented – just after the election – on the implications for the Labour Party of the controversy initiated by Harold Laski which had played so prominent a part in the election itself. Churchill had invited Attlee to accompany him to the first meeting of the Big Three in Potsdam which was to take place in July, just after polling day, and Attlee had agreed. Thereupon, in the midst of the election, Harold Laski, as Chairman of the National Executive, issued a statement urging that Attlee should attend the gathering 'in the role of observer only'. The Labour Party, he said, could not be committed to any decisions arrived at by the Three-Power Conference. 'Labour has a foreign policy which in many respects will not be continuous with that of a Tory-dominated Coalition. It has, in fact, a far sounder foreign policy.' Churchill used this declaration to protest that Attlee was a pawn of Laski and that a Labour Cabinet would be at the mercy of Labour's National Executive. Attlee skilfully rebutted the charge. Bevan's comment, however, was that the Laski warning had been well worth making. Churchill, he wrote, 'appears to take up the position that any attempt to interfere with his unfettered powers to commit us to anything he likes is a break with democratic tradition.' The idea could only be put forward by 'a man who is drunk with power and impatient of all democratic processes'. Bevan drew the deduction: 'All this goes to show that the break with the Coalition has not been finally accomplished. The formal severance must be followed by spiritual disentanglement. We can promise continuity of policy in nothing . . . We did not fight an election in order to perpetuate the spirit of the Coalition.'

The Laski controversy, however, did not influence events, despite Churchill's grotesque exploitation of it. He thought he had unearthed a Red Letter or a Savings Scare, as in 1924 or 1931. The nation, it seems, was more inclined to reflect on its whole history since 1918. The war had awakened a more radical impulse than anything Britain had known for generations. The Tories remained blinkered by the old traditions. Of course, Bevan did not believe that the Labour leaders he had attacked so mercilessly had overnight become clear-eyed revolutionaries. He could draw comfort, however, from the adage of Oliver Cromwell: 'No one goes so far as he who does not know where he is going.' If the currents of history were on his side, the lack of seamanship in the captain and his mates might still be remedied. Nor did he ever underrate the difficulties of achieving a Socialist revolution by democratic means. No one had truly attempted the task before. If it could be accomplished without bloodshed, what a boon it would be, not only for Britain, but for all mankind! And if it failed in Britain, where could it succeed? 'The watchword for Labour, therefore,' he wrote, while waiting for the results, 'is audacity. Audacity, whether we are in office or in opposition. Audacity if we are in opposition, because if not we shall never get power: audacity if we get a majority because if not we shan't keep it. In the Parliament of 1929 to 1931 the Labour Party failed not because it was too bold, but because it was too timid. In the years following it conducted the opposition in too muted a fashion. The times call for a different mood. Fortunately the men and women who stood for Labour are in the spirit of the times. Let the consciousness of this strengthen Attlee in the difficult weeks before him. For when he returns it will be to a House of Commons wholly different from the one to which he has been accustomed.'

On 26 July the results were announced. Labour had secured three hundred and ninety-three seats (or three hundred and ninety-seven if the three I.L.P. and one Common Wealth candidates are added) out of six hundred and forty. It had a total of 11,992,292 votes against 9,960,809 cast for the Conservative–Liberal National alliance, the Liberals having 2,239,668. In the needle contest at Ebbw Vale Bevan had 27,209 votes against 6,758 secured by his Conservative opponent.

After the count Aneurin discussed the political and personal prospects late into the night with Archie Lush in a way they had never done before. They had never talked in terms of office and personal advancement. But they heard on the radio that Churchill had gone to the Palace; a Labour Government was in the making. 'Do you think Attlee will offer you anything?' asked Archie. Aneurin was doubtful. But he was emphatic on two points. He would only accept a real job; he would not be content to answer as an Under-Secretary for policies which he had little power in shaping. More important still, it must be a real Labour Government pursuing Socialist aims; if the aims were abandoned he would leave. It was still true, as it had been so often in their previous discussions, that 'the texture of our lives shaped the question into a class and not an individual form'. Archie did manage to prise from him a more personal comment. If the choice was offered the Ministry of Health was the place where he would like to go. But their main debate ranged much more widely – over the whole field of what a Labour Government could *do*.

Back in London he continued the same discussion with Jennie Lee. His mind was not resolved easily. He knew what his enemies said of him – that he was a loud-mouthed demagogue who would soon be destroyed by a constructive job. The test, they hoped, would dispose of 'the squalid nuisance' for ever. Moreover, he himself had sometimes remarked that politicians could be corrupted by the offer of constructive work no less than by money, rank and the normal prizes. They could be tempted to leave the greatest issues to others and to find consolation in an agreeable, commendable backwater. This was another reason why he was so firmly resolved – even before the opportunity appeared likely to come – to accept nothing but a major Cabinet post. Even so, for him, after taking so many blows before and during the war, it would have been an unbearable deprivation if he had been given no chance to build.

A few days later Archie telephoned Aneurin in London. 'What do you think?' said Aneurin, 'I've got to see Attlee at nine-thirty.' 'But that means real office,' said a startled Archie, 'he can't have got down to the Under-Secretaries yet.' It was still barely credible. None of the speculation in the press had suggested that the incorrigible rebel would step into one of the chief posts in the Government. But next day the newspapers carried the announcement. At forty-seven years old, he was to be the Minister of Health and the youngest member of the Cabinet.

'I understand,' said Attlee to him at the brief interview, 'that you have much experience of negotiation. I am offering you the post where you will deal with health, housing and the local authorities.' Ernest Bevin claimed that he had persuaded Attlee to make the choice; [5] the votes of the much-despised constituency party delegates to Labour's 1944 Conference had probably been more influential. Some suspiciously noticed that he had been given one of the toughest jobs in the Government. For a full unravelment of the riddle the world had to wait until Mr Attlee produced his autobiography. 'For Health,' he wrote, 'I chose Aneurin Bevan whose abilities had up to now been displayed only in opposition, but I felt that he had it in him to do good service.' [6]

Aneurin Bevan, as we have seen, had his own ideas of what service he could do.

5. *Ernest Bevin* by Francis Williams.
6. *As It Happened* by C. R. Attlee.